MW01235524

UMI ANNUAL SUNDAY SCHOOL LESSON
C O M M E N T A R Y

PRECEPTS
FOR
LIVING®

M I S S I O N   S T A T E M E N T

*We are called
of God to create, produce, and distribute
quality Christian education products;
to deliver exemplary customer service;
and to provide quality Christian
educational services, which will empower
God's people, especially within the Black
community, to evangelize, disciple,
and equip people for serving Christ,
His kingdom, and church.*

UMI
Urban Ministries, Inc.
The African American Christian Publishing
& Communications Co.

UMI ANNUAL SUNDAY SCHOOL LESSON COMMENTARY
PRECEPTS FOR LIVING® 2007–2008
INTERNATIONAL SUNDAY SCHOOL LESSONS
VOLUME 10
UMI (URBAN MINISTRIES, INC.)

Melvin Banks Sr., Litt.D., Founder and Chairman
C. Jeffrey Wright, J.D., President and CEO

All art: Copyright© 2007 by UMI.
Bible art: Fred Carter

CONTRIBUTORS

Editorial Staff
Dr. Vincent Bacote,
Editor
Cheryl P. Clemetson,
Ph.D., Vice President
of Editorial
Cheryl Wilson,
Developmental Editor
Evangeline Carey, Staff
Writer
Megan Bell, Copy
Editor

Product Manager
Vicki Frye

Cover Design &
Layout
Trinidad D. Zavala

Bible Illustrations
Fred Carter

Contributing Writers
Essays/In Focus
Stories
Melvin Banks Sr., Litt.D.
Evangeline Carey
Cheryl Clemetson, Ph.D.
Dr. Judy Hull
Darcy Ingraham
Dr. A. Okeckukwu

Ogbonnaya
Kathy Steward
Cheryl Wilson
Dr. Louis H. Wilson

Bible Study Guide
Writers
Dr. Vincent Bacote
Lisa Crayton
Jennifer King
Vanessa Lovelace
LaTonya Mason
Keyonn Pope
Frederick Thomas
Dr. Rosa Sailes
Faith Waters
Charlesetta Watson-
Holmes
Jimmie Wilkerson-
Chaplin

More Light
On The Text
J. Ayodeji Adewuya,
Ph.D.
Evangeline Carey
Moussa Coulibaly, Ph.D.
Clay Daniel
Robert Dulin
Kevin Hrebik
Ransome Merith
Nathan P. Munn

James Rawdon
Dr. Rosa Sailes
Raedorah Steward
Virginia Stith
Dr. Louis H. Wilson

Dear *Precepts* Customer,

We are excited to bring you this year's *Precepts For Living*®. As you read and study God's Word through the lessons presented in *Precepts For Living*®, we know that you will continue to find this a valuable Bible study tool!

We are also pleased that in addition to the *Precepts For Living*® *Personal Study Guide* (the workbook) and the CD-ROM version of *Precepts*, we continue to offer *Precepts* in large print. You will also notice that the biblical text for each lesson now includes the *New Living Translation* in addition to the King James Version. On our Christian journey, *Precepts For Living*® not only serves as a witness through our learning and sharing more of the Bible, but helps us develop new tools and other ways to delve into a deeper understanding of God's Word. As Paul admonishes Timothy to "Study to shew thyself approved" (2 Timothy 2:15), Christians today are given the same responsibility. Challenging ourselves to learn and grow more in God's Word prepares us to be stronger Christians, and to witness to others about the saving power of Jesus Christ.

During your course of study for this year, you will be given the opportunity to discover or expand your understanding and knowledge through the following themes: "God Created A People"; "God's Call to the Christian Community"; "God, the People, and the Covenant"; and "Images of Christ." This year of study promises to be meaningful and enriching to your Christian walk.

Precepts For Living® will continue to evolve in an effort to meet our customers' needs. We appreciate your comments and feedback. Please e-mail your feedback to precepts@urbanministries.com or mail your comments to UMI, *Precepts For Living*®, P.O. Box 436987, Chicago, IL 60643-6987.

We hope that your spirit is edified and encouraged by the contents of this book.

Yours in Christ,

Dr. Vincent E. Bacote

Dr. Vincent E. Bacote,
Editor

TABLE OF CONTENTS

Contributors ii
Letter from the Editor iii
Cycle of 2007–2010 vi
God—Creator of All! vii

Fall Quarter, 2007

GOD CREATED A PEOPLE
September 2007 Quarter At-A-Glance 1
Thematic Essay: *In the Beginning, God Created. . .!* 3
Portrait of Christian Education Essay: *Creation* ..6
Point of View Essay: *God's Word—The Tie That Binds* 8
Heritage Profile: *Elijah McCoy* 10

LESSONS
Unit 1: God Created a People
SEPTEMBER
2 God Created the Heavens and the Earth
   Genesis 1:1–6, 8, 10, 12–15, 19–20, 22–23, 25 12
9 God Created Humankind
   Genesis 1:26–30 21
16 Abraham, Sarah, and Isaac
   Genesis 15:5–6; 18:11–14; 21:1–8....26
23 Abraham, Hagar, and Ishmael
   Genesis 21:9–21 35
30 Isaac and Rebekah
   Genesis 24:34–40, 42–45, 48........46

Unit 2: God's People Increased
OCTOBER
7 Esau and Jacob as Rivals
   Genesis 25:19–34.........................55
14 Jacob's Dream at Bethel
   Genesis 28:10–22 63
21 Jacob and Rachel
   Genesis 29:21–35 72
28 Esau and Jacob Reconciled
   Genesis 33:1–11 79

Unit 3: God's People Re-created
NOVEMBER
4 Joseph's Dream
   Genesis 37:5–11, 19–21, 23–24, 28 ..86
11 Joseph's Dream Began to Come True
   Genesis 41:25–40...........................93
18 God Preserved a Remnant
   Genesis 45:1–12...........................101

25 Jacob Blessed His Family
   Genesis 48:11–19........................108

Winter Quarter 2007–2008

GOD'S CALL TO THE CHRISTIAN COMMUNITY
December 2007 Quarter At-A-Glance 114
Thematic Essay: *Have You Heard God's Call?*..116
Portrait of Christian Education Essay: *Teaching the Adult Learner* 118
Point of View Essay: *The Call to Community: Our God-Given Responsibilities*..................119
Heritage Profile: *Patrick Francis Healy*....121

LESSONS
Unit 1: God's Call at Christmas and Beyond
DECEMBER
2 Called to Believe!
   Luke 1:8–23 123
9 Called to Be a Vessel!
   Luke 1:26–38 132
16 Called to Proclaim!
   Luke 1:67–80 140
23 Called to Rejoice!
   Luke 2:1–14 147
30 Called to Witness!
   Luke 2:22–35 154

Unit 2: The Awareness of God's Instruction
JANUARY
6 Inspired to Inquire!
   Luke 2:41–52 164
13 Inspired to Love!
   Luke 6:27–36 173
20 Inspired to Pray!
   Luke 11:5–13................................182
27 Inspired to Trust!
   Luke 12:22–34 191

Unit 3: God Summons Us to Respond!
FEBRUARY
3 Summoned to Labor!
   Luke 10:1–12, 17–20 202
10 Summoned to Repent!
   Luke 13:1–9 213
17 Summoned to Be Humble!
   Luke 14:1, 7–14 221
24 Summoned to Be a Disciple!
   Luke 14:25–33 231

Spring Quarter, 2008

GOD, THE PEOPLE, AND THE COVENANT
March 2008 Quarter-At-A-Glance 239
Thematic Essay: *Have You Kept Your Covenant Commitment with God?* 241
Portrait of Christian Education Essay: *Teaching That Changes Lives*.....................243
Point of View Essay: *God's Covenant: A Word That Cannot Come Back Void* 245
Heritage Profile: *Benjamin E. Mays*........246

LESSONS
Unit 1: Signs of God's Covenant
MARCH
2   The Ark Comes to Jerusalem
     1 Chronicles 15:1–3, 14–16, 25–28 ..248
9   God's Covenant with David
     1 Chronicles 17:1, 3–4, 6–15......256
16 God Calls Solomon to Build the Temple
     1 Chronicles 28:5–10, 20–21......265
23 Fulfillment of God's Promise
     2 Chronicles 6:12–17; Luke
     24:44–49 272
30 Josiah Renews the Covenant
     2 Chronicles 34:15, 18–19, 25–27,
     29, 31–33 280

Unit 2: Trusting God's Covenant in Hard Times
APRIL
6   Daniel Keeps Covenant in a Foreign Land
     Daniel 1:8–20 288
13 Three Refuse to Break Covenant
     Daniel 3:10–13, 16–18, 21, 24....297
20 Daniel's Life-and-Death Test
     Daniel 6:4–7, 10, 16, 19, 21, 25–26..305
27 Daniel's Prayer for the People
     Daniel 9:1–7, 17–19.....................313

Unit 3: Rebuilding the Walls and Renewing the Covenant
MAY
4   The Temple Rebuilt
     Haggai 1:1–4, 7–10, 12–15 322
11 Rebuilding the Wall
     Nehemiah 2:1–8, 11, 17–18 331
18 Up Against the Wall
     Nehemiah 4:1–3, 7–9, 13–15; 6:15 ..340
25 A Call to Renew the Covenant
     Nehemiah 8:1–3, 5–6, 13–14, 17–18....350

Summer Quarter, 2008

IMAGES OF CHRIST
June 2008 Quarter-At-A-Glance 359
Thematic Essay: *Jesus Christ—the Lamb Without Blemish* 361
Portrait of Christian Education Essay: *Motivating Christlike Behavior*..................363
Point of View Essay: *A Diverse Christ* 365
Heritage Profile: *Reverend Alexis Felder* ..367

LESSONS
Unit 1: Images of Christ in Hebrews
JUNE
1   Jesus as God's Son
     Hebrews 1:1–4, 8–12 369
8   Christ as Intercessor
     Hebrews 7:20–28 376
15 Christ as Redeemer
     Hebrews 9:11–18; 10:12–14, 17–18..384
22 Christ as Leader
     Hebrews 12:1–13 392
29 The Eternal Christ
     Hebrews 13:1–16 399

Unit 2: Images of Christ in the Gospels
JULY
6   Christ as Teacher
     Luke 4:31–37; 20:1–8 407
13 Christ as Healer
     Mark 1:29–45 416
20 Christ as Servant
     John 13:1–8, 12–20 426
27 Christ as Messiah
     Matthew 16:13–23 436

Unit 3: Images of Christ in Us
AUGUST
3   Doers of the Word
     James 1:17–27 445
10 Impartial Disciples
     James 2:1–13 455
17 Wise Speakers
     James 3:1–10, 13–18 463
24 People of Godly Behavior
     James 4:1–12 472
31 Prayerful Community
     James 5:13–18 481

CYCLE OF 2007–2010

Arrangement of Quarters According to the
Church School Year, September through August

	FALL	WINTER	SPRING	SUMMER
Year One 2007–08	Creation God Created a People (Genesis)	Call God's Call to the Christian Community (Luke)	Covenant God, the People, and the Covenant (1 and 2 Chronicles, Daniel, Haggai, Nehemiah)	Christ Images of Christ (Hebrews, Gospels
Year Two 2008–09	Community New Testament Survey	Commitment Human Commitment (Luke, Old Testament)	Creation Christ and Creation (Ezekiel, Luke, Acts, Ephesians)	Call Call of God's Covenant Community (Exodus, Leviticus, Numbers, Deuteronomy)
Year Three 2009–10	Covenant Covenant Communities (Joshua, Judges, Ezra, Nehemiah, Mark, 1 and 2 Peter)	Christ Christ the Fulfillment (Matthew)	Community Teachings on Community (John, Ruth, New Testament)	Commitment Christian Commitment in Today's World (1 and 2 Thessalonians, Philippians)

GOD— CREATOR OF ALL!

by Evangeline Carey

Study and appreciate the front cover of this year's *Precepts For Living® Annual Commentary*. Then be reminded that the God we serve, the God who is the Head of our lives, created everything that exists. He created so much beauty, and He is supreme over all He created. Without Him, nothing exists. Our graphics take us to the star-lit heavens, where the stars may equal *all* the grains of *all* the sands on *all* the beaches of the world. Those stars should remind you of God's covenant with Abraham. After an obedient Abraham was willing to sacrifice his son Isaac, God told him, "I will bless you richly. I will multiply your descendants into countless millions, like the stars of the sky and the sand on the sea shore" (22:17).

Now gaze on the captivating blue waters that should remind you of Genesis 1:6 where God Himself said, "Let there be a firmament in the midst of the waters, and let it divide the waters from the waters." Together, the stars and the waters should refresh your spirit and remind you that we serve an awesome God! He, and only He, is sovereign (in control of even history and never out of control).

These stars and the waters should also remind you of *transformation*—how Almighty God took "an earth without form and void" (Genesis 1:2) and made it into something magnificent! This same God can transform, or change, lives ravaged by sin and also make them beautiful. He can make them into lives that lift up holy hands and hearts and bring glory and honor to a Holy God. He can put His own Spirit in us so that we become the witnesses that He is calling for us to be. As His witnesses, we will proclaim His Good News of salvation in the highways, byways, and the uttermost parts of the earth and bring hope and beauty to other lives.

In the four quarters that we will study, we should see and appreciate that God created His universe, including His world (the heavens, earth, the seas, grass and herb yielding seeds, living creatures after his kind, cattle, creeping thing, beast of the earth after his kind, and finally humanity [Genesis 1:1–27]). Because of His unconditional love for us, it was only humans that He created in His own image—after His likeness (v. 27). This means that we are able to think, reason, and choose to have an intimate, personal relationship with our holy God. We are able to worship our God, who is more than enough in our times of trouble.

Specifically in the first quarter, we will explore the "book of beginnings"—Genesis. We will study the theme of "Creation." From our review, we learn just how powerful and mighty God is. Notice how He speaks and makes something out of nothing (1:3).

The second quarter takes us to the book of Luke and we examine "God's Call to the Christian Community"—which is made up of all believers, regardless of race, creed, color, or national origin (the universal church). Because we are to be God's light in a dark world plagued by evil and sin, this call summons us to unity and obedience.

Then the third quarter deals with the "Covenant" theme. From the Old Testament books of 1 and 2 Chronicles, Daniel, Haggai, and Nehemiah, we learn more about God (His attributes), the people (the Israelites—God's chosen people), and the Covenant (the old agreement that the Children of Israel were expected to obey and see how it leads into and differs from the New Covenant).

We should be grateful that under the New Covenant, Gentiles (you and me) are included. We are "grafted (inserted) into "The Olive Tree"—(a metaphor for God's chosen people, the Israelites—the parent tree). This simply means that the blessings that were first meant for only Israel, now includes all believers—

Jews and Gentiles. The crown jewel of this binding agreement is that God provides atonement for our sins in the person of Jesus Christ. He is our sin *eradicator—a terminator.* He is 100%God/100% man, sinless, and will die a substitutionary, sacrificial death on the Cross at Calvary to pay all believers' sin penalty. In other words, a Holy God deemed that the penalty for sin is death. However, Jesus took our place on that Cross. He took our punishment and by God's grace (favor) we are saved through believing on the Lord Jesus Christ (John 3:16).

The Old Testament Scriptures, covered in the first three quarters, laid the foundation for the Messiah, Jesus Christ, to come and the Israelites looked forward to His arrival. Now in the last quarter, we look at the New Testament and find that God continues His narrative saga or redemption for humanity. Here, we will study the Gospels and Hebrews where Jesus came and we are now looking forward to His Second Coming. He came the first time as a Suffering Servant—a Saviour who endured grave pain, bled, and died a cruel death for the sins of humanity (for your sins and mine). However, He's coming back the second time as Judge. The time to seek Him as Saviour will be no more. This season will be over.

As you study these four quarters, note that God is laying out His plan of salvation before us. In the given Scriptures, follow the thread of His redemptive plan as He builds His kingdom, which will consist of everyone who has believed on the Lord Jesus Christ as their personal Saviour. Follow in Genesis how He creates His world and declares that it was very good, including man (Genesis 1–3). Then notice how, after the fall of Adam and Eve, Almighty Sovereign God sets in motion His plan of salvation or redemption from sin by electing or choosing for Himself a people (the Israelites), who would act as role models to a lost and dying world and show us *how to* and *how not to* walk in intimate fellowship with a Holy God. Most of all, the "Messiah Seed" would come through this line. Finally be aware that Jesus came and He's coming back again.

The Old Testament believers looked forward to His coming. The Gospels tell us that He came. We must now answer the question, "Will we be ready for His Second Coming?"

Evangeline Carey is a staff writer for UMI and has been an adult Sunday School teacher for more than 25 years.

SEPTEMBER 2007
QUARTER AT-A-GLANCE
God Created a People

The overall focus for this quarter is creation. As we explore the book of Genesis, we trace God's creative power from the creation of the universe through human creation to the creation of a covenant people.

UNIT 1 . GOD CREATED A PEOPLE

In these five lessons, we explore God's work as He creates the universe, humankind, and a family of promise.

Lesson 1: September 2, 2007
God Created the Heavens and the Earth
Genesis 1:1–6, 8, 10, 12–15, 19–20, 22–23, 25

God is the Creator of the universe. He created the heavens, earth, and everything in it in an orderly fashion. Not only is He the Creator, but He is the sustainer of life. Upon surveying His creation, God deemed it "good."

Lesson 2: September 9, 2007
God Created Humankind
Genesis 1:26–30

After creating the heavens, earth, and all in it, God created humankind. Both man and woman were created and blessed by God in His image and given dominion over creation.

Lesson 3: September 16, 2007
Abraham, Sarah, and Isaac
Genesis 15:5–6; 18:11–14; 21:1–8

God promised Abraham that his descendants would be as numerous as the stars. Though elderly and having a wife past childbearing years, Abraham and Sarah bore Isaac, and from this line a covenant people were created.

Lesson 4: September 23, 2007
Abraham, Hagar, and Ishmael
Genesis 21:9–21

During Isaac's weaning ceremony, Sarah saw Ishmael mocking him. That, along with Sarah's partiality toward Isaac, caused her to demand that Abraham send Ishmael and Hagar away. Abraham was conflicted—after all Ishmael was his son too—but God instructed Abraham to listen to Sarah. God promised to make Ishmael into a great nation as well, and He was with Ishmael as he grew.

Lesson 5: September 30, 2007
Isaac and Rebekah
Genesis 24:34–40, 42–45, 48

Abraham's servant (Eliezer) was sent out to find a wife for Isaac. Both men trusted that God would guide the servant to the right woman for Isaac. God did. He led Eliezer to Rebekah.

UNIT 2 . GOD'S PEOPLE INCREASED

These four lessons follow the development of the family of promise from Jacob and Esau's rivalry to their reconciliation.

Lesson 6: October 7, 2007
Esau and Jacob as Rivals
Genesis 25:19–34

Esau and Jacob were twins born to Isaac and Rebekah. God told Rebekah that her children represented two nations. From birth (and fueled by parental favoritism) Esau and Jacob were rivals. This rivalry continued into adulthood, as Jacob traded a bowl of stew to a hungry Esau for his birthright.

Lesson 7: October 14, 2007
Jacob's Dream at Bethel
Genesis 28:10–22

Jacob had an encounter with God in a dream. In his dream, Jacob saw a ladder that ascended to heaven; God was at the top of the ladder. God confirmed His covenant with Jacob to create a covenant people through this family line and to be with Jacob at all times. Jacob responded faithfully by tithing.

1

Lesson 8: October 21, 2007
Jacob and Rachel
Genesis 29:21–35

Jacob worked for Laban for seven years in order to marry Rachel. When the time came, however, Laban deceived Jacob, and he wound up marrying Rachel's older sister, Leah. Jacob had to work for Laban seven more years in order to marry the woman he loved.

Lesson 9: October 28, 2007
Esau and Jacob Reconciled
Genesis 33:1–11

The last time Jacob saw Esau, Esau was ready to kill him. So, Jacob was apprehensive about seeing his brother again. Surprisingly, things were different. When the brothers met, Esau embraced Jacob, showing a forgiving attitude rather than a vengeful one. Both brothers showed a willingness to restore their broken relationship.

UNIT 3 .
GOD'S PEOPLE RE-CREATED

When the people were threatened with starvation and death, God preserved their lives and continued to bless them. These lessons begin with Joseph's dream and conclude with Jacob blessing his grandsons.

Lesson 10: November 4, 2007
Joseph's Dream
Genesis 37:5–11, 19–21, 23–24, 28

Joseph announced his dreams of greatness to his father and already jealous brothers. The brothers plotted to kill him, but rather than being racked with guilt of his blood on their hands, they sold him into slavery.

Lesson 11: November 11, 2007
Joseph's Dream Began to Come True
Genesis 41:25–40

Pharaoh had a dream that was puzzling him. God gave Joseph the ability to interpret Pharaoh's dream to mean that the land would experience seven years of abundance and seven years of famine. Joseph offered Pharaoh a solution, and in return, Pharaoh elevated Joseph to a position of power, which is what Joseph, himself, dreamed.

Lesson 12: November 18, 2007
God Preserved a Remnant
Genesis 45:1–12

Joseph identifies himself to his brothers and realizes that the events in his life—specifically their selling him into Egypt—were part of God's grand plan to preserve a remnant of the family of promise. God worked out for good what Joseph's brothers meant for evil.

Lesson 13: November 25, 2007
Jacob Blessed His Family
Genesis 48:11–19

Jacob moved to Egypt to live out his last days. There he pronounced blessings on Joseph's sons, Ephraim and Manasseh, giving the younger son, Ephraim, a greater blessing. Jacob's blessing continued the line of descendants promised to Abraham and Sarah.

THEMATIC ESSAY

IN THE BEGINNING, GOD CREATED..!

by Evangeline Carey

In this quarter, we will explore the book of Genesis, the very first book of the Canon (the 66 books of the Bible). Genesis means "beginnings" or "origin." It gives the biblical view of creation and explains the beginning of the world, including civilization—human history, marriage, family, and God's plan of salvation for humanity. It is here that the story begins of how God created everything that exists, and how He formed it from nothing (1:2). Emphatically and without revocation, the Word of God states that God created the world and everything in it, including all life. Without Him there is nothing that exists. Consequently, everything begins with God, and everything, as we know it, will end with God (Revelation 21).

In Unit I, we examine how "God Created a People." This is a five-lesson unit that tells Israel's earliest history. Unfortunately when Adam and Eve chose to disobey God in the Garden of Eden, they broke their intimate, personal relationship with Him. This caused momentous problems for all humanity. Specifically, sin came into the world. The facts are: God created a perfect earth and all its contents and said they were very good (1:31). He also created man and woman and they were perfect and good too. However, God chose to give us a "free will" so that we could choose or not choose to have an intimate relationship with Him. We could choose to obey Him or choose not to obey Him. Like Adam and Eve, too often humanity chooses not to obey our Creator, and we must suffer the dire consequences.

There is no doubt, then, that God created a universe He determined was very good, and humanity messed it up with their disobedience. You see, before they sinned, Adam and Eve were perfection themselves and were surrounded by it: they (1) were in a perfect paradise (Genesis 2:8–15); (2)

were protected by their innocence in the garden; (3) did not fear God because they had no sin, shame, or guilt (3:10); (4) were not separated from a holy God because of their sins; (5) were free from any pain and suffering; and (6) were comfortable in God's presence (3:8–10). However, the situation drastically changed after they disobeyed God's command not to eat from the Tree of Knowledge of Good and Evil. In fact, they had colossal losses: (1) their innocence—purity (now they had sin, shame, and guilt); (2) their comfort in the presence of a holy God (now, they had limited access to Him because their sin separated them from a holy God [3:8–10]); and (3) of their home (after they sinned, they were barred from the garden [v. 23]); plus, their rebellion against God opened the floodgates to suffering, pain, and death for all humanity.

Due to the fact that Adam and Eve, who were the highlight of God's creation, rebelled and disobeyed God in the Garden of Eden, God created a a people (the Israelites) whom He would use as examples to help restore our intimate relationship with a holy God. In essence, God established a line through which the "Messiah Seed" (Jesus Christ) would come. He would be the Saviour of humanity. He came to save us from our sins.

God's chosen people, then, are descendants of Shem, one of Noah's sons (Genesis 10:21–23). In fact, Abraham, David, and Jesus all descended from him. His progeny also included these Bible nations: "the Hebrews, Chaldeans, Assyrians, Persians and Syrians" (*Life Application Study Bible* 1996, 21). The Israelites were to show all nations *how to walk* and *how not to walk* with a holy God. Studies of the sacred Scriptures reveal the following:

Noah & His Wife

The Sons and Their Descendants

Shem	(Hebrews, Chaldeans, Assyrians, Persians, and Syrians) Abraham and the entire Jewish nation descended from Shem, including David and Jesus
Ham	(Canaanites, Egyptians, Philistines, Hittites, and Amorites) They settled in Canaan, Egypt, and the rest of Africa.
Japheth	(Greeks, Thracians, and Scythians) They settled in Europe and Asia Minor.

ABRAHAM & SARAH	Isaac & Ishmael
ISAAC & REBEKAH	Esau & Jacob

Thus, Abraham and Sarah had Isaac, the promised child. By Sarah's servant, Hagar, Abraham's son, Ishmael, was born. We will explore God's creation of these two different family lines from Abraham, but how the continuation of the family of promise was through Isaac (the child from Abraham and Sarah's union).

In Unit II, we see how "God's People Increased." The promised family grew through God blessing Jacob (Isaac and Rebekah's son). Even though Esau was the first born, he gave up the special honor that goes to the firstborn son for the immediate pleasure of satisfying his hunger for food (Genesis 25:31–34). This birthright included a double portion of the family inheritance and the chance of one day becoming the family's leader. Therefore, instead of Esau, the birthright went through Jacob. Subsequently, God's chosen people are the 12 tribes of Israel or Jacob's (Israel's) 12 sons. They are God's chosen people, who entered a covenant relationship with Him. The chart below shows the family line and some important descendants.

Finally, Unit III of our study explores "God's People Re-created." In this discussion, God directs the Children of Israel's movement to Egypt using Jacob (Israel) and his favorite wife Rachel's son, Joseph. Because Joseph was Jacob's preferred son, jealousy ensued between the brothers and they sold Joseph to "Ishmaelite traders taking a load of gum, balm, and aromatic resin from Gilead down to Egypt" (37:25, NLT). In Egypt, the traders sold Joseph to Potiphar, one of Pharaoh's (the king of Egypt) officers (v. 36). However, a sovereign God was still in control of these historical events. He used these negatives and turned them into positives. Joseph being sold into slavery put him in Egypt, where there was plenty of food during a seven-year famine. This also allowed Pharaoh to put Joseph in charge of Egypt and the food bank, and even make him ruler (41:37–41). At 30 years of age, Joseph became second to the pharaoh in command in Egypt.

The all-powerful God permitted this seven-year famine that brought Joseph and his brothers face to face again. This also brought God's chosen people to Egypt, where they multiplied to the point that many years later, a Pharaoh who did not know Joseph decreed that the Israelites would become slaves to the Egyptians (Exodus 1:8–11). They served them for approximately 400 years. Then God heard their cries and delivered them out with a mighty hand. Clearly, God sent Joseph to Egypt ahead of his family to preserve a remnant threatened with starvation. He brought them into Egypt and took them out of there too. They are His Covenant People, whom He promised to take to the Promised Land, the land flowing with milk and honey—the land flowing with God's goodness. All they had to do is follow, trust, and obey Him.

From the narrative of God's creation, His creating a people, and then re-creating them, we also see embedded themes and theological concepts that flow through the Scriptures. Some are:

God is *awesome*: He does what He does, what He wills, and needs help from no one. He answers to no one but Himself.

God is *creative* and *Creator*: He made everything that exists and without Him nothing exists.

God is *distinct from His creation*: He is higher, infinite, and superior than all His creation.

God is *eternal*: He always has existed and always will exist. Moses said in Psalm 90:2, KJV, "from everlasting to everlasting, thou art God."

God *has order*: He had a plan in creating and in saving humanity and He worked well His plan—He put it into place and is seeing it to fruition.

God is *holy*: God is set apart from sin. He will not tolerate it. He deemed that the penalty for sin is death (eternal separation from a holy God).

Jacob's Family Tree

The Wives

ZILPAH	LEAH	RACHEL	BILHAH
[Leah's servant]		[favorite]	[Rachel's servant]

The Children
(12 Sons and 1 daughter and their notable descendants)

Gad	Reuben	Joseph	Dan (Samson)
Asher	Simeon	Benjamin	Naphtali
	Levi		
	Judah		
	Issachar		
	Zebulun		
	Dinah		

God is *infinite*. He created time and space, but is outside of time and space. He is not contained by time and space.

God is *Judge*. He will judge sin. He judged Adam and Eve for their disobedience in the garden, He judged the evilness of Noah's time (chapter 6), and He will also judge us.

God is *love*. Because He loved us, He meticulously made His universe and all that is in it, including humanity.

God is *omnipotent (all-powerful)*: Through His creating, we see God's power and purpose. He spoke and things fell into place (Genesis 1:3, 6, 9–11).

God is *sovereign*: He is in control and never out of control of events and things that happen in His world, even history. He spoke, He said, He divided, He saw, and even He evaluated what He had done and said it was very good.

God is *Sustainer*. He keeps, cares for, and loves His creation. He protected Noah and his family in the ark (Genesis 6–8). That ark was the "Ark of Safety"—those who got into the ark were saved from the flood. Those outside of the ark died. Jesus is now our "Ark of Safety." Those who believe on Him or accept Him as their Lord and Saviour are saved—they are inside the Ark of Safety.

However, those who choose not to accept Jesus Christ are outside of the ark—they will be eternally separated from a holy God.

Remember that the book of Genesis sets the stage for the entire Bible—all 66 books. It shows an orderly God interrupting eternity with His grand program of creating. When the world as we know it now, with all its evil and violence, is destroyed and God creates a new heaven and new earth (Revelation 21), again He will be able to say, "It is very good!"

Sources:

Arnold, Bill T., and Bryan E. Beyer. *Encountering the Old Testament.* Grand Rapids, Mich.: Baker Book House Co., 1998. 1–101.

The Life Application Study Bible, King James Version. Wheaton, Ill.: Tyndale House Publishers. 1996.

The Life Application Study Bible, New Living Translation. Wheaton, Ill.: Tyndale House Publishers, 1996.

Evangeline Carey *is a staff writer for UMI and has been an adult Sunday School teacher for more than 25 years.*

CREATION

by Cheryl Clemetson, Ph.D.

God's creation is so awesome and amazing that we can marvel at its wonder and proclaim, "Only God." From the beginning of creation, the handiwork of God is vivid and so miraculous that we are reminded of the all-exclusive rights of the inception, the implementation, and the by-products of all creation. Only God could have created something of complexity out of nothingness and simplistic order out of chaos. (Genesis 1:1). We see the Lord's handiwork from the majestic mountain to the smallest grain of sand. There are many creation stories from various religious and cultural beliefs. Yet, the beauty and the excellence of how the Judeo-Christian story is expressed, is breathtaking. In the book of Genesis we are invited to share in the wondrous work of God's creation of all the world with words of pointed poetic excellence from the distinct and intentional difference of darkness and light to the luscious fruit and gentle waters. The Lord's creativity is embedded with mysteries that humanity is yet to fully discover or embrace in our lives.

The unknown complexities of God are unparalleled throughout the universe. Although science and technology have unlocked many secrets, we are left with more questions and concerns as to the mysteries of God and about the goodness and the power of nature that we cannot control or harness all for ourselves. As someone once asked, "Have you noticed how God gave man the control of everything but nature?" In God's infinite wisdom, the Lord knew not to give us control over nature so that we can command who can use what and when at our whim, which would be utterly disastrous and chaotic. Although we cannot have total control over nature, we do have the responsibility and opportunity to learn how we can work with nature and learn from it. Learning the secrets about our natural resources and embracing our distinctive role as caretakers of the world enables us to discover important information to help live healthier lives and to respect nature.

It is through the growing principle of reaping and sowing that we can apply biblical truths to our lives. What we choose to plant, the type of soil we plant in, when we plant, and how we nurture and care for what we plant are necessary components for yielding good crops. The significance of planting and reaping is found in the Bible in the many stories and choices that people make. For example, Jesus uses this basic principle of reaping and sowing from an agricultural vantage point to explain the planting of God's Word in our lives in Matthew 13. In this parable the creation of life in the Word of God is evidenced in what type of soil the seeds are planted in; it is a determining factor in the seeds' growth. The seeds thrown upon rocky soil and thorns do not have the nutrients to nourish the seed. Yet, the seeds that are given to the right soil for their development grow. This is a reminder to us that everyone can be touched by the Word of God; but what nourishing resources are we using to give life to the Word of God in us?

Some of the nourishing resources we have for us as Christians are the power of God's Word, prayer, and God's promises. Christianity is sometimes viewed as a weak religion, and we Christians are weak in our faith and belief in the Lord when we do not exercise the power we have in God's Word. The power we find in Christianity emerges from the ability to serve a God who is the creator of all creation. Therefore, we begin with our supreme God, whose power to create is immeasurable and inexhaustible. God's ability to speak and form creation cannot be compared or measured to any other. We do not know when the Lord decided to create the world as we know it or create us, but we do know that it is because of God that all of creation has its life.

One of the joys of being a part of God's creation is sharing in the power of God's Word. God's

"In the beginning God created the heaven and the earth" (from Genesis 1:1).

creation is not limited to the beauty or the complexities of nature. One of the many joys we have is power and creativity of God's Word. We can find peace and solace in the Word as we read Psalm 23 or Psalm 121. When we are afraid, we can read Psalm 27 or the story of Rahab and know that God can and does make a way for us. At the same time, we are reminded of our need to change and repent when we have left the comfort and direction of the Holy Spirit as we read in the Gospel of John and the book of Romans. Giving compassion and showing mercy to others through understanding and knowing what God expects from us as in the book of Micah reminds us how we are to walk and live our lives before the Lord. The power of God's Word is so real and awesome that we are always learning more about who the Lord is and our relationship with Him as we read and live the Holy Word.

The challenges in our lives and the lives of others speak volumes as to how we abuse the creative gifts that the Lord has blessed us with and the many blessings we have. Issues from homelessness to domestic violence to poverty are rampant and in every pocket of society around the world. Yet, we are blinded and do not see clearly because we choose to not see or do what we need to do for others.

Behold the beauty of the Lord and all of God's majesty when we are enticed by the lovely fragrance of a gentle rose, or see the gentle waves dance with delight against the warm grains of sand, or when we help a child who has been broken and is in pain because of abuse, or give food and shelter to those in need. As those created in God's image, creativity is a part of who we are. Let us be creative for the good and the glory of the Lord to make a difference in the world and bring hope and solutions to those who suffer throughout the world and in our own backyards.

Cheryl Clemetson, Ph.D., is the vice president of editorial at UMI.

GOD'S WORD—THE TIE THAT BINDS

by Darcy Ingraham

O Lord , my God. When I, in awesome wonder, consider all the world thy hands have made. I see the stars; I hear the rolling thunder. Thy power throughout the universe displayed," said Carl Boberg in 1886. Indeed, we are surrounded by God. We can see Him in the exquisiteness of all His creation, a world crafted by the hand of God. Humankind was created from the dust of the ground, and brought to life by His very breath. The book of Genesis illustrates, with written word, the birth of this earth and all that is on it (1:1–27). Despite the historical account that the Bible gives us, some people still doubt that the world was created by God. Perhaps those who doubt have not taken the time to look around and observe the intricacies and awe-inspiring beauty of God's masterpiece.

> *"Hidden within the pages of the Bible are many answers to life from beginning to end."*

It's easy to get caught up in our busy lives. Ironic is the fact that we become so preoccupied with life that we neglect the one who created us. Much like static on a radio station drowns out the music, the business in our lives drowns out God's voice of guidance and direction. Unable to hear His voice, we will lose our way. Nineteenth-century scholar, educator, and activist Anna Julia Cooper once said, "One needs occasionally to stand aside from the hum and rush of human interests and passions to hear the voices of God."

God often speaks to us through His own creation if we take the time to listen. After the great Flood, God used His creation to establish a covenant with Noah. "And I will establish my covenant with you; neither shall all flesh be cut off any more by the waters of a flood; neither shall there any more be a flood to destroy the earth. And God said, This is the token of the covenant which I make between me and you and every living creature that is with you, for perpetual generations: I do set my bow in the cloud, and it shall be for a token of a covenant between me and the earth. And it shall come to pass, when I bring a cloud over the earth, that the bow shall be seen in the cloud," (Genesis 9:11–14, KJV). Be it a gentle breeze, a babbling brook or the falling leaves, listen. He's whispering to you.

Another way God speaks to us is through His Word. One cannot pick and choose what parts of the Bible we want to believe. From Genesis and the beginning of creation to Revelation and Christ's second coming, it's all or nothing. The Bible as a whole is the tie that binds it all together from beginning to end. The Old Testament is a historical account of life before the birth of our Saviour that lays the groundwork for the teachings of Christ in the New Testament. English novelist, Charles Dickens grasped the connection between the Bible's account of creation and its relevance today when he said, "The whole difference between construction and creation is exactly this: that a thing constructed can only be loved after it is constructed; but a thing created is loved before it exists." Sin corrupted the heart of humankind in the Garden of Eden (Genesis 3). God sent His Son to be born of a virgin, walk among us, teach us, and ultimately die on the cross to save us from our sins. God sacrificed His own Son because He loved us so. Though our hearts are tainted with sin, God still loves us and wants us to spend eternity with him.

The Bible teaches us how to live a Christlike, purposeful life—a path that will lead us to our heavenly home and the throne of God.

When we accept God's gift of salvation through His Son, we are making a commitment. Our life is no longer about self, but rather how God can use our life for the furthering of His divine purposes. Colossians 1:14–17 reminds us of the magnificence of the One we serve: "In whom we have redemption through his blood, even the forgiveness of sins: Who is the image of the invisible God, the firstborn of every creature: For by him were all things created, that are in heaven, and that are in earth, visible and invisible, whether they be thrones, or dominions, or principalities, or powers: all things were created by him, and for him: And he is before all things, and by him all things consist." Living a life dedicated to serving the One who created us, the Lord our God, will take self-sacrifice, perseverance, and inner strength.

To remain a focused and faithful servant, we will need continuous spiritual refueling lest we grow weary and discouraged. We all know that God is unmovable, unshaken. Scientist and educator George Washington Carver once said, "Our Creator is the same and never changes despite the names given Him by people here and in all parts of the world. Even if we gave Him no name at all, He would still be there, within us, waiting to give us good on this earth." If one day we wake up feeling discouraged and find we have lost our nearness to God, He is not the one who moved. There are steps we can take to maintain our relationship with Him. Just as we refuel our physical bodies to remain healthy, we must also refuel the spiritual part of ourselves to remain healthy and strong.

There is so much sadness and suffering in this world that sometimes we wonder where God is. We could easily succumb to the pain and cry out in despair. In times such as this, we need to look closely for God because He is here. Singer and performer Pearl Bailey knew this too. She said, "People see God every day; they just don't recognize him." God's Word, the Bible, is a wonderful source of encouragement. Just as God is unmoved,

His Word is unchanged. In the Old Testament we can read about such things as the wondrous creation of the world and be awed. We can be comforted by the words of the Psalms. We can be encouraged by the courageousness of godly men and women. In the New Testament we can read about the miraculous birth, life, death, and resurrection of Christ. We can be edified by the teaching of the parables and strengthened by the faithfulness of the disciples. Reading the Bible every day will help keep us spiritually strong and better able to thwart Satan's attacks. Just like animals of prey will seek out weakened victims—so, too, will Satan. The sword of the Spirit may well be our greatest defense. It is that and so much more.

Hidden within the pages of the Bible are many answers to life from beginning to end. The Bible reveals every truth we need to know in order to live a God-honoring life. We need to believe its words, heed its instruction, and share its timeless truths.

Living a godly life and leaving a legacy of love and devotion to our Creator, our heavenly Father, our King, is the greatest treasure we can leave to our children. It will impact their lives and make a difference far beyond any monetary gain we bequeath to them.

There are many uncertainties in this world. Nothing we say or do in this life guarantees us a positive outcome, aside from living a godly life. "For the which cause I also suffer these things: nevertheless I am not ashamed: for I know whom I have believed, and am persuaded that he is able to keep that which I have committed unto him against that day" (2 Timothy 1:12). God alone is the one certainty we have, for He is not an ordinary God.

He is God the Father, God the Son, and God the Holy Spirit. He is our Creator and He is our King. Is this your King?

Darcy Ingraham is a freelance writer who lives in upstate New York. She resides with her husband of 23 years and four sons. She is a fill-in pianist and teaches Junior Church.

ELIJAH MCCOY

(1843–1929)

Inventor

In 1843, Elijah McCoy, the son of fugitive slaves, was born in Ontario, Canada. His parents, George and Mildred McCoy, had escaped on the Underground Railroad from Kentucky to Canada, where slavery had been abolished since 1833. George McCoy then served for the British force and was blessed to receive 160 acres of farmland. At a young age, Elijah began taking things apart and rebuilding them, demonstrating an interest in mechanics. Mr. McCoy's appreciation for education led him to send Elijah, the third of twelve children, to Scotland to study engineering. There, during his apprenticeship, he began to gain recognition of his gift for machinery and received Master of Mechanics and Engineering credentials.

Following his studies in Scotland and in pursuit of employment as an engineer, he traveled to Ypsilanti, Michigan. However, due to the prejudice that still existed, he was unable to find work in that particular field. In 1870, he became a locomotive fireman and an oiler for the Michigan Central Railroad, a job that had promising possibilities of promotion. McCoy was responsible for shoveling coal and servicing the locomotives as they came in. During his work with machinery, McCoy began to take notice of the limitations and disadvantages involved with locomotives. Although the late 1800s were times of great invention, the lubrication system of locomotives was taxing and inefficient. Locomotives had to be shut down consistently and all the parts oiled with an oilcan. On June 23, 1872, McCoy patented the "Lubricating Cup," a device that oiled moving parts, requiring less maintenance and making the machinery more durable.

While he worked as an industrial consultant for the Detroit Lubricator Company and other firms, McCoy continued to focus on his inventions. The railroad industry continued to improve and began building larger locomotives, some as much as four times larger. The larger machines required higher horsepower and burned lots of coal, so they used superheated steam, which improved the coal burned per mile, but once again created a problem in lubrication. The large locomotives required an oil and powered graphite mixture, which would sometimes clog engines. In 1915, McCoy patented the "Locomotive Lubricator," which took away the danger of clogging.

McCoy received over 50 patents in his lifetime. His contributions to the building of locomotives revolutionized the railroad industry. In spite of enormous success, McCoy was financially unable to manufacture his inventions in mass quantities, so he sold many of his patent rights. His inventions made millions of dollars, but he received only enough to continue his passion.

At 77, he founded the Elijah McCoy Manufacturing Company in Detroit with other investors. The company sold and manufactured the "Locomotive Lubricators." After God granted him a long life of fulfillment and inventions that changed America, Elijah McCoy died on October 10, 1929. He received recognition in 1975, when the city of Detroit celebrated Elijah McCoy Day by marking his home as a historical site and naming a street after him.

Sources:

Crudup, Byron. "Elijah McCoy." Blacks in Technology: Past and Present Website. http://www.users.fast.net/~blc/xlhome6.htm (accessed February 23, 2007).

"Elijah McCoy." Africa Within Website, 2001. www.africawithin.com/bios/elijah_mccoy.htm (accessed February 23, 2007).

"Elijah McCoy." The Black Inventor Online Museum Website. www.blackinventor.com/pages/elijahmccoy.html (accessed February 23, 2007).

Stephanie LaFlora is a college student and summer intern at Urban Ministries, Inc.

TEACHING TIPS

September 2
Bible Study Guide 1

1. Words You Should Know

A. Created (Genesis 1:1) *bara'* (Heb.)—To shape, form, or fashion; to make out of nothing.

B. Firmament (vv. 6, 8, 14–15, 20) *raqiya`* (Heb.)—Extended surface or solid expanse; sky.

2. Teacher Preparation

Unifying Principle—How Is Creation Possible? How the universe came into existence is a question still being asked today. Christians, however, know that God spoke Creation into existence. In Genesis 1, we learn that God is the originator and sustainer of life.

A. Read the Focal Verses. Begin to prepare to teach the lesson by spending time in prayer contemplating God's awesome handiwork in creating the universe.

B. Read the September Quarter Thematic Essay.

C. Read the Bible Background and study the Devotional Reading Scriptures in at least two different Bible versions, keeping the AIM for Change and the Unifying Principle in mind.

D. Outline the significant points of today's lesson based upon achieving the AIM for Change objectives. Be sensitive to the various perspectives regarding creationism versus evolution.

E. Complete lesson 1 for September 2 in the *Precepts For Living® Personal Study Guide.*

3. Starting the Lesson

A. Begin class time with prayer.

B. Introduce the quarterly theme, "God Created a People," by providing a brief overview of the September Quarter Thematic Essay.

C. Tell the class that the topic for today's lesson is "How Is Creation Possible?" (Unifying Principle).

D. Explain to the class the objectives of today's lesson by reinforcing the AIM for Change.

4. Getting into the Lesson

A. Get the class involved in the lesson by asking a volunteer to read the In Focus life application story.

B. Remind the class that the Creation story is the most significant story of the Bible, because on it hangs all the other truths of the Scriptures. If people do not believe what Genesis 1:1–15 teaches, they may have difficulty believing the rest of the Bible.

C. Have the class read the the Focal Verses and answer the Search the Scriptures and Discuss the Meaning questions.

D. If time allows, complete lesson 1 for September 2 in the *Precepts For Living® Personal Study Guide.*

5. Relating the Lesson to Life

A. Challenge the class members to look at their own lives and think about how the Creation story might relate to where they are in their walk with the Lord.

B. Engage the class in a discussion based on the questions in Lesson in Our Society.

6. Arousing Action

A. Have the students reflect on their own lives. What does the Creation story mean to them?

B. Ask a volunteer to share what he or she has learned from today's lesson.

C. Be sure to provide time for the class to discuss the Make It Happen activity.

D. Remind the class to read the Daily Bible Readings for September 9, and suggest that they complete lesson 2 from the *Precepts For Living® Personal Study Guide* in preparation for next week's lesson.

E. Close the class with prayer, thanking God for His beautiful creation.

Worship Guide

For the Superintendent or Teacher
Theme: God Created the Heavens and the Earth
Theme Song: "I Love to Tell the Story"
Devotional Reading: Psalm 8
Prayer

GOD CREATED THE HEAVENS AND THE EARTH

Bible Background • GENESIS 1:1–25
Printed Text • GENESIS 1:1–6, 8, 10, 12–15, 19–20, 22–23, 25   Devotional Reading • PSALM 8

AIM for Change

By the end of the lesson, we will:
EXPLORE the Genesis account of how the universe was created;
BELIEVE that God is the Creator and Sustainer of life; and
SHOW an appreciation for creation by being good stewards of God's creation.

Keep in Mind

"In the beginning God created the heaven and the earth. And the earth was without form, and void; and darkness was upon the face of the deep. And the spirit of God moved upon the face of the waters" (Genesis 1:1–2).

Focal Verses

KJV

Genesis 1:1 In the beginning God created the heaven and the earth.

2 And the earth was without form, and void; and darkness was upon the face of the deep. And the Spirit of God moved upon the face of the waters.

3 And God said, Let there be light: and there was light.

4 And God saw the light, that it was good: and God divided the light from the darkness.

5 And God called the light Day, and the darkness he called Night. And the evening and the morning were the first day.

6 And God said, Let there be a firmament in the midst of the waters, and let it divide the waters from the waters.

1:8 And God called the firmament Heaven. And the evening and the morning were the second day.

1:10 And God called the dry land Earth; and the gathering together of the waters called he Seas: and God saw that it was good.

1:12 And the earth brought forth grass, and herb yielding seed after his kind, and the tree yielding fruit, whose seed was in itself, after his kind: and God saw that it was good.

13 And the evening and the morning were the third day.

14 And God said, Let there be lights in the firmament of the heaven to divide the day from the night; and let them be for signs, and for seasons, and for days, and years:

15 And let them be for lights in the firmament of the heaven to give light upon the earth: and it was so.

NLT

Genesis 1:1 In the beginning God created the heavens and the earth.

2 The earth was formless and empty, and darkness covered the deep waters. And the Spirit of God was hovering over the surface of the waters.

3 Then God said, "Let there be light," and there was light.

4 And God saw that the light was good. Then he separated the light from the darkness.

5 God called the light "day" and the darkness "night." And evening passed and morning came, marking the first day.

6 Then God said, "Let there be a space between the waters, to separate the waters of the heavens from the waters of the earth."

1:8 God called the space "sky." And evening passed and morning came, marking the second day.

1:10 God called the dry ground "land" and the waters "seas." And God saw that it was good.

1:12 The land produced vegetation—all sorts of seed-bearing plants, and trees with seed-bearing fruit. Their seeds produced plants and trees of the same kind. And God saw that it was good.

13 And evening passed and morning came, marking the third day.

14 Then God said, "Let great lights appear in the sky to separate the day from the night. Let them mark off the seasons, days, and years.

15 Let these lights in the sky shine down on the earth." And that is what happened.

1:19 And the evening and the morning were the fourth day.

20 And God said, Let the waters bring forth abundantly the moving creature that hath life, and fowl that may fly above the earth in the open firmament of heaven.

1:22 And God blessed them, saying, Be fruitful, and multiply, and fill the waters in the seas, and let fowl multiply in the earth.

23 And the evening and the morning were the fifth day.

1:25 And God made the beast of the earth after his kind, and cattle after their kind, and every thing that creepeth upon the earth after his kind: and God saw that is was good.

1:19 And evening passed and morning came, marking the fourth day.

20 Then God said, "Let the waters swarm with fish and other life. Let the skies be filled with birds of every kind."

1:22 Then God blessed them, saying, "Be fruitful and multiply. Let the fish fill the seas, and let the birds multiply on the earth."

23 And evening passed and morning came, marking the fifth day.

1:25 God made all sorts of wild animals, livestock, and small animals, each able to produce offspring of the same kind. And God saw that it was good.

In Focus

Lois attends a university in the Pacific Northwest. Coming from a conservative evangelical background, she always believed the Creator of the universe was God. However, Lois's physical anthropology teacher insisted that God had no part in creating the universe; rather, the earth evolved from a cataclysmic explosion, and human beings evolved into their present state from the earliest life form.

Lois argued vehemently for her Christian belief, but to no avail. In fact, Lois's teacher threatened to fail her if she didn't stop talking about her Christian beliefs in the class and in her papers. But Lois knew what she believed and had no intentions of changing her views.

For centuries people have questioned and debated the origin of the universe. But for most Christians, whether or not God created the universe is not an issue for debate. The Bible says that God created the universe and everything within it. As we begin today's lesson, we will focus on the beginning of the universe and God's handiwork in the Creation story.

The People, Places, and Times

Creation. The act of God by which the universe came into being is Creation. The Bible's chief account of Creation is Genesis 1:1–2:3. Instead of divine combat and struggle with a willful prehistoric force, we find the sole, sovereign Master of the universe directing the work of Creation by verbal command. God is shown here making the world in six days and resting on the seventh. Bible scholars differ on whether the "days" were 24-hour days or longer periods.

Heaven. The firmament, or the massive transparent dome that covers the earth, is heaven. The blue color of the sky was attributed to the chaotic waters that the firmament separated from the earth (Genesis 1:7). The earth was thus surrounded by "waters" above and below (Deuteronomy 5:8). The firmament was thought to be substantial; when the windows of the firmament were opened, rain fell (Genesis 7:11–12).

In Hebrew, the word for "heaven" is always plural. At the same time, the Greek word for "heaven" in the New Testament also frequently appears in the plural. The use of the plural probably does not mean that the ancient Hebrews conceived of more than one heaven. Heaven was the place of the stars, sun, and moon and of the birds. It is also the abode of God (1 Kings 8:20) and where God is enthroned (Exodus 24:9–11).

Source:

Achtemeier, Paul J., ed. *Harper's Bible Dictionary*. New York: HarperCollins Publishers, 1985. 192–93, 377.

Background

Genesis is the first book of a larger work called the Pentateuch, the first five books of the Old Testament. Many people believe that Moses is the author of Genesis and the Pentateuch. The word "Genesis" is Greek, and it means "origin" or "beginning." This title was given to the book by the translators of the Greek Old Testament, known as the Septuagint.

Genesis reveals the origins of human history and gives us a glimpse of God's progressive self-revelation to the human race. The book is quoted more than 60 times in the New Testament, and Jesus Christ quotes from its many passages (cf. Matthew 19:4–6; Mark 10:4–9). Genesis provides the historical account of the beginning of God's relationship with humans; it also records the beginning of many things: the world, sin, civilization, the nations, and Israel.

Genesis also contains important theological themes, such as the doctrine of the living, personal God; the doctrine of humans who are made in the image of God; the doctrine of the Fall; the anticipation of a Redeemer; and the covenant promises made to the nation Israel. Genesis is a book unique among all the literature of the ancient Near East and is the foundation for all other books in the Bible.

Source:
Ryrie, Charles C. *Ryrie Study Bible*. Chicago: Moody Press, 1984. 5.

At - A - Glance

1. The Beginning of the Universe
(Genesis 1:1–2)
2. The Beginning of Light (vv. 3–5)
3. The Beginning of Heaven (vv. 6, 8)
4. The Beginning of the Earth (vv. 10, 12–13)
5. The Beginning of the Seasons (vv. 14–15, 19)
6. The Beginning of Life and Blessings
(vv. 20, 22–23, 25)

In Depth

1. The Beginning of the Universe (Genesis 1:1–2)

The Bible begins with the truth that "God created the heaven and the earth" (v. 1). We can learn much about God from this one statement. First, God is creative. Who but God could have brought into existence something from nothing? Second, we learn that God is eternal and in control of the world. In essence, God doesn't need anything or anyone to help Him be God. He is God all by Himself.

Science tells us that the vast galaxy in which we live is spinning at the speed of 490,000 miles an hour and needs 200 million light years just to make one rotation. In addition, there are over one billion other galaxies just like ours in the universe! Some scientists speculate that the number of stars in Creation is equal to all the grains of sand in the world. However, as Christians we believe that the universe didn't just *happen*. No, almighty God put all the pieces of our universe together in an intricate and marvelous fashion.

God gave form and shape to the universe that was previously void, dark, and uninhabited. Verse 2 tells us that God's Spirit moved over the waters and was actively involved in the creation of the world. The Hebrew word for "moved" is *rachaph* (**raw-KHAF**), and it means "to relax or hover." In essence, the universe came into shape as the Holy Spirit hovered over the waters.

2. The Beginning of Light (vv. 3–5)

How long did it take God to create the world? While the Bible tells us six days, it is not clear whether they are literal 24-hour time periods or whether they represent millions of years. However, the most important point is not how long it took God to create the world, but that He did so in an orderly fashion. So, the first element that God created was light. The Bible affirms that God spoke light into existence by saying, "Let there be. . ." and it was.

3. The Beginning of Heaven (vv. 6, 8)

The next element God created was a "firmament in the midst of the waters" (v. 1:6). The Hebrew word for "firmament" is *raqiya`* (**raw-KEE-ah**), which means "an extended surface or expanse." Apparently God began to separate the sky and waters so that there would be a distinction between the two, as there is a distinction between day and night. Charles Ryrie suggests that the firmament was an open expanse of the heavens, which appeared as a vast canopy or tent above the earth.

Because the universe was made up of water, God made a "dome," above which He formed the sky and beneath which He formed the oceans. Have you ever stood on a beach and looked out as far as the eye can see? It appears as though the sky and the water are touching one another. Perhaps at the beginning of the universe they merged before God separated the sky and waters during the second day of Creation.

4. The Beginning of the Earth (vv. 10, 12–13)

On the third day of Creation, God began to move the waters around so that the dry land could appear and the waters could be given their special place. The earth is made up mostly of water, so, in essence, God moved the waters around so the dry land could be seen. God called the dry land "earth." The Hebrew word is 'erets (EH-rets), and it means "earth," "country," and "ground."

Before God populated the earth with people, He created grass, herbs, fruit trees, and all the seeds needed to bring forth vegetation and other plant life. All the plants, grass, trees, and other greenery were made by God, though the evolutionists attempt to convince us that these things just "happened." We believe the world is too intricate to have just happened by chance. The Bible affirms that God made the vegetation on the earth and said that "it was good" (v. 1:12).

5. The Beginning of the Seasons (vv. 14–15, 19)

On the fourth day of Creation, the sun and moon appeared. Charles Ryrie suggests that the purpose of distinguishing day and night was to enable humans to get their bearings, to mark off the seasons, and to give light to the earth.

The sun and moon are much-needed heat and light sources, and each was created by God for a fixed time and purpose. Regardless of what many evolutionists teach, we know that God has been and continues to be in control of the universe and that all He has made is good.

Since we recognize God as the Creator of all that exists, we cannot only praise His genius and power, but we can do our part to preserve the earth's resources and use them for the glory of God and for the benefit of His creatures.

6. The Beginning of Life and Blessings (vv. 20, 22–23, 25)

The fifth day of Creation concerns the filling of the waters and the skies. Just as the creation of heavenly bodies on the fourth day corresponds to the creation of light on the first day of Creation, the creation of birds and fish on the fifth day matches the division of the waters by the firmament on the second day. It depicts God's creation of all living creatures.

Another distinctive feature of the fifth day is the first recorded blessing in the Bible (v. 22). It's interesting to note that throughout the book of Genesis, God's blessings always immediately follow His creating. Genesis shows that God has a blessing for all living creatures, animals (v. 22), mankind (v. 27), the Sabbath (2:3), Adam (5:2), Noah (9:1), and Abram (12:3; 17:16). God blessed the creatures by allowing them to procreate, again indicating His superior position.

Finally, Genesis is best described as the story of God's life-giving creation power. By simply speaking, God created everything that we hear, see, smell, and touch, and He deemed that everything was "good."

Source:
Ryrie, Charles C. *Ryrie Study Bible.* Chicago: Moody Press, 1984. 7, 8.

Search the Scriptures

1. What condition was the earth in when God began to create (Genesis 1:2)?

2. Who was responsible for the beginning of Creation (v. 2)?

3. How did God create light (v. 3)?

4. How did God create the heavens and water (vv. 6–8)?

5. What did God make on the third day (vv. 11–13)?

6. What did God do to divide the days and seasons (vv. 14–15)?

Discuss the Meaning

1. What does the Bible mean when it says "in the beginning"?

2. When, where, and how was the universe created?

3. Is it possible that evolutionists are correct about how the universe came into being? Why or why not?

4. What difference does it make whether we were created by God or came into being by an evolutionary process?

Lesson in Our Society

1. How does the Christian view—human beings are made in God's image—affect our view of non-Christian people in our community?

2. How does our belief that God is the Creator of all human beings—saved and unsaved—affect our views about unborn children? Physically disabled people? Criminals?

3. How does our belief in God as Creator of the material universe—plants, trees, birds, and animals—affect our attitudes toward the preservation of our forests and endangered species?

Make It Happen

Organize a class project to enhance an area within walking distance of your church. Some suggestions are to (1) clean up a vacant lot, (2) create or improve a playground, (3) start a recycling program, (4) paint or sponsor the painting of a nature or religious mural on a vacant wall, or (5) plant some grass or a tree or some trees.

Or spend some special time thanking God for His creation. Spend time at a community park or a beach—examine the natural elements around you. Can you see God's handiwork in the creation? What can you learn from the natural surroundings? Write down your observations in a prayer journal, and praise God for the beauty of His universe.

Follow the Spirit

What God wants me to do:

_____

_____

Remember Your Thoughts

Special insights I have learned:

_____

_____

More Light on the Text

Genesis 1:1–6, 8, 10, 12–15, 19–20, 22–23, 25

1 In the beginning God created the heaven and the earth.

The first verse of the Bible is notable for a couple of interesting reasons. First, the text does not set out to prove that God exists; it assumes God's existence. Second, it operates as a summary statement of all that follows. This statement invites us into the narrative that follows.

The text identifies the Creator as "God" (Heb. *'elohiym*, **el-o-HEEM**). The Hebrew term indicates plu-

rality; when we look back at the text through the entire message of the Bible, we can interpret this to refer to the Trinity; but in its original context it more accurately indicates God's transcendence, greatness, and majesty. This term helps identify the one, true God in contrast to the ancient world's notion of multiple gods. It is He who "created" (Heb. *bara'*, **baw-RAW**) the universe. This Hebrew term not only refers to God as the source of everything, but it also carries with it the fact that God assigns purpose and function to His created order.

2 And the earth was without form, and void; and darkness was upon the face of the deep. And the Spirit of God moved upon the face of the waters. 3 And God said, Let there be light: and there was light. 4 And God saw the light, that it was good: and God divided the light from the darkness. 5 And God called the light Day, and the darkness he called Night. And the evening and the morning were the first day. 6 And God said, Let there be a firmament in the midst of the waters, and let it divide the waters from the waters.

The Creation was "without form, and void" (Heb. *tohuw*, **TO-hoo** and *bohuw*, **BO-hoo**), which conveys the truth of the earth being in an early stage of chaos. The text presents the Creation as undifferentiated and disordered. The Creation is not yet capable of producing life.

The text goes on to report the gradual unfolding and development of the Creation. The Spirit "moved" (the Hebrew word *is rachaph*, **raw-KHAF**). This is the first reference to the Spirit of God in the Bible. The term *ruwach* (**ROO-akh**), also translated as "wind or breath," can be thought of as something like moving air. In this instance, the Spirit of God is present and ready to bring order to the formless Creation and to prepare the earth for habitation. This is the Spirit whose power is available to transform our sometimes formless, chaotic, and void lives.

"Light," from the common Hebrew word *'owr* (ore), implies God, who Himself is Light (1 John 1:5; Revelation 18:1). He spoke every aspect of known visible light into being, and it was so. What God commands, happens (Psalm 33:9). Today we know human, plant, and animal life are all impossible without light. Isaiah's words in 45:7 are matchless: "I form the light, and create darkness: I make peace, and create evil: I the LORD do all these things" (cf. 2 Corinthians 4:6).

"Darkness" is from the common Hebrew word *choshek* (**kho-SHEK**). Though some contend that darkness always represents evil, at Creation God took the darkness that covered the formless void and called it "night" (Heb. *layil,* **LAH-yil**). Today we know sleep is a vital part of life; we, as humans, not only need sleep, but the rest of creation requires regular rest cycles as well.

The light and darkness formed day and night. God continued to differentiate His creation and assign specific functions. He created for His world "morning" (Heb. *boqer,* **BO-ker**) and "evening" (Heb. *`ereb,* **EH-reb**). The combined cycle created the very first complete "day" or *yowm* (**yome**), a word that contains a concept of time.

There is much debate over the use of the word "day" in Genesis 1. Depending upon the context, it may mean what we conventionally understand to be a 24-hour period, or it may refer to an epoch or a period of time. In this text, it certainly refers to God's decision to act within an epoch or timeframe. With that in mind, we must think of the text as indicating that God created within a particular frame of time, which could have been seven days or epochs; but remember that the aim of the text is to tell us that the one, true God created everything, not to determine when He performed this act.

"Firmament," from the Hebrew *raqiya`,* (**raw-KEE-ah**) is used only 17 times in the Old Testament and usually refers to more than air. It is used as being "heavenly" in Psalm 150:1: "Praise ye the LORD. Praise God in his sanctuary: praise him in the firmament of his power." At the same time, *raqiya`* is the place where birds fly (see Genesis 1:20). At this stage of Creation, the waters separate, apparently making the distinction between liquid and vapor forms, and the atmosphere as we know it is called into existence.

1:8 And God called the firmament Heaven. And the evening and the morning were the second day.

Reinforcing the above use of *raqiya`,* God called the atmosphere "Heaven" (Heb. *shamayim,* **shaw-MAH-yim**), a word that is used 420 times in the Bible. Again, although "Heaven" clearly and most often is used in the same sense as "firmament" (i.e., "heav-

enly"; see Genesis 22:15; Psalms 8:1; 11:4), the distinction seems lost here, because *shamayim* is also a place where birds fly (Genesis 7:3; Job 35:11) and clouds can be seen (Job 38:37).

1:10 And God called the dry land Earth; and the gathering together of the waters called he Seas: and God saw that it was good.

Any modern syntax of "gathering together" would imply an orderly, even gentle act. The thought of the oceans of the world being gathered, while at the same time being separated from dry land, doesn't necessarily evoke the image of a gentle act; rather, it brings to mind a violent, explosive, even volcanic act given to giant, mountainous upheavals combined with equally deep gouging from the various waterways and bodies of water.

1:12 And the earth brought forth grass, and herb yielding seed after his kind, and the tree yielding fruit, whose seed was in itself, after his kind: and God saw that it was good. 13 And the evening and the morning were the third day. 14 And God said, Let there be lights in the firmament of the heaven to divide the day from the night; and let them be for signs, and for seasons, and for days, and years: 15 And let them be for lights in the firmament of the heaven to give light upon the earth: and it was so.

It is interesting to note that all the earth's vegetation wasn't created instantly, but grew out of the soil. Much as the evolutionary formula for wear and tear on rocks from passing water must be radically increased when all the water and dry land in the world is sorted out in a single day, so this stage of creation is conducted entirely by God's power. "Brought forth" is from the very common Hebrew word *yatsa* (**yaw-TSAW**), which among numerous other uses also is used in the normal sense of growing vegetation (Psalm 104:14). It should not surprise anyone that God could grow trees overnight any more than He could order land and soil into existence from a formless void. Although man doesn't exist yet, God knew for whom His creation was planned, and He knew man would need an abundant and self-replicating supply of nourishment. All plant life is created with seeds, the means of reproduction; again, God declared His work as good.

The creation of the sun, moon, and stars visible from Earth to specifically delight humankind and serve their needs continues the purposeful progression of God's custom-designed habitat for humanity. It is important to remember that in the original context, other religions viewed the sun and moon as deities, but here they are objects designed by God to serve humanity. God knew man (whom He had not created yet) would need to keep track of time and be able to navigate the earth. Having already created light, He made these particular elements of created light to appear in the sky (the "firmament of heaven") and begin their appointed tasks (see vv. 16–18). It is important to note here that the sun, moon, and stars appeared after God had created light. This leads some interpreters to conclude that Genesis 1 is presenting not a chronological but a comprehensive account of creation according to various categories.

1:19 And the evening and the morning were the fourth day. 20 And God said, Let the waters bring forth abundantly the moving creature that hath life, and fowl that may fly above the earth in the open firmament of heaven.

Now that the structure of man's habitat was complete, it was time for it to be occupied. In a single day, the entire variety of both air and sea creatures came into being as complete, living, and unique organisms. This use of "firmament" (Heb. *raqiya*), even within the Creation story, underscores the basic use of the atmosphere as a place for birds to fly. In His infinite wisdom God not only provided for man's initial needs but for future needs as well as for the needs of all the creatures within creation given to man for his survival and pleasure.

1:22 And God blessed them, saying, Be fruitful, and multiply, and fill the waters in the seas, and let fowl multiply in the earth. 23 And the evening and the morning were the fifth day.

Not only did God fill Earth's waters and skies with life, but on a separate day and by a separate command He caused them to be procreative. Just as He knew man would need to keep track of time, be able to navigate, and survive off of Earth's grain and fruit nutrients, He also knew man would need a steady supply of nourishment. God's blessing was significant since it was His first; His second would be on the first human male and female (Genesis 1:28)—also prior to a command to procreate. An almost duplicate blessing with the same procreative context would be bestowed on Noah and his family when they were told to replenish the population of Earth after the Flood (9:2).

1:25 And God made the beast of the earth after his kind, and cattle after their kind, and every thing that creepeth upon the earth after his kind: and God saw that it was good.

God declared land animals to be good, and later gives some as food.

Most Christians believe that those who have chosen to refuse meat in their diet, while entirely within their rights of free choice, negate God's intent and design for both animals and humankind. Prior to the fall of man and the Flood, humans didn't eat meat (Genesis 1:28–30). After the Fall, however, everything changed, and God actually ordained meat as food. Immediately after blessing Noah and telling him to replenish the earth's population, God said in Genesis 9:3: "Every moving thing that liveth shall be meat for you." The only injunction at the time was not to eat meat with lifeblood still in it (v. 4). (More rules were to come, but never again was meat banned from man's diet.) Various verses in the New Testament support both the Old Testament's specific approval of eating meat and freedom from numerous injunctions. From the Creation account, we see that God planned from the beginning only good things for man; He could just as easily have made beasts inedible, or useless nutritionally, and let them be used only to serve mankind, for example, as beasts of burden, transportation, and so on. Further, He could have made all types of animals edible for protein and nutrition but bland and tasteless. Instead, eating is more than functional; it is a central part of our existence as social creatures. This is an aspect seldom mentioned, but true for all sources of food—plants, animals, poultry, and seafood. Although there are exceptions and everyone has individual tastes, by far the majority of virtually all food created by God is not only nutritious and necessary but pleasurable to eat. There were no recalls to redesign or reinvent; from the beginning, God planned everything with perfec-

"In the beginning God created the heaven and the earth" (from Genesis 1:1).

tion for His marvelous habitat for humanity. What a loving and thoughtful God we serve! Indeed, all that God does is good!

Consider the following from Ashley Johnson, highlighting the increasing complexity of Creation:

> Observe the steady march from the lower to the higher, from the insensate to the intelligent, from the servitor to the sovereign. See the universe by God's hand touched to harmony; see the march of Creative power to its culmination in the making of the companion for Man, pure and innocent, the highest image of God, and hear the stars sing together and the sons of God shout for joy over the completion of the mighty and glorious work!

Source:
Johnson, Ashley S. "Creation." *Condensed Biblical Cyclopedia*, Blue Letter Bible, July 1, 2002. http://blueletterbible.org/study/cbc/cbc01.html

Daily Bible Readings

M: God the Creator
Psalm 8
T: The First Day
Genesis 1:1–5
W: The Sky
Genesis 1:6–8
T: The First Harvest
Genesis 1:9–13
F: The Sun and Moon
Genesis 1:14–19
S: The Birds and Sea Creatures
Genesis 1:20–23
S: The Animals
Genesis 1:24–25

TEACHING TIPS

September 9
Bible Study Guide 2

1. Words You Should Know

A. God (Genesis 1:26–29) *'elohiym* (Heb.)—Divine One; Ruler or Judge.

B. Replenish (v. 28) *male'* (Heb.)—To fill, satisfy.

2. Teacher Preparation

Unifying Principle—Why Are We Here? Humankind is God's special creation—created in His image and given dominion over this earth. Because all humankind is created in God's likeness, we must treat each other as the special creations that we are.

A. Begin preparing to teach today's lesson by spending time in prayer.

B. Read the Bible Background and Focal Verses, and study the Devotional Reading Scriptures in at least two different Bible translations, keeping the AIM for Change and Unifying Principle in mind.

C. Outline the significant points of the lesson based upon achieving the AIM for Change objectives.

D. For further preparation, complete lesson 2 for September 9 in the *Precepts For Living® Personal Study Guide.*

3. Starting the Lesson

A. Begin the class time with prayer.

B. Review last week's lesson and ask for volunteers to give their testimonies of how they applied the lesson to their lives during the past week. Remind the students that God made the earth according to His plan, and this week you will discuss how humankind fits into God's plan.

C. Tell the class that the focus of today's lesson is to answer the question "Why Are We Here?" (Unifying Principle). Instruct the class to follow along as you read aloud the Background section.

D. Review the Daily Bible Readings leading up to this week's lesson.

E. Point out today's learning objective by introducing the AIM for Change.

4. Getting into the Lesson

A. Using the In Focus story as a cornerstone, engage the class in a wider discussion on why we are here and the purpose for which we were created.

B. Instruct the class to silently read today's Focal Verses.

C. Discuss The People, Places, and Times section to help the students understand the importance of the Garden of Eden and Adam and Eve's responsibility in the garden.

5. Relating the Lesson to Life

A. Instruct the class to take a few minutes to ponder or answer the Discuss the Meaning questions.

B. Use the Lesson in Our Society and Discuss the Meaning questions to help the students connect the theological significance of this lesson with their social context. Ultimately, the students should understand that even though God created humankind from the dust of the ground, we should not treat one another like dirt. We are created in God's image, and God entrusted us with everything that He created and gave us dominion over it. Therefore, we should treat all of God's creations with dignity and care.

6. Arousing Action

A. Allow class members to share what they see of God's image reflected in one another and in their surrounding community, workplace, and home.

B. As review, engage the class in a question-and-answer session based on lesson 2 for September 9 in the *Precepts For Living® Personal Study Guide.*

C. Suggest the class read the Daily Bible Readings for September 16 and complete lesson 3 in the *Precepts For Living® Personal Study Guide* in preparation for next week's lesson.

D. Close the class in prayer, asking God for help in treating His creations with dignity and respect.

Worship Guide

For the Superintendent or Teacher
Theme: God Created Humankind
Theme Song: "What a Fellowship"
Devotional Reading: Isaiah 40:25–31
Prayer

GOD CREATED HUMANKIND

Bible Background • GENESIS 1:26–2:3
Printed Text • GENESIS 1:26–30   Devotional Reading • ISAIAH 40:25–31

AIM for Change

By the end of the lesson, we will:

DISCUSS what it means to be created in God's image;

CONSIDER how effective humankind has been in caring for what God entrusted to them; and

GIVE THANKS to God for creating humankind and PRAY for help in treating God's people as we should.

Keep in Mind

"And God said, Let us make man in our image, after our likenesss: and let them have dominion over the fish of the sea, and over the fowl of the air, and over the cattle, and over all the earth, and over every creeping thing that creepeth upon the earth" (Genesis 1:26).

Focal Verses

KJV

Genesis 1:26 And God said, Let us make man in our image, after our likeness: and let them have dominion over the fish of the sea, and over the fowl of the air, and over the cattle, and over all the earth, and over every creeping thing that creepeth upon the earth.

27 So God created man in his own image, in the image of God created he him; male and female created he them.

28 And God blessed them, and God said unto them, Be fruitful, and multiply, and replenish the earth, and subdue it: and have dominion over the fish of the sea, and over the fowl of the air, and over every living thing that moveth upon the earth.

29 And God said, Behold, I have given you every herb bearing seed, which is upon the face of all the earth, and every tree, in the which is the fruit of a tree yielding seed; to you it shall be for meat.

30 And to every beast of the earth, and to every fowl of the air, and to every thing that creepeth upon the earth, wherein there is life, I have given every green herb for meat: and it was so.

NLT

Genesis 1:26 Then God said, "Let us make human beings in our image, to be like us. They will reign over the fish in the sea, the birds in the sky, the livestock, all the wild animals on the earth, and the small animals that scurry along the ground."

27 So God created human beings in his own image. In the image of God he created them; male and female he created them.

28 Then God blessed them and said, "Be fruitful and multiply. Fill the earth and govern it. Reign over the fish in the sea, the birds in the sky, and all the animals that scurry along the ground."

29 Then God said, "Look! I have given you every seed-bearing plant throughout the earth and all the fruit trees for your food.

30 And I have given every green plant as food for all the wild animals, the birds in the sky, and the small animals that scurry along the ground—everything that has life." And that is what happened.

In Focus

Kim's son William asked his mother, "Where did I come from and why am I here?"

William was only 6 years old, and Kim wasn't sure whether her son would understand reproduction or the true value of human life. Nor did she want to lie to her son by telling him the *stork* story that she was told as a child. Instead, she made it clear to William that God created all people and creatures on Earth—including him. Because he is one of God's special creations, he was priceless to her and to God.

This week we will look at God's creation of human life and discover how we were created in God's image and entrusted with the stewardship of all creation.

The People, Places, and Times

Adam. In Genesis, God created man and woman in His image, separating them from the animals, to rule the earth. Yahweh (God) formed Adam from the earth, set him over the Garden of Eden, and allowed him to have dominion over everything God created.

Garden of Eden. In the book of Genesis, the Garden of Eden is mentioned more than 15 times. The Hebrew word '*Eden* (**AY-den**) means "luxury," "pleasure," or "delight." Eden was the source of four great rivers and the site of the Tree of Life and the Tree of Knowledge of Good and Evil. Eden was probably located on the continent of Africa.

Background

In last week's lesson we learned that God is the Creator of all things. God created the world in six days, including light, the heavens, the waters, the earth, vegetation, and the seasons. Everything God made He spoke into existence. Today's lesson focuses on the beginning of humankind, created in the image and after the likeness of God. As we begin our lesson today, God has made birds, cattle, all beasts, and every creeping thing in the world (see Genesis 1:24). When we look at God's handiwork, one realizes that each and every creature God made has a purpose—especially humankind.

At - A - Glance

1. God's Priority (Genesis 1:26)
2. God's Providence (v. 27)
3. God's Provision (vv. 28–30)

In Depth

1. God's Priority (Genesis 1:26)

The entire message of the Bible is set forth in this very first chapter of Genesis, with the supreme act being God's creation of man. The central message says that God regards humanity so highly that He gave us dominion over everything He created.

Humankind is a very special part of God's universe and plan. Some question why God spoke in plural terms when He stated, "Let *us* make man in *our* image." One theory is that God was referring to the Holy Trinity—God the Father, God the Son, and God the Holy Spirit. Another theory suggests that the usage of plural language denotes majesty and God was addressing His Spirit, who was present and active at the beginning of creation (see Genesis 1:2). However, neither of these theories appears plausible given further scrutiny of the original Hebrew text. What we can observe, however, is that the early church developed a Trinitarian view (the Father, Son, and Holy Spirit) based on the fact that the New Testament views Christ as divine and as an active participant in creation with the Father and the Holy Spirit.

Notice how God created humankind in His image and likeness. We know that God is not confined to a physical form like ours. However, this passage implies that we have certain capabilities (e.g., rational thought, emotional and spiritual capacities) that should reflect the attributes of God. It is in this sense that we were made in the image of God. While we will never be exactly like God, we can reflect His nature in our kindness, patience, forgiveness, and love for other people.

The greatest gift God gave man, besides salvation and His Son Jesus, who died on the cross for the remission of our sins, is dominion. Dominion was the very first promise God made to humanity. God made it clear that humanity is to have dominion over all things that inhabit the earth. As a result of man's special place in God's universe, we should consider it an honor to care for the things of the universe—things like our communities, schools, and businesses, as well as the environment. Just like Adam and Eve, the original man and woman, God holds us accountable for caring for one another and for His earth.

2. God's Providence (v. 27)

Scripture says that not only was man made in God's own image, but woman was made in His image as well. We should not overlook or try to minimize these words. Man and woman were made equal in God's creation. Neither sex is exalted nor depreciated in God's eyes. He gave them equal dominion to rule over the earth. Man and woman were to work together to carry out God's will.

3. God's Provision (vv. 28–30)

After creating the land animals and the sea, God created human beings. God blessed them and commanded them to be fruitful and multiply, fill the earth, and subdue it. God cares about His creatures so much that He does not desire we should ever go without. In essence, God gave dominion, or authority, to man and woman. They were to be God's stewards and watch over all the things that God made.

God gave us the assignment of having dominion or *radah* (Heb.), which means we have authority over all things that inhabit the earth. We are responsible for our environment and must not be careless or wasteful in taking care of God's planet. As He did with the original man and woman, God holds us accountable for neglecting or caring for His earth.

Search the Scriptures

1. How did God make man (Genesis 1:26)?
2. Over what things does humankind have dominion (v. 26)?
3. God creates humankind to reflect what about Himself (v. 27)?
4. What did God give man to maintain his sustenance (vv. 29–30)?

Discuss the Meaning

1. To whom was God referring when He said, "Let us . . ." (Genesis 1:26)?
2. What is the significance of God's blessing upon humankind?
3. What are some of the ways God's provisions are demonstrated in your life?
4. How might our understanding of creation and man's place in it affect our relationship with God? With others?

Lesson in Our Society

This week, take a closer look at your community and surrounding environment. Can you see God's handiwork? What can you do to take dominion over these areas to ensure that God's creation does not deteriorate as a result of humankind's carelessness and neglect?

Make It Happen

Do you accept God's provisions for your life? Does your daily Christian walk reflect God's image? Based on today's study, create a list of some of the things God created and how they directly affect your life. List some of the provisions of God in your life. Now, give thanks in prayer.

Follow the Spirit

What God wants me to do:

_____

_____

Remember Your Thoughts

Special insights I have learned:

_____

_____

More Light on the Text

Genesis 1:26–30

26 And God said, Let us make man in our image, after our likeness: and let them have dominion over the fish of the sea, and over the fowl of the air, and over the cattle, and over all the earth, and over every creeping thing that creepeth upon the earth.

Day six was the pinnacle of God's creation in that He created man. There has been much scholarly debate regarding the plural language God used here. Why did God speak in the plural ("let us," "our image," "our likeness")? Some scholars believe the language refers to God having an inner consultation with other divine beings (e.g., the angels), meaning those who are not God were called to participate in the act of creation. Other scholars suggest the plural language refers to the majesty, attributes, and powers within the Godhead (the Father, Son, and Holy Spirit); God was addressing His Spirit, who was present and active at the beginning of creation (Genesis 1:2).

The Hebrew word for "image" is *tselem* (**TSEH-lem**), which appears only 17 times in the Bible. Ten times it refers to various types of physical images (Numbers 33:52; 1 Samuel 6:5, 11; 2 Kings 11:18; 2 Chronicles 23:17; Ezekiel 7:20; 16:17; 23:14; Amos 5:26). Two passages in Psalms (39:6; 73:20) refer to shadows, and the other five occurrences are in Genesis (1:26–27; 5:3; 9:6). The limited use of this word in Scripture has made its interpretation difficult. However, this is not the case with the Hebrew word *demuwth* (**dem-OOTH**), or "likeness." As used here, the term means "to resemble, fashion, or to be like." Because we realize that God does not have a physical form, it is implied that the resemblance is one of mental and/or spiritual attributes that humanity shares with the Creator. Conceivably, then, the "likeness" or "image" of God toward man serves as a mirror to the rest of the world of God's divine nature.

27 So God created man in his own image, in the image of God created he him; male and female created he them. 28 And God blessed them, and God said unto them, Be fruitful, and multiply, and replenish the earth, and subdue it: and have dominion over the fish of the sea, and over the fowl of the air, and over every living thing that moveth upon the earth.

Immediately after God blessed man, He gave him power and authority. A study of the phrase "have dominion" (Heb. *radah*, meaning "to rule or prevail against") reveals that God gave man authority and stewardship over everything He created. Similar to the command to be fruitful and multiply that God gave the animals in verse 22, God's command to humanity draws upon His personal relationship with man. Thus, man was created in God's image, to rule over His creation on Earth on God's behalf. The purpose and function of humans involves the responsibility of caring for and cultivating the creation.

29 And God said, Behold, I have given you every herb bearing seed, which is upon the face of all the earth, and every tree, in the which is the fruit of a tree yielding seed; to you it shall be for meat.

One of the first communications between human beings and God was for them to see the many provisions God had for them. God said, "behold" (*hinneh*, **hin-NAY**), or "see." In other words, God was saying, "See all the provisions I have made for you." Look at and know how far God has gone to prepare for your survival and sustenance.

What were they to see? They were to see what God had given them for their well-being. The word "given" is translated from the Hebrew word *nathan* (**naw-THAN**). As used here, it refers to how much thoughtfulness God applies to the care of His creatures. The word also implies that the Divine Giver charges us as His creatures to take the same care that

He has taken. Here God pledged to distribute His wealth to meet our needs without fail. This, indeed, speaks to God's generosity. Another reference to God's provision is the use of the word "meat." The term simply means "food." It is derived from the Hebrew word *'oklah* (**ok-LAW**), which means "food" or "something to consume, devour, or eat." One could also play with the idea that this term is feminine and speaks of the nurture of the God who, like a mother, cares for, provides for, and nurtures His children.

30 And to every beast of the earth, and to every fowl of the air, and to every thing that creepeth upon the earth, wherein there is life, I have given every green herb for meat: and it was so.

Whereas verse 29 deals with God's good provision for human beings, in the same way verse 30 deals with God's provision for the animals.

Daily Bible Readings

M: The Creator of All
Isaiah 40:25–31
T: Created in God's Image
Genesis 1:26–27
W: God Provides
Genesis 1:28–31
T: A Hallowed Day
Genesis 2:1–3
F: God's Glory in Creation
Psalm 19:1–6
S: Thanksgiving for God's Greatness
Psalm 103:1–14
S: Remember God's Commandments
Psalm 103:15–22

TEACHING TIPS

September 16
Bible Study Guide 3

1. Words You Should Know

A. Too Hard (Genesis 18:14) *pala* (Heb.)—To make extraordinary; to act miraculously or marvelously; to sanctify. Denotes a clear-cut display of God's care for Israel.

B. Circumcised (21:4) *muwl* (Heb.)—The practice of cutting the foreskin of the male genital organ. Circumcision was and is very important to the Jews because it signifies God's covenant with Abraham.

2. Teacher Preparation

Unifying Principle—Our Place in the Family! Families are so important that God creates and has plans for families. We should celebrate the fact that we are part of both a human and God's family.

A. Begin your study by reading the Daily Bible Readings Scripture passages leading up to today's lesson.

B. Spend time in prayer, asking God for insight and wisdom to teach the lesson.

C. Read the Focal Verses, Bible Background, and Devotional Reading Scriptures in at least two different Bible translations.

D. Develop key questions regarding family and covenant based on the Unifying Principle and AIM for Change objectives.

E. Complete lesson 3 for September 16 in the *Precepts For Living® Personal Study Guide* for further insight on today's teaching.

3. Starting the Lesson

A. Tell the class that in today's lesson we will look at families and how important they are to God.

B. Lead the class in prayer, lifting up the AIM for Change objectives.

C. Lead into the lesson by giving a brief overview of The People, Places, and Times and Background sections.

4. Getting into the Lesson

A. Ask for a volunteer to read the In Focus story aloud, then have the class silently read the Focal Verses.

B. Spend a few moments answering the Search the Scripture questions.

C. Read and then solicit responses to the Discuss the Meaning questions.

D. Invite class members who have children or grandchildren to share how each child represents the promise and potential within both their family and God's family.

5. Relating the Lesson to Life

A. Today's lesson focuses on God's promise to increase Abraham's family, thus blessing his descendants. Discuss what impact the fulfillment of this promise has on the lives of those in your class.

B. Contemplate the Lesson in Our Society question. Ask the class to draw a time line that shows how they have seen God's promises manifest in their lives or in the lives of family members.

6. Arousing Action

A. Direct the students' attention to the Make It Happen section. Ask the class to invite an unsaved family member to church next Sunday.

B. Instruct the class to read the Daily Bible Readings for September 23 and complete lesson 4 from the *Precepts For Living® Personal Study Guide* to prepare for next week's lesson.

C. Ask a volunteer to close the class in prayer.

Worship Guide

For the Superintendent or Teacher
Theme: Abraham, Sarah, and Isaac
Theme Song: "What a Mighty God We Serve"
Devotional Reading: Isaiah 51:1–5
Prayer

ABRAHAM, SARAH, AND ISAAC

Bible Background • GENESIS 15:1–6; 18:1–15; 21:1–8
Printed Text • GENESIS 15:5–6; 18:11–14; 21:1–8   Devotional Reading • ISAIAH 51:1–5

AIM for Change

By the end of the lesson, we will:

SUMMARIZE God's covenant with Abraham and state how it was fulfilled;

REFLECT on our place in both our human and heavenly families; and

CELEBRATE being part of a family; and SECURE, if necessary, a place in God's family.

Focal Verses

Keep in Mind

"Is any thing too hard for the LORD?" (Genesis 18:14).

KJV
Genesis 15:5 And he brought him forth abroad, and said, Look now toward heaven, and tell the stars, if thou be able to number them: and he said unto him, So shall thy seed be.

6 And he believed in the LORD; and he counted it to him for righteousness.

18:11 Now Abraham and Sarah were old and well stricken in age; and it ceased to be with Sarah after the manner of women.

12 Therefore Sarah laughed within herself, saying, After I am waxed old shall I have pleasure, my lord being old also?

13 And the LORD said unto Abraham, Wherefore did Sarah laugh, saying, Shall I of a surety bear a child, which am old?

14 Is any thing too hard for the LORD?

21:1 And the LORD visited Sarah as he had said, and the LORD did unto Sarah as he had spoken.

2 For Sarah conceived, and bare Abraham a son in his old age, at the set time of which God had spoken to him.

3 And Abraham called the name of his son that was born unto him, whom Sarah bare to him, Isaac.

4 And Abraham circumcised his son Isaac being eight days old, as God had commanded him.

5 And Abraham was an hundred years old, when his son Isaac was born unto him.

6 And Sarah said, God hath made me to laugh, so that all that hear will laugh with me.

7 And she said, Who would have said unto Abraham, that Sarah should have given children suck? for I have born him a son in his old age.

8 And the child grew, and was weaned: and Abraham made a great feast the same day that Isaac was weaned.

NLT
Genesis 15:5 Then the LORD took Abram outside and said to him, "Look up into the sky and count the stars if you can. That's how many descendants you will have!"

6 And Abram believed the LORD, and the LORD counted him as righteous because of his faith.

18:11 Abraham and Sarah were both very old by this time, and Sarah was long past the age of having children.

12 So she laughed silently to herself and said, "How could a worn-out woman like me enjoy such pleasure, especially when my master—my husband—is also so old?"

13 Then the LORD said to Abraham, "Why did Sarah laugh? Why did she say, 'Can an old woman like me have a baby?'

14 Is anything too hard for the LORD?"

21:1 The LORD kept his word and did for Sarah exactly what he had promised.

2 She became pregnant, and she gave birth to a son for Abraham in his old age. This happened at just the time God had said it would.

3 And Abraham named their son Isaac.

4 Eight days after Isaac was born, Abraham circumcised him as God had commanded.

5 Abraham was 100 years old when Isaac was born.

6 And Sarah declared, "God has brought me laughter. All who hear about this will laugh with me.

7 Who would have said to Abraham that Sarah would nurse a baby? Yet I have given Abraham a son in his old age!"

8 When Isaac grew up and was about to be weaned, Abraham prepared a huge feast to celebrate the occasion.

In Focus

Jay and Linda had been trying for almost six years to get pregnant. They had visited doctor after doctor who told them they could find no medical reason why Linda had not conceived and that they should keep trying. Day after day, month after month, the couple prayed and asked God to bless them with a child, but still nothing happened. Then one day, much to their surprise, Linda became pregnant.

The special day finally came nine months later. Jay tiptoed slowly into the hospital room and looked at his wife, who opened her eyes. Linda smiled when she saw his wide grin, and even though she knew the answer, she asked him anyway: "Did you see your son?"

"I sure did, and he looks just like me," Jay replied as he leaned over to kiss his wife on the forehead.

"You think so? I thought he looked just like me," said Linda smiling. Just then, the nurse entered the room with their newborn son and handed him to the proud new papa. Linda's eyes filled with tears.

"What's wrong, baby? Why are you crying?" asked Jay.

Linda wiped her tears and responded, "Jay, you know you and I don't have any real family. We were both raised in foster homes and never knew who our parents were. When I was a little girl, I used to pray and ask God to allow me to grow up and have a loving husband and child so one day I could have a family all my own. After taking so long to get pregnant, I was beginning to think that God was not going to answer my prayers. I'm crying because with the birth of this little baby boy, God has finally answered and done what we thought was impossible."

Family is very important to God. In today's lesson we find God fulfilling His covenant promise to Abraham to increase his family with the birth of Isaac.

The People, Places, and Times

Covenant. Covenant was a frequent basis for human relationships that were not kinship ties. They were of great importance in Old Testament history and religion.

Abraham/Abram. Even after the Flood, immorality and sin continued to increase. God chose Abraham's family to establish a new covenant through which all families would be blessed.

Sarah/Sarai. Both are variations of the same name, which means "princess." Sarah was 90 years old when she gave birth to Isaac. In the New Testament, Sarah's conception of Isaac is cited as an example of God's power to fulfill His promises (Romans 9:9).

Ur. God called Abraham to leave his father's home and go to a new land. The Bible traces Abraham's steps from Ur to Haran, through Palestine, and into Egypt.

Source:
Packer, J. I., and M. C. Tenney. *Illustrated Manners and Customs of the Bible*. Nashville, Tenn.: Thomas Nelson Publishers, 1980. 27–28.

Background

When Abram was 75 years old, the Lord extended a call to him that contained the promise of great things to come. It would take an additional 25 years before Abram would see God's promise come to fruition. During that time, Abram and Sarai made their fair share of mistakes. They, at times, became restless as they waited for God's promise to be fulfilled. They even tried to give God a helping hand in fulfilling His promise. Nevertheless, God chose Abram to be the father for His special family, the Jews. It was through Abram that God promised to make a great nation with many descendants.

At-A-Glance

1. God Answered Abram (Genesis 15:5–6)
2. Sarah Laughed (18:11–14)
3. Isaac, the Promised Child, Was Born (21:1–8)

In Depth

1. God Answered Abram (Genesis 15:5–6)

Here, God assured Abram that his heir would not be adopted, but would be one he would father. To give Abram an idea of the number of heirs his seed would produce, God told him to look toward the sky and attempt to count the stars—that is how large his family would become. It is at this point that Abram truly accepted and believed God's promise.

When God saw Abram's faith, He counted it as righteous.

Being in right relationship with God is an important concept. Some scholars believe that verse 6 is the key verse of the entire Old Testament. When God told Abram that his heir would not be Eliezer, his servant, but would be his own seed, Abram believed God. In other words, God regarded Abram's faith in such a way that he was justified in God's eyes—Abram's belief finally corresponded to God's promises.

The apostle Paul talks about this type of righteousness: "But now the righteousness of God without the law is manifested, being witnessed by the law and the prophets; Even the righteousness of God which is by faith of Jesus Christ unto all and upon all them that believe: for there is no difference" (Romans 3:21–22). Paul shows that Abram's faith was based on more than simple knowledge; it stemmed from the promise of redemption in Christ Jesus.

2. Sarah Laughed (18:11–14)

In an earlier visit God had promised Abraham an heir. Now the angel of the Lord returned to Abraham to strengthen his faith and encourage him (Genesis 18:10). But Abraham's wife, Sarah, was not convinced. She could not find it in her heart to believe the angel's news, so she laughed to herself. Her laughter came from doubt and mistrust. The Bible identifies other different kinds of laughter: the laughter of joy (Genesis 21:6) and the laughter of defiance (Job 5:22). In her mind she could not imagine how she could possibly conceive when she had "waxed old" and was beyond childbearing years (Genesis 18:12).

The angel rebuked Sarah by asking Abraham, "Wherefore did Sarah laugh?. . Is any thing too hard for the LORD?" (vv. 13–14). It is worthy to note that Abraham laughed to himself when God told him the same thing (cf. Genesis 17:16–17). One could speculate that the angel's reproof was not meant to be rhetorical, but instead it was an attempt to engage Abraham in further conversation—an attempt to move Sarah and Abraham beyond their limited view of the future. In any case, God directed the question to Abraham and not Sarah, which implies that God held Abraham accountable for Sarah's response. In any event, in spite of seemingly insurmountable odds, God fulfilled His promise to Abraham.

3. Isaac, the Promised Child, Was Born (21:1–8)

At last Sarah and Abraham became parents. Just as promised, God caused Sarah to conceive and bear a son, Isaac, the child of the promise. God's promise to Abraham for an heir was accomplished. God had plans for this family. A covenant people were created from the line of Abraham.

The theme of laughter continues in these verses. When God first told Abraham that he would have an heir with Sarah, he laughed at the absurdity of such an impossible thing occurring (Genesis 17:17). Sarah's reaction was the same, although when questioned by God she tried to deny her laughter (18:12–15). One has only to remember the ages of Sarah (90) and Abraham (100) to understand why the couple was skeptical. After all, Isaac's birth emphasized what appeared to be impossible. However, the source of their laughter changed from absurd doubt to exceeding joy. Sarah's laughter gave honor to God for Isaac's birth.

Search the Scriptures

1. According to God, how numerous would the descendants of Abram be (Genesis 15:5)?

2. What was Abram's response to the Lord's assurances (v. 6)?

3. What was special about the descendants God promised Abraham he would have (18:11)?

4. How old was Sarah when she had her baby (21:1–2)?

5. How did Sarah feel about the birth of Isaac (vv. 6–7)?

Discuss the Meaning

Imagine Abraham and Sarah's delight when Isaac was born! After all the years of waiting, God had fulfilled His promise to Abraham to increase his seed more than the stars in the sky. Abraham and Sarah knew that through them and their son Isaac, God promised to create a covenant people. God promised to bless not only the descendants of Abraham but all the nations of the earth (Genesis 12:3). As a result, today *all* Christians are a part of Abraham's extended family.

Families are a very important part of God's plan. Take a few moments to think of your family dynamic. Are you a member of a traditional family (mother, father, sister, etc.)? A blended family (mixing of two different families through remarriage)? An adoptive family? A single-parent family? A foster family? What does it mean to have an earthly family? What is the significance of being a member of God's family?

Lesson in Our Society

As spiritual descendants of Abraham, we are all members of God's extended family. Take a few moments and think about the members of your family. Think about a time when you have seen God's faithfulness in action in your home, in your church, or in your community. Share your insight with the rest of the class.

Make It Happen

All born-again believers are members of a very unique family—God's family. However, there may be some member of your earthly family or a friend that has not accepted Christ. As you go about your daily task this upcoming week, think about someone to whom you would like to extend an invitation to join God's family.

Follow the Spirit

What God wants me to do:

_____

_____

Remember Your Thoughts

Special insights I have learned:

_____

_____

More Light on the Text

Genesis 15:5–6; 18:11–14; 21:1–8

While it may not be every day that we associate the promises given to Abraham with the Creation story, there is a direct and important connection that is relevant today. Even before God constructed His habitat for humanity, He had planned far into the future. Just as the countless ingredients of the Creation produced a planet capable of sustaining billions of humans for many thousands of years, so the formation of spiritual realities and truths began even before the act of creating the universe. Part of this master plan included the formation of a covenant people with whom God would interact to teach His ways, and through whom He would communicate to all of mankind. God chose Abraham to be the father of His covenant people and nation, and formed an unconditional covenant with him that is still active today. That is one big family!

As our lesson opens, God is delivering His covenant promise to Abraham for the third time (see Genesis 12:2–3; 13:14–15) in the third of seven visitations, informing him that his descendants would be as numberless as the stars over his head. Previously God had told him He would make of him a great nation and that all nations would be blessed through him. He had later told him that he would inherit a vast territory and his descendants would be as numberless as the dust particles under his feet (see also Acts 7:2–5; Hebrews 11:8–12). These promises soon came to fruition in Solomon's time: "Judah and Israel were many, as the sand which is by the sea in multitude" (1 Kings 4:20).

That God repeated His promises to Abraham a third time (at this point, with more repetitions to come) should speak volumes to believers today. Consider the words of Matthew Henry: "If God loves us, and has mercy in store for us, he will not suffer us to take up our rest anywhere short of Canaan, but will graciously repeat his calls, till the good work begun be performed, and our souls repose in God only. In the call itself we have a precept and a promise." We are human creatures, lacking faith and full of doubt; we're slow to believe. Thankfully, we serve a loving and patient God who often repeats His promises until His people clearly hear His voice and again take heart from His words and presence (see Psalms 85:8; 91:15; 138:3). God especially visits the disciple of faith with comfort, strength, and dependable promises;

Abraham was an eminent example of such a disciple, and therefore he was the recipient of those blessings.

5 And he brought him forth abroad, and said, Look now toward heaven, and tell the stars, if thou be able to number them: and he said unto him, So shall thy seed be. 6 And he believed in the LORD; and he counted it to him for righteousness.

When Scripture says Abraham "believed" in God (Heb. *'aman*, **aw-MAN**), the literal meaning is he "stayed himself" on the Lord; this speaks of a firm, supporting, even parental element. The word *'aman* also means "trusty, faithful, and reliable."

Any such clear, firm, and strong faith or belief in God will be rewarded by Him, just as Abraham's faith was. As will be shown in the lesson, Abraham had ample time and reason for unbelief and doubt; in fact, many today wouldn't even entertain such a promise from God (pregnancy) at such advanced ages. Abraham was 75 when he first received the promise (Genesis 12:4), and 100 when it was fulfilled (21:5); Sarah was 90 (Genesis 17:17). Scripture also reveals that Abraham was not perfect and his faith lapsed on several occasions; he did not pass but rather failed various tests of his faith. His failures, however, should teach us about his humanity; his victories should show us that they are attainable by other people who are flawed just as he was. It should not surprise us that such a stellar moment of faith in the face of directly contradictory circumstances became the benchmark for all those after Abraham who would believe in God by faith and, as he was, be granted righteousness.

New Testament believers may not realize that they actually follow Abraham's example to this day, or that Abraham's example, in essence, was the Gospel in the Old Testament (see Romans 4). When God "counted" (Heb. *chashab*, **khaw-SHAB**) "righteousness" (Heb. *tsedaqah*, **tsed-aw-KAW**) to Abraham in response to his faith, it meant He credited, or imputed, righteousness to him (He declares or counts us righteous). When Adam sinned, his guilt was imputed to us; when Christ died for our sins, our guilt was imputed to Him. When we repent and believe, Christ's righteousness is imputed to us.

The apostle Paul used the word "impute" in a succinct comparison of the believer's righteousness by faith with that of Abraham: "He staggered not at the promise of God through unbelief; but was strong in faith, giving glory to God; And being fully persuaded that, what he had promised, he was able also to perform. And therefore it was imputed to him for righteousness. Now it was not written for his sake alone, that it was imputed to him; But for us also, to whom it shall be imputed, if we believe on him that raised up Jesus our Lord from the dead" (Romans 4:20–24).

The New Testament uses the word "justified" (Gk. *dikaioo*, **dik-ah-YO-o**), which means "to render or declare righteous" (Romans 3:21–24; 4:18–25; 5:1). The Greek word for "righteousness," *dikaiosune* (**dik-ah-yos-OO-nay**) is a direct derivative of *dikaioo*. Justification is the legal aspect of salvation, much like a judge or jury in a court of law will make a legal declaration of innocence (righteousness) or guilt. The strength of the word "impute" also is seen in the fact that our sins were imputed to Christ on the cross. In literal terms, to count righteousness to someone means a wholesale transfer of a condition acceptable to God.

The uniqueness of Abraham's story is that he was the very first to be declared righteous in response to his faith—before he was circumcised, long before the law, ages before grace. At this moment, God's promise to Abraham sprouted—that he would become the father of many nations with descendants numberless as the stars because he led the way for everyone after him who would be justified by faith, including believers today (Romans 4:16).

While it is well known that God makes promises and covenants with us, they don't do us much good if we don't believe in His ability to fulfill them or if we don't reach out in faith and receive them. What would happen at a wedding, for example, if only one of the two at the altar made promises that then were neither acknowledged nor received by the other? For the marriage to work, the expressed promises would require not only a response but a return pledge. God requires us to receive His covenant promises by faith, after which He pours out His blessings on us, and we then find ourselves, in response, promising our lives to Him in praise and gratitude according to our faith. It must be understood that God, not Abraham, made the promise; but Abraham, by faith, received the promise and thus entered into God's covenant. Similarly, the new covenant of Christ stands inviolable (Hebrews 5:9; 9:12), regardless of the human

"Is any thing too hard for the LORD?"
(Genesis 18:14).

herself. Nothing is hidden from God, however, and through Abraham, He reproves Sarah for her unbelief. From a human perspective, circumstances may seem impossible, and when it seems as if God isn't doing anything in response to our prayers, it's easy to think God has forgotten about us. From God's perspective, the exact same circumstances may be a tool in His hands to demonstrate His power and glory. Warren Wiersbe, noted teacher and author, says it well: "Even when life is dark, you can still see the stars." He also says: "When the outlook is bleak, try the uplook." God faithfully loves and cares for us in spite of ourselves, in spite of our unbelief: "If we believe not, yet he abideth faithful: he cannot deny himself" (2 Timothy 2:13).

13 And the LORD said unto Abraham, Wherefore did Sarah laugh, saying, Shall I of a surety bear a child, which am old? 14 Is any thing too hard for the LORD?

A noted speaker once used an illustration about a ship in a bottle to illustrate faith. He asked the audience to imagine trying to get the ship out of the bottle in one piece. Naturally, everyone wondered how something like that would be possible without deconstructing the ship. Then he said, "Now simply imagine the ship outside the bottle, like turning a page and it's done. That's how faith works. We don't have to know the 'how' in order to believe in God's ability. Forget the 'how' and ask in faith for what you need." God didn't expect Abraham and Sarah to figure out how He was going to give them a child now that they were well past childbearing age; He expected them to have faith in Him and His ability. This is, in fact, what Abraham did—he believed God for a child even though his own body was "as good as dead" and Sarah's womb "was also dead" (Genesis 15:6; cf. Hebrews 11:12; Romans 4:19, NIV).

While Abraham believed, Sarah still struggled with the promise, but God questioned Abraham about Sarah's doubts. God's question created one of the all-time classic Old Testament passages. It must be remembered that this wasn't a question from a voice in the sky or in a dream or vision. The voice came from a rare *theophany*, a physical appearance of the Son of God, in the Old Testament.

Christ, in His pre-incarnate physical form, along with two angels, had come to visit Abraham in his

response or lack thereof. Yet all who believe in Christ and receive the new covenant promises by faith (Hebrews 9:15) will enter the covenant and will be declared righteous, or justified (Romans 5:1), as was Abraham, who led the way for us.

18:11 Now Abraham and Sarah were old and well stricken in age; and it ceased to be with Sarah after the manner of women. 12 Therefore Sarah laughed within herself, saying, After I am waxed old shall I have pleasure, my lord being old also?

Three men had visited Abraham and reminded him (for the fourth time) of God's promise of a son (Genesis 18:1–10). From her part of the tent just behind them, Sarah overheard and her reaction was to laugh "within herself" (silently). Sarah cannot get beyond the fact that she now is past menopause ("I am waxed old"). Some have said Sarah was indelicate on the matter, but we must remember that she didn't speak her words; rather, she thought them within tent on their way to the second part of their mission, which was to destroy Sodom and Gomorrah (Genesis 18:16). This was the third such physical appearance to Abraham (Genesis 12:7; 17:1) and the sixth visitation, including words and visions. Hebrews 13:2 is relevant here, which admonishes us to be careful how we welcome strangers, for we never know when we might entertain angels.

"Is any thing too hard for the LORD?" In Hebrew the word translated "too hard" (*pala'*, **paw-LAW**) means "wonderful or marvelous." In other words, God was asking Abraham: "Is anything too wonderful or marvelous for Me?" Amazingly, in Isaiah 9:6, a derivative of *pala'* is used for the word "Wonderful" (Heb. *pele'*, **PEH-leh**) in the familiar Messianic prophecy (and beloved Christmas passage): "For unto us a child is born, unto us a son is given: and the government shall be upon his shoulder: and his name shall be called Wonderful, Counsellor, The mighty God, The everlasting Father, The Prince of Peace" (Isaiah 9:6). Not only does nothing exceed God's power, but also nothing is too wonderful for God to be willing or able to do for those He loves. Neither the miraculous conception of this child for Abraham and Sarah nor the miraculous conception of His own Son for Joseph and Mary are too difficult for Him; by the same token, neither is the wonderful *giving* of this child of promise, the first of countless descendants, nor the wonderful *giving* of His own Son, whose very name is Wonderful, for the ongoing fulfillment of the promise to Abraham. It is by the birth of Isaac to Abraham and Sarah, and Jesus to Joseph and Mary, that God answers His own rhetorical question in truly wonderful ways.

21:1 And the LORD visited Sarah as he had said, and the LORD did unto Sarah as he had spoken. 22 For Sarah conceived, and bare Abraham a son in his old age, at the set time of which God had spoken to him.

God provided the promised heir "as he had spoken"; He fulfilled His promise to Abraham.

The birth of Isaac clearly is another vivid illustration of how there is nothing God either isn't able or willing to do for His children. In addition, there are numerous specific parallels between these two greatly celebrated births. Both were born at the time God had set: "But when the fulness of the time was come,

God sent forth his Son, made of a woman, made under the law" (Galatians 4:4). Both children were given names by God prior to their birth, and both names were rich with significance (Matthew 1:21). Both mothers received heavenly confirmation (Genesis 18:13–15; Luke 1:26–38). Both children came after extended delays: Abraham and Sarah waited 25 years from promise to birth (see also Hebrews 6:12). Both were miraculous births—contrary to nature, impossible for man—and thus were revelations of God's power (Luke 1:37). In both, God's plan of redemption for mankind rested on an infant. Both mothers rejoiced at the miracle: "And Mary said: My soul doth magnify the Lord" (v. 46). Both were an accomplishment of God's purpose and promise. Isaac became father to Jacob, who fathered the 12 tribes of Israel, and from Israel came the Messiah, mankind's redeemer. In the wise words of Warren Wiersbe, "No matter how long you may have to wait, you can trust God to accomplish His purpose." "How long is too long to wait on God? is a question each must answer individually, but all can learn a valuable lesson in patience and God's faithfulness from Abraham and Sarah.

Not only do God's children have the right to call on God's power, but also they are repeatedly encouraged not to lean on their own strength; they are rather to trust in God's strength, power, and ability (Zechariah 4:6). Abraham and Sarah placed their faith in a faithful God whose promises are trustworthy (Hebrews 11:11). The only way Isaac entered God's covenant family was through grace and faith—the same way every believer today enters the family of God.

3 And Abraham called the name of his son that was born unto him, whom Sarah bare to him, Isaac. 4 And Abraham circumcised his son Isaac being eight days old, as God had commanded him. 5 And Abraham was an hundred years old, when his son Isaac was born unto him.

God selected the name Isaac (Genesis 17:19), which literally means "he laughs" (Heb. *Yitschaq*, **yits-KHAWK**). This caused commentator Matthew Henry to wryly pen, "He might have designed him some other name of a more pompous signification." Nonetheless, God's ways are not our ways, and He knew before any of the coming events the reasons for naming Isaac as He did. Laughter of various types surrounded the life of Isaac, starting a year before he was born. In the same visitation, when God told Abraham to name his son Isaac, Abraham laughed for joy (Genesis 17:17). Shortly thereafter, during an appearance at Abraham's tent, Sarah laughed in disbelief (18:12). After Isaac's birth Sarah laughed again; this time it was for joy (see next section, 21:6). The thought of his birth had caused both his parents to laugh at different times and in different ways, and later Isaac's brother Ishmael laughed at him out of mockery (21:9). Ultimately the life of Isaac brought great joy to all who became heirs by faith to God's great promise to Abraham. Whenever we experience the joy of the Lord, we might do well to remember that God gave Isaac, the first child of promise (see also Luke 15:7, 10), the name that means "laughter."

6 And Sarah said, God hath made me to laugh, so that all that hear will laugh with me. 7 And she said, Who would have said unto Abraham, that Sarah should have given children suck? for I have born him a son in his old age. 8 And the child grew, and was weaned: and Abraham made a great feast the same day that Isaac was weaned.

God had specifically promised that Sarah, not Hagar, would be the mother of the promised son (Genesis 17:16–19; 18:9–15). The birth of Isaac, at long last, relieved Sarah of the burden of childlessness, which in ancient days was much more of a burden than it is today. It is only natural to be filled with joy, expressed in laughter, when relieved of a long-term burden; it is even more joyous when a long-held promise is fulfilled. Procreation today is much more optional depending on a couple's chosen lifestyle, but in Abraham's time infertile women faced social disparagement. As if to add insult to injury, God had already changed Abram's name ("exalted father") to Abraham, literally meaning "father of a multitude," promising that he would become the "father of many nations" (Genesis 17:5; also see Nehemiah 9:7). Even though he did have one son, Ishmael, Sarah had none, and Ishmael hardly constituted a multitude. Moreover, God changed the name of Abraham's wife, who would become a mother of many nations, from Sarai ("princess") to Sarah ("noblewoman") (Genesis 17:15–16). In a real sense, Sarai was Abram's princess; now she was to be the princess of many,

including royalty (v. 16, "kings of people shall be of her"). This promise eventually was fulfilled in the birth of the Prince of Peace (Isaiah 9:6) and King of kings (Revelation 17:14).

Neither Isaac's day of birth nor his day of circumcision (eight days later) were celebrated with feasting. Perhaps the former was in order to protect Sarah's health, and perhaps the latter was so as not to detract from this important ceremony that God had ordained, and as well out of consideration for the still very young infant's health. Rather, the day of celebration and feasting came when Sarah weaned Isaac. Weaning is something modern people take for granted, but in ancient days infant mortality was considerably higher; thus it was a time to celebrate and give thanks to God when a child survived until he or she could start ingesting solid food. With accompanying joy resounding through generations, the promise lives on!

Sources:

Henry, Matthew. "Commentary on Genesis 12." *Matthew Henry's Commentary on the Whole Bible.* Blue Letter Bible. March 1, 1996. http://www.blueletterbible.org/Comm/mhc/Gen/Gen012.html.

Wiersbe, Warren W. *Be Obedient (Abraham).* Wheaton, Ill.: Victor Books, 1991. 99.

———. *Be Obedient (Genesis 14–24).* Wheaton, Ill.: Victor Books, 1996.

Daily Bible Readings

M: Listen!
Isaiah 51:1–5
T: Abraham Believed
Genesis 15:1–6
W: Abraham Doubted
Genesis 17:15–22
T: Abraham, the Host
Genesis 18:1–8
F: Sarah's Laughter
Genesis 18:9–15
S: Sarah's Joy
Genesis 21:1–8
S: The Faith of Abraham
Hebrews 11:8–12

TEACHING TIPS

September 23
Bible Study Guide 4

1. Words You Should Know

A. Bondwoman (Genesis 21:10, 12–13) *'amah* (Heb.)—A maidservant or a female slave.

B. Seed (vv. 12–13, 17–18) *zera'* (Heb.)—A child, offspring, or descendant.

C. Child (vv. 14–16) *ye'ledh* (Heb.)—Term is often applied to a son or boy.

D. Bowshot (v. 16) *tachah* (Heb.)—To hurl or shoot.

2. Teacher Preparation

Unifying Principle—Dealing with Dissension in the Family! Seeds of dissension were sown in Abraham's family that continue to this day. Though the family was in conflict, it is important to note that God's love and provision were available to all parties involved. When dissension in a family occurs, we should do whatever we can to promote peace.

A. Read Genesis 16, 20, and 21 in their entirety to familiarize yourself with the content of this lesson.

B. Look at Galatians 4:21–31 for the New Testament application of today's Scripture text.

C. Complete lesson 4 for September 23 in the *Precepts For Living® Personal Study Guide* for more practical application of today's Scripture text.

3. Starting the Lesson

A. Ask a student to open the class with a prayer.

B. Say to the class that today's lesson will address dissension within the family (Unifying Principle) by looking at Abraham's relationship with Sarah, Hagar, and Ishmael.

C. Ask a volunteer to read the Focal Verses.

D. Introduce the AIM for Change objectives.

4. Getting into the Lesson

A. Instruct the class to silently read today's In Focus story.

B. Engage the class in a brief discussion regarding some of the problems blended families face.

C. Set the stage for today's text by reinforcing the Background and The People, Places, and Times sections.

D. Answer Search the Scriptures as a group.

5. Relating the Lesson to Life

A. Break the class into three equal groups and assign each group a question from the Discuss the Meaning section. Allow each group approximately 15 minutes for discussion.

B. Reconvene the class and ask a spokesperson from each group to briefly share the group's conclusion to the discussion question with the rest of the class.

C. After hearing each group take on the Discuss the Meaning questions, allow the class to share how the seeds of division and dissension have become manifest in their own families, and to discuss the impact these conflicts have on family members. Encourage them to talk about how God's love is available to all of the parties involved and how they can be of help in showing God's love and promoting a peaceful resolution.

6. Arousing Action

A. Instruct the class to silently read the Lesson in Our Society section and reflect on its meaning.

B. Read the Make It Happen section aloud. Encourage the class to follow through on the suggestion to be reconciled with a family member. Ask those not presently experiencing family problems to pray for those who are.

C. Remind the students to complete lesson 5 in the *Precepts For Living® Personal Study Guide* and to read the September 30 Daily Bible Readings in preparation for next week's lesson.

D. Take a moment to solicit personal prayer requests. Close the class in prayer.

Worship Guide

For the Superintendent or Teacher
Theme: Abraham, Hagar, and Ishmael
Theme Song: "I Have Decided to Follow Jesus"
Devotional Reading: Genesis 16
Prayer

ABRAHAM, HAGAR, AND ISHMAEL

Bible Background • GENESIS 21:9–21
Printed Text • GENESIS 21:9–21   Devotional Reading • GENESIS 16

AIM for Change

By the end of the lesson, we will:

DISCUSS the events that led to conflict in Abraham's family;

REFLECT ON God's promise and care for Ishmael and what it says to those who may feel rejected by their family; and

IDENTIFY conflict that may exist in our family and ENCOURAGE peace.

Keep in Mind

"And also of the son of the bondwoman will I make a nation, because he is thy seed" (Genesis 21:13).

Focal Verses

KJV **Genesis 21:9** And Sarah saw the son of Hagar the Egyptian, which she had born unto Abraham, mocking.

10 Wherefore she said unto Abraham, Cast out this bondwoman and her son: for the son of this bondwoman shall not be heir with my son, even with Isaac.

11 And the thing was very grievous in Abraham's sight because of his son.

12 And God said unto Abraham, Let it not be grievous in thy sight because of the lad, and because of thy bondwoman; in all that Sarah hath said unto thee, hearken unto her voice; for in Isaac shall thy seed be called.

13 And also of the son of the bondwoman will I make a nation, because he is thy seed.

14 And Abraham rose up early in the morning, and took bread, and a bottle of water, and gave it unto Hagar, putting it on her shoulder, and the child, and sent her away: and she departed, and wandered in the wilderness of Beersheba.

15 And the water was spent in the bottle, and she cast the child under one of the shrubs.

16 And she went, and sat her down over against him a good way off, as it were a bowshot: for she said, Let me not see the death of the child. And she sat over against him, and lift up her voice, and wept.

17 And God heard the voice of the lad; and the angel of God called Hagar out of heaven, and said unto her, What aileth thee, Hagar? fear not; for God hath heard the voice of the lad where he is.

18 Arise, lift up the lad, and hold him in thine hand; for I will make him a great nation.

NLT **Genesis 21:9** But Sarah saw Ishmael—the son of Abraham and her Egyptian servant Hagar—making fun of her son, Isaac.

10 So she turned to Abraham and demanded, "Get rid of that slave woman and her son. He is not going to share the inheritance with my son, Isaac. I won't have it!"

11 This upset Abraham very much because Ishmael was his son.

12 But God told Abraham, "Do not be upset over the boy and your servant. Do whatever Sarah tells you, for Isaac is the son through whom your descendants will be counted.

13 But I will also make a nation of the descendants of Hagar's son because he is your son, too."

14 So Abraham got up early the next morning, prepared food and a container of water, and strapped them on Hagar's shoulders. Then he sent her away with their son, and she wandered aimlessly in the wilderness of Beersheba.

15 When the water was gone, she put the boy in the shade of a bush.

16 Then she went and sat down by herself about a hundred yards away. "I don't want to watch the boy die," she said, as she burst into tears.

17 But God heard the boy crying, and the angel of God called to Hagar from heaven, "Hagar, what's wrong? Do not be afraid! God has heard the boy crying as he lies there.

18 Go to him and comfort him, for I will make a great nation from his descendants."

19 Then God opened Hagar's eyes, and she saw a well full of water. She quickly filled her water container and gave the boy a drink.

19 And God opened her eyes, and she saw a well of water; and she went, and filled the bottle with water, and gave the lad drink.

20 And God was with the lad; and he grew, and dwelt in the wilderness, and became an archer.

21 And he dwelt in the wilderness of Paran: and his mother took him a wife out of the land of Egypt.

20 And God was with the boy as he grew up in the wilderness. He became a skillful archer,

21 and he settled in the wilderness of Paran. His mother arranged for him to marry a woman from the land of Egypt.

In Focus

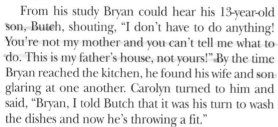

From his study Bryan could hear his 13-year-old son, Butch, shouting, "I don't have to do anything! You're not my mother and you can't tell me what to do. This is my father's house, not yours!" By the time Bryan reached the kitchen, he found his wife and son glaring at one another. Carolyn turned to him and said, "Bryan, I told Butch that it was his turn to wash the dishes and now he's throwing a fit."

"No, Dad," Butch interrupted, "she's always trying to boss me around. I've got homework to do and I don't have time to wash any stupid dishes."

This feuding between Butch and Carolyn had been going on for months. No matter what Carolyn said, Butch always found fault with it. When Butch's parents divorced three years ago, Butch took it hard. His grades in school dropped and he became sullen. After Bryan and Carolyn married, Bryan thought that bringing Butch to live with him would be best thing for his son—but no such luck.

Butch often ignored Carolyn and refused to speak to her. If his father and Carolyn were talking, Butch would interrupt. Just last week Carolyn had told Bryan she thought Butch being there with them was a mistake and that he ought to let Butch return to his mother. Bryan loved Butch, and he loved his new wife. Standing there now, looking at the two of them, Bryan knew that he needed to pray and ask God to help him decide what to do.

Today's lesson reminds us that although family conflict will arise, God's love and provision are still available; and we should do whatever we can to promote peace and show love toward one another.

The People, Places, and Times

The Wilderness of Paran. Paran is a desert area located in the northeastern section of the Sinai Peninsula, with the Arabah on the east and the wilderness of Shur on the west. The region experiences very little rainfall (less than 10 inches per year). The Wilderness of Paran or Desert of Paran is thought to be the place where the Israelites spent part of their 40 years of wandering. It was from Kadesh, in Paran, that the 12 scouts were sent into the Promised Land to gather information prior to what would have been the Israelites' entry just a little more than two years after the Exodus from Egypt (Numbers 10:11). King David spent some time in the wilderness of Paran after Samuel died (1 Samuel 25:1). This region is part of modern-day Egypt and Saudi Arabia.

Source:

Packer, J. I., and M. C. Tenney, eds. *Illustrated Manners and Customs of the Bible.* Nashville, Tenn.: Thomas Nelson Publishers, 1980. 592–94.

Background

The book of Genesis provides us with a revealing story of Abraham's faith walk with God. God promised Abraham that, through Sarah, he would have a child who would bring forth countless descendants. In spite of God's promise, years went by; Abraham was now 86 years old, and he and his wife, Sarah, remained childless. Blaming God for her failure to conceive, Sarah suggested that her slave, an Egyptian girl named Hagar, act as a surrogate mother, and she proceeded to give Hagar to her husband as a secondary wife (Genesis 16:2–3).

As was customary, any child born to Sarah's slave would be considered Sarah's child as well because she was Abram's first and true wife. Hagar became pregnant, and Abraham's home was quickly filled with angry tension. The Bible suggests that Hagar's behavior toward Sarah changed: "Her mistress was despised in her eyes" (v. 4). Instead of Abraham's home being filled with joy as they awaited the birth of a child, it was now marked by jealousy, hostility, and turmoil. Even though it was her idea, Sarah blamed Abraham. Abraham insisted, however, that the responsibility belonged to Sarah alone. Interestingly, neither of them petitioned the Lord for guidance. Instead, Sarah treated the pregnant Hagar so harshly that the Egyptian girl ran away into the wilderness. There, an angel of the Lord appeared to the abused Hagar and instructed her not only to return but to submit herself to Sarah! The angel promised Hagar that from her seed would come countless descendants. Hagar was told that the child she was carrying would be a son, and she was instructed: "Call his name Ishmael; because the LORD hath heard thy affliction" (v. 11).

What an interesting challenge God presented to Hagar. She was instructed to return to the very same abusive and painful situation that sent her to the wilderness in the first place. God's direction, while uncomfortable for the young girl, held the promise of wonderful blessings from the God who heard and responded to her crying in the middle of the desert.

At-A-Glance

1. The Cause of the Conflict
(Genesis 21:9–10)
2. The Effect of the Conflict (vv. 11–12)
3. The Comfort in the Conflict (v. 13)
4. The Cost in the Conflict (vv. 14–16)
5. The Provision in the Conflict (vv. 17–21)

In Depth

1. The Cause of the Conflict (Genesis 21:9–10)

Chapter 21 opens with God fulfilling His promise that Abraham and his wife Sarah will have a child of their own. This promise had been made many years earlier, and Sarah had grown anxious, and perhaps a little fearful, that God would not honor His Word. Rather than waiting on God, Sarah gave her Egyptian slave girl, Hagar, to her husband as a secondary wife and a surrogate mother. Abraham had acquired male and female slaves and livestock from Pharaoh during the time he spent in Egypt while a famine devastated the land of Canaan (see Genesis 12:10, 16). It was probably during this time that Hagar came to be

Sarah's maidservant, or bondwoman. Even though both Abraham and Sarah acknowledged that Sarah's inability to conceive was the will of God, notice that neither of them bothered to consult with God before they took matters into their own hands.

God had always treated Abraham as a friend. In this matter, however, Abraham seemed to discount his previous experiences with God. Throughout Genesis, God directed Abraham, telling him where to go, where to live, whom to associate with, and what to do. As a result, Abraham had become a very wealthy and highly esteemed man with a beautiful wife. Yet, with Sarah's persistent urging, Abraham decided to conceive a child on the strength of his own capability, rather than relying on the promises of God, who had always provided everything he needed.

As one might imagine, a household with one husband and two wives—one younger and pregnant—quickly became a tension-filled environment. Sarah and Hagar were antagonistic toward one another. This antagonism drove the pregnant Hagar to run away. While she was in the desert, an "angel of the LORD found her by a fountain of water in the wilderness" (Genesis 16:7). Interestingly, Hagar was the first person in the Bible to give God a name: "And she called the name of the LORD that spake unto her, Thou God seest me: for she said, Have I also here looked after him that seeth me?" (v. 13). This suggests that perhaps a personal relationship had already been established between Hagar and God. In any case, it was not comfort but direction that God offered the suffering slave girl.

Hagar was ordered to return to Sarah and to live under the hand of her mistress. God did not free Hagar from slavery, nor did He direct her away from the source of her hurt. We would do well to remember that God's solution to our problems may require us to humble ourselves and to be submissive. Although this may not always sit well with us, we must remember and understand that God alone holds the key to our future, and we must be willing to obey Him in all matters.

2. The Effect of the Conflict (vv. 11–12)

Hagar obeyed God and returned to the household of Abraham and Sarah, where she gave birth to a son. Following God's instructions, Hagar named the child Ishmael, a name that means "God will hear." At the age of 86, Abraham was finally a father. It would be another 13 years before God opened Sarah's womb and Isaac would be born to Sarah and Abraham. The promise that God made to Abraham some 25 years earlier had finally come to fruition. We can only imagine how happy Abraham must have been. He was 100 years old, and his wife, Sarah, was 90, and he now had two healthy sons living side by side.

When Genesis 21 opens, a feast is being held to celebrate the weaning of Isaac. Children tended to nurse longer in those days and in that culture, and Isaac may have been as old as 3 or 4 when he was finally weaned. The text implies that the enjoyment of the day was interrupted when, during the celebration, Sarah observed Ishmael mocking his little brother. She demanded that Abraham "cast out this bondwoman and her son: for the son of this bondwoman shall not be heir with my son" (v. 10). One should not be surprised at Sarah's request that Hagar and her son be banished from the tents of Abraham. Sarah's intense dislike for Hagar was, no doubt, fueling her antagonism toward Ishmael.

Though Ishmael's behavior seemed questionable, we must recognize that for the past 13 years he had been the only child of an aging man who desperately wanted children. No doubt Abraham had both loved and pampered Ishmael. One must also consider that Abraham was now a very wealthy and very powerful man, and Ishmael, his only son, had enjoyed a privileged childhood that he now had to share with a brother.

Though her motivation was wrong, Sarah was absolutely right on one key point—Ishmael was not the child of promise! It was Isaac, whom God had promised would bring Abraham a line of descendants more numerous than the stars in the sky. Ishmael was not the result of God's supernatural movement in the life of Abraham; he was the result of impatience and self-indulgence on the part of Sarah and Abraham. Isaac, not Ishmael, was God's choice.

3. The Comfort in the Conflict (v. 13)

Sarah's request that Abraham expel Hagar and Ishmael must have been heartbreaking to Abraham. After a lifetime of barrenness, Sarah's demand that he send his oldest child away must have hurt him

deeply. Abraham's genuine love for his oldest son, Ishmael, was clearly illustrated in Genesis 17. We see Abraham falling on his face and laughing at God's announcement of Isaac's future birth. Abraham told God, "O that Ishmael might live before thee!" (v. 18). At that point, it is clear that Abraham had grown content with his one son—Ishmael. God, however, was insisting that His covenant promise would be fulfilled through Isaac and not Ishmael (vv. 15–21).

Now, in the midst of the turmoil, God reminded Abraham of this, telling him to do as Sarah said and to send both Hagar and Ishmael away. In the face of this heart-wrenching pronouncement, God comforted Abraham by assuring him that His blessing toward Ishmael would mirror the blessing He had in store for Isaac.

Clearly, God recognized that Hagar and Ishmael were innocent victims of circumstance, and worthy of a promising future. As difficult as it must have been, Abraham chose to trust and believe that God was a covenant-keeping God!

What a powerful reminder that the God we serve is Master of time. Unlike God, you and I are linear thinkers. We can only remember the pain of our past and despair over the torment of our present. God, on the other hand, knows exactly what our future holds. He is in control of everything. We must develop a spirit of obedience—even when we don't understand what lies ahead. We must trust that God knows and that He cares. He requires that each of us commit to obediently trusting and following His Word. Even in the midst of our anguish, our comfort lies in knowing God loves us and wants what is best for us. God's will, not our immediate comfort, must reign supreme if we are to triumph.

4. The Cost of the Conflict (vv. 14–16)

After receiving provisions from Abraham—bread and water—Hagar and her son left the safety of the tents of Abraham and headed off into the desert. While it might appear that Sarah had won and rid her household of Hagar and Ishmael, we must stop here to recognize the enormity of the situation. First, she had allowed the spirits of jealousy and bitterness to take hold and direct her actions, thus spreading the seeds of dissension in her family. Second, Sarah had made a demand that deeply wounded her husband. To require that her husband cast away his firstborn son points to a self-indulgent spirit rather than a spirit of loving reconciliation. Surely, Sarah knew that Abraham loved Ishmael, yet her desire to be rid of the child and his mother took precedence over her husband's happiness.

Finally, Sarah's ill treatment of Hagar was unjustifiable. As mistress of the house Sarah was obligated to extend decent treatment to everyone, whether they were free or a slave. No doubt her jealousy toward Hagar would not allow her to exercise kindness or gentleness in her treatment of the slave girl.

After their expulsion from Abraham's tents, instead of heading west into Egypt, Hagar and Ishmael traveled east into the wilderness of Beersheba. Hagar may have known that her son's future lay not in her homeland of Egypt, but in the vast area of Arabia. In any case the text seems to imply that the water Hagar received from Abraham ran out and she and Ishmael now faced slow and agonizing death by dehydration.

What a pitiful predicament Hagar found herself in! First, she had been expelled by Abraham, and then the water had run out and with it all hopes of reaching safety. Hagar may even have feared that God Himself had abandoned her. No doubt faint with thirst and tired by the walking in the fierce heat of the desert sun, Ishmael appeared to his mother to be dying. Unwilling to watch her son die, Hagar moved a "bowshot" away from her son and began to cry.

5. The Provision in the Conflict (vv. 17–21)

God had not abandoned Hagar or her son. For the second time in her life, Hagar had a miraculous experience. "God heard the voice of the lad," and He began to comfort Hagar.

While His initial question—"What aileth thee, Hagar?"—may seem strange, a closer reading reveals the beauty of it. First, God, through His angel, addressed Hagar by name. God had never left Hagar. He knew her, and He knew all about her troubles. Second, the question implies that whenever God comes into a situation, the situation is transformed. Hagar was not given any answers to the present problem, nor was she directed what to do about the present problem; rather, she was called to trust God.

"Fear not," she was told, "God hath heard the voice of the lad." The same God who heard her voice

years ago was assuring her that He now heard the voice of her son. God responds when someone cries out from a situation of helplessness and hopelessness. Through His angel, God directed her to get up and "mother" Ishmael ("take up the lad"). He then renewed His promise regarding the descendants of Ishmael becoming a nation.

It is only when Hagar obeyed God that her eyes were "opened" and she saw a well from which she could draw the water to sustain both of them. God's blessing to her was made evident in a real and needed way.

The account ends with the indication that God's promise had been fulfilled. Ishmael's future had been accurately prophesied: Arabian nomads or Bedouins indeed roamed the wilds of the desert. In Genesis 16:12, NRSV, the term "wild ass" was used to describe Ishmael. Please note that this term is not derogatory. Wild asses were swift, powerful, and able to survive in the harshest of desert conditions. Like the wild asses, Ishmael and his descendants would survive. Ishmael became an archer and a skilled hunter who would be more than able to kill game for food and be a formidable opponent to any human enemy.

Hagar and Ishmael settled another 100 miles south, in the area we now know as the Sinai Peninsula. In this rugged and isolated area, Ishmael would develop his leadership skills and strengthen his control over Arab tribes. Here, Hagar arranged a marriage for him, selecting a wife for her son among her own people.

The exiled Ishmael would later return and assist his brother Isaac with the burial of their father Abraham (Genesis 25:9). The same chapter records the names of Ishmael's 12 sons, who became the founders of tribes that spread from Egypt to present-day Iraq. How interesting that many modern-day Arabs correctly recognize that they are descendants of Ishmael, and that Jews and the rest of the Israelites are descendants of Isaac—but they are all the seed of Abraham, the fulfillment of God's promises to him.

Search the Scriptures
1. Why did Sarah want Hagar cast out (Genesis 21:9–10)?
2. How did Abraham feel about Sarah's demand (v. 11)?

3. Why did God tell Abraham to listen to Sarah (v. 12)?

4. What provisions did Abraham make for Hagar and Ishmael (v. 14)?

5. What promise was made to Hagar in the desert (v. 18)?

Discuss the Meaning

1. In verse 9, it appears that Sarah wanted Hagar and Ishmael cast out because Ishmael posed a threat to Isaac's inheritance. Do you think there may have been other factors that caused Sarah to demand the eviction of Hagar and Ishmael? Are these types of issues still faced by families today? How are Christians expected to deal with these types of issues?

2. Compare and contrast the response of Abraham in Genesis 21:11–14 and his earlier response to a demand from Sarah when there was tension between Sarah and Hagar in Genesis 16:3–6. Where was Abraham's focus in each account? What do you think were Abraham's strengths and weaknesses as a husband?

3. Do you think that Hagar's Egyptian ethnicity contributed to her victimization? If you do, why do you believe this?

Lesson in Our Society

Believing that God is the source of all life is not a difficult concept for us. Many of us are quite certain that God has provided for us in our past. What some of us find challenging is trusting God to provide during periods of turmoil and hardship! Very often when we are feeling isolated, hurt, or even victimized, it is difficult to remember that the God we serve is omniscient, omnipresent, and omnipotent. He knows everything that is going on in our lives. He knows when we are hurt, and He knows who is hurting us. Our faith demands that we trust Him to reconcile every situation in His appointed time. God is everywhere all of the time. There is no situation that we endure alone. He is available to comfort us if we ask Him. God is all-powerful. When present trials make us anxious or fearful, we must remember that the provision for all we need rests in His hands. Christians are not immune from tests, trials, and tribulations, nor are Christian families immune from dysfunctions. Through these hardships, we must hold on to the promise and the hope that only God can provide.

Make It Happen

It is often difficult for us to recollect abusive incidents that have occurred in our families. It is much easier to maintain a safe distance between us and the offending relative. This week, ask God to provide an opportunity for you to be reconciled with someone in your family and begin the healing process that will allow you to fully embrace, rather than just tolerate, that family member. Spend time in prayer and Scripture study so that you may be prepared when this opportunity presents itself. If you are not presently at odds with a family member, think of what other types of families (or communities) you are a part of; think of someone you might be at odds with and reconcile your differences with that person.

Follow the Spirit

What God wants me to do:

_____

_____

Remember Your Thoughts

Special insights I have learned:

_____

_____

More Light on the Text
Genesis 21:9–21

It may be a revelation to some that the current conflict in the Middle East goes all the way back to these passages in Genesis, in particular the heartrending conflict in Abraham and Sarah's family regarding their oldest son, Ishmael, son of Sarah's Egyptian handmaiden Hagar, and Isaac, the long-awaited son of promise. It is a well-known fact to many that Ishmael is the father of the Arabian nations, and Muslims universally claim descent from him. That both Jews and Arab Muslims claim Abraham as their founding patriarch is an irony, but also a historical fact. The vast differences between their religions began with Ishmael, claimed by the Arabs, and Isaac, claimed by the Jews. Thus, the conflict that started in Genesis continues to this day.

"And also of the son of the bondwoman will I make a nation, because he is thy seed" (Genesis 21:13).

Ishmael was the elder son of the Hebrew patriarch Abraham and the reputed ancestor of a group of Arabian tribes. The region occupied by these Ishmaelites included most of central and northern Arabia.

The Ishmaelites are descendants of Ishmael, the son of Abraham and Hagar. The 12 sons of Ishmael and his Egyptian wife became princes and progenitors of as many tribes. All Arabs, following Mohammed's example, claim to be descendants of Ishmael.

The Ishmaelite people are frequently mentioned in the Bible (see Genesis 37:25; Judges 8:24). They were Arab nomads who traded with Egypt. According to Genesis 25:12–18, the Ishmaelites (like the Israelites) were divided into 12 tribes, and pitched their tents in northern Arabia as far as the borders of Egypt and Assyria. The Arabs themselves derived their descent from Ishmael.

First came the conflict in the home of Abraham, between Ishmael and Isaac, and then the ongoing next-generation conflict in the home of Isaac, between Esau and Jacob. Ishmael's descendants are directly related to Esau's descendants since Ishmael was Esau's uncle. The 12 tribes of Ishmael and the 12 tribes of Israel have been fighting ever since over the ownership of Israel, which God covenanted to Isaac and not Ishmael. It seems that not only have bloodlines been handed down through the generations, but also bloodthirstiness against Israel.

What seems plain in Scripture to Christians, a Muslim would consider distorted. According to the Muslims' account, Abraham took Ishmael, not Isaac, to Mecca, not Mount Moriah (the eventual site of the Jewish Temple Mount and current home of the Muslim Dome of the Rock) to sacrifice him. Moreover, the Koran (Qur'an) claims that Ishmael then inherited the title deed to Israel and not Isaac. However, the Muslim account has never been able to satisfactorily explain why the New Testament clearly supports the Old Testament (see Galatians 4:28–31), or how the Genesis account of God making Israel the promised land for the Hebrew children was written 2,500 years before the creation of Islam.

One of many practical applications can be made and an exhortation issued in a call for peace among families, for we never know how far our family disputes may travel, or what long-term consequences may result. At the same time, if we are to have a hope and a future, we always need to be alert for God's voice and His guidance, and to be obedient to Him when He speaks to us (Jeremiah 29:11).

9 And Sarah saw the son of Hagar the Egyptian, which she had born unto Abraham, mocking.

As mentioned previously, this event is part of the various types of laughter that surrounded Isaac's life, which God foresaw when He selected his name. Still, we aren't told exactly why Ishmael, who was 13 or 14 years older than Isaac, would act this way toward his baby brother. In Hebrew the term "mocking" is *tsachaq* (**tsaw-KHAK**). It is used 13 times in the Old Testament and means "to make fun of, or repeated laughing," as contrasted with a gentle teasing. Apparently, in Hebrew and several surrounding original languages, the word itself sounded like laughter (onomatopoeia). The word is used to describe what happened when Lot tried to get his family out of Sodom, telling them the city was going to be destroyed, and they thought he was joking with them (Genesis 19:14). Isaac here was about 3 to 4 years old, which most scholars agree was the age when children in ancient times were weaned. One could only imagine that with such a difference in their ages, nothing justified a teenager mocking a toddler, especially a family member. The greater reality of the events, however, is much more significant than what appears on the surface to be just another case of normal sibling rivalry.

The apostle Paul clearly explains the spiritual implications of this Old Testament story: "For it is written, that Abraham had two sons, the one by a bondmaid [Hagar], the other by a freewoman [Sarah]. But he who was of the bondwoman was born after the flesh [Ishmael]; but he of the freewoman was by promise [Isaac] . . . . he that was born after the flesh persecuted [mocked] him that was born after the Spirit . . . ." (Galatians 4:22–23, 29). The complete passage (Galatians 4:21–31) clearly outlines who the sons are, who their parents are, and which of them is

of the flesh versus of the Spirit. From the very beginning, Ishmael was to be a source of grief for his family, starting with Hagar's pregnancy, which apparently gave her an air of superiority around the still childless Sarah (Genesis 16:4–5). Sarah treated Hagar harshly as a result, and Hagar fled into the desert. God visited her there, selected Ishmael's name (Heb. *Yishma'el*, **yish-maw-ALE**, literally "God hears") in Genesis 16:11–12, and then informed her that her son would grow to become a "wild man" and would live a life of hostility. Even though Abraham loved his son (17:18), a reality to which God responded with the promise of making him a nation (v. 20), Ishmael never brought to his family the great joy that surrounded Isaac.

When the Jews began to preach a return to the law in opposition to Paul's teachings of grace, he informed the Galatian Christians what those Jews were like—they were like the children of Ishmael, not Isaac (Galatians 4). He was aware they all were children of Abraham, but he asked them whether their mother was a slave (Hagar) or a free woman (Sarah). Ishmael was born of a slave, according to the flesh (v. 23), while Isaac was born of a free woman, according to promise. Paul wanted them (the Judaizers: those who wanted all Christians to submit to the Jewish law) to realize what they preached was a return to slavery of the law, while what he preached was a reception of the promise of grace by faith. Flesh never will be at peace with Spirit, and there can be no coexistence between law and grace. What seems like just another Old Testament story of sibling rivalry really is a lesson for the ages.

10 Wherefore she said unto Abraham, Cast out this bondwoman and her son: for the son of this bondwoman shall not be heir with my son, even with Isaac.

As Sarah previously had done with Hagar (16:3–4), she asked Abraham once again to resolve the issue for her and cast Hagar out. In Hebrew, the phrase "cast out" is *garash* (**gaw-RASH**); it is used in the sense of driving out forcibly, as in driving out an enemy (see Joshua 24:12, 18) or the separation from a divorce (see Leviticus 21:14). Abraham had previously told Sarah that since Hagar was her handmaiden, she was free to do with her as she pleased. This time Sarah was asking her husband to cast out both Hagar and Ishmael, his son. This was a much weightier matter and was not within Sarah's sole discretion as before. Things had come to a head for Sarah, just as in our lives we often come to a point where a hard decision must be made regarding an element of the flesh, which continually vexes the Spirit (cf. Romans 7:19; Galatians 5:17). An even closer parallel is when we must come to terms with a family member who interferes or conflicts somehow with our pursuit of God, a case for which this lesson is very instructive.

11 And the thing was very grievous in Abraham's sight because of his son. 12 And God said unto Abraham, Let it not be grievous in thy sight because of the lad, and because of thy bondwoman; in all that Sarah hath said unto thee, hearken unto her voice; for in Isaac shall thy seed be called.

Even though he was well aware by now that Ishmael was not the promised heir, Abraham struggled with the difficult decision to cast out his own son. "Grievous" in Hebrew is *yara* (**yaw-RAH**); it signifies shaking or trembling. It is used during times when God is greatly displeased with Israel (1 Chronicles 21:7). Abraham was visibly shaken to consider such a drastic measure. Isaac was still a toddler, but Abraham had many years to get to know and love Ishmael; he understandably was torn. As any person of faith would do in the throes of a serious conflict, Abraham apparently prayed, because God responded during his struggle. Now the decision was God's, and by trusting God's wisdom, Abraham found the peace and courage to carry out even the most difficult of decisions, to cast out both his first-born son and the boy's mother. Surely it was God's reminder of His previous promise, repeated several times now, that made Abraham realize what was at stake. Sarah had previously made a mistake in encouraging her husband to have a child with Hagar; this time she was not wrong in wanting to protect the child of promise from the child of flesh, of whom God had not approved. By obeying, Abraham opened the door for God's higher purpose for all who would follow.

13 And also of the son of the bondwoman will I make a nation, because he is thy seed.

With this repeated pronouncement (see Genesis 17:20), God essentially created the Arab nations of the world, the vast majority of whom are Muslims, whose god is Allah of the Islamic religion. Though Muslims correctly claim their most ancient descendants are Ishmael and Abraham, they incorrectly believe Ishmael rather than Isaac originated the bloodline of the world's Saviour (and deny that Jesus Christ is that Saviour). From Ishmael's second son, Kedar, they attribute Muhammed, and through Muhammed came the Twelfth Imam.

Sunni Muslims call the Twelfth Imam Al-Mahdi, "The Guided One." In Shi'ite Islam eschatology, he is "The Promised One." The Twelfth Imam first appeared in A.D. 878 as a youth, but he then disappeared in a mosque in Samatra, Iraq. He is supposed to reappear near the end of the world—specifically during a time of great world disorder.

Out of respect for the seed of Abraham, God did make a nation of Ishmael as promised, but it was a nation born in conflict, destined to wage war with Israel in the Old Testament.

14 And Abraham rose up early in the morning, and took bread, and a bottle of water, and gave it unto Hagar, putting it on her shoulder, and the child, and sent her away: and she departed, and wandered in the wilderness of Beersheba.

It must be remembered that while Sarah came to Abraham with the problem of Ishmael mocking Isaac and asking him to cast them out, he wouldn't have done so because of his love for Ishmael had God not instructed him to do what Sarah asked. Abraham already had learned the rewards of faith, trust, and obedience. Little did he know, however, that even though this was a very difficult trial for him, he was to face a much greater trial when God would ask him later to sacrifice Isaac, the son of promise (22:1–19). Because Abraham obeyed God then, we can assume he also obeyed God by sending Hagar and Ishmael out with very limited provisions. It's also possible that God's intent, at least in part, was to punish Hagar for not disciplining Ishmael better or for not controlling her own haughtiness when she became pregnant ahead of Sarah. In any event, both mother and child were humbled at the hand of God for His purposes, an experience with which many are familiar. It is when we learn to be thankful for God's humbling and trust His hand even in the worst trials that we truly have begun to grow in understanding (Deuteronomy 8:2, 16; 2 Chronicles 34:17; Daniel 4:37).

15 And the water was spent in the bottle, and she cast the child under one of the shrubs. 16 And she went, and sat her down over against him a good way off, as it were a bowshot: for she said, Let me not see the death of the child. And she sat over against him, and lift up her voice, and wept.

Had Hagar remembered God's words to her the first time she was cast out (see Genesis 16:7–14), she might not have been so quick to despair. Like her own child of flesh, Hagar seemed to live by her senses and didn't see the spiritual aspect of her circumstances, nor did she demonstrate faith in God.

17 And God heard the voice of the lad; and the angel of God called Hagar out of heaven, and said unto her, What aileth thee, Hagar? fear not; for God hath heard the voice of the lad where he is. 18 Arise, lift up the lad, and hold him in thine hand; for I will make him a great nation.

Hagar was comforted out of God's mercy and grace, not in response to her faith. God responded to the voice of Ishmael, not to Hagar. Thus we finally discover the reason for God naming the child as He did, "God hears." God heard the cries of the child of flesh and responded with mercy. Even though we are born into the slavery of sin, God still hears our cries when we call out to Him and responds with His forgiving love and merciful grace. Like Hagar, though, we often fail to see God's providence, and we also easily forget His promises to us. In Wiersbe's inimitable words from the previously quoted discourse, "Hagar is certainly a picture of the needy multitudes in the world today: wandering, weary, thirsty, blind, and giving up in despair. How we need to tell them the good news that the Water of Life is available and the well is not far away!"

19 And God opened her eyes, and she saw a well of water; and she went, and filled the bottle with water, and gave the lad drink. 20 And God was with the lad; and he grew, and dwelt in the wilderness, and became an archer. 21 And he dwelt in the wilderness of Paran: and his mother took him a wife out of the land of Egypt.

In God's care for Ishmael in the desert, even though it was by His command that Abraham cast them out, He fulfilled His promise to Abraham to make a nation of Ishmael (Genesis 17:20). God preserved Ishmael's life, but that did not mean that Ishmael's character would change; God had also told Hagar that her child would be a "wild man" and would live a life of hostility "against every man" (16:12). This part of God's Word also came to fulfillment as promised, even as Ishmael became a huge nation. Ishmael's descendants were antagonistic throughout history toward Israel (God's chosen people), and to this very day they continue to cause dissension within the family by persecuting both Christians and Jews.

Sources:

Landman, Isaac, ed. "Ishmaelites." In *The Universal Jewish Encyclopedia*. Vol. 5. New York: The Universal Jewish Encyclopedia, Inc., 1941. 609–10.

Tenney, Merrill C., ed. "Ishmaelite." In *The Zondervan Pictorial Bible Dictionary*. Grand Rapids, Mich.: Zondervan Publishing House, 1963. 387.

Daily Bible Readings

M: Sarah Deals Harshly with Hagar
Genesis 16:1–6
T: God Protects Hagar
Genesis 16:7–16
W: Abraham's Offspring
Genesis 21:9–13
T: Waiting for Death
Genesis 21:14–16
F: Water from God
Genesis 21:17–19
S: Ishmael Grows Up
Genesis 21:20–21
S: Ishmael's Descendants
Genesis 25:12–18

TEACHING TIPS
September 30
Bible Study Guide 5

1. Words You Should Know

A. Daughters (Genesis 24:37) *bath* (Heb.)—Female children; implies women of Canaanite origin.

B. Speaking in mine heart (v. 45) *dabar leb* (Heb.)—This term implies an internal thought or utterance in the mind.

C. And I bowed down my head (v. 48) *qadad* (Heb.)—Denotes physical lowering of oneself or obeisance to God.

2. Teacher Preparation

Unifying Principle—Recognizing the Right Woman (Man) The choice of a spouse is a major life decision. God's guidance should be sought not only in the selection and recognition of the right spouse, but in all major life decisions.

A. Begin preparing for today's lesson by reading Genesis 23 and 24 in their entirety.

B. Study the Focal Verses, paying particular attention to the AIM for Change objectives.

C. Read the More Light on the Text section, and outline the biblical content based on the Unifying Principle.

D. Complete lesson 5 in the *Precepts For Living® Personal Study Guide* for further insight.

3. Starting the Lesson

A. Ask a student to open the class with prayer, using the Keep in Mind verse and Unifying Principle as a guide.

B. Ask your students what they think are the most important considerations in deciding whom they should or should not marry. Allow 10 minutes or so for them to share their ideas.

C. Tell the class that today's lesson will address "Recognizing the Right Woman (Man)."

D. Reinforce the Unifying Principle by focusing on AIM for Change objectives.

4. Getting into the Lesson

A. Have the class silently read the In Focus story.

B. Ask for a volunteer to read the Focal Verses aloud.

C. Ask the class to consider whether or not their choices and actions are guided by God's Word.

D. Brainstorm with the class on what other types of major life decisions they think require God's guidance.

5. Relating the Lesson to Life

Allow the students to work in groups of two or three to answer the Discuss the Meaning, Lesson in Our Society, and Make It Happen exercises for today. Discuss the points, and report back to the class when they finish.

6. Arousing Action

A. Ask the students to discuss recent life decisions they made, and to share how they made those decisions and how they sought the Lord's guidance in making them.

B. Remind the students to complete the Daily Bible Readings. Reading God's Word will remind them how critical it is for Christians to inquire of the Lord before they make major life commitments.

C. Instruct the class to read and study the Daily Bible Readings for October 7 and complete lesson 6 in the *Precepts For Living® Personal Study Guide* in preparation for next week's lesson.

D. Ask one of the students to close the class in prayer.

Worship Guide

For the Superintendent or Teacher
Theme: Isaac and Rebekah
Theme Song: "I Surrender All"
Devotional Reading: Psalm 100
Prayer

ISAAC AND REBEKAH

Bible Background • GENESIS 24
Printed Text • GENESIS 24:34–40, 42–45, 48   Devotional Reading • PSALM 100

AIM for Change

By the end of the lesson, we will:

KNOW that God's guidance was sought in the choice of Isaac's spouse;

CONSIDER whether or not our choices and actions are guided by God's Word; and

SEEK God's guidance in all major life decisions.

Keep in Mind

"And I bowed down my head, and worshipped the LORD, and blessed the LORD God of my master Abraham, which had led me in the right way to take my master's brother's daughter unto his son" (Genesis 24:48).

Focal Verses

KJV

Genesis 24:34 And he said, I am Abraham's servant.

35 And the LORD hath blessed my master greatly; and he is become great: and he hath given him flocks, and herds, and silver, and gold, and menservants, and maidservants, and camels, and asses.

36 And Sarah my master's wife bare a son to my master when she was old: and unto him hath he given all that he hath.

37 And my master made me swear, saying, Thou shalt not take a wife to my son of the daughters of the Canaanites, in whose land I dwell:

38 But thou shalt go unto my father's house, and to my kindred, and take a wife unto my son.

39 And I said unto my master, Peradventure the woman will not follow me.

40 And he said unto me, The LORD, before whom I walk, will send his angel with thee, and prosper thy way; and thou shalt take a wife for my son of my kindred, and of my father's house:

24:42 And I came this day unto the well, and said, O LORD God of my master Abraham, if now thou do prosper my way which I go;

43 Behold, I stand by the well of water; and it shall come to pass, that when the virgin cometh forth to draw water, and I say to her, Give me, I pray thee, a little water of thy pitcher to drink;

44 And she say to me, Both drink thou, and I will also draw for thy camels: let the same be the woman whom the LORD hath appointed out for my master's son.

45 And before I had done speaking in mine heart, behold, Rebekah came forth with her pitcher on her

NLT

Genesis 24:34 "I am Abraham's servant," he explained.

35 "And the LORD has greatly blessed my master; he has become a wealthy man. The LORD has given him flocks of sheep and goats, herds of cattle, a fortune in silver and gold, and many male and female servants and camels and donkeys.

36 When Sarah, my master's wife, was very old, she gave birth to my master's son, and my master has given him everything he owns.

37 And my master made me take an oath. He said, 'Do not allow my son to marry one of these local Canaanite women.

38 Go instead to my father's house, to my relatives, and find a wife there for my son.'

39 But I said to my master, 'What if I can't find a young woman who is willing to go back with me?'

40 He responded, 'The LORD, in whose presence I have lived, will send his angel with you and will make your mission successful. Yes, you must find a wife for my son from among my relatives, from my father's family'.

24:42 So today when I came to the spring, I prayed this prayer: 'O LORD, God of my master, Abraham, please give me success on this mission.

43 See, I am standing here beside this spring. This is my request. When a young woman comes to draw water, I will say to her, "Please give me a little drink of water from your jug."

44 If she says, "Yes, have a drink, and I will draw water for your camels, too," let her be the one you have selected to be the wife of my master's son.'

shoulder; and she went down unto the well, and drew water: and I said unto her, Let me drink, I pray thee.

24:48 And I bowed down my head, and worshipped the LORD, and blessed the LORD God of my master Abraham, which had led me in the right way to take my master's brother's daughter unto his son.

45 Before I had finished praying in my heart, I saw Rebekah coming out with her water jug on her shoulder. She went down to the spring and drew water. So I said to her, 'Please give me a drink.'

24:48 Then I bowed low and worshiped the LORD. I praised the LORD, the God of my master, Abraham, because he had led me straight to my master's niece to be his son's wife."

In Focus

Sharon waited until the last of her Sunday School students had arrived. She taught the young women's class for 18- to 35-year-olds. Sharon was happy to see that the class was full this morning. From the sound of things, they all seemed energetic and eager to get into the study of the lesson. Sharon began by asking the young women how many of them wanted to marry. All of their hands shot up quickly. She then asked how many of them wanted to marry Christian men. Again, every hand was raised. Sharon asked them to tell her why they thought it was important that their future husbands be Christians.

Nora explained that she would only marry a saved man because she knew that if her husband were a Christian, then they would share basic beliefs. Zaretta added that the only way to ensure that she raised Christian children would be if she and her future husband were both Christians. Sadie, the youngest member of the class, shared the story of her cousin who had married a man who did not know Christ; within a year or two her cousin no longer regularly attended church because her husband would get angry and start a fight every time she got dressed to go to church. Sadie laughed and said, "I know I don't want that kind of drama going on in my house when I'm married."

Sharon then asked the class members to reach into their purses and take out their house or car keys. Puzzled, the students looked at each other. One by one, they pulled keys out of their purses. Sharon instructed them to lay their keys in the middle of a table. The young women complied, and piled the keys on top of one another. Sharon then asked the class to step away from the table, while she scattered the keys on the table. She asked them, "Can you still see your key? Can you tell your keys from someone else's keys?" Each of them answered that they could still identify their own keys.

"Good," Sharon said, and then she walked over to the doorway and turned off the light switch. The small classroom, located in the church's basement, was immediately thrown into total darkness. There was a moment or two of nervous laughter from the students, and then Sharon said, "Now, I want each of you to go over to the table and select your keys."

The students began to protest. One asked, "How are we going to do that? We can't even see the table?"

Another moaned, "It's so dark in here; I'm scared I might trip and fall before I even reach the table!"

One of the students tentatively stepped toward the table. Everyone could hear her bumping into chairs and, when she finally reached the table, the sound of keys being knocked to the floor. One by one, the students told why they thought it was impossible for them to locate the keys in total darkness.

After a few minutes Sharon reached up and turned the light back on, and asked the students to take their seats. When she returned to the front of the class she looked at them and said, "Each one of you knows your keys, and you know what your keys look like, but when there was no light, all of you needed help to find the keys that belonged to you. How can you expect to select the man that God has for you in the darkness? Now, how many of you agree with me that when it comes to something as important as identifying a husband, you're going to need the guidance of God's Word to help you make the right decision?"

In today's lesson, Eliezer recognized that without the help of the Lord there would be no way that he could fulfill his oath to Abraham to find a godly wife for Isaac.

The People, Places, and Times

Wells. In the harsh desert climate of the Middle East, where there are few springs, the inhabitants have always depended on wells or cisterns for their water supply. Wells in Palestine were usually excavated from the solid limestone. Water for both humans and livestock had to be removed, or "drawn," from these wells and cisterns, which required various devices. If the well was shallow, an earthenware water pitcher, jar, or bucket made from tanned goatskin was lowered unto the water by a rope. The rope was then pulled, hand over hand, or run over a crude pulley fixed directly over the well or cistern. If the well was deep, the rope, attached to a much larger bucket, was run over the pulley so that the water could be raised by the drawers walking away from the well as they pulled on the ropes. If the bucket was large and heavy enough, this method required the use of animals hitched to the rope.

In some areas where the water level was not too deep, a flight of stairs leading down to the well was constructed. Such a flight of stairs is implied when the Bible tells us that Rebekah "went down to the well, and filled her pitcher, and came up" (Genesis 24:16). Some wells were furnished with a curb or low wall of stone. It was on such a stone that Jesus sat and talked with the Samaritan woman (John 4:6).

In the ancient world, drawing water was a task for women and men who were deemed unfit for other work. Drawing water was usually done in the late afternoon or early evening.

Source:

Packer, J. I., and M. C. Tenney, eds. *Illustrated Manners and Customs of the Bible*. Nashville, Tenn.: Thomas Nelson Publishers, 1980. 474–75.

Background

After the death of his wife, Sarah, the care and concern of his son Isaac was paramount in the life of Abraham. Abraham decided that the time had come for Isaac to have a wife of his own. Abraham called his most trusted servant, Eliezer, to him and considered the matter. Eliezer was well known, and apparently dear to Abraham. Recall that it was Eliezer who was designated as Abraham's heir prior to the birth of Ishmael (Genesis 15:2–4). Eliezer continued to hold a place of importance in Abraham's household: He "ruled over all that [Abraham] had" (24:2). Abraham now found himself in a difficult situation. On one hand, he was certain that Isaac's wife should not come from the tribes of Canaan, yet it would probably be dangerous for Isaac to leave the Promised Land in search of a bride. Away from his father and the land promised to him by God, Isaac would be vulnerable to enemy attack. So Abraham entrusted the task to Eliezer. "I will make thee swear by the LORD, the God of heaven, and the God of the earth, that thou shalt not take a wife unto my son of the daughters of the Canaanites, among whom I dwell: But thou shalt go unto my country, and to my kindred, and take a wife unto my son Isaac" (vv. 3–4). Eliezer, though he was willing to do as Abraham asked, had a legitimate question: What if the bride selected for Isaac does not want to leave Mesopotamia and return with me to Canaan?

Abraham told Eliezer that God had promised him that Isaac would inherit the Promised Land of Canaan and God would send an angel or a messenger to help find a wife for his son. Abraham assured Eliezer that if the woman he found would not consent to come to Canaan, then Eliezer would be released from the vow. Abraham insisted, however, that under no circumstances should Eliezer take Isaac out of Canaan and take him to Mesopotamia. Ever faithful, Eliezer swore to do just as Abraham had asked. We are then told that he "arose, and went to Mesopotamia, unto the city of Nahor" (v. 10).

At-A-Glance

1. Eliezer Entrusted to Find a Bride
(Genesis 24:34–40)
2. Eliezer Received Divine Confirmation
(vv. 42–45)
3. Eliezer Thanked God (v. 48)

In Depth

1. Eliezer Entrusted to Find a Bride (Genesis 24:34–40)

In his old age, Abraham expected to die soon, but he realized that there was one thing he had to do to secure the fulfillment of God's promise regarding his posterity. It had been divinely appointed that his son Isaac was to succeed him as the keeper of the law of God and the father of the chosen people, but Isaac had no wife. Because the people of Canaan were given to idolatry, God had forbidden intermarriage between His people and them, knowing that such marriages would lead to apostasy. Abraham was concerned, and rightly so, that if Isaac married a woman who did not fear God, he would be in danger of sacrificing his principles for the sake of harmony (cf. 1 Kings 11:1–8). The choice of a wife for Isaac is of paramount importance to Abraham. It was essential to Abraham that Isaac marry a woman who would not lead him away from God.

Abraham began to think of his father's people who lived in the land of Mesopotamia. Although they were not free from idolatry, they did acknowledge the existence of the one, true God. Abraham was hopeful that among his kinfolk he might find a bride for his son, a woman who would agree to leave her home and unite with Isaac in marriage and maintain the pure worship of the one, true living God. Abraham entrusted the task of finding Isaac's wife to Eliezer, "his eldest servant," a man who had rendered him many years of faithful service.

Eliezer took 10 camels with him. Such a large team of camels implies that he may have used them for the anticipated return of the bridal party. He also took "goods of his master." These were gifts for the intended bride and her family. Eliezer made the long journey beyond Damascus and onward to the rich plains that border on the great river of the East.

2. Eliezer Received Divine Confirmation (vv. 42–45)

The ensuing verses are Eliezer's recounting to Rebekah's family of his mission and how it led him to find Rebekah.

When he arrived at Haran, the city of Nahor, Eliezer told them that he stopped, perhaps resting, just outside the walls of the town, near the well where the women came in the evening for water. It must have been a time of anxious thought for Eliezer. The results of his mission would impact not only his master's household but future generations as well. His choice of a bride for Isaac was a difficult one. How was he to choose wisely among strangers? Remembering the words of Abraham, that God would send His angel with him, he prayed earnestly for positive guidance. No doubt in the tents of Abraham he was accustomed to the constant exercise of kindness and hospitality, and he now asked that an act of courtesy might indicate the woman whom God had chosen as Isaac's bride.

Eliezer's prayer was quickly answered. As he surveyed the women gathered at the well, his attention was drawn to the courteous manners of one young woman. As she came from the well, the stranger went to greet her and asked for some water from her pitcher. Eliezer's request for water was met, along with an offer to draw water for his camels. Immediately one can tell this offer was more than just an act of courtesy. Because of the nature of ancient wells, in order to provide the camels a drink of water, Rebekah would have had to climb down into the well, carry a heavy pitcher of water back up, and empty it into the watering trough. She would have had to repeat this climb 10 times until all the camels had been watered. One should also keep in mind that camels are desert creatures that can drink as much as 20 gallons of water. Eliezer had the sign he was looking for! Although the text is clear that the young woman "was very fair to look upon" (Genesis 24:16), note that it was her readiness to serve and her courtesy that gave Eliezer the evidence he sought. This woman possessed a kind heart and an extraordinary energetic nature. More than a mere beauty, Rebekah demonstrated that she was a woman of character and strength.

We would do well to remember that looks alone should never be the primary factor in our selection of a spouse. Instead, we should look closely to find evidence of kindness, gentleness, and a willingness to share. Solomon boldly declared, "Whoso findeth a wife findeth a good thing, and obtaineth favour of the Lord" (Proverbs 18:22). Our marriage commitments are sacred and lifelong covenants. They must never be entered into on the basis of romantic sentiment or careless fleshly desire.

3. Eliezer Thanked God (v. 48)

Eliezer rewarded Rebekah's generosity with rich gifts and asked about her family. He must have been delighted to discover that standing before him was the daughter of Bethuel, Abraham's nephew. He was so overwhelmed that he bowed down his head, and worshiped the Lord. Eliezer was aware that it was only through divine intervention that he had found a woman worthy to be the wife of the son of Abraham.

Search the Scriptures

1. Whom did Abraham ask to find a bride for Isaac (Genesis 24:34)?

2. What oath did Abraham make his servant swear (v. 37)?

3. From which family did Abraham want to find Isaac's wife (v. 38)?

4. Where was Eliezer when he first saw Rebekah (vv. 42–43)?

5. What acts of kindness did Rebekah display toward Eliezer (v. 44)?

Discuss the Meaning

1. Although it is clear from the text that Rebekah was an attractive woman, notice that it was her kind and gracious personality that impressed Eliezer. How important are looks and possessions to us when selecting a suitable life partner? Do you think we place more emphasis on these things than we do the personality of a potential spouse? If so, why do you think that is?

2. It is clear that Abraham was adamant that Isaac not have a Canaanite bride. Do you think that we are obligated to discuss the ramifications of marrying a nonbeliever with our Christian family members or friends who are contemplating marriage to nonbelievers? If you believe we do have the obligation, why is it that we are hesitant to enter these discussions?

3. We often hear people say that marriage is just between two people—the husband and the wife. Do you agree with this? If not, who do you believe is affected by one's decision to choose a spouse?

4. It has been said, "Love is a poor reason to marry." Do you agree or disagree? Are there other considerations that are more important than love? If so, what are they? How does the Bible support your belief?

Lesson in Our Society

In ancient times, marriage arrangements were usually made by the parents. Although men were required to marry a woman they could not love, young men were guided by the judgment of their experienced parents. It was considered a dishonor and disgrace to ignore the parents' wishes in the choice of a bride. In American culture, the decisions of when and whom to marry are generally the sole decision of the man or woman contemplating marriage. Very often the counsel of parents or guardians is never solicited. Long courtships tend to be a thing of the past, and all too often very little attention is given to the background of a potential spouse. Some men and women—even though they were raised in the church, they have studied this matter, and they know the will of God—still choose to marry someone they know is unsaved. Given this occurrence, the alarming rate and frequency of divorce in the church and in our country should not surprise us. Not only are we marrying outside of the will of God, but many of us are marrying virtual strangers!

How disappointing it must be to God that so many of us fail to trust Him when it comes to choosing a life partner. For those of us who are contemplating marriage, we must trust the Holy Spirit to bring the right person into our lives. Rather than rushing to the altar, we must be willing to wait on the Lord for His choice so that we do not miss His best for our lives.

Make It Happen

If you are single, take time this week to ask God for a discerning spirit that will enable you to prayerfully consider the qualities that are important to you in your future husband or wife. After doing this, pray and ask God to show you how you can improve those same qualities in your own life so that when the time is right, your future spouse might see these same qualities in you. Spend time in prayer and Scripture study so that you may be prepared when the opportunity presents itself.

Follow the Spirit

What God wants me to do:

_____

_____

Remember Your Thoughts

Special insights I have learned:

_____

_____

More Light on the Text

Genesis 24:34–40, 42–45, 48

It is all too easy to lose sight of the fact that God deals with flawed, free-willed humans throughout history, specifically throughout the creation and fulfillment of His several covenants with humankind. Nothing, however, reemphasizes the human element of man's relationship with God like a wedding or a funeral, as Abraham buried his wife, Sarah, just three years before these bright passages about finding a bride for Isaac. Although he had failed more than once, Abraham also had proven his faith several times, and he had learned much about God's faithfulness. Now, after 25 years of waiting for Isaac's birth, and another 40 years of life, including the poignant moment when God asked him to sacrifice his son, Abraham finally got to oversee the long-awaited wedding arrangements for his son of promise.

34 And he said, I am Abraham's servant. 35 And the LORD hath blessed my master greatly; and he is become great: and he hath given him flocks, and herds, and silver, and gold, and menservants, and maidservants, and camels, and asses. 36 And Sarah my master's wife bare a son to my master when she was old: and unto him hath he given all that he hath.

There are two theories regarding the identity of the servant Abraham selected for this most important mission to find and bring home a wife for Isaac. While some thought it could be Eliezer (Genesis 15:2), others didn't; they noted that the earlier mention of him was 60 years prior, and they claimed that he would be quite elderly for a two-month round-trip journey of about 450 miles to Nahor. On the other hand, Abraham selected the most elderly of his servants who "ruled over all that he had" (24:2). In addition, a person ranging in age from 80 to 100 years old in biblical times was not as frail as someone in that same age range today.

The servant talked about his father's house, highlighting Abraham's great wealth. More practically and directly, our story has much to teach about how a man should approach a woman, not with pressure or demands, seeking only his own pleasure and will, but humbly and respectfully asking for her free choice as well as the approval of her family. Moreover, families today are still a big factor in weddings: They can make or break not only the event but later the marriage itself.

The servant recounted the events leading him to his conversation with Laban, Rebekah's brother. The servant was making the transaction with Laban as per the customs of the day surrounding arranged marriages. Laban took care of Rebekah and was the spokesperson for the family. As the servant found out, Rebekah was not from the Canaanite tribes, which would have excluded her from Abraham's specific conditions (23:3–4); rather, her grandfather was Nahor, Abraham's brother. At this news—and because she fulfilled the requirements of his prayer (24:12–14)—the servant thanked God (v. 26) for confirming she indeed was the one he had prayed to find and who fulfilled the requirements of Abraham, to whom he had given a solemn oath to bring back none other.

37 And my master made me swear, saying, Thou shalt not take a wife to my son of the daughters of the Canaanites, in whose land I dwell: 38 But thou shalt go unto my father's house, and to my kindred, and take a wife unto my son.

The servant continued to explain to Laban the purpose and details of his mission. Even as he told Laban that the strongest directive from Abraham was that she not be from tribes of Canaan, he was confirming his choice of Rebekah, since she clearly belonged to the right people now. He already was convinced that she was the right bride for Isaac, but now he needed to convince her family of it as well.

It is significant that Abraham instructed the servant not to bring back a Canaanite woman, which today would be equivalent to an unsaved spouse. There always will be plenty of Canaanites to be found; they are all around us. What is better is to find someone who shares your beliefs, not someone with whom you are infatuated; someone who is going in the same direction, not merely someone who is physically desirable. A mind-set like this must be in place prior to venturing out in search of a spouse (and it applies to both men and women). It will be too late once infatuation strikes; logic alone will fail against the power of desire. What stands a better chance of not failing is a prior commitment and clear purpose—even better reinforced with a solemn oath to the Father to settle for nothing less than someone of a kindred spirit, someone from the family of faith. A lack of wisdom in the selection of a mate has caused inestimable suffering for countless people, and has caused untold suffering for all within their circle of influence, not the least of which are their innocent children.

39 And I said unto my master, Peradventure the woman will not follow me. 40 And he said unto me, The LORD, before whom I walk, will send his angel with thee, and prosper thy way; and thou shalt take a wife for my son of my kindred, and of my father's house:

Even with everything he had to offer, from the beginning the servant was aware of the possibility that the woman might not go with him, and asked to not be held responsible for his oath should this be the case (Genesis 24:5, 8). He was not going to force the issue with the prospective bride, nor should we ever attempt to force the Gospel on anyone. This is not the way of the Holy Spirit, nor is it part of God's nature to overpower our free will (cf. Deuteronomy 30:19; Joshua 24:15; 2 Kings 18:32). The decision is each person's to make, and for it to be genuine it must be freely made, just as both the choice and the timing clearly were Rebekah's to make, even though her family wanted her to stay with them a little longer (Genesis 24:57–58).

Since this particular wedding was part of God's promise to Abraham, an angel was sent with the servant to help ensure the success of his mission.

In acknowledging the need for God's guidance and the humility of our limited vision and wisdom, there is no reason to believe that we cannot find ourselves in the same position as the praying, humble servant in our passage, with whom God sends an angel to help ensure the mission's success. How much better is one who prays in submission and dependence on God from the outset than the one who insists on overseeing every aspect of an endeavor with finite human understanding, seeking God only in moments of desperation or failure (Proverbs 3:5; Isaiah 12:2).

24:42 And I came this day unto the well, and said, O LORD God of my master Abraham, if now thou do prosper my way which I go; 43 Behold, I stand by the well of water; and it shall come to pass, that when the virgin cometh forth to draw water, and I say to her, Give me, I pray thee, a little water of thy pitcher to drink; 44 And she say to me, Both drink thou, and I will also draw for thy camels: let the same be the woman whom the LORD hath appointed out for my master's son.

As the story is recounted, one can almost imagine the look of praise on this servant's face. He wasn't just telling a story, but was giving a testimony. In the most literal of interpretations, this is a classic example of praying before and during a godly mission, and then thanking and praising God afterward. Here he recounted the prayer that set requirements just strenuous enough to weed out all but the most generous and industrious women, but not impossible as to expect God to perform a miracle on demand. It is also noteworthy that the servant prayed in faith and was willing to accept the outcome, whatever it might have been.

In the ancient Middle East, it was considered women's work to fetch water for her family and their livestock. A stranger asking a woman for a drink was one thing, but expecting her to voluntarily offer to water his entire camel train was quite another. Camels drink a considerable amount of water at a time; thus Rebekah made quite a generous and unusual offer to draw several gallons of water for a total stranger.

45 And before I had done speaking in mine heart, behold, Rebekah came forth with her pitcher on her shoulder; and she went down unto the well, and drew water: and I said unto her, Let me drink, I pray thee.

From Rebekah's perspective, she didn't have any idea she was going to be rewarded beyond her dreams, or that her act of kindness would place her both in the lap of luxury and in the lineage of Christ. Likewise, we never know when our good deeds may be well rewarded, even beyond what we can imagine (Ephesians 3:20), or when we might even entertain or impress heavenly visitors (an angel accompanied the servant; see also Hebrews 13:2). From the servant's perspective, he prayed for character first, and only later was blessed with great beauty as a bonus.

In today's language, the servant went to the workplace; he prayed for inner beauty and was given both inner and outer beauty.

Yet another aspect is the timing of the appearance of Rebekah at the well; she "coincidentally" showed up even before the servant had finished praying. Something not often thought of in connection with prayer, God cares for the timing of things as much as the things themselves. Sometimes the timing is everything, but especially when it comes to answering prayers, God's reputation as the "eleventh-hour God" is high praise for Him. He does, in fact, come through. He does hear and respond to His children. He does care about each and every detail of our lives. As we mature, we learn to trust His timing as well as His provision. "Though we are backward to pray, God is forward to answer," says commentator Matthew Henry.

24:48 And I bowed down my head, and worshipped the LORD, and blessed the LORD God of my master Abraham, which had led me in the right way to take my master's brother's daughter unto his son.

In this passage, "way" (Heb. *derek*, **DEH-rek**) is used in the normal sense, which can include one's course of life and one's moral journey, but when combined with "right" (Heb. *'emeth*, **EH-meth**), which in the Hebrew refers to truth, becomes "way of truth or true way." It has been well said that it is much easier to steer a moving car than a parked car. Being in the "true way" means being in God's will, walking in the way of God, with the emphasis on being in motion, already having stepped out on faith, and presumably praying for God's guidance on the journey. In contemporary language, we would say "seeking God," "seeking God's heart," "following after God," or "walking in His steps." Scripture is full of guidance when our hearts are receptive to being steered, especially when it involves leaving our comfort zone and entering unfamiliar territory. "Thy word is a lamp unto my feet, and a light unto my path" (Psalm 119:105). Numerous Scriptures speak of trusting God's guidance, seeking His truth, and living a life of truth in the pursuit of God and His ways. We may never see a pillar of cloud or fire, but we can trust Him to lead and guide us as we seek Him with all our hearts and strive to walk in His ways (Deuteronomy 12:10; Joshua 22:5; 1 Kings 2:3; Psalm 128:1; Isaiah 2:3). It is when we are the most unsure of our direction that we would do ourselves the greatest service to humbly seek God's guidance. The more serious the

occasion, the greater the need for us to seek God's wisdom and not rely on our own wisdom. When it comes to the subject of marriage, as in this text, God desires a proper mate for us as much as we do; He wants us to be with someone who also trusts Him and worships Him as we do (2 Corinthians 6:14).

Considering some of the other versions of a difficult passage often helps underscore the meaning; "which had led me in the right way" has also been translated "who had led me in the way of truth" (NKJV), "he had led me straight" (NLT), "who had led me on the right road" (NIV), "who had guided me in the right way" (NASB), "who had led me by the right way" (RSV), "who hath led me in the true way" (Young's).

May we, like the servant, bow our heads in thankful worship whenever we realize God has led us in the way of truth.

Matthew Henry says it thus: "Providence sometimes wonderfully directs those that by faith and prayer seek direction from heaven in the choice of suitable yokefellows: happy marriages are likely to be that are made in the fear of God; and these, we are sure, are made in heaven."

Source:
Henry, Matthew. "Commentary on Genesis 24." *Matthew Henry's Commentary on the Whole Bible.* March 1, 1996. http://www.blue letterbible.org/Comm/mhc/Gen/Gen024.html.

Daily Bible Readings

M: Wanted: A Wife
Genesis 24:1–9

T: A Drink for the Camels
Genesis 24:10–21

W: The Daughter of Bethuel
Genesis 24:22–27

T: A Show of Hospitality
Genesis 24:28–32

F: The Errand
Genesis 24:33–41

S: A Wife for Isaac
Genesis 24:42–51

S: God's Steadfast Love
Psalm 100

TEACHING TIPS

October 7
Bible Study Guide 6

1. Words You Should Know

A. Intreated (Genesis 25:21) `athar (Heb.)—To pray, plead, or make supplication.

B. Birthright (vv. 31–34) bekorah (Heb.)—The right or privilege of being the firstborn.

2. Teacher Preparation

Unifying Principle—Sibling Rivalry! Sibling rivalry can be sparked by many things and can fester for years. If such a conflict affects a family, the family should work to find the root of the problem and to resolve it.

A. Read the Focal Verses and begin preparing to teach the lesson by spending time in prayer seeking guidance regarding matters of family conflict.

B. Study the Bible Background and Devotional Reading Scriptures focusing on the Unifying Principle and AIM for Change objectives.

C. Begin to identify various ways families deal with conflict, in particular sibling rivalry.

D. For a more in-depth study, complete lesson 6 for October 7 in the *Precepts For Living® Personal Study Guide*.

3. Starting the Lesson

A. Ask a volunteer to lead the class in prayer.

B. Tell the class the next four lessons for the month of October will focus on how God's people increased. The lessons follow the development of Abraham's family (the family of promise), including Jacob, Esau, and Rachel.

C. Introduce the Unifying Principle for today's lesson—Sibling Rivalry!

D. Allow a few moments for the class to silently read the In Focus story.

E. Engage the class in a brief discussion by asking if anyone has ever experienced any type of family conflict, especially hostility between brothers or sisters.

4. Getting into the Lesson

A. Explain that today's Scripture passage focuses on Jacob and Esau and the rivalry that existed between the two brothers.

B. Provide additional insight by giving a brief overview of the Background and The People, Places, and Times sections.

C. Write the At-A-Glance outline on the chalkboard. Divide the class into three groups and assign each group an In Depth section and a corresponding Discuss the Meaning question for discussion (e.g., In Depth section 1 corresponds with Discuss the Meaning question 1).

D. Reconvene the class and ask a spokesperson from each group to elaborate on their discussion question with the rest of the class as a whole.

5. Relating the Lesson to Life

Read the Make It Happen challenge. Instruct the class to join hands in a prayer circle and ask for prayer requests concerning family conflict. Begin to pray for healing and reconciliation for those individuals experiencing family conflict.

6. Arousing Action

A. Now that individual prayer concerns have been addressed, begin to petition the class for prayer concerns regarding the society at large.

B. Remind the class that today is World Communion Sunday, and consider the fact that the Lord's Supper is a time of reconciliation.

C. Instruct the class to read the Daily Bible Readings for next week, and suggest they complete lesson 7 for October 14 from the *Precepts For Living® Personal Study Guide* in preparation for next week's class.

Worship Guide

For the Superintendent or Teacher
Theme: Esau and Jacob as Rivals
Theme Song: "There's No Me, There's No You"
Devotional Scripture: 1 Corinthians 1:26–31
Prayer

ESAU AND JACOB AS RIVALS

Bible Background • GENESIS 25:19–34
Printed Text • GENESIS 25:19–34   Devotional Reading • 1 CORINTHIANS 1:26–31

AIM for Change

By the end of the lesson, we will:

EXPLAIN what fueled the rivalry between Esau and Jacob;

REFLECT on any conflict that may exist between our siblings or family, in general; and PRAY for any healing and reconciliation that may be needed in our family.

Keep in Mind

"And the LORD said unto her, Two nations are in thy womb, and two manner of people shall be separated from thy bowels; and the one people shall be stronger than the other people; and the elder shall serve the younger" (Genesis 25:23).

Focal Verses

KJV

Genesis 25:19 And these are the generations of Isaac, Abraham's son: Abraham begat Isaac:

20 And Isaac was forty years old when he took Rebekah to wife, the daughter of Bethuel the Syrian of Padanaram, the sister to Laban the Syrian.

21 And Isaac intreated the LORD for his wife, because she was barren: and the LORD was intreated of him, and Rebekah his wife conceived.

22 And the children struggled together within her; and she said, If it be so, why am I thus? And she went to enquire of the LORD.

23 And the LORD said unto her, Two nations are in thy womb, and two manner of people shall be separated from thy bowels; and the one people shall be stronger than the other people; and the elder shall serve the younger.

24 And when her days to be delivered were fulfilled, behold, there were twins in her womb.

25 And the first came out red, all over like an hairy garment; and they called his name Esau.

26 And after that came his brother out, and his hand took hold on Esau's heel; and his name was called Jacob: and Isaac was threescore years old when she bare them.

27 And the boys grew: and Esau was a cunning hunter, a man of the field; and Jacob was a plain man, dwelling in tents.

28 And Isaac loved Esau, because he did eat of his venison: but Rebekah loved Jacob.

29 And Jacob sod pottage: and Esau came from the field, and he was faint:

NLT

Genesis 25:19 This is the account of the family of Isaac, the son of Abraham.

20 When Isaac was forty years old, he married Rebekah, the daughter of Bethuel the Aramean from Paddan-aram and the sister of Laban the Aramean.

21 Isaac pleaded with the LORD on behalf of his wife, because she was unable to have children. The LORD answered Isaac's prayer, and Rebekah became pregnant with twins.

22 But the two children struggled with each other in her womb. So she went to ask the LORD about it. "Why is this happening to me?" she asked.

23 And the LORD told her, "The sons in your womb will become two nations. From the very beginning, the two nations will be rivals. One nation will be stronger than the other; and your older son will serve your younger son."

24 And when the time came to give birth, Rebekah discovered that she did indeed have twins!

25 The first one was very red at birth and covered with thick hair like a fur coat. So they named him Esau.

26 Then the other twin was born with his hand grasping Esau's heel. So they named him Jacob.

27 As the boys grew up, Esau became a skillful hunter. He was an outdoorsman, but Jacob had a quiet temperament, preferring to stay at home.

28 Isaac loved Esau because he enjoyed eating the wild game Esau brought home, but Rebekah loved Jacob.

29 One day when Jacob was cooking some stew, Esau arrived home from the wilderness exhausted and hungry.

30 And Esau said to Jacob, Feed me, I pray thee, with that same red pottage; for I am faint: therefore was his name called Edom.

31 And Jacob said, Sell me this day thy birthright.

32 And Esau said, Behold, I am at the point to die: and what profit shall this birthright do to me?

33 And Jacob said, Swear to me this day; and he sware unto him: and he sold his birthright unto Jacob.

34 Then Jacob gave Esau bread and pottage of lentiles; and he did eat and drink, and rose up, and went his way: thus Esau despised his birthright.

30 Esau said to Jacob, "I'm starved! Give me some of that red stew!" (This is how Esau got his other name, Edom, which means "red.")

31 "All right," Jacob replied, "but trade me your rights as the firstborn son."

32 "Look, I'm dying of starvation!" said Esau. "What good is my birthright to me now?"

33 But Jacob said, "First you must swear that your birthright is mine." So Esau swore an oath, thereby selling all his rights as the firstborn to his brother, Jacob.

34 Then Jacob gave Esau some bread and lentil stew. Esau ate the meal, then got up and left. He showed contempt for his rights as the firstborn.

In Focus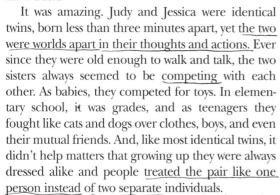

It was amazing. Judy and Jessica were identical twins, born less than three minutes apart, yet the two were worlds apart in their thoughts and actions. Ever since they were old enough to walk and talk, the two sisters always seemed to be competing with each other. As babies, they competed for toys. In elementary school, it was grades, and as teenagers they fought like cats and dogs over clothes, boys, and even their mutual friends. And, like most identical twins, it didn't help matters that growing up they were always dressed alike and people treated the pair like one person instead of two separate individuals.

The rivalry finally culminated in a permanent falling out between the two sisters five years ago when Judy accused Jessica of stealing her boyfriend and marrying him. Now Judy lives in Chicago and Jessica lives in Atlanta. Their children have never met, and the sisters never call each other except in "life-or-death emergencies." Even holidays are a problem because the two refuse to be in the same house at the same time. To make matters worse, in times of conflict the twins' mother always takes Judy's side and their father always sides with Jessica.

Siblings have clashed since the days of Cain and Abel. In today's lesson we will look at the roots of family conflict between Jacob and Esau, a rivalry that began at birth and continued into their adult years.

The People, Places, and Times

Rebekah. Like Sarah, Rebekah, too, was barren (Genesis 25:21). In biblical times barrenness was more than a physical or social problem; it was thought to be the result of disobeying God (Deuteronomy 7:14). However, unlike Abraham, Isaac prayed to God and she conceived, thus carrying two male children in her womb.

Jacob. He was the younger son of Isaac and Rebekah and Esau's twin brother. God changed his name from Jacob to Israel (which means "God prevails") after Jacob proved his perseverance by wrestling with an angel (Genesis 32:22–32).

Esau. He was the eldest son of Isaac and Rebekah and the twin brother of Jacob. A rugged outdoorsman, Esau was the eldest son and favored by his father. Originally, Esau went to live in a mountainous region south of Moab along the Dead Sea. The area came to be known as Edom, which means "red" or "ruddy," characterized by the red sandstone that covers much of the terrain as well as Esau's red hair and complexion.

Sources:

Butler, Trent C., gen. ed. *Holman Bible Dictionary*. Nashville, Tenn.: Broadman & Holman Publishers, 1991.

Packer, J. I., and M. C. Tenney, eds. *Illustrated Manners and Customs of the Bible*. Nashville, Tenn.: Thomas Nelson Publishers, 1980.

Background

The death of Abraham began the focus of attention on Isaac's household and lineage. Isaac grew to manhood and married a woman named Rebekah, who appeared unable to conceive. Isaac prayed and the Lord heard him, allowing Rebekah to give birth to twin boys, Esau and Jacob.

At - A - Glance

1. Family Prayers (Genesis 25:19–23)
2. Family Competition (vv. 24–28)
3. Family Choices (vv. 29–34)

In Depth

1. Family Prayers (Genesis 25:19–23)

Isaac and Rebekah had been married for 19 years, but still the couple didn't have any children. After Isaac prayed to God to allow his wife to have children, Rebekah conceived; but there was conflict within her womb. Rebekah became so frustrated with her difficult pregnancy that she asked the Lord what was happening inside of her. The Lord told her that she was carrying twin sons who were struggling with one another. The Lord told her that her twin sons were going to be the fathers of two competing nations, and the one who was born second was going to be stronger and rule over the firstborn.

2. Family Competition (vv. 24–28)

Even before their birth, the strife between Rebekah's twin sons, Jacob and Esau, had begun. Esau, the firstborn, was so covered with red hair that he looked like he was wearing a red fur coat. The second twin reached out and grabbed his brother's foot, so they called him Jacob, or the "heel grabber."

As the boys grew, Esau became a hunter, while Jacob was described as a quiet man, probably taking the time to think on life matters. The vast differences in the interests and personalities of the twin sons apparently fueled their parents' favoritism. Isaac favored Esau, the rough outdoorsman who could be depended on to get things done, while their mother, Rebekah, favored Jacob because he, unlike his brother, was more like her.

While it was not wrong for Isaac to prefer Esau or for Rebekah to prefer Jacob, what was wrong was for Isaac and Rebekah to treat one child better than the other. The sibling rivalry fueled by their parents continued not only throughout the brothers' lives but throughout the lives of their descendants as well.

Throughout the Old Testament we see that much of the suffering of the Israelites came at the hands of the Edomites (Numbers 20:20–21; 2 Samuel 8:13, 14; Psalm 137:7).

It is normal for us to prefer people who are like ourselves. As Christians we may prefer to spend time with other Christians, but as Jesus commanded, we must also minister to the lost, the hurting, the helpless, and the homeless (Luke 4:18–19). As Christians we must imitate our Father, who loved us so much that while we were yet sinners, He sent Christ to die for us (Romans 5:8).

3. Family Choices (vv. 29–34)

Jacob must have had his sights set on his brother's birthright for some time. As the opportunity presented itself, Jacob found himself in an advantageous bargaining position. Esau came in from the field and was extremely hungry. Jacob was cooking food, and his brother asked for something to eat. Instead of simply giving his brother some food, Jacob agreed to trade a meal for Esau's birthright.

Jacob is often accused of *stealing* Esau's birthright, although the text does not explain it in this fashion. As much as Jacob wanted his brother's birthright, it must be acknowledged that Esau did not fully recognize or appreciate the value of that birthright. Esau likely did not actually despise his birthright, but he certainly disregarded its significance. What was this birthright that Jacob felt was so important and Esau really didn't care much about?

According to Jewish culture, there were four rights, or privileges, allowed to the firstborn son:

• He exercised authority over the family. When the father died, usually the eldest son became the authority figure of the family. He made or approved all major decisions for the family including family location, work assignments, conflict resolution, marriages, burials, and asset distributions.

• He received a double portion of the family inheritance. When the father died and the family assets were distributed among the children, the eldest son received twice as much as the other family members.

• He received a special blessing from the father. During the time of the patriarchs, it was customary for the father to bless his children before he died. The blessing was a combination of a prophecy about the person's future and a pronouncement of God's blessing upon that individual.

• He became the family priest. Part of the eldest son's responsibility was to be the family's spiritual leader. He had the responsibility of passing on the family's spiritual history and traditions while guiding the family according to God's will by offering prayers and sacrifices on their behalf.

Did Jacob or Esau understand all that was involved in the birthright process? Probably not. At that moment, getting something to eat was more important to Esau than the birthright that would impact generations far beyond their physical existence. Since Esau so easily gave away his birthright, his actions indicated he had no real appreciation for the spiritual blessing that was considered the possession of the eldest son.

The writer of Hebrews declares Esau to be a *profane* man (Hebrews 12:16), caring little for that which is holy. By exchanging his birthright for something to eat, Esau was actually leaving God out of his life plans. Esau cared so little for his place as the elder son that he didn't even bother to find out what he was bargaining for.

Search the Scriptures

Fill in the blanks.

1. The three patriarchs mentioned in today's lesson are _____, _____, and _____ (Genesis 25:19–20).

2. Rebekah was the wife of _____ and the daughter of _____ (v. 20).

3. Isaac was ____ years old when he married and _____ years old when his twin sons were born (vv. 20, 26).

4. Esau means _____ and Jacob means _____ (vv. 25–26).

5. Esau is known for selling his _____ to Jacob for _____ (vv. 29–34).

Discuss the Meaning

1. Sarah, Rebekah, and later Rachel, Jacob's wife, were blessed with children in answer to prayer. Discuss a time when your prayers directly influenced or affected a family situation. God had already revealed the destiny of Rebekah's two sons (Genesis 25:23). Why, then, do you believe she resorted to deceit and trickery instead of praying and trusting God for the outcome?

2. Most adults can identify with the anguish of family conflict. For those individuals in the class who have children (grown or otherwise), ask them if they believe they favor one child over the other, and how that favoritism may have affected their children. For those individuals who do not have children, allow them to reflect on conflicts within their families and how they resolved the situation.

3. At some point, nearly every family has experienced some sort of family conflict. Engage your group in a debate based on the following two assumptions: (1) Esau was careless regarding the birthright; (2) Jacob was conniving in his quest to obtain the birthright.

Lesson in Our Society

This Sunday is World Communion Sunday. World Communion Sunday is celebrated on the first Sunday in October throughout the world. On this day Christians celebrate oneness in Christ in the midst of the world we are called to serve. Use the day to plan a communion service—the focus of which is healing of broken family relationships.

Make It Happen

When family conflicts occur, especially between siblings, the outcome may be determined by strength, experience or knowledge, cunning, intelligence, or some combination of all these factors. In order to heal broken relationships, consider how God's love might prevent us from taking advantage of another family member. List five or six ways that promote family unity at home, in your neighborhood, and among your church family. Take some time to plan a special service or activity for healing these broken relationships, and put it into practice in the upcoming week(s).

Follow the Spirit

What God wants me to do:

_____

_____

Remember Your Thoughts

Special insights I have learned:

_____

_____

More Light on the Text

Genesis 25:19–34

The section introduces the reader to the whole cycle of Jacob and Esau and offers us glimpses of three episodes in their early years that both determine and illustrate the subsequent course of their careers. In these 16 verses, we have their future lives in a nutshell.

19 And these are the generations of Isaac, Abraham's son: Abraham begat Isaac:

The opening, "These are the generations of Isaac" is one of the 10 headings marking a new division within Genesis (see Genesis 2:4; 5:1; 6:9; 11:27; 25:12). The purpose of the introduction here is designed specifically to connect Isaac's posterity with Abraham, his direct descendant. Isaac is the central character and the reader's attention is on him.

20 And Isaac was forty years old when he took Rebekah to wife, the daughter of Bethuel the Syrian of Padanaram, the sister to Laban the Syrian.

This verse summarizes the story of Isaac's marriage to Rebekah. It looks forward to Jacob's future journey to Paddan-Aram and his dealings with his uncle Laban (Genesis 29–31).

21 And Isaac intreated the Lord for his wife, because she was barren: and the Lord was intreated of him, and Rebekah his wife conceived.

"Isaac intreated the Lord for his wife." The word "intreated" (Heb. `athar, **aw-THAR**) is not commonly used for prayer in the Old Testament. It occurs most frequently in Exodus of Moses entreating God to send away the plagues (8:8–9, 28–30; 9:28). Its usage here probably suggests the earnestness with which

Isaac sought the Lord for the fulfillment of His promise. There is an important lesson to be learned here. Though God had already promised to multiply his family, Isaac prayed for it. It is also significant to note that although Isaac prayed for many years and his request seemed to go unnoticed, he did not stop praying or believing God for an answer. All too often believers today quit too soon. The fulfillment of God's promise is always sure, even though it may appear to be slow.

22 And the children struggled together within her; and she said, If it be so, why am I thus? And she went to enquire of the LORD.

Rebekah's happiness was soon clouded by the agonies of the twins that she carried, as the children struggled within her. The phrase "struggled together" (Heb. *ratsats*, **raw-tsats**) literally means "to oppress, to jostle each other, or to have a physical contest to gain a superior position over an opponent, as in a wrestling match." What a great burden for Rebekah to bear. The children in her womb dashed against or bruised each other, suggesting that there was a violent agitation occurring inside her, so much so that she was apprehensive both for her own safety and for the safety of her unborn children. Concerned about the situation, Rebekah went to inquire of the Lord. It is significant to note the uniqueness of the conflict here. It is a conflict between twins that rages so vehemently that their mother is driven to despair. "Why am I thus?" Rebekah wonders in despair. Even in the womb there didn't appear to be enough room for Esau and Jacob. Their mother's womb became their first battlefield, an ominous sign of what was to follow among their descendants.

23 And the Lord said unto her, Two nations are in thy womb, and two manner of people shall be separated from thy bowels; and the one people shall be stronger than the other people; and the elder shall serve the younger.

How the Lord communicated is not explicitly stated. More important was the message communicated to Rebekah: the "two nations" inside her womb were struggling with each other. The word "nations" (Heb. *gowy*, **GO-ee**), as used here, generally refers to "a people, tribe, or nation at large," particularly Gentiles (cf. Genesis 10:5). Rebekah had not one but two manner of "people" (Heb. *leom,* **leh-OME**) struggling inside her belly. The use of the Hebrew word *leom* has a particular significance. At its root, *leom* implies togetherness or a cohesive unit, and indicates an ethnic or cultural bond. This is of particular significance, because God was letting Rebekah know that the struggle between her unborn sons had implications far beyond mere sibling rivalry. The two were embarking upon a journey that would last throughout their lives and the lives of their descendants.

24 And when her days to be delivered were fulfilled, behold, there were twins in her womb. 25 And the first came out red, all over like an hairy garment; and they called his name Esau. 26 And after that came his brother out, and his hand took hold on Esau's heel; and his name was called Jacob: and Isaac was threescore years old when she bare them.

Esau was the firstborn: "And the first came out red." The word "red" (Heb. *admoniy,* **ad-mo-NEE**), of a reddish color, is probably an allusion to Adham, the red earth. They called his name Esau, the hairy one. This simply means that he was covered with red hair. The name Esau has a loose connection with a place called Seir, the early name for Edom to the southeast of the Dead Sea, where Esau later settled (Genesis 32:3; 36:8).

At birth Jacob did not simply follow close upon the heels of Esau, but seized Esau's heel, as if he would trip him up. He had his brother's heel by the hand while yet in his mother's womb; the name Jacob (Heb. *Ya`aqob,* **yah-ak-OBE**) means "heel-catcher." As with Esau, so too Jacob's name would take on a meaning later in life as his deceptive nature became evident. So from the very beginning, the twins' births had great significance for later events in their lives.

27 And the boys grew: and Esau was a cunning hunter, a man of the field; and Jacob was a plain man, dwelling in tents.

As the boys grew up, their different personalities began to emerge. On the one hand, Esau, the rough and hairy child, became the great hunter and sportsman. The Hebrew word for "hunter" (*tsayid,* **TSAH-yid**) means "one who supported himself and family by hunting and by agriculture." On the other hand,

Jacob is described as a "plain man," that is, someone who dwells in tents. Although this word has the moral connotation of uprightness or perfection (Genesis 6:9; Job 1:1, 8; 2:3), such description is certainly not applicable to Jacob at this point, and probably not until after his name was changed (Genesis 32:26–30).

28 And Isaac loved Esau, because he did eat of his venison: but Rebekah loved Jacob.

This verse concerns the parental attachment to one child in preference over another. Isaac loved Esau, and Rebekah loved Jacob. Parents must carefully guard against such partiality realizing it as both sinful and dangerous. The reason for Rachel's special love for Jacob is not stated. Nevertheless, whatever her motives, the scene is now set for Rebekah to use her husband's appetite to acquire the blessing for the son she admires most. The brothers are already moving inexorably toward realizing the prophetic announcement of their division.

The conduct of both parents was less than commendable. Their partiality gave occasion to the strife that existed between the two brothers. While it may be a fact that siblings can exhibit vastly different personalities, no one child should be slighted, neglected, or preferred by their parents.

29 And Jacob sod pottage: and Esau came from the field, and he was faint: 30 And Esau said to Jacob, Feed me, I pray thee, with that same red pottage; for I am faint: therefore was his name called Edom.

The phrase "sod pottage" (*zuwd naziyd,* **zood naw-ZEED**), literally translates as "he boiled boiled food or soup" or "he cooked something cooked," and this, according to Genesis 25:34, was the pottage that Esau exchanged for his birthright.

When Esau came from the field, he was faint— exhausted. The word "faint" (Heb. *'ayeph,* **aw-YAFE**) refers to being in a weakened physical condition, requiring food, drink, and rest to recuperate. In his excitement to gratify his appetite, Esau said to Jacob, "Feed (Heb. *la'at,* **law-AT**, literally, let me swallow— an expression for eating greedily) me." Notice the play on words: "red (Heb. *'adom,* **aw-DOME**) pottage" and the name "Edom" (Heb. *'Edom,* **ed-OME**).

31 And Jacob said, Sell me this day thy birthright.

Jacob's answer was cold and calculating. The word "birthright" (Heb. *bekorah*, **bek-o-RAW**) occurs four times in verses 31–34. In the Old Testament, the privileges of the firstborn were clearly defined. They included the official authority of the father, a double portion of the father's property, the functions of the domestic priesthood, and authority and superiority over the rest of the family (Genesis 27:19, 27–29; 49:3; Exodus 22:29; Numbers 8:14–17; Deuteronomy 21:17). The way Jacob stated his demand suggests a long premeditation and a ruthless exploitation of his brother's moment of weakness. Unbeknownst to him, Esau's readiness to forfeit the birthright would pave the way to greater loss, the loss of the blessing (see Genesis 27). In biblical times, the rights of a firstborn son were negotiable, but to sell them so cheaply was a clear mark of Esau's lack of knowledge of them. Although Jacob's character was not wholly admirable, at least he took the future seriously (cf. Hebrews 11:9 ff.).

32 And Esau said, Behold, I am at the point to die: and what profit shall this birthright do to me?

Esau continued speaking, belying his claim that he was on the verge of dying, thus displaying a careless indifference to a privilege that he ought to have held dear. He asked Jacob, "What profit shall this birthright do to me?" Esau was literally asking Jacob, "What use is this thing [birthright] to me?" It appears to Esau that the birthright was not likely to ever be of service to him, since he was almost certain to die because of hunger. Esau concluded that a birthright, whose enjoyment was in the future, had no benefit to someone who has only a short time to live. Esau, like many people today, preferred instant selfish gratification to deferred benefits or eternal enjoyments.

33 And Jacob said, Swear to me this day; and he sware unto him: and he sold his birthright unto Jacob.

Jacob's reply confirms that he was determined to take an undue advantage of brother's folly and lack of self-control. Though Jacob might have been aware of the prophecy about having precedence in his father's house, he was by no means justified using the wrong methods to both hasten and assure its fulfillment. The end does not always justify the means. By his action, Jacob verified his right to the name of supplanter, a name that at first appears to have had no other purpose other than the circumstance under which the two boys were born.

34 Then Jacob gave Esau bread and pottage of lentiles; and he did eat and drink, and rose up, and went his way: thus Esau despised his birthright.

This verse highlights the two-sided nature of the deal and draws attention to the inequity of the arrangement between the two brothers—Esau sold, but Jacob gave. What a tragedy. Esau ate, drank, and departed without any serious reflections about his ill-fated bargain, as reflected by the use of the Hebrew word for "despised": *bazah* (**baw-ZAW**, meaning "to hold in contempt or view as worthless"). This final statement is important because it emphasizes that Esau treated with flippancy something of great value and worth.

Daily Bible Readings

M: God Chose the Least
1 Corinthians 1:26–31
T: Rebekah Agrees to Marry Isaac
Genesis 24:50–61
W: Isaac Takes Rebekah as His Wife
Genesis 24:62–67
T: Rebekah's Twins Struggle in the Womb
Genesis 25:19–23
F: The Birth of Jacob and Esau
Genesis 25:24–28
S: Esau Sells His Birthright
Genesis 25:29–34
S: Esau's Lost Blessing
Genesis 27:30–40

TEACHING TIPS

October 14
Bible Study Guide 7

1. Words You Should Know
A. Lighted (Genesis 28:11) *paga'* (Heb.)—Denotes arriving or coming to.

B. Dreadful (v. 17) *yare'* (Heb.)—Implies a fearful reverence.

2. Teacher Preparation
Unifying Principle—Understanding Our Dreams! While dreams were a means by which God communicated during biblical times, today the Holy Spirit is present within us and provides a means for God to communicate with us. The key is to be open to receive God's messages to us and to trust in them.

A. Read Genesis 27 and 28 from a more modern-language version of the Bible to familiarize yourself with the characters and with the content of today's lesson.

B. Review the Background section and the Daily Bible Readings.

C. Complete lesson 7 from the *Precepts For Living® Personal Study Guide.*

D. Pray for the students in your class, asking God to open their hearts to today's lesson.

3. Starting the Lesson
A. After the students arrive and are settled, lead the class in prayer. Pray specifically for godly insights on the lesson and for blessings in the lives of the students.

B. Ask the class members to read the Keep in Mind Scripture verse in unison.

C. Allow 5–7 minutes of discussion to review last week's lesson to see if anyone completed the Make It Happen challenge.

D. Briefly go over the Background section for this week's lesson.

E. Put the AIM for Change on the chalkboard. Inform the class that today's lesson will focus on recognizing and trusting the Word of God when we hear it.

F. Instruct the class to silently read the In Focus story.

4. Getting into the Lesson
A. Review the concept of dreams as described in The People, Places, and Times section. Ask the class if God's will has ever been revealed to them (e.g., song, Scripture, person, dream, prophecy).

B. Ask for a volunteer to read the Focal Verses aloud from a modern-language translation such as *The Message* or *New International Version.*

C. Highlight key points of today's In Depth section by providing a brief overview of the Scripture text based on the At-A-Glance outline.

D. If time permits, complete the Search the Scriptures section.

5. Relating the Lesson to Life
A. Divide the class into two groups and assign each group a question from the Discuss the Meaning section. Allow 15 minutes for discussion

B. Reconvene the class and ask a representative from each group to share their group's findings with the rest of the class.

6. Arousing Action
A. Read the Lesson in Our Society section and engage the class in a discussion based on knowing when God is communicating to us.

B. Remind the students to complete the Daily Bible Readings for October 21 and complete lesson 8 from the *Precepts For Living® Personal Study Guide* in preparation for next week's class.

C. Close the class in prayer.

Worship Guide

For the Superintendent or Teacher
Theme: Jacob's Dream at Bethel
Theme Song: "Standing on the Promises"
Devotional Reading: Psalm 105:1–11
Prayer

JACOB'S DREAM AT BETHEL

Bible Background • GENESIS 27:41–28:22
Printed Text • GENESIS 28:10–22   Devotional Reading • PSALM 105:1–11

AIM for Change

By the end of the lesson, we will:

STATE the promise that God made to Jacob in his dream;

TRUST that God keeps His Word; and

RECOGNIZE when God is communicating with us and trust the words we receive.

Keep in Mind

"And, behold, I am with thee, and will keep thee in all places whither thou goest, and will bring thee again into this land; for I will not leave thee, until I have done that which I have spoken to thee of" (Genesis 28:15).

Focal Verses

KJV **Genesis 28:10** And Jacob went out from Beersheba, and went toward Haran.

11 And he lighted upon a certain place, and tarried there all night, because the sun was set; and he took of the stones of that place, and put them for his pillows, and lay down in that place to sleep.

12 And he dreamed, and behold a ladder set up on the earth, and the top of it reached to heaven: and behold the angels of God ascending and descending on it.

13 And, behold, the LORD stood above it, and said, I am the LORD God of Abraham thy father, and the God of Isaac: the land whereon thou liest, to thee will I give it, and to thy seed;

14 And thy seed shall be as the dust of the earth, and thou shalt spread abroad to the west, and to the east, and to the north, and to the south: and in thee and in thy seed shall all the families of the earth be blessed.

15 And, behold, I am with thee, and will keep thee in all places whither thou goest, and will bring thee again into this land; for I will not leave thee, until I have done that which I have spoken to thee of.

16 And Jacob awaked out of his sleep, and he said, Surely the LORD is in this place; and I knew it not.

17 And he was afraid, and said, How dreadful is this place! this is none other but the house of God, and this is the gate of heaven.

18 And Jacob rose up early in the morning, and took the stone that he had put for his pillows, and set it up for a pillar, and poured oil upon the top of it.

NLT **Genesis 28:10** Meanwhile, Jacob left Beersheba and traveled toward Haran.

11 At sundown he arrived at a good place to set up camp and stopped there for the night. Jacob found a stone to rest his head against and lay down to sleep.

12 As he slept, he dreamed of a stairway that reached from the earth up to heaven. And he saw the angels of God going up and down the stairway.

13 At the top of the stairway stood the LORD, and he said, "I am the LORD, the God of your grandfather Abraham, and the God of your father, Isaac. The ground you are lying on belongs to you. I am giving it to you and your descendants.

14 Your descendants will be as numerous as the dust of the earth! They will spread out in all directions—to the west and the east, to the north and the south. And all the families of the earth will be blessed through you and your descendants.

15 What's more, I am with you, and I will protect you wherever you go. One day I will bring you back to this land. I will not leave you until I have finished giving you everything I have promised you."

16 Then Jacob awoke from his sleep and said, "Surely the LORD is in this place, and I wasn't even aware of it!"

17 But he was also afraid and said, "What an awesome place this is! It is none other than the house of God, the very gateway to heaven!"

18 The next morning Jacob got up very early. He took the stone he had rested his head against, and set it upright as a memorial pillar. Then he poured olive oil over it.

19 And he called the name of that place Bethel: but the name of that city was called Luz at the first.

20 And Jacob vowed a vow, saying, If God will be with me, and will keep me in this way that I go, and will give me bread to eat, and raiment to put on,

21 So that I come again to my father's house in peace; then shall the LORD be my God:

22 And this stone, which I have set for a pillar, shall be God's house: and of all that thou shalt give me I will surely give the tenth unto thee.

19 He named that place Bethel (which means "house of God"), although the name of the nearby village was Luz.

20 Then Jacob made this vow: "If God will indeed be with me and protect me on this journey, and if he will provide me with food and clothing,

21 and if I return safely to my father's home, then the LORD will certainly be my God.

22 And this memorial pillar I have set up will become a place for worshiping God, and I will present to God a tenth of everything he gives me."

In Focus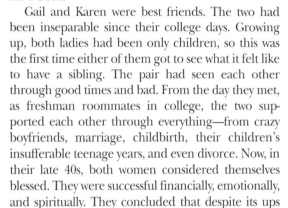

Gail and Karen were best friends. The two had been inseparable since their college days. Growing up, both ladies had been only children, so this was the first time either of them got to see what it felt like to have a sibling. The pair had seen each other through good times and bad. From the day they met, as freshman roommates in college, the two supported each other through everything—from crazy boyfriends, marriage, childbirth, their children's insufferable teenage years, and even divorce. Now, in their late 40s, both women considered themselves blessed. They were successful financially, emotionally, and spiritually. They concluded that despite its ups and downs, life was good.

One evening as Gail was getting ready to go to bed, her phone rang. It was Karen's mother calling her to tell her that Karen had been in a terrible accident on her way home from the airport and was killed. Gail couldn't believe it. Her best friend was gone? How could this be? She had just spoken to Karen the night before, and the two were planning to get together over the weekend for some serious girl talk about Karen's trip to LA. "How could she be gone? I just spoke with her yesterday," Gail told Karen's mom.

As Gail sat with Karen's family, she couldn't help but be sad at the loss of her best friend—no, her *sister*. How would she make it? Although she tried to stop them, tears began to run down her cheeks. Gail closed her eyes. Just then, the piano began to play, and the pianist began singing one of her and Karen's favorite gospel songs, "When Sunday Comes" by Donald Lawrence and the Tri-City Singers.

The soloist sang:
When Sunday comes, my trouble's gone,
As soon as it gets here, I'll have a new song.
When Sunday comes, I won't have to cry no more,
Jesus will soothe my troubled mind,
All of my heartaches will be left behind;
When Sunday comes.

As Gail heard the song, her heart filled with joy, and a sense of peace came over her. All of a sudden she knew that her friend was happy and at peace, and now so was she.

God speaks to us in many ways. In today's story we find Him speaking to a grieving friend through song. In today's Bible lesson we find God speaking to Jacob through a dream. No matter how the Word of the Lord comes to us, we must learn how to recognize it as God's Word and trust the Word we receive.

The People, Places, and Times

Bethel. Located about 12 miles north of Jerusalem and west of the Jordan River, Bethel has many significant connections to Old Testament events. Bethel was originally called Luz and belonged to the Canaanites. Upon his entry into Canaan, Abraham set up camp between Bethel and Ai (Genesis 12:8). It is here that Abraham "called on the name of the LORD" when he returned from Egypt (13:3–4). When Jacob fled from Beersheba to Haran, he spent the night here and dreamt of a ladder reaching to heaven with "angels of God ascending and descending on it" (28:11–12). It is Jacob who renamed the city Elbethel (35:6–7), a name that means "the God of the house of God." During times of trouble, the people of Israel went to Bethel to seek counsel of God (Judges 20:18; 21:2). It was also at Bethel that the Ark of the Covenant was entrusted to the care of Aaron's grandson, Phinehas. After the nation was divided, Bethel was included in the northern kingdom of Israel and became the official center of worship. Under King Jeroboam, Bethel became a site of idol worship (1 Kings 12:28–33). After the northern kingdom of Israel was exiled by the Assyrians, a handful of loyal priests continued to live and teach in Bethel. Bethel was not purged of its idols until the reign of King Josiah of Judah (2 Kings 23:15–18).

Dreams. In the Old Testament, dreams were very important, though not every dream was thought to be from God. Many divine revelations came through the dreams of various kings, prophets, and ordinary people. The dreams of kings, holy men, and women were considered to have national or international significance. While dreams were considered significant, many of God's prophets warned against relying solely on dreams to know and understand the will of God.

Sources:
Alexander, David, and Pat Alexander. *Eerdman's Handbook to the Bible.* Oxford, England: Lion Publishing, 1973. 296, 299, 666, 670.
Butler, Trent, gen. ed. *Holman Bible Dictionary.* Nashville, Tenn.: Broadman & Holman Publishers, 1991.

Background

In the preceding chapters we are introduced to an aging and frail Isaac. He is the father of twin sons, Esau and Jacob. Thinking that his death is imminent, Isaac asked that his older and favorite son, Esau, prepare him a dish made of freshly killed game. Isaac made arrangements with Esau to eat this meal and then bless his son before he died. However, unbeknownst to Isaac, the plan is overheard by his wife, Rebekah, who contrives with the younger son (Jacob: her favorite) to take advantage of Isaac's failing eyesight and trick Esau out of the birthright blessing.

With his mother's assistance, Jacob disguised himself and fooled his father into giving him the blessing that rightly belonged to his brother. The consequences of this act of deception were terrible. For her part, Rebekah had dishonored and mocked her husband (Genesis 27:12). Jacob had deceived his father and earned the bitter hatred of his older brother, who planned in his heart to kill his brother as soon as

"the days of mourning for [his] father [were] at hand" (v. 41). Fearing for her favorite son's life, Rebekah convinced Isaac that Jacob should be sent away to Haran, to the home of her brother Laban, to find a wife.

At-A-Glance

1. Jacob's Departure (Genesis 28:10)
2. Jacob's Dream (vv. 11–12)
3. Jacob's Blessing (vv. 13–15)
4. Jacob's Recognition of God (vv. 16–17)
5. Jacob's Decision to Honor God (vv. 18–22)

In Depth

1. Jacob's Departure (Genesis 28:10)

Isaac had given Jacob a second blessing and charged him to leave home: "Go to Padanaram, to the house of Bethuel thy mother's father; and take thee a wife from thence of the daughters of Laban thy mother's brother" (Genesis 28:2). As his father Abraham before him had been when he sent his servant to find Isaac a wife, Isaac was old and near death, and he was concerned and wanted to ensure that his son did not marry an idol-worshiping Canaanite woman. While the two narratives share these similarities, their differences are striking and noteworthy. First, while Isaac did bless Jacob and instruct him to obtain a wife, the real reason for Jacob's departure was to escape the wrath of his older brother, Esau. Jacob had tricked his brother into selling him his birthright and, at the urging of his mother, had deceived his father into giving him the blessing that belonged to his older brother. The theft of the birthright and blessing were no small matters. Ancient tradition called for the oldest son to become the official head of the family upon the death of the father. Additionally, the older son received two parts of the father's estate, twice as much as his brothers.

The second point of difference between the two narratives is that Abraham did not send his son to find his own wife; instead he dispatched his servant to find his son's bride. If one reads Abraham's reluctance to send Isaac away from him as a deep love for Isaac and a genuine concern for his safety as he would be traveling through the desert, then one must question why Isaac did not share the same concern for Jacob's well-being. The answer may lie in Jacob's treachery in the matter of deceiving his father and stealing his brother Esau's rights as the firstborn son. This is not to say that Isaac no longer loved Jacob, but it is understandable that he was painfully disappointed in him and his behavior.

Finally, when the servant of Abraham went to find a wife for Isaac, he was dispatched with a caravan of camels laden with many gifts. When Jacob left his father's tents, he left with no such dowry for the family of his future bride. We would do well to remember that while our sins are forgivable, we still must live with the consequences of our sins. When Jacob departed from his father, he was only carrying his walking staff (Genesis 32:10) and the memories of the hurt and pain he had caused his father and his brother.

His solitary journey certainly provided Jacob ample time to consider the consequences of his actions. He was now estranged from his brother—who hated him. It was unclear to him when, if ever, he would be able to return home to see his mother who loved him. Jacob certainly must have wondered what kind of reception he would receive from his uncle Laban. He would be arriving empty-handed and seeking a bride!

We want to remember that Jacob's grandfather, Abraham, did not die until Jacob was about 15 years old. In his youth, Jacob had had ample opportunities to hear about God's covenant right from the lips of his grandfather. No doubt Jacob was now coming to the realization that his participation in the fulfillment of God's promises would not come to him as a result of his own schemes. His attempt to seize the blessing had failed miserably.

2. Jacob's Dream (vv. 11–12)

The text implies that Jacob arrived just outside of the Judean hillside city of Luz in the evening. He had traveled some 62 miles by this point. It is possible that the gates of the city were closed for the evening, making it impossible for him to gain access. Like the shepherds, Jacob would have to spend the night sleeping outdoors and under the canopy of stars, with a hard stone for a pillow.

At some point during the night, Jacob dreamed of a ladder that stretched into the heavens. In his dream

he saw angels moving up and down the ladder. Remember that angels are messengers and that when we encounter them in the Scriptures, they are often delivering messages. In this vivid dream God was at the top of the ladder.

3. Jacob's Blessing (vv. 13–15)

God identified Himself as "LORD God of Abraham thy father, and the God of Isaac" (Genesis 28:13). There was to be no mistake. Jacob was in the presence of the God honored and revered by his father and his grandfather.

At this point God confirmed His covenant blessings that He had promised to both Abraham and Isaac. Here, God promised that the land on which Jacob now was sleeping would be given to him and to his posterity. God promised to watch over and protect Jacob until the land was his and until his "seed" was like the dust of the earth (v. 14), stretching in all directions, from the west to the east and from the north to the south. The descendants of Jacob would be everywhere and too numerous to count! It is interesting to note that Jacob had not experienced the blessing of God until he had arrived in the place that God had promised to bless. We would do well to remember that for some of us, our blessings will not happen until we get to the place where God wants to bless us.

What a wonderful comfort this covenant renewal must have been for Jacob. Here he was a fugitive, fleeing from the wrath of his brother. He was certainly not a likely candidate to be selected by God. Jacob's actions toward his father and brother clearly indicated he was a thief and a deceiver. Yet God had selected him to be the steward of the great covenant.

4. Jacob's Recognition of God (vv. 16–17)

When Jacob awakened from this dream, he was astonished. He had not only heard God, but he had seen God. Jacob did not have to rely on the testimony of his father or grandfather; he now knew without a doubt, "Surely the LORD is in this place" (Genesis 28:16). Up until this time, Jacob may have believed that the God worshiped by his father and grandfather was only present where they lived. Now he recognized that God was right there on the spot he was standing on! Not only was God present, but God had promised him the very blessings he had unsuccessfully tried to steal! No longer was Jacob alone or running away from his past. He now had God's promise: "I will not leave thee, until I have done that which I have spoken to thee of" (v. 15). Rather than escape his past, Jacob now had the hope of a future that was rightfully his.

It is with this understanding—that Jacob now had divine assurance that God would never leave him—that we understand Jacob's description of this place as "dreadful." The use of the word "dreadful" implies a reverential awe at what Jacob had experienced. Jacob understood, perhaps for the first time in his life, how awesome and powerful God was and how weak and ineffective he was.

5. Jacob's Decision to Honor God (vv. 18–22)

Here in the desert, outside of this Canaanite city, God had chosen to reveal His presence. It is no wonder that Jacob wanted to preserve the memory of this awesome experience and erect a memorial. He did not have the necessary materials to build a proper altar, and so he went about using the materials at hand: stones. This act is reminiscent of Jacob's grandfather Abraham, who similarly constructed altars in the places God had appeared to him. What a wonderful reminder to Christian parents, grandparents, and caregivers. Our children are always watching us. It is important that we model godly behavior, and it is also important that we provide them with models of godly worship and thanksgiving. Our praise and worship and our acts of thanksgiving are not private matters but ought to be demonstrated daily. God's presence in our lives has to be shown to them. If they see us build altars to God, they will know to build altars.

In memorializing the spot where he had discovered God, Jacob also swore to adopt his grandfather's practice in dedicating to God a tenth of all he received.

Search the Scriptures

Fill in the blanks.

1. "And Jacob went out from Beersheba, and went toward _____" (Genesis 28:10).

2. "And he dreamed, and behold a ladder set up on the earth, and the top of it reached to heaven: and behold the _____ of God ascending and descending on it" (v. 12).

3. "And, behold, the LORD stood above it, and said, I am the LORD God of _____ thy father, and the God of Isaac: the land whereon thou liest, to thee will I give it, and to thy seed" (v. 13).

4. "And he was _____, and said, How dreadful is this place! this is none other but the house of God, and this is the gate of heaven" (v. 17).

5. "And he called the name of that place Bethel: but the name of that city was called _____ at the first" (v. 19).

6. "And this stone, which I have set for a pillar, shall be God's house: and of all that thou shalt give me I will surely give the _____ unto thee" (v. 22).

Discuss the Meaning

1. In Genesis 28:15, God promised to be with Jacob and watch over him. In what ways did Jacob's dream affect God's covenant people?

2. Jacob received a great blessing from God at a time when his actions made him the least deserving. Discuss a time when you were certain that God had confirmed His promises to you.

Lesson in Our Society

God chose Jacob without regard to his past, but with complete regard to the past of his father and his grandfather. God is a covenant-keeping God. His promises to Abraham were eternal. The covenant did not end when Abraham died—the promises included Abraham's seed, Jacob. As Christians, we should rejoice: It is because of our covenant relationship with Jesus Christ that we can be assured God is always with us. Because of Jesus Christ, God chooses to look beyond our faults, forgive our sins, and continue to bless us.

Look at what's happening around the world today. The nightly news is replete with senseless acts of violence. Despite this fact, can you point to specific examples where you believe God's presence is at work?

Make It Happen

Our involvement in our careers and families make it difficult for many of us to spend "quiet time" with the Lord. Yet, if we are to hear Him, we have to make time. Determine to find time early in the morning or late in the evening that is just for you and God.

During this time close yourself away from others, and turn off any radios or televisions. Begin by praying, and then read the Scriptures. Allow God to speak to you through His Word.

Follow the Spirit

What God wants me to do:

_____

_____

Remember Your Thoughts

Special insights I have learned:

_____

_____

More Light on the Text

Genesis 28:10–22

10 And Jacob went out from Beersheba, and went toward Haran. 11 And he lighted upon a certain place, and tarried there all night, because the sun was set; and he took of the stones of that place, and put them for his pillows, and lay down in that place to sleep.

As Jacob was traveling from Beersheba to Haran, he came to a place where he was obliged to stop all night because the sun had set. Jacob had probably intended to reach Luz, but because the sun had set, he opted to stop and rest for the night. The phrase "he lighted upon a certain place" suggests that the stop was not anticipated. Rather, the stop was divinely appointed; the place where he stopped had already been consecrated by Abraham (see Genesis 12:8; 13:4).

12 And he dreamed, and behold a ladder set up on the earth, and the top of it reached to heaven: and behold the angels of God ascending and descending on it.

After making a pillow with the stones, Jacob fell asleep and had a dream where he saw a "ladder" (Heb. *cullam,* **sool-LAWM**) resting upon the earth with the top reaching to heaven and upon it angels of God going up and down, and Jehovah Himself standing above it. Although the etymology of the Hebrew word for "ladder" is not entirely certain, its symbolism is without doubt. It was a visible symbol of the real and uninterrupted fellowship between God in heaven and His people upon Earth.

Dreams often served as instruments of divine revelation in Old Testament times. As Jacob slept, he had a powerful dream that gave him insight into the realm of God's power. In ancient days gods were thought to be confined by certain physical boundaries. Through the dream, God revealed to Jacob that He has no boundaries. As Jacob saw the ladder stretched from heaven to Earth, God revealed to Jacob that he was available and accessible. The angels served to support the notion that God wanted to communicate with Jacob.

13 And, behold, the LORD stood above it, and said, I am the LORD God of Abraham thy father, and the God of Isaac: the land whereon thou liest, to thee will I give it, and to thy seed;

The vision was not just about angels. The Lord "stood" (Heb. *natsab,* **naw-TSAB**) above the ladder, which implies that this was more than simply a physical position at the top of a ladder; this was a personal revelation of Jehovah to Jacob. In proclaiming Himself to Jacob as the God of his fathers, God not only confirmed to him all the promises made to Abraham and the blessing for which Isaac had prayed (Genesis 28:3–4) in their fullest extent, but He also assured him of His protection on his dangerous journey and a safe return to his home (v. 14).

14 And thy seed shall be as the dust of the earth, and thou shalt spread abroad to the west, and to the east, and to the north, and to the south: and in thee and in thy seed shall all the families of the earth be blessed. 15 And, behold, I am with thee, and will keep thee in all places whither thou goest, and will bring thee again into this land; for I will not leave thee, until I have done that which I have spoken to thee of.

Jacob seems to have left home with a heavy heart. Through this dream, God reiterated His promise to Abraham and Isaac, relayed to Jacob the prosperity of his descendants, and reassured the fearful patriarch of His presence during this dangerous journey. God showed him the communication that exists between heaven and Earth—the guard of angels—and His ever-watchful eye looking down on him, whether awake or asleep. God confirmed Jacob's destiny as the heir of God's promise to his forefathers and to the world. What then has he to fear? No evil would

"And, behold, I am with thee, and will keep thee in all places whither thou goest...for I will not leave thee, until I have done that which I have spoken to thee of" (from Genesis 28:15).

happen to him while God was his guardian and strong defense. The Lord, in this dream, completely dispelled the fears of Jacob by confirming to him the covenant and promises made to Abraham and renewed with Isaac.

16 And Jacob awaked out of his sleep, and he said, Surely the Lord is in this place; and I knew it not.

Jacob had fallen asleep fearful, helpless, alone, sorrowful, and anxious, without any thought that he was especially cared for or watched by Abraham's God. He thought himself to be exiled from the presence of the Lord because of his cooperation in the deception of his brother Esau. Instead, God offered him promise, not condemnation. The Lord gave Jacob the promise of future generations and of His continued presence.

17 And he was afraid, and said, How dreadful is this place! This is none other but the house of God, and this is the gate of heaven.

As Jacob awoke, a feeling of awe came upon him. The dream had, no doubt, left a strong impression on Jacob. It was an impression so strong that he declared, "How dreadful is this place!" Here the word "dreadful" in Hebrew (*yare'*, **yaw-RAY**) means "to stand in awe or inspire reverence or godly fear." The appearance of the ladder, the Lord standing at its top, and the movement of the angels left Jacob with a true sense of God's commitment to keep His covenant with Jacob's forefathers. In that moment Jacob realized that God had been with him even when he hadn't been aware of it.

18 And Jacob rose up early in the morning, and took the stone that he had put for his pillows, and set it up for a pillar, and poured oil upon the top of it. 19 And he called the name of that place Bethel: but the name of that city was called Luz at the first.

The next morning Jacob turned the *pillow* into a *pillar*. He erected the stones upon which he had laid his head as a monument of the extraordinary vision he had had in this place. The pillow stones served to mark the place of his restoration. Jacob's experience moved him to worship and praise the Lord. He poured oil upon the top to consecrate it as a memorial of the mercy that had been shown him there. Jacob named the place where God called out to him Bethel, which means "house of God."

20 And Jacob vowed a vow, saying, If God will be with me, and will keep me in this way that I go, and will give me bread to eat, and raiment to put on, 21 So that I come again to my father's house in peace; then shall the LORD be my God: 22 And this stone, which I have set for a pillar, shall be God's house: and of all that thou shalt give me I will surely give the tenth unto thee.

Jacob made a vow. This was no ordinary vow, but a grand and solemn expression of Jacob's complete acceptance of the Lord to be his God, the significance of which is underscored by its mention again at key points in Genesis (see 31:13; 35:1–3, 7). God had already made an unconditional promise to Jacob to watch over him and bring him back to this land (28:15). Even though God had reached out to him, Jacob may have felt he needed to strike a deal with God. Apparently, Jacob thought he needed to

establish some conditions for this relationship, so he offered to build an altar and to tithe as a sign of his commitment. One thing is certainly clear from this passage of Scripture: Jacob learned that instead of relying on his abilities, he needed to stop being the "trickster," as his name implies, and to rely on God to supply his needs and to protect him.

The "if" in Jacob's vow does not imply doubt in God's promise; rather, it is the natural progression of Jacob taking God at His word: "If God is going to do so much for me, then I will do something for Him." In other words, if God were willing to prove Himself by fulfilling His covenant promise, then Jacob would acknowledge and worship God as his God, both by building an altar and by tithing all his possessions.

Finally, the circumstances in which Jacob made his vow are very striking. Typically, in the Old Testament, vows were made in situations of distress. Jacob's vow was no exception. He was in a distressed state. He was running away from home for participating in something that was the equivalent of being under threat of death. But now he had received an unexpected revelation announcing his return to his country and guaranteeing him safety on the journey. Here God showed Jacob the future and confirmed to him the covenant promise.

Daily Bible Readings

M: Remember God's Works
Psalm 105:1–6

T: An Everlasting Covenant
Psalm 105:7–11

W: The Conflict Deepens
Genesis 27:41–45

T: To Seek a Wife
Genesis 27:46–28:5

F: Esau Takes Another Wife
Genesis 28:6–9

S: God's Covenant with Jacob
Genesis 28:10–17

S: The Place Named Bethel
Genesis 28:18–22

TEACHING TIPS

October 21
Bible Study Guide 8

1. Words You Should Know

A. Leah (Genesis 29:23–25, 30–32) *Le'ah* (Heb.) —She was the first wife of Jacob. The name means "weary."

B. Week (vv. 27–28) *shabuwa'* (Heb.)—A period of seven (days, weeks, or years).

C. Hated (vv. 31, 33) *sane'* (Heb.)—To show a negative preference. Expresses the ill will and dislike that Jacob harbored for Leah.

2. Teacher Preparation

Unifying Principle—Dashed Hopes and Fond Wishes! Even in the most disappointing situations, God can work to bring about good and fulfill His plans for our lives. During these difficult times, we must not give in to feelings of hopelessness but have patience and faith in God.

A. Begin your preparation with prayer, asking God to open your mind to the teaching.

B. Read the Daily Bible Readings and Focal Verses for today's lesson.

C. Break the lesson down into three parts: observation, interpretation, and application. Begin to ask and answer questions like: What is happening in this passage of Scripture (observation)? What is the background of today's lesson (observation)? What is the cause and effect of the relationships between Jacob, Rachel, Leah, and Laban (interpretation)? What does this passage say about God (interpretation)? In what ways do the disappointing experiences I or the class have had parallel today's lesson (application)?

D. Complete lesson 8 from the *Precepts For Living® Personal Study Guide.*

3. Starting the Lesson

A. Write the AIM for Change objectives on the board.

B. Begin the class with prayer, keeping the AIM for Change objectives in mind.

C. Tell the class that today's lesson will focus on disappointments and dashed hopes (Unifying Principle).

D. Ask for a volunteer to read the In Focus story.

4. Getting into the Lesson

A. Instruct the class to silently read the Focal Verses.

B. Provide a brief overview of the Background and The People, Places, and Times sections.

C. In three columns, write the words "observation", "interpretation", and "application" on the board. Just like in your preparation to teach today's lesson, solicit answers from the class to the following questions in the Teacher Preparation section under C.

5. Relating the Lesson to Life

Instruct the class to get into pairs. Tell each person to write a sentence or two about a time when he or she was disappointed or upset. Have the partners exchange papers. After the partner writes a sentence in response from a positive perspective and passes it back to the owner, have each one read the response. Then join hands and pray for one another's concerns.

6. Arousing Action

A. Read the Lesson in Our Society section aloud. Ask volunteers to share their stories.

B. Challenge the students to commit to the Make It Happen exercise.

C. Remind the class to read the Daily Bible Readings in preparation for next week's lesson. Suggest that they complete lesson 9 in the *Precepts For Living® Personal Study Guide* as well.

JACOB AND RACHEL

Bible Background • GENESIS 29
Printed Text • GENESIS 29:21–35 Devotional Reading • PSALM 91

AIM for Change

By the end of the lesson, we will:

UNDERSTAND that God can work in disappointing situations to bring about good;

TRUST that God is working in our lives during disappointing times; and

PRAY for patience when it seems that our hopes and dreams aren't progressing as planned.

Keep in Mind

"And Jacob served seven years for Rachel; and they seemed unto him but a few days, for the love he had to her" (Genesis 29:20).

Focal Verses

KJV

Genesis 29:21 And Jacob said unto Laban, Give me my wife, for my days are fulfilled, that I may go in unto her.

22 And Laban gathered together all the men of the place, and made a feast.

23 And it came to pass in the evening, that he took Leah his daughter, and brought her to him; and he went in unto her.

24 And Laban gave unto his daughter Leah Zilpah his maid for an handmaid.

25 And it came to pass, that in the morning, behold, it was Leah: and he said to Laban, What is this thou hast done unto me? did not I serve with thee for Rachel? wherefore then hast thou beguiled me?

26 And Laban said, It must not be so done in our country, to give the younger before the firstborn.

27 Fulfil her week, and we will give thee this also for the service which thou shalt serve with me yet seven other years.

28 And Jacob did so, and fulfilled her week: and he gave him Rachel his daughter to wife also.

29 And Laban gave to Rachel his daughter Bilhah his handmaid to be her maid.

30 And he went in also unto Rachel, and he loved also Rachel more than Leah, and served with him yet seven other years.

31 And when the LORD saw that Leah was hated, he opened her womb: but Rachel was barren.

32 And Leah conceived, and bare a son, and she called his name Reuben: for she said, Surely the LORD hath looked upon my affliction; now therefore my husband will love me.

33 And she conceived again, and bare a son; and said, Because the LORD hath heard that I was hated,

NLT

Genesis 29:21 Finally, the time came for him to marry her. "I have fulfilled my agreement," Jacob said to Laban. "Now give me my wife so I can marry her."

22 So Laban invited everyone in the neighborhood and prepared a wedding feast.

23 But that night, when it was dark, Laban took Leah to Jacob, and he slept with her.

24 (Laban had given Leah a servant, Zilpah, to be her maid.)

25 But when Jacob woke up in the morning—it was Leah! "What have you done to me?" Jacob raged at Laban. "I worked seven years for Rachel! Why have you tricked me?"

26 "It's not our custom here to marry off a younger daughter ahead of the firstborn," Laban replied.

27 "But wait until the bridal week is over, then we'll give you Rachel, too—provided you promise to work another seven years for me."

28 So Jacob agreed to work seven more years. A week after Jacob had married Leah, Laban gave him Rachel, too.

29 (Laban gave Rachel a servant, Bilhah, to be her maid.)

30 So Jacob slept with Rachel, too, and he loved her much more than Leah. He then stayed and worked for Laban the additional seven years.

31 When the LORD saw that Leah was unloved, he enabled her to have children, but Rachel could not conceive.

32 So Leah became pregnant and gave birth to a son. She named him Reuben, for she said, "The LORD has noticed my misery, and now my husband will love me."

he hath therefore given me this son also: and she called his name Simeon.

34 And she conceived again, and bare a son; and said, Now this time will my husband be joined unto me, because I have born him three sons: therefore was his name called Levi.

35 And she conceived again, and bare a son: and she said, Now will I praise the LORD: therefore she called his name Judah; and left bearing.

33 She soon became pregnant again and gave birth to another son. She named him Simeon, for she said, "The LORD heard that I was unloved and has given me another son."

34 Then she became pregnant a third time and gave birth to another son. She named him Levi, for she said, "Surely this time my husband will feel affection for me, since I have given him three sons!"

35 Once again Leah became pregnant and gave birth to another son. She named him Judah, for she said, "Now I will praise the LORD!" And then she stopped having children.

In Focus

Scenario #1

Ever since September 11, 2001, Andre had not been able to get back to his former six-figure income. At one time he had been the top sales representative at a well-known insurance company, but after the World Trade Center attack, the bottom fell out, and Andre's career and his six-figure income fell right with it. Andre was forced to give up his comfortable lifestyle. He had lost it all—his lakefront condo, his Mercedes S-class automobile, expensive vacations, everything.

For over a year, Andre was unable to find steady work. Hopeless and helpless, he was at his wits' end. As Andre came home from yet another disappointing interview, he fell to his knees and prayed like he had never prayed before. He prayed for mercy, wisdom, and strength.

Scenario #2

Sherry wanted a child so badly. She was 34 years old, and her biological clock was ticking *loudly*. The problem: she had no husband; she didn't even have a good prospect in mind. The solution: adoption. How hard could it be? There were tons of babies out there that needed good homes, or so she thought. For months Sherry interviewed with adoption agencies and was set to adopt the child of a teenage mother. After the young mother gave birth to a healthy 7 lb., 2 oz. baby boy, everything went well; and three days later Sherry, an elated new mom, brought her son home.

About a month later, while she was preparing to bathe Jason, the phone rang. It was Sherry's attorney.

To Sherry's dismay, her newborn son's biological father had surfaced and was contesting the adoption. Apparently, the young girl had lied and falsified documents stating that her then-unborn child's father was deceased. How could this be happening? Sherry had done everything right. How could the young girl have lied about something so important? What was going to happen now?

Very few people reach adulthood without experiencing some sort of disappointment. It's a universal human experience. In the end you may even wonder if waiting a long time for something you desire is really worth it. In today's lesson we will review the story of Jacob and his marriage to Leah and see how God worked in the midst of deceit to increase the family of promise.

The People, Places, and Times

Biblical Marriage Customs. According to Hebrew custom, a man who had no sons often adopted a male heir, giving him his daughter as wife. The adopted son was required to labor in the household. Some scholars speculate that Laban may have intended to adopt Jacob; but then sons were born to Laban, and they perhaps grew jealous (Genesis 31:1).

Padanaram. This is the region of Mesopotamia from the Lebanon Mountains to beyond the Euphrates River on the north and Damascus on the south. This region comprised much of what is known as the Fertile Crescent, which stretched from the Persian Gulf to the Amanus Mountains.

Laban. He was the son of Bethuel, brother of Rebekah, father of Leah and Rachel. Laban was a member of the segment of the family of Terah that remained in Haran when Abraham and Lot migrated to Canaan.

Source:
Packer, J. I., and M. C. Tenney, eds. *Illustrated Manners and Customs of the Bible*. Nashville, Tenn.: Thomas Nelson Publishers, 1980. 433.

Background

After Jacob stole Esau's birthright blessing, Esau became so enraged that he threatened to kill Jacob, who then fled to his uncle Laban's in Padanaram. Frightened and alone, Jacob stopped on his journey to rest and had a dream reassuring him of God's covenant to his grandfather Abraham. Jacob then proclaimed that God was with him. Some consider this encounter Jacob's conversion from a worldly man to a spiritual man. It was only after his dream that he realized he was not alone, but he belonged to God.

As soon as Jacob arrived in the land of his kinfolk, he saw Rachel and was instantly smitten by her beauty. He arranged with Laban, her father, to serve him for seven years if he would allow Jacob to marry Rachel. The seven years of service were finally over.

It is here that today's lesson begins.

At-A-Glance

1. Jacob's Deception (Genesis 29:21–25)
2. Jacob's Disappointment (vv. 26–29)
3. Leah's Retribution—God's Promise Fulfilled (vv. 30–35)

In Depth

1. Jacob's Deception (Genesis 29:21–25)

Today's text continues the theme of family conflict and deception, which characterized Abraham's family. In order to win Rachel as his wife, Jacob agreed to serve Laban for seven years. At the end of this seven-year period, Jacob confronted Laban and asked for Rachel's hand in marriage. Laban agreed and planned a huge celebration to mark the occasion of his daughter's marriage (v. 22). Laban also marked the occasion by giving his daughter a handmaid (personal servant). In biblical times, it was customary for

a father who could afford it to give his daughter a maid of his on the day of her marriage. It was thought that the maid formed a link between the old household and the new. Laban went through all the formalities associated with presenting his daughter to her husband, but little did Jacob realize that the trickster had been tricked.

2. Jacob's Disappointment (vv. 26–29)

One can only imagine Jacob's disappointment when he discovered that his new bride was Leah and not his beloved Rachel. No doubt Laban's deception was made possible through the use of veils and Jacob's heavy drinking at the feast. Laban was quick to remind Jacob of the traditions, rights, and privileges afforded the firstborn child (v. 26). Ironically, Laban's ruse established an explicit link with Jacob's own deception of Esau. Jacob had deceived his own father, and now he himself was deceived. Now Jacob must have realized how Esau felt, and at the same time recognized himself in Laban's action. As a result Jacob agreed to work an additional seven years for his intended bride, Rachel, without so much as a quarrel or a quiver regarding Laban's deception.

3. Leah's Retribution—God's Promise Fulfilled (vv. 30–35)

Unfortunately, despite Laban's deception, Jacob still loved Rachel more (v. 30). In the midst of deception and disappointment, Leah cried out to the Lord, who had mercy upon her in her suffering and immediately blessed her with four sons born in succession (more than any of Jacob's other wives). Nevertheless, Leah, whom Jacob hated, was fruitful, while Rachel, his beloved, remained barren. In so doing, as time went on, the conflict between Rachel and Leah intensified.

How blessed we are to serve a God who does not insist on perfection. In today's text we see that despite all the lies, deception, and disappointments, God is able to work in disappointing situations to bring about good.

Source:
Exell, Rev. Joseph Samuel, and Rev. Thomas H. Leale Exell. *The Preacher's Complete Homiletic Commentary on the First Book Moses Called Genesis*. Grand Rapids, Mich.: Baker Books, 1996.

Search the Scriptures

1. Why did the Lord allow Leah to have children, but not Rachel (Genesis 29:31)?

2. Jacob and Leah's first children were _____, _____, _____, and _____ (vv. 32–33, 35)

Discuss the Meaning

1. Like Jacob, many people struggle with disappointment as a result of deception by someone they trust. How did Jacob's deception and disappointment still bring about God's good?

2. What effect did Rachel's barrenness have on her feelings toward Leah?

3. If something important doesn't turn out the way you had hoped, what are some helpful ways to deal with your disappointment?

Lesson in Our Society

Romans 8:28 says, "All things work together for good to them that love God." Given today's lesson on disappointment and deception, ask volunteers to share a story of positive results that grew out of disappointing circumstances.

Make It Happen

Everyone experiences disappointment at some time or another. This week, write a letter of encouragement or send an uplifting card to someone you know who's feeling disappointed.

Follow the Spirit

What God wants me to do:

_____

_____

Remember Your Thoughts

Special insights I have learned:

_____

_____

More Light on the Text

Genesis 29:21–35

21 And Jacob said unto Laban, Give me my wife, for my days are fulfilled, that I may go in unto her.

Jacob was the one who took the initiative to raise the subject of his wife; this shows his eagerness to con-

summate the marriage. It also suggests reluctance on Laban's part toward the union, inasmuch as he really did not need to be reminded that Jacob's years of service were completed. As in other occurrences of the word "give" (Heb. *yahab*, **yaw-HAB**) in Genesis, there is a sense of desperation and urgency.

22 And Laban gathered together all the men of the place, and made a feast.

Since there was no verbal reply from Laban recorded, it is difficult to know what he was thinking. His silence may indeed suggest his reluctance to give Rachel over at this point. Nevertheless, he invited his neighbors to celebrate the wedding banquet, or marriage "feast" (Heb. *mishteh*, **mish-TEH**). These feasts commonly lasted seven days, but the length appears to have varied according to the circumstances of the bridegroom.

23 And it came to pass in the evening, that he took Leah his daughter, and brought her to him; and he went in unto her.

Laban's deception of Jacob was possible because the bride usually entered the marriage chamber veiled, the veil being so long as to conceal not only the face but much of the body as well (cf. Genesis 24:65). Because the bride was always veiled, the bride's chamber was generally dark, and, of course, Leah was brought to Jacob in the evening, the deception might easily have gone undetected by Jacob.

24 And Laban gave unto his daughter Leah Zilpah his maid for an handmaid.

It was customary at marriages for the bride's father to give her a large present, often a handmaid who became her confidential servant (Genesis 24:59, 61). It is interesting to note that however unpleasant Laban was to Jacob, he still treated his daughters generously by presenting them each with a handmaid.

25 And it came to pass, that in the morning, behold, it was Leah: and he said to Laban, What is this thou hast done unto me? did not I serve with thee for Rachel? wherefore then hast thou beguiled me?

Imagine Jacob's shock. Seven years he had toiled and worked for Rachel, and now he found he had married her less-than-beautiful sister instead. Jacob's feelings are hinted at rather than analyzed. The question "What is this thou hast done unto me?" expresses Jacob's astonishment. The unthinkable had happened! In accusing Laban of deceit, Jacob was in fact condemning himself. The deceiver had himself been deceived. Jacob argued with Laban, but he could do nothing to alter the situation.

26 And Laban said, It must not be so done in our country, to give the younger before the firstborn.

Laban gave the reason for his action: it is not customary to put the younger sibling before the firstborn. Note that derivatives of the Hebrew term for "younger" (*tsa`iyr*, **tsaw-EER**) and "firstborn" (*bekiyrah*, **bek-ee-RAW**) have been used to describe the relationship of Esau and Jacob (Genesis 25:23, 32; 27:19, 32). Remember that Jacob, the younger, had put himself before the firstborn Esau, so there was a certain poetic justice in Laban's deception of Jacob. However, Laban's attempt to justify his action was weak. He could have made this known to Jacob much earlier.

27 Fulfil her week, and we will give thee this also for the service which thou shalt serve with me yet seven other years.

However unwilling Jacob may have been to continue celebrating his marriage to Leah, he could not opt out: He was isolated and without family support. Laban's only concession was that Jacob could take Rachel immediately as a second wife, and Jacob did want to marry Rachel. Realizing he had Jacob trapped, Laban then added another harsh demand: after marrying Rachel, Jacob had to work for Laban another seven years.

28 And Jacob did so, and fulfilled her week: and he gave him Rachel his daughter to wife also.

Jacob agreed to comply with Laban's terms. Rachel was the wife of Jacob's affections and intentions. Although taking of a second wife was not Jacob's original intent, his dream of having Rachel was not a dream denied but a dream deferred.

29 And Laban gave to Rachel his daughter Bilhah his handmaid to be her maid.

The abrupt end of the conversation indicates Jacob's grudging acceptance of Laban's new terms. Both Laban and Jacob did the correct thing: Jacob completed the first week of celebrations, and Laban gave him Rachel. And Rachel, like her sister Leah, was given a maid (cf. Genesis 29:24).

30 And he went in also unto Rachel, and he loved also Rachel more than Leah, and served with him yet seven other years.

Jacob did indeed serve another seven years, but unlike the first, they are not said to have "seemed unto him but a few days" (Genesis 29:20). Rather, they were days of sorrow and strife within the new family, as the account of the patriarchs' births now makes plain.

31 And when the LORD saw that Leah was hated, he opened her womb: but Rachel was barren.

Throughout the Old Testament motherhood is seen as the crowning joy of a woman's life, as it is in most traditional societies. Both Leah and Rachel had trials, though of different kinds. Because "the LORD saw"—the eye of the Lord was upon the sufferer—Leah bore four sons to Jacob. The word "hated" (Heb. *sane'*, **saw-NAY**) means "to be cold, loveless, and indifferent." It appears here in stark contrast to Jacob's love for Rachel in the previous verse. The verse is a significant statement of God's concern for the rejected. When the Lord "sees," He often acts decisively in defense of the weak and oppressed (cf. Genesis 6:5; 7:1; 18:21; 31:12; Exodus 2:25; 4:31).

32 And Leah conceived, and bare a son, and she called his name Reuben: for she said, Surely the LORD hath looked upon my affliction; now therefore my husband will love me.

This verse describes the birth of the first of Jacob's 12 sons, Reuben. The name Reuben is a wordplay on the Hebrew phrases *ra'ah* ("he saw") and *ben* ("son"), which are derived from the phrase *'elohiym ra'ah `oniy* ("God hath seen my affliction"), a sentiment spoken by Jacob about his treatment by Laban (Genesis 31:42).

33 And she conceived again, and bare a son; and said, Because the LORD hath heard that I was hated, he hath therefore given me this son also: and she called his name Simeon.

Leah named her second son Simeon, whose name is linked to the Hebrew term *shama'* (**shaw-MAH**), meaning "heard." Simeon's name shows that on the one hand God had heard Leah's prayers, but on the other hand, despite the birth of Reuben, the situation between Leah and Jacob had probably not improved.

34 And she conceived again, and bare a son; and said, Now this time will my husband be joined unto me, because I have born him three sons: therefore was his name called Levi.

Here Leah again explained her choice of name in terms of her forlorn hope that her husband would love her. In naming her son Levi, Leah showed that her desire was for love to finally bind her and Jacob together.

35 And she conceived again, and bare a son: and she said, Now will I praise the LORD: therefore she called his name Judah; and left bearing.

Like the names of her first three sons, Judah (meaning "praise") is a name that acknowledges the Lord's mercy toward Leah, but here she makes no mention of her hope for improved relations with her husband. Instead, she seemed to have accepted her situation and decided to praise God and be thankful. No explanation is provided for why Leah stopped bearing children. It goes without saying that of all the polygamous marriages in Genesis, Jacob's was told in the most detail. Although it was Laban who tricked Jacob into marrying Leah, Jacob, seemed never to have forgiven Leah for being an accomplice in deceiving him in this way. It appears that Jacob always regarded Rachel as his wife and treated Leah and her children as inferior; this distinction that persisted throughout the history of the family and culminated in Leah's sons attempted to eliminate Joseph, Rachel's firstborn and Jacob's favorite, from the family.

Daily Bible Readings

M: Assurance of God's Protection
Psalm 91
T: The Kiss That Brought Tears
Genesis 29:1–12
W: Seven Years of Labor
Genesis 29:13–20
T: The Trickster Is Tricked
Genesis 29:21–25
F: Seven More Years
Genesis 29:25–30
S: Four Sons Born to Leah
Genesis 29:31–35
S: Rachel's Sons
Genesis 30:22–24; 35:16–21

TEACHING TIPS

October 28
Bible Study Guide 9

1. Words You Should Know

A. Passed Over (Genesis 33:3) *'abar* (Heb.)—To lead along or lead through.

B. Drove (v. 8) *machaneh* (Heb.)—Encampment, army, or troop.

C. Blessing (v. 11) *berakah* (Heb.)—An offering, gift, or present to gain goodwill.

2. Teacher Preparation

Unifying Principle—Family Reunion! Relationships can sometimes seem irreparably broken, but that doesn't have to be if the parties involved show a desire and a willingness to be reconciled. We can seek to restore broken relationships through prayer.

A. Prepare to teach today's lesson by reading The People, Places, and Times, as well as the Background, In Depth, and More Light on the Text sections.

B. Refer to Day 20 of Rick Warren's *The Purpose Driven Life* for a study on reconciliation.

C. Make a list of some modern-day examples of family conflict as seen in the movies or television (e.g., the 1980 classic *Ordinary People*, the 1996 Spike Lee movie *Get on the Bus*).

D. *Optional:* Rent copies of the suggested movies above to give yourself and the class further insight on matters of family conflict and reconciliation.

3. Starting the Lesson

A. Write the following open-ended sentences on the chalkboard:

  1. Reconciliation is _____.
  2. Forgiveness is _____.

B. Start class with prayer.

C. Allow the class to fill in the blanks.

D. Relate the high points of Day 20 from Rick Warren's *The Purpose Driven Life.*

4. Getting into the Lesson

A. To round out the discussion on reconciliation versus forgiveness, ask a volunteer to read the In Focus section.

B. Instruct the class to share some of their answers to the open-ended question above.

C. Briefly go over the Background information and read today's Focal Verses. Engage the class in a discussion about family conflict and resolution using the In Depth section as a guide.

D. Reinforce today's AIM for Change by stating that even though some conflicts may seem irreparable, that does not have to be the case if the parties involved have a willingness to reconcile.

5. Relating the Lesson to Life

A. Review the Lesson in Our Society section and engage the class in a brief discussion on the two movies, *Ordinary People* and *Get on the Bus*, which deal with the issues of family conflict and racism.

B. Encourage class participants to talk about a personal conflict going on in their lives.

C. Brainstorm with the class on ways they could act as peacemakers between separated or estranged persons or groups.

6. Arousing Action

A. Explore the personal cost of reconciliation by asking yourself the question, "What has my lack of forgiveness or reconciliation cost me?"

B. Issue the Make It Happen challenge by asking the class to take the steps necessary to move toward forgiveness and reconciliation this week.

C. Instruct the class to prepare for next week's teaching by reading the Daily Bible Readings and completing lesson 10 for November 4 from the *Precepts For Living® Personal Study Guide.*

D. Close the class in prayer.

Worship Guide

For the Superintendent or Teacher
Theme: Esau and Jacob Reconciled
Theme Song: "He Looked Beyond My Faults"
Devotional Reading: Psalm 133
Prayer

ESAU AND JACOB RECONCILED

Bible Background • GENESIS 33
Printed Text • GENESIS 33:1–11   Devotional Reading • PSALM 133

AIM for Change

By the end of the lesson, we will:

KNOW that broken relationships can be restored;

REFLECT on any broken relationship we may currently be in; and

SEEK to restore those relationships starting with forgiveness through prayer.

Keep in Mind

"And Esau ran to meet him, and embraced him, and fell on his neck, and kissed him: and they wept" (Genesis 33:4).

Focal Verses

KJV Genesis 33:1 And Jacob lifted up his eyes, and looked, and, behold, Esau came, and with him four hundred men. And he divided the children unto Leah, and unto Rachel, and unto the two handmaids.

2 And he put the handmaids and their children foremost, and Leah and her children after, and Rachel and Joseph hindermost.

3 And he passed over before them, and bowed himself to the ground seven times, until he came near to his brother.

4 And Esau ran to meet him, and embraced him, and fell on his neck, and kissed him: and they wept.

5 And he lifted up his eyes, and saw the women and the children; and said, Who are those with thee? And he said, The children which God hath graciously given thy servant.

6 Then the handmaidens came near, they and their children, and they bowed themselves.

7 And Leah also with her children came near, and bowed themselves: and after came Joseph near and Rachel, and they bowed themselves.

8 And he said, What meanest thou by all this drove which I met? And he said, These are to find grace in the sight of my lord.

9 And Esau said, I have enough, my brother; keep that thou hast unto thyself.

10 And Jacob said, Nay, I pray thee, if now I have found grace in thy sight, then receive my present at my hand: for therefore I have seen thy face, as though I had seen the face of God, and thou wast pleased with me.

11 Take, I pray thee, my blessing that is brought to thee; because God hath dealt graciously with me, and because I have enough. And he urged him, and he took it.

NLT Genesis 33:1 Then Jacob looked up and saw Esau coming with his 400+ men. So he divided the children among Leah, Rachel, and his two servant wives.

2 He put the servant wives and their children at the front, Leah and her children next, and Rachel and Joseph last.

3 Then Jacob went on ahead. As he approached his brother, he bowed to the ground seven times before him.

4 Then Esau ran to meet him and embraced him, threw his arms around his neck, and kissed him. And they both wept.

5 Then Esau looked at the women and children and asked, "Who are these people with you?" "These are the children God has graciously given to me, your servant," Jacob replied.

6 Then the servant wives came forward with their children and bowed before him.

7 Next came Leah with her children, and they bowed before him. Finally, Joseph and Rachel came forward and bowed before him.

8 "And what were all the flocks and herds I met as I came?" Esau asked. Jacob replied, "They are a gift, my lord, to ensure your friendship."

9 "My brother, I have plenty," Esau answered. "Keep what you have for yourself."

10 But Jacob insisted, "No, if I have found favor with you, please accept this gift from me. And what a relief to see your friendly smile. It is like seeing the face of God!

11 Please take this gift I have brought you, for God has been very gracious to me. I have more than enough." And because Jacob insisted, Esau finally accepted the gift.

2 Cor. 5:18-20

In Focus

I'm sure you've heard the old saying, "You always hurt the one you love." Being hurt by a loved one is as old as the Bible itself. The book of Genesis is replete with instances of loved ones turning on one another. From Cain and Abel, to Joseph and his brothers, to Jacob and Esau, family members repeatedly (and many times intentionally) turned on one another. The question is, how does one begin the healing process? The answer is, through forgiveness and reconciliation.

In Matthew 6:5–15, Jesus says that through prayer we should seek to forgive those who sin against us, and in turn God will forgive us of our sins. While forgiveness may seem like a simple task, reconciliation is more difficult to accomplish. This is because forgiveness may involve only one person, but reconciliation always takes two people.

What is the difference between forgiveness and reconciliation? The dictionary defines "forgiveness" as the ability "to give up resentment against" someone. "Reconciliation" is defined as the act of "restoring friendship or harmony." The Hebrew word for "reconciliation" is *kaphar*, which means "to make atonement for." God is the one who initiated this reconciliation; He moved to reconcile sinful man to Himself (2 Corinthians 5:18–19). On the other hand, man is the object of reconciliation. In many cases, although forgiveness may have occurred, people are unsure of how to go about actually moving toward reconciliation.

In today's lesson, we learn from twin brothers Jacob and Esau that even though relationships may seem irreparably broken, if both parties have a willingness to forgive, reconciliation can begin.

The People, Places, and Times

Edom. Home to the Edomites, Edom was a mountainous region south of Moab that owed its existence to Isaac's son Esau. Even though the nations Edom and Israel came from the same family (Jacob and Esau) and shared a common border, the two were always bitter enemies.

Jabbok River. This is the place where Jacob and Esau met after 20 years of separation.

Exchange of gifts. In biblical times, it was customary to exchange gifts prior to two people meeting. Oftentimes these gifts were related to a person's occupation, which explains why Jacob sent sheep, goats, camels, cows, and bulls as gifts to Esau prior to the two meeting (Genesis 32).

Background

The story of dissention and animosity between twin brothers Jacob and Esau began when Jacob tricked his father, Isaac, into giving him the eldest son's birthright. Esau was furious and threatened to kill Jacob, who ran away to his uncle's home in Haran, where the deception continued. It was there that Jacob met and fell in love with Rachel, but Laban tricked Jacob into marrying the older sister, Leah, instead. How ironic—the trickster had been tricked! Just as Jacob deceived his father and acquired a blessing that was not rightfully his, Laban tricked Jacob into marrying a woman he did not want.

After 20 years, Jacob decided it was time for him to return to his homeland. Jacob's fear came from not knowing whether Esau still hated him enough to kill him or whether the past was forgiven. Our lesson today begins as Jacob sees Esau approaching.

At-A-Glance

1. Jacob Meets Esau (Genesis 33:1–3)
2. Esau Forgives Jacob (vv. 4–7)
3. Jacob and Esau Reconcile (vv. 8–11)

In Depth

1. Jacob Meets Esau (Genesis 33:1–3)

After sending a peace offering to his brother (Genesis 32:21), Jacob looked up to see Esau approaching with 400 men. Upon seeing his brother, Jacob quickly implemented a strategy to present himself and his children to his brother. Jacob lined up his family to present them to Esau. He placed his beloved Rachel and her son Joseph at the end of the receiving line, which indicated that Rachel and Joseph were the most important to him.

The scene is tense. Jacob approached his brother with trepidation and bowed before him seven times. Bowing was considered a sign of reverence and respect, which should have indicated to Esau Jacob's desire to reconcile their relationship.

2. Esau Forgives Jacob (vv. 4–7)

Esau ran to meet his brother and grabbed Jacob, kissed him, and hugged him, and then they both began to shed tears of joy. It would appear that Esau was ready to forgive his brother of his past transgressions. When Esau stepped back and saw Jacob's wives and children, he asked: "Who are all these folk?" (v. 5, paraphrased). Jacob responded by saying that this was his family, and he instructed them to bow before his brother. He had instructed his family to reverence his brother by bowing courteously, so the stage was set for the two brothers to attempt reconciliation.

3. Jacob and Esau Reconcile (vv. 8–11)

Jacob had no reason to expect his brother to forgive him. He had taken advantage of his brother not once but twice, and both times he had done it deliberately. This time Jacob had sent Esau a total of 550 goats, camels, donkeys, cows, and rams (Genesis 32:14–15) to try to obtain favor in his eyes (33:8).

Esau thanked his brother, but graciously declined his gift, saying that he had more than enough to sustain him. It is hard not to admire Esau's graciousness. He could have been angry with his brother and demanded all that he had. Instead, Esau told Jacob to keep what he had for himself.

Nevertheless, Jacob insisted that Esau receive his gift and he compared their reunion to the encounter he had had the night before, when he wrestled with God (32:22–32). The meeting with God and the meeting with his brother run parallel. Just as Jacob dealt with the crippling (and blessing) of God, so, too, was he prepared to deal with the outcome of the meeting with his brother.

The theme of forgiveness and reconciliation in today's text points to Paul's statement in 2 Corinthians 5:17: "Old things are passed away . . . all things are become new." One can only speculate whether Esau waited 20 years to forgive Jacob; but it did take Jacob 20 years to come back home, receive his brother's forgiveness, and start the journey toward reconciliation. Today we are more fortunate

than Jacob and Esau. Because Christ died on the cross to redeem us from our sins, we can expect God's forgiveness and reconciliation based on the promises found in His Word.

Search the Scriptures

1. Esau came to meet his brother _Jacob_ with _400+_ men (Genesis 33:1).
2. Jacob put his wife _Rachel_ and her son _Joseph_ at the end of the group (v. 2).
3. Jacob bowed before Esau _7_ times (v. 3).
4. How did Esau respond to Jacob's offer of gifts (vv. 9–11)? _Keep what you have. I have more than enough._

Discuss the Meaning

1. Many adults who have suffered betrayal or been deceived at the hand of a family member or close friend, have remained estranged from them for many years and have never attempted to restore the relationship. What do you believe the implications are to your spiritual walk if you continue to refuse to forgive? _You will suffer because if you refuse to restore the relation._
2. Many times, an attempt at reconciliation may not be well received by the offended party. What role does forgiveness play in restoring relationships and making peace? _It releases both parties of the offense and the guilt_

Lesson in Our Society

There is a popular quote by noted theologian Miroslav Volf that says, "The goal of pursuit of justice must not simply be that justice happens but that reconciliation also happens." It is easy to overlook the many ills that befall our society. The "isms" of life—racism, classism, sexism—have a unique way of reminding us that we live in a flawed, unjust society. Moreover, as Volf points out, justice without an attempt at reconciliation is an exercise in futility. God delights in forgiving and restoring His people. Although it may be difficult to take on societal ills individually, we Christians are all called to seek God, who forgives us of our sins, and to attempt reconciliation with our family members and fellowman (Matthew 5:21–24). We, too, must be willing to forgive and to restore any broken relationships, knowing that God can work through us in spite of our sinfulness.

Two popular movies that deal with conflict and reconciliation are the 1980 film *Ordinary People* and

Spike Lee's 1996 film *Get on the Bus*. If time permits, engage in a discussion around the main issues of the two films: family conflict (*Ordinary People*) and racism (*Get on the Bus*).

Make It Happen

Unlike forgiveness, which can be a singular act, reconciliation mostly involves two or more people talking to each other, and so it is not easy to achieve. Rather, it is among the most emotionally difficult things people are ever called on to do. Reconciliation is designed to lead individuals to change the way they think about their circumstances. Siblings have to forgive one another, wives have to forgive husbands (and vice versa), victims have to forgive oppressors, and the perpetrators of crimes have to admit their guilt. As part of your devotional time this week, set aside at least 30 minutes for prayer and reflection concerning how you might forgive and be reconciled with an estranged family member, friend, or situation.

Follow the Spirit

What God wants me to do:

_____

_____

Remember Your Thoughts

Special insights I have learned:

_____

_____

More Light on the Text
Genesis 33:1–11

The account of Jacob and Esau's reconciliation is one of the high points in the book of Genesis. The scene describes the long-dreaded meeting between Jacob and Esau. Jacob expected the worst from his brother and for days had been petrified by fears that now proved to be groundless. The time of strife between the two brothers was ending. The reunion brought the exiled Jacob back to his homeland—Canaan. As Jacob's new name (Israel) suggests, he was a transformed man with a new character at peace with God and man.

1 And Jacob lifted up his eyes, and looked, and, behold, Esau came, and with him four hundred men. And he divided the children unto Leah, and unto Rachel, and unto the two handmaids. 2 And he put the handmaids and their children foremost, and Leah and her children after, and Rachel and Joseph hindermost.

The last time Jacob had seen Esau, Esau had been ready to kill him. One can only imagine that Jacob would have been quite apprehensive seeing his brother coming over the horizon with 400 men in tow, but it turned out that he didn't need to be. Jacob divided his children among his wives and handmaids to present them to his brother. The reason for Jacob's arrangement of his family is not stated. Some scholars speculate that it was Jacob's intent to keep his beloved Rachel and her children at the end of the procession so they might stand a better chance of escaping danger at the hand of Esau and his men. Others say he was arranging his family so that he could present them to his brother in order of importance. In either case, the arrangement puts those whom he esteemed the least in front, and those whom he esteemed most in the rear.

3 And he passed over before them, and bowed himself to the ground seven times, until he came near to his brother.

Jacob "passed over" (Heb. *'abar*, **aw-BAR**, meaning "to pass over or march over") ahead of his family to meet Esau because he was indeed a changed man, as his new name, Israel, indicated. The one-time trickster and deceiver was now taking responsibility and leading the way, triumphing over the fear-dominated person he once was. What's more, as he approached Esau, he bowed down seven times. A sevenfold bowing was an act of respect given from a subordinate to his superior. In bowing before his brother, Jacob was doing more than acknowledging Esau's lordship; he was trying to make amends for the great act of deception whereby he had cheated Esau of his birthright blessing.

4 And Esau ran to meet him, and embraced him, and fell on his neck, and kissed him: and they wept.

Esau responded warmly. How magnanimous was Esau's action toward his brother! There was no hint of the anger or bitterness with which they had parted.

" And Esau ran to meet him, and embraced him, and fell on his neck, and kissed him: and they wept" (Genesis 33:4).

Instead, Esau greeted his long-lost brother with gestures of love and acceptance. Apparently, he had buried all his resentment and forgotten all his injuries, and he now received his brother with warm affection, as indicated by the Hebrew verbs "ran" (Heb. *ruwts*, **roots**), "embraced" (Heb. *chabaq*, **khaw-BAK**), "fell" (Heb. *naphal*, **naw-FAL**), and "kissed" (Heb. *nashaq*, **naw-SHAK**). Moreover, as the brothers "wept" (Heb. *bakah*, **baw-KAW**), the two could now begin the process of reconciliation.

5 And he lifted up his eyes, and saw the women and the children; and said, Who are those with thee? And he said, The children which God hath graciously given thy servant. 6 Then the handmaidens came near, they and their children, and they bowed themselves. 7 And Leah also with her children came near, and bowed themselves: and after came Joseph near and Rachel, and they bowed themselves.

Esau "lifted up" (Heb. *nasa'*, **naw-SAW**, meaning "to forgive") his eyes just as Jacob had earlier (v. 1), implying that the healing process between the two brothers had begun. A key phrase here is "hath graciously given," which translates as the Hebrew verb *chanan* (**khaw-NAN**), which suggests that Jehovah had shown favor, or kindness. So great was Jacob's desire to make peace with his brother that he implied that just as God has been gracious enough to show him favor, so, too, would Esau.

Jacob's respectful language in addressing Esau was striking in that Jacob referred to himself as "thy servant" (Heb. *'ebed*, **EH-bed**, meaning "bondservant or slave"). Jacob's opening words hint at his fearfulness and guilty conscience, or at the very least they constitute an attempt to reverse the former relationship between the brothers where Esau, the older brother, became Jacob's servant.

In biblical times, bowing was a sign of respect afforded only to a king. As such, Jacob "bowed" (Heb. *shachah*, **shaw-KHAW**, which means "to show reverence or to pay homage") in concert with the members of his entire family, which indicates that not only was he reverencing his brother, but he was giving his entire family permission to do so as well.

8 And he said, What meanest thou by all this drove which I met? And he said, These are to find grace in the sight of my lord.

Esau showed genuine pleasure at Jacob's success and greeted his wives and children with sincerity. However, Esau seemed a bit baffled by the gift Jacob had sent to him (see Genesis 32:14–21), as evidenced by the use of the word "drove" (Heb. *machaneh*, **makh-an-EH**), a Hebrew term for "encampment, army, or troop." Now Jacob had brought his entire family out to meet Esau. This implies that Jacob may have been using his family as a shield against his older brother's anticipated wrath, and he (Jacob) was now offering his most valuable possession—his family—to him as an act of kindness, as evidenced by use of the word "grace" (Heb. *chen*, **khane**, meaning "favor, charm, or elegance").

9 And Esau said, I have enough, my brother; keep that thou hast unto thyself.

It is impossible not to admire the generous and affectionate disposition of Esau both in his response to Jacob as "brother" (Heb. *'ach*, **awkh**), and his initial refusal to receive anything from him. His refusal implies that even though the brothers should have had a reciprocal relationship, Esau did not hold his brother's past sins against him.

10 And Jacob said, Nay, I pray thee, if now I have found grace in thy sight, then receive my present at my hand: for therefore I have seen thy face, as though I had seen the face of God, and thou wast pleased with me.

Jacob's relief knew no bounds. Here he compared his reunion with Esau to another meeting he had had in which God changed his name (cf. Genesis 32:22–32). Jacob urged his brother to receive his "present" (Heb. *minchah*, **min-KHAW**, meaning "gift, offering, or sacrifice"), which again shows that Jacob wanted to assure his brother that he was a changed man.

11 Take, I pray thee, my blessing that is brought to thee; because God hath dealt graciously with me, and because I have enough. And he urged him, and he took it.

According to custom, accepting a present or gift constituted tangible proof of reconciliation. As a result, Jacob would have still had some uncertainty about whether he had indeed found favor with his brother until Esau accepted his gift. If Esau accepted his gift, Jacob would be able to count on his brother's friendship and forgiveness. Otherwise, there would remain cause for uncertainty and fear. It is for this reason that Jacob insisted that Esau receive his gift, as evidenced by his use of the word "blessing" (Heb. *Berakah*, **ber-aw-KAW**). Here *Berakah* ("blessing") means "an offering, gift, or present to gain goodwill" and implies a sense of shalom (i.e., peace).

Daily Bible Readings

M: Jacob's Prayer
Genesis 32:3–12

T: Jacob's Presents to Esau
Genesis 32:13–21

W: The Brothers Wept Together
Genesis 33:1–4

T: The Gift of Reconciliation
Genesis 33:5–11

F: Their Separate Ways
Genesis 33:12–15

S: An Altar to God
Genesis 33:16–20

S: The Blessedness of Unity
Psalm 133

TEACHING TIPS

November 4
Bible Study Guide 10

1. Words You Should Know

A. Dream (Genesis 37:5) *chalowm* (Heb.)—A prophetic or ordinary dream.

B. Sheaves or sheaf (v. 7) *alummah* (Heb.)—Bound wheat or other crop.

C. Made obeisance (v. 7) *shachah* (Heb.)—To bow before a higher authority.

D. Pit (v. 20) *bowr* (Heb.)—A well used to hold water.

2. Teacher Preparation

Unifying Principle—Interpreting a Call! God has a calling for each of our lives; we may recognize what it is immediately or not be quite clear what it is. As we set out to answer God's call, we should know that we may face obstacles and barriers, but we should trust in God's help to overcome them.

A. Use the background materials on the *Precepts For Living® CD-ROM* and complete lesson 10 in the *Precepts For Living® Personal Study Guide* for this lesson.

B. Study the More Light on the Text, Background, and In Depth sections to gain insight on this familiar text.

C. Pay particular attention to the AIM for Change objectives and ask God for guidance in relating this lesson to your class and the specific issues they face.

3. Starting the Lesson

A. Instruct the class to silently read the In Focus story.

B. Ask class members to recall a dream or ambition they had as a child or that they have currently. Ask if they did or did not share their dream with others and why or why not.

C. Reinforce the AIM for Change objectives by explaining that Joseph shared his dream and perhaps faced some of the challenges the class mentioned in their own situations.

4. Getting into the Lesson

A. Begin class by placing three columns on a handout, flip chart, or chalkboard. Label the first column

"Event," the second column, "Result," and the third column, "Hidden Blessing."

B. As the class reads the Bible text, identify each event (Joseph tells his dream), its result (the brothers dislike him), and the hidden blessing (Joseph's journey to his destiny begins). Continue this process for the rest of the lesson. Refer to The People, Places, and Times section for additional background as needed.

5. Relating the Lesson to Life

A. Review the Discuss the Meaning questions.

B. Ask the class what they can do to nurture each other's dreams while avoiding jealousy.

6. Arousing Action

A. If possible, consider using a gift inventory to help class members determine their gift areas for use in the church.

B. Engage the class in a discussion of the differences between a call, a dream, and a wish.

C. Consider using time during class or having the students spend personal devotion time during the week to identify their calling by asking themselves a series of questions: (1) What am I passionate about doing? (2) What skills come easily to me? (3) After thinking about my pastor's vision, what do I see as the most serious need in the church? (4) How can my skill and passion help to meet the need I have identified?

Worship Guide

For the Superintendent or Teacher
Theme: Joseph's Dream
Theme Song: "I Surrender All"
Devotional Reading: Psalm 70
Prayer

JOSEPH'S DREAM

Bible Background • GENESIS 37
Printed Text • GENESIS 37:5–11, 19–21, 23–24, 28   Devotional Reading • PSALM 70

AIM for Change

By the end of the lesson, we will:

STATE the reasons that Joseph's brothers were jealous of him and what they did as a result;

CONSIDER whether or not God has a calling for our lives and, if so, what that calling might be; and

IDENTIFY barriers to answering God's call and take steps to overcome them.

Keep in Mind

"And Joseph dreamed a dream, and he told it his brethren: and they hated him yet the more" (Genesis 37:5).

Focal Verses

KJV **Genesis 37:5** And Joseph dreamed a dream, and he told it his brethren: and they hated him yet the more.

6 And he said unto them, Hear, I pray you, this dream which I have dreamed:

7 For, behold, we were binding sheaves in the field, and, lo, my sheaf arose, and also stood upright; and, behold, your sheaves stood round about, and made obeisance to my sheaf.

8 And his brethren said to him, Shalt thou indeed reign over us? or shalt thou indeed have dominion over us? And they hated him yet the more for his dreams, and for his words.

9 And he dreamed yet another dream, and told it his brethren, and said, Behold, I have dreamed a dream more; and, behold, the sun and the moon and the eleven stars made obeisance to me.

10 And he told it to his father, and to his brethren: and his father rebuked him, and said unto him, What is this dream that thou hast dreamed? Shall I and thy mother and thy brethren indeed come to bow down ourselves to thee to the earth?

11 And his brethren envied him; but his father observed the saying.

37:19 And they said one to another, Behold, this dreamer cometh.

20 Come now therefore, and let us slay him, and cast him into some pit, and we will say, Some evil beast hath devoured him: and we shall see what will become of his dreams.

21 And Reuben heard it, and he delivered him out of their hands; and said, Let us not kill him.

NLT **Genesis 37:5** One night Joseph had a dream, and when he told his brothers about it, they hated him more than ever.

6 "Listen to this dream," he said.

7 "We were out in the field, tying up bundles of grain. Suddenly my bundle stood up, and your bundles all gathered around and bowed low before mine!"

8 His brothers responded, "So you think you will be our king, do you? Do you actually think you will reign over us?" And they hated him all the more because of his dreams and the way he talked about them.

9 Soon Joseph had another dream, and again he told his brothers about it. "Listen, I have had another dream," he said. "The sun, moon, and eleven stars bowed low before me!"

10 This time he told the dream to his father as well as to his brothers, but his father scolded him. "What kind of dream is that?" he asked. "Will your mother and I and your brothers actually come and bow to the ground before you?"

11 But while his brothers were jealous of Joseph, his father wondered what the dreams meant.

37:19 "Here comes the dreamer!" they said.

20 "Come on, let's kill him and throw him into one of these cisterns. We can tell our father, 'A wild animal has eaten him.' Then we'll see what becomes of his dreams!"

21 But when Reuben heard of their scheme, he came to Joseph's rescue. "Let's not kill him," he said.

37:23 So when Joseph arrived, his brothers ripped off the beautiful robe he was wearing.

37:23 And it came to pass, when Joseph was come unto his brethren, that they stript Joseph out of his coat, his coat of many colours that was on him;

24 And they took him, and cast him into a pit: and the pit was empty, there was no water in it.

37:28 Then there passed by Midianites merchantmen; and they drew and lifted up Joseph out of the pit, and sold Joseph to the Ishmeelites for twenty pieces of silver: and they brought Joseph into Egypt.

24 Then they grabbed him and threw him into the cistern. Now the cistern was empty; there was no water in it.

37:28 So when the Ishmaelites, who were Midianite traders, came by, Joseph's brothers pulled him out of the cistern and sold him to them for twenty pieces of silver. And the traders took him to Egypt.

In Focus

Having grown up in the community, Kathy always felt that the church could provide greater encouragement and assistance to area residents who were facing occupational struggles because of a lack of educational opportunities. Her deep passion for this issue led her to approach the pastor and the church board. They were now granting her the opportunity to start a mentoring and literacy project for teen moms. Kathy knew that God had prepared her for this task because He had blessed her in college and graduate school. He had led her to a number of organizations that could support this vision, and now she was presenting the idea to the church and requesting volunteers to make the dream come true.

Her first hint that there was a problem came at the meeting when she realized people were questioning why young women, many of whom were unmarried, would be allowed to receive services in this church. Were the people she had known all her life really saying that the church should be providing assistance only to its members? Were they saying that Kathy should not head this project because she was under 30 years old? Were they really accusing her of pushing a personal career agenda and saying that her work was not valid community outreach? Kathy was stunned as she sank back in her seat. She knew God had given her the talent to help people and the opportunity to do so. How was she to act on her calling in the face of such opposition?

In today's lesson we will examine the content of Joseph's dream and his family's response to it.

The People, Places, and Times

Joseph and His Brothers. Joseph and his 11 brothers were the sons of Jacob (Israel) but had four different mothers (Leah, Rachel, Zilpah, and Bilhah). Reuben was the eldest of all the sons; Joseph was one of the youngest.

It was common for the family to graze animals in nearby valleys. It was also common to encounter groups of merchants on journeys to sell their goods. It was to such a group of merchants that Joseph's brothers sold him into bondage.

Background

Genesis 29–30 tells the story of Jacob's marriage to both Leah and Rachel. Jacob always declared that he loved Rachel. The competition of the two sisters for the love of this man created a rivalry that was always evident in the home. When Rachel was unable to bear sons for Jacob and Leah thought that her time of childbearing was over, they each gave Jacob a maidservant to bear children for Jacob in their stead. These maidservants were Zilpah and Bilhah. This practice was common and is reminiscent of Sarah giving Hagar to bear a son to Abraham.

Jacob's love for Joseph was well known in the family (Genesis 37:3). As a sign of his love, Jacob made Joseph a coat of many colors. This can be more accurately described as a colorful, long-sleeved robe that contrasted greatly with the short-sleeved, drab garments worn by most men. Joseph was 17 years old, far from a child and well into manhood, when this gift was given (37:2). In addition, at the time of our lesson text, the other brothers were tending to the difficult task of herding, but Joseph was at home with his father and was sent to the field only to bring back a report of how the work was going.

1. Joseph Tells His Dreams (Genesis 37:5–11)
2. Joseph's Brothers Conspire (vv. 19–21)
3. Joseph's Brothers Act (vv. 23–24, 28)

In Depth

1. Joseph Tells His Dreams (Genesis 37:5–11)

Joseph's status in his father's eyes had always created resentment among his brothers. They resented the preferential treatment Joseph received and the fact that he was known to "tattle" when the brothers were out of order (Genesis 37:2). When Joseph decided to tell his dream, he did not consider how others would accept it. Joseph's dream was from the Lord and was prophetic regarding the future of his family; however, because Joseph was already seen as "different" and "special," his dreams were not seen as signs of providence and blessing. The natural order of things required that the eldest sons be respected and honored by the younger. Joseph was one of the youngest of Jacob's 12 sons even though he was the oldest son of Jacob's favorite wife, Rachel. For Joseph to even hint that he would receive honor from his brothers was not according to tradition and intensified the animosity.

Joseph shared two dreams with his brothers. The first centered on a farming metaphor. In it Joseph and his brothers were gathering and bundling the harvest. Suddenly the bundles took on human qualities. Joseph's sheaf rose to a place and position of authority, while the sheaves that represented the brothers bowed before Joseph's sheaf. In another dream, Joseph saw the sun, the moon, and 11 stars bowing before him. As Jacob states (v. 9), the sun and moon represent Joseph's parents, and the 11 stars are his 11 brothers.

Joseph's brothers envied him. The Hebrew term for envy is *qana'* and means "to provoke to jealous anger." In verse 5, we are told that the brothers hated Joseph. This comes from a Hebrew term *sane'*, which means that they viewed Joseph as an enemy.

2. Joseph's Brothers Conspire (vv. 19–21)

The brothers saw Joseph in the distance as he came to the area where the animals were grazing (Genesis 37:18). This was probably because of Joseph's coat. They also referred to him as "a dreamer." Obviously, they still resented Joseph's vision of their giving honor to him. The term "dreamer" is the same term used later in the Old Testament for Baal, the false god. The word literally means "to be a lord or owner." The brothers not only resented the dream, but they resented the content of the dream.

The plan was to kill Joseph and throw his body in a well or pit. To cover their crime, the brothers would say that a wild beast killed Joseph. No doubt, the brothers thought it would seem plausible that Joseph was unable to defend himself against an attack from wild animals. He had ventured into dangerous territory in search of his brothers and had gone even deeper into danger when he had not found them in the expected area. The dangers of nomads, vandals, and animals were to be expected, but the danger Joseph was to encounter at the hand of his brothers was another matter.

It is interesting that the brothers were concerned with killing Joseph's dream. They seemed less worried that he would be dead than that his dream would be disrupted. Reuben, however, as the oldest son, had some compassion for his half brother and asked that Joseph's life be spared. Reuben's plan was to return at a later time and help Joseph. Reuben was the eldest, but he did not exercise his authority to stop the plot or to intervene to ensure that no harm would come to his brother. He did, however, help save Joseph's life.

3. Joseph's Brothers Act (vv. 23–24, 28)

In this section of the text Joseph's brothers moved to destroy his life and his dream. First, they removed the coat of many colors from his body. In essence, they stripped him of the authority and favor their father had placed in him. This was a symbolic gesture and a necessary action. The coat would later be used to identify Jacob's dead son. This action makes it obvious that Jacob's other sons did not care for their father. They had no consideration for the pain Jacob would suffer at the death of his favored son.

The plot to throw Joseph into an empty well would leave him starving and open to the heat of day, the fierce cold of night, and all other elements with no way of escape. At the last minute, Joseph was pulled from the pit, not because the brothers had a change of heart, but because they seized the opportunity to get rid of Joseph and make money from selling him into slavery. In a sense, Joseph was rescued from a physical pit and delivered into the pit of slavery and abandonment. By these actions we see that the hatred the brothers harbored was only tempered by the greed they possessed.

God was providing a place and a way for Joseph's dream to come true even in the midst of their plotting. No doubt Joseph saw the despair of his life as his brothers fell upon him. He probably began to doubt the dream that God had sent to him as he saw the hatred in his brothers' eyes and was bound and led away by a group of merchants who were traditional enemies to his family. Joseph was soon to learn a key life lesson: we may not see the road we will travel to reach our destiny, but God's promise will be fulfilled.

Search the Scriptures

1. What evidence can be found in the Scripture lesson that contrasts the lives of Joseph and his brothers?
2. What evidence in the text shows a growing resentment among members of Joseph's family?
3. Is there a difference in Jacob's reaction to Joseph's dreams and the reaction of the brothers? If so, what is the difference?

Discuss the Meaning

1. Joseph was called to greatness. Does a person's dream always have to meet with resentment and opposition? Why or why not?
2. What call has God placed in your life? What obstacles are you facing that might hinder fulfillment of that call?

Lesson in Our Society

When God accepts us into the body of Christ, He expects us to fulfill the vision He has for our lives. This is often referred to as a "call." Some people, like Joseph, may recognize that call immediately, while others might find it not so clear. A call is not necessarily to a public ministry such as preaching, but it is a mandate to do work that will help the body of Christ and serve others. Oftentimes, answering the call happens amidst obstacles and barriers that may be discouraging. We must trust God and seek His help in fulfilling the call He has for us.

Can you identify any ministries within your church or community that grew from God's call on individual persons?

Make It Happen

Take time this week to reflect on the call God has for your life. Pray about any obstacles you may be facing and any sidetracks you may have taken. See God's direction in moving forward regardless of the barriers you see before you.

Follow the Spirit

What God wants me to do:

_____

_____

Remember Your Thoughts

Special insights I have learned:

_____

More Light on the Text

Genesis 37:5–11, 19–21, 23–24, 28

Joseph's story is the next biographical installment in the patriarchal trilogy of faith through the descendants of Abraham, Isaac, and Jacob. In this story of call, redemption, and God's grace, God demonstrates that in spite of human arrogance, evil, and error, God's plans will be fulfilled.

5 And Joseph dreamed a dream, and he told it his brethren: and they hated him yet the more.

Before Joseph (Heb. *Yowceph*, **yow-SAFE**, meaning "Jehovah has added") dreamed the dream central to this saga, his brothers hated him for his prior indiscretions as a tattletale (Genesis 37:2). As a young lad of 17, and having been his father's favorite son since he was born in Jacob's old age, Joseph misused his favor and did not use discretion or humility in fostering relationships with his brothers. Not only was he guilty of parental preference, but Jacob (also Israel) demonstrated lack of discretion when he fueled the feud between the brothers by lavishing a visual reminder of his preference toward Joseph—a brightly colored coat. Seething with envy, the brothers hated Joseph greatly.

By the time Joseph had the aforementioned "dream" (Heb. *chalowm*, **khal-OME**, meaning "ordinary or prophetic dream"), hostility between the brothers was at an all-time high. Whereas maturity and wisdom might have prevented Joseph from telling this particular dream to his brothers, Joseph "told" (Heb. *nagad*, **naw-GAD**, meaning "to make known, expound") them, perhaps with immature joy at the thought, that the ones who now hated him would eventually bow down to him. Note that although Joseph dreamed of his promotion, he had not sensed that he was headed into a series of serious demotions on the journey up.

That Joseph's "brethren" (Heb. *'ach*, **awkh**, meaning "brother of same parents, half brother of the same father") hated him all the "more" (Heb. *yacaph*, **yaw-SAF**, meaning "to add, increase, or do again") set the stage for the subsequent events to unfold. Since dreams were regarded as a means of divine revelation and taken very seriously, it is not illogical that the brothers' anger increased, knowing that what Joseph dreamed would most likely come to pass.

6 And he said unto them, Hear, I pray you, this dream which I have dreamed: 7 For, behold, we were binding sheaves in the field, and, lo, my sheaf arose, and also stood upright; and, behold, your sheaves stood round about, and made obeisance to my sheaf.

Joseph called his brothers to "hear" (Heb. *shama`*, **shaw-MAH**) this dream. As the brothers were all binding their sheaves, the inanimate sheaves became animated and represented each brother and tribe. Joseph's sheaf "arose" (Heb. *quwm*, **koom**), implying a position of authority over the others. Furthermore, that his sheaf also "stood upright" (Heb. *natsab*, **naw-TSAB**, meaning "to be set over or to be appointed") let the brothers know that Joseph would again find favor to be promoted into a position of authority over them. In response to Joseph's sheaf being promoted over the others, the brothers' sheaves came "about" (Heb. *cabab*, **saw-BAB**, meaning "to assemble around") Joseph's upright sheaf in "obeisance" (Heb. *shachah*, **shaw-KHAW**, meaning "to bow down before a superior in homage"). This position of superiority and subordination further angered Joseph's brothers.

8 And his brethren said to him, Shalt thou indeed reign over us? or shalt thou indeed have dominion over us? And they hated him yet the more for his dreams, and for his words.

Perhaps compelled by disbelief or driven by anger, the brothers sought clarification concerning Joseph's

dreamed "reign" (Heb. *malak*, **maw-LAK**, meaning "to be or become king or queen") and "dominion" (Heb. *mashal*, **maw-SHAL**, meaning "to rule") over them. Hating Joseph for his prior indiscretions, favor with their father, and divine dreams, the brothers hated him even more for these "words" (Heb. *dabar*, **daw-BAW**).

9 And he dreamed yet another dream and told it his brethren, and said, Behold, I have dreamed a dream more; and, behold, the sun and the moon and the eleven stars made obeisance to me.

Dreaming another dream, Joseph told this dream to his brothers also, not only figuratively naming his brothers as subordinate to him, but telling that the "sun" (Heb. *shemesh*, **SHEH-mesh**), the "moon" (Heb. *yareach*, **yaw-RAY-akh**), and the "eleven" (Heb. *`asar 'echad*, **aw-SAWR ekh-AWD**) "stars" (Heb. *kowkab*, **ko-KAWB**) would bow down to him one after another. Here, the "sun," "moon," and "stars" represent his parents and brothers.

10 And he told it to his father, and to his brethren: and his father rebuked him, and said unto him, What is this dream that thou hast dreamed? Shall I and thy mother and thy brethren indeed come to bow down ourselves to thee to the earth?

When Joseph told this dream to his father in front of his brothers, his father "rebuked" (Heb. *ga`ar*, **gaw-AR**, meaning "reprove") him sharply, perhaps to encourage Joseph to be wise by not further inciting his brothers' obvious anger toward him. Joseph's father seemed mildly offended that his favored son would dream that he and his "mother" (Heb. *'em*, **ame**), who had been dead for some time at this point, would "bow down" (Heb. *shachah*, **shaw-KHAW**, meaning "to bow down before a superior in homage"; this is the same word as "obeisance" in verses 7 and 9) to him in a prostrate position with their faces to the ground or "earth" (Heb. *'erets*, **EH-rets**) in total submission. Or perhaps he was merely perplexed, wondering whether or not Joseph had accurately interpreted the dreams.

11 And his brethren envied him; but his father observed the saying.

Joseph's brothers "envied" (Heb. *qana'*, **kaw-NAW**, meaning "to be jealous") him, but his father "observed" (Heb. *shamar*, **shaw-MAR**, meaning "to give heed") or paid attention or kept in mind what Joseph was "saying" (Heb. *dabar*, **daw-BAW**, same word as "words" in verse 8).

37:19 And they said one to another Behold, this dreamer cometh. 20 Come now therefore, and let us slay him, and cast him into some pit, and we will say, Some evil beast hath devoured him: and we shall see what will become of his dreams.

As the story unfolds, Joseph's brothers conspired with one "another" (Heb. `ach*, **awkh**, meaning the same thing as "brethren" in verse 5) to get rid of this annoying younger brother—dreams and all! They conspired to slay Joseph and "cast" (Heb. *shalak*, **shaw-lak**, meaning "to throw") him into a pit. This pit, or cistern, usually stored rainwater during dry months and held prisoners when empty. The brothers further conspired to fabricate a lie to explain Joseph's absence when they returned to their father's house by saying that some evil "beast" (Heb. *chay*, **KHAH-ee**), or a particularly wild animal, devoured him. To have this be Joseph's fate would certainly aggrieve Jacob (see Genesis 37:31–35), but at least the brothers would be rid of the dreamer.

21 And Reuben heard it, and he delivered him out of their hands; and said, Let us not kill him.

When Reuben, the eldest brother, understood his brothers' diabolical plan, he offered an alternative option that would preserve Joseph's life and possibly win Reuben favor again with his father if he presented Joseph back to him unharmed. To prevent having Joseph's blood on their hands, Reuben "delivered" (Heb. *natsal*, **naw-TSAL**, meaning "to rescue or save") Joseph out of their "hands" (Heb. *yad*, **yawd**, figuratively meaning "strength or power"), or from their plans to kill him.

37:23 And it came to pass, when Joseph was come unto his brethren, that they stript Joseph out of his coat, his coat of many colours that was on him; 24 And they took him, and cast him into a pit: and the pit was empty, there was no water in it.

When Joseph unwittingly showed up where his brothers were herding their flocks, they stript Joseph out of his elaborate gift from his father: the coat of many colors. Taking Joseph's coat was to humiliate him and humble him from walking and talking so proudly as the favored son and dream interpreter. Also, taking the coat to his father would serve as validation of their story. The brothers threw Joseph into the empty cistern and conspired to leave him there to die alone and helpless.

37:28 Then there passed by Midianites merchantmen; and they drew and lifted up Joseph out of the pit, and sold Joseph to the Ishmeelites for twenty pieces of silver: and they brought Joseph into Egypt.

While the brothers sat down to eat, a band of Midianites merchantmen, or slave traders, arrived on the horizon. Knowing the lucrative business of slave trading in the Near East, the brothers took advantage of this opportunity to get rid of Joseph and make a profit. The brothers sold Joseph to a subgroup of Midianites called the Ishmeelites for 20 pieces of silver, an amount typical for a slave and the value of about two years of wages. Persons bought by slave traders seldom saw their freedom and were resold or traded in other areas. The traders eventually "brought Joseph into Egypt."

Source:
Kaplan, Aryeh. The Living Torah. New York: Mozniam Publishing, 1981.

Daily Bible Readings

M: The Favored Son
Genesis 37:1–4

T: The Jealous Brothers
Genesis 37:5–11

W: The Messenger
Genesis 37:12–17

T: The Dreamer
Genesis 37:18–24

F: Sold into Slavery
Genesis 37:25–28

S: A Father's Distress
Genesis 37:29–36

S: A Prayer for Deliverance
Psalm 70

TEACHING TIPS

November 11
Bible Study Guide 11

1. Words You Should Know

A. Pharaoh (Genesis 41:25, 28, 32–35, 37–39) *Par'oh* (Heb.)—A common title for the king of Egypt.

B. Kine (vv. 26–27) *parah* (Heb.)—A cow or heifer.

C. Famine (vv. 27, 30–31, 36) *ra'ab* (Heb.)—Hunger throughout a country.

2. Teacher Preparation

Unifying Principle—A Dream Unfolds! God's purposes are sometimes fulfilled in amazing ways, as shown with Joseph. We are encouraged to look in unlikely places or in unlikely ways to see God at work and remain confident that regardless of the situation, God is working.

A. Study the Focal Verses, More Light on the Text, Background, and In Depth sections to gain insight on this familiar text.

B. Pay attention to the AIM for Change and ask for God's guidance in addressing the faith and personal needs of your class.

C. Complete lesson 11 for November 11 in the *Precepts For Living® Personal Study Guide.*

3. Starting the Lesson

A. Review Joseph's dream from last week.

B. Read the In Focus story. Ask the students to share personal stories of God at work in unlikely places.

C. Either draw a time line or have class members act out a skit of the three major events in Joseph's life for the past 13 years (see the Background section).

4. Getting into the Lesson

A. Use the same pattern as last week to develop a three-column chart that the class will use to identify the events, results, and hidden blessings revealed in this week's study.

B. Pay special attention to The People, Places, and Times and In Depth sections for key points.

5. Relating the Lesson to Life

A. Review the Discuss the Meaning questions.

B. At the end of class, review the chart of today's lesson emphasizing that, as He did in Joseph's case, God is working on our behalf even when others fail us and our situations look bleak.

6. Arousing Action

A. Ask class members for "popcorn testimonies": 15 seconds in which they share an unexpected blessing God has placed in their lives. Begin by giving your own "popcorn testimony."

B. Challenge the class to complete the Make It Happen activities.

Worship Guide

For the Superintendent or Teacher
Theme: Joseph's Dream Began to Come True
Theme Song: "Love Lifted Me"
Devotional Reading: Psalm 105:16–22
Prayer

JOSEPH'S DREAM BEGAN TO COME TRUE

Bible Background • GENESIS 41:25–45
Printed Text • GENESIS 41:25–40   Devotional Reading • PSALM 105:16–22

AIM for Change

By the end of the lesson, we will:

STATE how the dream God gave to Joseph began to come true;

CONSIDER times when God worked in an unlikely way in our lives; and

BE CONFIDENT that God is working in our lives for good.

Keep in Mind

"And Pharaoh said unto Joseph, Forasmuch as God hath shewed thee all this, there is none so discreet and wise as thou art" (Genesis 41:39).

Focal Verses

KJV
Genesis 41:25 And Joseph said unto Pharaoh, The dream of Pharaoh is one: God hath shewed Pharaoh what he is about to do.

26 The seven good kine are seven years; and the seven good ears are seven years: the dream is one.

27 And the seven thin and ill favoured kine that came up after them are seven years; and the seven empty ears blasted with the east wind shall be seven years of famine.

28 This is the thing which I have spoken unto Pharaoh: What God is about to do he sheweth unto Pharaoh.

29 Behold, there come seven years of great plenty throughout all the land of Egypt:

30 And there shall arise after them seven years of famine; and all the plenty shall be forgotten in the land of Egypt; and the famine shall consume the land;

31 And the plenty shall not be known in the land by reason of that famine following; for it shall be very grievous.

32 And for that the dream was doubled unto Pharaoh twice; it is because the thing is established by God, and God will shortly bring it to pass.

33 Now therefore let Pharaoh look out a man discreet and wise, and set him over the land of Egypt.

34 Let Pharaoh do this, and let him appoint officers over the land, and take up the fifth part of the land of Egypt in the seven plenteous years.

35 And let them gather all the food of those good years that come, and lay up corn under the hand of Pharaoh, and let them keep food in the cities.

NLT
Genesis 41:25 Joseph responded, "Both of Pharaoh's dreams mean the same thing. God is telling Pharaoh in advance what he is about to do.

26 The seven healthy cows and the seven healthy heads of grain both represent seven years of prosperity.

27 The seven thin, scrawny cows that came up later and the seven thin heads of grain, withered by the east wind, represent seven years of famine.

28 This will happen just as I have described it, for God has revealed to Pharaoh in advance what he is about to do.

29 The next seven years will be a period of great prosperity throughout the land of Egypt.

30 But afterward there will be seven years of famine so great that all the prosperity will be forgotten in Egypt. Famine will destroy the land.

31 This famine will be so severe that even the memory of the good years will be erased.

32 As for having two similar dreams, it means that these events have been decreed by God, and he will soon make them happen.

33 Therefore, Pharaoh should find an intelligent and wise man and put him in charge of the entire land of Egypt.

34 Then Pharaoh should appoint supervisors over the land and let them collect one-fifth of all the crops during the seven good years.

35 Have them gather all the food produced in the good years that are just ahead and bring it to Pharaoh's storehouses. Store it away, and guard it so there will be food in the cities.

36 And that food shall be for store to the land against the seven years of famine, which shall be in the land of Egypt; that the land perish not through the famine.

37 And the thing was good in the eyes of Pharaoh, and in the eyes of all his servants.

38 And Pharaoh said unto his servants, Can we find such a one as this is, a man in whom the Spirit of God is?

39 And Pharaoh said unto Joseph, Forasmuch as God hath shewed thee all this, there is none so discreet and wise as thou art:

40 Thou shalt be over my house, and according unto thy word shall all my people be ruled: only in the throne will I be greater than thou.

36 That way there will be enough to eat when the seven years of famine come to the land of Egypt. Otherwise this famine will destroy the land."

37 Joseph's suggestions were well received by Pharaoh and his officials.

38 So Pharaoh asked his officials, "Can we find anyone else like this man so obviously filled with the spirit of God?"

39 Then Pharaoh said to Joseph, "Since God has revealed the meaning of the dreams to you, clearly no one else is as intelligent or wise as you are.

40 You will be in charge of my court, and all my people will take orders from you. Only I, sitting on my throne, will have a rank higher than yours."

In Focus

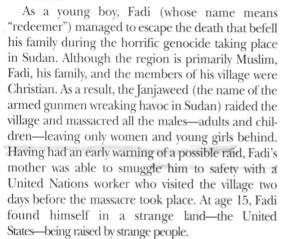

As a young boy, Fadi (whose name means "redeemer") managed to escape the death that befell his family during the horrific genocide taking place in Sudan. Although the region is primarily Muslim, Fadi, his family, and the members of his village were Christian. As a result, the Janjaweed (the name of the armed gunmen wreaking havoc in Sudan) raided the village and massacred all the males—adults and children—leaving only women and young girls behind. Having had an early warning of a possible raid, Fadi's mother was able to smuggle him to safety with a United Nations worker who visited the village two days before the massacre took place. At age 15, Fadi found himself in a strange land—the United States—being raised by strange people.

Now an adult, Fadi left medical school due to lack of funds. His ambition was to return to his homeland. He believed that like his name indicated, his life was spared for a reason; and that reason was to have a positive impact on the lives of the people he left behind in Sudan. Although he knew he could not stop the violence in the region, he could impact the lives of the survivors through medicine.

Unfortunately, Fadi, like most medical students, had a huge student-loan debt and had no way of making his dream of returning to his homeland come to pass. So he began his medical career at a small neighborhood hospital with the thought that he would save up enough money in a year to return to his homeland and set up a clinic. After three years, Fadi was still at the small hospital and had only managed to save $5,000, nowhere near enough to realize his dream.

One evening at church an organization called Doctors Without Borders visited and told of how they visit remote areas in third-world countries and set up hospitals to help fight the HIV/AIDS pandemic. After the service, Fadi approached the guest speaker, introduced himself, and asked if there was any way he could be of service to the organization. Elated at the offer, the speaker told Fadi that the next mission trip was leaving for Sudan in two months and he was more than welcome to join them. All he needed was a passport and a willingness to work hard. Tears filled Fadi's eyes—how could this man have known his dream? Finally he would be able to return to his homeland!

In today's lesson we see how Joseph's prophecy to Pharaoh led to the fulfillment of his dream.

The People, Places, and Times

Egypt. Egypt was a powerful nation. Its long history of rulers, coupled with its abilities in science, math, warfare, and economy, made it one of the greatest civilizations in history.

Ancient prisons. During Joseph's time, a person was placed in prison for an offense and left there for an indefinite and often arbitrary period of time. Release would only be possible if the debt to society or the offended person was paid. Potiphar would never have allowed Joseph to be released. The chief jailer was an official of Pharaoh's government and could dispense judgment as he saw fit. For him to turn all the prisoners and the administration of the prison over to Joseph was extraordinary.

Background

Joseph was only 17 when his brothers sold him into slavery. In today's lesson Joseph is 30 years old (Genesis 41:46). During the 13 years since he had been led away, Joseph had undergone deep hardship but had been given favor and deliverance in each case. Sold as a servant to Potiphar, the captain of the Egyptian army, the young Joseph was given authority over all household affairs. When Potiphar's wife falsely accused Joseph of attempted rape, he was thrown into prison indefinitely. He could have been killed, but the imprisonment was one more step toward fulfilling God's dream for him.

Once Joseph was in prison, the chief jailer recognized Joseph's administrative abilities and placed Joseph in charge of all prisoners and prison affairs. The recognition of Joseph's talent did not get him out of prison, but it did place him in a position to be used of God. When two of Pharaoh's household servants—the butler and the baker—were imprisoned, Joseph was able to interpret their dreams. When his interpretations were proven true, the butler was to mention Joseph to Pharaoh and seek his release; however, once the man was out of prison, he forgot about Joseph and did not keep his promise of help.

In today's lesson, Pharaoh, who not only was the king of Egypt but was, by Egyptian law, considered to be a god, had had a dream that puzzled him. God gave Joseph the ability to interpret Pharaoh's dream to mean that the land would experience seven years of abundance and seven years of famine. Joseph's encounter with Pharaoh was not to be taken lightly, since offering Pharaoh an interpretation that was inaccurate or even disliked by him could have resulted in Joseph's death. Only God could have given the correct answer and assured Pharaoh of its accuracy. Through this event God provided an opportunity for Joseph to find favor with Pharaoh and to give God credit for the interpretation. Joseph went before Pharaoh hoping for his release from prison, but God provided a much greater opportunity. Pharaoh elevated Joseph to a position of power, which is what Joseph himself had dreamed years earlier.

At-A-Glance

1. Joseph Interprets the Dream (Genesis 41:25–32)
2. Joseph Offers Godly Advice (vv. 33–36)
3. Joseph Receives Honor (vv. 37–40)

In Depth

1. Joseph Interprets the Dream (Genesis 41:25–32)

When Pharaoh was unable to gain a satisfactory answer to the dilemma presented by his dreams (Genesis 41:1–24), he called for someone to help him. It was then that the butler recalled Joseph and related the interpretation he received while in prison. Joseph was hastily brought before the king of Egypt. Here was the moment he had awaited, and yet it came so quickly that he barely had time to shave and change. Joseph was prepared, however, because he knew that God was able to deliver the interpretation. Had Joseph suddenly focused on himself and his ability, he may have met with a different outcome. Instead, Joseph relied on God to deliver him and to address Pharaoh's need.

The answer to Pharaoh's dream was a warning to prepare for a famine. Pharaoh had had two dreams, but Joseph realized that they were the same dream and that the repetition addressed the urgency with which Pharaoh should act. The nation of Egypt would have seven years of good crops and plenty, but those would be followed by a seven-year famine of equal proportion. Without this warning, Egypt would have been devastated as a world leader, and the nation would have been dissolved through the death of its people and the vulnerability of its government. The famine, however, was not to involve Egypt alone. All of the surrounding nations would also be in dire need.

It was God who gave Joseph favor to even be believed. Egypt was enjoying prosperity, and that situation would continue for another seven years. There was no indication that anything would change. Apparently God's touch on Pharaoh's heart through the dream made the king want to know the truth and to believe the truth despite what he saw around him. It is a wise leader who looks to the future in faith and is not persuaded by the seasons of plenty that appear to be permanent.

2. Joseph Offers Godly Advice (vv. 33–36)

Joseph not only interpreted the dream, but he gave the leader sage advice. This was a daring move. Generally one only tells a powerful person what the person asks. It was through his boldness in God that Joseph also proceeded to instruct Pharaoh in a plan that would spare the nation and its people. The plan called for finding able leadership, holding 20 percent of the crop in preparation for the lean years, and administering that reserve appropriately. Certainly Pharaoh was appreciative. He had just been hit with the news of the coming famine. He must have been grateful to have a well-thought-out suggestion.

3. Joseph Receives Honor (vv. 37–40)

Joseph was not asking to be made the person in charge. He recognized that Pharaoh did not know him and that he was only a man released from prison for this task with the hope of permanent release. Pharaoh, however, recognized that Joseph did not rely on his own cleverness and wisdom. Instead, Joseph followed God, who had revealed this great truth. By elevating Joseph, Pharaoh acknowledged that God was God! He recognized that the dream had come as a warning from God, and that Joseph had been placed in the right place for the right time to save an entire nation.

Joseph's brothers had mocked him and plotted to take his life because of a dream that would place them in subjection to him. They thought that by killing him they could kill his dream. They believed that if they got rid of him and sold him into slavery, the dream would be suppressed. They had no idea that by trying to keep him down they were moving him toward God's goal for him—the promise would be fulfilled! Now Joseph would be second only to Pharaoh. He would lead a nation and save the people from death and despair because he believed a dream that came from God—a dream that was now coming true.

Search the Scriptures

1. How many times in the text did Joseph give credit to God?
2. How did Pharaoh acknowledge God?
3. To what position was Joseph elevated?
4. What advice did Joseph offer Pharaoh?

Discuss the Meaning

1. How might Joseph's dream have kept him from despair during his captivity and imprisonment?
2. What evidence is there that Joseph was ready for his impromptu meeting with Pharaoh?
3. What accounts for Joseph's sphere of influence during the 13 years after he was held captive?
4. What lessons can Joseph's life teach us about God's ability to work in unlikely places and unlikely ways in our lives?

Lesson in Our Society

Each of us faces circumstances that can lead us to doubt our faith and plunge us into despair. It is important that, like Joseph, we find ways to give godly and practical encouragement to others whose situations seem bleak even when our own circumstance is dire.

We would also do well if we, like Joseph, were to see God at work in unlikely places in our own lives. When we seek God's wisdom in avoiding problems in areas such as our health and finance, we should be proactive and prepared for God to act rather than despondent when we face unexpected crises. When we ask God for a greater understanding of our lifestyle choices or seek Him for advice, we shouldn't be surprised when He fulfills the things He has promised us in His Word. We should, like Joseph, remain confident that God is working on our behalf as we prepare for His next move in our life.

Make It Happen

Take time this week to seek God's wisdom in facing issues. Give God credit for the positive choices you make.

This week deliberately seek someone to encourage despite your own situation. Ask God's help and wisdom in assisting others in seeking God in likely or unlikely places.

Follow the Spirit

What God wants me to do:

_____

_____

Remember Your Thoughts

Special insights I have learned:

_____

_____

More Light on the Text

Genesis 41:25–40

These events in Joseph's life occurred after Joseph's brothers conspired to kill him (Genesis 37:18–24), instead sold him to slave traders heading to Egypt (vv. 25–28), and caused their father to mourn deeply over his favorite son's ill fate (vv. 31–35); Joseph had also been sold to Potiphar, one of Pharaoh's generals. While in the custody of Potiphar (39:1–6), Joseph's apparent favor from God was evident to Pharaoh and all of his officials. His popularity soon ended, however, when he was falsely accused of sexual misconduct and found himself remanded once again to prison (39:6–23). While he was in prison, the Lord again was with him, and Joseph found favor and promotion at the hands of the prison warden. When the pharaoh sent his butler and baker to prison, they were disturbed by dreams, which Joseph accurately interpreted (40:1–23). At the time the pharaoh had his troubling dreams, Joseph was summoned to interpret them (41:1–24).

25 And Joseph said unto Pharaoh, The dream of Pharaoh is one: God hath shewed Pharaoh what he is about to do.

"Pharaoh" (Heb. *Par`oh*, **par-O**, meaning "great house") was also the common title of the king of Egypt. This pharaoh's exact name is unknown, but this is not unusual, as Pharaohs were regarded as gods; his subjects took care not to evoke his name casually. This "one" (Heb. *'echad*, **ekh-AWD**, meaning "a certain one") dream that Pharoah had was particularly disturbing and noteworthy as *God* revealed to Pharaoh exactly what He was about to "do" (Heb. *`asah*, **aw-SAW**, meaning "to accomplish") on Israel's behalf. Both dreams, of the same event, were to prompt the wise to prepare for a terrible famine by managing well their unparalled prosperity.

26 The seven good kine are seven years; and the seven good ears are seven years: the dream is one.

It is clarified here that although the pharaoh dreamed of seven "good" (Heb. *towb*, **tobe**, meaning "pleasant, agreeable") "kine" (Heb. *parah*, **paw-RAW**, meaning "cow, heifer") and of seven good "ears" (Heb. *shibbol*, **shib-bole**, meaning "as growing") to signify seven "years" (Heb. *shaneh*, **shaw-NEH**, meaning "as measure of time") the dream was one dream. This double message, perhaps even on different nights, added weight to the message and suggested gravity to its interpretation.

27 And the seven thin and ill favoured kine that came up after them are seven years; and the seven empty ears blasted with the east wind shall be seven years of famine.

Contrastingly, the dream evolved to include seven "thin" (Heb. *raq*, **rak**, meaning "lean") and "ill favoured" (Heb. *ra`*, **rah**, meaning "bad or evil") cows coupled in the dream with seven "empty" (Heb. *reyq*, **rake**, meaning "worthless") ears of corn "blasted" (Heb. *shadaph*, **shaw-DAF**, meaning "scorched") by the "wind" (Heb. *qadiym*, **kaw-DEEM**, meaning "east wind"). Such conditions would lead to a time of "famine" (Heb. *ra`ab*, **raw-AWB**, meaning "hunger of individuals"). This was particularly disturbing to the pharaoh, as Egypt consistently produced grain irrigated by the Nile floods.

28 This is the thing which I have spoken unto Pharaoh: What God is about to do he sheweth unto Pharaoh.

Joseph took care to humbly and responsibly interpret this dream and report this "thing" (Heb. *dabar*, **daw-BAW**, meaning "speech, word") to the pharaoh. Joseph's content and tone "spoken" (Heb. *dabar*, **daw-BAR**, meaning "declare, warn") told of the urgency and calamity forthcoming.

29 Behold, there come seven years of great plenty throughout all the land of Egypt: 30 And there shall arise after them seven years of famine;

and all the plenty shall be forgotten in the land of Egypt; and the famine shall consume the land;

Joseph interpreted the "plenty" (Heb. *saba'*, **saw-BAW**, meaning "satiety") as a season of prosperity and abundance throughout the "land" (Heb. *'erets*, **EH-rets**, meaning "earth") and for all of Egypt's inhabitants. Conversely, these seven years of satiety would be followed by seven years of famine so severe and devastating that the prosperity would be "forgotten" (Heb. *shakach*, **shaw-KAKH**, meaning "forget, to cease to care"). The people would not care to reminisce about the good old days as the severity of the seven years of famine would indeed "consume" (Heb. *kalah*, **kaw-LAW**, meaning "be complete") or completely destroy life, cattle, and crop.

31 And the plenty shall not be known in the land by reason of that famine following; for it shall be very grievous.

Joseph interpreted the pharaoh's dream to mean that a season of plenty would not be "known" (Heb. *yada'*, **yaw-DAH**, meaning "to perceive and see, find out and discern") or discerned by "reason" (Heb. *paniym*, **paw-NEEM**, meaning "presence, person") of such a severe and all-consuming famine that could only be described as "grievous" (Heb. *kabed*, **kaw-BADE**, meaning "very oppressive").

32 And for that the dream was doubled unto Pharaoh twice; it is because the thing is established by God, and God will shortly bring it to pass.

The repetition of a dream indicated its urgency. Therefore, that Pharaoh's dream was "doubled" (Heb. *shanah*, **shaw-NAW**, meaning "to repeat, do again") "twice" (Heb. *pa`am*, **PAH-am**, meaning "at one time . . . at another"), in essence, in a dream sequence that happened over and over, this proved that indeed these were prophetic dreams from God about the things He had "established" to occur "shortly" or "bring to pass" (Heb. *`asah*, **aw-SAW**, meaning "to do, accomplish") soon.

33 Now therefore let Pharaoh look out a man discreet and wise, and set him over the land of Egypt.

In preparation for these seasons of feast and famine, the pharaoh was instructed to participate in God's plan for Joseph's liberation and Israel's preservation. The pharaoh was instructed to "look out" (Heb. *ra'ah*, **raw-AW**, meaning "to see, perceive, consider") a "discreet" (Heb. *biyn*, **bene**, meaning "understanding") and "wise" (Heb. *chakam*, **khaw-KAWM**, meaning "wise ethically and religiously, wise in administration") man to "set" (Heb. *shiyth*, **sheeth**, meaning "to appoint") over these affairs during the feast and the famine. Such a man, or prophet, would be one who could see disaster and remedy. Joseph was one such man.

34 Let Pharaoh do this, and let him appoint officers over the land, and take up the fifth part of the land of Egypt in the seven plenteous years.

Additionally, the pharaoh was to appoint officers to implement the plans to stave off the famine by storing up a "fifth part" (Heb. *chamash*, **khaw-MASH**, meaning "to take one-fifth, tax a fifth of") of the harvest during the "plenteous" (Heb. *saba'*, **saw-BAW**, meaning "satiety") years for use during the prophesied famine years. Using this sensible advice, storehouses would be built and the grains would be harvested to sustain the nation during seven years of famine instead of selling the overflow to foreign corn merchants.

35 And let them gather all the food of those good years that come, and lay up corn under the hand of Pharaoh, and let them keep food in the cities.

The plans for survival included instructions to the officials to "gather" (Heb. *qabats*, **kaw-BATS**, meaning "collect, assemble") all the food, particularly the grain harvest, during the approaching seven good years, and to harvest all of the "corn" (Heb. *bar*, **bawr**) under the pharaoh's "hand" (Heb. *yad*, **yawd**, meaning "strength, power") and influence. They would "keep" (Heb. *shamar*, **shaw-MAR**, meaning "guarded") the food in the "cities" (Heb. *`iyr*, **eer**, meaning "a guarded city"), which perhaps refers to designated cities located throughout the region for the rare occasions when famine would be expected.

36 And that food shall be for store to the land against the seven years of famine, which shall be in the land of Egypt; that the land perish not through the famine.

They would have to "store" (Heb. *piqqadown*, **pik-kaw-DONE**, meaning "deposit, supply") the food during these seven years of famine to nourish the land and its inhabitants during the impending seven years of famine. Such measures and initiatives were feasible during times of famine. However, Pharaoh was mindful that the dream was doubly dreamed, so it is not inconceivable that these plans were executed urgently. Otherwise the land and its inhabitants would surely "perish" (Heb. *karath*, **kaw-RATH**, here meaning "to be eliminated") at the hand of famine.

37 And the thing was good in the eyes of Pharaoh, and in the eyes of all his servants.

Joseph's interpretation of this "thing" (Heb. *dabar*, **daw-BAW**, meaning "word") that God had revealed was "good" (Heb. *yatab*, **yaw-TAB**, meaning "pleasing") to Pharaoh. It was good in his "eyes" (Heb. `*ayin*, **AH-yin**, meaning "of mental and spiritual faculties") and in the eyes of his "servants" (Heb. `*ebed*, **EH-bed**, meaning "subjects").

38 And Pharaoh said unto his servants, Can we find such a one as this is, a man in whom the Spirit of God is?

The pharaoh implored of his officials and servants to "find" (Heb. *matsa'*, **maw-TSAW**, meaning "secure, acquire, get") the man who could manage such a nationwide plan of preservation and survival. To call for such a consensus was not unusual. Even the pharaoh understood that such a dream coming to him and being interpreted was an act of God; this was no premonition from any of the other gods worshiped in his kingdom. The pharaoh concluded that a man with the "Spirit" (Heb. *ruwach*, **ROO-akh**, meaning "breath, mind") of "God" (Heb. *'elohiym*, **el-o-HEEM**, meaning "the true God") would be the ideal and only one able to effect the plan.

39 And Pharaoh said unto Joseph, Forasmuch as God hath shewed thee all this, there is none so discreet and wise as thou art: 40 Thou shalt be over my house, and according unto thy word shall all my people be ruled: only in the throne will I be greater than thou.

It was not an uncommon practice for a commoner with skill to be appointed to the king's cabinet, as the pharaoh appointed Joseph as chief overseer. Securing the best man for the job, the pharaoh set Joseph over his house and gave him authority that by his "word" (Heb. *peh*, **peh**, meaning "mouth"), either a mere request or a command, the "people" (Heb. `*am*, **am**, meaning "nation") would be "ruled" (Heb. *nashaq*, **naw-SHAK**, meaning "to be handled") or under Joseph's reign. The pharaoh relinquished to Joseph all power except to the "throne" (Heb. *kicce'*, **kis-SAY**, meaning "seat of honor, authority, power"); only there would Pharaoh reserve veto power and be regarded as greater or more important than Joseph.

Daily Bible Readings

M: In Potiphar's House
Genesis 39:1–6
T: Joseph Refuses
Genesis 39:6–10
W: Revenge
Genesis 39:11–20
T: Pharaoh's Dream
Genesis 41:1–8
F: Joseph the Interpreter
Genesis 41:25–36
S: Second-in-Command
Genesis 41:37–45
S: God's Wonderful Works
Psalm 105:16–22

TEACHING TIPS

November 18
Bible Study Guide 12

1. Words You Should Know

A. Refrain (Genesis 45:1) *'aphaq* (Heb)—This term means "to hold or restrain."

B. Lord of all Egypt (v. 9) *'adown Mitsrayim* (Heb)—Implies a controller or ruler.

2. Teacher Preparation

Unifying Principle—Negative Actions, Positive Results! God is present and at work in our lives at all times. He can take the most negative, bleak circumstance and bring about something good.

A. Read Genesis 42–44 in their entirety to familiarize yourself with the history of Joseph and with the content of this lesson.

B. Create a time line to review the story of Joseph, identifying the high and low points of his life.

C. Review the AIM for Change objectives and highlight specific parts of the lesson that address the objectives.

3. Starting the Lesson

A. Ask a student to open the class with a prayer using the Keep in Mind verse as a guide.

B. Allow a few moments for the class to silently read the In Focus story.

C. Ask class members to share a time when a bad situation actually turned out to be a blessing in disguise.

4. Getting into the Lesson

A. Reinforce the AIM for Change.

B. Place the time line you prepared during your study time on the chalkboard or flip chart.

C. Ask a volunteer to read the Focal Verses in the NLT translation.

D. Point out that even though Joseph's life was filled with negative events that spanned over several years, God still brought about something good out of his tragedy.

5. Relating the Lesson to Life

Allow the students to work in groups of two or three to answer and discuss the questions in the Discuss the Meaning, Lesson in Our Society, and Make It Happen sections for today.

6. Arousing Action

A. Ask volunteers to share a time in their lives when a bad situation was used for good by God.

B. Remind the students to complete the Daily Bible Readings in preparation for next week's lesson. Remind the class how important it is to remember that God is in control of every situation.

C. Close the class in prayer.

How do we explain the good that comes out of terrible circumstances?

Worship Guide

For the Superintendent or Teacher
Theme: God Preserved a Remnant
Theme Song: "Jesus Is All the World to Me"
Scripture: Psalm 85
Prayer

GOD PRESERVED A REMNANT

Bible Background • GENESIS 43:1–45:15
Printed Text • GENESIS 45:1–12   Devotional Reading • PSALM 85

AIM for Change

By the end of the lesson, we will:

EXPLAIN how God used negative events in Joseph's life for a greater good;

REFLECT on times in our lives when God has transformed a negative situation into a good one; and

THANK God in challenging times, knowing He can turn any situation around.

Keep in Mind

"And God sent me before you to preserve you a posterity in the earth, and to save your lives by a great deliverance" (Genesis 45:7).

Focal Verses

KJV

Genesis 45:1 Then Joseph could not refrain himself before all them that stood by him; and he cried, Cause every man to go out from me. And there stood no man with him, while Joseph made himself known unto his brethren.

2 And he wept aloud: and the Egyptians and the house of Pharaoh heard.

3 And Joseph said unto his brethren, I am Joseph; doth my father yet live? And his brethren could not answer him; for they were troubled at his presence.

4 And Joseph said unto his brethren, Come near to me, I pray you. And they came near. And he said, I am Joseph your brother, whom ye sold into Egypt.

5 Now therefore be not grieved, nor angry with yourselves, that ye sold me hither: for God did send me before you to preserve life.

6 For these two years hath the famine been in the land: and yet there are five years, in the which there shall neither be earing nor harvest.

7 And God sent me before you to preserve you a posterity in the earth, and to save your lives by a great deliverance.

8 So now it was not you that sent me hither, but God: and he hath made me a father to Pharaoh, and lord of all his house, and a ruler throughout all the land of Egypt.

9 Haste ye, and go up to my father, and say unto him, Thus saith thy son Joseph, God hath made me lord of all Egypt: come down unto me, tarry not:

10 And thou shalt dwell in the land of Goshen, and thou shalt be near unto me, thou, and thy children, and thy children's children, and thy flocks, and thy herds, and all that thou hast:

NLT

Genesis 45:1 Joseph could stand it no longer. There were many people in the room, and he said to his attendants, "Out, all of you!" So he was alone with his brothers when he told them who he was.

2 Then he broke down and wept. He wept so loudly the Egyptians could hear him, and word of it quickly carried to Pharaoh's palace.

3 "I am Joseph!" he said to his brothers. "Is my father still alive?" But his brothers were speechless! They were stunned to realize that Joseph was standing there in front of them.

4 "Please, come closer," he said to them. So they came closer. And he said again, "I am Joseph, your brother, whom you sold into slavery in Egypt.

5 But don't be upset, and don't be angry with yourselves for selling me to this place. ~~It was God who sent me here ahead of you to preserve your lives.~~

6 This famine that has ravaged the land for two years will last five more years, and there will be neither plowing nor harvesting.

7 God has sent me ahead of you to keep you and your families alive and to preserve many survivors.

8 So it was God who sent me here, not you! And he is the one who made me an adviser to Pharaoh—the manager of his entire palace and the governor of all Egypt.

9 Now hurry back to my father and tell him, 'This is what your son Joseph says: God has made me master over all the land of Egypt. So come down to me immediately!

10 You can live in the region of Goshen, where you can be near me with all your children and grand-

11 And there will I nourish thee; for yet there are five years of famine; lest thou, and thy household, and all that thou hast, come to poverty.

12 And, behold, your eyes see, and the eyes of my brother Benjamin, that it is my mouth that speaketh unto you.

children, your flocks and herds, and everything you own.

11 I will take care of you there, for there are still five years of famine ahead of us. Otherwise you, your household, and all your animals will starve.'"

12 Then Joseph added, "Look! You can see for yourselves, and so can my brother Benjamin, that I really am Joseph!"

In Focus

Sabrina reached into her desk drawer and pulled out a box of tissues and pushed them across her desk to the young woman sitting across from her. Sabrina had been a licensed counselor for the past 20 years. She had heard it all, yet the stories her patients shared about their abusive experiences never ceased to break her heart. Joyce had laid her head down on Sabrina's desk and was crying her eyes out.

Joyce shared with Sabrina that her stepfather began sexually abusing her when she turned 12. When she had finally worked up the nerve to tell her mother, her mother called her a liar and a tramp and threw her out of the house. Joyce had initially stayed with some friends, but by the time she was 15 she was living on the streets, selling her body so that she could pay for an apartment and afford food. When she was 17, a friend took her to a Christian Women's shelter. There Joyce was introduced to Jesus, and she accepted Christ. The staff at the shelter assisted her in earning her GED, and now Joyce was about to graduate cum laude from law school with a job awaiting her as a victim's advocate. Despite everything that had gone wrong in her life, some good could now come out of her misfortune.

"Why do I still feel so empty and unfilled inside, Sabrina? What is it going to take? I've seen and done it all. I've been rejected by my family and my so-called friends have turned on me, and still I made it. But what good has it done? Why have I come through so much to end up feeling so lonely and rejected?" Joyce sobbed.

Sabrina got up from her chair and walked around to the other side of the desk. She put her arms around Joyce and told her to stop crying and to look at her. With tears still streaming down her face, Joyce looked up at Sabrina.

"Joyce, you've told me that you're a Christian. Is that true?" asked Sabrina. Joyce nodded her head yes.

Sabrina went on. "Then I need to ask you something. Do you really believe that you're saved?"

Joyce nodded her head again. "Oh, yes! I know Jesus saved me!"

"Joyce, when Jesus saves us, He forgives our sins too. Do you really think that if Jesus has forgiven you, He wants you to live the rest of your life in fear and shame about your past? Why do you think the Lord has allowed you to use your pain to help others?"

Victimization usually has two outcomes. Victims can identify themselves as victims and choose to spend their time and energy recounting past hurts, blaming themselves, and hating the persons who hurt them. Or they can be reconciled with their past by forgiving others' sins against them and live victoriously. In today's lesson we will see how Joseph lived out his dream despite his meager beginnings.

The People, Places, and Times

Joseph. Joseph was the fourth and final great biblical patriarch (Abraham, Isaac, and Jacob being the first three). Of Jacob's 12 sons, Joseph was his favorite. He was Jacob's eleventh son and the first son of his favored wife, Rachel. This designation by his father, and Joseph's God-given ability to prophesy, was what caused Joseph's older brothers to hate him. Eventually Joseph became a vizier, an officer second only to Pharaoh.

Source:
Packer, J. I., and M. C. Tenney, eds. *Illustrated Manners and Customs of the Bible.* Nashville, Tenn.: Thomas Nelson Publishers, 1980. 30, 122.

Background

Genesis 42–44 provides the necessary backdrop for today's lesson. A famine had struck Egypt and its surrounding countries, including Canaan. Facing starvation, Jacob had heard that there was plenty of food in Egypt and sent 10 of his sons to Egypt to obtain food. When the brothers had arrived in Egypt, they had been brought before Joseph—the vizier or governor—but none of them had recognized him as their brother, whom they had earlier sold into slavery. Joseph, however, had recognized them, but he had chosen to keep his identity hidden from them. Even though the brothers had told Joseph that they were only in Egypt to buy food, Joseph had accused them of being spies. The brothers had insisted on their innocence and told Joseph that they were the sons of Jacob of Canaan, sent by their father in search of food. It was at this point that Joseph had realized that his father might still be alive and had devised a plan to ensure that his brothers returned to him.

The food that Joseph's brothers had purchased from Egypt was now depleted, and Jacob asked his sons to return to Egypt to buy more. When he was reminded that the governor had insisted that Benjamin accompany them, Jacob was hesitant. The governor was already holding his son Simeon as a prisoner. Understandably, Jacob was reluctant to allow his youngest son, Benjamin (Rachel's other son and Joseph's full brother), to accompany the brothers to Egypt. It was only when his son Judah swore that he would protect Benjamin with his life that Jacob relented and allowed his youngest son to accompany his older brothers back into Egypt. Upon the brothers' return to Egypt with Benjamin, Joseph revealed himself to them.

At-A-Glance

1. Joseph Reveals Himself to His Brothers
(Genesis 45:1–2)
2. Joseph Forgives His Brothers (vv. 3–4)
3. Joseph Preserves His Brothers (vv. 5–12)

In Depth

1. Joseph Reveals Himself to His Brothers (Genesis 45:1–2)

Joseph now saw that his brothers had indeed changed. He ordered the Egyptians out of the room. It was at this point that Joseph finally revealed his true identity to his brothers. Any question we may have

had up until this point that Joseph had been cruelly manipulating his brothers is immediately dispelled when we look closely at the genuine poignancy of the moment. Just a short while earlier, Joseph's crying could be heard throughout the house (v. 2). This indicates that this was a highly emotional experience for Joseph. Perhaps it was the sight of his brother Benjamin that moved Joseph to tears. Or perhaps during the meal Joseph may have been testing his brothers to see if they would react jealously when he ordered that Benjamin be given five times the portion of food received by the others (Genesis 43:29–34). Either way, it appeared to Joseph that the men who were now before him had indeed changed. One can only speculate that Judah's offer to become a hostage rather than have Benjamin imprisoned may have touched Joseph's heart. It had been Judah's idea to sell Joseph into slavery years earlier. In either case, the text is clear that Joseph was unable to continue to hide his identity from his brothers.

2. Joseph Forgives His Brothers (vv. 3–4)

We are told that Joseph's brothers were "troubled at his presence" (v. 3). Their fear is understandable. The 17-year-old boy they had so cruelly abused and sold for silver now stood before them fully grown and holding the power of life and death in his hands. Their little brother was now a powerful ruler who could, with a single utterance, order them all killed. However, years of slavery and abuse had not hardened Joseph; vengeance was not what Joseph had in mind. It is important to note that Joseph's brothers had done nothing to earn his mercy; it was the grace of God at work in Joseph's life that allowed him to spare the lives of the very men who had wronged him.

As we navigate through life's painful and often unfair situations, it's important that we display an attitude of victory and not harbor a victim mentality. Rather than seeking to assign blame and exact punishment against those who have mistreated us, we should ask God to help us remain strong and faithful when things look bleak, knowing that God can bring about something good out of our pain.

3. Joseph Preserves His Brothers (vv. 5–12)

After reassuring his brothers that he bore no animosity toward them, Joseph declared that his being in Egypt was by the hand of God; it was not a result of his brothers' ill will toward him. Certainly the sins his brothers had committed against him were grievous, but Joseph was able to see that God's plan exceeded their evil purpose.

Joseph not only saw that it was God who had sent him to Egypt, but he also understood that his being in Egypt was a part of God's plan to preserve the seed of Abraham, Isaac, Jacob, and now Joseph himself! When Joseph declared, "God sent me before you to preserve you a posterity" (v. 7), he was declaring that God wanted this family to continue. At this time, Joseph probably did not understand just how his family would continue, but he did realize that he was being used by God to preserve his family.

Search the Scriptures

Fill in the blanks.

1. "And he wept aloud: and the _egyptians_ and the house of Pharaoh heard" (Genesis 45:2).

2. "And Joseph said unto his brethren, I am Joseph; doth my _father_ yet live?" (v. 3).

3. "Now therefore be not _grieved_, nor angry with yourselves, that ye sold me hither: for God did send me before you to preserve life," (v. 5).

4. "For these two years hath the _famine_ been in the land: and yet there are five years, in the which there shall neither be earing nor harvest" (v. 6).

Discuss the Meaning

1. Why do you think it is so difficult to try and understand God's greater purpose during difficult times?

2. Discuss the similarities between Joseph and Jesus as "suffering servants."

3. Read today's Devotional Reading Scripture, Psalm 85, and compare the psalmist's meaning in the context of today's lesson.

Lesson in Our Society

I once read a sign that said, "I never knew God was all I needed until God was all that I had." Surely, Joseph could identify with such a sentiment. Modern-day saints would do well to study the life of Joseph and to emulate his steadfast confidence in God. In whatever state we find ourselves, God is there and worthy of our praise. He has a plan and a purpose in

everything He allows us to go through. Whether we understand His plan or not, we must never forget that God is all we need.

Make It Happen

Our ability to respond to stressful and painful situations as victors, rather than victims, depends on our ability to recognize the hand of God in every situation. This week, set aside time each day for prayer. Begin to thank God for the challenging times you have faced and to allow Him to use you for His glory.

Follow the Spirit

What God wants me to do:

_____

_____

Remember Your Thoughts

Special insights I have learned:

_____

_____

More Light on the Text

Genesis 45:1–12

True to God's word, Egypt knew seven good years of prosperity and plenty (Genesis 41:46ff.), just as Joseph had said when he interpreted the dreams. As the good years ended and the seven years of famine began, all of the lands around Egypt experienced the famine, but Egypt did not. When the people began to feel the effects of the famine, they pleaded with the pharaoh to feed them. He directed them to do whatever Joseph instructed (vv. 53–57). Among the persons seeking food from the storehouses under Joseph's rule were 10 of his brothers (42:1ff.); he recognized them, but they did not recognize him. More humble in his position now, Joseph showed his brothers favor without revealing his identity and lavishly provided for his family. Each time the brothers returned to restock grain, they were laden with gifts from an anonymous donor (43:1–44:34).

1 Then Joseph could not refrain himself before all them that stood by him; and he cried, Cause every man to go out from me. And there stood no man with him, while Joseph made himself known unto his

brethren. 2 And he wept aloud: and the Egyptians and the house of Pharaoh heard.

Joseph was unable to restrain his emotions any longer or withhold his identity from his brothers or those overseers who "stood" (Heb. *natsab*, **naw-TSAB**, meaning "to be or set over") with him in this famine management program. He cried out to dismiss them all except his "brethren" (Heb. *'ach*, **awkh**, meaning "brother of same parents"). In this private moment, while also wanting to avoid shaming his brothers, Joseph wept aloud out of his loving devotion to his brothers in this dire situation. Joseph wept so uncontrollably that the pharaoh and the inhabitants "heard" (Heb. *shama`*, **shaw-MAH**, meaning "to listen to") their wise, prudent, discerning leader weeping.

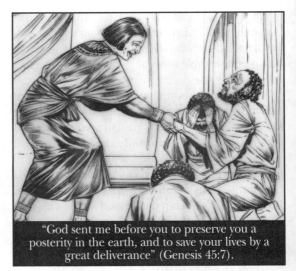

"God sent me before you to preserve you a posterity in the earth, and to save your lives by a great deliverance" (Genesis 45:7).

3 And Joseph said unto his brethren, I am Joseph; doth my father yet live? And his brethren could not answer him; for they were troubled at his presence.

Revealing who he was, Joseph immediately inquired of his father's condition and whether or not he was indeed alive. Even though the brothers had told him earlier that his father was indeed alive when they knew Joseph as an Egyptian official, perhaps Joseph was asking this of them again with the emphatic love and longing of a son inquiring about his father. Whatever his reasons, Joseph's brothers could not "answer" (Heb. *`anah*, **aw-NAW**, meaning "respond, speak") him because they were "troubled" (Heb. *bahal*, **baw-HAL**, meaning "disturbed, alarmed, terrified")—most likely they were terrified by Joseph's "presence" (Heb. *paniym*, **paw-NEEM**, meaning "face") and position. They surely remembered the occasion years ago when they had hated Joseph so and had conspired to kill him.

4 And Joseph said unto his brethren, Come near to me, I pray you. And they came near. And he said, I am Joseph your brother, whom ye sold into Egypt.

But Joseph, overjoyed to see them, called them to "come near" (Heb. *nagash*, **naw-GASH**, meaning "approach") him to get a closer look at the brother they had indeed "sold" (Heb. *maker*, **maw-KAR**, meaning "to sell or give up") to the Midianites when he was only a teenage boy. He did not remind them of their foolish indiscretion and diabolical plot to

embarrass them, but rather to impress upon them his true identity.

5 Now therefore be not grieved, nor angry with yourselves, that ye sold me hither: for God did send me before you to preserve life.

In a gracious turn of events, the same Joseph who had been left to die and eventually sold into slavery encouraged his brothers not to be "grieved" (Heb. *`atsab*, **aw-TSAB**, meaning "to hurt, vex") by his revelation and not to be "angry" (Heb. *charah*, **khaw-RAW**, meaning "kindled, incensed") against themselves for past actions. Joseph assured the brothers that God had used those very events to send him ahead of the famine "to preserve life" (Heb. *michyah*, **mikh-YAW**, meaning "sustenance") for them now. Although his brothers' actions had not been a dream, Joseph the dreamer interpreted them as critical to God's redemptive plan for Israel!

6 For these two years hath the famine been in the land: and yet there are five years, in the which there shall neither be earing nor harvest. 7 And God sent me before you to preserve you a posterity in the earth, and to save your lives by a great deliverance.

For the first two years of the famine, Joseph had kept his identity a secret. He now told his brothers that the ensuing five years would produce no "earing" (Heb. *chariysh*, **khaw-REESH**, meaning "ploughing time") and no harvest, assuring them that God, not their angry jealousy, had sent him ahead of the famine to "preserve" (Heb. *suwm*, **soom**, meaning "to put, place, or set") them a "posterity" (Heb. *sh'eriyth*, **sheh-ay-REETH**, meaning "remainder, remnant"), or portion, during the seven good years. Because Joseph had been established as overseer, their lives were going to be preserved as an act of great deliverance from an all-consuming famine then upon the land. This famine would most likely be the result of a severe drought.

8 So now it was not you that sent me hither, but God: and he hath made me a father to Pharaoh, and lord of all his house, and a ruler throughout all the land of Egypt.

Joseph again assured his brothers that even their actions had been part of God's act of redemption; because of it God had established him as a "father" (another title for a viceroy or vizier or official spiritual advisor) and "lord" (Heb. *'adown*, **aw-DONE**, meaning "firm, strong, master") over Pharaoh's immediate household and "ruler" (Heb. *mashal*, **maw-SHAL**, meaning "to have dominion") over all inhabitants of the land during the famine.

9 Haste ye, and go up to my father, and say unto him, Thus saith thy son Joseph, God hath made me lord of all Egypt: come down unto me, tarry not: 10 And thou shalt dwell in the land of Goshen, and thou shalt be near unto me, thou, and thy children, and thy children's children, and thy flocks, and thy herds, and all that thou hast:

Joseph then charged his brothers to hasten and return to their father with the good news of his life, appointment, and favor. Joseph sent his brothers away with this message of hope and celebration. He invited his brothers and father to come and dwell in the land of Goshen (Heb. *Goshen*, **GO-shen**, meaning "drawing near"), a region in northern Egypt east of the lower Nile, where they could be near him and enjoy all the rights, privileges, and protection suitable to his kin. (The Children of Israel lived there from the time of Joseph to the time of Moses.) Joseph's invitation extended to his brothers' "children" (Heb. *ben*, **bane**, meaning "son, grandson, child, member of a group"), their "flocks" (Heb. *tso'n*, **tsone**, meaning

"small cattle and flocks"), and their "herds" (Heb. *baqar*, **baw-KAWR**, meaning "large cattle and oxen").

11 And there will I nourish thee; for yet there are five years of famine; lest thou, and thy household, and all that thou hast, come to poverty.

It would be while they were in Goshen—or more importantly, in this nearer region to Joseph—that he would have a hands-on role to "nourish" (Heb. *kuwl*, **kool**, meaning "to sustain, maintain, contain") all of his brothers' and father's households lest they be overcome with "poverty" (Heb. *yarash*, **yaw-RASH**, meaning "be poor, disinherit") unnecessarily.

12 And, behold, your eyes see, and the eyes of my brother Benjamin, that it is my mouth that speaketh unto you.

Joseph appealed to his brothers to verify his identity, especially Benjamin. Joseph saw that his brothers treated Benjamin very similar to the way they treated him. Joseph urgently needed his brothers to understand that it was he, Joseph, who had "speaketh" to them (Heb. *dabar*, **daw-BAR**, meaning "to declare, promise, warn").

Daily Bible Readings

M: Restoration of God's Favor
Psalm 85
T: Food in Egypt
Genesis 42:1–20
W: Jacob's Difficult Decision
Genesis 43:1–15
T: Dining Together
Genesis 43:16–34
F: Joseph Tests His Brothers
Genesis 44:1–13
S: Judah's Plea
Genesis 44:14–34
S: Brothers Reconciled
Genesis 45:1–15

TEACHING TIPS

November 25
Bible Study Guide 13

1. Words You Should Know

A. Bowed (Genesis 48:12) *shachah* (Heb.)—To prostrate oneself in homage to loyalty or to God.

B. Blessed (v. 15) *barak* (Heb.)—To bend the knee, kneel down, or praise; to pray to, invoke, or ask a blessing of.

2. Teacher Preparation

Unifying Principle—Leaving a Legacy As one generation dies and another is born, what legacies do the younger generations have to look forward to? More than money or personal possessions, faith and Christlike character are worthwhile legacies to pass down, and have far greater value than tangible things.

A. This lesson marks the end of the quarter on Creation. This quarter's three units have traced the story of God's creative power from the creation of the universe, through human creation, to the creation of a covenant people. Before moving on to the next quarter, review the previous 12 lessons and prepare to act out the following activity.

B. Prepare the following activity: Wrap a shoe box with pretty gold or silver wrapping paper. Fill the shoe box with white tissue paper. On top of the tissue paper secure a small hand mirror and place the lid on the box. In addition, prepare several sheets of paper listing the "fruit of the Spirit"—love, joy, peace, longsuffering, gentleness, goodness, faith, meekness, and temperance (Galatians 5:22–23).

3. Starting the Lesson

A. As the students enter the classroom, have soft music playing and turn the lights down low (optional). Place the decorated shoe box in plain view of the entire class.

B. Lead the class in prayer. Tell the class that this is the final lesson for this quarter on God's creative power in which God assures Jacob that His legacy will continue to increase and grow.

C. Next, ask a volunteer to read the In Focus story.

D. Once the story is read, tell the class that today they will be attending a funeral; remove the lid from the shoe box and instruct the class to file past the mock casket (shoe box) and pay their last respects to the dearly departed. After the students have viewed the "body" and as they return to their seats, hand each person the list containing the fruit of the Spirit attributes.

E. After everyone is seated, invite the class to spend time detailing the legacy they hope to leave based on the Christlike attributes they hold in their hand.

4. Getting into the Lesson

A. Reinforce the AIM for Change objectives for today's lesson and summarize for the class the Background and The People, Places, and Times sections.

B. Ask several volunteers to read the Focal Verses aloud based on the At-A-Glance outline.

C. After reading the text, test the students' knowledge of the passage by answering the Search the Scriptures and Discuss the Meaning questions.

5. Relating the Lesson to Life

A. Read the Lesson in Our Society section.

B. Ask the students to compare and contrast how the legacies their parents and grandparents handed down to them (good or bad) compare with the legacies they will be able to leave to their children and grandchildren. Remind the class that a legacy can be more than money and possessions.

6. Arousing Action

Encourage the class to find out about their families' legacies by accepting the Make It Happen challenge for this week.

Worship Guide

For the Superintendent or Teacher
Theme: Jacob Blessed His Family
Theme Song: "I Will Bless Thee, O Lord"
Devotional Reading: Psalm 145:1–13
Prayer

JACOB BLESSED HIS FAMILY

Bible Background ● GENESIS 48:8–21
Printed Text ● GENESIS 48:11–19   Devotional Reading ● PSALM 145:1–13

AIM for Change

By the end of the lesson, we will:

EXAMINE the significance of Jacob's blessing to Joseph's sons Ephraim and Manasseh;

IDENTIFY the legacies that have been passed down from our ancestors; and

COMMIT to leaving our own faithful legacy for generations to follow.

Keep in Mind

"And Israel said unto Joseph, I had not thought to see thy face: and, lo, God hath shewed me also thy seed" (Genesis 48:11).

Focal Verses

KJV **Genesis 48:11** And Israel said unto Joseph, I had not thought to see thy face: and, lo, God hath shewed me also thy seed.

12 And Joseph brought them out from between his knees, and he bowed himself with his face to the earth.

13 And Joseph took them both, Ephraim in his right hand toward Israel's left hand, and Manasseh in his left hand toward Israel's right hand, and brought them near unto him.

14 And Israel stretched out his right hand, and laid it upon Ephraim's head, who was the younger, and his left hand upon Manasseh's head, guiding his hands wittingly; for Manasseh was the firstborn.

15 And he blessed Joseph, and said, God, before whom my fathers Abraham and Isaac did walk, the God which fed me all my life long unto this day,

16 The Angel which redeemed me from all evil, bless the lads; and let my name be named on them, and the name of my fathers Abraham and Isaac; and let them grow into a multitude in the midst of the earth.

17 And when Joseph saw that his father laid his right hand upon the head of Ephraim, it displeased him: and he held up his father's hand, to remove it from Ephraim's head unto Manasseh's head.

18 And Joseph said unto his father, Not so, my father: for this is the firstborn; put thy right hand upon his head.

19 And his father refused, and said, I know it, my son, I know it: he also shall become a people, and he also shall be great: but truly his younger brother

NLT **Genesis 48:11** Then Jacob said to Joseph, "I never thought I would see your face again, but now God has let me see your children, too!"

12 Joseph moved the boys, who were at their grandfather's knees, and he bowed with his face to the ground.

13 Then he positioned the boys in front of Jacob. With his right hand he directed Ephraim toward Jacob's left hand, and with his left hand he put Manasseh at Jacob's right hand.

14 But Jacob crossed his arms as he reached out to lay his hands on the boys' heads. He put his right hand on the head of Ephraim, though he was the younger boy, and his left hand on the head of Manasseh, though he was the firstborn.

15 Then he blessed Joseph and said, "May the God before whom my grandfather Abraham and my father, Isaac, walked—the God who has been my shepherd all my life, to this very day,

16 the Angel who has redeemed me from all harm—may he bless these boys. May they preserve my name and the names of Abraham and Isaac. And may their descendants multiply greatly throughout the earth."

17 But Joseph was upset when he saw that his father placed his right hand on Ephraim's head. So Joseph lifted it to move it from Ephraim's head to Manasseh's head.

18 "No, my father," he said. "This one is the firstborn. Put your right hand on his head."

19 But his father refused. "I know, my son; I know," he replied. "Manasseh will also become a great people, but his younger brother will become even greater.

shall be greater than he, and his seed shall become a multitude of nations.

And his descendants will become a multitude of nations."

In Focus

As a child, I loved going to Uncle Sam's house. His home was like a museum. It was chock-full of pictures and family memorabilia. At 90 years old, he was the family patriarch, and even though he was facing death, his mind was sharp as a tack.

One evening Uncle Sam's home health-care nurse called and told me I needed to come to Uncle Sam's bedside right away because he didn't have much longer to be with us. As I sat at his bedside, I realized that Uncle Sam's time with me was ending, and fond memories of a lifetime spent together flooded my mind.

Uncle Sam was great. Even though he never married or had any children, as the eldest child of his only sister I was the apple of his eye. He took me everywhere with him. We visited museums, attended plays, dined at expensive restaurants, and attended fancy parties.

One of my earliest childhood memories is of sitting in a fancy restaurant and being served escargot by a waiter in white gloves. Uncle Sam told me how to hold the metal contraption used to pull the meat out of the snail shell and not get juice all over my pretty dress.

It was Uncle Sam who fostered my love of books and reading. In his home library, there was an entire wall of books. He would let me read anything I could reach. To this day, I still don't believe I've read every book on that wall.

As I sat quietly reminiscing holding his hand the night I was called to his bedside, Uncle Sam opened his eyes and said, "Hi, Niecy, how long have you been here?

"Oh, about 45 minutes," I responded. "How do you feel?"

"For an old man, I've been better," he said softly. "Niecy, I need you to do me a favor."

"Of course, what do you need?"

In a voice just above a whisper he said, "I want you to go into the library, look on the top shelf in the far right corner and bring me that big, gold Bible."

As instructed, I went into the library and found a beautiful gold Bible that I had never seen before and brought it to him.

"Open it, and tell me what you see."

As I opened the Bible, my entire family history was laid out before me. In it were papers that dated back as far as the 1700s, when my ancestors were brought over on slave ships from Africa as indentured servants. Tears began to roll down my face. "Uncle, do you know how rare it is for a Black person to be able to trace their ancestry back this far?"

At its core, a legacy is a summation of a lifetime of achievement and the context in which that lifetime will be remembered. To make that happen, you must pass on more than just your money. You must also find ways to discern your family's values and to pass them on. In today's lesson, we see how Jacob handed down the legacy of his ancestors (God's promise to Abraham) to his grandsons, Ephraim and Manasseh.

The People, Places, and Times

Egypt. Historians date Joseph's arrival in Egypt as a slave around 1876 B.C. During this period, Egypt operated a highly skilled and sophisticated society. They traded in commercial goods with Crete, Palestine, and Syria.

Inheritance. The right of inheritance followed the eldest male in the family. He was expected to be the next head of the family and receive a double portion of the family inheritance (Deuteronomy 21:17; 2 Chronicles 21:2–3). Throughout Scripture the right-hand side is regarded as a place of honor and blessing (cf. Deuteronomy 11:29; Psalm 110:1; Matthew 25:23). The eldest male member of the family placed his right hand upon the eldest male child, thus passing along the inheritance to the next generation.

Allowances were made if the eldest male had only daughters and wanted to preserve his family inheritance. In such a case, his daughters had to marry within their tribe so the inheritance would not be transferred to another tribe (Numbers 36:5–9).

Ephraim. Ephraim, whose name means "doubly fruitful," received the double portion inheritance blessing from his grandfather, Israel, even though he was the younger of Joseph's two sons.

Source:
Packer, J. I., and M. C. Tenney. *Illustrated Manners and Customs of the Bible.* Nashville, Tenn.: Thomas Nelson, 1980.

Background

When Joseph was a young man, his brothers were jealous of him because their father, Jacob, favored Joseph above them. They hated him so much that they sold him into slavery in Egypt and told their father that Joseph was dead (Genesis 37:12–36). Over a period of years, Pharaoh made Joseph governor, and he became a man of power and influence in Egypt (41:42–49). When Joseph's brothers came to Egypt during the time of famine seeking grain, he revealed himself to them. Joseph made peace with his brothers and asked them to return to Canaan and come back to Egypt to live with their entire family, including Jacob, his father (see chapters 45–46).

In today's lesson, Jacob (now called Israel) is 147 years old, practically blind and very feeble. Joseph heard the news that his father's death was imminent, and so he brought his sons before their grandfather to receive their inheritance.

At-A-Glance

1. Joseph Presents His Sons to Be Blessed (Genesis 48:11–13)
2. Jacob Gives His Blessing (vv. 14–16)
3. Jacob Explains His Blessing (vv. 17–19)

In Depth

1. Joseph Presents His Sons to Be Blessed (Genesis 48:11–13)

Jacob was now 147 years old and practically blind. He knew that his life on Earth was ending (Genesis 47:29–31). Realizing that his father was in his last days, Joseph brought his sons to meet their grandfather to say farewell and receive the family blessing.

Jacob expressed his gratitude—he had never expected to see Joseph again, not to mention his grandsons, Ephraim and Manasseh. Jacob may have doubted that his favorite son was alive to carry out his legacy, but God never wavered in His promise to multiply Israel's seed (cf. Genesis 17:8; 28:3; 47:27).

2. Jacob Gives His Blessing (vv. 14–16)

Ephraim and Manasseh were now in position to receive their grandfather's blessing—Ephraim on Jacob's left and Manasseh on the right in the place of honor. They assumed that as the older of the two boys, Manasseh would receive Jacob's right-hand blessing. However, much to Joseph's surprise, Jacob crossed his hands and gave the greater blessing to Ephraim, the younger son. Joseph assumed that his father had unwittingly made a mistake (possibly due to his failing eyesight), and he attempted to correct his father's mistake. But Jacob assured Joseph that he knew what he was doing.

Jacob continued to bless his son by recounting God's divine providence and protection throughout his life. Having adopted both boys as his own (Genesis 48:5), Jacob now passed along the family's legacy to multiply and grow.

3. Jacob Explains His Blessing (vv. 17–19)

Joseph's attempt to correct his father's apparent mistake was met by Jacob's calm refusal. Jacob reassured his son that he was well aware of which son received the greater blessing. He told Joseph not to worry because Manasseh's descendants would be a great people, but Ephraim's descendants would go on to become a great nation. This is reminiscent of God's promise that Abraham would become the father of a multitude of nations (cf. Genesis 17:4–6; 35:11).

At the end of our journey of life, each of us needs to know that we have contributed to others and that our life has meaning. What we have contributed to others—to our families and to the larger community—is the legacy we leave. Far more than wealth, Jacob's legacy to his son and grandson was one concerning their destiny. Jacob was chosen by God to continue the patriarchal line that became the nation of Israel. From the beginning, God's promise to make His people a great nation had been handed down from Abraham, to Isaac, to Jacob, and to Joseph; and now it was being handed to Ephraim and Manasseh.

Search the Scriptures

1. What act did Jacob perform to switch the blessing from the elder to the younger son (Genesis 48:14)?

2. Jacob made three requests to God for Joseph's sons. What were they (v. 16)?

3. Why did Joseph want Manasseh to receive Jacob's right-hand blessing (v. 18)?

Discuss the Meaning

1. Why would Jacob bless Ephraim, the younger son? How does this pattern echo previous events in Genesis?

2. How can being left a legacy develop strength, character, responsibility, and competent family leadership?

Lesson in Our Society

Leaving a legacy means far more than bequeathing money and possessions to loved ones. It involves passing on economic success as well as emotional well-being. Healthy families demonstrate confidence and competency in their relationships, financial affairs, and social interactions. Unfortunately, many African American families still struggle when it comes to handing down a legacy of hope to future generations—financial or otherwise. It is not until we meet head-on the challenges, responsibilities, and opportunities of raising strong families, and we begin dealing appropriately with financial success and the importance of passing Christlike values down to our children and grandchildren, that we will begin to leave great legacies for future generations.

Make It Happen

Finding out how one's ancestors fit into world events is part of discovering your personal legacy. Unfortunately, slavery prohibited the majority of Blacks from learning how to read and write, voting, owning property, or legally marrying. Even after that horrific period in our nation's history ended, segregation and Jim Crow laws prevented accurate record keeping, resulting in the vast majority of African Americans' ancestry being lost.

Discovering your family history may seem intimidating, but it's not. The family in today's text was far from perfect, but each generation stood on God's promise of success. It became the duty of each generation to inspire faith and hope by passing on the promise (legacy) to future generations. In the weeks ahead, begin researching your family history. Seek out the elder members of your family and begin to learn about your family's shared values, goals, successes, and even failures. Ask questions. Gather old family photos, and utilize the Internet to search public records such as the federal census and birth and death records. There's an old expression that says, "If you don't know where you've been, you'll never understand how to get where you're going."

Follow the Spirit

What God wants me to do:

_____

_____

Remember Your Thoughts

Special insights I have learned:

_____

_____

More Light on the Text
Genesis 48:11–19

In this final biographical installment in the patriarchal trilogy of faith, Joseph is reunited with his father Jacob (now identified as Israel). This reunion is celebrated and commemorated by Pharaoh with lavish gifts (Genesis 45:16–20), the relocation of the brothers' family and herds (46:8–27), Israel blessing the pharaoh (47:7–10), and Israel's prosperity (47:27–28).

11 And Israel said unto Joseph, I had not thought to see thy face: and, lo, God hath shewed me also thy seed.

Joseph's father, Israel (Heb. *Yisra'el*, **yis-raw-ALE**, meaning "God prevails"), thought that he would never see his beloved and favorite son Joseph again. For years Jacob had lived under the assumption that his son was dead. Now, as he drew close to death, he was not only reunited with Joseph but with Joseph's sons as well. Overwhelmed at seeing Joseph, Israel acknowledged that it was God who allowed him to see even Joseph's "seed" (Heb. *zera*`, **ZEH-rah**, meaning "sowing, offspring") in his two grandsons, Ephraim and Manasseh.

12 And Joseph brought them out from between his knees, and he bowed himself with his face to the earth.

In a show of humility and gratitude, Joseph called his sons "out" (Heb. *yatsa'*, **yaw-TSAW**, meaning "to come forth") from between his knees as he joined them when they "bowed" (Heb. *shachah*, **shaw-KHAW**). Thus, Joseph was paying homage to his father while at the same time giving thanks to God for their reunion and the anticipated blessing to be bestowed on his sons.

13 And Joseph took them both, Ephraim in his right hand toward Israel's left hand, and Manasseh in his left hand toward Israel's right hand, and brought them near unto him.

Establishing the next generation of leaders in this legacy of faith, Joseph took his sons, Ephraim (Heb. *'Ephrayim*, **ef-RAH-yim**, meaning "doubly fruitful") and Manasseh (Heb. *Menashsheh*, **men-ash-SHEH**, meaning "causing to forget"). and brought them to Israel to lay his hand of blessing on them.

14 And Israel stretched out his right hand, and laid it upon Ephraim's head, who was the younger, and his left hand upon Manasseh's head, guiding his hands wittingly; for Manasseh was the firstborn.

Joseph's young sons were the culmination of Israel's life of joy and pain. To fulfill his legacy now, Israel needed to bestow on his grandsons the inheritance promised to their ancestors Abraham and Isaac (Genesis 35:11–12; 48:3–4), thereby instilling hope for the future.

Although Joseph positioned his sons according to their birthright (Ephraim on Israel's left and Manasseh on the right, in the place of honor), Israel instead switched hands and laid his right hand on the younger son, Ephraim, and his left hand upon Manasseh, the firstborn. The placement of the right hand indicated favor and esteem. The younger was given priority over the older, reminiscent of the deathbed blessing Jacob stole from his brother Esau (Genesis 27).

15 And he blessed Joseph, and said, God, before whom my fathers Abraham and Isaac did walk, the God which fed me all my life long unto this day,

By blessing his sons, Israel blessed Joseph with the legacy of faith and inheritance handed down by his ancestors Abraham and Isaac. Israel reminded Joseph that the same God who "did walk" (Heb. *halak*, **haw-LAK**, meaning "to go, walk, come") with

Abraham and Isaac was the same God who had "fed" (Heb. *ra'ah*, **raw-AW**, meaning "tend or feed") Israel throughout his entire life. The Hebrew word *halak*, (or "walk"), as used here, focuses on human walking and not on covenantal relationships. The metaphor is one of a shepherd who leads and protects his flock. Jacob indicated that because his ancestors (Abraham and Isaac) were faithful in their walk with God, so too God's involvement was faithful. He stated that it was God who had "shepherded" him; thus, Israel's blessing acknowledged God's faithfulness to past, present, and future generations.

16 The Angel which redeemed me from all evil, bless the lads; and let my name be named on them, and the name of my fathers Abraham and Isaac; and let them grow into a multitude in the midst of the earth.

Here Israel petitioned the Angel (Heb. *mal'ak*, **mal-AWK**, meaning "messenger or representative") assigned to him (cf. Genesis 31:11), the one who had "redeemed" (Heb. *ga'al*, **gaw-AL**, meaning "to act as kinsman–redeemer, to avenge") him and his household from evil, to again "bless" (Heb. *barak*, **baw-RAK**, meaning "to praise, salute, or adore") his grandsons. Could this have been the same angel that had appeared to Sarah and Abraham (cf. Genesis 18:1–15)? Perhaps it was the same one with whom Jacob had wrestled (32:22–32). By blessing them with the same promise that had been bestowed upon him, his father, and his grandfather, Israel was passing the promise to future generations.

Israel blessed them, asking God that they would "grow" (Heb. *dagah*, **daw-GAW**, meaning "to multiply or increase") into a "multitude" (Heb. *rob*, **robe**, meaning "abundance or greatness") in the "midst" (Heb. *qereb*, **KEH-reb**, meaning "from among a number of persons") of all their people.

17 And when Joseph saw that his father laid his right hand upon the head of Ephraim, it displeased him: and he held up his father's hand, to remove it from Ephraim's head unto Manasseh's head.

Obviously, in Joseph's mind, it was his father's poor eyesight that led him to make the mistake of blessing the younger boy with his right hand and the older son with his left. Therefore, Joseph sought to

"I had no thought to see thy face; and, lo, God hath shewed me also they seed" (from Genesis 48:11).

remove his father's hands and place them correctly. It's ironic that Joseph was inclined to reversing the favor and blessing Israel gave his grandsons even though he himself was favored over his older brothers, as was Isaac over Ishmael and Jacob over Esau. Once again, we see that God continues to amaze us by giving favor according to His plans rather than ours.

18 And Joseph said unto his father, Not so, my father: for this is the firstborn; put thy right hand upon his head. 19 And his father refused, and said, I know it, my son, I know it: he also shall become a people, and he also shall be great: but truly his younger brother shall be greater than he, and his seed shall become a multitude of nations.

Convinced that Israel had made a mistake, Joseph reminded his father which one of his sons was the firstborn. An undaunted Israel, however, refused to switch hands or rescind the blessing. Israel assured Joseph that he knew what he was doing, and he was doing it intentionally. Israel blessed Manasseh to become a great "people" (Heb. 'am, **am**, meaning "nation"), and blessed Ephraim, the younger brother, to be greater still, as his seed would prosper as a "multitude" (Heb. melo', **mel-O**, meaning "fullness, mass, or that which fills"). Thus, the legacy continues.

Daily Bible Readings

M: Bring Your Father
Genesis 45:16–20
T: God's Reassurance
Genesis 46:1–4
W: The Reunion
Genesis 46:28–34
T: A Blessing
Genesis 47:7–12
F: Joseph's Promise
Genesis 47:27–31
S: A Grandfather's Blessing
Genesis 48:8–21
S: The Greatness and Goodness of God
Psalm 145:1–13

DECEMBER 2007 QUARTER-AT-A-GLANCE
God's Call to the Christian Community

The study this quarter looks at various passages in the gospel of Luke as they deal directly or indirectly with the way that God calls the community of faith to live out the purpose for which it was created.

UNIT 1 . GOD'S CALL AT CHRISTMAS AND BEYOND

This unit explores how God's call was received and acted upon by Elisabeth and Zacharias, Mary the mother of Jesus, and Jesus.

Lesson 1: December 2, 2007
Called to Believe!
Luke 1:8–23

Zacharias, a priest on duty in the temple, was visited with the miraculous news that he and his wife Elisabeth would have a son who would be the forerunner of the Messiah. The angel told Zacharias God had heard his prayer. Zacharias questioned in fear and unbelief. And he is rendered speechless until the blessed event took place.

Lesson 2: December 9, 2007
Called to Be a Vessel!
Luke 1:26–38

A young virgin named Mary was visited by the angel Gabriel with the message that she was the chosen vessel through whom the Messiah would make His entrance into the human race. Mary questioned in wonder how such a thing could happen since she was a virgin.

Lesson 3: December 16, 2007
Called to Proclaim!
Luke 1:67–80

Elisabeth had delivered the miracle child of her old age. Suddenly, Zacharias's tongue was loosed and he began to bless the Lord and prophesy concerning his son. The boy grew up spending most of his time in the wilderness, much like Elijah, whose character John appeared to mirror.

Lesson 4: December 23, 2007
Called to Rejoice!
Luke 2:1–14

By order of Augustus Caesar, Joseph and Mary set out for the city of Bethlehem to register with the "census bureau" and pay taxes. The city was crowded—no room at the relatives' homes or at the legendary inn. The couple found themselves in a manger, a place where animals were kept. While there, Mary gave birth to Jesus. What more receptive audience for the news of the birth of the Lamb of God than shepherds? Upon receiving the news from angels, they ran to town and told others.

Lesson 5: December 30, 2007
Called to Witness!
Luke 2:22–35

The days of purification were 40 for the birth of a boy and 80 for the birth of a girl. On the eighth day, boys were to be taken to the temple for circumcision. In the temple are two people: Simeon, who has been promised by God that he would not die until he personally saw the Messiah, and Anna, a widow who had been in the temple for many years. Both blessed the child and the Lord for the privilege.

UNIT 2 . THE AWARENESS OF GOD'S INSTRUCTION

This unit has as its focus the inspiration that comes through God's call on us. Because we have been called to a partnership with God, we can find inspiration to learn, love, pray, and trust.

Lesson 6: January 6, 2008
Inspired to Inquire!
Luke 2:41–52

The caravan of relatives and friends had made an entire day's journey before they realized that Jesus was nowhere to be found among the company of travelers. Mary and Joseph headed back to

Jerusalem and discovered Jesus in the temple in discussion with the scribes—the teachers of the Law. Jesus' distraught parents wanted to know why Jesus had not kept up with them. Jesus' response appears to admonish them that they should have known He'd be somewhere on assignment for His Heavenly Father.

Lesson 7: January 13, 2008
Inspired to Love!
Luke 6:27–36

Israel was under oppression because of its sins and refusal to repent and return to God. To hear Jesus teach on loving one's enemies appeared to be a heresy! However, when one considers the impact of following Jesus' instructions concerning the treatment of one's enemies, it's worth a try.

Lesson 8: January 20, 2008
Inspired to Pray!
Luke 11:5–13

Jesus gave three examples of prayer in the parable of the persistent neighbor (intercession); asking, seeking, knocking (progressively intensifying levels of petition); and the speed and pleasure with which God assigns the work of the Holy Spirit into the lives of those who request it (spiritual development).

Lesson 9: January 27, 2008
Inspired to Trust!
Luke 12:22–34

Jesus points to nature, in all its splendor, as an example of things NOT worried about daily needs such as food, clothing, and shelter. Rather, Jesus admonishes us to focus on the kingdom and kingship of God in our lives—all else follows in divine order.

UNIT 3 . GOD SUMMONS US TO RESPOND!

This unit considers our cooperation with God by responding to the call to labor in extending the community of faith, to repent when we have failed or fallen short, to serve God with humility, and to be dedicated disciples.

Lesson 10: February 3, 2008
Summoned to Labor!
Luke 10:1–12, 17–20

Jesus gave practical advice to the disciples He was sending out to "labor": trust God for provision. He told them to find a spot and stay there; do the work and teach; don't force the Good News on anybody, and if their audience doesn't want to hear it, move on. The disciples followed Jesus' instructions and experienced great success.

Lesson 11: February 10, 2008
Summoned to Repent!
Luke 13:1–9

Jesus mentioned Pilate's slaughter of the Galileans in the temple and the Tower of Siloam falling on and killing others. Jesus compared these events to the Jews' own sinful state. In the parable of the fig tree, the tree should have been destroyed. Someone was merciful and wanted to fertilize it and give it another chance. God offers His people the same consideration when He allows circumstances to enter our lives to bring us to a place of repentance before our sins destroy us.

Lesson 12: February 17, 2008
Summoned to Be Humble!
Luke 14:1, 7–14

Jesus noticed folks vying for places of honor at the home of a well-to-do Pharisee. Jesus told them the parable of an invited guest at a banquet who goes to the seating reserved for more honored guests and gets bumped down. True humility, Jesus says, would be to purposely take the regular seating and be invited to the honored seating. Likewise, true humility would be to do for those who cannot possibly repay us for our kindness and not blow a horn about it (what God does).

Lesson 13: February 24, 2008
Summoned to Be a Disciple!
Luke 14:25–33

Jesus challenges us to seriously consider that to be His disciples, we must love and put God above all others. Jesus makes it plain that we have a purpose to fulfill and when we make the commitment to the fulfillment of that purpose, it's not some romantic notion—count the cost.

THEMATIC ESSAY

HAVE YOU HEARD GOD'S CALL?

by Evangeline Carey

The theme for this winter quarter is "God's Call to the Christian Community" and is taken from the gospel of Luke. As the thread of God's redemptive plan continues to weave through the Old Testament and crosses over into the New Testament, we find that God is still building His kingdom, which will reign forever.

Long ago, God called Abraham to leave the comfort zone of his familiar surroundings and go to a land unknown to him but very well known to an all-knowing God (Genesis 12:1–4). This land was Canaan—today's Israel. Abraham obeyed, and it was counted unto him as righteousness (Genesis 15:6). God delivered on His promise to make Abraham "a great nation." After the timeline moves through 42 generations, God continued to carry out His plan to bring the "Messiah Seed" into the world through the lineage of this great nation (Matthew 1:17).

In the Old Testament, God's chosen people—the 12 tribes of Israel—looked forward to the Messiah's coming. Now in the four Gospels found in the New Testament, the Messiah has come. His name is Jesus—"Emmanuel"; in the Hebrew, "Immanuel"—"God is with us" (Matthew 1:23, NLT). He has come to save His people from their sins.

As told again and again in the history books of the Old Testament, the 12 tribes of Israel went through cycles of covenant disobedience, suffering the consequences of God's punishment or wrath, repenting, and finally being restored by a loving God. In fact, to reestablish their personal, intimate relationship with Him, God used some of their enemies to capture and enslave them. Then, they repented and called out to God for deliverance. Subsequently, God raised up judges to deliver them. As long as the judges ruled over them, they tended to obey their God. However, when the judges died, the cycle began again: "And the chil-

dren of Israel again did evil in the sight of the LORD" (Judges 4:1, KJV).

The gospel of Luke tells how God prepared the way for the Messiah to come, establishing a new covenant, and how God would put His law "in their inward parts, and write it in their hearts" (Jeremiah 31:33, KJV). Luke tells his story of the virgin birth and announces that the Saviour has come (Luke 2:1–7).

A Call to Believe

Jesus has come, and all people are called to believe in Him and what He did for us on the Cross at Calvary. In fact, He is the only way by which we can be saved. His death on the Cross sealed the chasm that had been left between sinful humanity and the Holy God. Only Jesus Christ, the Lamb without blemish, could satisfy our sin penalty, which is death (eternal separation from a Holy God). Only He could pay our sin debt in full. He could have come down off the cross and saved Himself. In fact, He could have refused to go to the Cross at all. However, because of His unconditional love for us, He chose to die. Today He asks us to believe in Him and be saved (John 3:16).

A Call to Be a Vessel

Next, we explore the fact that God is calling the Christian community to be united as one in Christ and become a vessel—an instrument—that He can use. He wants us to show the world that He really is the one and only true God and that He loves us unconditionally. He calls the Christian community to minister to the lost (those who do not know Him as Lord and Saviour) and to the hurting and dying. He uses our minds, hands, and feet to do His work in His way to carry out His will. God uses people who are willing to walk in obedience and let Him carry out His kingdom-building initiative through them.

A Call to Be Faithful

Next we see how Zacharias and Elisabeth served as biblical examples of how to be faithful and trust a God who never lies and is Himself faithful to His own Word (Luke 1:5–25). Even though Elisabeth was barren and much older, she still gave birth to a son, John the Baptist, the forerunner of Jesus Christ. Again, God showed that He is the Sovereign God and has control even over the reproductive cycles of humanity—He can open and close wombs. John the Baptist paved the way for the "Messiah Seed," Jesus Christ, to come and save His people from their sins.

A Call to Proclaim His Word

God also calls believers to proclaim, or tell, His Good News of salvation to lost people. He mandates us to carry out the Great Commission, commanding us to "go and make disciples of all the nations, baptizing them in the name of the Father and the Son and the Holy Spirit. Teach these new disciples to obey all the commands I have given you" (Matthew 28:19–20, NLT). Therefore, at Christmas and beyond, He expects His church to worship Him in Spirit and in truth and to lift up Jesus so He can draw the spiritually lost to Himself (John 12:32). Clearly, the church's agenda is not about conferences, seminars, or programs that lift up people. The Christian community has the answers that so many who are going down the fast lanes of destruction are looking for. We have Jesus Christ as Head of our lives and the love of God operating in us. Consequently, we should reach out to others who need to know God and are still searching. God will give us His power to do what He is calling for us to do.

A Call to Rejoice

Luke tells us in 2:1–14 that God is calling whoever will believe to rejoice in Him both in good and bad times. Through Luke's account of Jesus' birth, God shows us that He is also concerned for the poor and the oppressed, as seen in the announcement of Jesus' birth first to lowly shepherds in the fields (vv. 8-20). We can rejoice because, regardless of our station in life, we can ask God to save us from our sins and to help us mentally, physically, and spiritually—and He will.

A Call to Be Witnesses

As Jesus walked among men for more than 30 years, we find that God spelled out His commands for the Christian community. Luke clarified that God calls the community of faith, the church, to live out the purpose for which she was created. The church was created to show a lost and dying world what it means to live in an intimate, personal relationship with a Holy God. God calls the Christian community, not just at Christmas but beyond, to step up to the plate and be the church—the bride of Christ. He is looking for a holy people (those set apart from evil) to be holy because He is holy (Leviticus 19:2).

Called to Obedience

As we study the life of Christ in Luke's gospel, we must be aware that Jesus Christ was obedient to the Father—He did His Father's will. Indeed, Jesus is our example. He went about His Father's business of teaching the Word (2:41–52). He loved even His enemies unconditionally, and He commanded us to do so as well (6:27–36). Throughout the Gospels, we learn that Jesus labored in the vineyard making disciples. He summoned all believers to do the same because "the harvest is great, but the workers are few" (10:2, NLT). If we are going to be in God's will, we must follow His directives. We must obey the One who is building His kingdom and who will decide who will spend eternity with Him in heaven or with Satan in hell.

Have you heard God's call? It is a call to salvation and to be a doer of His Word. It is a call to be faithful to Him and to our ministries—to be a vessel or instrument He can use in His kingdom-building initiative. Finally, it is a call to rejoice in Him and to obey His Word.

Source:

Life Application Study Bible, NLT. Wheaton, Ill.: Tyndale House Publishers, Inc., 1996.

Evangeline Carey is a staff writer for UMI and has been an adult Sunday School teacher for more than 25 years.

TEACHING THE ADULT LEARNER

by Dr. A. Okechukwu Ogbonnaya, Ph.D.

Because adults come to any learning situation with life experiences that have been fundamental in the formation of their identities, teaching adults is much more complex than teaching children. Christian education for adults is the process whereby, through the Scriptures, the power of the Holy Spirit's light shines upon the experiences of the adult. The purpose of Christian education is to transform the whole life of the adult Christian learner into conformity with the image of God as revealed in Christ.

To accomplish their transformation, adult Christian students need to receive tools and skills with which they can act out their Christian vocations in their everyday lives. Therefore, simply providing ready-made responses will be insufficient. The process of educating Christian adults must engage them at a level where the learning becomes theirs, not merely "what the Sunday School teacher said." The goal of educating Christian adults is to provide a process in which their faith becomes real and experiential.

Therefore, the adult educator must ask, "What does it mean to treat the learner as an adult?" A corollary question is, "What results can be expected from adult learning processes?" Further questions include: Are the students growing in their understanding of their Christian vocation? Are they conforming their everyday walk more and more to their understanding of the life of Christ? Is the education process helping to actualize the spiritual freedom promised in the Scripture?"

In order to develop the possibility of achieving these goals, adult Christian educators are called to practice several things. First, you should model maturity within your classroom, promoting the spirit of Christ by treating your students as adults. There is no substitute for the respect and dignity you offer adult learners. Second, model love and respect within the classroom. Both educators and students need love and respect in teaching and learning. Third, model enthusiasm for what you teach. If your teaching vocation fails to give you joy, chances are it will not be effective. Fourth, model freedom and grace. Adult learners need the sense that they have contributed to the process of their own learning. While time may constrain class participation and sharing, you as the educator are still responsible for creating a comfortable learning context. The worst enemy of effective learning is fear of being dismissed or even ridiculed for saying the "wrong thing."

Given the dynamic and experiential nature of adult learning, one effective way to educate is to ask for the students' experiences as they relate to the lesson. In this way you will discover some of the class members' needs and are better able to minister to them effectively.

There is a false notion in teaching circles that adults enjoy listening to lectures. While lecturing may be appropriate sometimes, it is not usually the most effective way to educate adult learners. Like children, adults appreciate variety in their learning environments. In response to this, you should develop a repertoire of a variety of methods for interacting with your class. No one method is sufficient for all times and circumstances. Only those that enhance a greater understanding of freedom in Christ will lead your students to discover deeper truths from the Word of God and orient them toward Christian action.

Jesus Himself taught by using parables, proverbs, riddles, and direct action, particularly as it related to the miraculous and silence. Sometimes He exhorted; at other times He was confrontational. However, His methods always related to the context and the people with whom He was communicating.

Dr. Ogbonnaya is a former VP of Editorial at UMI, a noted pastor, and speaker.

THE CALL TO COMMUNITY: OUR GOD-GIVEN RESPONSIBILITIES

by Dr. Louis H. Wilson

The phrase, "It takes a village to raise a child," has become a popular quote by politicians, civil service practitioners, and religious and community leaders. It is often used to bring attention to the need to care for our children holistically and to emphasize how communities ought to work together to accomplish common desirable goals.

So, what is a village, a community? What unites the people in these communities? Is an allegiance to common principles and values sufficient to define a community? After all, there are academic communities, gang communities, gay communities, ethnic communities, communities of recovering addicts, assisted-living communities. Many communities subdivide into smaller communities. One could say there are as many communities as there are causes or reasons that people decide to gather as a group.

Each of us belongs to more than one community. Some we choose; some are chosen for us by social or cultural realities. Then there is the calling of God to community.

Called by sovereign decree, Christians are in a community of faith—the family of God. It is our calling to God's community that defines how we embrace other communities.

Long before contemporary societies began discussing the meaning of community, the Bible provided a documented source of an essential task for every community—mutual responsibility. Beginning in the book of Genesis, the offspring of Adam and Eve were the first to demonstrate a breakdown in community. When God asked Cain about his brother, Cain responded, "Am I my brother's keeper?" (Genesis 4:9), we see a clear picture of what community is not.

Cain's sense of responsibility was not lost when he killed his brother. It was not even lost when he failed to bring a sacrifice worthy of the Lord's acceptance. As the text makes clear, the inability to understand community and positively affect those around us begins with a rejection of God, His Word, His grace, and the value He places on another created human being. Cain rejected God and became consumed with jealousy and dissatisfaction (Genesis 4:3–6). The tragic result was that he committed murder.

For the Christian, answering God's call to community begins with God's call to salvation and a call to love others. These two calls are indistinguishable. "Anyone who hates his brother is a murderer, and you know that no murderer has eternal life in him. This is how we know what love is: Jesus Christ laid down his life for us. And we ought to lay down our lives for our brothers. If anyone has material possessions and sees his brother in need but has no pity on him, how can the love of God be in him?" (1 John 3:15–17, NIV). Community begins with God and works its way out in functional and practical ways.

It is interesting to note that there is no word in the Bible that corresponds to our word for community. The closest we have is *chay* (**KHAH-ee**). *Chay* has a double meaning because of two overlapping root stems—to live and have life, and to give or restore life. Being a source of life and restoration is not about theological abstractions, however; it must be worked out in our daily living. The pattern established by the Lord is that our call to service, repentance, Christlikeness, and discipleship happen within specific cultural contexts where nurturing takes place that equips us to be effective kingdom witnesses. The implications of Acts 1:8 cannot be clearer: Reach those closest, reach those near, and then reach those who are far away.

With good intentions, some suggest the diversity represented in heaven implores us to ignore ethnic/cultural differences and embrace a universal call to be a united Christian community; these are lofty thoughts that escape practicality and biblical injunction. Building a loving community to exemplify the redeeming powers of the Lord requires an immediate cultural context. God's call to community and a united body of Christ is not to the exclusion of having an affinity for one's cultural group. The multitudes that bless the Lamb in heaven are not the proverbial American melting pot, people who are culturally indistinguishable. Just the opposite is true. The miracle of heaven is the recognition of diversity (Revelation 7:9). Applauding, recognizing, and embracing distinct communities is consistent with how God intends to further world evangelization (Revelation 14:6). Unless the Lord tarries or calls us home, He does not normally intend that we hurdle over or ignore the communities to which He calls us. Rather, a more consistent and typical pattern is that when we acknowledge Him and the precepts of the kingdom, we begin with our immediate context before moving on to others. Although called to the Gentiles, Paul maintained a concern for his own ethnic group, and rarely do we see him forsaking an opportunity to minister to his own people, the Jews.

Again, can it truly be said we love the God we cannot see and the neighbor who lives afar if we have no sense of commitment to those living within our own social/cultural and biological contexts, next door, and across the street? Can we refuse to meet the needs of specific ethnic, language, and people communities on earth that we will be assigned in heaven and call ourselves effective witnesses?

By God's decrees, communities of faith have irrevocable responsibilities to all of humanity. The call for our devotion and commitment to Him occur within the context of specific social/cultural communities. Nevertheless, being a community is more than recognizing a responsibility and sensitivity for humanity in general and our own specifically. As I like to say. "Without *organism* the church, or any community for that matter, is dead, without *organization* it will die."

Sustaining community is a call to be an organized organism, but not one that does not come with adversities and difficulties. The reality is, this side of heaven, community problems are a given. To rephrase a classic statement: If you ever find the perfect community, don't you join it, because you will mess it up. Effective and life-giving communities don't have to be perfect, just principled.

Look at the believers in the Corinthian church. Precipitated by a misunderstanding of the Cross of Christ and a reliance on worldly wisdom, they indulged in petty arguments about who's who. This was a community of believers burdened down by all kinds of stuff. Some were suing others, engaging in fornication, being discontent in marriage or singleness, behaving in ways that were offensive to others, or judging folk by their own hang-ups. Some even took the Lord's Supper without any sense of obligation for those of a lesser social class. In 1 Corinthians 12, however, Paul says there is a way to take this ragtag community and turn it into an effective instrument for the Lord in society.

If there is one thing that rings clear in chapter 12, it is this: When God assigns a role, play it. There is nothing as disruptive, detrimental, and unproductive than a community where individuals insist on not sticking to their heavenly assigned roles. There is nothing wrong with wanting to do something else, but wait to change your assignments with the understanding that He may need you to remain as you are. As a toe needs a head to know which way to go, a head needs a toe to get there. Both parts are obviously essential and obviously different. Everybody has a part to play, and for the community to advance, it is necessary that all the members play their parts.

In spite of the American and contemporary church's affinity for individual accomplishment and measurable success by worldly standards, God says in His community there is a need for everyone. To suggest otherwise is a direct refutation of God's law and an impediment to the well-being of the community (cf. 12:14–21). Even the less than honorable have a place in God's community. The community of God is for the up and coming, the down and out, and for those counted out.

While it helps to understand what unites a community, the more appropriate questions are: Are we willing to *be* what God has ordained? Are we willing to embrace His community, His world, His people, and are we willing to do it His way?

Dr. Wilson holds a doctorate in leadership and organizational development from the University of Phoenix, and has been involved in church leadership and development for the past 25 years.

PATRICK FRANCIS HEALY

Scholar, Educator, and University President

After the Civil War, the 10-year period known as the "Reconstruction" was a remarkable time in African American history. W.E.B. DuBois described this time as the "mystic years." It was a period of unprecedented upward mobility for African Americans and quite likely was the first time in American history when the country lived up to its constitutional mandate of "life, liberty and the pursuit of happiness" for all of its citizens.

During these "mystic years," public schools were opened up to Black people. Newly freed Blacks donated what they could to help build schools for Black children. Several colleges and universities for Blacks were also founded, including Atlanta University, Fisk University, Hampton Institute, Howard University, St. Augustine's College, Tougaloo College, and Tuskegee Institute.

The ballot box was opened to all males, regardless of race. It was discovered that Blacks outnumbered Whites in five southern states: Mississippi, South Carolina, Louisiana, Alabama, and Florida. In these and other southern states, Black men were elected to public office. Several Blacks were elected to the House of Representatives, and in 1880, Blanche K. Bruce was suggested as a possible vice presidential candidate.

One of the bright stars of this period was James Francis Healy. A mulatto, James was born in Macon, Georgia. His father, Michael Morris Healy, was a White slave owner; and his mother, Elisa, was Healy's Black household servant. Elisa, to whom Michael referred as his "trusty woman," bore him 10 children.

In 1837, Michael Healy, his "trusty woman," and their children moved north. There, Healy enrolled three of his children, two sons (James and Patrick) and a daughter, in the Franklin Park Quaker school in Burlington, New York. James, the eldest son, went on to become the first African American to be ordained a Roman Catholic priest. He was later named the bishop of Portland, Maine, the first Black bishop in America.

Patrick followed in his older brother's footsteps, graduating from Holy Cross College and becoming a Jesuit priest. With the help of some of his father's wealthy friends, Patrick went abroad to continue his education. He attended the Louvain in Belgium where on July 26, 1865, he became the first African American to earn a doctorate.

After completing his education, Patrick returned to the United States. Nine years later on July 31, 1874, he was inaugurated as president of Georgetown University, the first African American to head a predominantly white university. His nine-year tenure (1874–1882) was so successful that today he is still referred to as the "second founder of Georgetown." Patrick A. Healy was an outstanding Christian, scholar, educator, and administrator.

Sources:

Adams, Russell L. *Great Negroes: Past and Present.* Chicago: African American Images, 1984.

Bennett Jr., Lerone. *Before the Mayflower: A History of Black America.* Chicago: Johnson Publishing, 1988.

Ebony Pictorial History of Black America, Vol. 2. Chicago: Johnson Publishing Company, 1971.

Franklin, John Hope. *From Slavery to Freedom.* New York: McGraw-Hill, 1947.

TEACHING TIPS

December 2
Bible Study Guide 1

1. Words You Should Know

A. Lot (Luke 1:9) *lagchano* (Gk.)—To obtain or receive a divine allotment. A lot was a stone or some other object used to determine who would be selected for certain assignments.

B. Dumb (v. 20) *siopao* (Gk.)—Temporary loss of speech, sometimes attributed to an emotional upset. This happened to Zacharias.

2. Teacher Preparation

Unifying Principle—Surprising Opportunities People find it hard to believe that the miraculous could happen to them. What evidence do we have that miracles can happen in our lives? God promised Elisabeth and Zacharias a miracle, and God fulfilled that promise.

A. Pray and ask the Lord for insight while preparing to teach this lesson.

B. Begin to jot down some of the promises found in the Bible that God made and fulfilled.

C. Study The People, Places, and Times, Background, In Depth, and More Light on the Text and begin to take notes on how they relate to the AIM for Change and Unifying Principle.

3. Starting the Lesson

A. Begin class with prayer, thanking God for bringing the students and the teacher through another week.

B. Have the class silently read the In Focus story. Ask the class if they believe in miracles. Solicit a few examples from the class.

C. Explain that although many adults may find it difficult to believe in miracles, miracles can still happen to them.

4. Getting into the Lesson

A. Invite the class members to close their eyes and listen while you read the Scripture text. After the reading, ask the class to identify one word or phrase that touches their hearts. Encourage them to elaborate about how these words and/or phrases are significant to them.

B. Review the Search the Scriptures questions.

5. Relating the Lesson to Life

A. Break the class into two groups and assign each group a Discuss the Meaning question, allowing 10–15 minutes of discussion time.

B. Reassemble the class and ask each group to give a brief synopsis of their group's discussion question.

C. Instruct the class to reflect on the Lesson in Our Society section.

6. Arousing Action

A. Have the class read the Make It Happen section. Challenge the students to recommit themselves to a ministry of prayer. Include this challenge in a closing prayer.

B. If you have a *Precepts For Living® Personal Study Guide*, provide copies of lesson 2 for December 9th to prepare students for next week's Bible study.

Worship Guide

For the Superintendent or Teacher
Theme: Called to Believe!
Theme Song: "Standing on the Promises"
Devotional Reading: Psalm 66:1–4, 16–20
Prayer

CALLED TO BELIEVE!

Bible Background • LUKE 1:5–25
Printed Text • LUKE 1:8–23 Devotional Reading • PSALM 66:1–4, 16–20

AIM for Change

By the end of the lesson, we will:

CONSIDER the story of God's miraculous gift to Zacharias and Elisabeth;

REFLECT on the difference between the responses given by Zacharias and Elisabeth; and

GIVE thanks for the miracles God has worked in our lives.

Keep in Mind

"And, behold, thou shalt be dumb, and not able to speak, until the day that these things shall be performed, because thou believest not my words, which shall be fulfilled in their season" (Luke 1:20).

Focal Verses

KJV

Luke 1:8 And it came to pass, that while he executed the priest's office before God in the order of his course,

9 According to the custom of the priest's office, his lot was to burn incense when he went into the temple of the Lord.

10 And the whole multitude of the people were praying without at the time of incense.

11 And there appeared unto him an angel of the Lord standing on the right side of the altar of incense.

12 And when Zacharias saw him, he was troubled, and fear fell upon him.

13 But the angel said unto him, Fear not, Zacharias: for thy prayer is heard; and thy wife Elisabeth shall bear thee a son, and thou shalt call his name John.

14 And thou shalt have joy and gladness; and many shall rejoice at his birth.

15 For he shall be great in the sight of the Lord, and shall drink neither wine nor strong drink; and he shall be filled with the Holy Ghost, even from his mother's womb.

16 And many of the children of Israel shall he turn to the Lord their God.

17 And he shall go before him in the spirit and power of Elias, to turn the hearts of the fathers to the children, and the disobedient to the wisdom of the just; to make ready a people prepared for the Lord.

18 And Zacharias said unto the angel, Whereby shall I know this? for I am an old man, and my wife well stricken in years.

19 And the angel answering said unto him, I am Gabriel, that stand in the presence of God; and am

NLT

Luke 1:8 One day Zechariah was serving God in the Temple, for his order was on duty that week.

9 As was the custom of the priests, he was chosen by lot to enter the sanctuary of the Lord and burn incense.

10 While the incense was being burned, a great crowd stood outside, praying.

11 While Zechariah was in the sanctuary, an angel of the Lord appeared to him, standing to the right of the incense altar.

12 Zechariah was shaken and overwhelmed with fear when he saw him.

13 But the angel said, "Don't be afraid, Zechariah! God has heard your prayer. Your wife, Elizabeth, will give you a son, and you are to name him John.

14 You will have great joy and gladness, and many will rejoice at his birth,

15 for he will be great in the eyes of the Lord. He must never touch wine or other alcoholic drinks. He will be filled with the Holy Spirit, even before his birth.

16 And he will turn many Israelites to the Lord their God.

17 He will be a man with the spirit and power of Elijah. He will prepare the people for the coming of the Lord. He will turn the hearts of the fathers to their children, and he will cause those who are rebellious to accept the wisdom of the godly."

18 Zechariah said to the angel, "How can I be sure this will happen? I'm an old man now, and my wife is also well along in years."

sent to speak unto thee, and to shew thee these glad tidings.

20 And, behold, thou shalt be dumb, and not able to speak, until the day that these things shall be performed, because thou believest not my words, which shall be fulfilled in their season.

21 And the people waited for Zacharias, and marvelled that he tarried so long in the temple.

22 And when he came out, he could not speak unto them: and they perceived that he had seen a vision in the temple: for he beckoned unto them, and remained speechless.

23 And it came to pass, that, as soon as the days of his ministration were accomplished, he departed to his own house.

19 Then the angel said, "I am Gabriel! I stand in the very presence of God. It was he who sent me to bring you this good news!

20 But now, since you didn't believe what I said, you will be silent and unable to speak until the child is born. For my words will certainly be fulfilled at the proper time."

21 Meanwhile, the people were waiting for Zechariah to come out of the sanctuary, wondering why he was taking so long.

22 When he finally did come out, he couldn't speak to them. Then they realized from his gestures and his silence that he must have seen a vision in the sanctuary.

23 When Zechariah's week of service in the Temple was over, he returned home.

In Focus

George and his wife Annette were watching the evening news together when the anchorperson began to report on a story about two abused children.

"According to welfare officials, the children had been severely beaten and left alone . . ." the anchorperson reported.

Immediately, George grabbed the remote and turned to a different station.

"You didn't have to do that," said Annette.

"Yes, I did. I know how much that kind of stuff bothers you, even though you pretend it doesn't," said George. "It's not fair, hearing about parents who abuse and mistreat their children. And here we are, two people who love children and want to have our own so badly, but can't."

"I know, George, but all is not lost. Remember, the doctor said that he couldn't find anything medically wrong with either of us. So let's keep praying that one day we will have a child of our own. Give it time," said Annette.

For couples like George and Annette who love children and want to have their own, being childless is frustrating and discouraging. Certainly it must have also been frustrating for Zacharias and Elisabeth, but in today's lesson we see that their prayers for a child were miraculously answered at the hand of God.

The People, Places, and Times

The Gospel of Luke. Written by Luke, the beloved physician, sometime between A.D. 58 and 60, the book's primary focus is Jesus' concern for society's outcasts. More than any of the other gospels, Luke's account supplies more details about Christ's human life. He especially emphasizes prayer and focuses on the poor, the rich, and women.

Elisabeth. This woman, whose name means "oath of God," is the wife of Zacharias and the mother of John the Baptist. In biblical times, if a woman became pregnant after long years of waiting, there was great rejoicing when her baby was born.

Incense Offering. This was one of the most solemn duties for a priest to perform. Because of the number of priests at the time, one could expect to perform this function only once in his lifetime. The incense offering was brought twice a day, once in the early morning and again in the afternoon. To do so, the designated priest entered the part of the temple referred to as the holy place.

Sources:

Packer, J. I., and M. C. Tenney, eds. *Illustrated Manners and Customs of the Bible.* Nashville, Tenn.: Thomas Nelson Publishers, 1980.

Whyte, Alexander. *Bible Characters of the Old and New Testament.* Grand Rapids, Mich.: Zondervan Publishing House, 1967.

Background

As the parents of John the Baptist, Zacharias and his wife Elisabeth formed the link between the Old and New Testament. God's visit to Zacharias marked for Luke the beginning of the things that God promised to fulfill among His people. God, after 400 years, once again visited Israel and rose up a prophet who would prepare the people for the coming Messiah. Zacharias and Elisabeth's son John had a mission to announce the coming of the Messiah and Redeemer (cf. Luke 16:16).

Zacharias and his wife Elisabeth were both descendants of Aaron, a priestly family. This was considered a special distinction. Just as it was an honor for Mary to be chosen as the mother of Jesus, so too it was an honor for Zacharias and Elisabeth to be chosen as the parents of John the Baptist, the one whose voice cried in the wilderness, "Make straight in the desert a highway for our God" (Isaiah 40:3).

The names Zacharias and Elisabeth carry special meaning. Zacharias means "remembered of Jehovah," while Elisabeth means "oath of God." God's remembrance of His covenant and His faithfulness to His people are clearly central to understanding the coming of Christ in the fullness of time.

However, before the birth of Christ was the birth of the one who announced His coming, John the Baptist. Today's lesson will show how his birth was a miraculous gift to answered prayer.

At-A-Glance

1. The Angelic Announcement (Luke 1:8–12)
2. A Ministry Foretold (vv. 13–17)
3. An Unusual Visitor (vv. 18–23)

In Depth

1. The Angelic Announcement (Luke 1:8–12)

Zacharias and Elisabeth were a prayerful couple who followed the Lord's commandments. Nevertheless, as the years rolled on, they must have been very discouraged to find themselves childless after praying for so many years. In biblical times, children were considered a great blessing and a means of continuing the family name, thus perpetuating God's covenant with Israel. They may have wondered why their righteous lifestyle and their prayers were not rewarded with the gift of children. Clearly, they were not the kind of people who served God only because they wanted or expected something from Him, as evidenced by their long years of faithfulness to God in spite of their childlessness.

One cannot help but be reminded of similar instances in Scripture of childless couples such as Abraham and Sarah (Genesis 16:1; 18:11), Isaac and Rebekah (25:21), and Jacob and Rachel (30:1). Like Sarah, Elisabeth was beyond childbearing years, and much like Isaac and Rebekah, Zacharias and Elisabeth prayed to God for a miracle.

Twice a year, lots were cast to determine which priest would serve in the temple. On this occasion, the lot fell to Zacharias to burn incense in the temple. While Zacharias was burning the incense, the people were gathered for prayer in the temple court. When they saw the smoke of the incense offering go up, the symbol of a consecrated life, it was their signal to kneel and lift their hands in prayer. It was in this solemn moment that an angel of the Lord appeared to Zacharias.

The angel Gabriel's birth announcement followed a pattern typically found throughout the Old Testament (cf. Genesis 16:7–13; 17:1–21; Isaiah 7:10–14). First, an angel appeared (Luke 1:11), followed by a response of fear (v. 12), a word of reassurance (v. 13), a divine message (vv. 13–17), a request for a sign (v. 18), and finally a sign of assurance (vv. 19–20).

2. A Ministry Foretold (vv. 13–17)

The sight of the angel made Zacharias afraid. However, the angel told him not to fear because his prayers would be answered. The angel told Zacharias that his wife would have a son and that she would name him John, which means "Jehovah is a gracious giver" (v. 13).

The angel indicated that this child would be someone special. He would not be an ordinary son; rather, his birth would bring joy to his parents and to many others as well. This child, John, would call God's people back to righteousness. John would have true greatness, because he would be great in the sight of the Lord. The Scriptures affirm that from birth "he [would] be filled with the Holy Spirit" (v. 15, NLT).

The angel also said that John would turn the hearts of the fathers to the children and the disobedient to walk in wisdom of the just. Succeeding generations of Israelites had strayed further away from God. Their sinfulness was characterized by rebelliousness, which, when compared, is akin to that of a neglectful parent who ignores his children. John's role would be to restore sinful Israelites to the way of righteousness.

John's ministry is prophesied in Malachi 3:1. His special status as a prophet was further defined by his role as a forerunner of Christ, the one who would prepare His way. John the Baptist also was compared to Elijah because, like Elijah, he would be a strong man who would pronounce judgment on sinners without respect of persons (e.g., 1 Kings 21:17–29; Matthew 14:1–4).

3. An Unusual Visitor (vv. 18–23)

Like many before him, Zacharias found it hard to believe that he and his wife Elisabeth would conceive a child in their old age, so he asked the angel Gabriel for a sign of what was to come (cf. Genesis 15:8; 17:17). Because Zacharias did not believe Gabriel's news, the angel rendered him speechless until the child's birth.

The worshipers outside the temple were getting nervous because it was taking Zacharias so long to emerge (Luke 1:21). According to custom, the priest was not to tarry in the temple, but make the sacrificial offering and quickly exit. Zacharias's delay may have caused the worshipers outside to wonder if he had somehow been disrespectful and struck dead, thus placing their prayers in jeopardy. However, to the amazement of the crowd, when Zacharias emerged from the temple, he was gesturing with his hands and unable to speak.

Priests exiting the temple were expected to pronounce a blessing on the crowd, but when Zacharias came out and could not speak, the crowd immediately knew that something extraordinary had happened.

It was now time to reveal what happened to Zacharias and the plans God had for his family. Likewise, there are times in our lives when we are facing situations that God would have us not speak until

His will has been done. No doubt, Zacharias had concerns about what others thought about his reaction, but waiting for God's time was all he could do. His duty having ended, Zacharias and Elisabeth went home knowing that the unusual visit had forever changed their lives.

Search the Scriptures

1. By what method were priests assigned to specific duties in the temple (Luke 1:9)? *By Lot*

2. Where in the temple did the angel of the Lord appear (v. 11)? *The Holy Place*

3. How did Zacharias respond to the sight of the angel of the Lord (v. 12)? *With fear -*

4. What did the angel of the Lord tell Zacharias (vv. 13–17)?

Discuss the Meaning

1. Zacharias and Elisabeth were devout people who continued to serve the Lord, though their prayers for a child did not seem that they would ever be answered. What does this say to us about continually serving God when we think our prayers have gone unanswered?

2. Zacharias had doubts about the angel's prediction of a miraculous birth. What questions does this passage raise about the physical manifestations of God's Word? *We must pray with the Patience to wait on God's timing.*

Lesson in Our Society

Zacharias and Elisabeth received the answer to their prayers although the manifestation of the answer was not yet present. In the interim, they had prayed for years, and quite possibly had given up. While God's answers are not always "yes," there are many lessons that we can learn from this New Testament couple. As believers, our reaction to God's response to prayer is never passive. In some cases, we are amazed by God's power even when our request was made with the knowledge that God's power was beyond our understanding. At other times and despite our faith in God, circumstances and time render our reaction as weary and despondent.

Today's lesson reminds us that regardless of our degree of faith, we must always remember that God's sovereignty is at work on our behalf. Whether His answer is "yes" or "no," God will provide the answer that is best for our lives. When God requires us to wait for His response, we cannot look at that as a rejection or even as a sure assumption that a positive answer will come at a later time.

Like Zacharias and Elisabeth, our goal is to remain faithful regardless of God's response knowing that His will for our lives exceeds even our greatest desires.

Make It Happen

Today's lesson reminds us of the effectiveness of prayer and the patience needed to wait for God's answer. Sometimes we stop praying when God doesn't respond according to our timetable. Make a pledge today to recommit yourself to a ministry of prayer. Pray for yourself, for others in your home and family, and for your church and pastor. Consider starting a prayer journal if you don't already keep one. This will help you chart your prayers and God's answers to your prayers.

Follow the Spirit

What God wants me to do:

_____

_____

Remember Your Thoughts

Special insights I have learned:

_____

_____

More Light on the Text

Luke 1:8–23

8 And it came to pass, that while he executed the priest's office before God in the order of his course, 9 According to the custom of the priest's office, his lot was to burn incense when he went into the temple of the Lord.

There are two aspects of importance about Zacharias's serving in the temple to burn incense. First, he should have been prepared for this moment, and second, his service as priest was divinely ordained. "Executed the priest's office" is an English translation of a Greek infinitive. Infinitives stress not just the action implied in the verb, but also the attitude behind the action. To have been chosen to serve as a priest in God's sanctuary was reason enough for Zacharias to have an attitude of expectation. The

Greek word for "executed the priest's office is *hierateuo* (**hee-er-at-yoo-o**), which means "to serve as a priest."

His "lot" (Gk. *lagchano*, **lang-khan-o**) was to burn incense. Although the details are sketchy, God had clearly established a sacred lot (some suggest the stones on the high priest's breastplate were used) as a means to discern His will (see Leviticus 16:8; Numbers 34:13). In addition, lots were used to identify the apostle (see Acts 1:25–26) to replace the betrayer Judas.

This was a once-in-a-lifetime event for a priest of Zacharias's rank. Chosen among a potential and capable 18,000 priests, Zacharias had the honor of burning incense before the Lord. Zacharias's soul should have been burning with expectation.

10 And the whole multitude of the people were praying without at the time of incense.

The burning of incense along with the burnt offering during this biannual event occurred twice a day—at sunrise and dusk. The large multitude suggests this was the evening hour.

11 And there appeared unto him an angel of the Lord standing on the right side of the altar of incense. 12 And when Zacharias saw him, he was troubled, and fear fell upon him.

The text does not tell us if the angel appeared immediately after Zacharias entered the sanctuary or while he was burning incense or during the ritual prayers. But it is clear that not long before, an angel, Gabriel, appeared before Zacharias standing on the right side of the altar of incense.

Clearly, Zacharias did not go into the temple looking to "experience" anything out of the ordinary. Nevertheless, even though he was caught unaware, Zacharias should have known something was up when an angel appeared and stood on the right side of the altar.

Zacharias was troubled (Gk. *tarasso*, **tar-AS-so**), and fear fell upon him. Luke uses the same Greek word for "troubled" in 24:38 when he described the disciples as being perplexed or doubtful that Christ had manifested Himself among them. Could Zacharias have been wondering why he was having this experience? Again, the context is our clue, at least with reference to Gabriel's response.

13 But the angel said unto him, Fear not, Zacharias: for thy prayer is heard; and thy wife Elisabeth shall bear thee a son, and thou shalt call his name John. 14 And thou shalt have joy and gladness; and many shall rejoice at his birth.

Notice Gabriel did not address Zacharias's doubts, but his fears. Fear is not necessarily an unspiritual emotion. It is a proper response when mortality encounters immortality, whether it is the Divine, His representatives, or supernatural acts (see Exodus 15:16). In many instances, fear (Gk. *phobeo*, **fob-EH-o**) is used to denote respect for God. This cannot be its use in this context, however, because Gabriel commanded Zacharias not to fear. Your prayers are answered, Gabriel said, and your wife shall bear (Gk. *gennao*, **ghen-NAH-o**) a son.

This was a crucial point for Zacharias. The challenge to Zacharias was to step out in faith, to believe not in his situation but in His Saviour. Did you know that the Christian call to exercise faith is not an option? "For we walk by faith, not by sight" (2 Corinthians 5:7).

15 For he shall be great in the sight of the Lord, and shall drink neither wine nor strong drink; and he shall be filled with the Holy Ghost, even from his mother's womb.

John was called of God to a public ministry as defined not by outward accomplishments but by his relationship to the Lord. Look at verse 15 carefully. He will be great in the sight of the Lord. This puts our call and response in perspective. The size of the crowd around us, or even our ultimate fate in this life, does not qualify our usefulness or relationship with the Lord. Rather, our legacy, or reward, is united to our faithfully fulfilling God's purposes. Many of the religious leaders, who were John's peers, not only condemned his ministry, but they also condemned John to death. However, Christ said among men there was no greater (Luke 7:28), and John faithfully fulfilled His call as a Nazarite, one consecrated to the Lord (see Numbers 6:1–4; 1 Samuel 1:11) until the last days of his ministry and life.

John's miraculous birth and ministry was not an afterthought in God's plan. There is no such thing. Therefore, Zacharias had only to trust the word of God to believe the message of God sent via His angel.

If John were ordained of and empowered by God, he would be filled with the Holy Ghost from his mother's womb. Again, using a passive verb for "filled" (Gk. *pletho*, **PLAY-tho**), neither Zacharias nor John had anything to do with what God was about to do. The plan and the provision were all of His choosing and under His control. The goods news is that when God is in control, all things are possible.

16 And many of the children of Israel shall he turn to the Lord their God. 17 And he shall go before him in the spirit and power of Elias, to turn the hearts of the fathers to the children, and the disobedient to the wisdom of the just; to make ready a people prepared for the Lord.

There is a perfect union between God's purposes and His promises. What God says will happen, happens. John will be used to turn many to the Lord by "the spirit and power of Elias."

There are four instances where the Greek word for "turn," *epistrepho* (**ep-ee-stref-o**), meaning "to turn from something to something else," is used in which a clause (a group of words) is the object of the verb's action. The idea is the turning away from an improper relationship with someone (Luke 1:16) or something (v. 17; James 5:19–20) to a proper relationship. There is almost another lesson here by itself.

The New Testament books of James and Luke emphasize the themes of belief (Luke 1:4) and faith (see James 1:3). Having right relations with God and our apprehension of truth are irrevocable intertwined with having right relations with others and applying the godly wisdom of others. Using another infinitive, Gabriel told Zacharias how this would happen. The fathers' hearts would be turned toward their children and the disobedient to the wisdom of the just. Do you see it? By looking at godly models, fathers would begin parenting and the people would begin practicing their faith in their daily living.

Apeithes (**ap-i-thace**) is the Greek word for "disobedient." When so used, as in this verse, it refers to not complying. The context supports this because the Greek word that the adjective "disobedient" modifies is the noun "wisdom" (Gk. *phronesis*, **fron-ay-sis**). Only used twice in this verbal form, *phronesis* refers to practical, everyday wisdom manifested in those who are recipients of God's graces and acts of redemption. John's ministry would cause some to turn from sinful

"And, behold, thou shalt be dumb, and not able to speak, until the day that these things shall be performed" (from Luke 1:20).

ways of living to ways consistent with God's character as manifested by godly examples. The word translated "just" (Gk. *dikaios*, **dik-ah-yos**) is consistently used by Luke to identify a person or group's external behavior that is consistent with God's character.

People turn to the Lord because they are made ready and are prepared for and by Him. God starts it and will continue it and we participate in it, but God has already determined to finish it. The predetermined, unconditional result of people turning to the Lord is that they are guaranteed fellowship with God. Let's put it another way. God graciously takes us for a ride that does not end until we see Him as He is!

What does this have to do with Zacharias's faith? Everything. Gabriel had just informed Zacharias that God's plan of redemption and restoration was about to go to another level, and that Zacharias's family was playing a significant part. At the least, this was a "hallelujah time." Is it possible to miss the miracle of the tree because we cannot believe the miracle of the forest? Zacharias's following response says yes.

18 And Zacharias said unto the angel, Whereby shall I know this? for I am an old man, and my wife well stricken in years.

Zacharias could not believe God for a miracle in his life because He could not believe in a miracle-working God. "Whereby shall I know this?" is Zacharias's question. The word "know" is derived from the Greek word *ginosko* (**ghin-OCE-ko**), and is often associated with the concept of learning and understanding. Zacharias was clearly questioning God's power to cause he and Elizabeth to conceive,

which also implied disbelief in God's power to redeem and restore the nation. What is significant is how he came to this conclusion.

As is too often the case, we have a distorted view of what God can do to and through us. Zacharias was older ("an old man") and his wife was "well stricken in years." Disbelief was Zacharias's only option. The promise of redemption is at the core of the Gospel and at the core of our faith. When we cannot hear the Gospel, we listen to our personal limitations. Zacharias missed the message; consequently, he could not believe the miracle.

19 And the angel answering said unto him, I am Gabriel, that stand in the presence of God; and am sent to speak unto thee, and to shew thee these glad tidings.

Then, as if to rhetorically address Zacharias's response, the angel said in effect, "Zacharias, do you know this was a direct communication from God—the God that knew your limitations before sending the message? He is the one that sent me to you to show you these glad tidings." There is no doubt Zacharias had doubted the message.

"Glad tidings" is the translation of another Greek infinitive. The verb form is *euaggelizo* (**yoo-ang-ghel-ID-zo**), often rendered "good news." When used in this infinitive form, "glad tidings" always refers to some expression of God's plan of salvation. Our limitations do not bind us to unbelief; it is our unbelief that binds us to our limitations.

20 And, behold, thou shalt be dumb, and not able to speak, until the day that these things shall be performed, because thou believest not my words, which shall be fulfilled in their season.

The consequence that Zacharias must endure is that he would be dumb, that is, silent. He would even lack the capacity to communicate in a verbal way because he failed to believe. Again, belief is not optional; the call of the Christian is to believe. "And whosoever liveth and believeth in me shall never die. Believest thou this?" (John 11:26). That question is for you too: "Believest thou this?"

21 And the people waited for Zacharias, and marvelled that he tarried so long in the temple.

There is a contrast between the faith Zacharias should have expressed and the almost blind faith expressed by the people. The people were amazed that he was in the temple so long. It was thought that a person could be in the presence of God for only a short amount of time and remain alive. However, the word "marvelled" (Gk. *thaumazo*, **thou-MAD-zo**), as used here, does not convey a sense of fear but rather one of amazement, implying that something of divine origin had taken place. Remember, the crowd had been praying. Nothing prepares us to experience the mighty works of God like prayer.

22 And when he came out, he could not speak unto them: and they perceived that he had seen a vision in the temple: for he beckoned unto them, and remained speechless.

The first sight of Zacharias was probably received with a great deal of expectation. Zacharias would not have been the only priest in the sanctuary. It is possible that co-laborer priests came out of the temple prior to Zacharias and let the people know something out of the ordinary had happened, or they exited with Zacharias.

Whatever the specific circumstances, the truthfulness of the angel's words must have burned within Zacharias's soul. He could not speak, but he wanted to say something, "for he beckoned them" and the people correctly concluded he had seen a vision. The Greek word for "perceived," *epiginosko* (**ep-ig-in-OCE-ko**), suggests that the people at least accepted that something supernatural had taken place. Details may have been lacking, but they did respond positively to the knowledge they had been exposed to. What a challenge to the community of faith!

The call is not to believe and respond to all that there is possible to know; the call is to believe the essential essence of that which God provides (see Romans 1:19–20). The content of faith is to be received and believed. Anything less is just short of a demonic response. "Thou believest that there is one God; thou doest well: the devils also believe, and tremble" (James 2:19).

23 And it came to pass, that, as soon as the days of his ministration were accomplished, he departed to his own house.

It is not unusual in the infancy narratives of Luke that a journey or return home ends one event so that the readers can focus on another. Zacharias was to be commended. He persevered in fulfilling his designated and ordained duties as a priest. There is good news for the Christian here. We cannot change the mistakes of the past. We can make sure that nothing else remains within our power to do things in the present and future.

The Greek word for "accomplished" is *pletho* (**PLAY-tho**), and it has the connotation of complete satisfaction. In others words, God was still using Zacharias in full service of worship in the temple. God never throws us away! Another call of the Christian that requires trust in God, even when mistakes have been made and consequences are being endured, is to continue on! Do not let yesterday's failures and consequential hardships decide for you how God can use you today! Zacharias finished the administration of his service in the Lord's temple; then and only then did he depart to his own house.

Sources:
Bock, Darrell L. *Baker Exegetical Commentary on the New Testament: Luke 1:1–9:50*. Edited by Moises Silva. Grand Rapids, Mich.: Baker Books, 1994.
Packer, J. I., and M. C. Tenney. *Illustrated Manners and Customs of the Bible*. Nashville, Tenn.: Thomas Nelson Publishers, 1980.

Daily Bible Readings

M: Sing God's Praises
Psalm 66:1–4
T: Righteous before God
Luke 1:5–7
W: Incense Offering Interrupted
Luke 1:8–13
T: A Ministry Foretold
Luke 1:14–17
F: Zacharias Sees a Vision
Luke 1:18–23
S: Elisabeth Conceives
Luke 1:24–25
S: God Listened to My Prayer
Psalm 66:16–20

TEACHING TIPS

December 9
Bible Study Guide 2

1. Words You Should Know
A. Gabriel (Luke 1:26) *Gabriel* (Gk.)—An angel of the Lord, God's messenger.

B. Espoused (v. 27) *mnesteuo* (Gk.)—Betrothed or engaged to be wed.

C. Cousin (v. 36) *suggenes* (Gk.)—Other translations refer to Elisabeth as a relative of Mary. Their exact form of kinship is not known.

D. Barren (v. 36) *steiros* (Gk.)—Unable to conceive a child.

2. Teacher Preparation
Unifying Principle—Significance and Purpose Everyone wants to feel as though their life is significant and counts for something. How does God address these needs by calling us to serve? Mary, Jesus' mother, is an example of how God can call us to significance and purpose.

A. Study the background materials on the *Precepts For Living*® CD-ROM as well as the More Light on the Text, Background, and In Depth sections to gain insight on this familiar text.

B. Pay attention to the AIM for Change and ask God's guidance in how to focus this lesson for your specific class and the issues they face.

3. Starting the Lesson
A. Begin class by displaying a map, pictures, or a video of Galilee and Nazareth. Use information from The People, Places, and Times section to explain events in the life of Jesus that occurred there and in the surrounding areas.

B. Have the class discuss modern customs of engagement, the wedding ceremony, and an announcement of a birth. Lead a discussion of how these customs were followed in the families of the New Testament.

C. Consider having class members read the Focal Verses as a drama.

4. Getting into the Lesson
A. Ask the class to read 2 Samuel 7:13–16 and Isaiah 9:6–7. Discuss how Luke demonstrated that Jesus was the promised Messiah. Refer to The People, Places, and Times and the Background sections for additional information.

B. Follow the At-A-Glance outline to discuss the promises, blessings, and instructions presented in this lesson. Consider using the questions in Search the Scriptures to enhance a discussion of the verses.

5. Relating the Lesson to Life
A. Have the class respond to the In Focus story and identify situations that this story mirrors in their own lives.

B. Lead the class in a discussion of the Discuss the Meaning questions and the first two items in the Lesson in Our Society section. Allow the class to formulate ideas that could be used in their lives and the lives of others.

6. Arousing Action
A. Discuss how God employs people, as He did in this text, to bring His will into fruition in our lives.

B. Discuss number 3 in Lesson in Our Society. Allow the class to formulate ideas that could lead to addressing these issues individually, as a class, or as a part of the larger church agenda.

C. Give class members an opportunity to come up with ideas based on the Follow the Spirit and Remember Your Thoughts sections.

Worship Guide

For the Superintendent or Teacher
Theme: Called to Be a Vessel!
Theme Song: "Lord, I'm Available to You"
Devotional Reading: Psalm 40:1–5
Prayer

131

CALLED TO BE A VESSEL!

Bible Background • LUKE 1:26–38
Printed Text • LUKE 1:26–38 Devotional Reading • PSALM 40:1–5

AIM for Change

By the end of the lesson, we will:

REVIEW the powerful narrative in which Mary is called to be the mother of God's Son;

RECOGNIZE our significance and purpose in God's kingdom; and

RESPOND by identifying ways to live out God's plan for our lives.

Keep in Mind

"And Mary said, Behold the handmaid of the Lord; be it unto me according to thy word. And the angel departed from her" (Luke 1:38).

Focal Verses

KJV

Luke 1:26 And in the sixth month the angel Gabriel was sent from God unto a city of Galilee, named Nazareth,

27 To a virgin espoused to a man whose name was Joseph, of the house of David; and the virgin's name was Mary.

28 And the angel came in unto her, and said, Hail, thou that art highly favoured, the Lord is with thee: blessed art thou among women.

29 And when she saw him, she was troubled at his saying, and cast in her mind what manner of salutation this should be.

30 And the angel said unto her, Fear not, Mary: for thou hast found favour with God.

31 And, behold, thou shalt conceive in thy womb, and bring forth a son, and shalt call his name JESUS.

32 He shall be great, and shall be called the Son of the Highest: and the Lord God shall give unto him the throne of his father David:

33 And he shall reign over the house of Jacob for ever; and of his kingdom there shall be no end.

34 Then said Mary unto the angel, How shall this be, seeing I know not a man?

35 And the angel answered and said unto her, The Holy Ghost shall come upon thee, and the power of the Highest shall overshadow thee: therefore also that holy thing which shall be born of thee shall be called the Son of God.

36 And, behold, thy cousin Elisabeth, she hath also conceived a son in her old age: and this is the sixth month with her, who was called barren.

37 For with God nothing shall be impossible.

NLT

Luke 1:26 In the sixth month of Elizabeth's pregnancy, God sent the angel Gabriel to Nazareth, a village in Galilee,

27 to a virgin named Mary. She was engaged to be married to a man named Joseph, a descendant of King David.

28 Gabriel appeared to her and said, "Greetings, favored woman! The Lord is with you!"

29 Confused and disturbed, Mary tried to think what the angel could mean.

30 "Don't be afraid, Mary," the angel told her, "for you have found favor with God!

31 You will conceive and give birth to a son, and you will name him Jesus.

32 He will be very great and will be called the Son of the Most High. The Lord God will give him the throne of his ancestor David.

33 And he will reign over Israel forever; his Kingdom will never end!"

34 Mary asked the angel, "But how can this happen? I am a virgin."

35 The angel replied, "The Holy Spirit will come upon you, and the power of the Most High will overshadow you. So the baby to be born will be holy, and he will be called the Son of God.

36 What's more, your relative Elizabeth has become pregnant in her old age! People used to say she was barren, but she's now in her sixth month.

37 For nothing is impossible with God."

38 Mary responded, "I am the Lord's servant. May everything you have said about me come true." And then the angel left her.

38 And Mary said, Behold the handmaid of the Lord; be it unto me according to thy word. And the angel departed from her.

In Focus

When Ms. Vernon, the general manager, had her assistant call Jerome to make an appointment, he was a little afraid. *Uh-oh*, he first thought. *What did I do wrong?*

Much to his surprise, Ms. Vernon greeted him warmly. "I know a summons from the boss is a little scary," she said, "but I think I have some news that will excite you." Her words were so complimentary that Jerome felt she was leading up to something really bad. The company had been hiring a lot of college grads lately, and the workers without degrees were beginning to wonder if their jobs were secure. Silently he prayed that God would grant him favor to handle what was coming.

"I would like for you to consider entering a new training program as a first step to a promotion. I want other employees to know that we look at dedication and hard work, not just education. You've demonstrated a high level of commitment to your job, and you have a good attitude about your work. A lot of other employees who, like you, don't have a degree are going to be looking at you to see whether you can make it through," she explained.

"I know there is plenty riding on this. I'd love the opportunity. Thank you," Jerome said. "I'll work hard to make it a success."

In his heart he shouted, *Thank You, Lord, for giving me favor in this way.*

As he left her office he thought, *I didn't think that anyone noticed or even cared about me. I suppose God had a master plan all along.*

Everyone wants to feel that his or her life counts for something. In today's lesson, we will see that Mary is an example of how God can call us to significance and purpose.

The People, Places, and Times

Espousal. During biblical times, an engagement was just as binding as marriage. In the Old Testament, espousal is synonymous with marriage. The honor for the family came through the purity of the bride-to-be. Under the Law of Moses, if for any reason the woman was found to have violated her vow of chastity and marriage, she could be put to death and the family would be left in disgrace. Later, when the Jewish legal system allowed divorce, a man could divorce the woman even before the actual marriage if she was found to have disgraced the family or his honor through sexual impurity.

Galilee. Located in the northern area of Judah, Galilee was the site of Jesus' childhood and early ministry. At one point in its history, Galilee had a large Gentile population. Even though it was repopulated with Jews, southern Jews always viewed it negatively. Galilee is mentioned in the Old Testament, but it is of greatest prominence in the New Testament because of Jesus' ministry.

Nazareth. This city in lower Galilee became prominent following the birth of Jesus. The name itself means "the guarded one." Nazareth, located halfway between the Sea of Galilee and the Mediterranean Sea, was a small village with only one spring to supply fresh water to residents. (Today that spring is known as Mary's well.) Nazareth did not have a good reputation in Jesus' day, as reflected in Nathanael's question, "Can there any good thing come out of Nazareth?" (John 1:46). Jesus was rejected by His townspeople and was thrown out of the synagogue there (Matthew 13:54–58; Mark 6:1–6; Luke 4:16–30). The early church was also looked upon with disdain, being referred to as a sect of the Nazarenes (Acts 24:5). Part of the reason for Nazareth's lack of respect was likely due to the unpolished dialect of its inhabitants, a lack of culture, and possibly some immorality.

Background

Christianity faced important challenges in its early history. Luke's gospel, in part, is designed to counter certain false claims about Jesus by affirming that Jesus was Israel's long-awaited Messiah. Jesus was the fulfillment of God's promise to His people to send a Saviour. The first part of Luke's gospel is devoted to detailing the divinely orchestrated events that lead to the birth of the Messiah. Previous verses in Luke 1 tell how the angel Gabriel spoke to Zacharias and told him that his wife, Elisabeth, was going to bear him a son despite the couples' age. Their son was John the Baptist.

In the sixth month of Elisabeth's pregnancy, Gabriel appeared to Elisabeth's cousin, a young virgin named Mary who lived in Nazareth. Mary, who was probably no more than about 15 years old, was given the message that she was the chosen vessel through whom the Messiah would make His entrance into humanity. Mary questioned the angel based on her concerns for the laws of espousal and marriage, and her desire to honor God's grace upon her.

Controversy surrounding Jesus arose following His death, burial, and resurrection. There were those who said that Jesus was not human and that the crucifixion was not a real occurrence. To set the record straight, each of the Gospel writers narrated his message from a different perspective because they each wrote to a different audience. Luke's mention of a city of Galilee, named Nazareth, indicates that Luke's message was directed to a Gentile audience who were unfamiliar with Palestinian geography. He also tells his account of Jesus' birth from Mary's perspective. By contrast, Matthew's account focuses on Joseph's response. Luke alone records that Mary was a virgin. Other Gospel accounts do not take this fact into consideration, probably since it was the assumed norm. The word itself means "young woman" and by implication includes virginity until marriage. By stressing Mary's virginity, Luke affirmed Jesus' uniqueness—that He was both divine and human. God alone was responsible for His birth. Also, the virgin birth account affirmed that Jesus was born of a human mother, countering some claims that Jesus only appeared to be human.

At - A - Glance

1. Visit from the Angel (Luke 1:26–30)
2. Important Instructions (vv. 31–35)
3. All Things Are Possible (vv. 36–38)

In Depth

1. Visit from the Angel (Luke 1:26–30)

In the first part of chapter one, Luke wrote about the angel Gabriel's appearance to Zacharias and Elisabeth, and the divine declaration that the older couple would have a son. It was in the sixth month of Elisabeth's pregnancy that Gabriel appeared to Mary. The gospel writer begins with background information about Mary, her home, and her espousal to Joseph, who was of the house of David.

Gabriel announced first that Mary had found great favor with God, indicating that the Lord had a special purpose for her (v. 28). Second, he told her that God was with her. This would calm any fears she had. Finally he told her that she was to be praised among women. The news he was about to give her would shame her, Joseph, and her family; however, Gabriel let her know that the news he was bringing was an honor for her.

The sight of Gabriel and his announcement could be a fearful experience, especially for a young woman. Mary was understandably troubled and tried to figure out what Gabriel was talking about (v. 29). Mary was probably overwhelmed too. Picture an angel bringing accolades and a divine message! To calm her further, Gabriel told her that she must not be afraid (v. 30). She was not to let her imagination get ahead of her. God has a blessing beyond her imagination. She must have faith that God means her good. Gabriel's initial mission was to announce a blessing upon Mary.

2. Important Instructions (vv. 31–35)

Mary could never have imagined what the Lord had in store for her. She was about to conceive a child in her womb and bring forth a son. Gabriel even told her that the son's name would be Jesus. The name "Jesus" is the Greek equivalent of the Hebrew word for "Joshua," meaning "the Lord is salvation." The child to whom Mary would give birth would bring salvation to the world.

Gabriel pronounced a blessing and prophecy upon the child Mary would bring into the world. Mary's son would be great. Undoubtedly, every mother believes she has given birth to a wonderful child, but Gabriel wanted Mary to understand the full extent of whom her child would be. Her son, Jesus, would be called the Son of the Highest, meaning the

Most High God. Furthermore, the supreme God would give her son the throne of David. The promised Messiah would be from the lineage of David, which accounts for the mention of Joseph, who would raise this child as a member of the house of David. The Jews rested their hope in the Messiah's Davidic lineage, even though their hope was for an earthly kingdom and a politically powerful king. Gabriel's words recall the predictions of 2 Samuel 7:13–16 and Isaiah 9:6–7 regarding Israel's long-awaited king who would reign over all of the Jews (the house of Jacob) and whose reign would be forever. David reigned on a throne in Jerusalem for only a few years. Jesus reigns forever in the hearts of those who believe.

Knowing herself to be a virgin, Mary naturally questioned how she could conceive a child. Gabriel affirmed his message by explaining that Mary's son would come from a supernatural conception. The Holy Spirit would come upon Mary. The child would be holy; He would be the Son of God. Through the intervention of the Holy Spirit, Mary became the mother of God's Son. God fulfilled His promise to David through Jesus Christ. God's own Son would be the fulfillment of the Old Testament prophecy concerning the righteous reign of God.

3. All Things Are Possible (vv. 36–38)

Much to Mary's own surprise, God chose her to accomplish God's divine purpose. As if to confirm that miracles are possible, Gabriel told Mary about Elisabeth's pregnancy. Remember that Mary and Elisabeth were related. She no doubt knew that Elisabeth had never given birth and was considered barren. Mary also knew that Zacharias and Elisabeth had long given up hope for having a child of their own. This news confirmed that with God, nothing is impossible. At this point, Elisabeth was not going to conceive—she was almost ready to deliver! The same God who had allowed Elisabeth to conceive in her old age held the power to create life in Mary's womb. God keeps His promises to His people, no matter how difficult the circumstances may seem.

We do not know the degree of Mary's surprise, bewilderment, confusion, and any other emotion she may have experienced. We do know that Mary gave herself in humble submission to God's will. The Lord was able to use her because she was willing to accept whatever would follow as a result of doing God's will. She was willing to accept shame and ridicule in order for God to use her. For her obedience, Mary became the mother of the world's Saviour. She affirmed her humble status by referring to herself as the hand-maid of the Lord—a vessel. Mary put herself in the hands of God, whom she both trusted and served.

Search the Scriptures

1. When and where did Gabriel appear to Mary (Luke 1:26)?

2. What information does Luke give us about Mary's life (vv. 27–28)?

3. What is the significance of the first part of Gabriel's message to Mary (vv. 28–30)?

4. Identify the details of Gabriel's message regarding what would happen in Mary's life (vv. 31, 35).

5. What blessing and prophecy does Gabriel confirm about the child (vv. 31–33)?

6. What incident did Gabriel cite as affirmation of what was about to happen to Mary? Why was this incident important (vv. 36–37)?

7. What was Mary's reaction to all that Gabriel told her (vv. 29, 34, 38)?

Discuss the Meaning

1. God's blessings do not always come as we expect them. How does this statement prove true in this text, and how does Mary's submission to the will of God help us understand our own call to do God's will?

2. Mary was very young when Gabriel told her about God's plans for her life. While we cannot earn God's grace, what qualities did Mary possess that made her submissive to being used of God?

3. What issues of faith and trust can we take from this lesson for our own lives as we struggle with submitting to God in difficult situations?

4. In what areas of your life is God calling you to be more submissive to His will?

Lesson in Our Society

1. Mary was no doubt anxious in her encounter with Gabriel, but she did not recoil in fear. What are some of the areas in life where we often become afraid before we begin to see God's hand? Consider issues such as health, employment, and family concerns.

2. This lesson identifies two people (Elisabeth and Joseph) who will be important in Mary's support system. By implication, there are others in her community who will either affirm or reject her. What can Christians do to affirm one another in times of difficulty and trial? What importance should we connect to building a community of support among family, friends, and the church?

3. Consider Mary as a teen and compare her situation and sense of faith with teens today. Two facts are clear: (1) statistics today report that more teens wish to have a place in the church but feel rejected; (2) teen sexuality and pregnancy is an issue that cannot be ignored. What can the church community do to help teens face these issues? How can we welcome teens and make them part of the church community without causing them to feel that they are too young to be full members of the body of Christ? How can the church reach out to pregnant teens and teen mothers who are struggling? How can the church help so that the teens and their children will not fall prey to the negative future that often awaits them?

Make It Happen

1. How has your own life twisted and turned as you have allowed yourself to be shaped and molded in God's will? How different would your life have been if you had followed only your own plans for your life?

2. What can you do to be more open to hearing God's voice and being submissive to His direction?

Follow the Spirit

What God wants me to do:

_____

_____

Remember Your Thoughts

Special insights I have learned:

_____

_____

More Light on the Text

Luke 1:26–38

26 And in the sixth month the angel Gabriel was sent from God unto a city of Galilee, named Nazareth

"In the sixth month" is a reference to the sixth month of Elisabeth's pregnancy and should not be taken to mean the sixth month of the year. Luke's use of this phrase helps connect Mary's story with that of Elisabeth, as is also seen in verse 36. The connection between the two stories is further enhanced by the involvement of "the angel Gabriel," who was God's messenger to both Elisabeth (Luke 1:19) and Mary (v. 26).

Luke's reference to "a city of Galilee, named Nazareth" would have alerted the readers of his day to Mary's humble origins. Nazareth, though referred to here as a city, was an insignificant village located in the hills of the little-respected region of Galilee. Nazareth's claim to fame is best summarized in Nathanael's question to Philip, "Can there any good thing come out of Nazareth?" (John 1:46).

27 To a virgin espoused to a man whose name was Joseph, of the house of David; and the virgin's name was Mary.

A virgin is a young, unmarried female. As used here, the word implies a young girl who has not had sexual intercourse. This understanding of the word is further illustrated by Mary's question in Luke 1:34. The term "espoused" is more accurately translated as "pledged to be married."

By using the phrase "Joseph, of the house of David," Luke prepares his readers for what is to follow in Luke 1:32–33. Luke's aim is to show that Jesus is a descendant of the royal line of David. The significance of the Davidic descent of Jesus is also highlighted in Luke 2:4 and in Luke 3:23–38. It is also interesting to compare Romans 1:3 and 2 Timothy 2:8.

"And the virgin's name was Mary" is a thrice-repeated reference to Mary's virginity, twice here in verse 27 and once in verse 34. This repetition underscores the magnitude of Jesus' rare and miraculous conception.

28 And the angel came in unto her, and said, Hail, thou that art highly favoured, the Lord is with thee: blessed art thou among women.

The Greek translation for "And the angel came in unto her" implies that the angel came into the house where she was. Upon coming into the house, the angel greeted Mary with the common Grecian greeting, "Hail." This word for "greeting," in Greek, is *chairo* (**KHAH-ee-ro**). It would have been understood by Luke's readers as normal protocol, except that it was immediately followed by an unusual announcement: "thou that art highly favoured, the Lord is with thee: blessed art thou among women."

With this normal greeting and unique message, the angel informed Mary that she was the recipient of God's glorious grace—glorious in the sense that, of all women, she had been singled out for a special encounter with the nearness of the Lord and a once-in-history birthing experience.

29 And when she saw him, she was troubled at his saying, and cast in her mind what manner of salutation this should be.

The entrance of the angel into her house and the content of his message "troubled" (Gk. *diatarasso*, **dee-at-ar-AS-so**), or "perplexed" Mary. It is reasonable to think that Mary's confusion drove her to ask at least two silent questions: *What are you doing in my house? What kind of greeting is this?*

After all, Mary was not accustomed to having angels entering her house, not to mention speaking to her. Luke simply said that she "cast in her mind what manner of salutation this should be."

30 And the angel said unto her, Fear not, Mary: for thou hast found favour with God.

Mary's confusion and inquiries were met with the angel's words of reassurance. The Greek word *charis* (**KHAR-ece**), translated as "favour," literally means "grace." This implies an action and choice of God that has nothing to do with Mary's acceptability. Grace is the unearned and unmerited favor of God, which, when accepted, causes one to rejoice. Grace expects nothing in return. Grace's only motivation is the bountiful benevolence of God. It is this grace, says the angel, which God has bestowed upon Mary.

31 And, behold, thou shalt conceive in thy womb and bring forth a son, and shalt call his name JESUS.

The angel proceeded to inform Mary why the bestowal of God's grace was so necessary and significant for her. In short, the angel said, "Mary, you are going to have a baby, a male child, and you will name Him Jesus." Although Luke did not call attention to

it, the name "Jesus" means "Yahweh (or the Lord) saves."

32 He shall be great, and shall be called the Son of the Highest: and the Lord God shall give unto him the throne of his father David:

Here, and spilling over into verse 33, the angel described the great and royal role that the child to be born to Mary would play. He would be called "the Son of the Highest," which is a reference to the unique relationship that Jesus would have with the God of Israel. In other words, Jesus would be the Son of God.

"And the Lord God shall give unto him the throne of his father David" should be taken to mean that Jesus would fulfill the role of Israel's long-awaited Messiah.

33 And he shall reign over the house of Jacob for ever; and of his kingdom there shall be no end.

This verse reaffirms much of what has already been said in verse 32. As in verse 32, this verse describes Jesus as Israel's awaited Messiah. Like His earthly father before Him, Jesus would "reign over the house of Jacob." "The house of Jacob" refers to the nation of Israel (see Exodus 19:3; Isaiah 2:5–6; 8:17; 48:1).

The messianic nature of Jesus' reign makes His rule and His kingdom eternal: "he shall reign . . . for ever . . . and of his kingdom there shall be no end" (see 2 Samuel 7:16; 1 Kings 8:25; Micah 4:7).

34 Then said Mary unto the angel, How shall this be, seeing I know not a man?

It is difficult to ascertain Mary's reasoning and motivation for asking this question. At best, we can reason that Mary assumed that what the angel promised was to take place before the consummation of her marriage to Joseph. In view of this assumption and Mary's keen awareness of her virginity, along with her commitment to the custom of celibacy during the period of one's betrothal, the question in verse 34 makes logical sense.

35 And the angel answered and said unto her, The Holy Ghost shall come upon thee, and the power of the Highest shall overshadow thee: therefore also

"And Mary said, Behold the handmaid of the Lord; be it unto me according to thy word. And the angel departed from her" (Luke 1:38).

that holy thing which shall be born of thee shall be called the Son of God.

Luke, who was fond of talking about the power of the Holy Spirit (see Luke 1:41, 67, 80; 2:25–27), recorded that the angel answered Mary's question in verse 34 by saying that the Holy Spirit's overshadowing presence would be the causative factor for Mary's impregnation. Because of this connection with the Holy Spirit, the child to be born to Mary would be anointed and set apart for God's service. Indeed, He would be holy and therefore "called the Son of God."

36 And, behold, thy cousin Elisabeth, she hath also conceived a son in her old age: and this is the sixth month with her, who was called barren.

The angel's reference to Elisabeth's old age and barrenness was calculated to position Mary to believe that God can do the impossible. If God could cause Elisabeth to conceive in her old age, after leading a youthful life of barrenness, then surely God could cause Mary to conceive without the involvement of a sexual companion.

37 For with God nothing shall be impossible.

When God is at work, nothing is impossible for Him to accomplish. A variant translation is equally accurate: "No word from God will be powerless." In other words, whatever God chooses to make happen will happen, even if it appears to be impossible from our human point of view. Moreover, when His Word goes forth, it never returns to Him void. His Word always accomplishes what He desires, and it achieves the purpose for which He sends it (see Isaiah 55:11).

38 And Mary said, Behold the handmaid of the Lord; be it unto me according to thy word. And the angel departed from her.

Finally, Mary was convinced that God has spoken. She had moved from being confused (v. 29) to accepting a call from God. When she realized that it was God speaking to her, she humbled herself, accepted the call, and became submissive to His will. She quickly chose to become the Lord's "handmaid" and responded in agreement, "be it unto me according to thy word."

The concept of departure and return seems to be characteristic of Luke's writings when he wanted to bring closure to an event (see Luke 1:23, 56; 2:20; 5:25; 8:39; 24:12).

Obviously, Mary's experience was unique. But all who accept God's call are also in for a unique experience.

Sources:

Brown, Raymond. *The Birth of the Messiah.* New York: Doubleday, 1977. 303–309.

Fitzmyer, Joseph. *The Gospel According to Luke I–IX.* New York: Doubleday, 1981. 348–350.

Marshall, I. Howard. *The New International Greek Commentary on Luke.* Grand Rapids, Mich.: Eerdmans Publishing Company, 1978. 68–70.

Daily Bible Readings

M: God's Wondrous Deeds
Psalm 40:1–5
T: An Unexpected Visitor
Luke 1:26–29
W: Mary's Son's Future
Luke 1:30–33
T: The Miraculous Conception
Luke 1:34–35
F: Nothing Is Impossible!
Luke 1:36–38
S: Elisabeth Blesses Mary
Luke 1:39–45
S: Mary Sings to the Lord
Luke 1:46–56

TEACHING TIPS

December 16
Bible Study Guide 3

1. Words You Should Know

A. Horn (Luke 1:69) *keras* (Gk.)—Literally an animal's horn, this term symbolizes strength and courage.

B. Prophets (v. 70) *prophetes* (Gk.)—One who is moved by God's Spirit to explain the hidden truths of God.

C. Dayspring (v. 78) *anatole* (Gk.)—A rising light or the dawn.

2. Teacher Preparation

Unifying Principle—Life-Changing Events We often talk about life experiences that change us. But the question is, "What difference do these life-changing events make in how we live? At the birth of John the Baptist, Zacharias proclaimed the vision of God's future for his son, who would prepare the people for the coming Messiah.

A. Study the More Light on the Text, Background, and In Depth sections, and complete lesson 3 in the *Precepts For Living® Personal Study Guide* to gain insight on this familiar text.

B. Pay attention to the Lesson Aim and Unifying Principle. Ask God's guidance regarding how to focus this lesson for issues your class members are facing.

C. Prepare the At-A-Glance outline for display. This will help focus the class as you proceed through the activities for the day.

D. Assign one or more people to make three-minute reports based on the Background and The People, Places, and Times sections.

E. Have one or two people work as a team to prepare a skit based on the In Focus story.

F. Have one student prepare to read the Focal Verses as a dramatic monologue.

3. Starting the Lesson

A. Have the class members who prepared the In Focus story perform their skit.

B. Following the performance, engage the class in a quick summary of the skit and a brief discussion of how the main character's life was changed.

4. Getting into the Lesson

A. Have the class brainstorm a list of life-changing situations. This might include encountering health issues, facing a fear, having a child, moving away from familiar locations, losing a spouse, or changing jobs.

B. Have the selected class members present their mini reports on the Background and The People, Places, and Times sections.

C. Ask the class to be mindful of the life-changing events in today's text and how the Holy Spirit empowers us to face change.

D. Have a volunteer complete the dramatic reading of the Focal Verses.

5. Relating the Lesson to Life

A. Review the Discuss the Meaning and the Search the Scriptures questions.

B. Ask the class what strategies this lesson has inspired that will help them focus on the power of the Holy Spirit in facing life-changing issues.

6. Arousing Action

A. Have the class members place prayer requests on small sheets of paper and put these in a class prayer box. Lead the class in a general prayer asking God's victorious resolution for issues your class members face.

B. Have the students read the Make It Happen section. Ask them to identify specific applications of the section that speak to the needs of their lives.

CALLED TO PROCLAIM!

Bible Background • LUKE 1:57–80
Printed Text • LUKE 1:67–80 Devotional Reading • MALACHI 3:1–4

AIM for Change

By the end of the lesson, we will:

EXPLAIN how Zacharias's behavior changed as a result of the fulfillment of God's promise in John's birth;

REFLECT on the life-changing events that have occurred in your life; and

TELL others how believing in Jesus changes your life.

Keep in Mind

"And his mouth was opened immediately, and his tongue loosed, and he spake, and praised God" (Luke 1:64).

Focal Verses

KJV

Luke 1:67 And his father Zacharias was filled with the Holy Ghost, and prophesied, saying,

68 Blessed be the Lord God of Israel; for he hath visited and redeemed his people,

69 And hath raised up an horn of salvation for us in the house of his servant David;

70 As he spake by the mouth of his holy prophets, which have been since the world began:

71 That we should be saved from our enemies, and from the hand of all that hate us;

72 To perform the mercy promised to our fathers, and to remember his holy covenant;

73 The oath which he sware to our father Abraham,

74 That he would grant unto us, that we being delivered out of the hand of our enemies might serve him without fear,

75 In holiness and righteousness before him, all the days of our life.

76 And thou, child, shalt be called the prophet of the Highest: for thou shalt go before the face of the Lord to prepare his ways;

77 To give knowledge of salvation unto his people by the remission of their sins,

78 Through the tender mercy of our God; whereby the dayspring from on high hath visited us,

79 To give light to them that sit in darkness and in the shadow of death, to guide our feet into the way of peace.

80 And the child grew, and waxed strong in spirit, and was in the deserts till the day of his shewing unto Israel.

NLT

Luke 1:67 Then his father, Zechariah, was filled with the Holy Spirit and gave this prophecy:

68 "Praise the Lord, the God of Israel because he has visited and redeemed his people.

69 He has sent us a mighty Savior from the royal line of his servant David,

70 just as he promised through his holy prophets long ago.

71 Now we will be saved from our enemies and from all who hate us.

72 He has been merciful to our ancestors by remembering his sacred covenant—

73 the covenant he swore with an oath to our ancestor Abraham.

74 We have been rescued from our enemies so we can serve God without fear,

75 in holiness and righteousness for as long as we live.

76 "And you, my little son, will be called the prophet of the Most High, because you will prepare the way for the Lord.

77 You will tell his people how to find salvation through forgiveness of their sins.

78 Because of God's tender mercy, the morning light from heaven is about to break upon us,

79 to give light to those who sit in darkness and in the shadow of death, and to guide us to the path of peace."

80 John grew up and became strong in spirit. And he lived in the wilderness until he began his public ministry to Israel.

In Focus

Even though Gregory now had his own family, the responsibility of being the oldest continued to make him feel responsible for his aging parents and younger siblings. Fortunately, he had maintained a good job and was able to help his family, while taking excellent care of his wife and children. Gregory was also considered to be a person who was wise and could be called upon for advice.

When his company merged with another, Gregory had been assured of a position in upper management. The new owners, however, saw things differently and released a number of senior staff, leaving Gregory unemployed for the first time in his life. Despite his excellent qualifications, Gregory was unable to find employment. He refused to discuss the issue with his wife and family. He felt that discussing the challenges he was facing would only burden them and make him appear incapable.

In order to remain active, Gregory started volunteering at a senior center. One day while listening to an older resident, Gregory was encouraged by the fact that the older man had faced numerous challenges, but had never lost confidence that God would make a way. After prayer, Gregory talked with his wife, and he was able to also share some of his concerns with his siblings, who immediately took on some of the responsibilities of their aging parents. Feeling less burdened, Gregory continued to look for a job and to declare that God would deliver. Two weeks later, he was asked by the senior center to consider a position as director—a position he readily accepted.

Life is a continuing process of change: marriage, birth, jobs, divorce, death—the list goes on. The question is: How are your life-changing events shaping your Christian walk? Today's text reaffirms Zacharias's prophetic proclaim that their faith in Jesus is well-placed.

The People, Places, and Times

House of David. Prophets foretold that the Messiah would come from the House of David, meaning that the Messiah would be a Jew who would continue the reign of David's kingdom forever (2 Samuel 7:12–16; 1 Chronicles 17:11–14).

Background

When Elisabeth found out that she and her younger cousin, Mary, were both expecting children, they praised God together (Luke 1:36–56). Elisabeth delivered the miracle child in her old age. As directed by an angel (v. 13), Elisabeth declared that the child's name would be John (God's gift), but the elders refused to believe her. Because her husband, Zacharias, did not believe the prophecy that he would have a child in his old age, he was unable to speak at all until after the child was born (Luke 1:11–20). At the naming, Zacharias indicated that he agreed with his wife's name for the child. Suddenly, his tongue was loosed and he began to bless the Lord and prophesy concerning his own son. His prophecy and blessing are the content of today's lesson.

Prophets of the Bible would retreat to the desert to get closer to God and enhance their spiritual walk with the Lord. This private time kept their focus on the things of God and gave them little time to worry about the necessities of life. It also kept them separate from political and social ills. In similar fashion John's ministry took place primarily in the wilderness much like the Old Testament prophet Elijah. John, who was placed under a special Nazarite vow from birth, grew up knowing that his life was consecrated to the Lord (see The People, Places, and Times). Known as John the Baptist (or John the Baptizer), John declared the coming of the Lord and urged people to be baptized for the remission of their sins (Mark 1:4).

At-A-Glance

1. The Holy Spirit (Luke 1:67)
2. The Prophecy (vv. 68–75)
3. The Blessing (vv. 76–80)

In Depth

1. The Holy Spirit (Luke 1:67)

The Holy Spirit gives believers power to speak the promises of God with boldness. Throughout this chapter, the power of the Holy Spirit is manifested through various people. In this verse, Zacharias was moved by the Holy Spirit to proclaim the Spirit-given Word of God (see Joel 2:28) regarding God's plan for redemption.

The birth of John, the forerunner of Christ, was part of this plan and would change human destiny forever. The Holy Spirit had kept Zacharias from verbal communication, confining him to gestures and writing. Perhaps this was to circumvent Zacharias's own frailty, doubt, and unbelief. In any event, Zacharias watched in silent awe as his wife carried their firstborn child. When Elisabeth gave birth to a son, they followed custom by taking the child to the temple to be circumcised on the eighth day of life. The ceremony of circumcision was a celebration of the male child as part of God's covenant nation. It was at this ceremony that the child would be named. Relatives had planned to name the child Zacharias after his father, but Elisabeth objected and said the child's name should be John. Since it was customary to name a child after a relative, they turned to Zacharias, who quickly scribbled the name "John" on a tablet.

Immediately his voice was restored. Zacharias, filled with the indwelling power of the Holy Spirit, praised God and prophesied (Luke 1:59–67). Zacharias was no stranger to the Word of God. He was a priest, and he and his wife were obedient to the Law, upright in the sight of God (Luke 1:5–8). In his silence, Zacharias saw the accumulating series of events and their illuminating power of God. The knowledge of God's Word became a reality to Zacharias and through his life experiences his faith increased.

2. The Prophecy (vv. 68–75)

During the days of the prophets, Israel and Judah were under oppression by other nations. More than 400 years had passed since the last Old Testament prophet had spoken. It was natural then that the Jews, who had waited patiently to receive their King, thought their deliverance was connected to the overthrow of their enemies. They believed that God would change their situation by snatching them out of the hands of their oppressors. It was through the anointing of the Holy Spirit that Zacharias declared the Messiah would be the "horn" of salvation, meaning that the Messiah would be the power of God in the deliverance of God's people.

The Messiah is the fulfillment of the covenant God made with Abraham when He declared that Abraham would be the father of many nations. The Messiah was to come from the royal family of David, fulfilling God's promise that a descendant of David would rule forever. Jesus, as a descendant of Abraham and a direct descendant of David, was the fulfillment of Old Testament prophecy (2 Samuel 7:16).

Zacharias spoke of God's mercy on His chosen people and praised God for providing the long-awaited Messiah as the fulfillment of the Old Testament prophecy. Even though the nation of Israel had a history of disobedience, God kept His covenant promise to Abraham (Genesis 22:16–18). God's redemptive plan included the reconciliation of His people and the restoration of righteous fellowship with Him. The Messiah, at His first coming, would fight a spiritual war, not a physical battle: "That he would grant unto us, that we being delivered out of the hand of our enemies might serve him without fear, In holiness and righteousness before him, all the days of our life" (Luke 1:74–75). This would be accomplished through the new covenant in Christ, the Messiah (Hebrews 9:14–15).

3. The Blessing (vv. 76–80)

After praising God and recalling the years of God's promise and sovereign work, Zacharias rejoiced in knowing that God had granted favor upon his household. The knowledge that his child would usher in the coming Messiah must have filled Zacharias with indescribable joy. Out of all the generations of Jewish families, God chose Zacharias and his barren wife, Elisabeth, to bring forth the forerunner of Christ.

Zacharias was then led by the Holy Spirit to speak a blessing upon the child. God Almighty was declaring that John's ministry would prepare the people's hearts to receive the coming King. This was a tall order for such an innocent child, but the Lord always prepares His chosen ones for the task at hand. John would be set apart to do the Lord's work. His role would be similar to that of the Old Testament prophets: encouraging people to forsake their wicked ways and return to their first love, God. Operating in the power of the Holy Ghost, John would call people to repentance by declaring that they needed to be forgiven of sin. His voice would echo God's truth and convict hearts that had become hardened and resistant to the things of God. John's ministry would boldly show men the error of their ways as their hearts were softened to receive the Living Word in the form of Jesus Christ (Malachi 3:1; Matthew 11:9–10).

Search the Scriptures

1. In what ways does today's Scripture text reveal the fulfillment of God's covenant with Abraham?

2. Why was John called "the prophet of the Most High" (Luke 1:76)?

3. Zacharias, Elisabeth, and John were called to proclaim God's message. What roles did each play?

Discuss the Meaning

1. Zacharias was filled with the Holy Spirit when he prophesied. What does this tell us about proclaiming God's Holy Word?

2. John was separated, sent to the desert, before he ministered in public. What does this tell us about preparation for ministry as a vocation?

3. Since we are all called to be witnesses for the Lord, how can each of us strengthen our relationship with Christ, learn more about God's Word, and understand the message He would have us proclaim to our family and neighbors?

4. Zacharias doubted God's Word when the angel spoke to him in the temple. What do we learn about the promises of God through Zacharias's doubt and unbelief?

5. Identify the life-changing events in the lives of Zacharias and Elisabeth. Explain their initial reactions, how God prepared them to face the experience, and how they demonstrated powerful faith in their final responses.

Lesson in Our Society

Each of us faces situations and challenges that threaten to destroy our goals and dreams. In some cases, we are called upon to meet crises that threaten our lives or the lives of our loved ones. As those redeemed by Christ, we must find the strength in Jesus and the Bible to move forward even when we feel so weak that we are willing to accept despondency. The spiritual disciplines of committed Bible reading, daily prayer, and regular devotions

strengthen us so that we can declare God's deliverance even in the midst of our pain. Being able to encourage others and ourselves with wisdom from God's Word is important. In doing so, we realize our call to proclaim God's mercy and grace in ways that strengthen us and others.

Make It Happen

During this week, make a commitment to pray for the members of your class who have placed requests in the class prayer box. Also, make a commitment to renew your vigor in conducting daily devotions or prayer so that you can become stronger in exercising the spiritual discipline necessary to face life's challenges. If you have a regular spiritual routine of prayer, consider fasting or making a commitment to help someone in need. Seek God's direction for greater spiritual discipline and boldness in proclaiming His goodness to others.

Follow the Spirit

What God wants me to do:

_____

_____

Remember Your Thoughts

Special insights I have learned:

_____

_____

More Light on the Text

Luke 1:67–80

67 And his father Zacharias was filled with the Holy Ghost, and prophesied, saying,

The source of Zacharias's words was the Holy Spirit. He was completely under the control of or "filled" (Gk. *pletho*, **PLAY-tho**) with the Holy Spirit. He prophesied (Gk. *propheteuo*, **prof-ate-YOO-o**) from God.

68 Blessed be the Lord God of Israel; for he hath visited and redeemed his people,

"Blessed be the Lord God" is typically used throughout the Old Testament to introduce a thanksgiving or a benediction (e.g., Genesis 9:26; 14:20; 24:27), and became a standard phrase of prayer in

Jewish blessings. As such, Zacharias's blessing here is traditionally known as the Benedictus.

Zacharias gave thanks to the Lord because, after so many years, He had visited His people. The Greek verb *episkeptomai* (**ep-ee-SKEP-tom-ahee**), or "visited," denotes "visiting with help" or "to care for." It refers to God's interventions on behalf of His people, showing them mercy (see Matthew 25:36, 43; Luke 1:68, 78; 7:16; Acts 6:3; 7:23; 15:14, 36; Hebrews 2:6; James 1:27).

God visited His people and redeemed them. The Greek word for "redeemed" is *lutrosis* (**LOO-tro-sis**), and it literally means "made redemption." The word is commonly used to describe the salvation of the people of God. It implies deliverance or release. Jesus came to make the payment for the release of His people, a release from the guilt and power of sin.

69 And hath raised up an horn of salvation for us in the house of his servant David;

A "horn of salvation," (Gk. *keras soteria*, **KER-as so-tay-REE-ah**) describes the mighty deliverance God brought when He visited His people. The horn is the symbol of strength and might. The prophecy is referring to Christ, the Messiah, as "the horn of salvation" raised up "in the house of his servant David."

70 As he spake by the mouth of his holy prophets, which have been since the world began:

God's salvation happened in accordance with what He "spake" (Gk. *laleo*, **lal-EH-o**) through His prophets or through the mouths of His holy prophets. "Since the world began" in Greek is *apo aion* (**APO ahee-OHN**), and it refers to past years. Without defining how long, it implies that God has been working out His plan for a very long, almost endless, length of time.

71 That we should be saved from our enemies, and from the hand of all that hate us;

Here, the salvation that Luke alludes to concerns an individual's relationship with God. It involves a person's life and spiritual salvation. The Greek word for "saved" is *soteria* (**so-tay-REE-ah**). *Soteria* is also the Greek word for "salvation" (see v. 69). This verse serves to develop the thought of verse 69 in that it is

a parenthetical expression used by God to proclaim the coming of the Messiah from the line of David.

72 To perform the mercy promised to our fathers, and to remember his holy covenant; 73 The oath which he sware to our father Abraham,

In this verse, Luke connects the work of John to God's promises to Israel and the saving work of Jesus. Luke understood that the coming of Christ was the fulfillment of the covenant promise God made to Abraham (Genesis 12:1–3; 26:3) and David (2 Samuel 7:8–16). God made the promise by an "oath" (Gk. *horkos*, **HOR-kos**) to Abraham. Jesus was and still is the promised horn of salvation (v. 69).

74 That he would grant unto us, that we being delivered out of the hand of our enemies might serve him without fear, 75 In holiness and righteousness before him, all the days of our life.

The first part of Zacharias's Benedictus ends here. The ultimate goal of our deliverance from servitude is that we serve God wholeheartedly. To "serve" (Gk. *latreuo*, **lat-RYOO-o**) implies a total commitment to the one we serve (see Luke 2:37; see also 1 Peter 2:9; Revelation 1:6; 5:10).

Luke goes on to emphasize that because we are a covenant people, holiness (Gk. *hosiotes*, **hos-ee-OT-ace**, which denotes "purity in conduct and in motive") and righteousness (Gk. *dikaiosune*, **dik-ah-yos-OO-nay**, a "willingness to observe God's will") should be the standard for all of God's people all the days of their lives.

76 And thou, child, shalt be called the prophet of the Highest: for thou shalt go before the face of the Lord to prepare his ways;

Now Zacharias turned his praise from honoring the past to honoring the future—the future that recognizes the birth of his son, John, and John's place in God's redemptive work. John would assume the role of prophet. He would be known as "the prophet of the Highest" (Gk. *prophetes hupsistos*, **prof-AY-tace HOOP-sis-tos**). This title is more than a simple prediction of what John would be called; instead John would be a prophet who would go before the Lord fulfilling God's covenant promise (see Isaiah 40:3 and Malachi 3:1; 4:5).

"And his mouth was opened immediately, and his tongue loosed, and he spake, and praised God" (Luke 1:64).

77 To give knowledge of salvation unto his people by the remission of their sins, 78 Through the tender mercy of our God; whereby the dayspring from on high hath visited us,

Not only was John chosen to prepare the way of the Lord by calling the people to repentance, but he would also give them "knowledge of salvation." Here Luke contrasts John's role with that of Jesus, for repentance and baptism lead to forgiveness and salvation. Through the knowledge of salvation, the new covenant would be fulfilled. According to Jeremiah, that would mean every person would "Know the LORD . . . for I will forgive their iniquity, and I will remember their sin no more (Jeremiah 31:34).

The forgiveness of sins is made possible because of the Lord's mercy and His compassionate heart. The term "dayspring" (Gk. *anatole*, **an-at-ol-AY**), or "rising sun or stars," is interpreted in many ways due to it referring to sun or stars. Some scholars believe

it is a metaphor for Yahweh, the shoot or offspring of David or the star from Jacob (Numbers 24:17).

79 To give light to them that sit in darkness and in the shadow of death, to guide our feet into the way of peace.

Having knowledge of God should give light to those who sit in darkness. "To give light" (Gk. *epiphaino*, **ep-ee-FAH-ee-no**) is "to show oneself openly or before others." Conversely, one who sits in "darkness" (Gk. *skotos*, **SKOT-os**) operates in "spiritual darkness," implying "ignorance, or error." John's calling, then, was to prepare the way for the Messiah, "the way of peace" (Gk. *hodos eirene*, **ho-DOS i-RAY-nay**), which is "the plentiful life." Throughout the Gospel, peace is closely associated with God's redemptive work and the salvation that comes to God's people.

80 And the child grew, and waxed strong in spirit, and was in the deserts till the day of his shewing unto Israel.

John grew up and became strong in spirit, living out in the desert until the time set by God for him to begin his ministry.

Daily Bible Readings

M: A Messenger Is Coming
Malachi 3:1–4

T: Elisabeth Births a Son
Luke 1:57–61

W: His Name Is John
Luke 1:62–66

T: God Sends a Powerful Saviour
Luke 1:67–75

F: Preparing the Way
Luke 1:76–80

S: Warnings to the Crowds
Luke 3:7–14

S: A Powerful One Is Coming
Luke 3:15–20

TEACHING TIPS

December 23
Bible Study Guide 4

1. Words You Should Know

A. Lord (Luke 2:9, 11) *kurios* (Gk.)—The term *kurios* generally means "master," but here it is used for the title "Messiah."

B. Good tidings (v. 10) *euaggelizo* (Gk.)—To bring good news. It is also the root of the English word "evangelize."

2. Teacher Preparation

Unifying Principle—Reasons to Rejoice Everyone looks for reasons to rejoice. But how can we rejoice in the midst of all that life brings? The shepherds, whose lives were hard, received an announcement of God's fulfilled promise of the Messiah and declared their joy to all.

A. Read the Focal Verses several times, each time with a different version of the Bible.

B. Read the Daily Bible Readings as part of your daily devotions. Meditate on these verses, allowing God to reveal eternal truths to your heart concerning this week's lesson.

C. Complete lesson 4 from the *Precepts For Living® Personal Study Guide.* Review the information on the CD-ROM as well as The People, Places, and Times, Background, and In Depth sections of this guide to gather more insight for the lesson.

3. Starting the Lesson

A. Have a class member read the In Focus story as an introduction to prayer.

B. Lead in prayer by thanking God for His provision and asking for His guidance in helping class members realize that they all have been called and equipped to share the Good News of Christ with others.

C. Reinforce the AIM for Change objectives.

D. Based on the In Focus story, begin a discussion to see how many people know someone like Edith or Phyllis. Ask class participants to reflect on which personality most closely resembles their behavior.

4. Getting into the Lesson

A. Have the students share their experiences from last week's Make It Happen suggestions.

B. Instruct the class to read the Focal Verses. Consider doing this as a responsive reading with one person reading the first verse and the class reading the second verse. Continue this, alternating verses until the entire text has been read.

5. Relating the Lesson to Life

A. Discuss the Search the Scriptures questions.

B. Review the Discuss the Meaning and Lesson in Our Society sections to help the students apply eternal truths of today's lesson to their lives.

6. Arousing Action

A. Review the Make It Happen section. Ask the class members for suggestions regarding how to implement the ideas presented there. Encourage individual members to make personal commitments in this area in the coming weeks.

B. Remind the class of the importance of daily communication with God. Ask the class how they have used the Daily Bible Readings as a part of their devotions. Encourage those who have not done so to begin using this section of the lesson.

Worship Guide

For the Superintendent or Teacher
Theme: Called to Rejoice!
Theme Song: "Go Tell It on the Mountain"
Devotional Reading: Psalm 96:1–6
Prayer

CALLED TO REJOICE!

Bible Background • LUKE 2:1–20
Printed Text • LUKE 2:1–14 Devotional Reading • PSALM 96:1–6

AIM for Change

By the end of the lesson, we will:

INVESTIGATE the circumstances around Jesus' birth and the responses of persons to it;

EXPRESS joy at the good news of God's fulfilled promise; and

TELL someone about the good news of God's gift of the Messiah.

Keep in Mind

"For unto you is born this day in the city of David a Saviour, which is Christ the Lord" (Luke 2:11).

Focal Verses

KJV

Luke 2:1 And it came to pass in those days, that there went out a decree from Caesar Augustus, that all the world should be taxed.

2 (And this taxing was first made when Cyrenius was governor of Syria.)

3 And all went to be taxed, every one into his own city.

4 And Joseph also went up from Galilee, out of the city of Nazareth, into Judaea, unto the city of David, which is called Bethlehem; (because he was of the house and lineage of David:)

5 To be taxed with Mary his espoused wife, being great with child.

6 And so it was, that, while they were there, the days were accomplished that she should be delivered.

7 And she brought forth her firstborn son, and wrapped him in swaddling clothes, and laid him in a manger; because there was no room for them in the inn.

8 And there were in the same country shepherds abiding in the field, keeping watch over their flock by night.

9 And, lo, the angel of the Lord came upon them, and the glory of the Lord shone round about them: and they were sore afraid.

10 And the angel said unto them, Fear not: for, behold, I bring you good tidings of great joy, which shall be to all people.

11 For unto you is born this day in the city of David a Saviour, which is Christ the Lord.

12 And this shall be a sign unto you; Ye shall find the babe wrapped in swaddling clothes, lying in a manger.

NLT

Luke 2:1 At that time the Roman emperor, Augustus, decreed that a census should be taken throughout the Roman Empire.

2 (This was the first census taken when Quirinius was governor of Syria.)

3 All returned to their own ancestral towns to register for this census.

4 And because Joseph was a descendant of King David, he had to go to Bethlehem in Judea, David's ancient home. He traveled there from the village of Nazareth in Galilee.

5 He took with him Mary, his fiancée, who was now obviously pregnant.

6 And while they were there, the time came for her baby to be born.

7 She gave birth to her first child, a son. She wrapped him snugly in strips of cloth and laid him in a manger, because there was no lodging available for them.

8 That night there were shepherds staying in the fields nearby, guarding their flocks of sheep.

9 Suddenly, an angel of the Lord appeared among them, and the radiance of the Lord's glory surrounded them. They were terrified,

10 but the angel reassured them. "Don't be afraid!" he said. "I bring you good news that will bring great joy to all people.

11 The Savior—yes, the Messiah, the Lord—has been born today in Bethlehem, the city of David!

12 And you will recognize him by this sign: You will find a baby wrapped snugly in strips of cloth, lying in a manger."

13 And suddenly there was with the angel a multitude of the heavenly host praising God, and saying,

14 Glory to God in the highest, and on earth peace, good will toward men.

13 Suddenly, the angel was joined by a vast host of others—the armies of heaven—praising God and saying,

14 "Glory to God in highest heaven, and peace on earth to those with whom God is pleased."

In Focus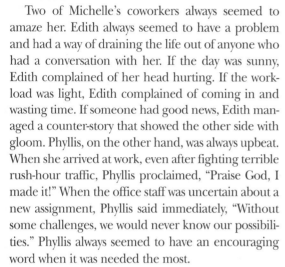

Two of Michelle's coworkers always seemed to amaze her. Edith always seemed to have a problem and had a way of draining the life out of anyone who had a conversation with her. If the day was sunny, Edith complained of her head hurting. If the workload was light, Edith complained of coming in and wasting time. If someone had good news, Edith managed a counter-story that showed the other side with gloom. Phyllis, on the other hand, was always upbeat. When she arrived at work, even after fighting terrible rush-hour traffic, Phyllis proclaimed, "Praise God, I made it!" When the office staff was uncertain about a new assignment, Phyllis said immediately, "Without some challenges, we would never know our possibilities." Phyllis always seemed to have an encouraging word when it was needed the most.

One day, while Michelle and several of her coworkers sat together at the lunch table, Michelle posed a question: "How do you get the strength to make it every day?" Edith was the first to speak.

"It's hard," she said. "Some days I wish I could find another job or do something different. All these folks say, 'Have a good day'; but, I tell you, life is hard and you have to be hard back."

After several other people at the table nodded their head in agreement, Phyllis said, "I get up in the morning and the first thing I do is thank God for another day and spend time in His Word. Once I've done that, I know that whatever comes my way won't be harsh enough to steal my joy. God is good, and I appreciate every day He gives me. I try to take that joy with me and pass it on to others, because life is too short to waste time complaining."

During this season, in particular, many people find it hard to rejoice and celebrate. The good news that today's lesson teaches us is that even in the midst of hardship, our reason to rejoice is found in Christ's coming.

The People, Places, and Times

Caesar Augustus. The Roman government ruled Judah harshly, and Caesar Augustus, the first emperor, was a tyrant who reigned in Rome from 27 B.C. to A.D. 14. While various emperors and other rulers gave Jewish religious leaders some freedom in religious matters and local governance, Rome ruled the entire known world at that time; thus, taxes were expected of "all the world."

Judea (Judaea). This was the southernmost part of what is known as the Promised Land. The monarchy was united under David and Solomon, but in the divided monarchy, Israel and Judah were split into northern and southern regions. One section of the southern area of Judah was known as Judea during the time of Jesus. Galilee was another geographical section.

The City of Nazareth and the City of David. There were two Bethlehems, one in Judea and one in Galilee, only seven miles northwest of Nazareth. Luke writes that Joseph and Mary went "into Judea, unto the city of David, which is called Bethlehem" (2:4). In order to pay taxes, the couple had to leave the City of Nazareth to be accounted for in Joseph's hometown of Bethlehem, the birthplace of King David called the City of David, which is where Jesus would be born. The journey from Nazareth to Bethlehem was about 80 miles.

Swaddling clothes. The Greek word for "swaddling clothes" (Luke 2:12) is *sparganoo* (**spar-gan-O-o**). It was traditional for a newborn baby to be tightly bound in strips of cloth. This helped to warm the child and to protect the newborn from the harsh elements. This was also symbolic of the love and protection the parents offered the child.

Source:
Beers, V. Gilbert. *The Victor Handbook of Bible Knowledge: Answers Your Questions on 300 Bible Stories.* Wheaton, Ill.: Victor Books, 1981.

Background

Luke begins his account of Christ's life by pointing out that the Saviour did not just step out of heaven and into history. Our Lord had a mother and an adopted father, Joseph. Luke ties Jesus' birth in Bethlehem to the figures of Herod the Great, Caesar Augustus, and Cyrenius, under whom the census took place. It is clear that Luke wrote mainly for Gentiles since the book is addressed to Theophilus who, like Luke, was a Gentile. Also, the Gospel itself is written so that Jewish customs are explained. This message would have been clear to a Gentile audience.

Luke painstakingly re-created the social history for the reader by explaining what was taking place at the time of the birth of Jesus in both the Hebrew and Gentile communities within the Roman Empire. In Luke 2:1–14, we have the angel's poignant and exhilarating pronouncement of the divine birth.

That the pronouncement came to shepherds is significant because it points to King David's origin as a shepherd. Also, the shepherds were looked down on by the "good Jews" of the day since most shepherds were not able to strictly follow the details of the ceremonial law regarding meticulous hand washing and other rules and regulations. The orthodox Jewish community looked down on them as a very common people.

The status of the shepherd's lifestyle offers encouragement to those who lack religious status. The shepherds' lifestyle is also typical of the life Jesus would lead during His ministry on Earth. Jesus would be unorthodox in many respects as He offered encouragement in His relationships with the common people.

At-A-Glance

1. Preparing for Christ's Birth (Luke 2:1–7)
2. Witnesses of Christ's Birth (vv. 8–9)
3. The Good News of Christ's Birth (vv. 10–14)

In Depth

1. Preparing for Christ's Birth (Luke 2:1–7)

Luke accomplished his intention of providing the historical, chronological, and prophetic setting of Jesus' birth. It was prophesied in Isaiah 9:6–7 that a child would be born to implement a righteous government based on judgment and justice. Through God's divine providence, Caesar Augustus issued an imperial order for a census or enrollment decree that forced everyone to be counted.

Since Joseph was from King David's bloodline, Joseph and Mary went to Bethlehem to register. The birth of Jesus in Bethlehem would fulfill Micah's prophecy about the Messiah (Micah 5:2). When the tired couple arrived in Bethlehem, Mary was about to go into labor and give birth to the child that would be the Saviour of the world. Since the inn was full, the couple was forced to find shelter in a stable. After Mary gave birth to Jesus, she wrapped Him in swaddling clothes and laid Him in a manger (a feeding trough).

2. Witnesses of Christ's Birth (vv. 8–9)

In the meantime, the angel of the Lord made the announcement to several shepherds who were attending to their duties on a clear, star-filled night. When the angel appeared before the shepherds, they were surrounded by the visible manifestation of God's glory. The shepherds were told to go to the City of David and see "a Saviour, which is Christ the Lord" (2:11). These shepherds, who thought nothing of defending their flocks from hungry wolves and lions, were shocked, awed, and afraid (2:9); still, they were eager to listen to the voice of the angel directing them to where they would find Jesus.

It is believed that the angel appeared to the group of shepherds near the watchtower of Edar, which was near Bethlehem (Genesis 35:21). If this is so, then these were no ordinary shepherds. The sheep that pastured in this area were destined for sacrifice in the temple. This would mean that the shepherds who supplied the lambs for the sin offering were the first to be made aware of the "Lamb of God" who would take away the sins of the world forever (John 1:36).

The fact that the angelic announcement came to shepherds is significant. A shepherd cares for flocks of sheep. He leads the sheep to pasture, to water, and, at night, to the fold for safety. The shepherd is responsible for protecting the flock from wild animals. The shepherd and sheep motif typifies the role of Jesus as Saviour. He was born to be the Messiah, to lead the "flock," God's people, and to serve the flock as the Lamb of God. Jesus referred to Himself as the "good shepherd" (John 10:11).

3. The Good News of Christ's Birth (vv. 10–14)

The angel ascribed three different titles to Jesus. The first title, Saviour, means "the one who would bring about salvation and deliverance." The second title, Christ, is the Greek equivalent of the Hebrew word "Messiah," which means "the anointed one of God." This term was used for the central figure of Jewish expectation. The final term, Lord, describes a superior, a master, or an owner. When applied to God or Christ, the word is used in place of the divine name.

The angel also gave the shepherds a sign to help them locate the divine child: they would find the baby wrapped in swaddling clothes and lying in a feeding trough. In other words, they would recognize God on Earth by the humbleness of the circumstances surrounding His birth.

As if one angel were not enough, a multitude of angels began to sing forth praise giving honor and glory to God. The announcement was not one of judgment and terror. The announcement of the birth of Christ meant that God was making a way for all people to have peace in Him. Life is filled with strife and persecution. Fear and anxiety were as prevalent in New Testament times as they are now. The governmental persecution of the people by Rome is evident in the backdrop of these verses and in the proclamation elsewhere that children would be killed in order to stop the Messiah's birth (Matthew 2:13–16). Most importantly, because of original sin, humans were separated from God eternally. God cannot look upon sin and fellowship with those who are born in sin. The good news meant that peace would be restored in place of the enmity that arose from the sin of Adam and Eve (Genesis 3:15–19). What joyous news that the birth of the Messiah would bring peace on Earth and would show God's goodwill toward all people. In our lesson text, heaven and Earth intermingled to proclaim the good news of Christ's birth.

The Christmas season is an especially good time to be thankful and to celebrate Jesus Christ. The shepherds are excellent examples for us to follow during this season. They received the Word of God from the angels by faith. They responded to the Word with immediate obedience. Then they took the place of the angels and spread the Word to others. Faith, obedience, and evangelism are three of the necessities for building the kingdom of God.

Search the Scriptures

1. Why did Joseph go to Bethlehem (Luke 2:4)?
2. What shone over the shepherds who were watching their flocks (v. 9)?
3. What news did the angels have for the shepherds (v. 10)?
4. What sign did the angels give the shepherds to identify the Christ (v. 12)?

Discuss the Meaning

1. What lessons from Jesus' humble birth can modern believers apply to their own circumstances?
2. What lessons can we learn from the encounter of the shepherds with the angel?

Lesson in Our Society

In today's society we are drawn to tragedy and bad news. We cause traffic jams by gaping at accidents. We buy magazines about scandals. We clog our conversations with negative things that we've heard concerning other people.

We are not asked to pretend that problems don't exist; nevertheless, the Bible tells Christians to rejoice. Jesus said to rejoice because our "names are written in heaven" (Luke 10:20). Peter says to rejoice with unspeakable joy (1 Peter 1:8). Each day we should look for opportunities to rejoice and share our faith with those who don't know the Lord.

There's no better way of embracing the spirit of Christmas than giving a bit of time to help others. Volunteering, especially during the Christmas season, is one way for you and your family to become active in helping spread the good news of Christ throughout your community.

Make It Happen

In the coming week, note all the opportunities that you may have to talk with people about Jesus. Make a point each day to tell people about wonderful things that have happened to you. Also, try to find out some good news about others. Greet people with the question, "What's the good news?" At the end of the week, note any changes in your perspective on life as a result of your new conversations.

Follow the Spirit

What God wants me to do:

_____

_____

Remember Your Thoughts

Special insights I have learned:

_____

_____

More Light on the Text

Luke 2:1–14

1 And it came to pass in those days, that there went out a decree from Caesar Augustus, that all the world should be taxed.

Luke mentions Emperor Augustus in order to establish a time frame for the birth of Jesus; thus, he writes a narrative and tells a story. Gaius Octavius ruled as emperor from 31 to 14 B.C. He was acclaimed "Augustus" (Gk. *Augoustos*, **OW-goos-tos**, meaning "venerable") in 27 B.C. The purpose of registration decreed by Augustus was to establish control

"For unto you is born this day in the city of David a Saviour, which is Christ the Lord" (Luke 2:11).

for conscription and to collect taxes. Taxes were used to support the state, particularly to provide for the emperor and his needs.

2 (And this taxing was first made when Cyrenius was governor of Syria.)

Luke was establishing historicity in order to connect the birth of Jesus to the world at-large. Cyrenius ruled Syria, a large Roman province, from A.D. 6 to 7. Subsequently, there is a gap in Luke's chronology; however, Luke's story should not be discounted.

3 And all went to be taxed, every one into his own city.

In order for the proper tax to be levied, people had to go back to their birth towns. Luke reported that it was the census that forced Joseph to return to his hometown of Bethlehem.

4 And Joseph also went up from Galilee, out of the city of Nazareth, into Judaea, unto the city of David, which is called Bethlehem; (because he was of the house and lineage of David:)

Joseph went to Bethlehem, the City of David, because he was a descendant of David. Bethlehem was the Judean village of David's origin.

5 To be taxed with Mary his espoused wife, being great with child.

Luke did not refer to Mary as Joseph's wife, although technically Jewish law states that he could have since they were engaged. Unlike in Matthew (1:18–25), he was primarily silent about Joseph's reactions to this pregnancy.

6 And so it was, that, while they were there, the days were accomplished that she should be delivered.

To add validity to His messianic identity, the child was born in Bethlehem. The timing of the census and the pregnancy set the occasion for Luke's story.

7 And she brought forth her firstborn son, and wrapped him in swaddling clothes, and laid him in a manger; because there was no room for them in the inn.

A firstborn son was considered a special blessing in Jewish families and had a privileged role. One would think that Joseph would stay with family members since he was from Bethlehem, but Luke continued to establish the story and the meekness of the birth of the Messiah by stating that not a main room in a home nor even an attached room for guests was available for the Messiah. The Greek word for "inn" (*kataluma*, **kat-AL-oo-mah**) implies lodging and could refer to either place.

8 And there were in the same country shepherds abiding in the field, keeping watch over their flock by night.

Luke continued to describe the setting into which the "Anointed One" was born. His place of birth was merely a feeding area for animals. Luke connected the City of David with the shepherds, since David was also a shepherd before he was anointed king.

9 And, lo, the angel of the Lord came upon them, and the glory of the Lord shone round about them: and they were sore afraid.

Luke included this third appearance by angels (see 1:5–23, 26–38). This appearance, however, was to all people. Also, the shepherds did not protest what the angels told them. The "glory" (Gk.*doxa*, **DOX-ah**) indicates splendor.

10 And the angel said unto them, Fear not: for, behold, I bring you good tidings of great joy, which shall be to all people.

Recognizing the shepherds' fear, the angels tried to assuage them. They brought the news of the visitation of God among His people in an authoritative, yet calming fashion. The angels brought news that would bring "joy" (Gk. *chara*, **khar-AH**).

11 For unto you is born this day in the city of David a Saviour, which is Christ the Lord.

The City of David was mentioned again to add credibility to Jesus' role as the Messiah. He is not only the Messiah, but the Saviour. This refers to His role as both messianic king and heir to David's throne. He is Saviour because as king He can grant forgiveness of sin.

12 And this shall be a sign unto you; Ye shall find the babe wrapped in swaddling clothes, lying in a manger.

The sign was not the child's circumstances, but the fact that what the angels had described to the shepherds was true. It was the fulfilling of a prophecy about Jesus (Isaiah 7:14).

13 And suddenly there was with the angel a multitude of the heavenly host praising God, and saying,

"Heavenly host" (Gk. *ouranios stratia*, **oo-RAN-ee-os strat-EE-ah**) implies a large, gathered number. It is the armies of heaven whose testimony reveals the divine meaning of this birth.

14 Glory to God in the highest, and on earth peace, good will toward men.

The Greek word *eudokia* (**yoo-dok-EE-ah**) can be read as "good will" or "benevolence." Where the peace of God is present, there is good will and benevolence.

Daily Bible Readings

M: Sing a New Song
Psalm 96:1–6
T: Joseph and Mary
Matthew 1:18–21
W: Traveling to Bethlehem
Luke 2:1–5
T: Jesus, Firstborn Son
Luke 2:6–7
F: Angels Proclaim the News
Luke 2:8–14
S: Shepherds Visit the King
Luke 2:15–20
S: Judging with God's Truth
Psalm 96:7–13

TEACHING TIPS

December 30
Bible Study Guide 5

1. Words You Should Know

A. Christ (Luke 2:26) *Christos* (Gk.)—The anointed one, the Messiah.

B. Salvation (Luke 2:30) *soterion* (Gk.)—The promised deliverance that God brings through the Messiah.

2. Teacher Preparation

Unifying Principle—Hearing and Telling Good News We all like to hear and tell good news. How do we respond to the good news of Christmas? Simeon responded to the birth of Jesus the Messiah by declaring that God was keeping the promise of salvation.

A. Read Chapters 1 and 2 of Luke to familiarize yourself with the context of this lesson.

B. Read the Focal Verses in their entirety and the Jewish laws concerning purification and infant dedication to place this particular lesson in context.

C. Research the role of the Holy Spirit in Luke's gospel and His role in Simon's providing reliable witness to the person and work of God's Son.

3. Starting the Lesson

A. Open the class with a prayer using the Lesson Aim and Keep in Mind Scripture as a guide.

B. Reinforce the concepts of the AIM for Change and the Unifying Principle.

C. Share the story of Dr. Melvin Banks Sr., from today's In Focus story.

D. Ask the class to cite examples when God fulfilled His promises in their lives.

4. Getting into the Lesson

A. Summarize the Jewish laws concerning purification and infant dedication. Emphasize the role of the Holy Spirit in the conception and ministry of Jesus, along with the Spirit's role in confirming that Jesus is the Messiah.

B. Ask several students to summarize the Focal Verses and relate the significance of Simon's witness.

5. Relating the Lesson to Life

A. Read the Discuss the Meaning, Lesson in Our Society, and Make It Happen exercises for today.

B. Allow the students to work in groups of two or three to answer the Search the Scriptures questions, discuss the points, and report back to the class when they finish.

6. Arousing Action

A. Read the Lesson in Our Society section. Next, ask students to respond to the question from the Make It Happen challenge.

B. Remind the students to complete the Daily Bible Readings to prepare for next week's lesson.

C. Close the class in prayer. Be sure to take time to solicit personal prayer requests.

CALLED TO WITNESS!

Bible Background • LUKE 2:22–38
Printed Text • LUKE 22:22-35 Devotional Reading • ISAIAH 49:5–6

AIM for Change

By the end of the lesson, we will

CONSIDER Simeon's response to the birth of the Messiah;

TRUST God because the birth of the Messiah shows that God keeps promises; and

WITNESS to the promises that God fulfills in our lives.

Keep in Mind

"And Simeon blessed them, and said unto Mary his mother, Behold, this child is set for the fall and rising again of many in Israel; and for a sign which shall be spoken against" (Luke 2:34).

Focal Verses

KJV

Luke 2:22 And when the days of her purification according to the law of Moses were accomplished, they brought him to Jerusalem, to present him to the Lord;

23 (As it is written in the law of the Lord, Every male that openeth the womb shall be called holy to the Lord;)

24 And to offer a sacrifice according to that which is said in the law of the Lord, A pair of turtledoves, or two young pigeons.

25 And, behold, there was a man in Jerusalem, whose name was Simeon; and the same man was just and devout, waiting for the consolation of Israel: and the Holy Ghost was upon him.

26 And it was revealed unto him by the Holy Ghost, that he should not see death, before he had seen the Lord's Christ.

27 And he came by the Spirit into the temple: and when the parents brought in the child Jesus, to do for him after the custom of the law,

28 Then took he him up in his arms, and blessed God, and said,

29 Lord, now lettest thou thy servant depart in peace, according to thy word:

30 For mine eyes have seen thy salvation,

31 Which thou hast prepared before the face of all people;

32 A light to lighten the Gentiles, and the glory of thy people Israel.

33 And Joseph and his mother marvelled at those things which were spoken of him.

34 And Simeon blessed them, and said unto Mary his mother, Behold, this child is set for the fall and rising again of many in Israel; and for a sign which shall be spoken against;

NLT

Luke 2:22 Then it was time for their purification offering, as required by the law of Moses after the birth of a child; so his parents took him to Jerusalem to present him to the Lord.

23 The law of the Lord says, "If a woman's first child is a boy, he must be dedicated to the LORD."

24 So they offered the sacrifice required in the law of the Lord—"either a pair of turtledoves or two young pigeons."

25 At that time there was a man in Jerusalem named Simeon. He was righteous and devout and was eagerly waiting for the Messiah to come and rescue Israel. The Holy Spirit was upon him

26 and had revealed to him that he would not die until he had seen the Lord's Messiah.

27 That day the Spirit led him to the Temple. So when Mary and Joseph came to present the baby Jesus to the Lord as the law required,

28 Simeon was there. He took the child in his arms and praised God, saying,

29 "Sovereign Lord, now let your servant die in peace, as you have promised.

30 I have seen your salvation,

31 which you have prepared for all people.

32 He is a light to reveal God to the nations, and he is the glory of your people Israel!"

33 Jesus' parents were amazed at what was being said about him.

34 Then Simeon blessed them, and he said to Mary, the baby's mother, "This child is destined to cause many in Israel to fall, but he will be a joy to many others. He has been sent as a sign from God, but many will oppose him.

35 (Yea, a sword shall pierce through thy own soul also,) that the thoughts of many hearts may be revealed.

35 As a result, the deepest thoughts of many hearts will be revealed. And a sword will pierce your very soul."

In Focus

Many of you may not realize it, but Urban Ministries, Inc. (UMI) was founded on the promise of God to Dr. Melvin E. Banks Sr. as a young boy in Birmingham, Alabama. When Dr. Banks was just 12 years old he heard an aged African American man speak movingly about the great spiritual needs within the Black community. At that moment, Melvin dedicated himself to the task of uplifting Christ within the African American community and fulfilling the call God placed on his heart.

In 1970, Dr. Banks started Urban Ministries, Inc. (UMI) in the basement of his home. With his wife, Olive, by his side, the pair began producing Sunday School material specifically geared for the needs and life concerns of urban people in general and for African Americans in particular.

Today, under Banks's direction, UMI has grown to be one of the leading publishers of Christian education resources for churches in the African American community, serving nearly 100,000 teachers with Sunday School and Vacation Bible School materials. Dr. Banks is also the author of a number of books and Bible studies, and the founder of the Urban Outreach Foundation, an organization that conducts leadership training institutes. He is an elder in his local church, serves on the board of trustees of Wheaton College and Circle Y Ranch, a summer camp for children and youth.

Dr. Banks is often asked how he accomplished these tasks; he simply smiles and responds, "God didn't give me these tasks because He thought it would be easy, but because He knew I would see it through." Today, UMI stands as a testament to the promises that God continues to fulfill in his life and the lives of others.

As we take a look at the promises that God has made to us, these promises stretch back to the beginning of time, and they continue to unfold, even to this day. Today's lesson is about the promises that God kept to His servant Simeon.

The People, Places, and Times

Joseph and Mary. Joseph and Mary are the earthly parents of Jesus, though Joseph is more like Jesus' stepfather since Jesus was conceived by the Holy Spirit in Mary's womb. Mary, the mother of Jesus, was mostly likely a young teenager (possibly as young as 14 or 15), but she humbly accepted God's will for her to be the mother of the Messiah.

Simeon. A righteous and pious layperson who received a revelation by the Holy Spirit that he would see the Messiah before he died.

Background

Luke's gospel gives attention to the numerous circumstances surrounding the coming of the Messiah. He particularly emphasizes the role of the Holy Spirit in the conception and ministry of Jesus, along with the Spirit's role in confirming that Jesus is the Messiah to His parents through a revelation given to Simeon. In today's text, Joseph and Mary are revealed to observant Jewish people who follow the laws related to purification (40 days after the birth of a male child—Leviticus 12:1–4) and dedication of the firstborn to God (Exodus 13:2, 12, 15). Simeon's testimony is significant because the Jewish people were living under the reign of the Roman empire and were longing for the day when their deliverer, the Messiah, would come. Simeon's chorus of praise is the response that declares that the era has arrived.

Source:
Bock, Darrell L. *Baker Exegetical Commentary on the New Testament: Luke 1:1–9:50.* Edited by Moises Silva. Grand Rapids, Mich.: Baker Books, 1996.

At-A-Glance

1. Jesus Is Dedicated (Luke 2:22–24)
2. Simeon Encounters the Messiah (vv. 25–27)
3. Simeon Praises God and Speaks a Prophecy (vv. 28–35)

In Depth

1. Jesus Is Dedicated (Luke 2:22–24)

Jewish law required women to go through a process of purification after giving birth to a child. In the case of a male child like Jesus, this was a period of forty days. Upon the completion of this process, Joseph and Mary went to the temple in Jerusalem to dedicate their firstborn to the Lord. Their strict observance of the law reveals that they took God's revelation through His Word and law very seriously. Joseph and Mary sought to obey God's law. Their example shows us that it is important to take God's revelation seriously. In the history of Israel and even today, God's people do not always treat divine directives with the seriousness that they require. The Bible gives us commands to be obeyed, not mere suggestions to follow when it suits our whim.

It is also notable that Joseph and Mary offered a sacrifice of a pair of doves and two young pigeons instead of a lamb and a young pigeon or turtledove. This reveals that Joseph and Mary are poor people; it also places Jesus in an environment where He directly identifies with those He came to save. The good news of the Gospel goes to the poor and the oppressed, and this goes beyond a merely spiritual sense of the words. The Messiah comes to bring deliverance to us from the spiritual slavery of Satan as well as to address the brokenness in our experiences, including the very real difficulties of poverty. God has not forgotten the poor, and the coming of the Messiah reveals the divine intent to care for "the least of these" (Matthew 25:40, 45).

2. Simeon Encounters the Messiah (vv. 25–27)

Luke introduces us to Simeon, a man who is a model of faithfulness to God. He is unique because he is someone who has experienced the Holy Spirit, which was not a common experience of the Jewish people. The Holy Spirit was not a common possession of the people of God until after Pentecost, so this emphasis in the text helps to highlight Simeon's significance. We should regard Simeon as a prophet, especially in light of his words to come. The role of the Holy Spirit in prophecy is also significant in light of what is to come as the narrative of Jesus' life and ministry unfolds. Described as someone who was waiting for the Israel's consolation, Simeon was like the rest of the Jewish people who were living in a

Jerusalem occupied by Rome. Messianic prophecies (e.g. Isaiah 40:1; 49:13) indicated that God would bring comfort or consolation to His people, and there was a great longing among the Jews for the time when God would deliver on His promises. Simeon had been told through a revelation by the Holy Spirit that he would not die until he had seen the Lord's Christ. "Christ" means anointed one ("Messiah" comes from the Hebrew word with the same meaning). Simeon was then moved by the Holy Spirit (v. 27) to go to the temple, where he crossed paths with Joseph and Mary who were there to fulfill their obligation to the law.

The emphasis on the Holy Spirit in Luke's Gospel should not be overlooked. The Holy Spirit is often overlooked when we talk about Jesus, but it is impossible to avoid the centrality of the Spirit here. From Jesus' conception through His ministry, the Holy Spirit is present and involved. In fact, what makes Jesus "the anointed one" is the presence of the Spirit upon Him. The same Holy Spirit so central to the life of Jesus is also central to God's promise to Simeon, the fulfillment of that promise, and the prophecy that follows.

3. Simeon Praises God and Speaks a Prophecy (vv. 28–35)

When Joseph and Mary arrived in the temple courts, they encountered Simeon who took Jesus into his arms and praised God. Simeon's praise consisted of exulting in the fact that God had finally fulfilled His promise to Simeon about seeing the Messiah. Now this prophet could die in peace because the promise had been fulfilled. Simeon was not asking to be struck down, but he was proclaiming that he could depart this life because he had seen what God wanted him to see. Significantly, Simeon spoke of seeing the salvation that comes from God. Most likely, Simeon was thinking of the deliverance that would come to Zion and physically deliver the Jewish people from the Roman empire. It is true that the Messiah will set all things right when Jesus returns, but His first coming accomplishes the work that reconciles humans to God and begins to correct the disorder in creation, but not in the fullness that Jesus' second coming will accomplish. Simeon also referred to Jesus as the light. Jesus will bring light to the darkness that is in the world and His salvation will extend to include all people. It is a glory to the people of Israel because this salvation

comes through God's chosen people. This is a fulfillment of the promise made to Abraham that in Him
all the nations would be blessed (Genesis 12:1–3).

The response of Joseph and Mary is quite revealing. Although Mary was told by the angel Gabriel that
she would be the mother of the Messiah, and Joseph
learned this from an angelic message in a dream
(Matthew 1:20–21), they were clearly surprised by this
revelatory praise that identified their son as the
Messiah who would bring salvation. This shows us that
even though they "knew" their son was special, they
really did not completely understand the cosmic significance of Jesus' birth. Mary and Joseph are not
alone in failing to completely grasp the magnitude of
the person and work of Jesus. Even the 12 disciples
have to be reminded over and over again that Jesus is
far more extraordinary than they think.

A prophetic message follows Simeon's praise to
God. The prophecy indicated that Jesus would be
someone who will be source of division in Israel. He
would be a cause for some to stumble and a cause for
the vindication of those who truly believe that He is
the Messiah. This will reveal what lies in the hearts of
many people. Jesus is the messianic hope who fulfills
the promises of salvation that God made, but His
reception would not be one of universal acceptance.
Furthermore, Simeon told Mary that she would also
suffer, a reference to the maternal pain she would
experience when it turns out that her son is a suffering Messiah who will die a painful, humiliating death
on a cross.

Today's passage shows that God is a God who delivers on His promises, though we do not know when or
exactly how He will do it. When we experience God's
fulfillment of His promises, we should respond like
Simeon and be an exultant witness to the greatness of
God.

Search the Scriptures

1. Why did Mary and Joseph go to the temple, and
what did this say about their relationship with God
(Luke 2:22–24)?

2. What makes Simeon significant in this passage
(vv. 25–26)?

3. What is notable about Simeon's prophecy and
the response of Mary and Joseph (vv. 30–35)?

Discuss the Meaning

1. Why is it important to follow the examples of
people like Joseph, Mary, and Simeon?

2. Simeon's prophecy reveals a lot of information
about Jesus as the Messiah. What are some aspects of
his prophecy that tell you something new about Jesus?
What might make your own witness to Jesus more
potent as a result of this information?

3. The text links the mission of Jesus and Mary's life
experience. How should we think about Mary in light
of the prophecy?

Lesson in Our Society

In the era of reality TV, YouTube, and MySpace,
people are nearly tripping over themselves to give witness to various details about their lives and about what
they find to be of great importance. Many times people reveal things about themselves that are less than
flattering, but the desire to have exposure and attention seems to intensify the eagerness to make oneself
known. As Christians, we have a responsibility as witnesses to proclaim and demonstrate to the world that
the Messiah, Jesus Christ, has come and has brought
salvation for the world. Yet, for various reasons,
Christians are often less than eager to reveal their allegiance to Jesus as opposed to their dedication to an
athletic team or a political or social cause. More than
ever, our society needs to see us speaking and living as
witnesses to Jesus in the same enthusiastic way that
Simeon did.

Make It Happen

How can you improve as a witness to Jesus? This
week, examine how your words and actions "speak"
about what is most important in your life and pursue
ways to improve your own presentation of the Gospel.
One of the best ways to improve your witness is by
seeking out someone gifted in evangelism to help you
discover ways you can be more effective in sharing the
truth about Jesus.

Follow the Spirit

What God wants me to do:

_____

_____

Remember Your Thoughts

Special insights I have learned:

_____

_____

More Light on the Text

Luke 2:22–35

22 And when the days of her purification according to the law of Moses were accomplished, they brought him to Jerusalem, to present him to the Lord;

The laws of the Old Testament required three things of the parents of a firstborn male: circumcision, redemption, and purification. Verse 21 tells us that Mary and Joseph had Jesus circumcised on the eighth day after His birth according to the stipulations of the law.

Purification was actually for the mother of the child. The law of purification after childbirth is found in Leviticus 12. A woman was considered unclean for seven days after giving birth to a male child. On the eighth day the child was to be circumcised, then she was to "continue in the blood of her purifying" for 33 days—for a total of 40 days. She was not to touch anything holy or enter the temple during this time. The sacrifice of purification was to occur at the end of the 40-day period.

Interestingly enough, the word the KJV translates "her" (Gk. *autos*, **ow-TOS**) is masculine plural in the Greek, so it actually means "their." This catches our attention because according to the law, Joseph and Jesus were not considered unclean (unless perhaps Joseph had become unclean through involvement in the delivery, but that appears unlikely). Commentators agree that this is Luke's way of pointing out the piety of both of Jesus' parents. Although Mary was technically the one obligated under the law, Joseph considered her obligation to be his obligation. He was thoroughly committed to upholding the law of God in his household.

Joseph and Mary brought Jesus to the temple in Jerusalem in order to present him to the Lord. The word "present" (Gk. *paristemi*, **par-IS-tay-mee**) means "to place beside, to present, stand by, or appear." It is used elsewhere in the New Testament to exhort Christians to present ourselves to God for spiritual service and moral purity (cf. Romans 12:1; 2 Corinthians 11:2; Colossians 1:22; 2 Timothy 2:15).

It seems likely, but not definite, that the "presentation" of Jesus is a reference to the payment of his redemption price (see below). The law did not require that the price be paid at the temple, but it is possible that Mary and Joseph decided to take care of the issue since they had to be there anyway for the sacrifice of purification.

23 (As it is written in the law of the Lord, Every male that openeth the womb shall be called holy to the Lord;)

This passage is a reference to Exodus 13:2, 12, 15; 34:20 and Numbers 18:15–17, which require the redemption, or purchase, of every firstborn son. The Exodus command requires the sacrifice of a lamb; Numbers gives an amount of silver as an alternate redemption price.

The rationale for the redemption command is straightforward: The Lord claims ownership of His people. To teach the Israelites to see themselves as belonging to Him, He requires that firstborn males be purchased.

Not only the people are His, but their possessions are His—even the firstborn of the livestock were to be redeemed. If an Israelite did not want to redeem his firstborn donkey, he was to break its neck. The firstborn of clean livestock, such as sheep, cattle, and goats, were to be sacrificed.

The people of God are to understand that we belong to Him because He has purchased us at a great price. God's action to release the people of Israel from their slavery in the land of Egypt was a "purchase" (Leviticus 25:42). In fact, the redemption command's focus on the firstborn is intended to remind the people of the plague of the firstborn—the keystone event in that purchase (Exodus 13:15). However, the Exodus itself was a foretaste of an even greater act of redemption at an even greater cost: Christ's purchase of His people from sin and death by His death and resurrection (Acts 20:28; 1 Corinthians 6:20; Titus 2:14; 1 Peter 1:18–19; Revelation 5:9).

24 And to offer a sacrifice according to that which is said in the law of the Lord, A pair of turtledoves, or two young pigeons.

The offering of Mary's purification mentioned here—two turtledoves or pigeons—was specifically authorized if the parents of a newborn could not afford the ordinary requirement—a lamb plus either one pigeon or turtledove.

The offering was required in order for a woman to be considered ceremonially clean after undergoing childbirth. The laws that required this cleansing were part of a body of ritual law that regulated practices that were not sinful in themselves. However, the ordinary Israelite's life was ordered by these laws that required, among other things, that a woman be cleansed after her menstrual period, that a man be considered unclean after a nocturnal emission, and that anyone who touched a dead body would need to be cleansed.

The cleanliness laws do not teach us that activities—some of which were involuntary or unavoidable—that cause ceremonial uncleanness are wrong. However, they do establish the principle that the people of God are to distinguish between the ordinary and the holy. They were to take great care that they did not bring anything less than holy, including themselves, into the presence of God.

25 And, behold, there was a man in Jerusalem, whose name was Simeon; and the same man was just and devout, waiting for the consolation of Israel: and the Holy Ghost was upon him.

Simeon is described as a "just" (Gk. *dikaios*, **DIK-ah-yos**) man, meaning that he was known as upright and righteous. *Dikaios* was used in the Greco-Roman world to refer to model citizens. Luke is using the term to describe him as a model citizen of the kingdom of God—one who cared deeply about obeying the commands of the Lord. He is also described as "devout" (Gk. *eulabes*, **yoo-lab-ACE**), meaning "God-fearing" or "reverent." Simeon was a man who took God at His word and cared more about what God thought about him than what others thought.

Simeon was waiting for the "consolation" (Gk. *paraklesis*, **par-AK-lay-sis**) of Israel. *Paraklesis* has a variety of meanings, most notably (1) a call for help, or (2) the consolation, comfort, and solace that comes in response to a call for help. Rabbis used this term to refer to the salvation that the Messiah would bring. Just as the Jews of Moses' day cried out for deliverance from their Egyptian taskmasters, so too Simeon and the pious Jews of his day were crying out for deliverance from their oppression. Many expected the Messiah to be a mighty military conqueror who would overthrow the Roman empire and lead Israel to political independence. However, Simeon understood the Messiah more in terms of the suffering servant predicted by Isaiah. He was expecting that Jesus would save the people of God from their bondage to sin and death.

26 And it was revealed unto him by the Holy Ghost, that he should not see death, before he had seen the Lord's Christ.

The word "revealed" in this instance (Gk. *chrematizo*, **khray-mat-ID-zo**) means to be divinely commanded, admonished, or instructed. It is the same word used to describe Joseph receiving the Lord's command to flee to Egypt when Herod plotted Jesus' murder, and again to go to Galilee to avoid Archelaus (Matthew 2:12, 22).

The revelation Simeon had received was no mere gut feeling or lucky prediction. God—perhaps in a dream or vision—had promised him an important role in the history of redemption. Simeon's words that follow indicate he had understood the Lord to mean that he would in fact die soon after seeing the Christ. This is why teachers have traditionally portrayed Simeon as an old man, even though the text never actually says he was old as it does for Anna in verse 36.

27 And he came by the Spirit into the temple: and when the parents brought in the child Jesus, to do for him after the custom of the law,

Luke does not indulge our curiosity by telling us how the Holy Spirit communicated with Simeon as Joseph, Mary, and Jesus enter the temple grounds, but he wants us to notice that even his steps were guided by God. (Perhaps Simeon was old, and walking was not easy.)

Whereas earlier in the passage, Mary and Joseph were said to be accomplishing their purification, here Luke emphasizes that their action is intended for Jesus; he and Simeon now take center stage. From this point on we are to think about Jesus' identity and purpose.

28 Then took he him up in his arms, and blessed God, and said,

Upon receiving the baby Jesus into his arms, Simeon began to speak. The word "blessed" (Gk. *eulogeo*, **yoo-log-EH-o**) literally means "to speak well of, or to praise."

29 Lord, now lettest thou thy servant depart in peace, according to thy word:

This phrase could also be translated, "Lord, you are now releasing your servant." The form of the verb "lettest depart" (Gk. *apoluo*, **ap-ol-OO-o**), which means "to release," is used to describe an ongoing action. Simeon had interpreted God's promise to mean that he would in fact die soon after seeing the Messiah.

"Lord" (Gk. *despotes*, **des-POT-ace**) is only used twice to refer to God in the New Testament. It could also be translated "master." Simeon's life was consumed by service to God.

Simeon refers to himself as "servant" (Gk. *doulos*, **DOO-los**) of the Lord. The word could also be translated "bondservant" or "slave." In the social order of the day, the position of bondservant was humble to say the least. However, Simeon does not use the term to express his low position. To be a "servant of the Lord" was to be tasked with special orders from God—a high honor! The expression "servant of the Lord" was applied in the Old Testament to such heroes of faith as Moses (Joshua 14:7), David (2 Samuel 7:5), and Elijah (2 Kings 10:10), as well as to the people of Israel as a whole (Isaiah 43:10).

30 For mine eyes have seen thy salvation,

Simeon had taken to heart passages of Scripture such as Psalm 119:81: "My soul fainteth for thy salvation." "Salvation" (Gk. *soterion*, **so-TAY-ree-on**) in the Bible strongly parallels the concept of deliverance—deliverance from anything that keeps the people of God from experiencing God's best. Simeon, filled with longing for the coming of the Messiah, understood that the greatest threat to the well-being of the people of Israel was not their political oppression at the hands of the Roman Empire. The greatest threat was the spiritual oppression of their enemy—Satan, who had succeeded in blinding many to the true purpose of the promised Messiah.

31 Which thou hast prepared before the face of all people;

The Old Testament promises the worldwide revelation of the Lord's salvation (cf. Isaiah 52:10; Psalm 98:3). If the coming of the Lord's salvation were to be conceived of as the rising of the sun, Simeon was declaring that the first glimmers of light have appeared on the horizon. The day is at hand! Simeon's words are later echoed by John the Baptist in Luke 3:6.

32 A light to lighten the Gentiles, and the glory of thy people Israel.

Simeon here makes a clear reference to Isaiah 42:6 and 49:6, in which the Suffering Servant is declared to be God's instrument for bringing truth, justice, and mercy not only to the people of Israel but to all the nations of the world. In fact, God had promised from the time of man's fall into sin to redeem men and women from every ethnic group and nation in the world. In Genesis 12:3 He promised Abraham "in thee shall all families of the earth be blessed" (cf. Genesis 18:18; 22:18). That promise was then repeated to Isaac and Jacob (Genesis 26:4; 28:14). We see the ultimate fulfillment of this promise in Revelation 7:9–17. A great multitude "of all nations, and kindreds, and people, and tongues" stands before God enthroned in heaven, worshiping God for His great salvation, which was accomplished by the blood of Jesus.

Although the salvation that Jesus purchased was for the blessing of all people, the people of Israel are still accorded a place of honor in the family of God. Paul writes in Romans 3:1–18 that Jews have no advantage over Gentiles with regard to salvation (cf. Romans 10:12). Jews are just as much under the curse of death as Gentiles, and need to receive the saving work of Jesus by faith in the same way as Gentiles. Furthermore, the distinctive Jewish rites of the old covenant such as circumcision have no impact on one's relationship with God. They can earn no one any special divine favor.

However, the physical descendants of Abraham, Isaac, and Jacob have an incredible and unique ancestral legacy. Their ancient fathers were the ones entrusted with the oracles of God (Romans 3:2). Their family history is the history of the people of God: adoption into God's household, the covenants, the giving of the Law, the temple worship, the patriarchs, the kings, the prophets and, of course, the birth of our Lord and Saviour Jesus Christ (Romans 9:4–5).

33 And Joseph and his mother marvelled at those things which were spoken of him.

The word "marvelled" (Gk. *thaumazo*, **thou-MAD-zo**) means to wonder or to be amazed. The Greek verb construction indicates that their marveling was an ongoing process—they probably remembered what Simeon had said for some time and were awestruck whenever they reflected on it.

Their amazement could have been based on several factors. First, Mary and Joseph were probably caught by surprise when Simeon approached them. They expected to simply go about their business at the temple and return home. Secondly, they would have been part of a vast crowd in the temple courts; the fact that Simeon singled them out for this pronouncement about their child was either an incredible coincidence or a divine arrangement. Third, this pronouncement by Simeon was just the latest in a series of extraordinary occurrences, none of which Mary and Joseph had ever expected to happen to them.

Mary and Joseph were simple people. Although Joseph was descended from the line of David (1:27; 2:4), they were not members of the religious or social elite. Joseph was a carpenter (Matthew 13:55), hardly an occupation that was esteemed when it came to matters of religion (cf. Mark 6:1–3). While the Scriptures give us no reason to question whether or not they believed God's word concerning the extraordinary nature of their son, that doesn't mean it was easy for them to understand or explain. Doubtless they realized it was an incredible privilege to bear the Messiah as their own son, but it was also awe-inspiring—even intimidating—in a way that none of us could ever imagine. It seems most likely that they were simply overwhelmed by all that happened to them in the months before and after Jesus' birth.

34 And Simeon blessed them, and said unto Mary his mother, Behold, this child is set for the fall and rising again of many in Israel; and for a sign which shall be spoken against;

The word "blessed" (Gk. *eulogeo*, **yoo-log-EH-o**) is the same word used in verse 28 to recount Simeon's words to God. Perhaps Simeon sensed Mary and Joseph's apprehension at all that they had experienced and recognized that words of blessing would encourage them to continue trusting the Lord.

The blessing Simeon offered was actually a prayer to God on behalf of Mary and Joseph. When one person blesses another in Scripture, he is asking for God to look kindly upon the other. It is considered to be a powerful and effective outpouring of God's grace to be blessed by a righteous or influential person (cf. Genesis 27, 48).

The verb "is set" (Gk. *keimai*, **KI-mahee**) literally means "to lie or recline" but is used figuratively here to mean "to be appointed or destined." Christ's coming, as well as the response of the people of Israel to Him, was not happenstance.

The word "fall" (Gk. *ptosis*, **PTO-sis**) is used only one other time in the New Testament—by Jesus to describe the collapse of a house built upon the sand (Matthew 7:27). However, the word is used in the Septuagint (the Greek translation of the Old Testament that was well known in the first century) to mean "downfall." It appears six times in passages that predict the Lord's judgment on the pagan nations of Tyre and Egypt (Ezekiel 26–32). The person or nation that has "fallen" is in a condition of utter ruin and complete misery as a consequence of being aligned against God and experiencing His righteous judgment. That Simeon uses this word to describe "many in Israel" is no accident. Israelites who fail to receive and trust in Jesus Christ will be just like the pagan nations in the days of their fathers who suffered God's wrath for their unrepentant opposition to the people of Israel.

The word translated "rising again" (Gk. *anastasis*, **an-AS-tas-is**) can refer to a rising such as getting up from a chair, but it is used frequently in the New Testament to mean resurrection from the dead. Strictly speaking, Simeon probably only intended to use the fall/rise contrast as a pointed illustration of the distinction between those cursed because of their rebellion against the Messiah and those blessed for their acceptance of His message. However, his words beautifully foreshadow the resurrection of Christ and the promise of resurrection for all who receive Him.

The concept of a division between those who reject Christ and those who receive Him, along with dramatic judgment for the former and divine blessing for the latter, is a prominent feature of several Old Testament prophecies. In fact, Simeon may be alluding to passages such as Isaiah 8:14–15; 28:13–16 and Psalm 118:22–23. Other passages in the New Testament apply and expand on this concept. In telling the parable of the tenants, Jesus directly quotes Psalm 118:22, clearly referring to Himself as the cornerstone (Matthew 21:42). Peter follows His example in confronting the Jewish council over their role in Jesus' crucifixion (Acts 4:11). While many stumble on the cornerstone, those who hope in Him will not be put to shame. First Peter 2:4–8 is a message of inspiration and hope for those who believe in Jesus. In fact, those who hope in Christ are "stones" in the "spiritual house" of which Christ is the cornerstone.

The verb translated "spoken against" (Gk. *antilego*, **an-TIL-eg-o**) can also mean "to oppose or contradict," so some English translations use the phrase "sign to be opposed" or "sign to be rejected." As the primary representative of God's kingdom on earth and the agent of redemption for God's people, Jesus would become the primary target of the enemies of God. Simeon is predicting an onslaught of verbal and nonverbal opposition.

35 (Yea, a sword shall pierce through thy own soul also,) that the thoughts of many hearts may be revealed.

The consequences of the opposition to God's kingdom would result in tremendous grief for Mary—a clear foreshadowing of the crucifixion. The fact that Joseph is not mentioned in the Gospels after the beginning of Jesus' ministry has led to the widespread assumption that Joseph died either in Jesus' childhood or young adulthood. Such a scenario would explain why Simeon's prophecy only concerns Mary, as the crucifixion would no doubt have been a painful experience for Joseph as well had he been alive.

The events that cause Mary heart-rending grief will also bring about the revelation of the thoughts of many hearts. The theme or phrase "revelation of thoughts" is one way the Scriptures refer to the final judgment. The Old Testament frequently portrays God as a judge from whom nothing can be hidden (cf. Psalm 7:8–10; Ecclesiastes 12:14; Jeremiah

17:10). And the theme of hidden things being revealed appears to be especially important to Luke, as it appears several more times before the end of his Gospel. Jesus says, "For nothing is secret, that shall not be made manifest; neither any thing hid, that shall not be known and come abroad" (Luke 8:17). While talking about the Pharisees with His disciples, Jesus says, "For there is nothing covered, that shall not be revealed; neither hid, that shall not be known" (12:2). Jesus later warns the Pharisees directly: "Ye are they which justify yourselves before men; but God knoweth your hearts" (16:15).

The enemies of God believed that by killing Jesus they would get rid of Him once and for all. Little did they know, however, that in so doing they were accomplishing God's purpose: the vindication of Christ, so that He might judge the living and the dead (cf. Acts 17:31). The construction of the Greek phrase "may be revealed" indicates that the revelation of hearts is actually dependent on the events that will cause a sword to pierce Mary's soul. The judgment cannot occur as God has ordained it unless Christ is first offered as sacrifice for sin and rises from the dead.

Daily Bible Readings

M: A Light to All Nations
Isaiah 49:5–6

T: The Presentation to God
Luke 2:22–24

W: The Consolation of Israel
Luke 2:25–26

T: A Sign from the Spirit
Luke 2:27–28

F: A Light to the Gentiles
Luke 2:29–33

S: A Sign of Opposition
Luke 2:34–35

S: A Sign of Redemption
Luke 2:36–38

TEACHING TIPS

January 6
Bible Study Guide 6

1. Words You Should Know

A. Passover (Luke 2:41) *pascha* (Gk.)—The meal, the day, the festival, or the special sacrifices connected with the Passover feast.

B. Wisdom (v. 52) *sophia* (Gk.)—Knowledge of very diverse matters.

2. Teacher Preparation

Unifying Principle—Questions and Answers We all have questions for which we seek answers. How does inquiry within the community of faith lead to maturity? Entering into dialogue in the temple, Jesus gave us an example of how to grow in faith and wisdom.

A. Research the celebration of Passover and learn about the customs associated with celebrating the feast.

B. Read the Background Scriptures and Focal Verses.

C. During your preparation time, begin to reflect and jot down possible responses to the following questions found throughout the In Depth section: What helps us to mature spiritually? How many of us actively seek to understand the revelation that God has given us with the kind of passion Jesus exhibited as a 12-year-old? Are we people who have a faith that truly seeks understanding, or are we perhaps too content with the level of knowledge we already have?

3. Starting the Lesson

A. Open the class with prayer, using the Keep in Mind Scripture and AIM for Change objectives as guides.

B. Reiterate the Unifying Principle and the objectives for today's lesson.

C. Briefly summarize the Background and The People, Places, and Times sections.

D. Ask for a volunteer to read the In Focus story aloud as the rest of the class follows along.

4. Getting into the Lesson

A. Ask for a volunteer to summarize the Focal Verses pointing out the Keep in Mind verse.

B. Divide the class into three small groups of two or three and assign each group an In Depth section to review and discuss. Make sure to have one person in the group act as recorder to capture the responses of their group.

C. Allow the students to remain in their groups and assign each group the appropriate Search the Scripture questions as well as one Discuss the Meaning question.

5. Relating the Lesson to Life

A. Reconvene the class and ask the group recorder to report to the class their conclusions.

B. Have the students discuss the times when they were most enthusiastic about learning and discovery, whether what they learned related to their job, a hobby, or school. Discuss how they might also have the same passion for learning about God.

6. Arousing Action

A. Ask students to consider the Make It Happen challenge and think of ways to develop a deeper relationship with God, keeping in mind that reading God's Word is one of the most important ways to increase our knowledge of God.

B. Remind the students to complete the Daily Bible Readings, and for those who have one, complete lesson 7 from the *Precepts For Living® Personal Study Guide* in preparation for next week's class.

C. Close the class in prayer. Be sure to take a minute or two to solicit personal prayer requests.

Worship Guide

For the Superintendent or Teacher
Theme: Inspired to Inquire!
Theme Song: "Guide Me Through, O Great Jehovah"
Devotional Reading: Psalm 148:7–14
Prayer

INSPIRED TO INQUIRE!

Bible Background • LUKE 2:41–52
Printed Text • LUKE 2:41–52 Devotional Reading• PSALM 148:7–14

AIM for Change

By the end of the lesson, we will:

EXAMINE the story of Jesus' time spent in the temple;

UNDERSTAND the relationship between inquiry and spiritual growth; and

COMMIT to lifelong learning in the community of faith.

Keep in Mind

"And he said unto them, How is it that ye sought me? wist ye not that I must be about my Father's business?" (Luke 2:49).

Focal Verses

KJV

Luke 2:41 Now his parents went to Jerusalem every year at the feast of the passover.

42 And when he was twelve years old, they went up to Jerusalem after the custom of the feast.

43 And when they had fulfilled the days, as they returned, the child Jesus tarried behind in Jerusalem; and Joseph and his mother knew not of it.

44 But they, supposing him to have been in the company, went a day's journey; and they sought him among their kinsfolk and acquaintance.

45 And when they found him not, they turned back again to Jerusalem, seeking him.

46 And it came to pass, that after three days they found him in the temple, sitting in the midst of the doctors, both hearing them, and asking them questions.

47 And all that heard him were astonished at his understanding and answers.

48 And when they saw him, they were amazed: and his mother said unto him, Son, why hast thou thus dealt with us? behold, thy father and I have sought thee sorrowing.

49 And he said unto them, How is it that ye sought me? wist ye not that I must be about my Father's business?

50 And they understood not the saying which he spake unto them.

51 And he went down with them, and came to Nazareth, and was subject unto them: but his mother kept all these sayings in her heart.

52 And Jesus increased in wisdom and stature, and in favour with God and man.

NLT

Luke 2:41 Every year Jesus' parents went to Jerusalem for the Passover festival.

42 When Jesus was twelve years old, they attended the festival as usual.

43 After the celebration was over, they started home to Nazareth, but Jesus stayed behind in Jerusalem. His parents didn't miss him at first,

44 because they assumed he was among the other travelers. But when he didn't show up that evening, they started looking for him among their relatives and friends.

45 When they couldn't find him, they went back to Jerusalem to search for him there.

46 Three days later they finally discovered him in the Temple, sitting among the religious teachers, listening to them and asking questions.

47 All who heard him were amazed at his understanding and his answers.

48 His parents didn't know what to think. "Son," his mother said to him, "why have you done this to us? Your father and I have been frantic, searching for you everywhere."

49 "But why did you need to search?" he asked. "Didn't you know that I must be in my Father's house?"

50 But they didn't understand what he meant.

51 Then he returned to Nazareth with them and was obedient to them. And his mother stored all these things in her heart.

52 Jesus grew in wisdom and in stature and in favor with God and all the people.

In Focus

One evening as Yvonne sat watching television, the telephone rang. She picked it up and said, "Hello."

"Auntie, what does God look like?"

On the other end of the phone was her inquisitive 6-year-old nephew, Alexander. Caught a little off guard by the question, Yvonne responded, "What did you say?"

Again, he said, "What does God look like?"

Immediately Yvonne's mind went racing, trying to figure out how to explain to a 6-year-old what God looks like. Finally, she responded, "Well, Alex, God is invisible, and no one knows what He really looks like. But we can learn about God and see what God acts like by learning about His Son, Jesus, in the Bible."

After a few moments of silence, Yvonne heard the phone drop and suddenly her sister Diane was on the phone.

"How does He come up with these questions?" Yvonne asked her sister, laughing.

"I don't know," replied Diane, "he just does. I had no idea what he wanted to ask you. He simply told me he wanted to ask you a question, so I dialed your number. You know what they say, 'out of the mouths of babes and sucklings.'"

"I suppose you're right. I guess my answer was sufficient?"

"I guess it was. He went back to his room to play."

Seeking answers to spiritual questions is a healthy component of our faith. The Christian community of faith should provide a safe place for spiritual inquiry; a place where children as well as adults can ask questions about how God is working in our lives and in the world. In today's lesson, we see Jesus as a young boy in the temple asking as well as answering questions.

The People, Places, and Times

Feast of Passover. The Feast of Passover celebrates the Jews' passage from slavery to freedom and commemorates the occasion in which the death angel passed over the Hebrew households in Egypt (see Exodus 12–13). Jews are commanded to remember the night of their liberation by partaking of the seder. During biblical times, the seven-day celebration was held in Jerusalem and attendance by the entire family was required (see Exodus 23:14–17).

Doctors. In today's text, doctors are teachers—men trained to understand the Torah and who also guided students in their understanding of the Law of God and the traditions of the Jews.

Background

Luke's gospel emphasizes the uniqueness of Jesus in numerous ways. One notable way is the contrast between Jesus and John the Baptist.

Today's text also reveals that Jesus' development was uniquely superior as seen through His activity in the temple and His response to His parents. John and Jesus have important roles to play, but Luke's gospel helps us see the extraordinary person that Jesus is by showing us an episode where He is no ordinary inquirer in matters of God's Word. While Jesus is unique, His eagerness to inquire of the teachers in the temple should stimulate us to be those who hunger after wisdom and long to grow as God's people.

Sources:

Bock, Darrell L. *Baker Exegetical Commentary on the New Testament: Luke 1:1—9:50*. Edited by Moises Silva. Grand Rapids, Mich.: Baker Books, 1994.

Packer, J. I. and M. C. Tenney eds., *Illustrated Manners and Customs of the Bible*. Nashville, Tenn.: Thomas Nelson Publishers, 1980.

At - A - Glance

1. The Passover Journey (Luke 2:41–44)
2. The Encounter in the Temple (vv. 45–50)
3. Jesus Returns Home and Grows Up (vv. 51–52)

In Depth

1. The Passover Journey (Luke 2:41–44)

As in the previous lesson, today's passage begins by indicating the faithfulness and obedience of Joseph and Mary. Typical of observant Jewish people, they made an annual trip to Jerusalem for the Passover, where they would recall God's miraculous deliverance of the Israelites from slavery in Egypt. This observance was required by the law (Exodus 23:14–17).

Luke 2:40 states that Jesus grew in wisdom and with God's grace upon Him, and indicates the 12 years that have passed leading up to this particular

Passover journey. Some scholars suggest that this may have been the first time Jesus made the trip with His family, but there are no clear indications as to whether this was His first time or not.

After completing the Feast of Passover, Joseph and Mary made the return trip, only to find after a day's travel that Jesus was not with them. The reason they may not have noticed initially is that they were traveling with a large caravan that included other relatives. In the midst of such a large group it would have been easy for Jesus to go unnoticed as they made the trip back to Jerusalem.

Large caravans were typical for such trips, as the road to Jerusalem would have been dangerous for a small family traveling alone. As it turns out, Jesus did not really get lost on the journey, but instead stayed in Jerusalem to be with the teachers in the temple.

2. The Encounter in the Temple (vv. 45–50)

After discovering that Jesus was not with any of their relatives, Joseph and Mary went back to Jerusalem in search of their son. Three days later, they found Him in the temple, listening attentively to the teachers of the Law and asking them questions. In His interactions with the teachers of the Law, Jesus demonstrated that He is not a typical 12-year-old inquiring about the Law. His questions and answers showed Him to be Someone of such remarkable insight that He amazed everyone.

While there is a clear difference between Jesus and the rest of us, His eagerness for and pursuit of knowledge about God's revelation serves as an important example. How many of us who regard ourselves as followers of Christ actively seek to understand the revelation that God has given us with the kind of passion Jesus exhibited as a 12 year-old? Are we people who truly seek understanding, or are we perhaps too content with the level of knowledge we already have?

Upon finding Jesus in the temple, His parents expressed their concern about His absence on the return trip home. In reply, Jesus gave an answer that revealed His ultimate priorities and allegiance. When Mary told Him, "Thy father and I have sought thee," Jesus responded that they should not have been surprised that He has been in His true Father's house. This answer should not be seen as if Jesus was being disrespectful to Mary and Joseph, but rather as an indicator of the kind of piety that Jesus possesses as

well as a reminder of His mission. While the trip to Jerusalem indicates the faithfulness of Joseph and Mary, Jesus' decision to remain in the temple and to inquire in the temple shows that His dedication is of a greater kind than that of His parents. Remaining in Jerusalem demonstrates a commitment to God's purpose that goes beyond familial loyalty. Later in His ministry, Jesus will express this commitment with statements such as "Anyone who loves his father or mother more than me is not worthy of me; anyone who loves his son or daughter more than me is not worthy of me" (Mathew 10:37, NIV). Faithfulness to God requires a commitment that trumps all other loyalties.

As in the previous lesson, Joseph and Mary did not understand the meaning of what had been said. Although they had been told about Jesus in angelic visitations, they did not fully grasp who Jesus was. In a manner similar to the disciples who walked with Jesus but were often surprised by events or sayings that indicated the fullness of Jesus' identity, Mary and Joseph were as perplexed by the words of Jesus as the teachers in the temple were by His questions and insightful answers. The fact that it took time for those who lived among Jesus to understand who He was should prompt us to inquire as to how much we really know our Saviour. Are we really as familiar with Jesus as we might assume?

3. Jesus Returns Home and Grows Up (vv. 51–52)

Jesus did not make the temple His new residence, but returned to Nazareth with Mary and Joseph and lived as an obedient son. The text goes on to tell us that Mary treasured the things she learned about Jesus in her heart, just as she did when He was born and visitors came from afar to worship Him (Matthew 2:1–12). While Mary may not have completely understood everything about Jesus, her act of treasuring the truth she learned about Him indicates a mind-set that serves as an example for us. Mary reminds us that the things we learn about Jesus should be regarded as treasures we hold in the depths of our hearts. Even if we do not completely understand everything about Jesus, we should reflect deeply on the magnificent things we learn about Him, as well as the rest of God's revelation to us in the Bible.

The final verse tells us that Jesus increased in wisdom, stature, and in favor with God and others. For some it may seem perplexing to think that Jesus needed to acquire wisdom, since He is both fully divine as well as fully human. What we must keep in mind is that when Jesus became flesh, He took on limitations, and willfully set aside unlimited omniscience. In the Gospels we see that Jesus operates in submission to the Father—as One who has come to do the Father's will, and who will only do what He is told to do. In the book of Luke it will also become clear that Jesus operates as One guided by the Holy Spirit. As a person under submission to God, Jesus only expresses His divinity when directed to do so. Since Jesus took on this limitation, it should be no surprise that He learns about the Law like other Jewish people, though neither should we be surprised that He has greater insight than others.

Search the Scriptures

1. Why did Jesus' parents travel to Jerusalem every year? What was different about this trip (Luke 2:41–44)?

2. What made Jesus so intriguing when He was among the teachers of the Law (vv. 46–47)?

3. What did Jesus say to His parents when they asked Him why He stayed in the temple? What was their response (vv. 48–50)?

Discuss the Meaning

1. What is significant about Jesus being found in the temple? Would it have made any difference if Joseph and Mary found Him in a marketplace? Why or why not?

2. When Jesus sits among the teachers, He is not content to merely listen. What kind of example does the young Jesus provide for us by His behavior in the temple?

3. Today's text ends by telling us that Jesus' parents didn't understand what He said and that He eventually grew up and increased in wisdom. What does this seem to say about Joseph and Mary?

Lesson in Our Society

These days there is a lot of talk about pursuing one's passion. Many people say that the key to the best life is finding your passion and living it out. While the pursuit of one's passions is laudable in most cases, how much of a passion for us is seeking to know God as best we can? Are we attempting to

inquire after God and His ways in the manner that Jesus does in today's text? While Jesus is different from us, it is because of Him that we can also talk about learning about our Father. How passionate are you about knowing God and pursuing His agenda?

Make It Happen

This week, make an effort to learn more about your faith. Whether it is learning more about Jesus, about God's character, or about God's agenda for His people, look into the Scriptures to take your relationship with God to a deeper place.

Follow the Spirit

What God wants me to do:

_____

_____

Remember Your Thoughts

Special insights I learned:

_____

_____

More Light on the Text

Luke 2:41–52

41 Now his parents went to Jerusalem every year at the feast of the Passover.

The Jews came into existence as a people who possessed unique and divinely ordained customs and practices. They had special God-given rights; they were the most privileged of all peoples to worship the only true God; and they had all it took to serve God in the way acceptable to Him. The apostle Paul, describing the divine heritage of the Jews, aptly puts it this way: "Who are the Israelites; to whom pertaineth the adoption, and the glory, and the covenants, and the giving of the law, and the service of God, and the promises; Whose are the fathers, and of whom as concerning the flesh Christ came, who is over all, God blessed forever. Amen" (Romans 9:4–5).

The feasts were part of the Jewish customs and practices. Celebrating the feasts was in fulfillment of the covenant God had with them. The Passover feast mentioned in this verse was the first of the three major annual festivals of the Jews; it was celebrated in Jerusalem in the month of Nisan (March–April), from the 14th to the 21st. The first day, being the 14th, was the actual Passover feast, while the remaining days were called Feast of Unleavened Bread. The Passover commemorated the miraculous deliverance of the Israelites from Egyptian bondage and the sparing of their firstborn when the destroying angel smote the firstborn of the Egyptians.

The Greek word translated "Passover" *pascha* (**PAS-khah**) in this verse is used to refer to the meal, the day, the festival, or the special sacrifices connected with the Passover feast. But specifically, it refers to the *paschal supper* eaten on the first day of the feast, the 14th of Nisan. The Hebrew word translated "Passover" is *pacach* (**PEH-sakh**); it means "to pass over, skip over or to spare."

Later observances of the Passover differ in certain respects from the first and original celebrated in Egypt on the night before the deliverance. The first Passover was observed at home; the head of the family slew the lamb in his own house, and the blood was sprinkled on the doorway. After the first Passover, the priests regulated the service at the tabernacle; this created a fully developed ceremonial law. Under this perfected law, the priests altered details in order to assimilate the Passover to the standard religious service. The Passover was celebrated by the Jews annually and incorporated these distinctions from the first and original: the Passover lamb was slain in the temple, the place where God would choose to put His name, rather than at home (Deuteronomy 16:5–6); the blood was sprinkled on the altar instead of the door posts; and apart from the family sacrifice for the Passover meal, there were public and national sacrifices offered each of the seven days of the Feast of Unleavened Bread. Each year the people recited the meaning of the Passover; they later started singing the Hallel (Psalms 113–118) during the meal. A second Passover on the 14th day of the second month was observed by those ceremonially unclean or away on a journey at the time of its regular celebration on the 14th of Nisan.

These changes made to the Passover, and the fact that it became a perpetual ordinance, made it last through generations even to the time of Jesus. Solomon built the temple in Jerusalem—the place where God had put His name. For this reason, the Passover was celebrated in Jerusalem. In keeping with the yearly observance, every devout Jew, including Jesus' parents, was expected to go to Jerusalem for the Passover.

42 And when he was twelve years old, they went up to Jerusalem after the custom of the feast. 43 And when they had fulfilled the days, as they returned, the child Jesus tarried behind in Jerusalem; and Joseph and his mother knew not of it.

Jesus' parents observed the Passover from year to year. In the course of time, as indicated by the stage of Jesus' growth, He became 12 years old.

At this time, He went to Jerusalem for the Passover according to the custom of the feast. The Greek word translated "custom" is *ethos* (**ETH-os**); it signifies "usage prescribed by law; a manner, habit; a rite or ceremony." The word translated "feast" is *heorte* (**heh-or-TAY**); it means a "holy day." Making the journey to Jerusalem, performing the special sacrifices, eating the Passover meal, and all that is done in observing the Passover had become a habit or rite prescribed by law for the Jews. All these acts were performed during holy days—specific seasons or days set apart unto the Lord. The feast lasted over a period of eight days. The first and the last days were Sabbath days in which no one was required to do any servile work other than make preparations for the meal. Those who traveled to Jerusalem from other towns, like Jesus and His parents, had to stay in Jerusalem during the period of the feast. This is what is meant by " they . . . fulfilled the days. "

Before Jesus was 12, He could possibly have attended the Passover feast with His parents. For Luke to make special reference concerning Jesus being 12 years old could mean something significant. According to the Jewish custom, bar mitzvah is a ceremony and celebration for a Jewish boy who has attained the age of 13, at which he accepts the religious responsibilities of an adult. At age 12, Jesus was getting close to experiencing this ceremony; He was about to be a bar mitzvah (as the celebrant is called), to be introduced into Jewish society as a responsible male.

After they had observed the days of the feast, they returned home, but Jesus tarried behind in Jerusalem. The Greek word translated "tarried" (*hupomeno*, **hoop-om-EN-o**) means "to endure or to wait." The boy Jesus waited behind in Jerusalem while His parents headed back home. As someone who had a divine mission to accomplish and a purpose to fulfill on earth, His waiting behind in Jerusalem immediately after Passover was certainly in accordance with His mission. Consequently, the Passover of Jesus' twelfth year on Earth occasioned His first purposeful interaction with the Jewish public.

As the Son of God who came to fulfill God's will, Jesus' tarrying wasn't an act of His own will but of God's. There was a heavenly outpouring of spiritual virtue upon the boy Jesus at the age of 12 to reveal His divine nature. In the meantime, His parents didn't realize they left Him behind as they journeyed home.

Jesus Christ Himself is a fulfillment of the law (Matthew 5:17), the law that prescribes the Passover. As the apostle Paul writes to the Corinthians, he refers to Christ as our passover who is sacrificed for us (1 Corinthians 5:7). The Passover typologically represents Christ; while the feast is a type, Christ became its Antitype; the law that instituted the Passover was a shadow (Colossians 2:16–17), but Jesus Christ is its reality—the fulfillment.

44 But they, supposing him to have been in the company, went a day's journey; and they sought him among their kinsfolk and acquaintance. 45 And when they found him not, they turned back again to Jerusalem, seeking him.

In the course of the journey, assumption gave way to awareness. Mary and Joseph became aware that Jesus was not in the group after traveling an entire day. The Greek word for "company" (*sunodia*, **soon-od-EE-ah**) denotes "companionship on a journey" or a "company of travelers." Because the boy Jesus was fulfilling something of a notable spiritual importance back in Jerusalem, it took a whole day for His parents to realize they were missing His companionship. When they discovered that He was not in their group, they started searching for Him among their relatives. The Greek word translated "sought" (*anazeteo*, **an-ad-zay-TEH-o**) denotes "to seek carefully," that is, to search out someone while having some difficulty in the process. This means it was quite an effort trying to search for Jesus through the group of travelers.

46 And it came to pass, that after three days they found him in the temple, sitting in the midst of the doctors, both hearing them, and asking them ques-

tions. **47 And all that heard him were astonished at his understanding and answers.**

After three days of searching for Jesus, His parents eventually found Him in the temple in discussion with the doctors. The Greek word translated "doctors" (*didaskalos*, **did-AS-kal-os**) signifies "instructor, teacher, or master." These doctors were teachers of the Law who taught the Jewish religion; they were also called scribes, professional expositors of the laws of Judaism. The scribes underwent special training and had to pass rigid examinations before being officially recognized. They were highly respected within the Jewish community. These were the caliber of people with whom the boy Jesus was having an intellectual discussion at age twelve. He was "hearing them" and "asking them" questions. The word translated "hearing" (*akouo*, **ak-OO-o**) conveys the idea of hearing the meaning or message of what is spoken, the thing perceived, which forms an understanding in the hearer, as opposed to hearing a sound. As Jesus heard from the doctors, He understood matters pertaining to their laws. The Greek word translated "asking" (*eperotao*, **ep-er-o-TAH-o**) signifies "to demand, inquire or desire" and suggests asking with some eagerness. Jesus seemed to demand answers from the doctors based on what He desired to know.

A time of inquiry is a standard practice in observing the Passover. When the meal has been prepared, the family sits around the table with the head of the family taking a place of honor. The first cup of wine is served, then everyone eats a portion of the bitter herbs. The unleavened bread is handed out next; afterward, the lamb is placed on the table in front of the head of the family. Before eating this paschal meal, a second cup of wine is served; at this point the son, in accordance with Exodus 12:26, asks the father the meaning and significance of the feast. Jesus could have been extended this practice of making inquiries about the feast to the doctors in the temple.

An impartation by the Holy Spirit certainly inspired Him at that age to make intelligent inquiries that astonished these learned doctors. He exhibited profound understanding; He gave them amazing answers. To them, He was a sort of prodigy. They didn't know He had a divine nature, which was actually manifesting.

He did not only inquire of them, He also gave them answers. The Greek word translated "answers" (*apokrisis*, **ap-OK-ree-sis**), meaning "a response," tells us that Jesus was also asked questions to which He gave responses. By His answers, He revealed an understanding that astonished the doctors in the temple. With such understanding at His age, He revealed to the doctors that He was a responsible male, mature enough to be introduced to the Jewish society, and as one capable of imparting the true knowledge of God on the people.

This first public encounter with these Jewish leaders helped to give Jesus an intimate knowledge of the Jewish religion and how the people served God. While teaching in later years, He denounced the way the Jews used their tradition to make the commandment of God ineffective (Matthew 15:3). He also denounced other aspects of their customs and practices.

It is of great spiritual benefit to be inquisitive about spiritual matters. This will cause us to make inquiries about God, His Word, and the life we possess in Him. An inquisitive disposition is sure to bring inspiration, and by inspiration we get illuminating knowledge that leads to growth and spiritual maturity. Within the community of faith, it is therefore advisable to dialogue with others and to make inquiries from those whom the Lord has ordained to teach us His Word. This might require us to voice our convictions about certain issues of the faith, and to accept correction when we are wrong. In this way, we will grow in faith and wisdom. This is why we have to commit ourselves to a lifelong learning in the community of faith.

48 And when they saw him, they were amazed: and his mother said unto him, Son, why hast thou thus dealt with us? behold, thy father and I have sought thee sorrowing.

Amazement follows discovery. We will also always be amazed when Jesus Christ becomes the object of our aspiration and search. The Greek word translated "amazed" (*ekplesso*, **ek-PLACE-so**) means "to be exceedingly struck in mind, to be struck with astonishment." This was how Jesus' parents felt upon discovering Him in the temple. They didn't expect to see Him in the temple with the teachers of the Law. The fact that He was unperturbed and feeling comfortable with these learned men inflamed their amazement and was in sharp contrast to their feel-

ings of anxiety that had mounted over the period of a three-day search for Him.

Anxiety made Jesus' mother upset about His actions. She probably fathomed that Jesus' actions were in some way wrong. In an outburst of emotions typical of mothers, she inquired why He had done this to them. The Greek word translated "dealt" (*poieo* (**poy-EH-o**) simply means "to be" and connotes "hath done unto us." Though she knew that her son was the Messiah, the Son of God, she was still puzzled as to what the reason could be for His unusual behavior.

49 And he said unto them, How it is that ye sought me? Wist ye not that I must be about my Father's business? 50 And they understood not the saying which he spake unto them.

Here we see a striking commitment to kingdom business at an early age. Jesus replied to His mother with a question that offered an explanation: a question that justified His presence in the temple, and explained His absence from the caravan of travelers. The Greek word translated "wist" (*eido*, **I-do**) means "to know, to be aware," hence "Wist ye not" can be translated, "Don't you know?" or "Are you not aware?" Jesus' response appears to admonish His parents that they should have known He would be somewhere on assignment for His Heavenly Father. His reply reveals His willingness and commitment to his Father's business while making them aware of its importance.

In His question, He speaks of an inner compulsion. He says, "I must...." The Greek word for "must" (*dei*, **die**) denotes "it is necessary"; it is used to indicate a necessity brought about by certain circumstances. In this case, Jesus is saying, by reason of His Father's will He had to do His Father's business. It was necessary for a divine purpose to be fulfilled, which made every other thing less significant—even traveling back home with His parents.

51 And he went down with them, and came to Nazareth, and was subject unto them: but his mother kept all these sayings in her heart.

The arrival of Jesus' parents seemed to mark the end of His three-day mission in the temple. In his reply to His mother in verse 49, He questioned her with His spiritual authority as the Christ, the Son of

God, who came from heaven to fulfill God's work on earth. But His full awareness of the fact that He was human, a boy of 12, and still under parental care, made Him conduct Himself in the most appropriate manner: He went back to Nazareth with His parents and became subject to them. The Greek word translated "subject" (*hupotasso*, **hoop-ot-AS-so**) means "to submit oneself to, to obey or make oneself a subordinate." Since He was still a child, Jesus complied with natural order by submitting Himself to the authority and protection of His parents.

His mother became a repository of His sayings. The Greek word translated "kept" (*diatereo*, **dee-at-ay-REH-o**) signifies "to keep carefully, to observe strictly." This gives us the idea of Jesus' mother meticulously collecting every saying of Jesus and storing them in her heart.

52 And Jesus increased in wisdom and stature, and in favour with God and man.

Every child is expected to grow into adulthood. Growth in children is characterized by physical, mental, and spiritual development. As Jesus grew up, He increased in wisdom. The Greek word for "wisdom" (*sophia*, **sof-EE-ah**) is used in a broad sense to mean "human and spiritual wisdom." Increasing in wisdom is an indication of spiritual development and growing in the Holy Spirit, for the wisdom of God is one of the principal manifestations of the Spirit in one's life. Other attributes accompanied wisdom to bring about Jesus' spiritual development. The prophecy of Isaiah reveals these attributes to us: "And the spirit of the Lord shall rest upon Him, the spirit of wisdom and understanding, the spirit of counsel and might, the spirit of knowledge and of the fear of the Lord" (Isaiah 11:2). Isaiah further tells us what He will be made into as a result of this wisdom: "And shall make him of quick understanding in the fear of the Lord: and he shall not judge after the sight of his eyes, neither reprove after the hearing of his ears" (v. 3).

Jesus increased in stature. The Greek word for "stature" (*helikia*, **hay-lik-EE-ah**) signifies "age, maturity in years or size." Jesus grew normally, physically; His growth was not stunted, and this is an indication that He grew up to full human size. He also increased in favour. The word translated "favour" (Gk. *charis*, **KHAR-ece**) denotes "graciousness, grace in a person." It speaks of the divine influence upon the heart, and its reflection in the life of a person. This graciousness or divine influence in Jesus' life continuously attracted benefits, gifts, pleasure, and acceptability from God and man.

Daily Bible Readings

M: A Horn for God's People
Psalm 148:7–14
T: The Passover Feast Instituted
Numbers 9:1–5
W: First Passover Observed
Exodus 12:11–14
T: The Annual Pilgrimage
Luke 2:41–45
F: About the Father's Business
Luke 2:46–50
S: Growing Up in Nazareth
Luke 2:51–52
S: Praise the Lord!
Psalm 148:1–6

TEACHING TIPS

January 13
Bible Study Guide 7

1. Words You Should Know
A. Love (Luke 6:27) *agapao* (Gk.)—A selfless concern for the welfare of others.

B. Bless (v. 28) *eulogeo* (Gk.)—To invoke God's favor.

C. Do good (vv. 33, 35) *agathopoieo* (Gk.)—To be benevolent; to do good so that someone derives advantage from it.

2. Teacher Preparation
Unifying Principle—Responding to Opposition Every person needs to learn how to express love to others. What does Jesus teach us about loving our enemies? Jesus taught His disciples to love their enemies, do good to those who hate them, and do to others as they would have others do to them.

A. Read today's Focal Verses, The People, Places, and Times, and Background sections to familiarize yourself with today's lesson.

B. Obtain a copy of *Strength to Love* by Dr. Martin Luther King Jr. The work is a compilation of 16 sermons and one essay written by Dr. Martin Luther King Jr. Pay particular attention to the sermon for chapter five titled "Love Your Enemies." Or read the excerpt from today's In Focus story taken from Dr. King's Nobel Peace Prize acceptance speech.

3. Starting the Lesson
A. Ask a student to open the class with a prayer using the Keep in Mind verse and AIM for Change section.

B. Next, set the scene for a visualization exercise. Instruct the students to sit quietly, close their eyes, take a few deep breaths, and relax as they imagine themselves sitting in church listening to a sermon by a young Dr. King. Begin to read selected excerpts from Dr. King's sermon "Love Your Enemies" or excerpts from his Nobel Peace Prize acceptance speech found in today's In Focus story.

C. After the reading, ask the class to answer the following question: "How can I express love to my enemies?"

4. Getting into the Lesson
A. Reinforce the AIM for Change by telling the class that even though many people may find it difficult to practice the concept of loving one's enemies, today's Focal Verses hold up Jesus' ideals of love, forgiveness, and generosity.

B. Break the class into two groups and assign each group an In Depth and corresponding Focal Verses to read, review, and discuss.

5. Relating the Lesson to Life
A. Allow the class to remain in their work groups to answer the Search the Scriptures and Discuss the Meaning questions. Ask for a volunteer within each group to act as group recorder. Allow several minutes for both groups to discuss the points and report back to the class when they finish.

B. Reconvene the class and go over the Lesson in Our Society exercises for today.

6. Arousing Action
A. Allow students time to discuss situations when it was clear that they were being mistreated by someone or when it was clear that someone had become their enemy.

B. Encourage the students to follow through on the Make It Happen suggestion.

C. Close the class in prayer. Be sure to take time to solicit personal prayer requests.

Worship Guide

For the Superintendent or Teacher
Theme: Inspired to Love!
Theme Song: "Love Lifted Me"
Devotional Reading: Psalm 37:1–11
Prayer

INSPIRED TO LOVE!

Bible Background • LUKE 6:27–36
Printed Text • LUKE 6:27–36 Devotional Reading • PSALM 37:1–11

AIM for Change

By the end of the lesson, we will:

EXPLORE the meaning of the love that Jesus taught;

REALIZE that people we do not like deserve to be loved; and

DO something for others that we would like to have done for us.

Keep in Mind

"But love ye your enemies, and do good, and lend, hoping for nothing again; and your reward shall be great, and ye shall be the children of the Highest: for he is kind unto the unthankful and to the evil" (Luke 6:35).

Focal Verses

KJV

Luke 6:27 But I say unto you which hear, Love your enemies, do good to them which hate you,

28 Bless them that curse you, and pray for them which despitefully use you.

29 And unto him that smiteth thee on the one cheek offer also the other; and him that taketh away thy cloak forbid not to take thy coat also.

30 Give to every man that asketh of thee; and of him that taketh away thy goods ask them not again.

31 And as ye would that men should do to you, do ye also to them likewise.

32 For if ye love them which love you, what thank have ye? for sinners also love those that love them.

33 And if ye do good to them which do good to you, what thank have ye? for sinners also do even the same.

34 And if ye lend to them of whom ye hope to receive, what thank have ye? for sinners also lend to sinners, to receive as much again.

35 But love ye your enemies, and do good, and lend, hoping for nothing again; and your reward shall be great, and ye shall be the children of the Highest: for he is kind unto the unthankful and to the evil.

36 Be ye therefore merciful, as your Father also is merciful.

NLT

Luke 6:27 "But to you who are willing to listen, I say, love your enemies! Do good to those who hate you.

28 Bless those who curse you. Pray for those who hurt you.

29 If someone slaps you on one cheek, offer the other cheek also. If someone demands your coat, offer your shirt also.

30 Give to anyone who asks; and when things are taken away from you, don't try to get them back.

31 Do to others as you would like them to do to you.

32 If you love only those who love you, why should you get credit for that? Even sinners love those who love them!

33 And if you do good only to those who do good to you, why should you get credit? Even sinners do that much!

34 And if you lend money only to those who can repay you, why should you get credit? Even sinners will lend to other sinners for a full return.

35 "Love your enemies! Do good to them. Lend to them without expecting to be repaid. Then your reward from heaven will be very great, and you will truly be acting as children of the Most High, for he is kind to those who are unthankful and wicked.

36 You must be compassionate, just as your Father is compassionate.

In Focus

As we approach the King holiday, it is worthwhile to note that Dr. Martin Luther King Jr. was one of the most notable figures of the twentieth century. During the Civil Rights Movement of the 1950s and '60s, Dr. King captured the hearts and minds of people throughout the world with his commitment to love and nonviolent resistance. It was Dr. King's belief that even though nonviolence may be perceived as cowardly, it is not. He believed that the racial tension only existed between good and evil and not between peo-

ple, and that our only means of survival was to love one another. Consider the following excerpt from Dr. King's Nobel Peace Prize acceptance speech:

Sooner or later all the people of the world will have to discover a way to live together in peace, and thereby transform this pending cosmic elegy into a creative psalm of brotherhood. . . .If this is to be achieved, man must evolve for all human conflict a method which rejects revenge, aggression and retaliation. The foundation of such a method is love. . . . I believe that unarmed truth and unconditional love will have the final word in reality. This is why right temporarily defeated is stronger than evil triumphant.

I still believe that one day mankind will bow before the altars of God and be crowned triumphant over war and bloodshed, and nonviolent redemptive goodwill will proclaim the rule of the land. . . . I still believe that we shall overcome.

To begin the process of loving one's enemies, Dr. King admonished believers to begin a journey of self-examination followed by an earnest effort to look for the good in others. He believed that "within the best of us, there is some evil, and within the worst of us, there is some good." He believed that to love one's enemy meant to show *agape* or unconditional love that seeks nothing in return. According to Dr. King, "Love is understanding, redemptive goodwill for all men, so that you love everybody, because God loves them. You refuse to do anything that will defeat an individual, because you have *agape* in your soul. This is what Jesus means when he says, 'Love your enemy.'"

Today's lesson reinforces the ideal that Jesus taught His disciples to love their enemies, do good to those who hate them, and do to others as they would have others do to them.

Source:

Excerpt reprinted by arrangement with the Heirs to the estate of Martin Luther King Jr, c/o Writers House as agent for the proprietor, New York, NY. Copyright 1964 Martin Luther King Jr., copyright renewed 1992 Coretta Scott King.

The People, Places, and Times

The Sermon on the Plain. Today's text is a portion of what scholars refer to as the Sermon on the Plain, Luke's equivalent to Matthew's Sermon on the Mount. The content of the sermon in Luke emphasizes the ethical aspects of following Jesus. Since Luke's audience was primarily Gentile, the aspects of Jesus' teachings that emphasized the Mosaic Law are not present, whereas Matthew's audience was Jewish.

Background

Today's text presents Jesus to us in His role as a teacher who is articulating the ethical requirements of those who live in a way that reflects God's character. Jesus is God's ultimate revelation to us, and He shows in His actions and His words what God is like as well as what true humanity looks like. Today's lesson presents some of the most challenging teachings of Jesus—the practice of love toward those who are against us. At the time when Jesus presents these ethical requirements, it was common for Jews to experience persecution at the hands of the Romans, so the commands given are not just nice ideas, but intensely practical advice.

Source:

Bock, Darrell L. *Baker Exegetical Commentary on the New Testament: Luke 1:1–9:50*. Edited by Moises Silva. Grand Rapids, Mich.: Baker Books, 1994.

At-A-Glance

1. Seek the Good of Everyone
(Luke 6:27–31)
2. Love Others and Be Merciful Like God
(vv. 32–36)

In Depth

1. Seek the Good of Everyone (Luke 6:27–31)

After declaring blessings and woes, Jesus presents a command that could only have been perceived as extraordinary. Introducing it by beckoning those with ears to hear, Jesus commands those who would follow God to do seemingly unnatural things. We are commanded to love our enemies, do good to those who hate us, bless those who curse us, and pray for those who mistreat us. This is a stunning call to live in a way

that ordinary people cannot. From a natural point of view, loving one's enemies or seeking the good of those who hate us would seem to be strange, yet here Jesus calls those who would follow Him to behave in ways that go beyond "normal" expectations.

Jesus follows these commands with four examples. First, He says we should not retaliate against those who insult or harm us. "Turning the other cheek" means that the love Christ commands is one that refuses to defend one's rights or fight back in retaliation, but instead to be willing to forgive.

The second example is one set within the context of robbery. If someone takes something from you, one should not seek revenge but remain vulnerable. In the first century where travel was dangerous, this example emphasized that God's people should be those who seek to love their neighbor even if the neighbor acts more like a thief than a neighbor. The third example is that followers of Jesus should be ready to give in all circumstances without reference to matters of class, ethnicity, or even poor relationships. The final example is to not demand something be returned if it is taken. This reflects an absence of retribution. It is important here to point out that Jesus' command and the examples He gives are intended to represent the radical nature of being His follower. It is turning the way of the world on its head. Those who follow Jesus are to exemplify the way of love as ones who trust God to take care of them as they seek to faithfully follow Him. It is also important to point out that the examples given are not to be taken as commands to put oneself in danger or disadvantage, but to emphasize that the ethics of the world are to be far surpassed by following God. Finally, Jesus offers the Golden Rule as a basis for radical Christian living: We should treat others as we would like to be treated—this ethic applies to everyone, perhaps especially one's enemies. How can this happen? How is it possible to live in radical opposition to the ways of the world? The only way it will be possible to carry out these commands is through the work of God in our lives, which we have because the Holy Spirit lives in us.

2. Love Others and Be Merciful Like God (vv. 32–36)

After giving examples of the command for radical Christian love, Jesus proceeds to give negative examples. First, He asks what is radical or distinctive about loving those who love you in return, since this is even what sinners do? Why should God be inclined to give favor to those who love others in a way that is nothing more than typical? The second example is like the first: if you perform good deeds for those whom you know will return good on your behalf, how is that different from the way of the world? Loving those who love us and doing good to those who do the same for us is a limited way of expressing love in contrast to the radical command that refuses to establish boundaries for loving conduct. The third example looks back to the example about giving. If we only lend or give money to those who will repay us (even, or perhaps especially, with interest), there is no difference between us and the sinful world. We should not link our incentive for giving with our expectation of repayment. Followers of Jesus should be those who are willing to give to others without various "strings attached."

Jesus then repeats His command that His followers demonstrate radical love that seeks the good of one's enemies and contributes to others without the expectation of repayment. This is followed by the promise that God will reward those who live in such a radical way and that followers of Jesus will be truly God's children. This does not mean that salvation is the result of our good works; indeed, as Paul indicates in Ephesians 2:10, we are saved so we can do these good works. Why such a great promise? Jesus says this is because we show ourselves to be like God, who is kind to those who are ungrateful and wicked. Even though sinful humans (especially those in rebellion against God) don't deserve anything other than punishment, God is disposed to be loving, merciful, and generous toward them. Jesus closes this section of His sermon with the command that we be merciful just as our Father God is merciful.

Today's lesson clearly displays the truth that following Jesus means a commitment to a distinctive lifestyle exemplified by love for all of our neighbors, including those who may be our enemies. The command to conform our character to correspond to God's merciful nature calls us to go against all of the worldly advice which tells us that if we want to have the best life possible, we will have to be self-protective and only give our time to relationships that will benefit our own prospects for success. Jesus calls us to

something radically different: a life of self-giving love and mercy and trust in God that He will provide for us and grant us a good life. It is not easy, but if we want to be like Jesus, then like Him, we must seek the good of everyone, including those who may not deserve it.

Search the Scriptures

1. Jesus commands His followers to _____, _____, _____, and _____ (vv. 27–28).

2. What examples does Jesus give to make His point (vv. 29–30)?

3. Who are we acting like if we follow Jesus' commands (vv. 35–36)?

Discuss the Meaning

1. How does Jesus want us to be different from the world? What does He mean by the four commands given in verses 27–28?

2. How far do we take the examples that Jesus gives us? Are we supposed to put ourselves in danger in order to follow God faithfully?

3. What does Jesus mean when He says that we will be children of God when we obey these commands?

4. Why is it difficult to express love to one's enemies? What creative ways have you found to show love to an enemy?

Lesson in Our Society

One of the most natural things for humans is to seek to protect ourselves and our possessions. We want to look out for ourselves and for those who are like us, and sometimes our commitment to protection may mean that we will need to retaliate against those who are against us. This is all quite natural, yet Jesus calls us to a different standard. For African Americans, one way to think about this is in regard to the legacy of slavery and racism, which has victimized many people. The natural thing is to want to protect ourselves and "our people" and to seek for ways to put ourselves in power so we can retaliate against the agents of oppression. Today's lesson presents a great challenge: radically love your enemies and seek their good. It is very easy to desire to "get a turn" at being the oppressor, yet those of us who are followers of Jesus will only reveal ourselves to be such when we demonstrate the radical lifestyle of the Gospel and seek the best for others while knowing that God will

also care for us. This does not mean that we ignore injustice; rather, it means that as we seek justice we exhibit the radical love of Jesus.

Make It Happen

In commemoration of the upcoming Dr. Martin Luther King Jr. holiday and Dr. King's commitment to show unconditional love for one's enemies, this week think about people in your past and present who have either been enemies or who have harmed you in some way. Commit to pray for them or even seek them out for the purposes of forgiveness and reconciliation. Ask God to help you become the kind of person who exhibits a merciful nature, particularly when it is hard to pray for those who have been against you in some way.

Follow the Spirit

What God wants me to do:

_____

_____

Remember Your Thoughts

Special insights I have learned:

_____

_____

More Light on the Text

Luke 6:27–36

Luke 6:27 But I say unto you which hear, Love your enemies, do good to them which hate you.

During the course of Jesus' ministry, there were times when He came under the intense heat of opposition. Experts in Jewish law from the various religious sects (the Pharisees and the Sadducees) challenged Him with some technical questions about the law and their beliefs in an effort to trap Him and debunk His teachings. Nevertheless He always replied with answers that confounded and silenced them. In one of those instances, a Pharisee, an expert in the law, tested Jesus with the question of which was the greatest commandment of the law. Jesus replied that love for God and for one's neighbor were the two greatest commandments (Matthew 22:37–39). He said that the whole law and the prophets (v. 40) hung on these two commands. In other words, these two commandments form the pivot of all the laws handed down to the Israelites by God; and the proclamations and works of the prophets were meant to inspire the people to love.

Immediately before making this new command, Jesus proclaimed four blessings and four woes (Luke 6:20–26) to different categories of people who experience the two contrasting conditions of life. He gives this commandment of loving enemies to everyone who could hear Him—to the recipients of the blessings, and the recipients of the woes. He was talking to a large crowd of His disciples who came to hear Him and be healed.

This commandment came at a time of Israel's oppression. Israel was under Roman rule during the lifetime of Jesus. Because of her sins and refusal to repent and return to God, Israel had come under Roman oppression, which established enmity and hostility between them. Thus in this state of enmity characterized by hatred, exploitation, bitterness, and malice, Jesus taught them to love their enemies. This teaching appeared to be heresy, because the Jews felt it was justifiable to reciprocate hatred with hatred. Some believers today are under the oppression of antagonists or superiors who act as masters to them. The treatment they are receiving makes it difficult for them to respond in love. However, when we consider the impact of following Jesus' instructions to love our enemies, we must comply because loving our enemies enables us to live the kind of life acceptable to God—a life of love.

The Greek word translated "love" (*agapao*, **ag-ap-AH-o**) denotes "to love in a social or moral sense." This word is used to express the essential nature of God that is to be found in every disciple of Christ, and must be shown to a fellow human being. There is a human tendency to hate one's enemy, but Jesus tells us that our attitudes should transcend this tendency in order to fulfill God's requirements. He mentions that love for our neighbors is the second greatest command; one's neighbor is not just the person living next door, or the colleague with whom one works, or relatives, friends, acquaintances, and comrades, but, our fellow human being. In this sense, an enemy, no matter how great the antagonism or hostility existing between us is a fellow human being who deserves to be loved.

The command to love, the intrinsic nature of God, and the fact that every human being needs love are three factors meant to prompt the Christian to obey the commandment of love and to exhibit God's nature of love. Love should be an exercise of the divine will fulfilled by a deliberate choice made in obedience and service to God.

Jesus Christ was addressing His disciples, they were members of His fold, subject to His teachings and commandments, and so they were meant to know the higher laws of life. He commanded His disciples to show goodness in response to hatred. The Greek word translated "good" (*agathopoieo*, **ag-ath-op-oy-EH-o**), meaning "to do well, to be of benefit to another," conveys an injunction to do good to others as a matter of favor or duty.

28 Bless them that curse you, and pray for them which despitefully use you.

Jesus continues to infuse the right spirit, the right attitude of heart, the right way to respond to harsh treatment from others. He is conditioning His disciples with a positive attitude to enable them to fulfill the law of love against the negative tide of maltreatment from evil people. In our world of evil, curses abound in the mouths of the ungodly. Disciples of Christ who find themselves in the workplace, the family, or other social settings will be subjected to insults, criticisms, slander, and curses from the people of the world. But this commandment of the Lord Jesus is meant to indicate the desired condition of the heart of a disciple of Christ. Each disciple must have in themselves the spirit of love: because with this spirit, they can tolerate harsh treatment from people, resist the pangs of offense, and develop the capacity, desire, and willingness to bless the one who curses them. The Greek word translated "bless" (*eulogeo*, **yoo-log-EH-o**) means "to speak well of, to invoke a benediction upon a person, to praise." Jesus said, "For out of the abundance of the heart the mouth speaketh" (Matthew 12:34). This commandment to bless those who curse us is also meant to create a positive attitude in us from which an abundance of blessings can flow from our months.

The Greek word translated "'curse" (*kataraomai*, **kat-ar-AH-om-ahee**) means "'to pray against, to wish evil against a person." The disciple of Christ is required to counter the person who wishes them evil or prays against them with a blessing, and not to curse them in reply. The Lord Jesus says to pray for them. In addition we are given the responsibility of praying for those who use us. The Greek word translated "pray" (*proseuchomai*, **pros-YOO-khom-ahee**) always refers to prayer to God. Jesus commands us to pray to God for the souls of those who maltreat us. God hears prayers about someone when we have obeyed Him concerning that person. The Greek word translated "despitefully use" (*epereazo*, **ep-ay-reh-AD-zo**) denotes "to insult, slander or accuse falsely." Despiteful use is an opposition against us, and we are required to express love to those who oppose us in this manner.

29 And unto him that smiteth thee on the one cheek offer also the other; and him that taketh away thy cloke forbid not to take thy coat also.

This is a command to not resist violence. When maltreatment degenerates to physical attack against us, Jesus still commands us not to resist or retaliate. The Greek word translated "smiteth" (*tupto*, **TOOP-to**), meaning "to strike, beat," conveys the idea of being struck or beaten repeatedly with the hand or a stick. This is why Jesus urges us to offer the other cheek for a repeated beating. Maltreatment from others stirs up anger, bitterness, malice, hatred, and a vengeful spirit, but all these are contrary to the spirit of love. God wants us as His children to exhibit His love in a world of evil filled with hatred and violence. With the spirit of love in our hearts, we are to distinguish ourselves from followers of other gods. This is how God has set the order: when curses and violence are shown to us, we should respond with love, blessing, prayer. We should yield to the discomfort of the maltreatment and allow vengeance against those who hurt us to come from Him alone. Naturally, we are disposed to mete out vengeance against our enemies, but vengeance belongs to God alone (Hebrew 10:30). So we should take the insults, and let God do the payback for us. The love of God guards us so jealously that He wants us to gratefully accept His defensive, vengeful might, as we respond in love to curses. "Seeing it is a righteous thing with God to recompense tribulation to them that trouble you" (2 Thessalonians 1:6).

The second part of the Luke passage tells us not to resist extortion. Jesus says if someone takes away our cloak we shouldn't stop him from taking our coat also. The Greek word translated "forbid" (*koluo* **ko-LOO-o**) means "to hinder restrain or withhold." In the process of yielding to extortion, Jesus tells us not to stop a person from taking additional property we own. We are not to withhold from him whatever else he wants from us.

30 Give to every man that asketh of thee; and of him that taketh away thy goods ask them not again.

The spirit of love should make us munificent without discrimination. The interdependence among people and the need for assistance prompts us to ask for help from one another. Jesus knows that we are likely to get into the position where we can give help to other people. He commands us to give. The Greek word translated "give" (*didomi*, **DID-omee**) means "to bestow, render, minister, offer, grant, commit." In the sense of "to minister," it connotes the idea of providing or supplying one's needs. The "every man" denotes any kind of person: the poor, the rich, the old, and the young; relatives, friends, enemies, or strangers; irrespective of religion, background, race, color, beliefs, or social class.

Based on this command, the thief and the cheat become objects of the love of God that is meant to emanate from the believer who happens to be their victim. Jesus commands the believing merchant not to ask for his merchandise back from those who stole from him. This is a passive form of giving: by either an act of theft or cheating, the believing merchant is deprived of his goods, and instead of taking it as an offense, he is commanded to consider it an act of giving and a way of showing love to the thief. This commandment, undoubtedly, expresses an indirect form of showing love, particularly when it ought to be considered an offense.

31 And as ye would that men should do to you, do ye also to them likewise.

This verse is considered the Golden Rule: Do unto others as you would want them to do unto you. There is always a natural desire in us to receive good treatment from other people. We love to be spoken well of; we love to be accorded respect and honor; we love to be given our dues; we love to hear kind words; to be encouraged; and to be given gifts. Jesus says that whatever kind of treatment we love to receive from other people, we should also desire to give to them. The Greek word translated "would" (*thelo*, **THEL-o**)

"But love ye your enemies, and do good, and lend, hoping for nothing again; and your reward shall be great, and ye shall be the children of the Highest: for he is kind unto the unthankful and to the evil" (Luke 6:35).

is a word that expresses a wish. What you wish for yourself is what you should wish for others. God's relationship with us is an example: Although we are sinful in nature and do not have the capacity to love Him or do anything good, He loves us because He wants us to love Him in return.

32 For if ye love them which love you, what thank have ye? for sinners also love those that love them. 33 And if ye do good to them which do good to you, what thank have ye? for sinners also do even the same. 34 And if ye lend to them of whom ye hope to receive, what thank have ye? for sinners also lend to sinners, to receive as much again.

Jesus teaches unconditional love. Love for others should not be spurred on by the fact that the other person is capable of reciprocating our love. The Greek word translated "grace" (*charis*, **KHAR-ece**) is the same word rendered "thanks" in this verse. It connotes "'favor, benefit, pleasure." This means we derive favor and benefit by loving people who are unable to reciprocate. Our acts of love should not be based on favoritism; this attitude is found among sinners who are controlled by the carnal mind and those who gratify the desires of the flesh. Sinners show their acts of love to people whom they believe

are capable of paying them back, because they consider it an investment into the lives of these beneficiaries.

At rebirth, the Holy Spirit was given to us as a gift from God, by this we have the spirit of love, and we bear in us the capacity to love. "The love of God is shed abroad in our hearts by the Holy Ghost which is given unto us" (Romans 5:5). The Bible urges us to walk after the Spirit and not after the flesh (Romans 8:9). When we show love, do good, and lend to all—to those who can reciprocate and to those who cannot—we are walking after the Spirit. Walking in the Spirit is compliance to God; walking in the flesh is enmity to God.

Jesus spoke of "treasure in the heavens" (Luke 12:33). He tells us that our deeds of love, particularly those shown to the poor, create a treasure for us in heaven that cannot wear out or be stolen. He says this treasure is of the utmost importance and we should all strive to obtain it. To practice love toward all is an investment that has benefits that last for eternity.

35 But love ye your enemies, and do good, and lend, hoping for nothing again; and your reward shall be great, and ye shall be the children of the

Highest: for he is kind unto the unthankful and to the evil.

We are inclined to believe that bad people, those who have hurt us or have been cruel to us, are undeserving of our love or our acts of kindness. This mentality definitely fosters enmity; it is a barrier that debars us from entering the realm of love; and it hardens our hearts from adopting the spirit of love. Jesus' command to love our enemies enables us to break down this barrier in our hearts to love. While it may be easy or convenient for us to love those we are pleased with or those with whom we have some affinity, it is naturally impossible to love our enemies. But according to God's economy, this difficult or impossible aspect is what actually brings about the greatest reward from Him. That we might be beneficiaries of this great reward, Jesus commands us to love, to do good, and to lend without expecting anything. The Greek word translated "reward" (*misthos*, **mis-THOS**) means "pay for services, wages" that are received later. This signifies our rewards in heaven.

According to Jesus, our acts of love firmly establish our stand as children of the Highest. The Greek word translated "highest" (*hupsistos*, **HOOP-sis-tos**) is used to refer to God as "the Supreme or the Most High." Referring to God by His most exalted status always indicates a need to compare Him with other gods; He is the highest, the one, true God. These specific acts of love commanded by Him are peculiar to Him alone; other false gods would rather empower their subjects or adherents to harm their enemies, making them do evil things to people who offend them. God desires a distinction between His people and the people who serve other gods; the command to love our enemies is one of the ways of creating this distinction.

The Bible urges us to be imitators of God and live a life of love, because God is love (Ephesians 5:1–2; 1 John 4:8). Because God is "kind unto the unthankful and to the evil," He wants us to do the same to our enemies. Sinners are born enemies to God, but He is loving, gracious, and kind to them. For those of us who are saved today, we were once sinners. "But God commendeth his love toward us, in that, while we were yet sinners, Christ died for us" (Romans 5:8).

36 Be ye therefore merciful, as your Father also is merciful.

Mercy is a positive reaction in which we show forgiveness and kindness to one who has offended us. Being merciful is the character of God, and so showing mercy to our offenders means manifesting God's character to them. When we desire to take punitive measures against those who have done evil to us, we are urged to be merciful to them. Mercy can be regarded as one side of a coin of which love is the other side: while love gives, mercy forgives. The Greek word translated "merciful" (*oiktirmon*, **oyk-TIR-mone**) means "to be compassionate or be pitiful to others." Since we are imperfect, liable to err, and likely to be subjected to adverse conditions of life, we inadvertently offend one another and become beset by ills. Mercy comes as a gracious gift that averts punitive measures or judgment on anyone who has committed an offense. We all err and we all need mercy from one another. The child of God is supposed to be a merciful Christian like his Father in heaven.

Daily Bible Readings

M: Trust in the Lord
Psalm 37:1–11
T: Love Your Neighbor
Leviticus 19:17–18
W: Love Your Enemies
Luke 6:27–28
T: Absorb Injustice
Luke 6:29–30
F: Set the Standard
Luke 6:31
S: Expect Nothing in Return
Luke 6:34–36
S: Posterity for the Peaceable
Psalm 37:35–40

TEACHING TIPS

January 20
Bible Study Guide 8

1. Words You Should Know

A. Importunity (Luke 11:8) *anaideia* (Gk.)—Boldness, shamelessness.

B. Gifts (v. 13) *doma* (Gk.)—Presents.

2. Teacher Preparation

Unifying Principle—Finding a Listening Ear Everyone longs to have a relationship with someone who cares enough to listen to and respond to our needs. To whom can we go? Jesus taught that we have a loving heavenly Parent to whom we can persistently bring our needs and the desires of our heart.

A. Read through the entire lesson, paying special attention to the AIM for Change and the Unifying Principle.

B. Complete lesson 8 in the *Precepts For Living® Personal Study Guide.*

C. Prepare a sign-up sheet to pass out to the class for establishing prayer groups that list e-mail addresses and or phone numbers.

3. Starting the Lesson

A. Ask a student to open the class with a prayer using the Keep in Mind verse as a guide.

B. Have the students follow along as you read and explain the AIM for Change for today's lesson.

C. Ask a volunteer to read the In Focus story. Ask class members to share situations that they have taken to God in prayer but their prayers have seemingly gone unanswered.

D. Discuss the meaning of the Keep in Mind verse and how it might affect our faith development.

4. Getting into the Lesson

A. Briefly review the Background information to set the stage for today's text.

B. Ask several volunteers to summarize the Focal Verses in their own words.

C. Engage the students in a discussion regarding the In Depth content.

5. Relating the Lesson to Life

A. Pass out the sign-up sheet and instruct students who wish to participate to list their e-mail address or phone numbers to encourage interaction based on the Make It Happen exercise.

B. Allow the students to work in groups of two or three to answer the Discuss the Meaning questions and Lesson in Our Society.

6. Arousing Action

A. Have the students discuss their prayer lives, and ask them to recall a time when God answered their prayers after they waited a long period of time.

B. Remind the students to complete the Daily Bible Readings or complete lesson 9 from the *Precepts For Living® Personal Study Guide* in preparation for next week's teaching.

C. Close the class in prayer. Be sure to take a minute or two to solicit personal prayer requests.

Worship Guide

For the Superintendent or Teacher
Theme: Inspired to Pray!
Theme Song: "Let the Words of My Mouth"
Devotional Reading: Psalm 28:6–9
Prayer

INSPIRED TO PRAY!

Bible Background • LUKE 11:5–13
Printed Text • LUKE 11:5–13 Devotional Reading • PSALM 28:6–9

AIM for Change

By the end of the lesson, we will:

EXPLORE Jesus' teachings on being persistent in taking our needs to God;

EXPERIENCE trust and security while praying to God; and

APPROACH God with perseverance, trusting Him to respond.

Keep in Mind

"And I say unto you, Ask, and it shall be given you; seek, and ye shall find; knock, and it shall be opened unto you" (Luke 11:9).

Focal Verses

KJV **Luke 11:5** And he said unto them, Which of you shall have a friend, and shall go unto him at midnight, and say unto him, Friend, lend me three loaves;

6 For a friend of mine in his journey is come to me, and I have nothing to set before him?

7 And he from within shall answer and say, Trouble me not: the door is now shut, and my children are with me in bed; I cannot rise and give thee.

8 I say unto you, Though he will not rise and give him, because he is his friend, yet because of his importunity he will rise and give him as many as he needeth.

9 And I say unto you, Ask, and it shall be given you; seek, and ye shall find; knock, and it shall be opened unto you.

10 For every one that asketh receiveth; and he that seeketh findeth; and to him that knocketh it shall be opened.

11 If a son shall ask bread of any of you that is a father, will he give him a stone? or if he ask a fish, will he for a fish give him a serpent?

12 Or if he shall ask an egg, will he offer him a scorpion?

13 If ye then, being evil, know how to give good gifts unto your children: how much more shall your heavenly Father give the Holy Spirit to them that ask him?

NLT **Luke 11:5** Then, teaching them more about prayer, he used this story: "Suppose you went to a friend's house at midnight, wanting to borrow three loaves of bread. You say to him,

6 'A friend of mine has just arrived for a visit, and I have nothing for him to eat.'

7 And suppose he calls out from his bedroom, 'Don't bother me. The door is locked for the night, and my family and I are all in bed. I can't help you.'

8 But I tell you this—though he won't do it for friendship's sake, if you keep knocking long enough, he will get up and give you whatever you need because of your shameless persistence.

9 "And so I tell you, keep on asking, and you will receive what you ask for. Keep on seeking, and you will find. Keep on knocking, and the door will be opened to you.

10 For everyone who asks, receives. Everyone who seeks, finds. And to everyone who knocks, the door will be opened.

11 "You fathers—if your children ask for a fish, do you give them a snake instead?

12 Or if they ask for an egg, do you give them a scorpion? Of course not!

13 So if you sinful people know how to give good gifts to your children, how much more will your heavenly Father give the Holy Spirit to those who ask him."

In Focus

For years Kenny watched as his fellow coworkers either were promoted or moved on to better paying jobs. For the life of him, he could not understand why after five years on the job he had not been promoted. He showed up on time, he did his job properly, and he was always upbeat and positive; he had even trained some of the people who moved up the ladder ahead of him. What was the problem? Troubled by this situation, he began to share his frustrations with a friend one evening while attending mid-week Bible study.

"I don't get it, man. What am I doing wrong? I like my job. I like the company, but they just won't give me a break. I apply for new and better positions, but I can't seem to move up. I'm qualified; I've got the skills; I just don't get it," Kenny told his friend Brad.

"Um," replied Brad. "How's your prayer life?"

"My prayer life? What's my prayer life got to do with it? I pray. I pray for my wife, my family, my children, my health… you know, the usual stuff."

"Yeah, but do you pray about your job? Have you asked God what *He* wants you to do and where *He* wants you to be?"

"You know what? No. Initially, I prayed for God to lead me to the right employer and He did, but after I got the job, I stopped praying about it."

"Well, I think it's time you started praying about it, my brother. I'll tell you what—there are three of us who get together every morning at 6:30 on a conference call for prayer. You should join us."

"That's a good idea. I think I will join you brothers. Let me get your number."

In today's text, Jesus taught that persistent prayer is one of the best ways to find answers to life's many twists and turns. He taught His disciples that we have a loving Heavenly Father to whom we can persistently bring our needs in prayer.

The People, Places, and Times

The Disciples. Today's lesson contains one part of a teaching on prayer that Jesus gave to His disciples. The disciples in today's text are the inner circle of Jesus, those who were willing to drop everything and walk with Jesus. The Greek term for "disciple" is *mathetes* (**mah-THAY-tayss**), which means a learner who is under a teacher. The Gospels portray the disciples as those who were dedicated to Jesus, although they were often slow to learn, quick to seek retaliation—not unlike the rest of us. The fact that such unlikely people were those whom God used to turn the world upside down after Christ's resurrection and the advent of the Holy Spirit should be an encouragement to us, especially in times when we may feel we don't merit the title of disciple. Yet the context of today's lesson is one where we see that in spite of immaturity and imperfections, the disciples had a strong desire to learn from Jesus, and today we learn with them the importance of confidently and consistently approaching God in prayer.

Background

Today's text opens with a parable. The entire text itself is one part of an episode where the disciples had come upon Jesus at prayer and asked Him to teach them how to pray. The parable follows Jesus' teaching of the Lord's Prayer. Jesus often used parables as ways to communicate what He wanted people to learn by telling a story. Not all parables were easily understood, especially when Jesus told parables to large crowds, but in such cases Jesus would take the time with His inner circle of disciples to explain the meaning of the parable. Scholars debate whether or not parables are intended to communicate one point or many, but today's text is a clear example of a parable intended to demonstrate a specific point about prayer. The disciples wanted Jesus to teach them to pray, and the parable in today's lesson serves to illuminate the point that Jesus wants to make about coming to God confidently and expectantly in prayer.

Source:

Green, Joel B., and Gordon Fee, eds. *The New International Commentary on the New Testament: The Gospel of Luke*. Grand Rapids, Mich.: Eerdmans, 1997.

At-A-Glance

1. The Parable of the Friend at Midnight (Luke 11:5–8)
2. The Encouragement to Pray (vv. 9–13)

In Depth

1. The Parable of the Friend at Midnight (Luke 11:5–8)

Jesus wanted to teach His disciples, and us, the importance of prayer. He began with a parable about a friend who has a guest, but who is unable to offer the hospitality expected when one has visitors.

In Jesus' day, guests were to be cared for no matter what time they showed up. If there was no bread left (it was baked daily), a host had a serious dilemma. What does such a host do? In the parable, the host goes to his friend's house and requests three loaves of bread in order to care for and feed his guest. His friend initially refuses his request because attending to the request would likely rouse the children who are already asleep. Since most homes only had one large room, this posed a very real problem. The result is that the friend does rise and give his friend the bread he has requested, which he would do for reasons beyond their preexisting friendship.

One ongoing scholarly dispute concerns the reason for the friend's positive response. Is it because the friend is persistent and bold in making a request at such an hour, or is it because the host responds to the request because of a desire to maintain his honor? The debate revolves around the meaning of the word often translated as "persistence" (Gk. *anaideia*). Does this word refer to the condition of the petitioner or the concern of the one receiving the request? There are good arguments for both views, but in light of the overall context where Jesus is teaching the disciples about prayer and their approach to God, it makes sense that *anaideia* refers to the boldness of the petitioner who strongly desires to have this request met as soon as possible.

This parable presents a tension-filled situation that the original audience would have immediately grasped. The resolution to the dilemma highlights the bold disposition that the disciples should have been coming to God in prayer. This is not a type of boldness that disrespects others, but a confidence that leads one to intensely focus on God who provides for all of our needs.

2. The Encouragement to Pray (vv. 9–13)

After presenting this parable, Jesus sought to strongly encourage the disciples to pray. He pointed out three different ways of speaking about our prayers as they come to God. Coming to God with our needs is like asking, seeking, or knocking, and the disciples are encouraged to boldly approach God just like the friend approached his neighbor in the parable. If a friend will provide for the basic needs of one who comes to him at night, how much more will God provide for the needs of His disciples who come before Him in prayer? It is important to emphasize that the point of boldly and confidently approaching God in prayer is not so we can get God to give a "rubber stamp" to our elaborately crafted agendas for material prosperity and worldly success. Rather, this text emphasizes that just as the neighbor provided for the basic needs of his friend, so, too, God will provide for our needs. This is an important distinction in a time when many teach that texts such as this one show that God will give us the American dream if we only have enough faith. God certainly wants to bless us, but He does not promise to give everyone the lifestyle of the rich and famous. God will care for us and bless us beyond expectation, but He decides what these blessings will look like, not us.

Jesus used a second illustration to explain why we should be confident in approaching God. If earthly parents give good things to their children, then certainly God would. Jesus used very interesting examples. What parent would give a child something harmful or poisonous when the child is asking for fish or for an egg? In today's society, it would indeed be newsworthy if a news reporter discovered that there was a family where the children had consistently asked their parents for meat and eggs, but were given snakes and scorpions instead. It would be a story of amazing child abuse that would shock all of us, because our expectation is that even troubled parents will take care of the basic needs of their children, and even delight to do so. If sinful humans respond positively to such requests, God will certainly do so and more. How do you regard God when you think about approaching Him? Is it possible that you actually have greater expectations of what humans will do in meeting your needs rather than what God will do? Are you afraid, at least some of the time, that God is not someone who wants to meet your basic spiritual needs?

The last verse is very important. Not only is God concerned about meeting our basic needs, but here Jesus told the disciples that God will give the Holy

Spirit to those who ask. It is important to understand that until the coming of the Spirit in Acts 2, the Holy Spirit did not reside within God's people. The Spirit came upon people for certain occasions, such as the anointing of the king (a constant presence), a prophecy, or tasks like building the tabernacle (Exodus 35:30–35). The possession of the Holy Spirit is absolutely central to all of our spiritual needs. Apart from the Holy Spirit, it is basically impossible to truly live in the way that God intends.

In Romans 8:1–16, Paul strongly emphasizes the centrality of the Holy Spirit to Christian living and conquering sin. In today's text, Jesus lets the disciples know that God is willing to provide exactly what they need so that all of their spiritual needs can be met. They do not experience the fulfillment of the promise offered in verse 13 until Pentecost, but this shows that God is indeed a loving Father who will provide what we need the most. To give the gift of the Holy Spirit is superior to any human gift.

Search the Scriptures

1. The _____ of the host is the reason why his friend gives him three loaves (Luke 11:8).

2. Jesus encourages the disciples to ____, ____, and _____ in prayer to God (v. 9).

Discuss the Meaning

1. What should we really expect from God in prayer?

2. Is God only concerned with "spiritual" things or does He want to give us more than that? What is the emphasis of today's text?

3. What does it mean when the text says that God will give the Holy Spirit to those who ask? Do we still need to ask for the Holy Spirit after we are saved?

Lesson in Our Society

We live in a celebrity-obsessed, consumer-focused society where many of the messages we receive tell us that if we follow a certain formula, we are guaranteed to have the life we have always wanted. This thinking has also crept into the church, and many churches are modern-day success stories, because they proclaim the message that the Gospel is ultimately about God providing you with whatever you want once you "crack the code" and learn the right way to pray so that you can "release" your blessing. It is very important for us to make sure we understand that the

Gospel is good news that turns our focus toward God, not on our selfish motivations. Our prayer lives should flow out of a loving response to a God who has reconciled us to Himself and who invites us to trust that He will give us many blessings, even if we don't know what they will look like. We need to look lovingly at our Heavenly Father and make our requests to Him even as we submit our destiny to His will.

Make It Happen

This week, seek to enhance your prayer life by daily asking God to give you the blessings He wants to give you. How often do you pray with others? If you have never been part of a prayer group or had a prayer partner, begin the process of finding a prayer group or a friend with whom you can pray regularly and share answers to prayer as God provides them.

Follow the Spirit

What God wants me to do:

_____

_____

Remember Your Thoughts

Special insights I have learned:

_____

_____

More Light on the Text

Luke 11:5–13

5 And he said unto them, which of you shall have a friend, and shall go unto him at midnight, and say unto him, Friend, lend me three loaves; 6. For a friend of mine in his journey is come to me, and I have nothing to set before him?

Jesus had just finished teaching His disciples how to pray. He taught them a model prayer, which we refer to today as the Lord's Prayer. Needs give rise to prayers, which are usually in the form of supplication (or requests). This verse begins with a parable in which Jesus portrays a typical situation where a need arises and a neighbor has to ask a friend for help. *Philos* (**FEE-los**) is the Greek word translated "friend"; it denotes a "loved one, a dear and friendly person, associate or neighbor." Supplication or request is always made to somebody—it could be a friend, a relative, or God. The person to whom supplication is made is usually seen as a source of our needs—though God is the ultimate source of all human needs.

Sometimes, a need arises when the circumstances are not favorable: it could be a lack of supplies or a wrong time of the day or season in which one cannot generate income to meet the pressing need. The neighbor went to meet his friend at midnight (wrong hour of the day) to make a request. Midnight is a time of darkness and in the parable darkness may signify a time of calamity, sorrow, or unfavorable situations. When encompassed by some or all of these, the resultant effect could be some pressing needs, urgent special attention, an awkward state of affairs, and the like. This is most likely a time when we are inspired to pray. At midnight, the man went to his friend to make supplication. The Bible abounds with the phrase, "I pray thee," which denotes the act of beseeching someone or making an entreaty to someone for help or favor. He went to beseech his friend to lend him three loaves.

The man seeking to borrow three loaves has a sense of obligation. He feels obligated to provide refreshment for his friend who has come to visit him. At that midnight hour, he was short of supplies and had to beseech his friend. We should be motivated to pray by a proper sense of obligation, apart from a sense of need. Jesus enjoined us to pray without fainting (Luke 18:1). When we are motivated by a sense of obligation to pray, then we feel a sense of duty to pray for others—this is intercession. However, if we are motivated by a sense of need, we pray for ourselves.

In his letter to the Ephesians, the apostle Paul urges us to be alert and to always keep on praying (interceding) for all the saints (6:18). Interceding for other brethren means standing in the gap for them—that is, standing between them and God—and making yourself a channel of blessing unto them.

7 And he from within shall answer and say, Trouble me not: the door is now shut, and my children are with me in bed; I cannot rise and give thee.

A response of refusal from the friend to whom the man made supplication came as an initial impediment to his chances of having his needs met. In most cases, there are certain odds against

our efforts to get what we need; when we pray it seems answers are not forthcoming. The man felt troubled by his friend's request. The word translated "trouble" is *kopos* (**KOP-os**), which means "weariness, laborious toil." This gives us the idea that the supplicant's request was a disturbance to his friend and will make the friend weary himself or give him such laborious toil in the process of opening the door and going to give the supplicant what he requests.

8 I say unto you, Though he will not rise and give him, because he is his friend, yet because of his importunity he will rise and give him as many as he needeth.

Our supplication may frequently meet with resistance as a result of the unwillingness from the one we consider capable of rendering help to us. According to this parable, the man (the source) was unwilling to give his friend what he requested. Some people are unwilling to attend to others' requests for reasons like stinginess, cruelty, lack, or reluctance. In this verse, Jesus points out another reason: due to his familiarity with his friend, he couldn't esteem him enough to make him take the troubles.

The Greek word for "importunity" is *anaideia* (**ahn-EYE-day-ah**); it denotes "shamelessness." It is also translated as "persistence" in many English versions of the Bible. Commentators debate whether the word refers to the persistence of the friend at the door or whether it refers to the one who is receiving the request and concerned about his reputation. In the former sense, we would understand that the word used in this illustration points out the supplicant's attitude of persistently asking his friend for help without being shy. When one has a pressing need, sometimes, he goes beyond certain bounds of modesty, undermining his dignity or pride and shamelessly and persistently requests a friend to meet his need at that time. This is the case with the supplicant.

This view of the parable would emphasize the need for earnestness and perseverance in prayer to God. Therefore, if the man refuses to attend to his friend because of reluctance or the fact that he has become familiar with his friend, then according to Jesus, he must attend to the man because of his importunity (or persistence). Importunity can weary the one considered to be the source of one's needs; it can break down barriers of refusal or unwillingness in a person, thereby making him a reluctant benefactor. When this happens, the benefactor will eventually give to the supplicant as much as he needs. In the latter understanding of *anaideia*, the request is honored because the reputation of the giver is at stake. From this vantage point, the focus of the parable is on God's nature as a generous giver who responds to all manner of requests, even those that arise under less-than-ideal circumstances. On either interpretation of the parable, we are strongly encouraged to bring all of our requests to God, particularly those that are the most dire.

9 And I say unto you, Ask, and it shall be given you; seek, and ye shall find; knock, and it shall be opened unto you.

Here we are made to know three forms of outward actions that can be exhibited in the process of requesting: asking, seeking, and knocking. In this

"And I say unto you, Ask, and it shall be given you; seek, and ye shall find; knock, and it shall be opened unto you" (Luke 11:9).

passage, Jesus places emphasis on these actions as a way of encouraging us to do them, and elevating them to the status of a command backed by divine authority. Obviously, before He made this statement, people must have been asking, seeking, and knocking. By making this encouraging command, Jesus provides the substance of faith for the believer to make requests of God. Hebrews 11:1 says, "Faith is the substance of things hoped for, the evidence of things not seen." With the command in Luke 11:9, the believer is able to access the realm of possibilities occasioned by the power of God responding to faith resulting from obedience. Asking, seeking, and knocking are different forms of petition. There are a number of Greek words that are translated "ask," each describing the various attitudes of asking. *Aiteo* (**eye-TEH-oh**), used here, which means "to ask," suggests the attitude of a supplicant, the petition of one who is lesser in position than to whom the petition is made.

The Greek word translated "seek" is *zeteo* (**dzay-TEH-oh**), signifying "to strive after, endeavor, to desire." It denotes the idea of going about to seek and making enquiry. *Krouo* (**KROO-oh**) is the Greek word translated "knock." When we knock at others' doors, we are close to their place of abode. As we knock with regard to petitioning God, it's like we are knocking on the door of heaven. It is suggestive of coming to the Lord in prayer on a consistent basis. According to Jesus, the gift requested shall be received with certainty by the one who asks, discovery is certain for the one who seeks, and the door will be opened to the one who knocks.

10 For every one that asketh receiveth; and he that seeketh findeth; and to him that knocketh it shall be opened.

The coveted privileges of receiving, finding, and experiencing an open door is for everyone, without discrimination. Though Jesus was speaking to His disciples, His statement seems to apply to a general audience—believers and nonbelievers—because of its axiomatic nature. In practice, followers of Christ are instructed to make petitions in the name of Jesus. A fundamental belief in Jesus (John 14:12–14), the reality of abiding in Him and His words abiding in us (John 15:7), the fact that He chose us, ordained us, and that we should bear fruit (John 15:16)—all of these give us authentic grounds to petition God in the name of Jesus.

God is the ultimate source of our needs, He is Jehovah-jireh, meaning "God is our Provider." The believer is meant to be oriented toward God alone as far as petitioning is concerned. The carnal inclination to trust in man is denounced by God in Jeremiah 17:5 where He said, "Cursed be the man that trusteth in man, and maketh flesh his arm, and whose heart departeth from the LORD." Any true believer must endeavor to rid his Christian practice of this carnality, for it is like the moth that causes destruction to the fabrics of his spirituality and his relationship with God. Verse 7 says, "Blessed is the man that trusteth in the LORD, and whose hope the LORD is." A consistent attitude of petitioning God in times of need is sure to breed trust and reliance on Him. As we go through the challenges of life, getting to various junctures in the course of living our lives where we need something, we can always petition our Heavenly Father, being fully assured that we will definitely receive what we ask of Him.

11 If a son shall ask bread of any of you that is a father, will he give him a stone? Or if he ask a fish, will he for a fish give him a serpent? 12 Or if he shall ask an egg, will he offer him a scorpion?

Jesus used a comparison here to point out God's generosity to respond with the exact demand of a petition. Naturally, within the bounds of normalcy, no father would give his son stone in place of bread, except a cruel and wicked father. The Greek word translated "father" is *pater* (**pat-AYR**); this word is from a root signifying "a nourisher, protector, upholder," and is used in various senses. This root meaning explains the functions and responsibilities of a father. As a nourisher a father is expected to give his son the appropriate thing the son needs to nourish himself. There is the responsibility of fatherhood—the loving care of a father and the willingness of a father to please his son—these should essentially make any father give what is right and pleasing to his son.

In the son there will always be a vacuum of need that should be filled by the father. The choice of need varies, and can be determined by either of them, but basically, the son is at the receiving end and he determines what he needs. The son's choice of need used by Jesus in this illustration is very significant—bread, fish, and egg. The supposed father's gift that turns out to be harmful—stone, serpent, or scorpion—also has some significance. The Greek word translated "bread" is *artos* (**AR-tos**); this is a loaf or cake made out of flour and water and baked into round or oblong shapes. Bread is used figuratively of food in general—the necessities for the sustenance of life— and of spiritual sustenance, or of eternal life (Jesus is the Bread of Life). An innate tendency to live a sustainable life would make a child petition his father for bread. But if the quest for the sustenance of life is seen as evil by a cruel father (which is abnormal), he will offer a stone. Stones were used as a means of punishing offenders; those who committed certain evils were stoned to death.

The Greek word *ichthus* (**ikh-THOOS**) is translated "fish." In biblical times fish constituted one of the staple foods of man, and the fish trade was highly developed in those times. Some of the apostles of Christ were fishermen. The offering of a serpent in place of a fish would be indicative of giving the son something that could bring death instead of sustenance.

The word translated "egg" is *oon* (**oh-ON**). The offering of a scorpion in place of an egg is another way of providing that which brings harm instead of life.

13 If ye then, being evil, know how to give good gifts unto your children: how much more shall your heavenly Father give the Holy Spirit to them that ask him?

Man is evil from birth (Psalm 15:5), and as such he is prone to evil. *Poneros* (**pon-ay-ROS**) is the Greek word translated "evil." It denotes "wicked, bad, vicious" and is used to describe the moral or ethical condition of people. It also denotes "evil that causes labor, pain, and sorrow." Jesus addressed His disciples by making them acknowledge the fact that they are evil as a result of the fall; yet they still have the capacity to give good gifts to their children. This is indicative of their fatherly love, their willingness to do good to their children, and the fact that they feel the imperative to perform their fatherly responsibilities. Jesus then compared their essential character of evil, which produces such good with the essential charac-

ter of goodness, love, generosity, and kindness with which God, our Heavenly Father, abounds.

Therefore, based on God's intrinsic nature, and the fact that He is our Father, He will give us what is good for us. In concluding His explanation of the parable, Jesus encouraged His followers to come to God with their requests and with the expectation that God will provide for them, because God desires to give good things to His children.

Spiritual development is essential for every child of God, and the Holy Spirit is the Agent of this development. In every believer, development should begin with an aspiration to grow; it is upon the basis of this aspiration that we should petition God. Spiritual development is characterized by an increase in the anointing (the sanctifying influence of the Holy Spirit), growing in and exhibiting the fruit of the Spirit, yielding to the leading of the Holy Spirit, desiring and receiving the gifts of the Spirit, consistently receiving the revelation of truth as guided by the Spirit as well as growing in the knowledge of Christ, growing in wisdom and understanding, and progressively experiencing actual change in one's situation and condition. These are laudable areas upon which we should petition God, and He will be readily disposed to grant our requests.

Daily Bible Readings

M: Answered Prayer
Psalm 28:6–9
T: Teach Us to Pray
Luke 11:1–4
W: A Friend's Request
Luke 11:5–8
T: Ask and Receive
Luke 11:9–12
F: Persistent in Prayer
Luke 18:1–17
S: God's Gift of the Holy Spirit
Luke 11:13; Acts 2:1–4
S: Praise the Lord!
Psalm 138:1–3

TEACHING TIPS

January 27
Bible Study Guide 9

1. Words You Should Know

A. Life (Luke 12:22–23) *psuche* (Gk.)—The soul is that part of a person distinct from his or her body, and includes the will and emotions.

B. God (vv. 24, 28, 31) *theos* (Gk.)—Used in reference to the God of Israel.

C. Fear (v. 32) *phobeo* (Gk.)—To be afraid.

2. Teacher Preparation

Unifying Principle—Combating Anxiety and Worry We all face pressure and may experience anxiety. What can we do to combat anxiety and worry? Jesus says that when we trust in God, we have no need to worry

A. Read Psalm 55:22.

B. Read Luke 11 and 12 to familiarize yourself with the background for Jesus' teaching on trust.

C. Prior to class, contact three class members to act out the parts of Susan, Melinda, and Carla as a role-play of today's In Focus story. Be prepared to discuss ways God provides for our basic needs and answers our emergency petitions.

D. Complete lesson 9 in the *Precepts For Living® Personal Study Guide.*

3. Starting the Lesson

A. Begin the class with prayer.

B. Ask volunteers to read the AIM for Change and the Keep in Mind verse.

C. Have the student volunteers act out the In Focus story for the rest of the class.

D. Ask the students to briefly discuss if they have ever been in a similar situation and how they fared.

4. Getting into the Lesson

A. Read the Background section and discuss how God cares about all of His creation, including people, birds, and flora.

B. Summarize the Focal Verses.

C. Solicit answers to the Search the Scriptures questions

5. Relating the Lesson to Life

A. Briefly discuss things that people worry about.

B. Jesus says that anxiety about possessions reflects a lack of trust in God, a lack of interest in the kingdom, and a lack of generosity toward those in need. Due you believe generosity reduces anxiety?

6. Arousing Action

A. Read the Make It Happen section. Ask the students to briefly define "wants" and "needs." Then discuss how these affect one's prayer life, and can spark worry or fear.

B. Instruct the students that while trusting God may not be easy, it is essential to living a joyful Christian life.

C. Have the students write down one area in their lives where they want to trust God more. Encourage them to pray for this daily.

Worship Guide

For the Superintendent or Teacher
Theme: Inspired to Trust!
Theme Song: "I Will Trust in the Lord"
Devotional Reading: Psalm 31:1–5
Prayer

INSPIRED TO TRUST!

Bible Background • LUKE 12:22–34
Printed Text • LUKE 12:22–34 Devotional Reading • PSALM 31:1–5

AIM for Change

By the end of the lesson, we will:

EXPLORE Jesus' teaching on trusting God;

ACKNOWLEDGE that we can trust God for everything; and

PURSUE a relationship with God that will alleviate worry and anxiety.

Keep in Mind

"And he said unto his disciples, Therefore I say unto you, Take no thought for your life, what ye shall eat; neither for the body, what ye shall put on" (Luke 12:22).

Focal Verses

KJV

Luke 12:22 And he said unto his disciples, Therefore I say unto you, Take no thought for your life, what ye shall eat; neither for the body, what ye shall put on.

23 The life is more than meat, and the body is more than raiment.

24 Consider the ravens: for they neither sow nor reap; which neither have storehouse nor barn; and God feedeth them: how much more are ye better than the fowls?

25 And which of you with taking thought can add to his stature one cubit?

26 If ye then be not able to do that thing which is least, why take ye thought for the rest?

27 Consider the lilies how they grow: they toil not, they spin not; and yet I say unto you, that Solomon in all his glory was not arrayed like one of these.

28 If then God so clothe the grass, which is to day in the field, and to morrow is cast into the oven; how much more will he clothe you, O ye of little faith?

29 And seek not ye what ye shall eat, or what ye shall drink, neither be ye of doubtful mind.

30 For all these things do the nations of the world seek after: and your Father knoweth that ye have need of these things.

31 But rather seek ye the kingdom of God; and all these things shall be added unto you.

32 Fear not, little flock; for it is your Father's good pleasure to give you the kingdom.

33 Sell that ye have, and give alms; provide yourselves bags which wax not old, a treasure in the heavens that faileth not, where no thief approacheth, neither moth corrupteth.

34 For where your treasure is, there will your heart be also.

NLT

Luke 12:22 Then, turning to his disciples, Jesus said, "That is why I tell you not to worry about everyday life—whether you have enough food to eat or enough clothes to wear.

23 For life is more than food, and your body more than clothing.

24 Look at the ravens. They don't plant or harvest or store food in barns, for God feeds them. And you are far more valuable to him than any birds!

25 Can all your worries add a single moment to your life?

26 And if worry can't accomplish a little thing like that, what's the use of worrying over bigger things?

27 Look at the lilies and how they grow. They don't work or make their clothing, yet Solomon in all his glory was not dressed as beautifully as they are.

28 And if God cares so wonderfully for flowers that are here today and thrown into the fire tomorrow, he will certainly care for you. Why do you have so little faith?

29 "And don't be concerned about what to eat and what to drink. Don't worry about such things.

30 These things dominate the thoughts of unbelievers all over the world, but your Father already knows your needs.

31 Seek the Kingdom of God above all else, and he will give you everything you need.

32 "So don't be afraid, little flock. For it gives your Father great happiness to give you the Kingdom.

33 "Sell your possessions and give to those in need. This will store up treasure for you in heaven! And the purses of heaven never get old or develop holes. Your treasure will be safe; no thief can steal it and no moth can destroy it.

34 Wherever your treasure is, there the desires of your heart will also be.

In Focus

Susan flicked her wrist, releasing the piles of bills she tightly held. Some dropped on the table while others landed on the floor. Despair washed over her as she glanced again at her journal. She frowned at the neat row of figures that represented each bill and other items she needed for the next two weeks. Unfortunately, the paycheck she received at work that day would not cover the full amount. She wouldn't even have enough to buy groceries or pay for next week's bus pass. Thinking about those things made her cry.

"Lord, I need help here," she prayed, wiping away the tears pooling in her eyes. "Please increase my faith."

For a few minutes, she sat with head bowed. Soon her favorite Bible verses, Psalm 37:3–4, poured into her heart. She softly recited the verses to herself: "Trust in the LORD, and do good; so shalt thou dwell in the land, and verily thou shalt be fed. Delight thyself also in the LORD; and he shall give thee the desires of thine heart."

"Lord," she prayed, "I will trust in You for the things I need. And I will delight myself in You." She prayed for a few more minutes, then picked up the bills and headed to bed to read for a while. She turned her telephone off so as not to be disturbed.

Thirty minutes later, the beep of her cell phone startled her. It was her best friend and prayer partner, Melinda.

"Girl, where have you been?" Melinda asked. "I've been trying to reach you for, like, forever. I'm at that new mega warehouse food place. I was picking up meat, veggies, and other stuff. The prices are so good that I decided to get you something, but I didn't know what you might need. When you didn't answer your telephone, I decided to pick you up one of everything I got myself, except the broccoli, of course."

Chuckling at the reference to the despised vegetable, Susan thanked Melinda, bringing her up-to-date on her bills situation. She agreed to stay awake until Melinda dropped by with the groceries.

A short while later her cell phone beeped again. This time it was a text message from a coworker. "Didn't get to tell you before you left work today," Carla texted. "I have an emergency out of town. Feel free to use my bus pass until I get back. It might take more than a week. I left it in my desk drawer. See ya."

Susan had to read the message twice before it sank in. In less than an hour, God had provided for two of her most pressing needs. She sent a text message back to Carla. Dropping to her knees she began to pray. She had so much to be thankful for.

In today's lesson Jesus encouraged the disciples to trust God for everyday needs, and in impossible situations. Like Susan, we can experience God's provision when we trust Him, even when it seems there is no way out.

The People, Places, and Times

Ravens. Related to crows, ravens are large, black birds. They are scavengers, feeding on dead and weak animals, and have the ability to locate food in some of the hardest to find areas. Despite their feeding habits, ravens are considered very intelligent birds. Ravens first appear in Scripture in Genesis 8:7 when Noah sent out a raven to determine whether the land was beginning to dry up as the flood receded. Sending out a raven made sense for two reasons: (1) the bird's instinct to locate food in hard-to-find places would enable it to persevere until food was located; and (2) since the Flood destroyed all living things, only carcasses would be available to the hungry bird. The raven did not return, an indication that it did find food. Because of their propensity to eat dead things, ravens were considered "dirty birds," and the Israelites were prohibited from eating or offering them for sacrifice (Leviticus 11:15; Deuteronomy 14:14).

Solomon. The Son of King David and heir to his father's throne, Solomon was the wisest king in Israelite history. He reigned for 40 years. At the beginning of his reign, he pleased God by humbly asking for wisdom, rather than riches or prestige. God was so pleased that He declared, "Wisdom and knowledge is granted unto thee; and I will give thee riches, and wealth, and honour, such as none of the kings have had that have been before thee, neither shall there any after thee have the like" (2 Chronicles 1:12). God fulfilled His promise to Solomon, who became known for his expansive wisdom (some of which is revealed in the books of Ecclesiastes and Proverbs) and wealth. News of both spread to other regions. Doubtful if the accounts were true, the queen of Sheba visited Solomon (2 Chronicles 9:1–12). During her visit, the queen was overwhelmed by what she heard and saw, specifically even noting the clothing that Solomon's servants wore. During Solomon's reign, Israel enjoyed long seasons of peace. Solomon's greatest achievement was the building of the temple of God (2 Chronicles 3–5). His greatest failure was his forbidden love for foreign women who introduced him to idolatrous worship.

Kingdom of God. The concept of kingdom was not a new one to the assembled hearers. Their past and present history included rule by kings; some followed God completely, while others were evil. By referring to the kingdom of God, Jesus specifically encouraged hearers to seek allegiance to a higher authority than those they currently served. It was a message that John the Baptist had preached, and one that Jesus reiterated when John was thrown in prison. At that time, Jesus said, "The time is fulfilled, and the kingdom of God is at hand: repent ye, and believe the gospel" (Mark 1:15). The coming of Jesus signaled the beginning of God's reign, which will not come fully until Christ returns. Moreover, it was a kingdom that could not be dethroned, touched with hands, or entered through human endeavor. "Once, having been asked by the Pharisees when the kingdom of God would come, Jesus replied, 'The kingdom of God does not come with your careful observation, nor will people say, "Here it is," or "There it is," because the kingdom of God is within you'" (Luke 17:20–21, NIV). The reign of God refers to our own status with God as well as the final victory over the forces that oppose God.

Background

Luke, a physician, was a companion of the apostle Paul, and was regarded as a valued ministry team leader. Paul called him the "the beloved physician." Being the only non-Jewish Gospel writer, Luke provided his perspective on the things he discovered as he researched the events about which he wrote. In fact, he recorded more miracles than the other Gospel writers, and some of the parables he recorded are only found in his account.

Luke notes, "And it came to pass afterward, that [Jesus] went throughout every city and village, preaching and shewing the glad tidings of the kingdom of God: and the twelve were with him" (Luke

8:1). During these travels, the "shewing" included healings and other miracles Jesus did, and those He charged the disciples to do. Much of that preaching included parables, as well as teaching on issues Jesus felt important, or those raised by the crowd.

For example, a wealthy farmer concerned about an inheritance told Jesus, "Master, speak to my brother, that he divide the inheritance with me" (12:13). Jesus used the request to speak to the crowd about covetousness. Jesus warned, "Take heed, and beware of covetousness: for a man's life consisteth not in the abundance of the things which he possesseth" (v. 15). Jesus used that warning as a springboard to share a parable of a stingy, rich farmer, and to also warn the disciples not to worry about basic human needs (the focus of today's lesson). Worrying can be a sign that they were not trusting God to fulfill those needs, and can also lead to the type of selfishness portrayed in the parable of the rich farmer.

At-A-Glance

1. Banish Life's Worries
(Luke 12:22–23, 29, 30)
2. Life's Impossibilities (vv. 25–26)
3. Lessons in Nature (vv. 24, 27–28)
4. Trust God (vv. 31–34)

In Depth

1. Banish Life's Worries (Luke 12:22–23, 29, 30)

As thousands gathered to listen to Him speak, Jesus taught a variety of parables that covered a wide spectrum of life issues. Then in these verses we learn how He brought the message closer to home by focusing on worry. Both Luke and Matthew recorded this message, but Luke's version made it clear that this topic was specifically for the disciples, not the multitude, as Jesus encouraged His closest followers to banish life's worries.

Jesus told them to "take no thought" (v. 22). The NIV translates this phrase as "do not worry." In the original Greek, the word for "thought" is *merimnao* (**mer-im-NAH-o**), and it can also be translated as "to be troubled." Jesus wanted His disciples free from worries and cares that could make their lives less fulfilling and their ministries less effective.

Worry is a consistent and often progressive negative meditation. It takes root in our hearts, but it is our minds that play, rewind, and replay concerns. As we "take thought" about those concerns, they begin to seem larger than life as fear, doubt, and unbelief magnify the situation. When addressing His disciples, Jesus made it clear that He knew worry was not only a possibility but also a reality. Anyone choosing to make the deeper commitment to follow Him would experience many of the same challenges that Jesus did, including possible ostracization and physical harm. Those, like Peter and his friends, who gave up business ventures temporarily or permanently, could also experience a reduction in income.

Jesus specifically exhorted His disciples to "take no thought" for four things: (1) their lives, (2) their food, (3) their bodies, and (4) their clothing. Basically, He covered every area that impacts a person, and from which worries can arise. The command seems impossible to follow until we read the remaining related verses that clearly assure us that God is aware of our needs; and as God Almighty, He is ready, able, and willing to meet those.

There was only one way the disciples could banish life's worries: trusting God completely with their lives, and for their provision. "Trust" denotes dependence, relying solely on someone or something without any need for one's own input. Jesus explained how this works in a disciple's life. He said, "I am the vine, ye are the branches: He that abideth in me, and I in him, the same bringeth forth much fruit: for without me ye can do nothing" (John 15:5). The analogy of the vine and branches provides a glimpse of the intimate relationship we should have with God, trusting Him for everything.

2. Life's Impossibilities (vv. 25–26)

While the previous verses addressed basic needs of life, Jesus took His message on living a worry-free life a step further in these verses by addressing the "impossible" issues. These issues are those we worry about, even though we know we can't do anything about them. In this case, Jesus used worries about height to bring home His point. In spite of our feelings about our stature, none of us can make ourselves taller or shorter. Despite this fact, people worry about how short or tall they are, or the future height of their children. What a waste of time and energy. "If ye

then be not able to do that thing which is least, why take ye thought for the rest?" (Luke 12:26).

Jesus knew that, ironically, it is the impossible things that people tend to worry about more. He simply reminded the disciples that while some things are beyond human control or ability, they are "least" or minor to the almighty God! After all, in the case of height, God is the One who determines our stature; our very DNA that affects height is God-given.

Scripture records many seemingly impossible things that were able to be accomplished. Elisha, for example, was an Old Testament prophet. Upon request, he received a double portion of Elijah's spirit when his mentor, Elijah, was taken into heaven (2 Kings 2:9–11). Thus he was able to do even greater works than Elijah. In one instance the prophets, under his command, decided to build a facility because the existing one was too small to house them. As one of the prophets worked on the project, his borrowed axe fell in the Jordan River and began sinking. Distraught, he asked Elisha for help. After learning where the axe had fallen, Elisha cut a stick and threw it in the water. The axe immediately floated to the top of the water, and the young prophet was able to retrieve it (2 Kings 6:1–7). This was an impossible situation made possible only by the prophet's total reliance on Elisha and his ability to work miracles.

Our problem is that, generally, we do not fully trust God to care and provide for us. This is evident by our relying on our own natural abilities and resources until we reach a situation we can't handle. Then, like the prophet, we cry out for help. That's not the trust Jesus inspired the disciples to have. He wants us to rely on God for even our basic needs. He wants us to seek Him even in seemingly impossible situations, and trust Him alone for the outcome. And instead of us wrestling with worry, He invites, "Come unto me, all ye that labour and are heavy laden, and I will give you rest. Take my yoke upon you and learn of me; for I am meek and lowly in heart: and ye shall find rest unto your souls. For my yoke is easy, and my burden is light" (Matthew 11:28–30).

3. Lessons in Nature (vv. 24, 27–28)

To a people whose basic livelihoods depended on agriculture and livestock, Jesus directed their attention to nature to understand what worry-free living looked like. He specifically turned their attention to two things: ravens and lilies.

Jesus teaches that, as scavengers, ravens do not sow, reap, or gather in storehouses. In other words, they do not provide for themselves by working, or saving for the future. Despite this they always have food to eat. The species continues to survive and thrive for one primary reason: God feeds them! Jesus asks, "Are ye better than the fowls?" (Luke 12:24). God's chosen people, the Israelites, prevented from eating or offering the birds for sacrifice, would readily understand that the answer to this question is yes.

Lilies are beautiful, colorful flowers. Like all flora, lilies depend on God for rain to grow and flourish. By referring to them, Jesus again pointed to the fact that these creations do not care for themselves. By comparing their splendor to Solomon's, Jesus showed that material things can never rival God-given creations. Indeed, even if we have the greatest riches on Earth we, like the ravens and lilies, would still need God to thrive. And like the splendor of the lilies, our trust in God outshines any material thing we have.

4. Trust God (vv. 31–34)

Jesus wrapped up His teaching on worry by redirecting the priorities of His disciples. He exhorted them to seek the kingdom of God, and promised that those who did would not lack material possessions. Yet, He challenged them to put so little confidence in their material goods that they would be willing to sell it or give it away.

Many Christians struggle with these verses. Does God really want us to sell everything we have? Must we then give it all away? Jesus answered this when He noted, "For where your treasure is, there will your heart be also" (Luke 12:34). In other words, if you have a generous heart and would willingly give up everything, should you feel Jesus requires you to, then it is apparent that you own things rather than living for and serving them. That is the message of the parable of the rich farmer. Jesus' main concern was with the condition of the man's heart, rather than the expansiveness of his possessions. Instead of wanting to give away his surplus, the farmer thought to build a bigger barn to house his extra goods. Be not deceived. God does not mind that we have possessions. He does mind that we begin to trust solely on them, to the point of selfishness and hoarding.

How can we circumvent this? By learning to trust God more fully, relying on Him to help us combat anxiety and worry, and developing an active worship and prayer life. Previously, upon request of His disciples, Jesus had taught His disciples how to pray. On that occasion, He told them to pray for: (1) God's will to be done; (2) daily bread, or provision; (3) forgiveness of sins; and (4) the ability to withstand temptation (Luke 11:1–14). Then Jesus remarked, "If a son shall ask bread of any of you that is a father, will he give him a stone? or if he ask a fish, will he for a fish give a serpent? Of if he shall ask an egg, will he offer him a scorpion? If ye then, being evil, know how to give good gifts unto your children: how much more shall your heavenly Father give the Holy Spirit to them that ask him?" (Luke 11:11–13).

God is our provider. He cares for us and wants us to trust Him in every area of our lives. Yet we will never completely trust God while relying on our own inner strength or possessions. Instead we need to rely on the Holy Spirit to guide our hearts in prayer, while helping us keep our minds from mulling over worries.

Search the Scriptures

1. What three things are we told not to be worried about, and why (Luke 12:22, 29–30)?

2. What is more important than our natural needs or possessions (v. 23)?

3. How does the beauty of lilies compare to Solomon's attire (v. 27)?

4. To what did Jesus equate worries about clothing (v. 28)?

Discuss the Meaning

1. Why was it important to know that God cares for ravens and lilies?

2. Why do you think Jesus specifically noted the short life span of a lily when referring to our need for clothing?

3. How can we tell if we are trusting God or exercising little faith?

4. Why do you think God equated "treasure" with material things?

Lesson in Our Society

In our technology-rich, debt-driven society, it is becoming increasingly difficult to trust God. Instead of praying for provision, we can pick up the telephone or send an e-mail to ask a friend or family member to borrow money or other needed items. We can use a credit card to pay for needs or wants, without ever waiting for God's answer to materialize. While these things are possible, they are not God's best. As Jesus taught, God wants us to trust Him, but not just for everyday needs or in emergencies. Instead He wants us to trust Him 24 hours, seven days a week. What about you? What impediments stand in the way to your complete trust in God?

Make It Happen

Some forms of depression and some other mental and physical illnesses are directly related to worry. Today's lesson specifically encourages us not to worry about anything, including our basic needs. Distinguishing between wants and needs can help us defeat worry. Fold a piece of paper in half. Write down the word "needs" on one half, and the word "wants" on another. Brainstorm areas of need in your life, noting their urgency. For example, "Money for utility bills— ASAP." As you work through the list, honestly ask yourself, "Is this a need or a want?" Commit to waiting on God to provide your needs, and seek His help in being patient for your desires to be fulfilled without going into debt.

Follow the Spirit

What God wants me to do:

_____

_____

Remember Your Thoughts

Special insights I have learned:

_____

_____

More Light on the Text

Luke 12:22–34

22 And he said unto his disciples, Therefore I say unto you, Take no thought for your life, what ye shall eat; neither for the body, what ye shall put on.

Jesus was speaking to His disciples. He had just taught them the parable of the rich fool whose barn was filled with goods; because he had no more room for more goods, he was going to build a bigger barn. Jesus used this parable to help us re-prioritize storing goods, or making financial savings, and to emphasize a greater value—the need to be rich toward God. One of the aims of savings is financial security; a lack of financial security can cause people to worry. And so to humans who are subject to various natural conditions that agitate them, Jesus offers this word of

"Therefore I say unto you, Take no thought for your life, what ye shall eat; neither for the body what ye shall put on" (from Luke 12:22).

admonition. The Greek word for "thought" is *merimnao* (**mer-im-NAH-o**), meaning "to be anxious, be careful"; by this He enjoined us not to be anxious about our lives concerning what to eat and what to wear. The need to feed and be clothed is a fundamental cause of human worries. These represent the basic necessities for survival. With this statement, Jesus was discouraging any form of anxiety over material needs, because He knew how potent these needs could be on the human mind.

23 The life is more than meat, and the body is more than raiment.

In comparison, Jesus said life as a gift is greater than its sustenance. The Greek word *psuche* (**psoo-KHAY**) is translated as "life"; *psuche* primarily refers to life in a very broad sense, but further denotes "the breath of life, the natural life." In this context, it refers to our life in its entirety, from being sustained by God to the full range of human experiences and pursuits. Life is a gift from God alone; no man has the power to create it. For this reason life is greater than meat. The Greek word translated as "meat" is *trophe* (**trof-AY**), and it simply means "food, nourishment." In the contrast expressed here, it refers to the food we need to consume in order to live; the absence of it may cause anxiety or some irrational conduct, particularly when it seems that our survival is at stake. In this comparison, Jesus was not demeaning our need for food, but He was reorienting the priorities of His disciples so that they recognize their life depends on God as opposed to their own efforts to ensure survival or a "good" life.

The Greek word for "body" is *soma* (**SO-mah**); it denotes "the body as a whole, the instrument of life." It is sometimes used to refer to the physical nature of man as distinct from *psuche* (**psoo-KHAY**), "the soul." The body is the vessel that contains the spirit and the soul; it bears the natural physical form of the individual. It cannot be done away with—unless at death—nor is it replaceable. The word translated "raiment" is *enduma* (**EN-doo-mah**), meaning "clothing, a garment of any kind that is put on." Though clothes cover the body, they wear out; they are artificial and cannot be compared with the body that is created by God.

24 Consider the ravens: for they neither sow nor reap; which neither have storehouse nor barn; and God feedeth them: how much more are ye better than the fowls?

Reference is made to ravens, which are lesser creatures and yet are objects of God's providing care. Ravens are birds in the habit of flying restlessly about in search for food to satisfy their voracious appetite; they are scavengers. The raven's way of feeding is being used here by Jesus to describe people with an excessive disposition for sustenance—people who have a voracious appetite, people who excessively seek food for survival, and/or people who worry themselves over getting food.

The Greek word for "sow" is *speiro* (**SPI-ro**), meaning "to sow seed, to scatter abroad." It gives us the idea of laboring, working, or putting in some kind of effort that leads to wages. The Greek word *therizo* (**ther-ID-zo**) is translated as "reap"; it means "to harvest." This is usually the outcome of sowing. *Therizo* is synonymous with "wages, recompense, or rewards." The Greek word *tameion* (**tam-I-on**) is translated as "storehouse"; while *apotheke* (**ap-oth-AY-kay**) is translated as "barn." Both words are synonymous: *tameion* denotes primarily "a store chamber," and secondarily "a private room or secret chamber"; *apotheke* denotes "a repository, a place where anything is stored." Both words give us a general idea of an inner chamber where things are stored or where one can get some privacy.

Ravens don't labor or work like we do. They have no means of livelihood, they don't receive wages, they don't have store chambers where they can store food for a rainy day, they don't have a place to store their income to give them financial security, yet God satisfies their voracious appetite. The question Christ infers in this verse is this: If God feeds lesser creatures like ravens that lack a developed mode of living that features the process of working, earning wages, and storing or saving, but have such voracity, will He not do much more for us who are higher creatures? Therefore, we are meant to trust Him to provide our needs. Our encouragement to depend on God is echoed in the words "Casting all your care upon him; for he careth for you" (1 Peter 5:7).

25 And which of you with taking thought can add to his stature one cubit? 26 If ye then be not able to

do that thing which is least, why take ye thought for the rest?

Jesus used these rhetorical questions to expose our inability to increase our stature in spite of the anxieties we may have over our general well-being. The Greek word translated as "stature" (*helikia*, **hay-lik-EE-ah**) denotes "maturity in years or size"; but in this verse, Jesus refers specifically to size (height). The mention of a unit of measurement indicates this. *Pechus* (**PAY-khoos**) is the Greek word for "cubit"; it denotes the forearm, the part between the hand and the elbow, used as a "measure of length." Many things cause us to worry, from health, food, clothes, relationships, work, to physical form or appearance, but Jesus says we cannot do the least thing, that is, increase our height by one cubit. Increase of height is by a natural process. Jesus calls it "the least" because we seem to have control over other things that pertain to our physical bodies: weight, cleanliness, bodily form, healing, changing our hair color, or cutting our hair, but we are unable to affect our height.

27 Consider the lilies how they grow: they toil not, they spin not; and yet I say unto you, that Solomon in all his glory was not arrayed like one of these.

Jesus next referred to lilies and how they grow. For the second time, He presented the blessed natural state of being one of God's creatures as a picture that reveals His providing care, a picture that enables us to acknowledge God's care and trust in Him. *Krinon* (**KREE-non**) is the Greek word for "lilies" in this verse. The word "lilies" refers to various species of flowers: the chamomile, tulip, gladiolus, asphodel, iris, and the like. The gladiolus species are of brilliant, rich colors, shading from pinkish purple to deep violet purple and blue; the chamomile, white daisy like, with delicate beauty; and the iris, looking gorgeous. Jesus' comparison would therefore be a composite picture, revealing the splendid colors and beautiful shapes of the numerous species of the lily.

The Greek word translated as "toil" is *kopiao* (**kop-ee-AH-o**), meaning "to labour, to work hard, to be weary," while "spin" is *netho* (**NAY-tho**). *Kopiao* denotes to work or labor in a general sense, but *netho* denotes a specific kind of work: to make yarn out of cotton, wool, or silk for use in making cloth. The idea is that lilies are beautifully arrayed and gorgeous in their appearance, yet they don't labor or make

clothes. And Solomon in all of his material glory can't be compared with any of them.

28 If then God so clothe the grass, which is to day in the field, and to morrow is cast into the oven; how much more will he clothe you, O ye of little faith?

Amphiennumi (**am-fee-EN-noo-mee**) is the Greek verb translated as "clothe"; it means "to put clothes on." The adorning colors and beautiful forms of the lilies are clothes God has put on them. The word "grass" is a generic term meaning plants, vegetation, vegetables, herbs, and green growing things. But Jesus used this term to classify and depict it as a lower creature in comparison to man; and although it has an ephemeral existence, it is worthy of receiving God's generous care. God's act of care in providing clothing for us is displayed after the Fall. He clothed Adam and Eve with animal skins when they realized they were naked and felt the need to be clothed (Genesis 3:21). This goes to show that God takes the responsibility of clothing us and providing for our needs.

In the latter part of this passage, Jesus reproved His audience for having little faith. *Oligopistos* (**ol-ig-OP-is-tos**) is the Greek word translated as "little faith"; it is a combination of the prefix *oligos*, meaning "little" and *pistis*, meaning "faith." *Oligopistos* denotes "trusting too little." Jesus used this phrase as a reproof for anxiety. Our ability to trust God to provide our needs should be based absolutely on our confidence in God's ability to provide for us. Jesus challenges the faith of His followers by pointing to God's care for His creation. In response, we should be confident that He will supply our needs.

29 And seek not ye what ye shall eat, or what ye shall drink, neither be ye of doubtful mind.

Superficially, the statement may be taken as an outright discouragement from seeking food and drink. The Greek word *zeteo* (**dzay-TEH-o**) is translated as "seek"; it is used metaphorically, to "seek" by thinking or to "seek" how to do something, or what to obtain. This verse reiterates verse 22, using the word "seek" to convey a similar idea with "take no thought." In this case, "seek" depicts the process of thinking about or finding a way of obtaining what is needed. It speaks of active seeking: making a determined and laborious effort to seek for food and drink, getting wholly involved in the process of seeking for sustenance. With this kind of attitude, we take full responsibility for our sustenance and do not allow God to take the responsibility of providing. This attitude also encourages self-reliance and a lack of confidence in God.

Jesus discourages a lack of confidence in God with the statement "neither be ye of doubtful mind." *Meteorizo* (**met-eh-o-RID-zo**) is the Greek word translated as "doubtful mind." This word literarily means "to raise in midair, raised on high," but in this context it connotes "fluctuating, being anxious, wavering," or "vacillating, wavering between hope and fear." If we have this state of mind, we cannot trust in God. Doubt is the opposite of faith.

30 For all these things do the nations of the world seek after: and your Father knoweth that ye have need of these things.

The admonition not to actively seek food, drink, and clothing is meant to enable us to fulfill a divine purpose: to make us distinguish ourselves from the people of the world. The Greek word translated as "nations" is *ethnos* (**ETH-nos**); it is used to refer to "gentiles, heathen, pagans"—people who don't serve God. Non-Christians often devote their time and energy to seeking after material comfort in a way that portrays worship for materialism and the belief that all of our provisions come from our own hands. Jesus discourages us from such misguided seeking that results from forgetting that God is the One who knows our needs and willfully provides for us.

Our Heavenly Father is omniscient—He knows everything. His complete knowledge that encompasses the whole of creation and everything therein includes our needs. The Greek word for "knoweth" is *oida* (**OY-da**); this word is a perfect tense with a present meaning; it signifies primarily, "to have seen or perceived"; hence, "to know, to have knowledge of"; it suggests fullness of "knowledge." As One who knows, He is willing and able to provide; therefore, trusting in Him means placing our confidence in His willingness and ability to provide food, drink, and clothing for us. Because of His love and care, He shows particular concern for humans, the crown of creation.

31 But rather seek ye the kingdom of God; and all these things shall be added unto you.

The best alternative of what to seek is offered here, the ultimate object of human search is presented, and the greatest and worthiest pursuit of life that attracts divine commendation and approval is hereby mentioned—the kingdom of God. For the sake of this, we ought to trouble ourselves, inconvenience ourselves, and seek after it. The figurative use of the Greek word *zeteo* (**dzay-TEH-o**), meaning "to seek by thinking" and "to seek how to do something, or what to obtain," applies to the process of seeking the kingdom. Also, the resultant connotation—actively seeking by making a determined and laborious effort—rightly applies to the process of seeking the kingdom of God.

"All these things" refers to all material sustenance. Material things are not to be the ultimate object of our pursuits in life; according to Jesus, they shall be added. The Greek word translated "added" is *prostithemi* (**pros-TITH-ay-mee**), meaning "to place additionally, to put to something." This conveys the idea that something else holds first priority, and the pursuit of material sustenance (food, drink, and clothing) becomes something else that is placed additionally. That which is in first place becomes the focus of our seeking (the kingdom of God), while the additional thing becomes the "supplement" (material sustenance). Jesus enjoins us to actively seek the priorities of the kingdom, and to direct our energies toward God. He provokes us to focus on the kingdom and Kingship of God in our lives, because these are the things that have eternal value for us—not food, drink, and shelter. Material sustenance and all else follows in divine order; God will always make all these things available for us.

32 Fear not, little flock; for it is your Father's good pleasure to give you the kingdom.

This is a word of encouragement to dispel fear. *Poimnion* (**POYM-nee-on**) is the Greek word translated as "flock"; this word is used figuratively to mean "a group of Christ's believers." "Mixed multitude" (Exodus 12:38) is used metaphorically in the Bible to describe the multitude of believers all over the world today, comprised of various denominations and diverse Christian practices. In contrast to the mixed multitude, the little flock can be used to refer to the group of believers—out of all believers in the world—who eventually make it to heaven. They are those who run the race and eventually receive heavenly rewards, those who seek the kingdom and actually take hold of it. This is the background concept behind the statement Jesus made: "For many are called, but few are chosen" (Matthew 22:14). Thus, the little flock constitutes the chosen ones who earnestly and actively seek the kingdom; and God is pleased to give it to them.

These words of the Lord Jesus are meant to dispel fear from the minds of the little flock. Their position as a little flock pleases the Lord, but they are further counseled not to entertain fear, for fear is the direct opposite of faith.

33 Sell that ye have, and give alms; provide yourselves bags which wax not old, a treasure in the heavens that faileth not, where no thief approacheth, neither moth corrupteth.

Jesus instructs us in this verse to give alms, because this act enables us to create treasure bags in heaven. He proposes a rather radical notion: to sell all we have to give to the poor. This might be hard to accept, but it signifies the cost of following Jesus—that we shouldn't place importance on material things. The Greek word translated as "alms" is *eleemosune* (**el-eh-ay-mos-OO-nay**); this word signifies "mercy or compassion," as in showing mercy to the poor particularly when giving alms to them. *Balantion* (**bal-AN-tee-on**) is translated as "bags"; it is a "depository, a pouch for money, a money box or purse." Obviously, there is no material money box in heaven, but this word is used here figuratively to refer to a form of depository, or a heavenly account, or treasure box in heaven where our wealth is being stored. When we reflect God's character by being merciful in giving alms to the poor, we are making a deposit in this heavenly account. "He that hath pity upon the poor lendeth unto the LORD; and that which he hath given will he pay him again" (Proverbs 19:17).

The characteristic nature of the treasure in heaven is that it doesn't wax old. *Palaioo* (**pal-ah-YO-o**) is translated as "wax"; it means "to become old or to make worn." *Anekleiptos* (**an-EK-lipe-tos**), meaning "unfailing, inexhaustible," is translated as "faileth not." Jesus speaks of a treasure bag that cannot be exhausted or fail to make its contents available. The fact that thieves cannot approach our treasure bags in heaven, and moths

cannot corrupt them, also makes them immune to destruction.

34 For where your treasure is, there will your heart be also.

This statement reveals that our hearts dwell in the same place as our treasures. This treasure has a strong magnetic force that attracts our hearts. The Greek word for "heart" is *kardia* (**kar-DEE-ah**); here this word is used figuratively to mean "thoughts, affections, desires, imagination." The treasure base attracts our desires, thoughts, and affections. And so we are encouraged to lay up treasures in heaven so that our hearts will constantly be drawn heavenward. "Set your affection on things above [in heaven], not on things on the earth" (Colossians 3:2). We must not become so attached to earthly treasures that our heavenly treasure chest can be found empty when we arrive in glory.

Daily Bible Readings

M: Trust God
Psalm 31:1–5

T: Valuable to God
Luke 12:22–24

W: Worry Won't Help!
Luke 12:25–26

T: Clothed by God
Luke 12:27–28

F: God Knows Your Needs
Luke 12:29–31

S: Receive the Kingdom
Luke 12:32–34

S: Trust God, not Princes
Psalm 146:1–7

TEACHING TIPS

February 3
Bible Study Guide 10

1. Words You Should Know

A. Labourers (Luke 10:2, 7) *ergates* (Gk.)—Usually one who works for hire, especially an agricultural worker.

B. Kingdom (v. 9) *basileia* (Gk.)—Royal dominion. The sphere of God's rule.

2. Teacher Preparation

Unifying Principle—Response Requires Work We are often summoned to struggle for purposes greater than ourselves. How do we respond to the summons? When Jesus appointed seventy disciples to prepare His way, they obeyed despite the probability of hardship and rejection.

A. Read the Background, In Depth, and More Light on the Text sections, highlighting the sections that directly connect to the AIM for Change objectives.

B. Begin to jot down possible answers to the Discuss the Meaning questions and Make It Happen suggestions.

C. Gather information about the various outreach ministries within your church or community-at-large (e.g., homeless shelter, food pantry, or American Red Cross) for distribution among the class.

3. Starting the Lesson

A. Assign a student to lead the class in prayer, focusing on the AIM for Change objectives and thanking God for the opportunity of studying His Word this week.

B. Review the highlights of last week's lesson. Have a few students share their experiences from last week's Make It Happen suggestion.

C. Allow several minutes for the class to silently read today's Focal Verses and In Focus story. After the class has finished reading, explain that today's lesson deals with the believer's call to work in God's kingdom.

4. Getting into the Lesson

A. Pass out sheets of lined paper and use the questions in the Search the Scriptures as a closed Bible quiz for those who studied the lesson in advance and as a means of introducing the lesson to those who did not. Have the students write their answers on the paper, and then review the answers together.

B. Break the class into four groups and assign each group a question from the Discuss the Meaning questions. After the groups discuss their questions, have a representative from each group present their conclusions to the rest of the class.

5. Relating the Lesson to Life

A. Share your testimony of salvation with the class and explain how you came upon the decision to teach in your present capacity.

B. The Lesson in Our Society can help the students see how this lesson parallels with many present-day situations. Using today's lesson, ask students if they feel that all believers are summoned by God to share the Good News of salvation with others. Then ask how they plan to execute their summons over the upcoming weeks.

6. Arousing Action

A. The Make It Happen challenge encourages class participants to become active in ministry. Use this opportunity to pass out any information you have collected concerning your church's outreach ministries or those of any national outreach organizations.

B. Instruct the students to read the Daily Bible Readings in preparation for next week's lesson.

C. Close the class with prayer.

Worship Guide

For the Superintendent or Teacher
Theme: Summoned to Labor!
Theme Song: "Harvest Time"
Devotional Reading: Psalm 78:1-4
Prayer

SUMMONED TO LABOR!

Bible Background • LUKE 10:1–12, 17–20
Printed Text • LUKE 10:1–12, 17–20 Devotional Reading • PSALM 78:1–4

AIM for Change

By the end of the lesson, we will:

CONSIDER Jesus' call to labor for the kingdom;

BECOME CONVINCED we should participate in working in God's kingdom; and

RESPOND obediently to God's call to work for the kingdom.

Keep in Mind

"Therefore said he unto them, The harvest truly is great, but the labourers are few: pray ye therefore the Lord of the harvest, that he would send forth labourers into his harvest" (Luke 10:2).

Focal Verses

KJV

Luke 10:1 After these things the Lord appointed other seventy also, and sent them two and two before his face into every city and place, whither he himself would come.

2 Therefore said he unto them, The harvest truly is great, but the labourers are few: pray ye therefore the Lord of the harvest, that he would send forth labourers into his harvest.

3 Go your ways: behold, I send you forth as lambs among wolves.

4 Carry neither purse, nor scrip, nor shoes: and salute no man by the way.

5 And into whatsoever house ye enter, first say, Peace be to this house.

6 And if the son of peace be there, your peace shall rest upon it: if not, it shall turn to you again.

7 And in the same house remain, eating and drinking such things as they give: for the labourer is worthy of his hire. Go not from house to house.

8 And into whatsoever city ye enter, and they receive you, eat such things as are set before you:

9 And heal the sick that are therein, and say unto them, The kingdom of God is come nigh unto you.

10 But into whatsoever city ye enter, and they receive you not, go your ways out into the streets of the same, and say,

11 Even the very dust of your city, which cleaveth on us, we do wipe off against you: notwithstanding be ye sure of this, that the kingdom of God is come nigh unto you.

12 But I say unto you, that it shall be more tolerable in that day for Sodom, than for that city.

NLT

Luke 10:1 The Lord now chose seventy-two other disciples and sent them ahead in pairs to all the towns and places he planned to visit.

2 These were his instructions to them: "The harvest is great, but the workers are few. So pray to the Lord who is in charge of the harvest; ask him to send more workers into his fields.

3 Now go, and remember that I am sending you out as lambs among wolves.

4 Don't take any money with you, nor a traveler's bag, nor an extra pair of sandals. And don't stop to greet anyone on the road.

5 "Whenever you enter someone's home, first say, 'May God's peace be on this house.'

6 If those who live there are peaceful, the blessing will stand; if they are not, the blessing will return to you.

7 Don't move around from home to home. Stay in one place, eating and drinking what they provide. Don't hesitate to accept hospitality, because those who work deserve their pay.

8 "If you enter a town and it welcomes you, eat whatever is set before you.

9 Heal the sick, and tell them, 'The Kingdom of God is near you now.'

10 But if a town refuses to welcome you, go out into its streets and say,

11 'We wipe even the dust of your town from our feet to show that we have abandoned you to your fate. And know this—the Kingdom of God is near!'

10:17 And the seventy returned again with joy, saying, Lord, even the devils are subject unto us through thy name.

18 And he said unto them, I beheld Satan as lightning fall from heaven.

19 Behold, I give unto you power to tread on serpents and scorpions, and over all the power of the enemy: and nothing shall by any means hurt you.

20 Notwithstanding in this rejoice not, that the spirits are subject unto you; but rather rejoice, because your names are written in heaven.

12 I assure you, even wicked Sodom will be better off than such a town on judgment day.

10:17 When the seventy-two disciples returned, they joyfully reported to him, "Lord, even the demons obey us when we use your name!"

18 "Yes," he told them, "I saw Satan fall from heaven like lightning!

19 Look, I have given you authority over all the power of the enemy, and you can walk among snakes and scorpions and crush them. Nothing will injure you.

20 But don't rejoice because evil spirits obey you; rejoice because your names are registered in heaven."

In Focus

One day a preacher and an atheistic barber were walking through the city streets. The barber said to the preacher: "This is why I cannot believe in a God of love. If God was as kind as you say, He would not allow these poor bums to be addicted to dope, alcohol, and other life-destroying habits. No, I cannot believe in a God who permits these things."

The minister was silent until they met a man who was especially unkempt and filthy. His hair was hanging down his neck and he had a half inch of stubble on his face. The preacher turned to the barber and said: "See that man over there? Why don't you go over and offer him a free shave and a haircut?"

Indignantly the barber answered, "Why blame me for that man's condition? I can't help it that he is like that. He has never come into my shop where I could fix him up and make him look like a gentleman!"

Giving the barber a penetrating look, the minister said: "To follow God means to become involved in the work God calls us to do. How can you blame God for this man's condition if you aren't willing to help him?"

The invitation of God is issued to all, but many remain unaware of the invitation because of a lack of messengers to spread the Word. Today's lesson focuses on the believers, summons to serve by spreading the Good News.

The People, Places, and Times

Messengers. Sending messengers in pairs was traditional among the Jews and early Christians. The practice is first mentioned in Luke 9:51–52 by Jesus when He sent James and John into the Samaritan village. The practice not only provided companionship and protection but also provided the double witness prescribed in Deuteronomy 17:6 and 19:15 to render a testimony as credible.

Chorazin. A coastal city along the Sea of Galilee where Jesus performed many miracles.

Bethsaida. A fishing town on the Sea of Galilee and the birthplace of Philip, Andrew, and Simon. It was also near the place where Jesus performed the miracle of the feeding the five thousand (Luke 9:10–17).

Tyre and Sidon. Two well-known cities that Isaiah prophesied would suffer God's judgment and condemnation because of their sin (Isaiah 24:1–18).

Harvest. The Israelite farmer considered his land to be a gift from God (Deuteronomy 11:8–12) and was faithful in his stewardship of it. Christ and the New Testament writers used the images of the harvest to depict the condition of humanity. In Matthew 13:30, 36–42 Jesus used the image of the harvest to explain God's final judgment. In the epistles, Paul uses planting and harvesting to explain Christian giving (2 Corinthians 9:6–11), and righteousness (Galatians 6:7–10). The writer of Hebrews illustrates how divine correction produces a harvest of righteousness and peace (12:5–11).

In today's lesson the Lord returns to the harvest metaphor to explain to the teams of disciples to go before Him to the villages He planned to visit.

Background

In Luke 9:1–2, Jesus had already sent forth the 12 apostles, and here He is sending 70 more to spread the Good News message. We know from Matthew 15:38 and Luke 9:14 that Jesus' followers at one time numbered in the thousands if not the tens of thousands. So, you may wonder, why were only 70 disciples sent out? The significance of the 70 can be traced to the Table of Nations found in Genesis 10 where 70 Hebrew nations are named. Alternatively, Moses, in the book of Numbers, appointed 70 of Israel's elders to help him manage the large multitude (11:16–17). In today's lesson, Jesus calls 70 others and sends them out with the same good news of His kingdom.

At-A-Glance

1. Jesus Chooses the Seventy
(Luke 10:1–3)
2. Jesus Gives Instruction for the Mission
(vv. 4–12)
3. Jesus Enlightens the Seventy
(vv. 17–20)

In Depth

1. Jesus Chooses the Seventy (Luke 10:1–3)

The Lord visited as many places in person as possible. After the death of John the Baptist, the 12 apostles and the 70 took up the task of preparing the way for Jesus' entry in every city and place He planned to go and preach the kingdom message.

Verse two contains the commission to the 70 laborers. In His instructions, Jesus gave the imperatives to pray and go. Prayer was necessary for two reasons: first, any work of ministry begins with prayer as an expression of our complete dependence on God; second, Jesus explained that although the field was full and ripe there were not many people willing to work in the field. Therefore, He told His followers to pray and ask the Lord of the harvest to send workers into the harvest field.

Jesus saw the world as a gigantic field ready for harvesting. He explained to the laborers that He was sending them on their mission as lambs among wolves. As lambs, they must be completely dependent on the Shepherd to care for their needs and to protect them from the wolves who would try to destroy them and their testimony.

2. Jesus Gives Instruction for the Mission (vv. 4–12)

As part of their dependence on Jesus to provide for their needs, they were told not to carry any money or even an extra pair of shoes. Because of the urgency of their message, they were not to engage in long greetings that were common during that time.

Jesus gave them instructions for entering a house and for entering a town for the first time: When entering a house, they were to announce a blessing of peace. When used in greeting, peace denotes a state of harmonious, untroubled well-being. This state of well-being was brought about by God's mercy, granting the house freedom from all sorrows that are experienced because of sin. If the residents of the house were peaceful, the blessing would stay with them. If the people were not peaceful, the blessing would return to the disciple.

One sign of a peaceful residence was the desire of the residents to share their blessings. When the disciples came upon such a house, they were not to move from house to house, but to stay in the house where they were welcomed and allow the residents of the house to bless them with shelter and food.

Upon entering a town for the first time, Jesus instructed them to again accept the blessing offered to them. However, their mission was to announce that the kingdom of God is near and heal the sick as confirmation of their message. In the case where they were not welcomed in a town, they were to stand in the middle of the street and announce: "Even the dust of your town that sticks to our feet we wipe off against you" (v. 11, NIV). This act and statement constituted a curse on the town for rejecting the Good News. The town and people who rejected the Good News would suffer an end times fate far worse than the people of Tyre, Sidon, and Sodom when God destroyed that sinful city (cf. Genesis 19:24; Isaiah 24:1–18).

The commission that Jesus gave to the 70 is almost identical to the commission He gave to the 12 apostles (Luke 9:1–6). Jesus gives the same commission to all His people. This reminds us that the Gospel is not just for those we find socially acceptable, but for all who would answer the call regardless of their situation in life. For these 70 to go, they had to trust the presence of Jesus even though He was not with them physically. They had to be ready to suffer in humility knowing that their suffering would be for a divine purpose.

Here Luke illustrates our role in spreading the Gospel of Jesus Christ. Our first mission may be to our family and friends, but from there we must branch out into the world. We are the ones sent out into the world, into the highways and high-rises, into the cities, into corporate America, and beyond to bring a global population to a decision to follow Christ. They will either answer the call faithfully, just like the disciples and the 70, or they will reject it.

Jesus sends us all out with the same commission. We are to pray for those who have not accepted Christ as Lord and Savior and ask Him to send more workers into the field. Then we are to get up off our knees and go and announce that Jesus has paid the cost for all our sins and we now have the privilege of becoming children of God and citizens of the kingdom.

3. Jesus Enlightens the Seventy (vv. 17–20)

Scripture does not tell us how long the 70 were away on their missions but we know the missions were successful beyond their wildest dreams. They returned to Jesus filled with joy and amazement and reported, "Lord, even the demons obey us when we use your name" (v. 17, NLT).

It is easy to understand how excited the 70 must have been, to think that God used them as instruments of His will. They had seen the sick and infirmed healed, they had experienced victory over demons by calling on the authority of the Name of Jesus. More importantly, however, was the fact that Jesus said because of their newfound authority their names would be written in heaven (v. 20).

Jesus uses the metaphor of the harvest to describe the idea of bringing people into the reign of God. All Christians are called to harvest God's vineyard, and we who are co-laborers with Jesus in the kingdom of God cannot sit still and watch the ripened harvest die on the vine. Jesus Himself tells us that the reason we must go into the field is that the laborers are few.

God has given us authority to labor in the vineyard, and it is a work for which we must be ready to sacrifice even our lives. Understand that we are critical to the accomplishment of the task of the kingdom. When we first decided to accept Jesus as our Savior, we became candidates for service. Disciples not only follow the Master, they learn His teachings and imitate Him putting what they have learned into practice. Consequently, if we have chosen to follow where He leads, then we must be ready to take on the task of spreading the Gospel of the kingdom of God.

Search the Scriptures

1. Of the thousands of people who followed Jesus, how many did Jesus appoint to go ahead of Him and announce His coming (Luke 10:1)?

2. When entering a house, what blessing were the disciples to proclaim on the house (v. 5)?

3. What were the disciples to do when the town they entered did not welcome them and their message (vv. 10–11)?

4. When the 70 returned to Jesus, what part of their mission most excited them (v. 17)?

5. What should be the believer's greatest source of joy (v. 20)?

Discuss the Meaning

1. *(Group 1)* The key word in today's text is "labourers," which is repeated three times in the Scripture (Luke 10:2, 7). Read the definition of the word from the Words You Should Know section and explain how the definition applies to sharing the Gospel.

2. *(Group 2)* Discuss how the harvest metaphor relates to taking the Gospel to the world.

3. *(Group 3)* In verses two and three Jesus gives the 70 two commands. What were these commands, and how do these two imperatives relate your personal views on evangelism and outreach ministry?

4. *(Group 4)* Discuss why you believe it is difficult for the average Christian to share his or her faith with unbelievers, and begin to brainstorm ways to overcome this apprehension.

Lesson in Our Society

When Jesus appointed 70 disciples to prepare his way, they obeyed despite the probability of hardship and rejection. Oftentimes, we are summoned to struggle for purposes greater than ourselves. How do we respond to God's command to "go" and labor in the vineyard in a society that largely shuns outward displays of one's Christian beliefs in the marketplace? You may not always be allowed to place a Bible on your desk or hang a cross in your cubicle, but you can be, as the apostle Paul said, a living epistle (2 Corinthians 3:2–3), where the Word of God is written on your heart and manifests itself in the way you walk, the way you talk, and the manner in which you treat others.

Make It Happen

Christianity needs people who will answer the call to labor for the kingdom, and the first place one can begin to build God's kingdom is by tending your own vineyard. To what, if any, evangelistic or outreach ministries do you belong? If you have yet to become active in an outreach ministry, purpose in your heart today to pray and ask God where your skills, talents, and service are needed most outside the four walls of your church, and go where God commands.

Follow the Spirit

What God wants me to do:

_____

_____

Remember Your Thoughts

Special insights I have learned:

_____

_____

More Light on the Text

Luke 10:1–12, 17–20

That Luke opens this account with "after these things" is significant, since this phrase is meant to draw our attention to the pivotal happenings of chapter 9. That chapter begins with a mission that sounds remarkably like the one reported here, except that those sent are only Jesus' inner circle of 12. The miraculous feeding of thousands at Bethsaida comes next, demonstrating to the disciples that Jesus could

and would provide for all their needs as they ministered on His behalf. After that Jesus establishes His identity as the Messiah sent from God in three ways: first by coaxing Peter into a believing confession of Jesus' Messiahship; then through the Transfiguration, during which Jesus shone with His true glory, appearing with His forerunners Moses and Elijah, and heard the very voice of God the Father confirming that Jesus was His Son; and finally through a demonstration of His own power over supernatural demonic forces. But instead of taking His rightful place as king, Jesus then speaks about life connected to Him as filled with suffering and self-denial, as shown by the fact that "His face was as though he would go to Jerusalem" (where He would suffer and die [Luke 9:53]).

1 After these things the Lord appointed other seventy also, and sent them two and two before his face into every city and place, whither he himself would come.

Since the mission was to take place "after these things," the 70 missionaries of Luke 10:1–20 would have known (or at least should have known) that their mission would be successful because of Jesus' lordly authority, but that it would also likely involve suffering and rejection. They were sent out in pairs, probably for safety (traveling alone in Palestine was dangerous, as suggested by the parable of the Good Samaritan later in this chapter), but perhaps also so that they could fulfill Deuteronomy 19:15: "One witness shall not rise up against a man for any iniquity, or for any sin, in any sin that he sinneth: at the mouth of two witnesses, or at the mouth of three witnesses, shall the matter be established." This *double witness* would have strengthened their testimony to those they encountered during their mission.

Equally important is the phrase "before his face" (Gk. *pro prosopou autou*, **pro proh-SOH-poo ow-TOO**). The Greek language uses this phrase to mean "[sent] ahead of him," but the words used show how closely Jesus was tying the mission of the disciples to His own mission (as we will see later in the passage). The fact that He would let them go first to a place where He was going speaks volumes about Jesus' purpose to entrust His holy message to the mouths of men and women.

2 Therefore said he unto them, The harvest truly is great, but the labourers are few: pray ye therefore the Lord of the harvest, that he would send forth labourers into his harvest.

Jesus began His commission of the disciples by setting the stage for the task ahead of them. Using a favorite metaphor (the "harvest," see also John 4:35), Jesus revealed the scope and difficulty of the mission. Jesus' response to the enormity of the task is profound. Even though He had already shown Himself to be the all-powerful Son of God, He nevertheless directed the disciples to ask His Father to "send" (Gk. *ekballo*, **ek-BALL-oh**, showing power and purposefulness) more harvesters. Jesus' use of the term "Lord of the harvest" underlines the absolute sovereignty of God over the mission; Jesus left no room for the disciples to believe that the burden rests oppressively on their shoulders.

3 Go your ways: behold, I send you forth as lambs among wolves.

The solemn task given to these missionaries becomes yet clearer in this verse. For one thing, Jesus used the verb *apostello* (**ah-po-STELL-oh**) from which the word *apostle* is derived; we see that the mission of these "sent ones" has great and foundational importance. More significant, though, is the metaphor used for those being sent; they are not even full-grown sheep (as helpless as those creatures are!), but "lambs" (Gk. *aren*, **ar-AYN**), young offspring who would be helpless among ravenous wolves. To use a similar phrase, it would appear that these emissaries are no better than sacrificial lambs. Their only hope is in the all-seeing, all-powerful, all-loving care of their Shepherd, as promised in Isaiah 40:11: "He shall feed his flock like a shepherd: he shall gather the lambs with his arm, and carry them in his bosom, and shall gently lead those that are with young." This image of the Shepherd Jesus takes for Himself in John 10, and the apostles reinforce the image in Hebrews 13:20 and 1 Peter 5:4. Paradoxically, both the danger and the security of the disciples' mission come from their connection to Jesus.

4 Carry neither purse, nor scrip, nor shoes: and salute no man by the way.

Once again, Jesus gave instructions that would appear foolish if it were not for God's own protecting presence. The lack of a purse meant that no money would be taken for the journey; the scrip was a sort of knapsack for ones' belongings. To have neither of these resources would leave the disciples utterly dependent on their hosts. Rejection by a prospective host meant danger to their very lives. Further, the prohibition against taking a pair of shoes (this probably meant not to take an extra pair) would make the journey more arduous and dangerous. In all this the 70 would be displaying quite graphically not only their absolute dependence upon God and the kindness of others, but also a kinship with the poor (a common theme in the book of Luke). If they returned safely and bearing any marks of missionary success, the credit would be due to their Sender.

5 And into whatsoever house ye enter, first say, Peace be to this house.

The greeting that Jesus commanded here finds rich background in the Hebrew concept of *shalom* (**shah-LOHM**). This word refers not simply to the absence of conflict or to good relations between people, but to a much deeper idea that includes wholeness, blessing, and overall well-being, all due to the favor of God upon a particular nation, family, or individual. To say, "Peace to this house" would be similar to saying, "The Lord be with you" or "God bless you" in our day. Understanding this idea makes the possibility of rejection mentioned in the next verse more understandable; after all, very few people would reject a generic wish or offer of peace, but the connection of these emissaries to God—and ultimately to Jesus—made their cause much more precarious.

6 And if the son of peace be there, your peace shall rest upon it: if not, it shall turn to you again.

Again, the rejection described here would be puzzling if the "peace" in mind were only a fleeting formality or a casual greeting. Clearly, the 70 would be bringing a much more substantial message, and only those who are "sons of peace" would accept it. The Bible abounds with the use of *huios* (**hooy-OS**) or its Hebrew counterpart *ben* (**ben**) with a genitive construction, so that "son of" really means that the person is characterized by, or the recipient of, what follows. For example, Nabal in 1 Samuel 25:25 is called a "son of folly," meaning that he is the epitome of foolishness. In Ephesians 2:3 we see the phrase "children of wrath"—not meaning that such people are full of wrath but that they are *objects* of wrath. It would not seem an exaggeration to say that both senses of the phrase are operative here; these "sons of peace" are both characterized by *shalom* and objects of the *shalom* that comes from God.

The second part of this verse seems foreign to us modern readers; we are not accustomed to speaking of mere words as "resting upon" someone or "returning to" someone. The Ancient Near East was much more in tune with the power of the spoken word (particularly given the rarity of written documents). In addition, the Scriptures are full of descriptions of God's word as a creative power that actually brings about concrete results; one need look no further than Genesis 1, where God simply says "Let there be . . ." and entire realms come into existence. In this context, these 70 are emissaries of the Word Himself, the final and fundamental message of God; so their words are invested with great significance. To reject the offer of God's blessing brought by these missionaries was to reject God Himself.

7 And in the same house remain, eating and drinking such things as they give: for the labourer is worthy of his hire. Go not from house to house.

By commanding long sojourns with the "sons of peace" instead of completely itinerant wandering,

"The harvest truly is great, but the labourers are few: pray ye therefore the Lord of the harvest, that he would send forth labourers into his harvest" (from Luke 10:2).

Jesus reinforced the fact that the disciples' ministry of *shalom* would bless those who received it. While it is not specified what the disciples' ministry within each home might look like, we can safely assume that they spoke of the One who sent them, since the purpose of their trip was to be utterly identified with Him, and to prepare the way for His own visit. The phrase "the labourer is worthy of his hire" appears here, and a variation of it occurs in Matthew 10:10, in 1 Corinthians 9:14, and in 1 Timothy 5:18. These last two occurrences make clear that a minister is to be paid by those he serves. What is noteworthy here is that although the disciples took almost nothing on their trip and thereby identified with the poor, they were not to be beggars. Rather, they were seen as workers who received their due for their difficult labor.

8 And into whatsoever city ye enter, and they receive you, eat such things as are set before you:

This verse is largely a repetition of the preceding command, but it expands the area of acceptance and blessing from "house" to "city." As Jesus' condemnations of certain cities in verses 13–15 make clear, God views His creatures in larger groupings than individuals or even families. From the days of Sodom and Gomorrah to the mission in view here, God's covenantal eyes see humanity corporately and not just individually.

9 And heal the sick that are therein, and say unto them, The kingdom of God is come nigh unto you.

Here we find two more evidences that the 70 are truly commissioned by Jesus, so that their ministry is tied directly with His: first, they will heal just as He healed, and second, their message boils down to the same central point: "The kingdom of God is come nigh unto you" (see also Matthew 4:17). We might do well to ask at this point, which is more important: the miracles or the message? Though the former is more dramatic and was no doubt considered more impressive by those who witnessed such miracles, all four Gospels make clear that the purpose of miracles is to be signposts pointing to the Miracle Worker, the King Himself. So both miracles and message had an identical purpose: whether by deed or by word, they point to the coming of the long-expected King. But while miracles can be misleading or misunderstood (see

Luke 11:14–23, where Jesus is accused of doing miracles through Satan's power, and vv. 29–32, where Jesus condemns His hearers for seeking miraculous signs instead of the One to whom they point), it is ultimately the message—the good news of the Gospel—that God chooses to use to bring about the deepest and truest rescue of the souls of men and women. As Paul will later say, "it pleased God by the foolishness of preaching to save them that believe" (1 Corinthians 1:21).

The word *eggizo* (**en-GID-zoh**), here translated "has come nigh," is in the Greek perfect tense, which means that even though the central event has already happened (in this case, Jesus had already come upon the seen), the focus is often on the continuing effects of such an event. Note that Jesus did not say, "The kingdom of God *will* come upon you," but rather that it has already come in the sense that the King has arrived on the scene. We might compare it to the day that David took his seat in Jerusalem after ruling for seven years in Hebron over a divided Israel (see 2 Samuel 5). At that time David might have said to all Israel, "My kingdom *has come* upon you." The hearers would have known that the kingdom was *now*, for they stood in the presence of their beloved king. But in fact it was also true that they had many years to enjoy the advance of David's kingdom, during which he subdued Israel's enemies and put his people in a much more secure position. In the same way, though the coming of Jesus means that the kingdom has arrived, it does not mean that the kingdom is as victorious at that moment as it ever will be. Not only must the key events still take place (the death, resurrection, and ascension of Christ, and the subsequent giving of the Holy Spirit to the church), but then that kingdom must advance to cover all the earth as God intends—a process that is still going on today.

10 But into whatsoever city ye enter, and they receive you not, go your ways out into the streets of the same, and say,

These instructions from Jesus are very significant in that they showed the disciples how to handle the sort of rejection they faced in 9:51–56. There, when rejected by the people of a Samaritan village, James and John asked Jesus if they should rain fire from heaven on those of the village! They clearly had some sense of the power available to them through their association with Jesus, but little wisdom as to how to handle rejection. Jesus did not deny that rejection of those He sent was a dire and dangerous thing, but pointed out that those rejected were not to seek vengeance themselves. Instead, they were to withhold the miracles that they would otherwise perform, and in a "show and tell" sort of way, leave the town with a sobering warning, as the next verse shows.

11 Even the very dust of your city, which cleaveth on us, we do wipe off against you: notwithstanding be ye sure of this, that the kingdom of God is come nigh unto you.

The disciples' actions in a town that rejected them were to graphically portray the threatened judgment of God. The wiping off of dust from their feet is a way of saying, "We separate ourselves (and therefore the King Himself) from you so radically that we will not even allow a tiny remnant of your city to leave with us" (see Acts 13:51 for a similar event surrounding the rejection of the Gospel). At the same time, Jesus still called the disciples to announce the message of the kingdom to them; however, there is a key difference in this announcement from that of verse 9, a difference which is not reflected in the King James translation. The words "unto you" are not present in the original Greek; the announcement should simply have read, "The kingdom of God has come." The implication is obvious: Though the great news of the kingdom has come to the earth, it has not come *to you*, the rebellious ones who rejected it. The following verse reveals just how serious this rejection is.

12 But I say unto you, that it shall be more tolerable in that day for Sodom, than for that city.

This sort of proclamation often puzzles readers of the Bible, as an example of times when God seems to be overly harsh in His judgment. (For other examples, consider Achan's sin in Joshua 7, or the death of Ananias and Sapphira in Acts 5.) This event seems to fall in that category; it makes us ask, why should this town be judged so harshly simply for lack of hospitality? What these events often have in common is that they occur at crucial

moments in salvation history—times at which it is absolutely vital to be found on God's side. And since there is no greater moment in the history of God's redemption than the entry of the Son of God into history, there is likewise no more crucial time to answer the call of God. And, as Luke 10:12–15 ominously shows, there is no more dangerous time to reject the call of the Gospel.

In referring to the notorious city of Sodom, Jesus may have been using hyperbole (a sort of exaggeration) to show the seriousness of rejecting His ministry, but we also find a clue to His meaning in the phrase "in that day." Jesus' use of this phrase always pointed to the end-times Day of Judgment, during which some will be welcomed into His presence and others rejected, having rejected Him. The point here is that while Sodom received a terribly earthly judgment, its people will nevertheless have a better chance in the final end-times judgment than those of the town that rejects the Messiah.

10:17 And the seventy returned again with joy, saying, Lord, even the devils are subject unto us through thy name.

Luke does not tell us if the disciples experienced any of the rejection about which Jesus spoke (though they certainly would later, as the book of Acts shows). The focus here is on their joy in being connected with the power and authority of Jesus; Jesus experienced joy in this fact as well (see verse 21–24). Though at other times the disciples sought to make names for themselves, at this juncture their words demonstrated a basic humility; they addressed Jesus as "Lord" and make clear that the supernatural events that took place did so because of the name of Jesus. The reader is meant to experience the same sort of astonished joy as the point is once again driven home: those Jesus sends really do represent Jesus! They are, to use a popular phrase, His "hands and feet" in the world.

18 And he said unto them, I beheld Satan as lightning fall from heaven.

The language of this verse recalls Isaiah 14:12–20, where the fall of "the Day Star, the Son of Dawn" is described; though the great kingdom of Babylon is being described, it is implied that

Satan is the one at work behind the evil kingdoms of the world. These verses perhaps refer to that shadowy event otherwise not described in the Bible: the fall of Satan from angelic fellowship with God into rebellion against God. It may be that Jesus was talking here about witnessing that very event. More likely, however, Jesus was saying something even more astonishing: that the cosmic, final defeat of Satan is tied to the ministry of those He sends into the world. The verb tense used here suggests vividness, as if Jesus had just been observing the event, while the disciples were away on their mission. In addition, the word *pipto* (**PIP-toh**), "fall" or "falling," is placed an emphatic position in the Greek, so that the focus is on the Devil's crushing defeat, which is suggested again in the following verse.

19 Behold, I give unto you power to tread on serpents and scorpions, and over all the power of the enemy: and nothing shall by any means hurt you.

Once again, a perfect tense verb (*dedoka*, **DED-oh-kah**) is used to show that Jesus' "gift" is one that will endure throughout the disciples' ministry; it is an enduring, rather than a temporary, endowment. The disciples would have recognized the reference to "serpents and scorpions" as calling back all the way to Genesis 3, where the serpent tempted Adam and Eve into sin, but where also God promised to overcome the devastating effects of their sin through the "seed" of the woman (see Genesis 3:15). Throughout the Bible God's people are shown to triumph over the dangerous wilderness, where such creatures prevail (see Deuteronomy 8:15). Jesus now included His own disciples in this history of redemption, for He is indeed the "seed" of Eve. The history of those who follow Jesus, like His own history, shows that the promise here is not invincibility, but that ultimately Jesus and those who follow Him will triumph, and that they will always be protected from true evil. For the battle will be won in the death and resurrection of the promised One; the glorious victory will be made sure. As one commentator puts it, "In the war with Satan, Jesus' ministry is D day."

20 Notwithstanding in this rejoice not, that the spirits are subject unto you; but rather rejoice, because your names are written in heaven.

An account full of surprises takes one final surprise twist: despite the assurance of victory over those who reject them and even over the spiritual forces who oppose them, the disciples have a much better reason to rejoice: they belong to God, no matter what. The Greek verb *grapho* (**GRAHF-oh**) was typically used to a formal kind of writing, like a census. In other words, God has not casually written down the disciples' names on a scrap of paper in pencil that it might be erased, but has finally and certainly written down their names in indelible ink in an eternal book. In contrast to the Devil, whose defeat is sure though at times his will seems to dominate, these disciples would know the certainly of their inheritance, even at the bleakest moments. In this way Jesus redirected the disciples' joy (v. 17) and made it more like His own; yet once more, they were bound and united to their Lord and Master.

Source:

Bock, Darrell L. *Baker Exegetical Commentary of the New Testament: Luke 9:51–24:53*. Edited by Moises Silva. Grand Rapids, Mich.: Baker Books, 1996.

Daily Bible Readings

M Instruct the Believers
Psalm 78:1–4

T: The Twelve on a Mission
Luke 9:1–10

W: The Seventy Go in Pairs
Luke 10:1–3

T: Travel Lightly in Peace
Luke 10:4–7

F: Proclaim God's Kingdom
Luke 10:8–12

S: They Returned with Joy
Luke 10:17–20

S: See God's Work
Psalm 66:1–7

TEACHING TIPS

February 10
Bible Study Guide 11

1. Words You Should Know

A. Sinners (Luke 13:2) *hamartolos* (Gk.)—Those who deviate. Commonly used in the New Testament in connection to publicans or tax collectors.

B. Perish (vv. 3, 5) *apollumi* (Gk.)—Utter destruction; to destroy.

2. Teacher Preparation

Unifying Principle—Turning Our Lives Around As we look at our lives, we see things about us that we would like to change. How do we change our behavior so that we are better people? Jesus called people to repent and to allow God to transform their lives.

A. Explore the meaning of the word "repent" using several different sources (e.g., dictionary, Bible dictionary, concordance). The *Precepts For Living®* CD-ROM will help in your search.

B. Read the Focal Verses. In addition, review The People, Places, and Times, Background, In Depth, and More Light on the Text.

3. Starting the Lesson

A. Prior to the students entering the class, write the following question on the chalkboard: *What would you do if you only had a year left to live?*

B. Assign a student to lead the class in prayer, focusing on the AIM for Change.

C. Review last week's lesson. Allow several minutes for the students to share their decisions to become active in outreach ministry based on last week's Make It Happen and Lesson in Our Society suggestions.

D. Instruct the class to take out a sheet of paper and jot down their thoughts to the question on the chalkboard.

E. After they have answered the question, allow the class several minutes to read the Focal Verses and In Focus story for today's lesson silently.

F. Give a brief review of the In Depth section based on the At-A-Glance outline, highlighting Jesus' motives for telling the parable of the fig tree.

G. Jesus uses the parable of the fig tree as a metaphor to warn of coming judgment and spiritual death as a result of sin. Ask the class to give their thoughts on what it means to perish spiritually.

4. Getting into the Lesson

A. Ask for volunteers to share their responses to the question on the chalkboard. Allow several minutes for student interaction.

B. Give a brief synopsis of The People, Places, and Times and Background sections. Pay special attention to the comments on the fig tree and repentance.

5. Relating the Lesson to Life

A. Invite the class to discuss their views on why it appears that bad things always seem to happen to good people.

B. The Lesson in Our Society section can help the students see how the lesson parallels with many present-day calamities.

6. Arousing Action

A. Ask if anyone has prayer requests based on the Make It Happen suggestion. If so, jot down their requests and make sure to include them during closing prayers.

B. Instruct the class to read the Daily Bible Readings and, for those who have it, complete lesson 12 in the *Precepts For Living® Personal Study Guide* in preparation for next week's lesson.

C. Close the class in prayer thanking God for His redemption, making sure to include students' prayer requests.

Worship Guide

For the Superintendent or Teacher
Theme: Summoned to Repent!
Theme Song: "Redeemed by the Blood"
Devotional Reading: Psalm 63:1–6
Prayer

SUMMONED TO REPENT!

Bible Background • LUKE 13:1–9
Printed Text • LUKE 13:1–9 Devotional Reading • PSALM 63:1–6

AIM for Change

By the end of the lesson, we will:

GRASP the biblical concept of repentance;

EXAMINE areas of our lives where we need to make changes; and

REPENT and allow God to transform their lives.

Keep in Mind

"I tell you, Nay: but, except ye repent, ye shall all likewise perish" (Luke 13:3).

Focal Verses

KJV **Luke 13:1** There were present at that season some that told him of the Galileans, whose blood Pilate had mingled with their sacrifices.

2 And Jesus answering said unto them, Suppose ye that these Galileans were sinners above all the Galileans, because they suffered such things?

3 I tell you, Nay: but, except ye repent, ye shall all likewise perish.

4 Or those eighteen, upon whom the tower in Siloam fell, and slew them, think ye that they were sinners above all men that dwelt in Jerusalem?

5 I tell you, Nay: but, except ye repent, ye shall all likewise perish.

6 He spake also this parable; A certain man had a fig tree planted in his vineyard; and he came and sought fruit thereon, and found none.

7 Then said he unto the dresser of his vineyard, Behold, these three years I come seeking fruit on this fig tree, and find none: cut it down; why cumbereth it the ground?

8 And he answering said unto him, Lord, let it alone this year also, till I shall dig about it, and dung it:

9 And if it bear fruit, well: and if not, then after that thou shalt cut it down.

NLT **Luke 13:1** About this time Jesus was informed that Pilate had murdered some people from Galilee as they were offering sacrifices at the Temple.

2 "Do you think those Galileans were worse sinners than all the other people from Galilee?" Jesus asked. "Is that why they suffered?

3 Not at all! And you will perish, too, unless you repent of your sins and turn to God.

4 And what about the eighteen people who died when the tower in Siloam fell on them? Were they the worst sinners in Jerusalem?

5 No, and I tell you again that unless you repent, you will perish, too."

6 Then Jesus told this story: "A man planted a fig tree in his garden and came again and again to see if there was any fruit on it, but he was always disappointed.

7 Finally, he said to his gardener, 'I've waited three years, and there hasn't been a single fig! Cut it down. It's just taking up space in the garden.'

8 "The gardener answered, 'Sir, give it one more chance. Leave it another year, and I'll give it special attention and plenty of fertilizer.

9 If we get figs next year, fine. If not, then you can cut it down.'"

In Focus

There is a story of a Hindu who was seeking God. When he heard about how Jesus came to live on Earth, he could not understand why the Creator of the universe would want to humble Himself in such a way.

Because of his religious background, the Hindu had a reverence for all forms of life. One day as he was walking in a field, he noticed a large anthill. The Hindu stopped to observe the activity of these amazing creatures.

Suddenly he heard the noise of a tractor plowing the field. The plow would soon make its way to the

would perish in a similar kind of earthly tragedy. Considering the previous context and Jesus' focus on the judgment in the last day, He was much more likely referring to that judgment here. So, in fact, apart from repentance, the fate of His hearers could be much worse than those who experience bodily death. However, Jesus was gracious and hopeful even in His warning; His use of a certain word for "if" (Gk. *kan*, kan) allows that repentance to be a distinct possibility and so provided a note of hope even in the seriousness of this part of the passage.

4 Or those eighteen, upon whom the tower in Siloam fell, and slew them, think ye that they were sinners above all men that dwelt in Jerusalem?

Jesus introduced a second example, not just to drive His point home but also to introduce a second dimension in the concept of theodicy: what even modern-day insurance companies refer to as "acts of God." In other words, people who are killed through sinful acts of violence are not themselves worse sinners than anyone else, but what about those to whom natural disasters or accidents happen? Since God allowed (or caused) such things to take place and no sinful human intention was involved, does this not mean that the victims in some way got what was coming to them? The "Siloam" to which Jesus referred was probably a reservoir for Jerusalem located near the intersection of the south and east walls of the city. This incident would have been especially significant in that it took place in Israel's capital, near the temple—the heart of Jewish piety. If this was God's judgment, and Jerusalem was not exempt from it, then the people would have been frightened indeed.

On another note, Jesus used a Greek word for "sinners" (Gk. *opheiletes*, **of-i-LET-ace**) that is connected to the verb for "to owe a debt." The use of this word connects this dialogue once again with the warning that came before it in 12:57–59. The question left open the possibility that the victims of this tragedy were just the kind of people who failed to "settle their accounts" with God.

5 I tell you, Nay: but, except ye repent, ye shall all likewise perish.

Jesus responded to His own question in the same way He had to the previous question—by denying that these victims were any worse sinners than anyone

else in their midst. The only difference in the wording of His two responses is that here for "likewise" Jesus used the word *homoios* (Gk. **hom-OY-oce**), which is even stronger than the word used previously. At this point, Jesus was ramping up the urgency, showing that the key question for His hearers was not, "Why did such-and-so happen to them?" but rather, "What will happen to me?" In light of the universal human destiny of death and judgment (see Hebrews 9:27), Jesus made it clear that the response of His followers to tragedy should be to examine their lives and to turn from sin and to God in repentance to salvation.

6 He spake also this parable; A certain man had a fig tree planted in his vineyard; and he came and sought fruit thereon, and found none.

Luke apparently places this parable with the preceding dialogue not only to reinforce the theme of urgency, but also to emphasize the tremendous grace afforded to God's people by His patience. The parable has many features that are common to Jesus' parables: first, its generic character (it does not reference a specific person but only "a certain man"); second, its use of agricultural images (the fig tree, the vineyard); and finally, a central message (rather than many messages), which we will discover in the verses below.

Both the vineyard and the fig tree were common images used by the Lord (for the vineyard, see Mark 12:1–11; for the fig tree, see Matthew 21:18–21; both of these are repeated or share similar stories in other Gospels). In this parable, the vineyard does not hold much significance; it is only the setting for the story. Rather, the focus is on the fig tree. Given that the fig tree in Jesus' other uses of the metaphor (including the cursing of the fig tree in Matthew 21) represented Israel, and given Jesus' audience, it clearly represented Israel here as well. The other similarity with the "cursing" stories is that the man in this parable looks for fruit on the tree but finds none. However, in the other accounts the authors are relating the historical event in which Jesus encounters the fig tree; here, that event is encapsulated within a parable. All of these events bear a striking similarity to the words of God found through the prophet Micah in Micah 7:1, which is worth quoting here: "Woe is me! for I am as when they have gathered the summer fruits, as the grapegleanings of the vintage: there is no cluster to eat: my soul desired the firstripe fruit." The parable here, when considered in light of this "woe," concerns the danger to Israel as a nation and to unfaithful individual Israelites who reject the message of Jesus' kingdom.

7 Then said he unto the dresser of his vineyard, Behold, these three years I come seeking fruit on this fig tree, and find none: cut it down; why cumbereth it the ground?

The owner of the vineyard is rightly distressed that his fig tree has borne no fruit, because healthy fig trees usually took three years to bear fruit. Thus it would be wrong for us to picture the owner as cruel and impatient in contrast to the vinedresser's compassion. Instead, the picture is of a righteous and holy God taking stock of His fig tree (Israel) and seeing that, though it should have long since borne fruit for Him, it has not done so. To return to the language of the parable, the vineyard owner is justifiably disturbed because the fig tree is soaking up nutrients that other healthy, fruit-bearing plants could be using. Having allowed more than enough time for the fig tree to blossom as it should, his verdict is clear: cut it down, and as an implied idea, give its space to a plant that will bear fruit.

8 And he answering said unto him, Lord, let it alone this year also, till I shall dig about it, and dung it:

The vinedresser brings in the element of compassion and patience alongside the vineyard owner's righteous and justified judgment. (Note that this is not a picture of conflict between the two men in the parable, but rather the display of complementary aspects of God's character.) Beyond all reasonable expectation (and certainly despite the apparent worthlessness of the fig tree), he asks for permission to tend and fertilize it for one more year. Note the exceeding grace that is suggested here; not only does the vinedresser intercede to save the fig tree, but also he plans to tenderly care for the tree and do everything in his power to assure that it bears fruit.

9 And if it bear fruit, well: and if not, then after that thou shalt cut it down.

Yet even with this gracious offer present, there are ominous notes here. First, there is the fact that only one year of extension is granted to the fig tree. Though we need not take this as Jesus granting to Israel a literal 365 days to repent, the message is clear: time is short and the need to respond to God could hardly be more urgent. Also, there is an interesting grammatical construction here; two different Greek words for "if" are used so that the first clause ("if it bear fruit") is viewed as less likely than the second ("if not").

Finally, note that the parable is a bit of a cliffhanger; we do not find a response from the vineyard owner, and so at first glance it seems we do not know if he will even let the tree continue to exist at all. This open-endedness is meant to leave the decision up to the hearer and to put the suspense on the hearer's response. For in fact we do know that the offer of grace is indeed extended; after all, it is the Lord who is telling the parable, and in doing so He represents both owner and vinedresser. It is He who warns of judgment but also promises forgiveness and life upon repentance and faith and who will go to the ultimate length at the Cross to make such life secure.

Daily Bible Readings

M: My Soul Is Satisfied
Psalm 63:1–6

T: Turn from Your Ways
Luke 3:7–14

W: Jesus Calls for Repentance
Mark 1:14–15

T: Repent or Perish
Luke 13:1–5

F: Bear Fruit of Repentance
Luke 13:6–9

S: Paul Calls for Repentance
Acts 26:19–23

S: Choose God's Way
Psalm 1:1–6

TEACHING TIPS

February 17
Bible Study Guide 12

1. Words You Should Know

A. Parable (Luke 14:7) *parabole* (Gk.)—Natural, or earthly, stories that illustrated spiritual truths.

B. Which were bidden (v. 7) *kaleo* (Gk.)—To invite, or call by name; in the case of a wedding denotes an invited guest.

C. Shame (v. 9) *aischune* (Gk.)—Denotes disgrace or dishonesty; the feeling of being made ashamed.

D. Exalteth (v. 11) *hupsoo* (Gk.)—To lift up, honor, or to lift up/increase in dignity.

2. Teacher Preparation

Unifying Principle—The Necessity of Humility
Our society values and rewards people who put themselves first. What is a better way to live? At a meal where people are clamoring for the best seats, Jesus tells a parable about humility.

A. Read the Focal Verses and Background.

B. Use a dictionary to study and contrast the terms humility/humble, and pride.

C. Read Psalm 25:9.

D. Be mindful that *biblical* humility differs vastly from what most people think humility denotes. Consider the positive and negative meanings of humility and pride, and come prepared to discuss these, as well as the rewards of humility and the consequences of pride.

E. Prior to class, contact four students and ask if they would perform the In Focus story as a role-play. (roles: Alfred, Alfred's wife, Joseph, the pastor).

3. Starting the Lesson

A. Begin the class with prayer. Focus on the AIM for Change, and the need for humility, regardless of what position we hold, or gifts and talents we have.

B. Read the Keep in Mind verse.

C. Ask a volunteer to read Psalm 25:9.

D. Briefly discuss the questions "What does humility mean to you?" and "Why do people associate humility with weakness?"

4. Getting into the Lesson

A. Write the words "humility" and "pride" on the chalkboard. Ask for brief examples of any rewards and/or consequences that the Bible promises for humility or pride.

B. Briefly share the dictionary definitions of humility/humble and pride. Discuss how these differ or are comparable to humility and pride as depicted in the parable.

C. Summarize the content of today's Focal Verses.

D. Discuss ways Jesus Christ exemplified intentional humility and how students can follow His example.

5. Relating the Lesson to Life

A. Briefly discuss situations that lend themselves to people being humbled and exalted.

B. Review the Keep in Mind verse, reminding the students of the necessity of humility and that when we place the needs of others above our own needs, we leave room for God to bless, exalt, and promote us.

6. Arousing Action

A. Ask the students to commit to being intentionally humble this week by building up or serving others, rather than exalting themselves.

B. Invite the students to share any concerns or prayer requests they may have concerning the lesson.

C. Close the class with prayer, making specific petitions addressing students' concerns.

Worship Guide

For the Superintendent or Teacher
Theme: Summoned to Be Humble!
Theme Song: "Have Thine Own Way, Lord"
Devotional Reading: Psalm 25:1–10
Prayer

SUMMONED TO BE HUMBLE!

Background • LUKE 14:1, 7–14
Printed Text • LUKE 14:1, 7–14 Devotional Reading • PSALM 25:1–10

AIM for Change

By the end of the lesson, we will:

EXPLORE humility as Jesus depicted it in the parable;

EXAMINE our feelings about being intentionally humble; and

CARRY OUT an act of kindness that shifts the focus from self to others.

Keep in Mind

"For whosoever exalteth himself shall be abased; and he that humbleth himself shall be exalted" (Luke 14:11, KJV).

Focal Verses

KJV

Luke 14:1 And it came to pass, as he went into the house of one of the chief Pharisees to eat bread on the sabbath day, that they watched him.

14:7 And he put forth a parable to those which were bidden, when he marked how they chose out the chief rooms; saying unto them,

8 When thou art bidden of any man to a wedding, sit not down in the highest room; lest a more honourable man than thou be bidden of him;

9 And he that bade thee and him come and say to thee, Give this man place; and thou begin with shame to take the lowest room.

10 But when thou art bidden, go and sit down in the lowest room; that when he that bade thee cometh, he may say unto thee, Friend, go up higher: then shalt thou have worship in the presence of them that sit at meat with thee.

11 For whosoever exalteth himself shall be abased; and he that humbleth himself shall be exalted.

12 Then said he also to him that bade him, When thou makest a dinner or a supper, call not thy friends, nor thy brethren, neither thy kinsmen, nor thy rich neighbours; lest they also bid thee again, and a recompence be made thee.

13 But when thou makest a feast, call the poor, the maimed, the lame, the blind:

14 And thou shalt be blessed; for they cannot recompense thee: for thou shalt be recompensed at the resurrection of the just.

NLT

Luke 14:1 One Sabbath day Jesus went to eat dinner in the home of a leader of the Pharisees, and the people were watching him closely.

7 When Jesus noticed that all who had come to the dinner were trying to sit in the seats of honor near the head of the table, he gave them this advice:

8 "When you are invited to a wedding feast, don't sit in the seat of honor. What if someone who is more distinguished than you has also been invited?

9 The host will come and say, 'Give this person your seat.' Then you will be embarrassed, and you will have to take whatever seat is left at the foot of the table!

10 "Instead, take the lowest place at the foot of the table. Then when your host sees you, he will come and say, 'Friend, we have a better place for you!' Then you will be honored in front of all the other guests.

11 For those who exalt themselves will be humbled, and those who humble themselves will be exalted."

12 Then he turned to his host. "When you put on a luncheon or a banquet," he said, "don't invite your friends, brothers, relatives, and rich neighbors. For they will invite you back, and that will be your only reward.

13 Instead, invite the poor, the crippled, the lame, and the blind.

14 Then at the resurrection of the righteous, God will reward you for inviting those who could not repay you."

In Focus

Joseph and Alfred were excited. Of all the men's ministry leaders, they were handpicked to accompany their pastor to an international ministry summit that would be aired live on a renowned Christian television network. Before going, they were informed that only one would be allowed to sit in the special reserved area on the stage with their pastor; the other could pick any other seat in the vast auditorium.

Alfred packed his bags with care, assuring that his newly purchased suit would not wrinkle and that the new matching tie, hankie, and cuff links were safely secured. "I'm a shoe-in to sit with the pastor, so make sure you watch me live" he told his wife as she assisted him.

"But honey," she said, "how can you be sure? There are two of you, and Brother Joseph may be chosen instead."

"No way," he joked. "Do you notice how he dresses and that dorky haircut? Trust me. Pastor will want me sitting next to him so I can make him look good."

The flight to the event went smoothly, and the day of the summit arrived. Alfred smirked to himself when he noticed Joseph wearing the suit he usually wore to special functions at the church. "Man, I love the brother," Alfred thought to himself, "but he sure doesn't have a clue about how to dress, or how to get in the pastor's good graces."

As they ventured to find seats, the two men were separated by the crowd trying to find seats before the summit began. Joseph headed for the non-reserved area, while Alfred sought out a place with easy access to the stage. As the proceeding began the pastor came to the podium and said, "Please take your seats, we will begin shortly once everyone is in place." Then he looked down at the paper in his hand. "Also, if I call your name, please come immediately to the pulpit. Joseph, come and sit beside me." Joseph's head snapped when he heard his name. Jumping to his feet, he exited the aisle and headed for the stairs leading up to the right side of the stage. As he mounted the stairs, he smiled down at Alfred.

In today's lesson, Jesus tells a parable about humility that teaches humble people should not assume the best seats for themselves.

The People, Places, and Times

Pharisees. A major religious party in Jesus' time, the Pharisees were known for their strict observance of the Law of Moses and reliance on tradition. Portrayed as Jesus' adversaries in all four Gospels, the Pharisees often were outraged at Jesus' teachings and actions that portrayed a loving God who offered grace, while commanding salvation by faith (not works) alone.

Lawyers. This professional group was charged with studying, interpreting, and applying the Law of Moses. In many ways, their work mirrored that of the scribes who were originally priests, but whose roles included these same responsibilities, as well as copying the Law, writing documents, and other tasks.

Weddings. Like today, weddings were festive social gatherings of which a variety of people from different social backgrounds were invited. It's ironic to note that in the parable guests were vying for honor instead of remembering their purpose for attending the wedding: to honor the bride and bridegroom and their families.

Background

Jesus often taught in parables and performed miracles that displayed God's grace at work. He used parables to provoke hearers to seek deeper spiritual truth and understanding. Privately, Jesus would explain the meaning of these stories to His disciples, but others were not so privileged. Interestingly, Jesus' parables and miracles (cf. Luke 14:2–6) often seemed to conflict greatly with the strict adherence to the Law of Moses. Yet, Jesus noted that this was not the case. He explained, "Think not that I am come to destroy the law, or the prophets: I am not come to destroy, but to fulfill" (Matthew 5:17).

The paradox of Jesus fulfilling the Law was key to the discord between the Pharisees and Jesus. Unfortunately, it was not the only one. The Pharisees felt that Jesus upset the social structures of the day by not adhering to prominent attitudes about class, gender, or race. Instead, Jesus specifically demonstrated love and compassion for ALL people, as evidenced by His caring for society's outcasts (including lepers) and mingling with society's supposed "underdogs" (like Zacchaeus the tax collector, Luke 19:1–10).

Jesus exemplified humility, something that was not of great importance to the Pharisees who constantly jockeyed for position, authority, and power.

In word and deed, Jesus constantly challenged the Pharisees' manner of ruling and strict adherence to the law. In Luke 14 this becomes apparent yet again as Jesus resorts to telling parables to share spiritual truths. Specifically, He advocates humility over pride, generosity over stinginess.

At-A-Glance

1. Watching the Son of Man (Luke 14:1)
2. Necessity of Humility (vv. 7–10)
3. Serving the Underserved (vv. 12–13)
4. Heavenly Rewards (v. 14)

In Depth

1. Watching the Son of Man (Luke 14:1)

On the Sabbath, Jesus visited the home of a chief Pharisee to "eat bread." It was not unusual for Jesus to be among those who opposed His views. During these times, Jesus, undaunted by the opposition, continued His earthly ministry, teaching about God's grace, healing the sick, and performing miracles. Unfortunately, His ministry's effectiveness and compassion caused controversy amongst the Jewish leaders.

Luke makes a point of noting it was the Sabbath. On other occasions Jesus had butted heads with the religious leaders who strictly adhered to the law's instructions concerning what was and was not allowable Sabbath activities. In each prior case, Jesus was able to quell opposition by proving that while His actions may not have seemed appropriate or lawful, they were in fact so. For instance, in verse 5 after healing a man suffering with dropsy Jesus asks, "Which of you shall have an ass or an ox fallen into a pit, and will not straightway pull him out on the [S]abbath day?" Luke notes, "And they could not answer him again to these things." Why not? Because they knew they would help their prized animal had they found it in such a dilemma.

On this occasion, as with others, it is clear that while the chief Pharisee may have welcomed Jesus to his home, others within the group were not as welcoming, for "they watched him" (v. 1). Generally, this wasn't because they respected him or wanted to learn His ways. Instead, as Mark aptly noted, "Some of them were looking for a reason to accuse Jesus, so they watched him closely to see if he would heal him on the Sabbath" (Mark 3:2, NIV).

2. Necessity of Humility (vv. 7–10)

Ironically, as the Pharisees were watching Jesus, He, too, was marking—or intensely watching how those gathered to eat were selecting the more honored positions at the table. In the Greek, "marked" is the word *epecho* (ep-EKH-o), meaning to observe closely, pay close attention to. So while others hustled to get prominent seats for themselves, Jesus keenly watched their actions. What He saw greatly displeased the King of kings, who Himself was worthy of honored places, but instead chose to be a servant (cf. Philippians 2:7–8).

Scripture does not tell us which seat Jesus selected, or if He even sat to eat. What is clear is that Jesus used this opportunity to rebuke the Pharisees' actions while commending humility. For ambitious religious leaders then, and even leaders today, such instruction would have been difficult to swallow, mainly because most people do not associate humility with success. In fact, the higher many people go in a career or ministry, the less humble they often become. For example, those who hold high-level positions may begin treating subordinates with disdain and may even give them trivial assignments just to reinforce a sense of superiority. Scripture repeatedly warns of such attitudes or behaviors. Proverbs 16:18 reminds us, "Pride goeth before destruction, and an haughty spirit before a fall."

Even though Jesus was God's own Son, He remained humble. Because Jesus did not allow His eloquence, gifts of healing, or spiritual power to pollute His spirit, He never became haughty or arrogant. Moreover, Jesus was neither swayed by financial gifts, nor was He tempted by the promise of worldwide fame that the adversary dangled in His face on one occasion (see Matthew 4:1–11).

As Christians, it is imperative that we check ourselves to make sure we are walking in the humble image of Jesus Christ, our Lord and Saviour. We must make a conscious decision to remain humble no matter what it takes, keeping in mind that by biblical standards, a person can be both successful and humble. Biblical humility provides room for a person to confidently use his or her gifts and talents in a non-conceited, non-obnoxious fashion. A truly humble person, therefore, will not be conceited or feel it necessary to "lord it over others" as he or she serves and leads in the church, community, or workplace.

3. Serving the Underserved (vv. 12–13)

In biblical times, as in today's society, not too many people volunteered for the unglamorous position that entails serving the underserved, or those individuals who are the neediest based on economic, physical, or social limitations. In these verses, Jesus instructs us to reach out to those who are least likely to be exalted on earth.

A test of humility, therefore, may be our willingness to serve and care for those who cannot repay us. This is only possible when we keep in mind that everything we have comes directly from God. As the apostle Paul noted, this fact should keep us from becoming overly confident (see Romans 12:3; 1 Corinthians 4:7).

In His parable, Jesus warned of both the pitfalls and blessings of humility. Interestingly, the Greek word *tapeinoo* (**tap-i-NO-o**) denotes demotion, assigning (or assuming) a lower position than others. The term can be both positive—to deliberately humble oneself, as Jesus did, or negative—to be humbled by someone else. In life, we can serve humbly and confidently and enjoy the fruits of our labors spiritually, materially, financially, or socially, or we can walk haughtily and encounter situations that humble us. The choice is ours, but every Christian should understand that God's desire is for us to exemplify biblical humility, allowing God to work in and through us. We can accomplish this by: (1) taking on the mind of Christ (Philippians 2:5); (2) not becoming "weary in well doing" (Galatians 6:9; 2 Thessalonians 3:13); and (3) recognizing our greatest rewards come from God who is the ultimate promoter.

4. Heavenly Rewards (v. 14)

What motivates a person to help others may also contribute to their ability to serve without recognition or compensation. For example, if we help others as detailed in the parable simply as a means of

expressing our gratitude to and love for God, we won't be overly concerned whether we have a title, corner office, or seat on the podium. Instead, we will willingly assist with any task and consider no job too menial.

Having such a focus reaps heavenly rewards. Jesus noted that we will be "recompensed at the resurrection of the just" (v. 14). Recompense means to repay. In a positive sense it means repay or reward; in a negative sense it means penalty. Thus, Jesus was noting that God notices our good deeds and will reward us accordingly. We may not receive natural benefits on this side of heaven, but they will come because God will not be indebted to anyone.

While the guests watched Jesus, Jesus watched them. As children of God, we acknowledge that God is omniscient, or all-knowing, but do we really believe that He is watching every action, weighing the motives of our heart? If we do, we would strive to walk humbly before our God—and man!

Search the Scriptures

1. For which specific purpose did the people gather on this particular Sabbath (Luke 14:1)?

2. Why did Jesus feel compelled to share the parable He did at the time He did (v. 7)?

3. What specific things did Jesus say humble hearers would do (vv. 10, 12–13)?

Discuss the Meaning

1. Why was it significant that Jesus watched the guests (v. 7)?

2. Why do you think Jesus used a wedding rather than another social setting as the background for the parable He taught (v. 8)?

3. How do you think those who were considered inferior felt after hearing the parable? What about those who considered themselves "superior"?

Lesson in Our Society

In today's status-conscious society it is not always easy to exude humility, but it is necessary—and possible. God exhorted us to be humble, provided Jesus as a living example of humility, and gave us a part of Himself in the form of the Holy Spirit to give us the courage, strength, and tenacity to remain humble. But do not be deceived. Being humble does not mean shunning high-level leadership positions in the church or community, or walking around with our heads bowed as if adopting a humble posture. Instead, it means being assured of who we are in Jesus Christ, serving Him with our whole hearts, and allowing Him to direct our steps, purge our attitudes, and serve others.

Make It Happen

No one is 100 percent humble all the time. Yet, we can strive to speak and act more humbly every day. A good first step is to memorize Galatians 5:22-23, which details the "fruit of the Spirit." As you take these verses to heart, you'll notice that the attributes of the fruit are designed to make us less self-seeking and more service-oriented.

Over the next week, choose at least one aspect of the Spirit's fruit to "major" in. Ask God to show you ways you can be more humble as you ask for specific opportunities to put the fruit in practice at home, work, or church.

Follow the Spirit

What God wants me to do:

_____

_____

Remember Your Thoughts

Special insights I have learned:

_____

_____

More Light on the Text

Luke 14:1, 7-14

In Luke's narrative, Christ had been heading toward Jerusalem—and the Cross—since 9:51. With every step, the tension builds, and chapter 13 only adds fuel to the fire. As He had done on previous occasions, to the chagrin of the Jewish leaders, Jesus healed on the Sabbath. But Jesus didn't stop there. He called His followers for a commitment to a kingdom where humble beginnings produce something of enormous and lasting value (cf. 13:18-21). As Jesus said, the door to this kingdom is narrow. The point is not how many can come in at one time or how many come in. The narrow door refers to the conditions necessary for admittance.

The statements in 13:26-27 must have been—and should be—piercing to the soul. "Then shall ye begin to say, We have eaten and drunk in thy presence, and thou hast taught in our streets. But he shall say, I tell you, I know you not whence ye are; depart from me, all ye workers of iniquity."

Is it possible to be in His presence, listen to His teaching, and miss Him? The answer is yes. Religious activity and obedience for obedience's sake can numb us to what God is doing and saying; and in a worst-case scenario, even separate us from God (cf. 13:31-35).

Luke presents to us in chapter 14 Christ's way of using a lesson on humility and the attitudes of the heart by exposing how superficial the actions of some in His audience are at common social events such as a wedding, a breakfast, a dinner, or a banquet.

1 And it came to pass, as he went into the house of one of the chief Pharisees to eat bread on the sabbath day, that they watched him.

Luke, as each Gospel writer, is unique in his style. Luke likes to carry his readers along one event to the next. In doing so he often uses the phrase "it came to pass" to introduce a new discussion, to draw attention to events that are about to take place, or to highlight or further explain in a dramatic way the preceding story. The context of chapter 14 implies it may be a continuation and further illustration of the themes presented in chapter 13.

As depicted in chapter 13, kingdom commitment is not about religious compliance that derives from tradition (cf. 13:10-17) or association (vv. 23-27). Rather, true kingdom commitment negates any ideas that religious, social, and cultural conformity are necessarily expressions of faith in Christ. What is right and normal to most might be anathema to God. One thing is for sure; those who dare to be different will always have a crowd of naysayers closely watching their every move, waiting to exploit any exposed or assumed weaknesses.

Our opening verse of this lesson contains a phrase that is a lesson in itself. They watched Him! It is one thing to go into a house where there is a gathering of friends. It is quite another to go into a house with mixed company—friends and foes.

The text suggests Jesus did have some friends among the Pharisees (cf. 13:31). Nevertheless there would always be a few Pharisees present, seeking to find reason to accuse Him of not complying with what was considered proper and fitting for a religious leader or any God-fearing Jew (see Mark 7; Luke 7). Persistently, Christ uses these confrontations to expose hypocrisy. Luke's personal note in 14:1 is already debunking that status quo.

Christ's actions do not support a non-confrontational Christianity. In fact, just the opposite is true. It takes humility to confront hypocrisy because the result often leads to isolation, condemnation, and the reproach by the religious-minded (see Mark 2:16). Christ was more concerned about making a case for God than establishing a favorable view of Himself. This is essence of humility because it requires total dependence on God.

Verses 2–6 elaborate and continue exposing the hypocrisy of traditional views on the Sabbath. Keeping the Sabbath to the Pharisees, along with other laws, was a sign of personal virtue apart from God, rather than a sign of dependence on God. If personal virtue is our standard of holiness, then the actions of others is the measuring rod. We know that we have arrived when others recognize us. It may be in this light that the following eight verses, 7–14, are to be understood.

7 And he put forth a parable to those which were bidden, when he marked how they chose out the chief rooms; saying unto them,

At the end of the day, unqualified obedience to social mores reflects inward spiritual realities. Luke says Christ put forth a parable. Parables always, always have spiritual implications (see Matthew 13:53; 21:33; Mark 4:13; 7:17; Luke 8: 9–11; 18:1). The implication is the business of making it day-to-day is somehow distinct from how kingdom residents are to live. Nothing is further from the truth.

This upcoming practical lesson has significant spiritual overtures. For where we think we ought to stand in relation to others is in all likelihood an indication of where we think we stand before God.

Even before reporting Christ's words, Luke begins preparing us for what is to come. Rather than "bidden," the NKJV uses the word "invited." This is an appropriate translation of the Greek passive form of the word *kaleo* (**kal-EH-o**), meaning "to call, specifi-

cally by name." Each guest received a personal invitation to attend the wedding.

Just as the guest list was determined by the host, so were the seating arrangements. The decision of who sat at the best seats, the seats of honor (Gk. *protoklisia*, pro-tok-lis-EE-ah), was at the discretion of the host. Humility begins by being thankful to have received an invitation. A much different attitude than "Now that I am here, who can see me?" It can be safely assumed that even for this Sabbath meal, the invited guests took concerted efforts to select for themselves seats of honor, places where others might assume they were important and had a special relationship to the host, and his special guest Jesus. Christ decided to use this particular social gathering as an opportunity to give a spiritual lesson on humility before God and man.

8 When thou art bidden of any man to a wedding, sit not down in the highest room; lest a more honourable man than thou be bidden of him;

Sometimes the most profound truths are simply stated. Let's offer a contemporary paraphrase: *Stop assuming just because you got an invitation that you are to be honored in a special way.* Now, notice it does not say, you cannot be an honored guest. That is the host's decision. Yes, the Bible does say give "honour to whom honour" (Romans 13:7), and hosts have every right to honor whomever they choose, as the next phrase indicates. Christ is not forbidding the honoring of people. He is saying that we ought not to seek our own honor and self-aggrandizement, which only leads to shame and humiliation, the very opposite of humility.

9 And he that bade thee and him come and say to thee, Give this man place; and thou begin with shame to take the lowest room.

Verse 9 reinforces the idea that the host decides who should take the seats of honor—"he that bade thee and him." There is nothing said about the rank or stature of those invited.

It is probably safe to assume the described set of circumstances were not beyond the comprehension of those within Jesus' hearing. Jockeying for status was not, and is not, a new phenomenon. However, liv-

"For whosoever exalteth himself shall be abased; and he that humbleth himself shall be exalted" (Luke 14:11).

ing for status and position has all the potential to lead to embarrassment and depression.

To seek honor and acclaim and then be denied reaches into the soul of a person and strips away the comfort that comes from being created in the image of God. The word *aischune* (**ahee-SKHOO-nay**), or "shame," literally means the revealing of those things associated with weaknesses or sins.

Can you imagine the embarrassment? The chief seats were normally elevated and positioned in the center of the room. Publicly requested by the host to step down and go to the back of the room, however discretely, would leave the other guests second-guessing not the intentions of the hosts, but your worthiness. Imagine the shame of it all—being asked to give up your seat for someone else, and then told to go sit in the place farthest (Gk. *eschatos*, **ES-khat-os**) from the center of attention.

Peter says, "Humble yourselves under the mighty hand of God, that He may exalt you in due time" (1 Peter 5:6, NKJV). Our protection from shame is the mighty hand of God. When we strike to achieve or acquire recognition for ourselves, we are on our own. Godly humility is our only defense and remedy against the scarring pains of emotional and public humiliation.

A preventive and curing medicine for shame is self-imposed humility. The ingredients are patience and trust that if we step down God will raise us up. The documentation that points out the antagonistic relations between Christ and His Pharisaic listeners is overwhelming. Still, Christ never leaves even the most hardened of heart without hope. Let us look at verse 10 carefully.

10 But when thou art bidden, go and sit down in the lowest room; that when he that bade thee cometh, he may say unto thee, Friend, go up higher: then shalt thou have worship in the presence of them that sit at meat with thee.

The word "but" in this sentence is a translation of a very powerful Greek conjunction, *alla* (**al-LAH**), meaning in contrast to what has just preceded. *Alla* in this context means in contrast to exalting yourself there is another way—live in such a way that is recognized by the only One who really matters.

First step is to make sure your attitude is that everyone else in the room is more important than yourself (see Philippians 2:3); then decide that the lowest seat in the house is your seat; now sit there. What a contrast to popular thinking, even among Christians.

Humility is not contrary to knowing what our position is in Christ. Working out our humility, however, may be contrary to us maintaining our position in the world.

An uplifted head and standing tall has nothing to do with being in a position of prominence or status. Living as a child of the King encourages service and sacrifice for others' benefit, not personal quests to

be out front (see Philippians 2:5–9). In other words, yes, you have God-given abilities; but humility says God defines when, where, and how you use them and how others see His power displayed in you.

The second half of the verse says that when we take the low road, God is in a position to place us on the high road. Introduced by the purpose conjunction *hina* (Gk. **HIN-ah**), this part of the verse says God has a goal to exalt us. "Friend, go up higher." Isn't that good news? Again, the issue is trust and patience. God will honor us when the time is right, "Then you will have glory in the presence of those who sit at the table with you" (v. 10, NKJV).

11 For whosoever exalteth himself shall be abased; and he that humbleth himself shall be exalted.

It is a good study reminder to note these telling Greek conjunctions. *The Precepts For Living*® CD-ROM is an excellent tool to take your understanding to another level. Up to this point in the lesson, we have noted the Greek conjunctions *alla* and *hina*, contrasting and purpose conjunctions respectively. Now Luke introduces verse 11 with another conjunction, *hoti* (**HOT-ee**). This conjunction is used to suggest that what is about to be said explains what preceded or provides the logical reasoning behind the previous statement.

Can Christ make it any plainer? The person who humbles or does not humble him or herself will either incur public humiliation in this world or affirmation in heaven and maybe now. The word "whosoever" is a translation of the word *pas* meaning "all." This biblical principle applies to everyone.

It does not matter what the media, the job title, or even the Christian community says, everyone who lifts themselves up *hupsoo* (Gk. **hoop-SO-o**) suffers the inevitable fate of humiliation, or as translated here, abased. Interestingly, this word *tapeinoo* (Gk. t**ap-i-NO-o**), meaning "humble," is the same word used of Christ when He humbled Himself to the point of shame and death on a Cross (Philippians 2:6–8).

There is only one difference in how "humbled" is used in passages. One is passive and one is active. Simply put, we can either passively wait for God to humble us in ways that reveal His purposes and our sinfulness, or we can actively humble ourselves and take joy in His purposes and how He chooses to exalt us.

12 Then said he also to him that bade him, When thou makest a dinner or a supper, call not thy friends, nor thy brethren, neither thy kinsmen, nor thy rich neighbours; lest they also bid thee again, and a recompence be made thee.

It is easy to camouflage a self-centered heart in the presence of matching standards of significance, affirmation, and acceptance. Camouflage only works when colors match the surroundings. Religious people can look humble around other religious people. A better test of humility is when we are among people who do not fit our standards of nobility and importance.

Make a note of observing not just who is around but who is not. Christ cautioned His host to stop inviting only those who could do something in return for him. Rather, Jesus said to consider providing an opportunity to give joy to those who normally do not receive an invitation.

13 But when thou makest a feast, call the poor, the maimed, the lame, the blind:

Notice the types of gatherings Christ used to make His point. In verses 8 and 12 it was a wedding, and/or dinner. Here in verse 13 Christ referred to a feast.

A feast is more than a common meal or an expected celebratory gathering such as a wedding. Feasts, literally a banquet, were special gatherings called by the host to celebrate in a grand way a particular event. These were important gatherings. Those attending were a list of the most important people in the local community, region, or nation.

Christ says to invite to these occasions those who depend on others, those in obvious need, and those who require assistance from others, such as the maimed, lame, and blind. These are the types of individuals who you and your guests know can never return the favor. Why would anyone celebrate his or her good fortunes with those who probably lack the capacity to appreciate it? Verse 14 tells us why.

14 And thou shalt be blessed; for they cannot recompense thee: for thou shalt be recompensed at the resurrection of the just.

Humility pays incomprehensible dividends immeasurable by human standards because the investment is a manifestation of Christlikeness. The Greek word for "blessed" is *makarios* (**mak-AR-ee-os**). This is the same word Christ used in His Sermon on the Mount to describe those with a commitment to the King and His kingdom (see Matthew 5).

Those who humble themselves in their thoughts and actions are blessed because they are not looking for temporal rewards. Rather, their focus is on Him who rewards His faithful followers for all eternity. The humble are blessed because they are faithfully content knowing that their *full* payment is yet to come and not from someone or something in this life!

The summons to humility is not easy. The price of humility can be everything you hold dear in this life. Does this mean earthly recognition is forbidden to all Christians? Rarely is this the case. But it does mean that social, religious, and cultural affirmation and acceptance ought not to be the motives behind our actions.

Daily Bible Readings

M: Prayer of Humility
Psalm 25:1–10

T: Jesus Heals on the Sabbath
Luke 14:1–6

W: Disgraced at a Banquet
Luke 14:7–9

T: Exalted though Humble
Luke 14:10–11

F: The Guest List
Luke 14:12–14

S: A Life of Humility
Ephesians 3:1–10

S: Tending the Flock with Humility
1 Peter 5:1–5

TEACHING TIPS

February 24
Bible Study Guide 13

1. Words You Should Know

A. Disciple (Luke 14:26–27) *mathetes* (Gk.)—A student or learner, one who disciplines him or herself in order to emulate the work of a master.

B. Cross (v. 27) *stauros* (Gk.)—An upright stake used for cruel punishment in Jesus' time.

C. Forsaketh (v. 33) *apotassomai* (Gk.)—Denotes a voluntary separation from something or someone.

2. Teacher Preparation

Unifying Principle—Becoming Passionate Supporters People look for a cause or a purpose that they can passionately support. What is worth giving up everything for? Jesus challenged the crowd to leave everything behind and become His disciples.

A. Read the Focal Verses.

B. Read Matthew 10:37, noting the emphasis placed on loving family more than God, and how this further clarifies Jesus' statements in today's lesson.

C. Complete lesson 13 in the *Precepts For Living® Personal Study Guide*.

D. Come prepared to discuss the items or activities the students are willing to give up for their loved ones.

3. Starting the Lesson

A. Begin the class with prayer, asking God to help the students understand the importance of loving Him above all people and things in their lives.

B. Have a volunteer read the Keep in Mind verse.

C. Discuss the meaning of "cross" in that verse, and ask for examples of crosses people bear today.

4. Getting into the Lesson

A. Ask the students for good and bad examples of passionate discipleship from current events, keeping in mind such situations as September 11, suicide bombers, and political kidnappings.

B. Briefly summarize The People, Places, and Times, Background, and Focal Verses.

5. Relating the Lesson to Life

A. Poll the class for reasons people align themselves to specific causes or leaders.

B. Discuss the items or activities people voluntarily give up based on their commitment to a person or cause.

C. Invite the students to share what they believe are the hallmarks of a passionate Christian as described in the Scriptures.

D. Have a volunteer read the In Focus story, and discuss how it relates to sacrificial discipleship.

6. Arousing Action

A. Challenge the students to become more committed to Christ as evidenced by the sacrifices they make to love Him more deeply and to serve others.

B. Ask the students to consider the following question: What are you doing today to make sure your contributions to family, society, etc. are positive and memorable?

C. Challenge the students to examine and reorder their priorities.

D. Close with prayer.

Worship Guide

For the Superintendent or Teacher
Theme: Summoned to Be a Disciple!
Theme Song: "Only What You Do for Christ Will Last"
Devotional Reading: Psalm 139:1–6
Prayer

SUMMONED TO BE A DISCIPLE!

Background • LUKE 14:25–33
Printed Text • LUKE 14:25–33 Devotional Reading • PSALM 139:1–6

AIM for Change

By the end of the lesson, we will:

UNDERSTAND the meaning of being a disciple of Christ;

REFLECT on the sacrifice Jesus expects of His disciples; and

REORDER our priorities in light of Jesus' call to take up our cross and follow Him.

Keep in Mind

"And whosoever doth not bear his cross, and come after me, cannot be my disciple" (Luke 14:27, KJV).

Focal Verses

KJV **Luke 14:25** And there went great multitudes with him: and he turned, and said unto them,

26 If any man come to me, and hate not his father, and mother, and wife, and children, and brethren, and sisters, yea, and his own life also, he cannot be my disciple.

27 And whosoever doth not bear his cross, and come after me, cannot be my disciple.

28 For which of you, intending to build a tower, sitteth not down first, and counteth the cost, whether he have sufficient to finish it?

29 Lest haply, after he hath laid the foundation, and is not able to finish it, all that behold it begin to mock him,

30 Saying, This man began to build, and was not able to finish.

31 Or what king, going to make war against another king, sitteth not down first, and consulteth whether he be able with ten thousand to meet him that cometh against him with twenty thousand?

32 Or else, while the other is yet a great way off, he sendeth an ambassage, and desireth conditions of peace.

33 So likewise, whosoever he be of you that forsaketh not all that he hath, he cannot be my disciple.

NLT **Luke 14:25** A large crowd was following Jesus. He turned around and said to them,

26 "If you want to be my disciple, you must hate everyone else by comparison—your father and mother, wife and children, brothers and sisters—yes, even your own life. Otherwise, you cannot be my disciple.

27 And if you do not carry your own cross and follow me, you cannot be my disciple.

28 "But don't begin until you count the cost. For who would begin construction of a building without first calculating the cost to see if there is enough money to finish it?

29 Otherwise, you might complete only the foundation before running out of money, and then everyone would laugh at you.

30 They would say, 'There's the person who started that building and couldn't afford to finish it!'

31 "Or what king would go to war against another king without first sitting down with his counselors to discuss whether his army of 10,000 could defeat the 20,000 soldiers marching against him?

32 And if he can't, he will send a delegation to discuss terms of peace while the enemy is still far away.

33 So you cannot become my disciple without giving up everything you own.

In Focus

Professor Thompson peered over his glasses at the graduating senior seated in front of him. Jared was one of his favorite undergrads, which made his decision even tougher to share.

"Jared," he began, "as you know, you are eligible for the fellowship that includes everything you would need to study under me for your master's degree. It's a full ride: tuition, room and board, books and expenses, and a monthly stipend."

"Yes, sir," Jared interrupted. "And I am excited about

the opportunity. I always dreamed of working more closely with you. You're the best in the field."

"Thanks. Well, I have some bad news. Although you were the top contender for the fellowship, I have had to make the tough decision and select someone else."

Jared stammered. "I don't understand. How can that be? I thought the rules said the best candidate has to be chosen."

"As department chair, I have the final say and academics is only one benchmark. There are other factors to consider."

Professor Thompson paused. He silently asked God to give him the right words to express himself without demoralizing the young man.

"Jared," he began again, "you're bright, extremely gifted, and very personable. But there's one thing you lack."

"What's that?"

"Conviction," Professor Thompson sighed. "You are not passionate enough about this area of religious study, and I'm afraid that halfway through, you'll quit. If that happens, not only do we lose you, we lose the opportunity to prepare someone who will be ready to go to the mission field in two years. I'm sorry."

"You're sorry? I'm sorry. I really needed the money to get my master's degree."

"See my point," Professor Thompson said. "You really aren't passionate about the program. Your main focus is provision. If you ask God, He will provide the funds for your further study and also reveal exactly where *He* wants you. Looking back ten years from now, you'll be happy I didn't give you that fellowship."

"You might have a point, but I'm still disappointed," Jared muttered.

"I know you are, but I have a feeling God has great plans for you. Here's my card; keep in touch. I'd love to know what God is doing in your life. Now . . . why don't we pray and ask Him to show you the open window behind this closed door? I am sure there is one."

In today's lesson, Jesus explains the necessity for passionate discipleship. It is not enough to merely name Jesus as Saviour. He must also be our Lord, for whom we are willing to forsake everyone and everything. Jesus taught that only individuals with that level of commitment could be His true disciples.

The People, Places, and Times

Cross. A tall, heavy stake with a crossbeam used to hang, torture, and execute criminals. Criminals were charged with carrying the crossbeam to the place set aside for the execution. By referring to the cross, Jesus hinted that His disciples should be willing to lay down their lives and reputations to fully commit to Him. They needed to be aware that being one of His disciples would not prove popular or even easy. Further, Jesus also foreshadowed the type of death He would endure: one that involved being falsely accused of crimes He did not commit.

Ambassador. An ambassador is a representative of a country or kingdom. Ambassadors were sent forth for specific purposes. They may, for example, go forth to negotiate a peace treaty. As official representatives, they exercised considerable authority and had the full resources of their homeland at their disposal while conducting business. Further, they were mindful that everything they said or did would reflect positively or negatively on their country or kingdom. Thus, they were required to be highly disciplined and circumspect, always putting the goals, objectives, and plans of their country or kingdom above their individual needs or wants. Of himself the apostle Paul noted, "I am an ambassador in bonds" (Ephesians 6:20), a reference to his imprisonment during the time of writing his epistle to the Ephesians. And he reminds us that we, too, are "ambassadors for Christ" (2 Corinthians 5:20).

Background

In Bible times, people would train under a master or teacher accomplished in spiritual, legal, or political matters. The goal: to advance in a chosen field by receiving hands-on tutelage, and by observing and emulating the master's life. The student would closely follow the master, keenly observing the master's way of life and manner of conducting business. Being associated with a renowned master improved the student's chances for advancement, and afforded greater prestige. The apostle Paul, for example, noted his training under Gamaliel, a highly regarded teacher of the Law (Acts 22:3). It was an honor to be selected as a student, but also a responsibility not to be taken lightly. Much commitment was required to discipline oneself to study, work, and serve.

As a radical teacher of His day, Jesus was generally thronged by multitudes—thousands of interested individuals who followed Him to witness miraculous happenings or receive miraculous provisions. While many of them followed Jesus from town to town, He was not deceived. Jesus knew that not all possessed the level of commitment needed to be a dedicated, passionate follower of the Son of Man. Jesus chose 12 men (Matthew 10:2–4). These men became known as disciples—committed to Jesus, His ministry, and His Word.

They represented men from different socioeconomic backgrounds, but they all had one thing in common initially: they were committed to following Christ and spreading the good news of the kingdom of God. Interestingly, in Matthew's Gospel we see that once Jesus called the Twelve aside to give them special miracle-working abilities, they became known as apostles. The term *apóstolos* (ap-OS-tol-os) means "sent forth" as an ambassador. The Twelve had so distinguished themselves based on their level of commitment that they, basically, were promoted. Given a command to reach the Jews, they were given additional authority, responsibilities, and giftings (Matthew 10:1, 7–8).

While this may seem like a tall order, the disciples had served alongside Jesus and witnessed Him doing these same miracles. Being charged to emulate His works, the apostles would have to commit to a deeper level of discipleship—one that recognized that while they had such abilities, they still had to answer their master Jesus, and their sole allegiance must be to Him alone.

At-A-Glance

1. The Cross of Discipleship (Luke 14:27)
2. The Cost of Discipleship (vv. 28–32)
3. The Conviction of Discipleship (v. 33)

In Depth

1. The Cross of Discipleship (Luke 14:27)

When multitudes thronged Him, Jesus took the opportunity to discuss the conditions of discipleship for those eager to learn from Him. Upon hearing these, the multitudes could easily have misunderstood the term "hate." Jesus did not mean that they literally had to despise their families or lives, but that they needed to completely overhaul their priorities. Instead of living a life focused on themselves or their families, disciples must live to love God, even if that meant putting their families and lives second.

It is probable that those assembled did not expect for Him to label discipleship with Christ as a cross. This instrument of punishment and cruelty was difficult to bear, and was the epitome of painful, humiliating death. Jesus used the reference to cross-bearing to provide an honest—albeit, not necessarily comforting—assessment of what disciples could expect to find. The reference conjured a picture of complete surrender and self-imposed humility. Jesus was looking for students who would be willing to conduct their business as He did: in meekness and peace, even in the face of opposition. In fact, on a previous occasion the Prince of Peace specifically explained: "Behold, I send you forth as sheep in the midst of wolves: be ye therefore wise as serpents, and harmless as doves. But beware of men: for they will deliver you up to the councils, and they will scourge you in their synagogues; And ye shall be brought before governors and kings for my sake, for a testimony against them and the Gentiles" (Matthew 10:16–18).

Today, people still yearn to be taught at the feet of great men and women. Whom we choose to follow will determine whether our passionate discipleship will become a tool for good or evil.

2. The Cost of Discipleship (vv. 28–32)

Second Samuel 24 tells of the time when King David took a census without God's permission. His disobedience led to a plague. In order to stop the plague, David was ordered to build an altar at the threshing floor of Araunah. When hearing of the need, Araunah offered it to the king, along with oxen and other items. David refused the offer. He explained, "Nay; but I will surely buy it of thee at a price: neither will I offer burnt offerings unto the LORD my God of that which cost me nothing" (v. 24). David understood that simply offering something he had received for free would not meet the Law's requirement for a sacrificial offering. Burnt offerings were completely consumed. After an offering burned all night, nothing remained but ashes (Leviticus 6:9). This offering signified a complete and utter "loss," but one that was wholly acceptable to God.

Obviously, in the case of the burnt offering, there was no provision made for getting any part of it back. This is the kind of discipleship commitment God wants from us. He demands that we be totally devoted to Him, His kingdom, and His commission to reach the lost. That is why Jesus reminded the multitude to "count the cost" before committing to Him. There would be no provision for turning back. There would be no possibility of simultaneously serving Him and the adversary. It was, and is, an all-or-nothing commitment.

In Luke 14:28–32, Jesus used the analogy of building a tower because the multitudes could readily relate to building homes and temples that required, time, energy, and money to complete. And He reminded them that the inability to complete the project would result in mocking or other forms of public humiliation. Is not this the case of Christians who follow God, but later slip back into destructive or compromising behaviors? Worldly friends and family members are quick to mock, pointing out the hypocrisy. Likewise, Jesus evoked the imagery of kings going to war because His listeners could understand the need for a king to be completely prepared for war before embarking on such an expensive and potentially life-threatening event.

As some have joked, "The Gospel is free, but it costs money to share it." Following Christ will cost us something. We have to examine and reprioritize our commitments so that our lives become a burnt offering acceptable to God. Further, we are to emulate the love, compassion, and fruitfulness of the Prince of Peace as we strive to be "worthy disciples." Indeed, as Christians, we must choose to follow Jesus first, forsaking everyone and everything that would hinder our service to Him. By doing so, we will reach more people for Christ by sharing an unpolluted message

"And whosoever doth not bear his cross, and come after me, cannot be my disciple (Luke 14:27).

of passionate discipleship evidenced by our total allegiance to, and love for, God.

3. The Conviction of Discipleship (v. 33)

In this verse, Jesus notes, "Whosoever he be of you that forsaketh not all that he hath, he cannot be my disciple" (v. 33). "Forsaketh" is *apotassomai* (Gk. **ap-ot-AS-som-ahee**), and denotes a voluntary separation from something or someone. It is the first time in today's lesson that we see this term. It sums up the expected conviction of those willing to be Jesus' disciples. We must voluntarily put Jesus first in our lives. We must consider Him both Saviour and Lord, giving Him full reign over our hearts, minds, and bodies as we become willing and obedient servants of God. And we must understand that God will not force us to do anything. He has blessed mankind with a will; unless we voluntarily become more dedicated disciples, He won't compel us to. The key, therefore, is to ask God to help us pray, "Not my will, but thine, be done" (Luke 22:42).

Additionally, Jesus did not mince words. He told the multitude that unless they were willing to put everything on the line for Him and His kingdom they *cannot* be disciples. Through the ages, Christians have passed this test under some of the most extreme circumstances. They have not compromised their faith nor denied their Master. Their conviction has helped them face firing squads, false imprisonments, physical and mental abuses, and even death. Many, as they died, praised God for the opportunity to show the world what passionate discipleship looks like. Even today, there are places in the world where the body of Christ is persecuted, and churches must go underground as they secretly meet for fellowship and to get renewed strength to stick to their discipleship conviction.

Like our brothers and sisters in Christ have discovered, passionate discipleship requires conviction. It is not pretty. It is not easy. But it assures a believer an eternal place with Christ, seated among others in the "cloud of witnesses" (Hebrews 12:1) who have loved Jesus more than life, family, or possessions.

What will discipleship cost us? It is difficult to say. We know that Jesus prepared us by warning that the world would hate us as it hated Him. We know that our brethren have suffered, and still do suffer, for the cause of Christ. But how our conviction will play out

is in God's hand. We must be less concerned with the "what ifs" and more concerned with obeying Jesus' command to forsake all. Only then, when our heart is not totally wrapped up in our families and possessions, will we be able to be the most effective disciples possible. Is it worth it? Definitely.

Search the Scriptures

1. What thing must a disciple of Christ hate or forsake (Luke 14:26, 33)?

2. And _____ doth not _____ his _____, and come after _____, cannot be my _____ (v. 27).

3. This ____ began to ____, and was not ____ to ____ (v. 30).

Discuss the Meaning

1. How can one both love and "hate" their family in the context of today's lesson?

2. Explain what Jesus meant by "counteth the cost."

3. What happens to people who cannot finish the commitments they begin?

4. In what specific ways can we forsake all and follow after Jesus?

Lesson in Our Society

The fanatical actions of individuals are aired daily on television and radio—people so committed to their cause that they willingly engage in destructive behavior causing harm to innocent victims. While their actions are not to be applauded or duplicated, these individuals do have enviable zeal. They are totally sold out to their leaders and causes.

Maybe you have struggled with complacency and wondered how to show more commitment to Christ. Jesus can help you take your commitment to the next level while helping you let go of people and things that cause you to "water down your witness."

Make It Happen

It's been said that an ounce of prevention is better than a pound of cure. This week, examine your life and lifestyle as they relate to your being a passionate disciple of Christ. Ask God to help you reorder your priorities, bringing balance to your life. If necessary, enroll in an evening Bible study to dig deeper into God's Word, which must be the foundation of any disciple's life. Also, commit to becoming more active in your church or community. No, this won't happen overnight, but your involvement can inspire others to live more passionate, Christ-centered lives.

Follow the Spirit

What God wants me to do:

_____

_____

Remember Your Thoughts

Special insights I have learned:

_____

_____

More Light on the Text

Luke 14:25–33

25 And there went great multitudes with him: and he turned, and said unto them,

There were those even among the elite who were willing to accept the challenge to be humble; after all, how difficult could it be to honor others and temporarily refrain from being the center of attention?

As for the masses, is there any doubt that they joyously and hopefully responded to Christ when He concluded His parable?

Allegiance to Christ is about being a disciple, and a disciple of Christ is like the melting ice in a glass of water. Slowly the form of the ice is lost and the ice takes on the properties of the water in which it was placed. This is our calling. Christ turned to the following multitudes and said: *We must be so much like Christ that we could be mistaken for Christ.*

26 If any man come to me, and hate not his father, and mother, and wife, and children, and brethren, and sisters, yea, and his own life also, he cannot be my disciple.

Have you ever heard someone say, "You do it *if* you want to"? Immediately we know there may be costly consequences to whatever action we are thinking about taking. Or, in some cases we use *if* to suggest something that possibly might happen. If I go looking for a job, I might find one. Grammatically speaking, these are conditional sentences. The question we need to answer to understand this lesson is whether or not being a disciple is optional for the Christian and if not, what does being a disciple mean day to day?

There are two words used to introduce conditional sentences in the Greek. If (Gk. *ean*, **eh-AN**) you do this or if this is true, this *might* happen or be true, or if (Gk. *ei*, **i**) you do this or if this is true . . . this *will* happen or these are the facts. There is the *if* of probability, and the *if* of factuality. Does it need to be said?

Christ completely understood the soul-stirring statement He was about to make. Christ said if you choose, if you make a decision to follow, to enter into a relationship with Him, then these are the conditions: If you do not hate your father, mother, wife, children, brethren, sisters, and even own life, you cannot be His disciples.

27 And whosoever doth not bear his cross, and come after me, cannot be my disciple.

Verse 27 just may be a parabolic phrase that eludes Christ's listeners and many in the church today. To "bear" means to endure and carry in such a way that exposes a necessary unity between the load being carried and the burden bearer (see Luke 22:10; Acts 9:15; Galatians 6:2). Moreover, only in a few occasions outside the Bible does the word "cross" (Gk. *stauros*—**stow-ROS**) mean anything other than an instrument—most often a wooden stake used to torture and inflect unimaginable pain.

When Christ said that we must bear our cross, He was saying without qualification, that disciples must take it upon themselves to carry the thing that tells the world they are ready and willing to die to all that does not come from Him. Before we move on, let's step back for a minute.

Verse 27 opens with these two Greek words: *hostis* (Gk. **HOS-tis**)—a relative pronoun—and the adverb *ouch* (Gk. **oo**). Literally, the one that does not bear (see below) his own cross cannot be . . . . His own is a reflective pronoun *heautou* (Gk. **heh-w-TOO**) that conveys mutual possession; in this case the pronoun refers to the cross. Using contemporary language, the one who refuses to bear the cross assigned by God cannot be His disciple. This is a difficult undertaking and maybe the reason why Paul said, "I die daily" (1 Corinthians 15:31). Could this be where we go wrong? Do we think death to personal agendas is done with at conversion and with the stopping of a few bad habits? Taking up our cross is a daily and persistent calling and a mark of being His disciple.

The word for "bear" is a present active verb. We never stop bearing the cross of pain and suffering this side of heaven when we are Jesus' disciples. We may make light of these words, but Jesus' audience probably did not. Some surely would have seen and heard the cries and pain of someone bearing a cross. Is Christ's call to discipleship different today? What cross is Christ calling you to bear?

28 For which of you, intending to build a tower, sitteth not down first, and counteth the cost, whether he have sufficient to finish it?

Have you ever signed up for a college class just for credit? In other words, the subject matter was inconsequential. You took the class for one reason: to get the necessary credits to complete the semester and/or graduate. Then after a few days, you discover that the subject matter was not easy and failing was a real possibility.

Christ wants us to avoid this dilemma by encouraging us to take some time and think about the call to be His disciple. If you're looking for kingdom credits without getting involved in a jealously guarded and intense relationship with the dean of the school, be a disciple of Jesus Christ.

If you think being Jesus' disciple is an easy path to heaven's throne, you are sorely mistaken. This is a costly road. Do yourself a favor—just as you would not begin the construction of a building without prior knowledge of what it was going take to finish—do not begin the disciple's journey without reflection on what will finish the journey.

The particular word for "count" used here and in Revelation 13:18 suggests counting with the intent of fully understanding the consequences, good or bad. Think about it. Not being a disciple is to have no other option but to depend on other fallible human beings for acceptance and guidance. To be a disciple is to have the assurance that the One who knows all has covered all the bases and always has your greatest good properly in focus.

The world would say count what you have in your hand. Christ would say, "Count what I have in My hand." The decision you make will change your life and maybe where you spend eternity. Be sure to calculate carefully.

29 Lest haply, after he hath laid the foundation, and is not able to finish it, all that behold it begin to mock him, 30 Saying, This man began to build, and was not able to finish.

Is it possible we make it too easy to come to Jesus? The answer is no. Redemption is free. There is no price to pay, no work to do. God did it all. Our salvation is by grace and that though faith; it is a gift of God (see Ephesians 2:8). Christ has not stated that this is what you must do to become His disciple. He has said if you come after Him, this is what it means to be His disciple. James says, "Faith without works is dead" (2:20). Pretending to have a relationship with Christ where none exists only leads to public ridicule.

There is an important contrast between this verse and verse 25. As was noted in verse 25, "is able" is a present passive form of the Greek word *dunamai*. Here in verse 29 the Greek word for "able" is *ischuo* (Gk. **is-KHOO-o**). *Ischuo* in this context is present active, meaning the subject—the one doing the building—is performing the action. *Dunamai* denotes having the ability to experience something; *ischuo* denotes having the internal capacity or ability to do something.

31 Or what king, going to make war against another king, sitteth not down first, and consulteth whether he be able with ten thousand to meet him that cometh against him with twenty thousand? 32 Or else, while the other is yet a great way off, he sendeth an ambassage, and desireth conditions of peace.

At first glance, these last few verses in our lesson appear to be a restatement of all that has been said before. Using the phrase "cannot be my disciple" (v. 27) helps demonstrate that these verses are not just thrown in. Rather, Christ has moved us from one level of understanding the call of the disciple to another.

In verse 26 Christ addressed the issue of what it means to be a disciple. In verses 27–30 Christ discussed a need to reflect on the costs of being a disciple. In these last few verses, Christ challenges us in our mission as disciples.

Using contemporary language to paraphrase verse 31, we could say that when we are on the job and there are more against us than for us, are we willing to go all the way for Jesus? If God calls you to a ministry in a drug-infested community, will you hang in there regardless? Do we see opportunities for manifestations of God and His glory when we are surrounded by the enemies of our minds, hearts, and souls? Christ rhetorically answers these questions in these verses. Do not quickly make a jump on the discipleship bandwagon unless you have a clear idea of whose music you are being asked to play and how the concert will end. The question is, "Do we want in?"

The Greek word *sumballo* (Gk. **soom-BAL-lo**) means "to consider, to converse, or debate," and *kathizo* (Gk. **kath-ID-zo**) means "to sit down." The word order in Greek puts the consulting before the sitting down. It may be that Christ is saying that accepting the call to be a disciple is a matter of careful thought and unhurried reflection, in order to fully digest all that is at stake.

There are many barriers in life to being a disciple. Some relational barriers have been mentioned (cf. 26) and some are circumstantial (cf. 28–32). The illustration that Christ uses to bring the point home is graphic—two to one, ten thousand troops against twenty thousand troops. Whatever the barriers, are we ready? It is not uncommon in today's world to publicly affirm relationships when in reality mutual commitment is lacking. Christ's disciple should be fully aware that becoming a disciple is a costly endeavor and not to be entered into lightly. Being a disciple changes us and affects everything around us.

Notice well that Christ has moved from illustrations directed at people, to possibly small groups, and on to an obviously significantly larger group. An individual who ignores the mandates of being a disciple puts him or herself and everybody around him or her in a position to be hurt. While the enemy is a long way off a "wise" king will *erotao* (Gk. **er-o-TAH-o**), ask (literally request or beg), for *eirene* (Gk. **i-RAH-nay**)! *Eirene* is the same word used for the peace that only comes from God (see John 14:27; Romans 1:7) or peace that comes from those changed by God (see 1 Corinthians 16:11; Hebrews 11:31)!

33 So likewise, whosoever he be of you that forsaketh not all that he hath, he cannot be my disciple.

Using one of the most explanatory conjunctions of the Greek language—*oun* (Gk. **oon**), Christ may very well be referring not just to the immediate preceding statement but all that has been said in chapter 14. What a wonderful and gracious. term Luke uses to cite the Lord's statement here in verse 33 and in the following phrase.

The Greek word *apotassomai* (Gk. **ap-ot-AS-som-ahee**) is used six times in the New Testament and literally means to say good-bye with the idea of separation. Are you willing to say good-bye to everything for the sake of the King and His kingdom? Two Greek words bring this text into focus: *pas* (Gk. **PAS**) and *huparchonta* (Gk. **hoop-AR-khon-tah**). *Pas* means "all" and *huparchonta* means "goods," "wealth," and/or "all that is at one's disposal animate or inanimate."

Christ's disciples are to say good-bye to all means not provided by God to attain and maintain a personal sense of worth and purpose in this world. Whether it is a job, a person, a ministry, or self (cf. 26), you cannot, again using the word *dunamai*, experience what it means to be Christ's disciple. The person who is not willing to view relationships from Christ's vantage point; he or she who does not carry his or her cross; he or she who does not consider the cost; and he or she who is not willing to lay down his or her life, that Christ might give them life more abundantly—cannot be His disciple.

Daily Bible Readings

M: You Know Me
Psalm 139:1–6
T: Conditions of Discipleship
Luke 14:25–27
W: First, Count the Cost
Luke 14:28–33
T: The Rich Ruler's Response
Luke 18:18–25
F: Rewards of Discipleship
Luke 18:28–30
S: First Disciples Called
Luke 5:1–11
S: Saul Called to Be a Disciple
Acts 9:1–16

MARCH 2008
QUARTER-AT-A-GLANCE
God, the People, and the Covenant

This quarter is a study in the books of 1 Chronicles, 2 Chronicles, Daniel, Nehemiah, Ezra, and Haggai. It is intended to focus on God's covenant with the people of Israel.

UNIT 1 . GOD MAKES A COVENANT

Lessons 1–4 begin with a direct focus on the symbolism of the Ark of the Covenant and end with a discussion of God's fulfilled promises.

Lesson 1: March 2, 2008
The Ark Comes to Jerusalem
1 Chronicles 15:1–3, 14–16, 25–28

King David was seeking to deliver the Ark of the Covenant to a temporary tent where it would be housed. The ark itself is a symbol of the importance of worship in the lives of God's people.

Lesson 2: March 9, 2008
God's Covenant with David
1 Chronicles 17:1, 3–4, 6–15

David was the beneficiary of the many blessings that had resulted from God's promises to him. David wanted to build a place to house the ark and the Lord constrained him, but reminded him of his covenant with him.

Lesson 3: March 16, 2008
God Calls Solomon to Build the Temple
1 Chronicles 28:5–10, 20–21

The Lord had chosen Solomon to build the temple that would house the ark. It was the temple that David sought to build.

Lesson 4: March 23, 2008
Fulfillment of God's Promise
2 Chronicles 6:12–17; Luke 24:44–49

God made David a promise—that his son would build the temple he had hoped to build for the Lord. Here we see the dedication of the temple, pointing to the fulfillment of God's promise.

UNIT 2 . TRUSTING GOD'S COVENANT IN HARD TIMES

Lessons 5–9 focus on trusting God when things get rough. This is a study in 2 Chronicles and the book of Daniel.

Lesson 5: March 30, 2008
Josiah Renews the Covenant
2 Chronicles 34:15, 18–19, 25–27, 29, 31–33

Josiah made a covenant to God—to keep His commandments and statutes.

Lesson 6: April 6, 2008
Daniel Keeps Covenant in a Foreign Land
Daniel 1:8–20

Daniel held fast to his conviction when offered the royal rations of food and wine. The Babylonian king, Nebuchadnezzar, did not observe the Jewish dietary laws to which Daniel had committed.

Lesson 7: April 13, 2008
Three Refuse to Break Covenant
Daniel 3:10–13, 16–18, 21, 24

Daniel and his friends determined that it was better to trust God to deliver them from the fiery furnace than to bow to the king's golden statue.

Lesson 8: April 20, 2008
Daniel's Life-and-Death Test
Daniel 6:4–7, 10, 16, 19, 21, 25–26

A decree was published by the king. Those who prayed to any other god aside from the king should be thrown into the lions' den.

Lesson 9: April 27, 2008
Daniel's Prayer for the People
Daniel 9:1–7, 17–19

Daniel was so overcome by grief over the devastation of Jerusalem and exile of his people that he made intercession and confession on their behalf for their sin against God.

UNIT 3 . REBUILDING THE WALLS AND RENEWING THE COVENANT

Lessons 10–13 focus on the exile of the Israelites and the rebuilding of Jerusalem.

Lesson 10: May 4, 2008
The Temple Rebuilt
Haggai 1:1–4, 7–10, 12–15

The prophet Haggai reminded the Israelites of their first priority: to keep their covenant with God and rebuild the temple in Jerusalem.

Lesson 11: May 11, 2008
Rebuilding the Wall
Nehemiah 2:1–8, 11, 17–18

In the face of the ruins of Jerusalem, Nehemiah decided to rebuild the wall in Jerusalem with the support of God and the king.

Lesson 12: May 18, 2008
Up Against the Wall
Nehemiah 4:1–3, 7–9, 13–15; 6:15

The wall of Jerusalem was being rebuilt because the people assisting with the vision had a mind to accomplish the task.

Lesson 13: May 25, 2008
Call to Renew the Covenant
Nehemiah 8:1–3, 5–6, 13–14, 17–18

Ezra read the Book of the Law aloud to the community for the purpose of renewing their covenant with the Father.

THEMATIC ESSAY

HAVE YOU KEPT YOUR COVENANT COMMITMENT WITH GOD?

by Evangeline Carey

Wycliffe Bible Dictionary defines "covenant" as "an agreement between two or more persons in which the following four factors, or elements, are present: parties, conditions, results, security." An omniscient (all-knowing) God initiated binding covenants with Adam (Genesis 2:16–17), with Noah before and after the Flood (9:8–17), and later with Abraham and God's chosen people (the Israelites) as He launched His awesome plan of salvation to save humanity from our sins (12:1–3).

In this quarter, we will focus on some of the covenants God made with the people of Israel, the descendants of Jacob: the Ten Commandments, the Davidic Covenant, and the prophet Daniel and his assistants.

The Ten Commandments were instructions given by God at Mount Sinai, one of the most sacred locations in Israel's history (Exodus 34:4–28). This occurred before the Children of Israel went into the Promised Land (Canaan). God designed these commandments, or laws, to lead the Israelites to a life of practical holiness before a holy God. He spelled out what He expected from His chosen people.

God emphasized to them, "I am the LORD your God, who rescued you from the land of Egypt, the place of your slavery. You must not have any other god but me" (20:2, NLT). Because throughout their history the Children of Israel engaged in apostasy (spiritual adultery, worshiping idols, chasing after other gods), they were often in serious trouble with God. Their blatant disobedience ignited His hot anger against them and initiated His divine discipline. He judged and punished them by allowing their enemies to take them into slavery.

In short, all 10 laws (the Ten Commandments) were put on two stone tablets by God Himself. Exodus 32:15–16 declares: "Then Moses turned and went down the mountain. He held in his hands the two stone tablets inscribed with the terms of the covenant. They were inscribed on both sides, front and back. These tablets were God's work; the words on them were written by God himself" (NLT).

Recall that Moses, after receiving the Ten Commandments the first time, was so overwhelmed with Israel's unrestrained idolatry with the gold calf that "he threw the stone tablets to the ground, smashing them at the foot of the mountain" (Exodus 32:19, NLT). Consequently, God later gave Moses another copy of the Ten Commandments on two more stone tablets. God told Moses to prepare "two stone tablets like the first ones. Also make a wooden Ark—a sacred chest to store them in. Come up to me on the mountain, and I will write on the tablets the same words that were on the ones you smashed. Then place the tablets in the Ark" (Deuteronomy 10:1–2, NLT). These were the ones that were placed in the ark at Mount Sinai. This ark served as a guide to Israel in the wilderness and was a symbol of the very presence of Almighty God with them. In fact, the *Life Application Study Bible Commentary* says, "The tablets of the law were still in the Ark about 500 years later when Solomon put it in his newly built Temple" (1 Kings 8:9).

According to the *Wycliffe Bible Dictionary*, the Ark of the Covenant was "a chest made of acacia wood, about four feet long, two and a half feet wide, and two and a half feet high" (141). Exodus 25:11–22 tells us that it was overlaid with gold inside and out. It had a ring of gold at each corner, or foot, through which poles were passed to carry it. The lid of the ark, or "mercy seat," was made of pure gold, as were the cherubim that stood at each end of the mercy seat. This Ark of the Covenant, then, was also a sign of God's covenant with the Israelites. It was this sacred chest that King David brought to Jerusalem.

God also made a covenant with King David, called the "Davidic Covenant." According to 1 Chronicles 17:8–14, "God did not want a warrior to build his Temple and David had shed much blood in unifying the nation."

Therefore, because David was a warrior whose job was to unify Israel and destroy her enemies, God did not want him to build His house. Instead, God promised David that He would do the following for David and his descendants: (1) make David famous throughout the earth; (2) provide a permanent, secure homeland for God's chosen people, Israel, so that they would never be disturbed—it would be their own land; (3) subdue all their enemies; (4) build David a house—a dynasty of kings; (5) raise up one of David's descendants (Solomon) to be heir to the throne and build God's house after David died; (6) make Solomon's kingdom strong; (7) be David's Father; (8) not take His unfailing love from David as He did with King Saul; and (9) see to it that David's dynasty and kingdom would continue for an eternity and be secured. According to prophecy, King Jesus will occupy this throne forever and ever in the New Jerusalem—on the new earth (Psalms 10:7; 146:10; Revelation 21:1–3).

God was and always is true to His word. He fulfilled His promise to David when Solomon became king. Solomon did build God's temple, and the Ark of the Covenant was brought to the temple (2 Chronicles 6:10).

The prophet Daniel and his three Hebrew assistants—Shadrach, Meshach, and Abednego—showed how to be God's covenant keepers in hard times. In 605 B.C., Nebuchadnezzar, king of Babylon, swept through Palestine conquering all in his path. In fact, he destroyed Jerusalem and made Judah his vassal state. In other words, the people of Judah were granted the use of the land, but in return they had to pay homage or serve Nebuchadnezzar and the Babylonians. To show how powerful he was, King Nebuchadnezzar took many of Jerusalem's wisest men and most beautiful women to Babylon and put them in slavery for approximately 70 years. Among these captives were Daniel and the three Hebrew young men.

While exiled in a foreign land, in captivity under an egocentric despot, Daniel and his three Hebrew friends remained faithful to God by honoring their covenant commitment to Him (Daniel 3:10–13, 16–18, 21, 24). Regardless of life-threatening consequences, they resolved not to eat from the king's table, drink his wine, or worship his idol of pure gold. Shadrach, Meshach, and Abednego were thrown into the fiery furnace, but God saved them (3:19–28). Later, Daniel was thrown into a den of lions, and the all-powerful God saved him too (6:16–23). They all passed their life-and-death tests. They would not compromise their faith. They were covenant keepers, not covenant breakers.

Finally, after the Israelites had perpetuated a cycle of disobedience, punishment, and repentance, they cried out to God and were restored. In fact, after the armies of Babylon destroyed God's temple—the symbol of God's presence—in Jerusalem in 586 B.C. and the Children of Israel had been punished for disobeying God yet again, it was time to return home to Judah. It was time to rebuild Jerusalem's walls and temple, and it was time for covenant renewal. Not only did the walls and building have to be restored, but so did the people. They had been through much.

In this post-exilic period, God used the prophets Nehemiah, Ezra, and Haggai to speak to His chosen people, Israel. These spokesmen for God urged the people to get on the job and build God's house.

Have you kept your covenant commitment with God? If not, learn from this quarter. See what positive character traits Daniel and his three assistants displayed that would help us even today in our walk with God. If you are keeping your covenant commitment, then be reminded that God will reward those who are faithful and obedient to His commands.

Sources:

Arnold, Bill T., and Beyer, Bryan E. *Encountering the Old Testament.* Grand Rapids, Mich.: Baker Books,1999.

Life Application Study Bible, NLT. Wheaton, Ill.: Tyndale House Publishers, Inc., 1996.

Pfeiffer, Charles F., Howard F. Vos, and John Rea, eds. *Wycliffe Bible Dictionary.* Peabody, Mass.: Hendrickson Publishers, Inc., 1998.

Evangeline Carey is a staff writer for UMI and has been an adult Sunday School teacher for more than 25 years.

TEACHING THAT CHANGES LIVES

by Melvin E. Banks Sr., Litt.D.

The goal of teaching is transformation. Human beings change as their life situations change. And since we believe the purpose of God's Word is to help us know and do God's will, we believe Bible study materials should enable people to come to grips with their life needs—the situations they encounter every day. Unless the teachers of Bible study curriculum are sufficiently knowledgeable of those needs, they will not be able to raise the right issues and help students see the relevance of that truth to their lives. Any person conversant with Scripture may be able to expound the text. But exposition alone does not get us to application and obedience.

These are learning principles that are widely accepted in educational circles of which teachers must be cognizant. Such principles must be adapted to the unique lifestyles of the learners. Teaching as transformation is seen in the manner Jesus communicated with the woman of Samaria as recorded in John 4. Notice how Jesus led this woman from one degree of spirituality to another, from her sin to the Saviour.

1. JESUS SECURED THE WOMAN'S ATTENTION

To secure the attention and readiness of the Samaritan woman, Jesus first affirmed her self-identity and worth by asking her for a drink of water. Since Jews never spoke to Samaritans, the mere fact of His speaking to her communicated to the woman that He respected her. By addressing her in public and as a Samaritan, Jesus conveyed to the woman what He thought of her and other Samaritans.

But Jesus went further. He requested from her a drink of water. In so doing, Jesus totally disarmed the woman and eliminated any misgivings or apprehension she may have had concerning Him. She now knew that this Jew accepted her. She would now have an attentive ear to accept whatever He subsequently said.

In the same way, to communicate with students, provoking interest in learning is more readily achieved when we begin where students are—at their point of need. That is not to say one begins and ends with the student's felt need. That is, a class designed to teach the Bible does not become reduced to a discussion of hot topics as an end in itself. Rather, we begin with felt needs in order to provoke interest in a subject about which they know very little.

2. JESUS PROMISED TO SATISFY HER FELT NEED

Next, Jesus promised the woman a source of water that made coming to the well unnecessary. In so doing, Christ piqued her interest. Jesus told her that the water in the well was temporary and ineffective in quenching the deeply felt spiritual thirst she was experiencing. He assured her that He could give water that was not in the well. This promise to satisfy a deeply felt need really excited her. She exclaimed, "Please, Sir. . .give me some of that water!" (John 4:15, LBT).

In a similar way, the teacher who promises students that their keenly felt need will be satisfied through a study of the Word of God will find greater interest. Of course, to sustain interest, the subsequent class discussion must live up to the promise.

3. JESUS PRESENTED NEW INFORMATION IN AN INTERESTING WAY

By building on the knowledge the woman already possessed, Jesus presented her with the new information: He could give her water that was not in the well. To clarify what He meant by water "not in the well" Jesus engaged the woman in dialogue. The new information she needed to hear was about eternal life, where and how to worship God, and about Jesus' own identity. While He started the conversation with water, He did not end there. Jesus knew that He was sent to represent His Father, to present words of eternal life. He would have compromised His mission had He allowed the dialogue to dissipate into frivolous chatter.

That point needs to be made, because some Sunday School teachers have been known to allow a class to degenerate into nothing more than the latest gossip. Such people are perhaps unmindful that while small talk has a place in a class, ultimately people must be confronted with "Thus saith the Lord." God has made Himself known in the Scriptures and our task as teachers is to guide others into exploring what He has to say about our life situation.

4. JESUS APPLIED THE NEW TRUTH TO THE SPIRITUAL NEED

Jesus was not satisfied in just presenting new information to the woman. He knew she needed to see the relationship of His identity to her own life situation. So Jesus invited her to call her husband. Applying truth to life is one of the critical components of effective teaching. Unless students can see the relationship of the Bible to the issues and problems they face today, the relevance of the Scriptures will appear very remote.

Indeed, it is very remarkable how each book is directed at a specific need among the people of God. Matthew was written to help Jews understand that the arrival of Jesus was a fulfillment of Old Testament prophecies concerning the Messiah. Paul's epistles to the Corinthians were written to answer questions they had about the Christian life. This is especially true of the epistles, but is discernible in all the Bible books. So exploring how Scripture relates to life is both imbedded within the Bible itself as well as in the learning needs of students.

5. JESUS MOTIVATED THE WOMAN TO ACT ON WHAT SHE KNEW

The action that the woman took reenforced her new convictions. She left her water pot to spread the news in the village. It was as though the woman said, "Now that I believe You could be the Messiah, let me do something with this information. Let me go tell the people back in the town." Immediately, therefore, she dropped her water pot, ran back into the city to tell the townspeople to come investigate this Stranger in town. "Could this be the Messiah?" she asked them.

The teacher who motivates students to take action from the study of the Scriptures has indeed been effective. That's because the ultimate objective of Bible study is not just to increase knowledge, but to impact a person's behavior, to motivate them to do the will of God (1 John 2:17). This is accomplished best not just from lecturing or exhorting them to obey, but by guiding them to discover the information themselves from the Word, by impacting the emotions through worship of God, and by providing opportunities to take action—to implement the truth to be learned.

That is what UMI aims to accomplish in its Bible study materials. These principles are imbedded into every lesson we produce.

Melvin E. Banks Sr., Litt.D., is the Founder and Chairman of UMI.

GOD'S COVENANT: A WORD THAT CANNOT COME BACK VOID

by Louis H. Wilson, Ph.D.

Promises, promises, promises. We live in a day when it seems a person's word reflects more of what is expedient than one's character, when circumstances, rather than commitments, define relationships. But according to Scripture it is not to be this way. From God's point of view, we are members of a covenantal community, unconditionally ratified by God, a community bound to God and His people.

Many passages in Scripture provide us with a foundation for understanding what it means to have covenant relationships with God and others.

To understand the essence of what a covenant is, we begin by citing the first two contexts of the word "covenant." In Genesis 6:18 (KJV), God tells Noah, "With thee will I establish my covenant; and thou shalt come into the ark, thou, and thy sons, and thy wife, and thy sons' wives with thee." God affirms the covenant in 8:20–22 and 9:8–11. After the Flood, God tells Noah that never again will He destroy the world and all living creatures.

Our call to a covenant relationship with God is also a call to a covenant relationship with His family. God's covenant words must be confirmed by deeds. Whether by omission or commission, when we say yes to Jesus, we are making a promise to God and His people that we will do our best to be a positive influence on the body.

Christians are not to live in a world of double-talk and hidden agendas. Christ calls us to keep it simple: "Let your communication be, Yea, yea; Nay, nay" (Matthew 5:37, KJV). Say it and mean it. If you promise to do something, do it!

This leads to something else that influences how we live out covenants with each other—the unconditional aspect of godly covenants. God does His part by bringing us into relationship with Himself; our part is to believe in what God is doing.

Taken as a complete section, God makes direct promises to Abraham in Genesis 12; 15; and 17. In chapter 12, Abraham leaves Haran, following God day by day. In chapter 15, God clarifies the covenant by providing more details, promising to give Abraham a son through whom the nations will be blessed. Nine times in chapter 17, God says to Abraham, "This is my covenant." Seven times He says, "I will." This covenant is about God. It is for Him and by Him, and it is by His power that covenant promises are fulfilled. Once again, Abraham responds in faith, doing as God asks by making an open confession—the rite of circumcision. He believes in all that God has said and acted on it.

Do we ask for commitments too quickly? From the time of Abraham's calling to God's request that he demonstrate complete surrender of all that was his was 15 years (12:4; 17:1). With purposeful persistence, God led Abraham to discover Him on a deeper level before taking him to another level of commitment. Covenantal relationships of substance do not happen overnight.

In the same way, when we promise fellow believers to walk, pray, and be used of God to see them through, are we really willing to covenant with them until God works it out? (Abraham made a few mistakes along with way.) Are we there for others unconditionally? Ready to stand with them when they embarrass themselves and those around them (12:10–20; 20)? We must also be willing to speak life, to share what God has said, and then, having done all, to stand (see Ephesians 6:13).

Louis H. Wilson, Ph.D., *holds a doctorate in leadership and organizational development from the University of Phoenix, and has been involved in church leadership and development for the past 25 years.*

BENJAMIN E. MAYS
(1895–1984)
Preacher, Educator, Leader

Part One

Before 500,000 people could march on Washington, DC, before 30,000 people could march from Selma, before there could be rebellion in Black America and renewal in the White church, before SNCC could sit-in, before Stokely Carmichael could talk about "Black Power," before Martin Luther King Jr. could dream, history had to take the flesh and form of certain Black men who were bold enough, wise enough, and selfless enough to assume the awesome responsibility of preparing the ground for a harvest, the fruits of which they themselves would probably never taste.

Of the handful of men called by history to this delicate and dangerous task, none tilled more ground or harvested a more bountiful crop than Benjamin Elijah Mays, a lean, beautiful Black preacher–prophet who served as schoolmaster of the Civil Rights Movement during a ministry that spanned some 60 years. During this period, Mays helped lay the foundation for the new world of Black and White Americans.

Master of a variety of roles—teacher, preacher, scholar, author, newspaper columnist, activist—Mays was enormously effective in the formative years of the Black Revolution in structures of power, such as serving on executive committees of the World Council of Churches and the International YMCA, as president of the United Negro College Fund, and as vice president and board member of the NAACP. In these roles, he had a direct and pervasive influence on the Black Church, the White Church, the Black college, the White college, and the Freedom Movement.

Part Two

Samuel DuBois Cook, president of Dillard University, recalled that Dr. Mays said, "It isn't how long one lives, but how well." Dr. Benjamin E. Mays, King's dear friend and former teacher, was himself an example of his own words.

Born on August 1, 1895, Dr. Mays was a native of Epworth, South Carolina, and grew up as the last of seven children of ex-slaves and semi-literate farmers. Stunned by the assertion that Blacks were intellectually inferior to Whites, he was determined to destroy this myth. After completing elementary and high school in the state, Mays entered Virginia Union University. After a year, however, he was able to enter Bates College in Maine, where he settled for himself the question of inferiority by winning a Phi Beta Kappa key and graduating in 1920. In 1925, he entered the University of Chicago where he earned a master's degree. A decade later, he was awarded a Ph.D. by the same university. In 1934, Dr. Mays joined Howard University as dean of its school of religion, and in 1940 he was named president of Morehouse College. During his presidency, the college came to be dubbed the "Black Oxford of the South," with an expanded physical plant, academically improved staff, a sound financial base, and spawning a disproportionate share of Black doctors, lawyers, Ph.D.'s, college presidents, teachers, and activists.

Two years after his retirement, at the age of 67, he became the first Black president of the Atlanta Board of Education, and at the age of 83, he was elected to his third term, which he served until the term ended in 1982.

Sources:

Adams, Russell L. "Benjamin E. Mays: 1895–1984, Preacher, Educator, Leader." *Great Negroes Past and Present.* Chicago: Afro-American Publishing Co., 1984.

Bennett Jr., Lerone. "Benjamin E. Mays: The Last of the Great Schoolmasters." *Ebony,* October 1994.

TEACHING TIPS

March 2
Bible Study Guide 1

1. Words You Should Know

A. Minister (1 Chronicles 15:2) *sharath* (Heb.)—To contribute to, serve, or wait on.

B. Sanctified (v. 14) *qadash* (Heb.)—To make clean or to consecrate an object or person; to be set apart for God and His purpose.

C. Ephod (v. 27) *'ephowd* (Heb.)—An outer garment often worn over the shoulder.

2. Teacher Preparation

Unifying Principle—A Symbol of God's Presence We must seek out symbols of God's presence to remind ourselves of the importance of worship.

A. Pray for the students in your class.

B. Review the Bible Study Guide as well as the material on the *Precepts For Living*® CD-ROM to become familiar with the significance of the Ark of the Covenant.

C. If possible, secure pictures or a model of the Ark of the Covenant. Find pictures of items that call us to worship, such as Bibles, altars, or churches.

D. Prepare a piece of chart paper by dividing it into three columns labeled "Reminders," "Hindrances," and "Resolve."

3. Starting the Lesson

A. Before the class arrives, prepare a display of the pictures of worship items or replicas of the ark you gathered during the week.

B. Lead the class to pray specifically for godly insights into the significance of worship.

C. Ask the class to respond to the display. Save the Ark of the Covenant for last. Share key information regarding the ark's place in worship.

4. Getting into the Lesson

A. For a small-group approach, assign six groups the task of searching the Bible text and the lesson and reporting on one of these six areas: (1) Obededom and the death of Uzza, (2) the stolen ark and the Philistines, (3) the instruments and music, (4) David's actions in verses 1–3, (5) carrying the ark in verses 14–16, and (6) the procession in verses 25–28. For a large-group approach, present material on the six areas yourself.

B. Ask each group (or the large group) to answer these questions: (1) What happened? (2) What did it mean for Israel? (3) What do you think that says to our church family?

C. Have a volunteer read the In Focus story aloud. Ask class members to share about an artifact, place, or situation that reminds them of the sacredness of worship. Record the responses in the "Reminders" column of the chart.

5. Relating the Lesson to Life

A. Have the class brainstorm things that hinder their worship and daily devotion. List these in the "Hindrances" column of the chart. Ask class members how they can give more time to worship and daily devotion. List their suggestions in the "Resolve" column.

B. Ask if any student has any insight to share regarding today's lesson.

6. Arousing Action

A. Have class members discuss how they could encourage those they influence to be more active in worship and daily devotion.

B. Share a personal thought about steps you have taken in preparation for ministry. Discuss whether the process was easy and/or why it was necessary.

Worship Guide

For the Superintendent or Teacher
Theme: The Ark Comes to Jerusalem
Theme Song: "Is Your All on the Altar?"
Devotional Reading: Psalm 150
Prayer

THE ARK COMES TO JERUSALEM

Bible Background • 1 CHRONICLES 15:1–28
Printed Text • 1 CHRONICLES 15:1–3, 14–16, 25–28 Devotional Reading • PSALM 150

AIM for Change

By the end of the lesson, we will:

EXPLORE the purpose and significance of the Ark of the Covenant;

REFLECT on the sacredness of worship; and

RECOGNIZE and respond to those things that invite us to worship God.

Keep in Mind

"And David gathered all Israel together to Jerusalem, to bring up the ark of the LORD unto his place, which he had prepared for it" (1 Chronicles 15:3).

Focal Verses

KJV 1 Chronicles 15:1 And David made him houses in the city of David, and prepared a place for the ark of God, and pitched for it a tent.

2 Then David said, None ought to carry the ark of God but the Levites: for them hath the LORD chosen to carry the ark of God, and to minister unto him for ever.

3 And David gathered all Israel together to Jerusalem, to bring up the ark of the LORD unto his place, which he had prepared for it.

15:14 So the priests and the Levites sanctified themselves to bring up the ark of the LORD God of Israel.

15 And the children of the Levites bare the ark of God upon their shoulders with the staves thereon, as Moses commanded according to the word of the LORD.

16 And David spake to the chief of the Levites to appoint their brethren to be the singers with instruments of musick, psalteries and harps and cymbals, sounding, by lifting up the voice with joy.

15:25 So David, and the elders of Israel, and the captains over thousands, went to bring up the ark of the covenant of the LORD out of the house of Obededom with joy.

26 And it came to pass, when God helped the Levites that bare the ark of the covenant of the LORD, that they offered seven bullocks and seven rams.

27 And David was clothed with a robe of fine linen, and all the Levites that bare the ark, and the singers, and Chenaniah the master of the song with the singers: David also had upon him an ephod of linen.

NLT 1 Chronicles 15:1 David now built several buildings for himself in the City of David. He also prepared a place for the Ark of God and set up a special tent for it.

2 Then he commanded, "No one except the Levites may carry the Ark of God. The LORD has chosen them to carry the Ark of the LORD and to serve him forever."

3 Then David summoned all Israel to Jerusalem to bring the Ark of the LORD to the place he had prepared for it.

15:14 So the priests and the Levites purified themselves in order to bring the Ark of the LORD, the God of Israel, to Jerusalem.

15 Then the Levites carried the Ark of God on their shoulders with its carrying poles, just as the LORD had instructed Moses.

16 David also ordered the Levite leaders to appoint a choir of Levites who were singers and musicians to sing joyful songs to the accompaniment of harps, lyres, and cymbals.

15:25 Then David and the elders of Israel and the generals of the army went to the house of Obededom to bring the Ark of the LORD's Covenant up to Jerusalem with a great celebration.

26 And because God was clearly helping the Levites as they carried the Ark of the LORD's Covenant, they sacrificed seven bulls and seven rams.

27 David was dressed in a robe of fine linen, as were all the Levites who carried the Ark, and also the singers, and Kenaniah the choir leader. David was also wearing a priestly garment.

28 Thus all Israel brought up the ark of the covenant of the LORD with shouting, and with sound of the cornet, and with trumpets, and with cymbals, making a noise with psalteries and harps.

28 So all Israel brought up the Ark of the LORD's Covenant with shouts of joy, the blowing of rams' horns and trumpets, the crashing of cymbals, and loud playing on harps and lyres.

In Focus

As a child, Elijah had watched His grandmother take the Bible from her nightstand and walk to the tree in her backyard each evening before settling herself to read. This was one of his most vivid memories of his summer visits to his grandparents' house in rural Tennessee. Nanna's devotions were like clockwork—at 4:30 each evening, she was reading Scripture. He could hear her humming or singing an old hymn as she gazed across the yard after reading a portion of the Scripture.

When the call came that Nanna had died, Elijah, now a grown man, and his father traveled to Tennessee to make arrangements and prepare the house for the inevitable selling. Their home was now in the North and their lives were too busy to even consider keeping Nanna's old house.

Elijah thought he would be strong in facing Nanna's death. She had lived a good life and reached more than the fourscore years and 10 that the Bible promised. However, when he arrived at the house and looked at the nightstand, the memories of Nanna's Bible came to him. He recalled the sacred moments she had spent holding it, and the regularity of her worship. As he remembered the old songs she sang as she held the Bible, his father entered the room and the two decided to pray. They thanked God for Nanna's example. They asked forgiveness for the crowdedness of their lives, which often caused them to neglect prayer and Bible meditation. They asked for God's strength in the days ahead and for His direction. They thanked God that the sacred book had called them to worship, just as it had called Nanna.

Our lesson reminds us that in our lives there are people, places, and items that represent God's presence and remind us of the worship we are to give Him. Worship is a life-changing experience, but we must honor God's presence properly in order to receive the intended impact. Today's lesson reminds us to regard worship with the utmost care.

The People, Places, and Times

The Ark of the Covenant. God instructed the Children of Israel to build a Tabernacle and several pieces of furniture for it after their exodus from captivity in Egypt (Exodus 25:10–22). One piece of furniture, the ark, measured two and a half cubits in length, and a cubit and a half in both width and height. A cubit is an ancient unit of measurement believed to equal about 18 inches. This wooden box was then covered in gold and was carried by two staffs made also of acacia wood, covered with gold. Mounted upon the ark was the mercy seat, a slightly raised platform, covered with pure gold. The mercy seat was surrounded by two cherubim made of gold, one mounted at each side of the seat.

The Ark of the Covenant resided within the Holy of Holies, the innermost room of the Tabernacle. Access was only permitted once per year, on the Day of Atonement. Access was restricted to one person, the high priest, who would enter the Holy of Holies with the blood of a goat, on behalf of his own and the people of Israel's sins. The goat's blood was sprinkled onto the mercy seat to make atonement for the sins of the people of Israel.

Background

The Ark of the Covenant had been a mainstay in the spiritual lives of the Children of Israel following their flight from Egypt. However, during the reign of King Saul, God's people had become disconnected from the ark, which represented God's presence. David, upon capturing Jerusalem and making it the capital city of Israel, sought to cure this disconnection by reuniting the people with the ark.

King David's first attempt at transporting the Ark of the Covenant to Jerusalem was a failure. Not only was the attempt unsuccessful, but it resulted in the death of one of the men, Uzza, assisting with its transporting. God had stricken Uzza to convey His anger toward David and Israel for not following His prescribed orders for transporting the ark (Exodus 25:14–15; Numbers 4:4–15; 7:9). Although David and Israel made what they may have considered adequate preparations for handling the ark, they were in essence inadequate, because they were not according to God's specific instructions. As a consequence of David and Israel's disobedience and carelessness, they were forced to temporarily store the ark with the family of Obededom for three months (1 Chronicles 13:14).

This point is not to be taken lightly by believers today. Often we choose to make seemingly "good" plans concerning various areas of our lives, only to have the plans fail miserably because they were not God's plans! However, God is so merciful that He often grants us, as He did David and Israel, a second chance by allowing us another opportunity to follow His plan in the manner He originally dictated.

At-A-Glance

1. Preparing for the Ark of the Covenant (1 Chronicles 15:1–3, 14–16)
2. Bringing the Ark to Jerusalem (vv. 25–28)

In Depth

1. Preparing for the Ark of the Covenant (1 Chronicles 15:1–3, 14–16)

David took extra care to prepare the place for the Ark of the Covenant. It is noteworthy that David pitched the tent that the ark was to inhabit at the same time he erected a home for himself and his family. After preparing the place where the ark would dwell, David gave specific instructions concerning those who should carry the ark (v. 2). David was obviously applying the lessons learned from his previously failed attempt to transport the ark that resulted in the death of Uzza (13:6–10). The wisdom of David in this instance is often overlooked by modern believers. Instead of following the example of David and learning from past failures, we prefer to repeatedly learn lessons by enrolling and re-enrolling in the school of hard knocks.

David displayed leadership qualities by ensuring that the ark was carried by the proper personnel. As leaders, in any capacity but especially in ministry, we can never expect to yield optimal results if the proper pieces are in improper places! On a basketball team, only an unskilled coach would allow a center to play the position of point guard, as this would hinder the flow of the offense. Similarly, in ministry, leaders should not have unfriendly persons serving as ushers, tone-deaf individuals serving as song leaders, or those lacking in knowledge of God's Word serving in teaching capacities.

Equally as important as making certain that one is called for the task is being careful not to defile God's Word while operating in that capacity. The Levites and the priests, who had been called by God, sanctified and cleansed themselves prior to touching the ark. Romans 3:23 tells us that "all have sinned, and come short of the glory of God." This declaration is inclusive of the parishioner, the preacher, and everyone in between. Therefore, we have an obligation to seek forgiveness and to undergo a spiritual cleansing process prior to engaging in ministry, so as not to pollute God's work with our own imperfections. Just as we were taught as children to thoroughly wash our hands prior to eating, we should exercise the same care when it comes to cleansing ourselves spiritually before partaking in ministry.

2. Bringing the Ark to Jerusalem (vv. 25–28)

Only after a failed attempt, the death of a servant, and much prayer and preparation did David and Israel successfully transport the ark to Jerusalem. Therefore, it should be no surprise that the demeanor of David and Israel was one of reverence, praise, and worship to God. It is common courtesy to express gratitude when someone does a kind gesture toward you. Depending on the nature of the act, the gratitude might range anywhere from a simple word of thanks to an expensive gift of thanks. Similarly, when God proves Himself faithful to us as believers, it is only appropriate to display some form of gratitude. This might be a monetary offering, a shout of praise, a song, or a dance. However, it is most important that the gratitude be genuine, so that God will receive it accordingly.

Search the Scriptures

1. Who did David designate to carry the ark and why (1 Chronicles 15:2)?

2. What instruments were used in the processional (vv. 16, 28)?

3. What people were included in the processional and celebration of the return of the ark (vv. 3, 14, 25)?

4. What was David clothed in as the ark was carried into Jerusalem (v. 27)?

Discuss the Meaning

1. What does the preparation David made for the ark indicate about the sacred nature of God's presence?

2. What is the significance of the Levites cleansing themselves prior to handling the ark?

3. What is the significance of David and Israel ushering in the ark with praise in song and with instruments?

Lesson in Our Society

All of us lead lives that are full of responsibilities, chores, and tasks that must be carried out. Often these obligations make for extremely action-packed days in which we rush from one thing to another, not giving each item the care that it deserves. As Christians we must always remember to give God's dealings the utmost care and concern, because God does not bless us haphazardly. He gives us only His best.

Make It Happen

Identify a time when you took part in ministry but afterward were seemingly unchanged. Now ask yourself if there was something you could have done, or not done, to assist in ushering in God's presence? Jot down three things that you can do, or not do, in order to enhance your worship experience. Implement these things the next time you have an opportunity.

Follow the Spirit

What God wants me to do:

_____

_____

Remember Your Thoughts

Special insights I have learned:

_____

_____

More Light on the Text

1 Chronicles 15:1–3, 14–16, 25–28

1 And David made him houses in the city of David, and prepared a place for the ark of God, and pitched for it a tent. 2 Then David said, None ought to carry the ark of God but the Levites: for them hath the LORD chosen to carry the ark of God, and to minister unto him for ever. 3 And David gathered all Israel together to Jerusalem, to bring up the ark of the LORD unto his place, which he had prepared for it.

In order to understand the significance of the ark it is important to examine its placement, construction, contents, and purpose. The ark, which was to have been placed permanently in the inner sanctuary of the Tabernacle, had no lid. Instead, it was covered by the mercy seat, a solid sheet of pure gold beaten or pounded into shape. In this way, God's mercy was the vehicle by which the priest was able to come before God on behalf of the people.

Moses was also instructed to place three items inside the finished ark: Aaron's rod, a container of the manna, that the Children of Israel had been fed in the wilderness, and the stone tablets inscribed with the terms of the covenant. These three items served as symbols of God's selection, provision, and relationship with His chosen people (see Exodus 16:32–34; Numbers 17:10–11; Deuteronomy 10:2–5).

David built houses in Jerusalem for himself and his family. He also prepared a place for the ark in Jerusalem, which is also referred to as the City of David (see 2 Samuel 5:5–7.) In explaining how to transport the ark, David made sure that the instructions given to Moses were followed. First, only the Levites were to take responsibility for the ark (see 1 Chronicles 15:2). One of the 12 tribes of Israel, the Levites were the tribal descendants of Levi, the third son of Jacob and Leah. They were set apart by God to fulfill their duties including ministering to God on behalf of the people. The priests were the descendants of Aaron, the brother of Moses and the man God had assigned as the first priest. In the wilderness, the Levites had the responsibility for moving the Ark of the Covenant along with all of the furnishings of the Tabernacle. The priests had the responsibility of conducting the worship through offering of sacrifices. The law clearly specified which animals were to be used for sacrifice and the manner in which the

"And David gathered all Israel together to Jerusalem, to bring up the ark of the LORD unto his place, which he had prepared for it" (1 Chronicles 15:3).

sacrifice was to be made. Because he knew the role of the Levites and priests was to lead people in the sacrifices and worship of God, David assigned the Levites the task of moving the ark and gave them the additional responsibility for the ministry of music.

David's preparation for returning the ark included involving all of the people of Israel in what we would call corporate worship. This was a momentous occasion. It symbolized the restoration of worship to the nation and victory over Israel's enemies. God had prospered the Levite, Obededom, when the ark resided with him (see 2 Samuel 6:11). David was certain that God would prosper the nation when this symbol of communion with God was restored to national prominence. Furthermore, God was not just the God of the leaders. He was God of the nation. All of the people were to participate and to witness what was done in that day. Through this procession, celebration, and worship, David established his kingdom as being loyal only to Jehovah, the self-existent God, who had chosen Abraham and his descendants and later taken the Children of Israel out of bondage and through the wilderness. The return of

the ark would be celebrated and the beauty of the procession would be discussed throughout Israel's generations.

15:14 So the priests and the Levites sanctified themselves to bring up the ark of the LORD God of Israel. 15 And the children of the Levites bare the ark of God upon their shoulders with the staves thereon, as Moses commanded according to the word of the LORD. 16 And David spake to the chief of the Levites to appoint their brethren to be the singers with instruments of musick, psalteries and harps and cymbals, sounding, by lifting up the voice with joy.

Before the ark could be moved, the priests and Levites had to sanctify themselves. In the Hebrew, the term "sanctify" (*qadash*, **kah-DAHSH**) means "to become ceremonially clean or to wash oneself in preparation for service to the Lord." The manner in which this sanctification takes place is described in Exodus 29:1–37. Strict adherence to the ritual of washing and sacrifice was necessary in order to avoid the penalty of death when approaching the ark and the Tabernacle.

It was also critical that the ark be carried in a specific manner. David had seen firsthand what transgression of God's instructions meant (see 2 Samuel 6). In this second attempt, the Levites followed God's instructions explicitly. According to the law, the ark was to be carried. It was to be laid upon the shoulders of the Levites as symbols of their carrying the worship of the Lord before the people. It was to be held only by its staffs, which, like the ark, were made of Acacia or shittim wood overlaid with gold. The staffs were placed through rings of pure gold, which were affixed to each corner of the ark. Through its materials and construction, the ark represented the protection and covering of God over His chosen people. The rings represented God's direction. Its symbolism for the nation of Israel and the people of God in the twenty-first century cannot be overlooked.

David's own ability as a musician was well known, and his reign was marked by his devotion to God. The return of the ark must be accompanied by praise; the worship of God must be accompanied by music and singing—a joyful noise. The instruments of David's time are described in these verses. The "psaltery" (Heb. *nebel*, **NEH-behl**) was similar in body style to a lyre and was probably played like its modern sister, the guitar. The "harp" (Heb. *kinnowr*, **ki-NOHR**) was named because of its "twanging" sound. The cymbals (Heb. *metseleth*, **mets-AY-leth**) were probably double cymbals and gave a high pitch as they would today. This music accompanied the voices of the singers of the tribe of Levi. This entire musical praise is described as a "sounding" and uses the Hebrew term *shama* (**shah-MAH**), which means "to listen attentively." At this resounding music and song, the nation was to pay strict attention and to rejoice because of the return of God's presence.

15:25 So David, and the elders of Israel, and the captains over thousands, went to bring up the ark of the covenant of the LORD out of the house of Obededom with joy. 26 And it came to pass, when God helped the Levites that bare the ark of the covenant of the LORD, that they offered seven bullocks and seven rams. 27 And David was clothed with a robe of fine linen, and all the Levites that bare the ark, and the singers, and Chenaniah the master of the song with the singers: David also had upon him an ephod of linen. 28 Thus all Israel brought up the ark of the covenant of the LORD with shouting, and with sound of the cornet, and with trumpets, and with cymbals, making a noise with psalteries and harps.

David led the return of the ark with a joyous and orderly procession, which included Israel's older leaders and captains (Heb. *sar*, **sar**).

The Israelites offered sacrifices to express their gratitude to God and to ask His blessing upon their nation as the ark was returned to prominence in the worship of the people. This voluntary gesture was made in accordance with the law for the sins of the people (see Leviticus 1:1–7). A sacrifice of seven animals of each type was made. In Scripture, the number seven refers to completeness and corresponds to the number of days in creation. The sacrifice, therefore, symbolized the complete atonement of the people as they sought the complete forgiveness and presence of God in their nation and national affairs.

The leaders followed strict guidelines even regarding attire. David, as well as the Levites, wore fine linen, and he also wore an ephod (Heb. *ephowd*, **ay-FOHD**), or "mantle or outer garment." David was not attempting to step into the place of the priest. Rather, his attire represented him as the leader and as a worshiper who had donned the finest vestments in this celebration of restoration. Interestingly, it is this ephod that David is famous for having danced out of, earning the scorn of his wife, Michal, Saul's daughter (see 2 Samuel 6:15–23).

Verse 28 summarizes the mood of the celebration and symbolizes the restored relationship between God and the nation of Israel. The "shouting" (Heb. *teruwah*, **ter-oo-AH**) is a term that means "battle cry." This was a historic moment in the nation's history. All surrounding nations would know by the sound that God had given victory to Israel. Here, additional instruments are mentioned. The "cornet" (Heb. *showphar*, **shoh-FAR**) is a ram's horn, which was blown in battle and to sound the alarm as a warning. The "trumpet" (Heb. *chatsotserah*, **khahts-oh-tser-AH**) added to the sound of the cymbals, the harps, and the voices to signify that God had returned to Israel and that the symbol of His presence would reside with His people.

The procession of the ark into the city of Jerusalem took three days. David knew that he was declaring the restored prominence of worship. His installation of the ark using worship with singers, musicians, and apparently dancers was not just a spectacle. David was ushering in God's presence and ushering in a new direction for the nation.

The Bible clearly tells us that the violence and bloodshed of David's reign did not stop with the entrance of the ark, but David's action in restoring the priority of worship not only took precedence over the violence, it created a mind-set among the people. In the return of the ark, the great Jehovah, who had chosen Abraham and promised him a great nation, was being honored. In this procession, the nation was remembering that Jehovah had delivered their fathers from Pharaoh's hand and brought them across the Red Sea. Through the restoration of worship, the nation was declaring before their enemies that the one, true God who had brought their forefathers out of the wilderness and across the Jordan had indeed delivered the Promised Land into their hands. David was shown to be a great king who was dependent upon the Lord and in whom the Lord was pleased.

As we reflect on today's lesson, we must remember that whether we are worshiping God in the church building or in our home, we should respond to God with expressions of praise and gratitude for who He is in our lives, for His power in the universe, and for what He has done for us. In Jesus Christ, God has fulfilled the promise of the Ark of the Covenant. In Him, God has made His abode with humanity and brought to earth the divinity that enables us to offer true worship and praise.

Daily Bible Readings

M: Praise the Lord!
Psalm 150
T: The Ark of God
1 Chronicles 15:1–3, 11–15
W: Music, Joy, and Celebration
1 Chronicles 15:16–24
T: Bringing the Ark of the Covenant
1 Chronicles 15:25–29
F: Before the Ark
1 Chronicles 16:1–6
S: A Psalm of Thanksgiving
1 Chronicles 16:7–36
S: Worship before the Ark
1 Chronicles 16:37–43

TEACHING TIPS

March 9

Bible Study Guide 2

1. Words You Should Know

A. Prophet (1 Chronicles 17:1) *nabiy'* (Heb.)—A person ordained by God to speak God's truth to the people.

B. House (vv. 1, 4, 6, 10, 12, 14) *bayith* (Heb.)—A family abode or the establishment of a household through the descendants of a particular person.

C. Covenant (v. 1) *beriyth* (Heb.)—A binding agreement.

D. Sheepcote (v. 7) *naveh* (Heb.)—A sheep pen or holding area for shepherds and sheep as they travel from place to place in search of pasture.

2. Teacher Preparation

Unifying Principle—Covenanting As Christians, it should bring us great joy to know that we live in covenant with God. We can find great comfort in knowing that God delivers on His promises—heaven and Earth shall pass away, but God's Word will never be void.

A. Pray for the students in your class, asking God to open their hearts to today's lesson.

B. Carefully review the Bible Study Guide and the material on the *Precepts For Living®* CD-ROM to familiarize yourself with more on David's background and with the key Hebrew terms (see Words You Should Know).

3. Starting the Lesson

A. Have each class member think of a promise they intended to keep, but later were unable to. Have a few people share the circumstances surrounding their broken promises.

B. Briefly discuss how we feel and how others feel when promises are broken.

4. Getting into the Lesson

A. Explain that today's lesson is about God's promise to David, and that it provides us with the confidence to depend on God to keep His promises.

B. Have the class brainstorm what they know about David's life. Record their responses on a flip chart.

C. After explaining Nathan's role in David's life, discuss the lesson following the outline in the At-A-Glance section. Incorporate the questions from the Search the Scriptures and Discuss the Meaning sections, as well as the list of Hebrew terms you created.

5. Relating the Lesson to Life

A. Have class members read the In Focus story. Ask everyone to think of a promise God has kept to them. Ask individuals to give one- or two-word descriptions of the promises such as "a family," "a job," or "restored health."

B. Have a volunteer read Lesson in Our Society aloud. Then ask the students to share (1) how God helps them develop faith by sending others to encourage them (as with David and Nathan) or (2) how counting one's blessings from the past helps us to wait on God's promises for our future (as when God reminded David of his past).

6. Arousing Action

A. Have class members respond aloud to the closing sentence in Lesson in Our Society.

B. Ask the entire class to respond to the Make It Happen challenge.

C. Ask the students to complete the Daily Bible Readings and lesson 3 in the *Precepts For Living® Personal Study Guide* in preparation for next week's lesson.

D. End the class with prayer.

Worship Guide

For the Superintendent or Teacher
Theme: God's Covenant with David
Theme Song: "Lord, Make Me a Sanctuary"
Devotional Reading: Psalm 78:67–72
Prayer

GOD'S COVENANT WITH DAVID

Bible Background • 1 CHRONICLES 17:1–27
Printed Text • 1 CHRONICLES 17:1, 3–4, 6–15 Devotional Reading • PSALM 78:67–72

AIM for Change

By the end of the lesson, we will:

KNOW the importance of covenant relationships;

APPRECIATE God's promises to His people; and

CELEBRATE the fulfillment of His Word.

Keep in Mind

"Now therefore thus shalt thou say unto my servant David, Thus saith the LORD of hosts, I took thee from the sheepcote, even from following the sheep, that thou shouldest be ruler over my people Israel: And I have been with thee whithersoever thou hast walked, and have cut off all thine enemies from before thee, and have made thee a name like the name of the great men that are in the earth" (1 Chronicles 17:7–8).

Focal Verses

KJV **1 Chronicles 17:1** Now it came to pass, as David sat in his house, that David said to Nathan the prophet, Lo, I dwell in an house of cedars, but the ark of the covenant of the LORD remaineth under curtains.

17:3 And it came to pass the same night, that the word of God came to Nathan, saying,

4 Go and tell David my servant, Thus saith the LORD, Thou shalt not build me an house to dwell in:

17:6 Wheresoever I have walked with all Israel, spake I a word to any of the judges of Israel, whom I commanded to feed my people, saying, Why have ye not built me an house of cedars?

7 Now therefore thus shalt thou say unto my servant David, Thus saith the LORD of hosts, I took thee from the sheepcote, even from following the sheep, that thou shouldest be ruler over my people Israel:

8 And I have been with thee whithersoever thou hast walked, and have cut off all thine enemies from before thee, and have made thee a name like the name of the great men that are in the earth.

9 Also I will ordain a place for my people Israel, and will plant them, and they shall dwell in their place, and shall be moved no more; neither shall the children of wickedness waste them any more, as at the beginning,

10 And since the time that I commanded judges to be over my people Israel. Moreover I will subdue all thine enemies. Furthermore I tell thee that the LORD will build thee an house.

NLT **1 Chronicles 17:1** When David was settled in his palace, he summoned Nathan the prophet. "Look," David said, "I am living in a beautiful cedar palace, but the Ark of the LORD's Covenant is out there under a tent!"

3 But that same night God said to Nathan,

4 Go and tell my servant David, 'This is what the LORD has declared: You are not the one to build a house for me to live in.

17:6 Yet no matter where I have gone with the Israelites, I have never once complained to Israel's leaders, the shepherds of my people. I have never asked them, "Why haven't you built me a beautiful cedar house?"'

7 Now go and say to my servant David, 'This is what the LORD of Heaven's Armies has declared: I took you from tending sheep in the pasture and selected you to be the leader of my people Israel.

8 I have been with you wherever you have gone, and I have destroyed all your enemies before your eyes. Now I will make your name as famous as anyone who has ever lived on the earth!

9 And I will provide a homeland for my people Israel, planting them in a secure place where they will never be disturbed. Evil nations won't oppress them as they've done in the past,

10 starting from the time I appointed judges to rule my people Israel. And I will defeat all your enemies. "'Furthermore, I declare that the LORD will build a house for you—a dynasty of kings!

11 And it shall come to pass, when thy days be expired that thou must go to be with thy fathers, that I will raise up thy seed after thee, which shall be of thy sons; and I will establish his kingdom.

12 He shall build me an house, and I will stablish his throne for ever.

13 I will be his father, and he shall be my son: and I will not take my mercy away from him, as I took it from him that was before thee:

14 But I will settle him in mine house and in my kingdom for ever: and his throne shall be established for evermore.

15 According to all these words, and according to all this vision, so did Nathan speak unto David.

11 For when you die and join your ancestors, I will raise up one of your descendants, one of your sons, and I will make his kingdom strong.

12 He is the one who will build a house—a temple—for me. And I will secure his throne forever.

13 I will be his father, and he will be my son. I will never take my favor from him as I took it from the one who ruled before you.

14 I will confirm him as king over my house and my kingdom for all time, and his throne will be secure forever.'"

15 So Nathan went back to David and told him everything the LORD had said in this vision.

In Focus

Each year Shawn and a group of men from the church take a fishing trip together as a kind of retreat. They use this as a time to get away, fellowship together, and spend some serious time in the wilderness at one with nature. This year, the group asked Richard, a new Christian, and a few other brothers to accompany them. Because more brothers were going than usual, the group rented two vans for the 350-mile trip.

While driving along a dark stretch of interstate, a deer stepped into the road directly in front of Shawn. Shawn, being a skilled driver, attempted to swerve but could not avoid colliding with the deer. The impact sent the deer flying into the ditch and sent the vehicle into a frenzy of twists, turns, and spins as it slid across the interstate and finally to a complete stop. After checking to make sure that everyone was safe, the men jumped out of the van to survey the situation.

When they saw the damage, a few men immediately began to worry as they considered the cost associated with repairing the rented vehicle. As the reality of the accident started to settle in, it was obvious that Richard was the most shook up about the ordeal.

Shawn and the others told him not to worry. One by one the brothers talked about how God had kept His promise to be with them and how their prayer for a safe trip had been answered. Needless to say, Richard still had concerns. "Don't you see the condition of that car? We could have been killed!"

Shawn smiled and said, "Not to worry. We took advantage of the unconditional road insurance policy for the vehicle, and it was God's unconditional grace that gave us protection! You see, man, we're covered on all sides."

God's unconditional promises are similar to the unconditional road insurance policy. We can always take God at His Word. His unconditional promises will cover us even when we feel hopeless and helpless, because God never fails.

The People, Places, and Times

Covenant. A covenant is a formal agreement or promise between two parties. In the Old Testament the word for "covenant" (Heb. *beriyth*, **ber-EETH**) is derived from a root word that means "to cut." Hence, a covenant is a "cutting," with reference to the cutting or dividing of animals into two parts, as the contracting parties passed between the animals in making a covenant agreement (see Jeremiah 34:18–19). The act signified that if one of the parties was not able to keep his agreement, he was submitting that what had been done to the animals would also be done unto him.

Throughout Scripture there are a number of covenants made between God and humanity. These many covenants fall into one of two categories: conditional or unconditional. Conditional covenants require one or both parties to perform certain duties before the covenant can be fulfilled. Conversely, unconditional covenants require no action to fulfill the promise(s) made in the covenant. For example, God sealed His covenant with Abraham by allowing His presence to pass between the animal halves (see Genesis 15:17–18). The covenant God made with David in today's lesson is also an unconditional covenant.

Background

The book of Chronicles is believed to have been written between 450 and 435 B.C. as one book. The book began appearing as two part (1 and 2 Chronicles) in the fifteenth century. The book may have been split to make the scroll sizes more manageable, as the original Bible texts were produced on scrolls. Some theologians advocate that the text should be divided into four parts: (1) The first part, composed of the first nine chapters of 1 Chronicles, contains a list of genealogies in the line of Israel down to the time of King David. (2) The remainder of 1 Chronicles contains a history of the reign of David. (3) The first nine chapters of 2 Chronicles contain the history of the reign of King Solomon. (4) The remaining chapters of 2 Chronicles contain the history of the separate kingdom of Judah to the time of the return from Babylonian exile. Some scholars would divide a study of Chronicles into three parts, combining the sections referring to David and Solomon since they represent rule over all the tribes of Israel. The link between David and Solomon is evident, in that God's covenant with David foreshadows the commanding presence of Solomon as David's successor as king.

At-A-Glance

1. David's Consultation with Nathan (1 Chronicles 17:1)
2. Nathan's Encounter with the Word of God (vv. 3–4)
3. God's Covenant with David (vv. 6–15)

In Depth

1. David's Consultation with Nathan (1 Chronicles 17:1)

Although David was the king of Israel, he was very careful to do nothing without prior consultation with the Lord through a priest or prophet (Nathan in this case). Nathan was an important link in communicating the will of God to David. It is notable that David, in all of his royalty, was humble enough to seek the guidance of Nathan concerning his desire to build a house. David could have easily sent out a decree that a house be constructed for the ark; instead, he sought the counsel of the prophet Nathan. This proved to be a wise decision for David as he quickly found that his desire was contradictory to God's will.

Regardless of how much wealth, success, or fame God allows us to acquire in our life, we should always remain humble and be willing to heed the advice of godly individuals He places in our lives.

2. Nathan's Encounter with the Word of God (vv. 3–4)

Nathan had an encounter with God on the same night that he learned of David's desire to build a house for the ark. This was no coincidence or happenstance. This was a case of God illustrating through Nathan's vision how detailed and well-orchestrated His plans were.

When God-fearing individuals, like David and Nathan, sincerely seek the face of God concerning an issue, God will provide an answer. As believers, we need to follow David's example and seek God's guidance concerning all matters, whether they seem trivial or pivotal. When we are operating in God's will in all capacities, then and only then are we able to live life to its fullest.

3. God's Covenant with David (vv. 6–15)

God reminded David that He had never predicated His love on whether or not He had a house of cedar. God further reminded David of how far He had already brought him, from his father's fields as a shepherd to being shepherd over the people of Israel. God had allowed David to reign victorious over all Israel's enemies. As if all He had done for David and Israel up until this point were not enough, God began to make more promises to David. The covenant that God made is an unconditional one, in that it does not hinge on the actions of David or the Children of Israel. In other words, regardless of how bad David and the Children of Israel messed up, they could not forfeit the promises of God.

God's promises to David began with the assurance that God would prepare a place for Israel. The covenant continued with the promise that God would take care of David's offspring, namely his son Solomon. Few things could have made David's heart happier than to know that his seed would continue to prosper even after his time on earth had ended.

God's reference to "thy sons" is not only a reference to Solomon (David's son) but also to Jesus Christ (God's Son). This becomes evident when in verse 14 when God says, "and his throne shall be established for evermore." Clearly, God was not stating that Solomon would rule as king of Israel forever; instead, God was referring to Jesus Christ, who would come and reign as the Saviour of the world forever.

Although covenants are often made between men and women on earth, it is extremely rare that one is made with no conditions. Standard practice assumes that both parties entering into a covenant have expectations which they must meet in order to validate the covenant. However, God gives us His grace and mercy freely without fail. He keeps His word every day. How wonderful it is to know that when we enter God's covenant through Jesus Christ, His promises are forever! *When we accept Jesus as our Lord/Savior, we enter into God's covenant and the covenant lasts forever.*

Search the Scriptures

1. With whom did David consult concerning his desire to build a house for the ark (1 Chronicles 17:1)?

2. What role did God give to the leaders of Israel before David's time (v. 6)?

3. What reminders did God give to David regarding His faithfulness in David's life (vv. 7–8)?

4. What did God mean when He promised David that he would "ordain a place" (v. 9)?

5. What did God promise not to take away from David's son (v. 13)?

Discuss the Meaning

1. What does David's willingness to discuss his plans with Nathan say to us as believers?

2. Why did God mention to David where He had brought him from?

3. What importance can Christians attach to the fact that God's covenant with David stretched beyond David's reign and death?

Lesson in Our Society

As society continues to advance in the areas of education and technology, people are becoming increasingly self-sufficient. This self-sufficiency often causes us to intermingle less and less. More importantly, our contemporary notion of self-sufficiency can create the deception that we have no need to recall God's promises to take care of us. The challenge today is for us to live in a way that models our dependency on God and gives Him gratitude for His unfailing promises. Today, count your blessings and make a promise to seek God's direction and guidance in all things.

Make It Happen

Identify a time where you thought you knew the answer to something important, but after double-checking, you realized that you were wrong. What lesson did you learn as a result of that situation?

Follow the Spirit

What God wants me to do:

_____

_____

Remember Your Thoughts

Special insights I have learned:

_____

_____

More Light on the Text
1 Chronicles 17:1, 3–4, 6–15

David devoted his monarchy to the restoration of public worship. He instituted liturgical worship and praise with the introduction of the musicianship of the Levites. The entrance of the ark into the national capital of Jerusalem moved the people into a realm of prominence among the other nations in ways that Israel had never before experienced. All of this was centered on their worship and praise of Jehovah, the one, true God. Our text today moves beyond David's restoration of worship as a national practice and introduces the idea that David had come to a point in his life where he felt uncomfortable living in secure surroundings that were, in his opinion, more grand than where the ark was kept.

1 Now it came to pass, as David sat in his house, that David said to Nathan the prophet, Lo, I dwell in an house of cedars, but the ark of the covenant of the LORD remaineth under curtains. 17:3 And it came to pass the same night, that the word of God came to Nathan, saying, 4 Go and tell David my servant, Thus saith the LORD, Thou shalt not build me an house to dwell in:

David's home may have been built with timber that comes from a species of Pinus (cedar), an evergreen that grows to a huge size and is known for its durability. Evidence is not clear regarding how grand David's house may have been. However, it is not likely that David's house was at all what we might envision for a king. The Hebrew word for "house" (*bayith*, **BAH-yith**) simply refers to a family abode of the type common in David's time. David's reference to "cedar" (Heb. *'erez*, **EHR-ets**, which means firm or strong) probably refers as much to the strength of his dwelling as to the materials used. In any event, we cannot conclude that David's house was a palace in the modern sense. The text simply states that David "lived" (Heb. *yashab*, **yah-SHAHB**) or dwelt in a well-constructed and permanent home and that he was comfortable in his life.

David's introductory remark to Nathan, "Lo," comes from the Hebrew word *hinneh* (**HIN-eh**), and means "behold." The root of this word is actually another Hebrew term, *hen* (**hayn**), which indicates surprise. David's statement to Nathan, therefore, implies that the idea of the Lord's dwelling being insufficient had either been bothering him or was a revelation that now took hold and caused him concern. David had done for the Lord what he thought was good. In fact, the return of the ark and the new priority of worship were very good. Now, however, being less concerned with external enemies, David realized that he could do better and wanted to fully honor the dwelling place of the Ark of the Covenant.

Part of David's concern was probably that the entire tabernacle and its furnishings were not in Jerusalem. The Levites had continued to worship God in Jerusalem before the ark, but the priests were presenting the offerings and sacrifices of the people before the brazen altar in Gibeon (see 1 Chronicles 16: 37-43). Theologians and biblical scholars alike are at a loss regarding why David did not return the tabernacle and all of its furnishings to Jerusalem at the same time he returned the ark. Perhaps the focus was on restoring the prominence of the ark by showing those who had taken it that the nation was now unified under God. Whatever the reason, only the ark itself resided in Jerusalem, and now David expressed his concerned for unified worship in a more appropriate place.

The Bible refers to five different people by the name of Nathan. The Nathan in this text is David's chief advisor and, on this occasion, David shares his innermost thoughts with Nathan regarding the place of the ark. Nathan is a prophet about whom little is known except for his role as advisor to David and later to Solomon and his mother, Bathsheba. Nathan was not afraid to speak the truth to David and had always spoken to the king with sound counsel based on his own faithfulness to God. It was Nathan whose prophetic gift brought God's accusation against David for having taken Bathsheba and killing her husband, Uriah (see 2 Samuel 11). Nathan sought God before giving David advice and David obviously respected Nathan as a confidant and friend.

Nathan's original response was to tell David to move forward with his plans (v. 2). Apparently it seemed to both Nathan and David that David's heart was in the right place. But when the Lord visited Nathan that night, the prophet was told to go back to David and tell him not to build the house because God was not in the plan. This was not to imply that God was not with David; God refers to David as his "servant" (Heb. *`ebed*, **EH-bed**). But it does make clear that God does not want the establishment of a permanent dwelling place for the ark and the furnishings of the tabernacle to be built by David.

17:6 Wheresoever I have walked with all Israel, spake I a word to any of the judges of Israel, whom I commanded to feed my people, saying, Why have ye not built me an house of cedars?

Jehovah is emphatic in explaining what the goal of human leadership over Israel has been. God forms this question with several Hebrew terms, "wheresoever" or *kol* (**kohl**), meaning "totality" and *asher* (**ah-SHEHR**), which means "what" or "that which." Coupled with the Hebrew word *halak* (**hah-LAHK**) or "walked," these words convey the idea of the totality of the Lord's dealings with Israel.

God never asked or commanded a house to be built for the ark. Basically, the Lord asked whether He had ever spoken or given cause for anyone who served as a leader or judge over Israel to think that a dwelling place for the Lord was needed. During the days of sojourn in the wilderness and later into the Promised Land, such a dwelling for the ark would have been fruitless since the Israelites were constantly on the move. Now that the nation was stable, apparently God had not changed His mind.

Jehovah presented a rhetorical question in order to reiterate the purpose for which He allowed human

"Now go and say to my servant David, 'This is what the LORD of Heaven's Armies has declared: I took you from tending sheep in the pasture and selected you to be the leader of my people Israel" (1 Chronicles 17:7, NLT)

house would not be brick and mortar. By using the term *bayith* coupled with the word "cedar," God made it clear that the house of the Lord would far exceed what David or anyone else could build. Cedar, like human effort, would be insufficient because God's house would become a house of people, generations who would follow Him. This statement looks beyond the reign of David and his son Solomon. It looks forward to the work of Jesus Christ in establishing the house of the Lord.

7 Now therefore thus shalt thou say unto my servant David, Thus saith the LORD of hosts, I took thee from the sheepcote, even from following the sheep, that thou shouldest be ruler over my people Israel: 8 And I have been with thee whithersoever thou hast walked, and have cut off all thine enemies from before thee, and have made thee a name like the name of the great men that are in the earth.

Here God reminded David from whence he came. This may very well have been God's way of both comforting and humbling David. God had prepared David for his current role as a leader. The "sheepcote" (Heb. *naveh*, **nah-VEH**) is a temporary dwelling or abode for sheep and shepherds as they moved from pasture to pasture. While the place in which David slept as king may have been comfortable (not royal), "following the sheep" (Heb. `*achar*, **akh-AR**) reminded David of the years when he had to walk behind the sheep. Of course this was not the most pleasant task since sheep walk in mud, manure, and

leadership over His people. God had "commanded" (Heb. *tsavah*, **tsah-VAH**) or given charge to all of the nation's previous leaders to feed His nation. God's leaders were expected to care for God's people. Again, God's use of the Hebrew term for "feed" (*ra'ah*, **rah-AH**) gave emphasis to this statement. The word actually means "to shepherd." God called His leaders and judges to shepherd, not to build. As shepherds they were to feed, protect, lead, and guide God's people.

David, too, was to be a shepherd, not a builder, and God's use of the phrase "built me an house of cedar" helps to clarify why. The Hebrew word for "house" (*bayith*, **BAH-yith**) also means to establish a household or family. The house of Jehovah was not to be in a stationary place or a single dwelling. God's anything else that may be on the ground. David's development into a leader had come through the muck and mire of life. His experience as a shepherd over sheep had given David the necessary tools to be an effective shepherd to the Children of Israel.

God's response to David said that David was doing exactly what God had called him to do. David, like the previous leaders of the nation, was to shepherd God's flock—Israel. This must have actually been a comforting word because David knew how to shepherd. David understood that the shepherd protected the flock and made sure that the grazing land was rich. By bringing the ark to Jerusalem and instituting worship, David had indeed shepherded God's people.

David had come a long way—from shepherd to king; from lion slayer to great warrior; from anonymity to great fame. God reminded David of all the great things He had done for him. David had seen God's protection and had received many blessings. As a shepherd, David lived a life of relative obscurity before becoming king. David's father, Jesse, had apparently been a man of prominence since references to David are usually accompanied by his father's name. But as a lad, David was the youngest brother and did not achieve the stature of his older siblings (see 1 Samuel 16). God pointed out (v. 8) that He had been with David through the hazards of his days as a shepherd, through his arduous trials as he fled from Saul's sword, and in his many battles with enemy nations. King David had become a great man, esteemed like the leaders of surrounding nations. Through all of this, God had been with David. All of the accolades and honor David received were made possible by God.

9 Also I will ordain a place for my people Israel, and will plant them, and they shall dwell in their place, and shall be moved no more; neither shall the children of wickedness waste them any more, as at the beginning, 10 And since the time that I commanded judges to be over my people Israel. Moreover I will subdue all thine enemies. Furthermore I tell thee that the LORD will build thee an house.

The word "ordain" is translated from the Hebrew word *suwm* (**soom**), which means "to establish." The term "place" is taken from the Hebrew word *maqowm* (**mah-KOHM**), which means "a standing place" such

as a city or even a position of leadership. David's concern had been a permanent home for God's presence, but God said that He alone will establish the permanent home—not for Himself but for His people. God will "plant" (Heb. *nata‘*, **nah-TAH**) His people, meaning that He will establish them physically as well as establishing them as a nation under Him. God also promised David that the nation of Israel would no longer be "moved" (Heb. *ragaz*, **rah-GAHTS**); they would not continue to be disquieted or disturbed. These terms bring to mind the image of planting a tree with roots that will enable it to grow tall, strong, and stable. Furthermore, God said that the people will "dwell" (Heb. *shakan*, **shah-KAHN**), meaning they will be settled as in a permanent residence. These phrases taken together paint a picture for modern Christians of our permanent residence in heaven and even call to mind the residence of the Holy Spirit in the hearts of believers.

God's statement went far beyond the establishment of the nation. He spoke to the relationship of Israel among its neighbors, with whom they had constantly been at war. God referred to the enemies of Israel as "the children of wickedness" (Heb. *bene ‘evelah*, **ben-AY eh-vel-AH**). This term is often translated as unrighteousness or perverseness, and refers to violent deeds of the surrounding nations that followed other gods. The Lord promised in this verse that the opposing nations will not "waste" (Heb. *balah*, **bah-LAH**) or wear upon the Israelites as they had from the "beginning" (Heb. *ri'shown*, **ree-SHOHN**) or in times past. This included when Israel had crossed into the Promised Land, since God made specific reference to the time when the various judges had been appointed to care for Israel.

God also clarified that it will not be David's prowess in war nor the leadership of any other king or chief warrior who will deliver His people. Not unlike the old Negro spiritual whose lyrics say, "Ain't going to study war no more," God told Israel that one day they will not have to be moved. God said that He will subdue for "all" (Heb. *kol*, **kohl**, meaning the totality) of the enemies (Heb. *'oyeb*, **oh-YAYB**) of Israel. The word for "subdue" (Heb. *kana‘*, **kah-NAH**) means to "bend the knee." In other words, it is before Jehovah, the God of Israel, that all nations shall bow. The phrase also carries the connation of humiliation, as God will humiliate the belief of all nations in their false gods. The prophet Isaiah (Isaiah 45:23), and later the apostle Paul (Romans 14:11), picked up this idea in stating that "every knee shall bow" before God.

God's assurances in verses 9 and 10 ended with God's promise to David. While the promise was specifically to David, it also applied to the nation of Israel because David was the king. God told David, who had apparently agonized over building a house for the Lord, that He, Jehovah, the Creator of the universe and all-powerful God, would build a house for David! This is the same Hebrew term, *bayith* (**BAH-yith**), which was used in verses 1 and 6 of our text; but here it carries more specifically the meaning it had in verse 6 and refers to the establishment of the household or descendants of David. For David, this is the ultimate blessing. The Israelites understood that the highest honor was paid to those whose children carried on the legacy of the father's house. God would not only build a physical house for David's family, He would build a heritage of greatness for the children of this king. This covenant continues the promises given to Abraham, Isaac, and Jacob for the greatness of the nation, but it also establishes David's line as rulers of the kingdom. The specific reference in verse 11 is to the reign of Solomon as successor to his father, David.

11 And it shall come to pass, when thy days be expired that thou must go to be with thy fathers, that I will raise up thy seed after thee, which shall be of thy sons; and I will establish his kingdom. 12 He shall build me an house, and I will stablish his throne for ever. 13 I will be his father, and he shall be my son: and I will not take my mercy away from him, as I took it from him that was before thee: 14 But I will settle him in mine house and in my kingdom for ever: and his throne shall be established for evermore.

David's son, Solomon, would build a house for the ark and the throne of Solomon will be established "forever" (Heb. *'owlam*, **oh-LAHM**). This Hebrew phrase means without ending and for an indefinite period. Although David is denied the privilege of building a house for the ark, God let him know that the ark would continue to be a focal point of worship for the Israelites. Solomon would be the one to build the house for the ark. God promised that unlike Saul, from whom God took the kingdom, Solomon would always have God's mercy. These are powerful words that Nathan delivers to David. God always keeps His promises: "God is not a man, that He should tell or act a lie, neither the son of man, that He should feel repentance or compunction [for what He has promised]" (Numbers 23:19, AMP).

In addition, these verses indicate that ultimately, through David's lineage, Christ would come, who would rule forever. As Christians, it should bring us great joy to know that we can and do live in covenant with God. Moreover, we can find great comfort in knowing that God delivers on His promises—nothing can occur that will void God's Word.

15 According to all these words, and according to all this vision, so did Nathan speak unto David.

David probably did not expect this response from the Lord. Certainly, his expression of desire to Nathan and Nathan's response indicate that the two men thought they were operating in God's will; but God does not always allow us to do what we feel is the right thing. Building a home for the ark was not in God's plan for David. Through this story of God's promise to David, Christians can find comfort in knowing that God will intervene in our lives, also, to keep us from going against His will. Many times He will use another person, as He did with Nathan and David, to help us realize His will for our lives. Like David we must be attentive when God allows others to speak His direction and wisdom to us.

Daily Bible Readings

M: God Chose David
Psalm 78:67–72

T: No House for God
1 Chronicles 17:1–6

W: God's House for David
1 Chronicles 17:7–10

T: A House of Ancestors
1 Chronicles 17:11–15

F: Great Deeds of God
1 Chronicles 17:16–19

S: A House of Israel
1 Chronicles 17:20–22

S: The House of David
1 Chronicles 17:23–27

TEACHING TIPS

March 16
Bible Study Guide 3

1. Words You Should Know
A. Commandments (1 Chronicles 28:7–8) *mitsvah* (Heb.)—The ordinances and precepts that compose the Law given to Moses.

B. Judgments (v. 7) *mishpat* (Heb.)—The decision of the Lord, which may be part of or apart from the written Law of Moses.

2. Teacher Preparation
Unifying Principle—Chosen for a Specific Task We all desire to do something worthwhile. Still, we must be aware of our limitations and our gifts—using them only for tasks to which God has called us.

A. Pray for the students in your class.

B. Carefully review the Bible Study Guide, taking notes for clarification. Consult the *Precepts For Living®* CD-ROM and complete lesson 3 in the *Precepts For Living® Personal Study Guide* for more information on David's life.

C. Before class, prepare an outline using the At-A-Glance topics.

3. Starting the Lesson
A. Lead the class in prayer.

B. Have the class read the In Focus story. Ask class members to recall a time when they had their hearts set on doing something, but never got to do it because of circumstances, or did it anyway and regretted not heeding God's warnings. Make the connection to David's situation: God had a better plan and would use Solomon to fulfill the task.

4. Getting into the Lesson
A. If possible, have a class member or an invited guest present today's Focal Verses as a dramatic reading.

B. Teach the lesson using the outline you prepared. Encourage class participation by using the Search the Scriptures and Discuss the Meaning questions.

5. Relating the Lesson to Life
A. Summarize the lesson by explaining that Solomon was told to do three things: (1) "keep and seek for all the commandments of the LORD"—1 Chronicles 28:8; (2) "serve him with a perfect heart and with a willing mind"—v. 9; (3) "Be strong and of good courage, and do it: fear not, nor be dismayed"—v. 20. Give small groups of students one of the three statements and ask the groups to identify at least three ways we can use this advice in our own lives.

B. Have the class summarize the promises and warnings God made to Solomon. Ask for comments on how God is keeping those promises and warnings in the lives of class members.

C. Ask if any student has an insight that he or she would like to share.

6. Arousing Action
A. Remind the class that, ultimately, today's lesson is advice from a father to a son. Have the class read Lesson in Our Society and determine what advice they might give to their children about the importance of following God's Word.

B. Allow class members to meditate privately for a few moments on their responses to the Make It Happen section.

C. Remind the class to read the Daily Bible Readings.

D. End the class with prayer.

Worship Guide

For the Superintendent or Teacher
Theme: God Calls Solomon to Build the Temple
Theme Song: "Lord, Make Me a Sanctuary"
Devotional Reading: Psalm 132
Prayer

GOD CALLS SOLOMON TO BUILD THE TEMPLE

Bible Background • 1 CHRONICLES 28:1–28
Printed Text • 1 CHRONICLES 28:5–10, 20–21 Devotional Reading • PSALM 132

AIM for Change

By the end of the lesson, we will:

UNDERSTAND our limitations, knowing what things God has not given us permission to do;

BE CONVINCED that God can enable us to use whatever abilities He has given us; and

PRAY for direction and strength to perform our assigned tasks.

Keep in Mind

"Take heed now; for the Lord hath chosen thee to build an house for the sanctuary: be strong, and do it" (1 Chronicles 28:10).

Focal Verses

KJV 1 Chronicles 28:5 And of all my sons, (for the LORD hath given me many sons,) he hath chosen Solomon my son to sit upon the throne of the kingdom of the LORD over Israel.

6 And he said unto me, Solomon thy son, he shall build my house and my courts: for I have chosen him to be my son, and I will be his father.

7 Moreover I will establish his kingdom for ever, if he be constant to do my commandments and my judgments, as at this day.

8 Now therefore in the sight of all Israel the congregation of the LORD, and in the audience of our God, keep and seek for all the commandments of the LORD your God: that ye may possess this good land, and leave it for an inheritance for your children after you for ever.

9 And thou, Solomon my son, know thou the God of thy father, and serve him with a perfect heart and with a willing mind: for the LORD searcheth all hearts, and understandeth all the imaginations of the thoughts: if thou seek him, he will be found of thee; but if thou forsake him, he will cast thee off for ever.

10 Take heed now; for the LORD hath chosen thee to build an house for the sanctuary: be strong, and do it.

28:20 And David said to Solomon his son, Be strong and of good courage, and do it: fear not, nor be dismayed: for the LORD God, even my God, will be with thee; he will not fail thee, nor forsake

NLT 1 Chronicles 28:5 And from among my sons—for the LORD has given me many—he chose Solomon to succeed me on the throne of Israel and to rule over the LORD's kingdom.

6 He said to me, 'Your son Solomon will build my Temple and its courtyards, for I have chosen him as my son, and I will be his father.

7 And if he continues to obey my commands and regulations as he does now, I will make his kingdom last forever.'

8 "So now, with God as our witness, and in the sight of all Israel—the LORD's assembly—I give you this charge. Be careful to obey all the commands of the LORD your God, so that you may continue to possess this good land and leave it to your children as a permanent inheritance.

9 "And Solomon, my son, learn to know the God of your ancestors intimately. Worship and serve him with your whole heart and a willing mind. For the LORD sees every heart and knows every plan and thought. If you seek him, you will find him. But if you forsake him, he will reject you forever.

10 So take this seriously. The LORD has chosen you to build a Temple as his sanctuary. Be strong, and do the work."

28:20 Then David continued, "Be strong and courageous, and do the work. Don't be afraid or discouraged, for the LORD God, my God, is with you. He will not fail you or forsake you. He will see to it that all the thee, until thou hast finished all the work for the service of the house of the LORD.

21 And, behold, the courses of the priests and the Levites, even they shall be with thee for all the service of the house of God: and there shall be with thee for all manner of workmanship every willing skilful man, for any manner of service: also the princes and all the people will be wholly at thy commandment.

In Focus

A major nonprofit corporation wanted to "give back" to the community and make a real difference for the city. If the project was successful, it would become a prototype for cities around the country. For the first four months, things went very well, but at midyear the project was losing ground. The fallout was starting to impact other projects and affect the corporation's reputation for providing services to the community. The project supervisor, Margaret, was pushing people to work harder and talking about what she wanted the team to do and how she wanted to be the first team to make the goal, but her approach wasn't working. New ideas were definitely needed.

Within three months, the management moved Margaret, and Barbara, a new manager, came on board. Barbara's style was just different enough that team members felt more included in the vision. Team meetings took on new life as people began to see this as an achievable goal for the team and not just the leader.

After reaching new goals and receiving recognition from the national office, the vice president of the division hosted a luncheon to recognize each team member. Barbara was thanked for reenergizing the team, but a special commendation was given to the previous supervisor, Margaret, for her vision and direction. In his speech, the vice president acknowledged that Margaret had taken the team from an idea to a prototype and the organization had benefited by her effort.

"However," the vice president said, "when Margaret felt that she had taken it as far as she could, she asked that we consider Barbara and we did. It takes a true leader to accept when it is time to pass the work to the person who can take it to the next level. Margaret laid a good foundation and because of that Barbara and the team were able to succeed."

Regardless of how talented, gifted, or anointed we may be, we should be more than willing to put our own agenda aside for the

work related to the Temple of the LORD is finished correctly.

21 The various divisions of priests and Levites will serve in the Temple of God. Others with skills of every kind will volunteer, and the officials and the entire nation are at your command."

sake of seeing God's will done. When in your life has God said for you to "pass the torch" for the greater glory of God's mission?

The People, Places, and Times

Conditional Covenant. God's covenants with humanity were of two types: conditional and unconditional (see lesson 2, March 9). David's words indicate that God's promises to Solomon are conditional, meaning that Solomon must follow the guidelines in order to receive God's continued blessing.

Background

By the time Solomon is introduced as the successor to the throne of Israel, David is nearing the end of his life. At his death, a relatively short time after Solomon's reign began, David was 70 years old. David was 30 years old when he assumed the throne of Israel, which means his rule lasted for approximately 40 years. After so many years as the leader of Israel, David had gained the respect, love, and admiration of the people. Today's lesson begins with David officially introducing his successor and son, Solomon, as the new king of the people of Israel.

At-A-Glance

1. The Royal Charge to Solomon Regarding the People of Israel (1 Chronicles 28:5–10)
2. The Spiritual Challenge and Encouragement to Solomon (vv. 20–21)

In Depth

1. The Royal Charge to Solomon Regarding the People of Israel (1 Chronicles 28:5–10)

David, being advanced in age, realized that his season was ending and his purposes concerning Israel had been fulfilled. After 40 years as ruler of Israel, this must have been a difficult time for David. However, he exudes his characteristic courage and uses his last days to make Solomon's first days (and ultimately his entire reign) as fruitful as possible. David's behavior is a prime example of the mind-set we should have when we are called to serve.

While introducing Solomon as the new ruler of Israel, David took time to explain to Solomon the king's responsibility to continue to keep God's commandments. Only obedience to the Lord would allow Solomon to complete God's chosen path for him and allow the people to remain in the land. Their obedience would also insure that their descendants would possess the land. This admonition from David gave the people of Israel the fundamental formula by which David had been successful for the previous 40 years.

Regardless to the nature of our task, whether at home, church, school, or work, our assignments are not for an infinite period of time. We all have an obligation to accomplish the tasks at hand during our respective assignments. Furthermore, we have an obligation to leave things in such a way that the entity (the family, the ministry, the club, etc.) can continue to make strides even after our season has lapsed. In fact, if we are successful at completing our task, those who come behind us will have no excuse for falling into the same potholes, traps, and snares that we fell into because our example should warn them and teach them how to prevent such pitfalls.

2. The Spiritual Challenge and Encouragement to Solomon (vv. 20–21)

David was compelled to give further instructions to Solomon. Having spent the last 40 years as king of Israel, David knew firsthand the struggle that leadership entails; therefore, he warned Solomon of the tough days ahead and encouraged him to be steadfast. In verse 20, David alludes to the time when Solomon will have "finished all the work for the service of the house of the Lord." In this statement, David subtly reminds Solomon that one day his season as ruler, like David, will also come to an end. Nevertheless, the great hope in this statement is that the Lord will be with Solomon throughout the process, ensuring that Solomon will be able to complete the task that God had given him.

Most of us have a desire to do something significant with our lives. However, being called or chosen by God has more to do with availability than ability, because God often calls upon us to accomplish tasks far beyond our imagination. David, although he was quite capable of building a temple to God, was not called to do so. Instead, God choose Solomon, David's son, to accomplish the task. This is profound. In passing the torch, David was telling the leaders and the people that their hope must not be in him, but in God. David was reminding the people that it was God who chose the house of David, God who determined who would build the temple, and God who would remain when David was gone.

Search the Scriptures

1. What must Solomon do in order for God to establish his kingdom forever (1 Chronicles 28:7–8)?

2. What instructions does David give Solomon regarding his heart and his service to God (v. 9)?

3. How long did David tell Solomon that God would be with him (v. 20)?

Discuss the Meaning

1. Take this opportunity to share your "calling" with your fellow classmates.

2. Ministry is a team effort requiring the participation, cooperation, and input of all parties in order for it to be the most effective. Begin to identify some of the strengths of fellow class members and how those strengths can be used to serve God and one another.

Lesson in Our Society

More and more, American culture has embraced a theme of self-centeredness and greed. Everyone is seemingly pursuing material possessions, notoriety, fortune, and fame, and doing so at the cost of forsaking everything else in their lives. Although these pursuits are not wicked in themselves, the pursuit of these things can cause believers to stray farther and farther away from God's will. In fact, if we are not careful to remain in God's will as we pursue the things we desire, we will forfeit the blessings God desires to give us. The pursuit of our goals should be guided by God's principles so that our successes result in a desire to serve God and others more than just ourselves.

Make It Happen

Think of an area of ministry you are excited about. Now ask yourself if you have consulted God in prayer regarding whether or not that is the ministry where

He would have you to operate. If you are already committed to a ministry, seek God's direction in how to better serve Him and others in that capacity.

Follow the Spirit

What God wants me to do:

_____

_____

Remember Your Thoughts

Special insights I have learned:

_____

_____

More Light On The Text

1 Chronicles 28:5–10, 20–21

5 And of all my sons, (for the LORD hath given me many sons,) he hath chosen Solomon my son to sit upon the throne of the kingdom of the LORD over Israel. 6 And he said unto me, Solomon thy son, he shall build my house and my courts: for I have chosen him to be my son, and I will be his father. 7 Moreover I will establish his kingdom for ever, if he be constant to do my commandments and my judgments, as at this day.

Our text today comes as David's life was drawing to an end. The chapter begins with David's assembly of the princes and leaders of the nation. Before the ent-ire congregation of Israel, David explained that he once had a desire to build a house for the Lord, but that God had denied his request because David's reign was bloody. This is a reference to the many people who had died in wars as David fought for Israel, but it is also a declaration against the innocent blood David spilled in the murder of Uriah (see 2 Samuel 11).

David recounted that of all his sons, Solomon, whose name means "peace" (Heb. *shelomoh*, **shel-oh-MOH**, from the Heb. *shalowm*, **shah-LOHM**), had been chosen by God to ascend to the throne at David's death and to build the house of the Lord. God had chosen and David was making a public declaration so that the entire nation would know that Solomon was not just David's choice; he was God's choice. Notice, too, that David did not say, "Solomon shall sit upon my throne." Instead Solomon would dwell on the "throne of the kingdom of the Lord (Jehovah) over Israel." Throughout his reign and despite wars, rebellions, and personal strife, David kept the worship of Jehovah as the central focus of the kingdom. Now David publicly stated once more that the kingdom belonged to God. Jehovah reigned over Israel, and Solomon would occupy the seat of human government over God's people.

David addressed Solomon face-to-face as he publicly declared his desire and God's instructions regarding the building of the Temple. This was not the first time David had instructed Solomon regarding this building for the Lord (see 1 Chronicles 22). In verse six, however, David began with the promise of God to him for Solomon. First, "Solomon thy son" was selected by God for this work. Second, Solomon was to build the house and the courts. The magnitude of the project was beginning to take shape. Third, God's choice of Solomon was not just that he should be king. Solomon would be God's son and God would be his father. What a magnificent and intimate statement! David's life was at a close but his son would not be fatherless. Jehovah Himself would be Solomon's father. The Hebrew term for "father" (*ab*, **ahb**) goes beyond God's being the father of Solomon alone. This is a declaration that God would be the father of the nation of Israel.

David explained that God promised not only to place Solomon on the throne but also to "establish his kingdom forever" (v. 7). However, the blessing of Jehovah upon Solomon was conditional. Solomon would only enjoy God's favor "if." He and his children would remain on the throne only *if* he was able to be "constant" (Heb. *chazaq*, **khah-ZAHK**) "to do" (*'asah*, **ah-SAH**) God's commandments and judgments. Or, Solomon had to be persistent and willing to follow Jehovah resolutely in spite of opposition or circumstance.

God did not want Solomon to just make public declarations of God's goodness. Solomon was specifically instructed to do—to make, to produce, to participate fully in accomplishing—God's Law. The term "commandments" (Heb. *mitsvah*, **mits-VAH**) refers to the ordinances and precepts that compose the Law, which was given to Moses. The word for "judgments" (Heb. *mishpat*, **mish-PAHT**) refers to the decisions of the Lord. God had a master plan for Solomon's reign, and Solomon was to remain as faithful to that during all the days of his life as he was on the day he stood before his father, David, to take responsibility for the nation.

8 Now therefore in the sight of all Israel the congregation of the LORD, and in the audience of our God, keep and seek for all the commandments of the

LORD your God: that ye may possess this good land, and leave it for an inheritance for your children after you forever.

Now that David had reported God's statement, he gave a personal charge to his son. David named the witnesses present at this confirmation of Solomon's acceptance of God's will. David said that Solomon was standing before "all of Israel," which is "the congregation of the Lord." Solomon's audience was not a nameless mass of underlings. The entire nation was represented, and the responsibility would be to care for the congregation of the Lord. David did not call these people Solomon's constituents or subjects. These were the people who Jehovah, the self-existent God, delivered and called to Himself. They were the offspring of Abraham, Isaac, and Jacob. They were collectively the people God delivered from Egypt; the people He placed in the Promised Land.

Furthermore, David said that Solomon's ascent to the throne was taking place before the audience of God. "Audience" is from the Hebrew term *ozen* (**OH-zen**), which literally means the ear of God (Heb. *Elohiym*, **el-oh-HEEM**), the divine judge and ruler. Solomon's acceptance of leadership was much more than pomp; it was a declaration before the Almighty Judge.

Solomon was first to "keep" (Heb. *shamar*, **shah-MAR**) or guard God's commandments. The Hebrew term means that Solomon was to reverence God's Law as precious and dear. He was to observe God's Law and even celebrate it among the people and in his own life. Second, Solomon was to "seek for" (Heb. *darash*, **dah-RAHSH**) God's presence and direction in everything he did. This does not mean that Solomon was to walk about looking as if God and God's Law were lost. Instead it means that Solomon was to make careful inquiry through prayer and worship. The two phrases cannot be separated. In order to keep the Law, Solomon had to seek God's guidance through worship and prayer so that he could apply God's precepts in proper judgment as he ruled God's people. If he were to do this faithfully and consistently, God had promised that Solomon would "possess this good land, and leave it for an inheritance for your children." The responsibility of Solomon was not just for himself, but for the generations to come. Without Solomon's faithfulness, his children would not enjoy the continued blessings of God in leadership over Israel.

9 And thou, Solomon my son, know thou the God of thy father, and serve him with a perfect heart and with a willing mind: for the LORD searcheth all hearts, and understandeth all the imaginations of the thoughts: if thou seek him, he will be found of thee; but if thou forsake him, he will cast thee off for ever. 10 Take heed now; for the LORD hath chosen thee to build an house for the sanctuary: be strong, and do it.

Verses 9 and 10 present sound advice and an ultimatum. "If thou seek him, he will be found," but "if thou forsake him, he will cast thee off for ever." David's fatherly advice was that Solomon must follow God with a "perfect heart" (Heb. *leb shalem*, **layb shah-LAYM**). This implies that in order to keep a covenant relationship with God, Solomon had to demonstrate determination and moral character. Solomon was also told to have a "willing mind" (Heb. *nephesh chaphetsah*, **NEH-fesh khah-fayts-AH**) to "serve" (Heb. *'abad*, **ah-BAHD**) God. This means that Solomon's entire being, including his emotions, was to be used to delight God and fulfill God's purpose on behalf of the nation of Israel.

David also assured Solomon that the Lord "searches" (Heb. *darash*, **dah-RAHSH**) the human heart. He assured him that God would search his heart to discern Solomon's faithfulness. God also "understands" (Heb. *biyn*, **been**) fully what our thoughts and intentions are. God cannot be deceived, and He will not accept half-hearted lip service. Therefore David urged Solomon to "Take heed now; for the LORD hath chosen thee to build an house for the sanctuary: be strong, and do it" (v. 10). God's selection of Solomon and His purpose for Solomon's reign was now established. It was up to Solomon to make a declaration, a promise, and a decision. "Now" (Heb. *'attah*, **ah-TAH**) means "immediately." Solomon did not need to seek advice or get a consensus. He had to make up his mind and be governed by his decision for the rest of his life. As if to keep Solomon from becoming too confident in his own righteousness, David warned Solomon that problems and temptations would come his way during the building of the Temple; but David told his son to "be strong and do it."

We are advised, like Solomon, not to make foolish decisions. There are times when we dare to believe that God is not paying attention to us, and we think we can get away with many things. But David lets us know that the Lord seeks with care to know, not just our hearts, but our thoughts as well, which in turn includes our "imaginations" (Heb. *yetser*, **YAY-tser**). Nothing is concealed from God. He knows our limitations far better than we ever do, and we can trust that He will not give us an assignment beyond our capabilities. We, too, must remember that the enemy of our souls will surely do all manner of things to discourage us when we are about the business of our Lord. It is necessary that we continually pray for direction and strength to perform the tasks that God has assigned to us.

28:20 And David said to Solomon his son, Be strong and of good courage, and do it: fear not, nor be dismayed: for the LORD God, even my God, will be with thee; he will not fail thee, nor forsake thee, until thou hast finished all the work for the service of the house of the LORD.

Again Solomon was encouraged to be strong, but also of "good courage" (Heb. *'amats*, **ah-MAHTS**). Solomon was to be alert, courageous, brave, stout, bold, solid, and hard. The task of building God's temple would take strength and courage. Solomon would face many things that could go wrong, both in construction and with the actions of humankind, yet he was told not to "fear" or "be dismayed" (Heb. *chathath*, **khah-THAHTH**). Solomon was not to allow his spirit and resolve to be shattered, broken, or afraid, because God would not fail or forsake him. The work he was undertaking for the Lord would come to pass, and it would meet the end God had ordained.

21 And, behold, the courses of the priests and the Levites, even they shall be with thee for all the service of the house of God: and there shall be with thee for all manner of workmanship every willing skilful man, for any manner of service: also the princes and all the people will be wholly at thy commandment.

When God has a plan, He pays attention to detail. The word "courses" (Heb. *machaloqeth*, **mahkh-ahl-OH-keth**) is a technical term of organization. The priests and Levites were organized into groups in order to undertake the continued service needed for the worship before the ark and the sacrifices before the brazen altar. David explained that all of the priests and Levites were behind Solomon and would serve in any capacity to see this place of worship built and consecrated to God's service.

The men and others throughout the nation were available for "all manner of workmanship." "Workmanship" (Heb. *mela'kah*, **mel-aw-KAW**) connotes occupation or business. While these men served as ministers in worship, they were also skilled laborers and artisans. Verse 21 makes it clear that all the people who had been set in place to help with the building are "were" (Heb. *nadiyb*, **nah-DEEB**), meaning that their hearts had been inclined by God. They were also noble in mind and of good character. The entire nation was available for whatever was needed and awaited Solomon's direction and command.

What powerful lessons we can learn from today's text! God has a plan for how His worship should be conducted and how His followers should live their lives. We have only to be willing to give the talents He has given us to bring His kingdom to fruition.

Daily Bible Readings

M: God's Promise to David
Psalm 132:1–12
T: God Chose Solomon
1 Chronicles 28:1–5
W: David Advises Solomon
1 Chronicles 28:6–8
T: With Single Mind and Willing Heart
1 Chronicles 28:9–10
F: David's Plan for the Temple
1 Chronicles 28:11–19
S: God Is with You
1 Chronicles 28:20–21
S: For God's Chosen
Psalm 132:13–18

TEACHING TIPS

March 23
Bible Study Guide 4

1. Words You Should Know

A. Cubits (2 Chronicles 6:13) *'ammah* (Heb.)—An ancient measurement believed to equal about 18 inches, drawn from the length of the forearm below the elbow.

B. Kneeled down (v. 13) *barak* (Heb.)—To "bless God" by bending or bowing before the Lord.

C. Behoved (Luke 24:46) *dei* (Gk.)—To be necessary, to be bound, to be needful.

D. Repentance (v. 47) *metanoia* (Gk.)—To change your mind regarding your purpose or actions.

2. Teacher Preparation

Unifying Principle—Whose Promises Can You Trust? Promises are to be kept, but many never come to fulfillment. God is faithful in keeping promises. It was many years in the making, but ultimately the temple was built. It was many centuries in coming, but the Messiah did come and the resurrection of Christ changed life forever. God, indeed, fulfills His promises.

A. Pray for the students in your class.

B. Carefully review the Bible Study Guide to prepare for today's lesson. Use the information on the *Precepts For Living*® CD-ROM and lesson 4 in the *Precepts For Living*® Personal Study Guide.

C. Secure a diagram of Solomon's temple and a drawing of the open tomb to display in class this week. If possible, find a drawing of the tabernacle.

D. Spend part of your devotional time this week in meditation on God's promises.

3. Starting the Lesson

A. Ask a volunteer to read the In Focus story and then lead the class in brainstorming a list of promises God has kept in their lives.

B. Lead the class in prayer, giving thanks for God's faithfulness in keeping His promises.

4. Getting into the Lesson

A. After having the class read the Focal Verses, display the pictures of Solomon's temple and the tabernacle. Explain how the temple followed the general pattern given to Moses for the design of the tabernacle.

B. Continue discussion of 2 Chronicles, recording on chart paper the class response to the major items in Solomon's speech.

C. Turn to the Scripture from Luke and display the picture of the open tomb.

5. Relating the Lesson to Life

A. Spend time answering the questions in Discuss the Meaning.

B. As you close, ask the class to determine how the open tomb is the fulfillment of the temple and how the promises to David and Solomon are fulfilled in Christ.

C. Ask if any student has an insight that he or she would like to share regarding today's lesson.

6. Arousing Action

A. Read the Lesson in Our Society section to the class. Invite the students to share opinions of this issue. Brainstorm a list of suggestions that will help us to keep our promises to God and others.

B. Lead the class in responding to the Make It Happen challenge.

C. Encourage your class to complete the Daily Bible Readings in preparation for next week's class time.

D. End the class with prayer.

Worship Guide

For the Superintendent or Teacher
Theme: Fulfillment of God's Promise
Theme Song: "Thank You, Lord"
Devotional Reading: Psalm 135:1–5
Prayer

FULFILLMENT OF GOD'S PROMISE

Bible Background • 2 CHRONICLES 6; LUKE 24
Printed Text • 2 CHRONICLES 6:12–17; LUKE 24:44–49 Devotional Reading • PSALM 135:1–5

AIM for Change

By the end of the lesson, we will:

LEARN that God keeps His Word;

TRUST God more than humans; and

IDENTIFY and celebrate fulfilled promises.

Keep in Mind

"The LORD therefore hath performed his word that he hath spoken: for I am risen up in the room of David my father, and am set on the throne of Israel, as the LORD promised, and have built the house for the name of the LORD God of Israel" (2 Chronicles 6:10).

Focal Verses

KJV **2 Chronicles 6:12** And he stood before the altar of the LORD in the presence of all the congregation of Israel, and spread forth his hands:

13 For Solomon had made a brasen scaffold, of five cubits long, and five cubits broad, and three cubits high, and had set it in the midst of the court: and upon it he stood, and kneeled down upon his knees before all the congregation of Israel, and spread forth his hands toward heaven,

14 And said, O LORD God of Israel, there is no God like thee in the heaven, nor in the earth; which keepest covenant, and shewest mercy unto thy servants, that walk before thee with all their hearts:

15 Thou which hast kept with thy servant David my father that which thou hast promised him; and spakest with thy mouth, and hast fulfilled it with thine hand, as it is this day.

16 Now therefore, O LORD God of Israel, keep with thy servant David my father that which thou hast promised him, saying, There shall not fail thee a man in my sight to sit upon the throne of Israel; yet so that thy children take heed to their way to walk in my law, as thou hast walked before me.

17 Now then, O LORD God of Israel, let thy word be verified, which thou hast spoken unto thy servant David.

Luke 24:44 And he said unto them, These are the words which I spake

unto you, while I was yet with you, that all things must be fulfilled, which were written in the law of Moses, and in the prophets, and in the psalms, concerning me.

NLT **2 Chronicles 6:12** Then Solomon stood before the altar of the LORD in front of the entire community of Israel, and he lifted his hands in prayer.

13 Now Solomon had made a bronze platform 7 1/2 feet long, 7 1/2 feet wide, and 4 1/2 feet high and had placed it at the center of the Temple's outer courtyard. He stood on the platform, and then he knelt in front of the entire community of Israel and lifted his hands toward heaven.

14 He prayed, "O LORD, God of Israel, there is no God like you in all of heaven and earth. You keep your covenant and show unfailing love to all who walk before you in wholehearted devotion.

15 You have kept your promise to your servant David, my father. You made that promise with your own mouth, and with your own hands you have fulfilled it today.

16 "And now, O LORD, God of Israel, carry out the additional promise you made to your servant David, my father. For you said to him, 'If your descendants guard their behavior and faithfully follow my Law as you have done, one of them will always sit on the throne of Israel.'

17 Now, O LORD, God of Israel, fulfill this promise to your servant David.

Luke 24:44 Then he said, "When I was with you before, I told you that everything written about me in the law of Moses and the prophets and in the Psalms must be fulfilled."

45 Then he opened their minds to understand the Scriptures.

45 Then opened he their understanding, that they might understand the scriptures,

46 And said unto them, Thus it is written, and thus it behoved Christ to suffer, and to rise from the dead the third day:

47 And that repentance and remission of sins should be preached in his name among all nations, beginning at Jerusalem.

48 And ye are witnesses of these things.

49 And, behold, I send the promise of my Father upon you: but tarry ye in the city of Jerusalem, until ye be endued with power from on high.

46 And he said, "Yes, it was written long ago that the Messiah would suffer and die and rise from the dead on the third day.

47 It was also written that this message would be proclaimed in the authority of his name to all the nations, beginning in Jerusalem: 'There is forgiveness of sins for all who repent.'

48 You are witnesses of all these things.

49 "And now I will send the Holy Spirit, just as my Father promised. But stay here in the city until the Holy Spirit comes and fills you with power from heaven."

In Focus

Sarah grew up having no relationship with her biological father. Her parents divorced when she was only 3 years old and her father never made an effort to be in her life since that time. For many years Sarah yearned to know her father. She felt that there must be a way for her to earn his love and admiration. Nevertheless, Sarah managed to remain focused and not get deterred as she pursued excellence in her life.

Her relentless attitude placed her at the top of her profession. Sarah was a firefighter, one of the few women in that role in her city. Her outstanding performance and hard work earned her a special commendation and promotion, which were announced in the media. On the eve of the ceremony, Sarah was cleaning out her old office as her telephone rang. She answered in her usual professional voice. A man asked, "Is this Sarah?"

Hesitantly she responded, "Yes, this is Sarah. Who's calling?"

The voice said, "Sarah, this is your father. I read about you in the paper. You looked so much like your mother that I knew it was you. I've been afraid all these years to call, but seeing your picture, I knew I could wait no longer."

Sarah was overwhelmed and overjoyed. She spent the next hour conversing with her father and finally invited him to come to the public ceremony.

Following the commendation, Sarah made a brief speech and then returned to her seat. She scanned the massive audience but had no way of knowing which person was her father. As Sarah left the platform, a man approached her with flowers and said, "Sarah. I'm Ray. I'm your dad."

The two embraced. She told her father how glad she was that he was there and she silently thanked God for remembering the prayer she had prayed since childhood.

Some prayers are answered immediately, and others may not be answered until the time God ordains in the future. Regardless of how long it takes, God will come through just like He promised. What promises has He already kept in your life? Which promises do you believe for in the future?

The People, Places, and Times

Solomon's Temple. Solomon's temple is also known as the "first temple," because it was the first temple to be built in Jerusalem. Building the temple was no small undertaking. It took a substantial amount of time to merely accumulate the materials needed to construct it. The materials David purchased for the temple during his reign were passed on to Solomon upon his ascent to the throne. David bequeathed to Solomon the financial resources of 100,000 talents of gold and 1,000,000 talents of silver toward construction of the temple (1 Chronicles 22:14). It is estimated that it took approximately three years to fully prepare for building the temple. Construction of the "first temple" began during the fourth year of Solomon's reign (2 Chronicles 3:2) and was completed in the eleventh year, a period of about seven and one half years.

The Resurrected Christ. As children, many of us learned the Easter story and got the idea that once Christ was risen, He was not seen again. This is far from true. The resurrected Christ was seen by Mary Magdalene (Mark 16:9), the disciples on the Emmaus road (Luke 24:13–32), the Eleven (Luke

24:36–49), and others (1 Corinthians 15:5–8). In fact, Jesus spent 40 days living with the disciples before His final ascension into heaven (Acts 1:3). The events listed in our lesson text take place during the 40-day period following the Resurrection.

Background

Solomon's construction of the temple for the Ark of the Covenant was a project that had been desired for quite sometime. David, Solomon's father, originally had the desire; however, God commanded David not to undertake the task. Instead, God promised David that his son would build the resting place for the ark. The temple followed the pattern given to Moses in the construction of the tabernacle, the portable worship center carried by the Children of Israel as they wandered in the wilderness. Although the temple built by Solomon was more elaborate, it still had all of the basic rooms and furnishings of the original tabernacle.

Today's lesson begins with Solomon publicly addressing the people of Israel concerning the recently completed temple. Solomon acknowledges the fulfillment of the promises God made to David. Then Solomon gives thanks to God for making good on His promises and asks God for His continued blessings.

The events described in our Scripture reference from Luke take place during the 40 days following the Resurrection. After Jesus' ascent, the disciples were told to wait in Jerusalem. On the fiftieth day, the Day of Pentecost, the Holy Spirit descended (see Acts 2). The teaching Jesus shares with His disciples during the 40-day period is recorded in today's text.

At-A-Glance

1. Solomon's Public Acknowledgment of God's Fulfilled Promise (2 Chronicles 6:12–17)
2. Christ's Promises to the Disciples (Luke 24:44–49)

In Depth

1. Solomon's Public Acknowledgment of God's Fulfilled Promise (2 Chronicles 6:12–17)

The construction of the temple required a large amount of time, as well as huge financial, physical,

psychological, and spiritual resources. The demands of building the temple weighed heavily upon Solomon as the leader of the kingdom, and upon the people of Israel. The magnitude of this mission and the responsibility to fulfill the wishes of his father, David, were no doubt equal pressures. It is understandable then that Solomon was humbled and prayerful after the completion of the temple. Similarly, when we as believers face and overcome an overwhelming and seemingly insurmountable obstacle, we ought to celebrate our victory and God's grace in a prayerful posture.

Solomon gave his prayer of thanksgiving and dedication in the presence of all of Israel. This was a key action for making certain that the people of Israel kept their faith and focus on God rather than on Solomon. As human beings, we have a tendency to incorrectly shift our faith and focus from God to the individual through whom God has chosen to do great things. Regardless of what great things people accomplish, we must remember that only with God's anointing and blessing can those things be done. Solomon provides a prime example of how we should behave if God has chosen to use us do great things. By immediately and publicly giving reverence to God, Solomon declared before the people that building the temple had been God's work.

2. Christ's Promises to the Disciples (Luke 24:44–49)

In 2 Chronicles, we saw the fulfillment of God's promises to Solomon's father, David, by way of completion of the temple. In the Scripture from Luke, we see Jesus Christ, the manifestation of promises made centuries before, as He proclaimed to His disciples that the promise of the Father would come as "power from on high," a reference to the Holy Spirit.

The promise of the Holy Spirit is still available to believers. Through God's power we are able to accept Jesus' Great Commission and become "fishers of men." Jesus stressed that although the disciples were to spread His Gospel throughout all nations, He wanted them to begin in Jerusalem. This can also be applied to us as believers, because we must be bold in allowing our ministry to begin within our families, friends, and others who are near to us. *We need to build our confidence before we go out to total strangers.*

Search the Scriptures

1. What are the dimensions and the purpose of the scaffold on which Solomon stood (2 Chronicles 6:13)?

2. What were the conditions God gave for continuing to bless Israel (v. 16)?

3. Where does Jesus tell the disciples to tarry (wait) (Luke 24:49)?

Discuss the Meaning

1. What promise does Solomon discuss in each verse?

2. Why were those promises important to Solomon, the people, and the nation?

3. Why are the promises discussed by Solomon important to us as Christians today?

After reading the passage from Luke, ask:

4. What promises did Jesus make and why were they important to the disciples?

5. How and why are the promises of Jesus important to us as Christians today?

6. Why did Christ specifically state to the disciples the importance of preaching the Gospel "among all nations, beginning at Jerusalem"?

Lesson in Our Society

There was once a time where a person's word really counted for something. If someone promised you something, you could fully believe them. However, as time progresses the value of a person's word is diminishing more rapidly than the ozone layer. Are you a contributing factor in warding off or adding to the depreciation of the promise? As Christians, we should make good on our promises, because this is the precedent that God has set forth— He always makes good on His promises.

Make It Happen

Has God made you a promise concerning something in your life that has yet to come to fruition? Today, spend time celebrating the promises God has kept to you. You will soon find that meditating on God's faithfulness will help you recognize that even though you may not have the answer you wanted, God is still keeping His promises to you. Give praise to God, allowing the words of your mouth, the mediations of your heart, and your actions before others to show your faith that God's promises are true.

Follow the Spirit

What God wants me to do:

_____

_____

Remember Your Thoughts

Special insights I have learned:

_____

_____

More Light on the Text

2 Chronicles 6:12–17; Luke 24:44–49

12 And he stood before the altar of the LORD in the presence of all the congregation of Israel, and spread forth his hands: 13 For Solomon had made a brasen scaffold, of five cubits long, and five cubits broad, and three cubits high, and had set it in the midst of the court: and upon it he stood, and kneeled down upon his knees before all the congregation of Israel, and spread forth his hands toward heaven,

In the opening verses of chapter 6, Solomon rehearses before the congregation of Israel the events his father, David, had shared regarding his own desire to build a house for the Lord and the promise of God that Solomon would build the house. Our lesson begins as Solomon completes his summary of how the temple was built and blesses the people who have assembled for the celebration of this historic event.

The "brasen scaffold" (Heb. *kiyowr nechosheth*, **kee-YOR nekh-OH-sheth**) or bronze platform, served much like a modern-day pulpit and allowed Solomon to be seen by all the congregation. The platform's measurements are recorded in "cubits" (Heb. *'ammah*, **ahm-MAH**). The term, which was used for linear measurements throughout the nations dating from antiquity, is roughly equivalent to the distance from the elbow to the end of the middle finger, about 18 inches. The measurement first appears in the Bible in the instructions given to Noah for building the ark for the flood (see Genesis 6:16). Both the Egyptians and the Babylonians attempted to create more precise standards for cubit length. Nevertheless, the writer's intent is to help us visualize the scaffold's measurements in order to understand the magnitude and importance of the structure to this historic event. Regardless of our inability to grasp the full scope of the size for the platform, it is here that Solomon leads the congregation into worship as he lifts his hands toward heaven and kneels in praise and thanksgiving to God.

Solomon's posture of kneeling is very important. Solomon was the king of Israel and his monarchy had been established for 11 years, since his father's death in 971 BC. The building of the temple took about seven and a half years. In light of his position as king, the length of his reign, and the magnitude of his work, we would expect that the people would knelt before Solomon. Instead, Solomon kneels (**Heb.** *barak,* **bah-RAHK**), meaning "to bless God" by bending or bowing before the Lord. Thus Solomon set the example of how the people should reverence God and declared as his father, David, had that Jehovah was the central figure in Israel's life. By kneeling, Solomon declared himself a servant of the Most High God.

14 And said, O LORD God of Israel, there is no God like thee in the heaven, nor in the earth; which keepest covenant, and shewest mercy unto thy servants, that walk before thee with all their hearts:

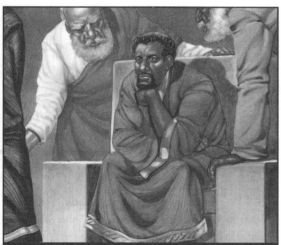

"And now the LORD has fulfilled the promise he made, for I have become king in my father's place, and now I sit on the throne of Israel, just as the LORD promised. I have built this Temple to honor the name of the LORD, the God of Israel" (2 Chronicles 6:10, NLT).

Solomon began by stating that the Lord Jehovah is the one, true God. This is a declaration that Israel will remain faithful to Jehovah despite their interactions with the surrounding nations that worshiped multiple gods. It was impossible for Israel to not interact with other countries. In fact, David had subdued the surrounding nations and many had become loyal to his authority. It was from these surrounding nations, either as tribute or spoil, that David had gathered much of the material he stored for Solomon to use in starting the building project, including a "hundred thousand talents of gold, and a thousand talents of silver." Solomon himself purchased or received gifts from other nations to reinforce the materials necessary for this massive building project. Second Chronicles 1:15 states that "the king made silver and gold at Jerusalem as plenteous as stones." Given the interaction of Israel with its neighbors, the declaration of God's authority served as a promise of continued faithfulness to the God of the nation.

Solomon's prayer began with adoration unto the Lord. Solomon honored God for keeping His promise to his father, David. The implication, however, goes beyond the promise to David. This nation was founded through the promise to Abraham. It was reinforced with God's promise to Jacob, whose very name was changed to Israel (see Genesis 32:28). By remembering God's faithfulness in making and keeping covenants, Solomon rehearsed the covenant faithfulness of God throughout the history of the nation.

But God not only kept His promises, He also showed "mercy" (Heb. *chesed,* **KHEH-sed**) or favor and kindness to His "servants" (Heb. *'ebed,* **EH-bed**). God loved Israel despite Israel's errors and sins. His loving-kindness and tenderness prevailed despite Israel's unfaithfulness through the wandering in the wilderness and the transgression in the Promised Land. Through all of this, Israel remained the servants of God. Throughout the history of the nation, there had been leaders such as Abraham, Isaac, Jacob, Moses, Joshua, Samuel, and David whose "walk" (Heb. *halak,* **hah-LAHK**) or behavior before God had been executed with all their "hearts" (Heb. *kol lebam,* **kohl leb-AHM**), which means with their entire minds and beings. This is not to imply that only the leaders were faithful or that the leaders did not err. Solomon's statement does declare that the hearts of the leaders and the people—their loyalty, their love, their desire to seek God's will, forgiveness, and direction—remained steadfast.

15 Thou which hast kept with thy servant David my father that which thou hast promised him; and spakest with thy mouth, and hast fulfilled it with thine hand, as it is this day.

In verse 15, Solomon turns more specifically to the promises of God to David. First, Solomon says that God "kept" (Heb. *shamar*, **shah-MAR**) His promises to David. This Hebrew term generally means to build a hedge around something in order to guard and protect it. In this case, it also refers to God remembering the promises He made to David. Through David's life and through Solomon's reign, God kept the promises He made to David. Solomon reminds God and the people that God's own mouth had "spoken" (Heb. *dabar*, **dah-BAR**) the covenant promises for David. Now, Solomon declared, God's own hand had brought these things to pass! The nation was standing in the place where God's promise regarding the building of the temple had been fulfilled.

16 Now therefore, O LORD God of Israel, keep with thy servant David my father that which thou hast promised him, saying, There shall not fail thee a man in my sight to sit upon the throne of Israel; yet so that thy children take heed to their way to walk in my law, as thou hast walked before me.

In verse 16, Solomon asks God to remember the next part of the covenant promise. Interestingly, Solomon included the conditional portion of the promise. God's promise was that the sons of David would reign upon Israel's throne as long as they were faithful to the Law and sought God with their whole hearts. By asking God to remember His promise, Solomon acknowledged the conditions that must be met in order to secure the throne for his own children.

17 Now then, O LORD God of Israel, let thy word be verified, which thou hast spoken unto thy servant David.

In our final verse of this text, Solomon appears to need reassurance from God as he asks Him to let His word be "verified" (**Heb.** *'aman*, **ah-MAHN**), which means "to support, confirm, and be faithful." In real-

ity, Solomon was asking that God remain faithful, that He be with Solomon as He had been with David. This is not a statement of doubt regarding God's ability; it is a plea for God's presence and continued mercy upon the king and the nation. This is not an uncommon request since, like Solomon and his father David before him, we, too, often feel the need for God to confirm His Word to us.

Luke 24:44 And he said unto them, These are the words which I spake unto you, while I was yet with you, that all things must be fulfilled, which were written in the law of Moses, and in the prophets, and in the psalms, concerning me.

The lesson text now jumps to the New Testament as we leave the site of the dedication of Solomon's temple and move to the place where the resurrected Jesus was speaking to His disciples. Jesus reminded the Eleven that during His three years as their teacher and leader, He had always taught them what was to come in order to "fulfill" (Gk. *pleroo*, **play-RO-oh**) what was written in the Hebrew Bible or Old Testament Scriptures. The reference is to "all" (Gk. *pas*, **pahs**) of the prophecies that declared from the beginning that the Messiah would come. Jesus explained that His presence as the Saviour had been referenced in the writings of the Law, which God had given to Moses, in the prophetic writings and speeches, and in the praise songs ("psalms"—Gk. *psalmos*, **psahl-MOSS**). In other words, all of the sacred Scriptures foretold His coming and His mission.

Jesus said that these things were written about "me" (Gk. *emou*, **em-OO**). Jesus let the disciples know that God's will had been made known in the Law of Moses (i.e., the first five books of the Bible) and the many prophesies about Him had to be fulfilled in His life, death, and Resurrection.

45 Then opened he their understanding, that they might understand the scriptures, 46 And said unto them, Thus it is written, and thus it behoved Christ to suffer, and to rise from the dead the third day: 47 And that repentance and remission of sins should be preached in his name among all nations, beginning at Jerusalem. 48 And ye are witnesses of these things. 49 And, behold, I send the promise of my Father upon

you: but tarry ye in the city of Jerusalem, until ye be endued with power from on high.

The disciples could not comprehend the words of Jesus until He opened their "understanding" (Gk. *nous*, **noos**), meaning that He opened their minds, their faculties of perception and understanding, their abilities to feel, judge, and determine what was presented to them. In verse 46, Jesus uses the term "behooved" (Gk. *dei*, **day**). Thus the death and resurrection of Jesus was a necessity established by the counsel and decree of God and disclosed in the Old Testament prophecies.

The duty of the disciples was to relate to humanity that salvation came only by the intervention of Christ. Christ had to suffer, die, and be resurrected in order for us to be able to receive and preach "repentance" (Gk. *metanoia*, **met-AHN-oi-ah**). God alone can "remit" or take away sin (Gk. *aphesis*, **AHF-ays-is**). Repentance means a change of mind and action regarding a purpose that person has formed or something the person has done. To have the remission of sins means to be released from bondage or imprisonment of sin. Jesus declares that the Gospel message must be preached in His name—the Messiah, the Christ—because no other person could claim credit for fulfilling the prophecies of God. Further-more, the declaration of the Gospel was not something that could be told only in Israel. The declaration of God's power must be preached "among all nations, beginning at Jerusalem."

Here lies the physical connection between the 2 Chronicles account of Solomon and the words spoken by Jesus, the resurrected Christ. All begins in Jerusalem. This was the place where God chose to place His name (see 2 Chronicles 6:6). It was in Jerusalem that Solomon built the temple. It was in Jerusalem that Christ was delivered for trial and crucifixion. It was in Jerusalem that the resurrected Christ met with His faithful followers who were "witnesses of these things." Finally Jesus told His disciples to remain in Jerusalem because it would be there that He would "send the promise of my Father upon you" so that the disciples would be "endued with power from on high."

In our humanness we might feel that the suffering of Christ was enough, but He told the disciples to "tarry" (Gk. *kathizo*, **kahth-ID-zoh**), meaning "to settle down until they are endued" (Gk. *enduo*, **en-DOO-oh**) with "power" (Gk. *dunamis*, **DOO-nahm-iss**). This Greek word *enduo* means "to sink into" in the sense of sinking into your clothes, while *dunamis* means "strength, power, or ability." The implication is that the power they would receive from God would become part of them. It would engulf them and cover them as a garment. This was the power promised to them in this text and again in Acts 1:8: "you shall receive power, after that the Holy Ghost is come upon you." The Holy Spirit was promised as God's presence within His followers. After Christ ascended to heaven, His followers received the Holy Spirit so that they would be powerful witnesses for Christ.

The final connection between the two texts in today's lesson is in the promises of God. With the power of God all things are possible. When He gives us a task to perform and makes promises to us, we need His strength in order to reach the goal. Solomon experienced this as he cried out to the Lord at the dedication of the temple, which marked the fulfillment of God's promise to David. The disciples learned this as they listened carefully to the words of Jesus Christ and as they experienced on the Day of Pentecost as the promises of God were fulfilled.

Daily Bible Readings

M: Praise for God's Goodness
Psalm 135:1–5

T: Dedication of the Temple
2 Chronicles 6:1–11

W: Solomon's Prayer
2 Chronicles 6:12–17

T: Pray Toward This Place
2 Chronicles 6:18–31

F: Repent and Pray
2 Chronicles 6:36–39

S: God's Promise Remembered
2 Chronicles 6:40–42

S: God's Promise Fulfilled
Luke 24:44–49

TEACHING TIPS

March 30
Bible Study Guide 5

1. Words You Should Know

A. Law (2 Chronicles 34:15, 19, 26) *towrah* (Heb.)—The Book of the Law was given by God to Moses. Generally this is a reference to not only the Ten Commandments but all of the Law of God included in the first five books of the Bible, the Pentateuch.

B. Abominations (v. 33) *tow'ebah* (Heb.)—To detest or find something disgusting. This reference is to the ceremonially unclean practices that were part of pagan worship rituals. Judah included, and in some cases substituted, these practices for their worship of God. Josiah removed all idol worship.

2. Teacher Preparation

Unifying Principle—Mending a Broken Relationship What does it take for a relationship to be reestablished? Josiah was grieved by the people's broken covenant with God and in humility took steps to restore their relationship with God.

A. Pray for all the students in your class.

B. Read the Bible Study Guide. Examine the *Precepts For Living*® CD-ROM if you find areas where you have additional questions regarding the biblical content.

C. Familiarize yourself with the AIM for Change objectives and Unifying Principle and review them as you plan the activities for today's lesson.

D. Prepare: (1) A large poster sheet with the statement: "When I discovered I was wrong, . . ." (2) A handout entitled "Things People Say" on which you have recorded statements such as "You're just like your daddy."

E. Prepare a list of verses that describe the legacy of Josiah's father, grandfather, and great-grandfather (see 2 Chronicles 32:32–33; 2 Chronicles 33:1–4, 20–23).

F. Early in the week, contact three or four of the class members and work with them to prepare a modern language skit depicting 2 Chronicles 34:1–19.

3. Starting the Lesson

A. After prayer, ask the class to complete the sentence on the poster sheet.

B. Before reading the Focal Verses, have the members present their skit.

C. After the skit, explain the divided kingdom and have several students read the Scriptures identifying the legacy of Josiah's forefathers.

4. Getting into the Lesson

A. Follow the At-A-Glance outline as you lead the class through the discussion of the remaining Focal Verses.

B. Use the Search the Scriptures and Discuss the Meaning questions to drive class discussion.

5. Relating the Lesson to Life

A. Have the class respond to the statements on the "Things People Say" sheet. Ask if such statements applied in Josiah's case and how such statements can positively or negatively impact our lives.

B. Have the group read the In Focus story and relate it to the "Things People Say" exercise. Have the class respond to the questions at the end of the story.

6. Arousing Action

A. Have the class read the Make It Happen section. Ask for further suggestions.

B. Remind the class to utilize next week's Daily Bible Readings during their time of devotion.

C. Ask a class member to close the class in prayer.

Worship Guide

For the Superintendent or Teacher
Theme: Josiah Renews the Covenant
Theme Song: "We Have Come Into This House"
Devotional Reading: Psalm 119:25–40
Prayer

JOSIAH RENEWS THE COVENANT

Bible Background ● 2 CHRONICLES 34
Printed Text ● 2 CHRONICLES 34:15, 18–19, 25–27, 29, 31–33 Devotional Reading ● PSALM 119:25–40

AIM for Change

By the end of the lesson, we will:

ANALYZE the true meaning of covenant;

REFLECT on our commitment to obey God; and

SURRENDER our desires in order to obey God's Word.

Keep in Mind

"And the king stood in his place, and made a covenant before the LORD, to walk after the LORD, and to keep his commandments, and his testimonies, and his statutes, with all his heart, and with all his soul, to perform the words of the covenant which are written in this book" (2 Chronicles 34:31).

Focal Verses

KJV **2 Chronicles 34:15** And Hilkiah answered and said to Shaphan the scribe, I have found the book of the law in the house of the LORD. And Hilkiah delivered the book to Shaphan.

34:18 Then Shaphan the scribe told the king, saying, Hilkiah the priest hath given me a book. And Shaphan read it before the king.

19 And it came to pass, when the king had heard the words of the law, that he rent his clothes.

34:25 Because they have forsaken me, and have burned incense unto other gods, that they might provoke me to anger with all the works of their hands; therefore my wrath shall be poured out upon this place, and shall not be quenched.

26 And as for the king of Judah, who sent you to enquire of the LORD, so shall ye say unto him, Thus saith the LORD God of Israel concerning the words which thou hast heard;

27 Because thine heart was tender, and thou didst humble thyself before God, when thou heardest his words against this place, and against the inhabitants thereof, and humbledst thyself before me, and didst rend thy clothes, and weep before me; I have even heard thee also, saith the LORD.

34:29 Then the king sent and gathered together all the elders of Judah and Jerusalem.

34:31 And the king stood in his place, and made a covenant before the LORD, to walk after the LORD, and to keep his commandments, and his testimonies, and his statutes, with all his heart, and with all his soul, to perform the words of the covenant which are written in this book.

NLT **2 Chronicles 34:15** Hilkiah said to Shaphan the court secretary, "I have found the Book of the Law in the LORD's Temple!" Then Hilkiah gave the scroll to Shaphan.

34:18 Shaphan also told the king, "Hilkiah the priest has given me a scroll." So Shaphan read it to the king.

19 When the king heard what was written in the Law, he tore his clothes in despair.

34:25 For my people have abandoned me and offered sacrifices to pagan gods, and I am very angry with them for everything they have done. My anger will be poured out on this place, and it will not be quenched.'

26 But go to the king of Judah who sent you to seek the LORD and tell him: 'This is what the LORD, the God of Israel, says concerning the message you have just heard:

27 You were sorry and humbled yourself before God when you heard his words against this city and its people. You humbled yourself and tore your clothing in despair and wept before me in repentance. And I have indeed heard you, says the LORD.

34:29 Then the king summoned all the elders of Judah and Jerusalem.

34:31 The king took his place of authority beside the pillar and renewed the covenant in the LORD's presence. He pledged to obey the LORD by keeping all his commands, laws, and decrees with all his heart and soul. He promised to obey all the terms of the covenant that were written in the scroll.

32 And he caused all that were present in Jerusalem and Benjamin to stand to it. And the inhabitants of Jerusalem did according to the covenant of God, the God of their fathers.

33 And Josiah took away all the abominations out of all the countries that pertained to the children of Israel, and made all that were present in Israel to serve, even to serve the LORD their God. And all his days they departed not from following the LORD, the God of their fathers.

32 And he required everyone in Jerusalem and the people of Benjamin to make a similar pledge. The people of Jerusalem did so, renewing their covenant with God, the God of their ancestors.

33 So Josiah removed all detestable idols from the entire land of Israel and required everyone to worship the LORD their God. And throughout the rest of his lifetime, they did not turn away from the LORD, the God of their ancestors.

In Focus

Barry waited outside on a cold, snowy evening for his father to pick him up from the spot where the Greyhound bus had dropped him. Finally, he was out of prison. Barry had spent the past 12 years of his life locked away from his family, his friends, and society. For the average 32-year-old male, those 12 years would have been spent getting a college degree, starting down a career path, finding a wife, and possibly having children; unfortunately, that was not the path Barry had chosen. Instead, 12 years ago, he decided to get behind the wheel of a car after having several beers and drive drunk. This resulted in a three-car collision that seriously injured two people and killed two people. In the end, Barry was sentenced to 12 years in prison.

Now having served his debt to society, Barry was a free man. Although he was glad to see this day come, he was also apprehensive. A lot had changed in 12 years. Barry went into prison an angry 20-year-old thug and now, 12 years later, a much wiser, much calmer 32-year-old man emerged.

Like most guys in prison, Barry sought out and found spiritual guidance. He began attending church services and reading the Bible. He quickly discovered that the people in the Bible were far from perfect. There were many who were thieves, murderers, adulterers, and liars; yet despite their unfaithfulness, God still desired a relationship with His people. Time after time the people sinned, and still God looked out for them. This was amazing to Barry. He never knew that such faithfulness existed. Once he realized that God could transform his life, he began to study the Bible more intently to identify ways he could begin life anew. Eventually, Barry accepted Christ as his Saviour.

Barry knew that God had forgiven him for his past but now as he stood on the corner, a free man, he wondered how he would go about mending the broken relationships of his past. What would people say about him? How would his old friends react to him? Would his family accept him? How would he begin to reestablish his life?

Like Barry, many people have a past that is far from perfect. Today's lesson is about Josiah, who rediscovered the Book of the Law and used it to develop a standard by which the Children of Israel could begin to rebuild and reestablish their covenant relationship with God.

The People, Places, and Times

Josiah. Josiah was a godly king who ruled Judah from 640 B.C. until 609 B.C.

Hilkiah. Hilkiah was a Levite and the high priest who aided in Josiah's reform movement. He was the father of the prophet Jeremiah.

Background

Following the death of Solomon in 930 B.C., his son, Rehoboam, inherited the throne of Israel. Solomon's extensive building program had been a great burden to the people physically and financially. When a representative group asked the new king for leniency, Rehoboam arrogantly opposed their suggestion (see 2 Chronicles 10).

Because of this, the people of the north chose Jeroboam to rule over the 10 tribes of Israel, leaving Rehoboam to rule the remaining tribes under the banner of Judah. Fearing that Israel would eventually return to Jerusalem, Jeroboam built places of worship in the north. This split of the nation led to a history of sin and idol worship (see 1 Kings 11–14).

Josiah's grandfather, Manasseh, and father, Amon, were wicked leaders who led the people of Judah deeper into idolatry. Josiah was anointed king of Judah when he was 8 years old. Because he sought God's direction for his life, he made a covenant, a promise to keep God's commandments and statutes.

At-A-Glance

1. The Discovery of God's Law
   (2 Chronicles 34:15, 18–19)
2. God's Servant Consulted (vv. 25–27)
3. Josiah Renews the Covenant
   (vv. 29, 31–33)

In Depth

1. The Discovery of God's Law (2 Chronicles 34:15, 18–19)

Josiah recognized the idolatry within the land and at the age of 20 started to remove the signs and places of idol worship. He removed the poles built by his grandfather that were dedicated to Asherah, a Canaanite fertility goddess. Josiah destroyed and scattered the idolatrous images in various areas in Judah including Bethel, Simeon, and Naphtali. In addition, Josiah began a renovation of the temple that had been built by Solomon.

Josiah funded the temple restoration through the collection of a temple tax. The restoration involved repairing the foundation, walls, and various sections of the building. This was an extensive repair of the place of Jewish worship. During this process, Shaphan, the King's scribe, was responsible for keeping the records that included the specifications of the temple, the record of daily repairs, and funds collected and spent.

During the renovation, Hilkiah, the high priest, was responsible for oversight of the temple work. It was during this task that he discovered the Book of the Law that was given to Moses. This particular discovery was believed to have been the book of Deuteronomy. In the modern Bible as well as the Jewish Scriptures, the first five books of the Bible, the Pentateuch, are included in the Law. God had allowed the Book of the Law to survive the wicked, idolatrous periods

of the kings before Josiah, and He allowed Hilkiah to find it.

This discovery of the Book of the Law began a revival throughout Judah. Following protocol, Hilkiah took the book to Shaphan to be recorded and then taken to the king. When the contents of the book were read to him, Josiah tore his clothes in despair and repentance. He realized the depth of Israel's spiritual misconduct was far greater than he imagined. Josiah wanted to know what God desired him to do in order to restore the nation to godly living. So he humbled himself before the Lord and sought godly counsel.

Josiah respected and feared God. His effort to remove the signs of idolatry and return the people to wholehearted reverence of Jehovah was proven by the destruction of the high places and the remodeling of the temple. It is not known who Josiah's teachers were. Obviously, his ascent to the throne at age 8 meant that someone godly taught him about David and the history of the nation as followers of Jehovah. Undoubtedly, what this verse makes very clear is that Josiah and those who were faithful to the Lord were faithful based on their *hearing* about the deeds God had performed in the past. They had not read the Law!

2. God's Servant Consulted (vv. 25–27)

The Old Testament speaks of four women who functioned as prophetesses speaking God's word to the people. These were Miriam (Exodus 15:20), Deborah (Judges 4:4), Noadiah (Nehemiah 6:14), and Huldah, who is mentioned in today's lesson. Hilkiah, Shaphan, and other emissaries were sent by Josiah to ask Huldah to consult God on behalf of the nation. God told Huldah to say that all the curses in the book would befall Judah because of the sin the people had committed. But, she continued, because Josiah humbled himself before the Lord, Judah would not incur God's wrath during his reign.

3. Josiah Renews the Covenant (vv. 29, 31–33)

Josiah realized that the first step in reestablishing God's covenant was for the people to recommit to God's standards and commandments. Josiah gathered the people, read them the Book of the Law, and challenged them to follow God edicts. Upon reading the Law, Josiah was the first to recommit to keeping

God's laws, thus leading the way for all the people to recommit themselves to God's covenant. In the final verses of our lesson, Josiah read the Book of the Law before the nation, and led Judah to recommit their lives to God.

After Josiah's reform, Israel continued to keep the covenant during his 31-year reign. Josiah was a good leader. Even as a young ruler, he sought to be upright before God. When he was confronted with the Word of God, he repented and surrendered himself before the Lord. His humility and conviction turned God's heart, and as a result Josiah was even more determined to turn the nation back to the worship of God. Because of Josiah's obedience, the people remained faithful to their covenant during the remainder of Josiah's rule.

Search the Scriptures

1. Why did Josiah tear his clothes (2 Chronicles 34:19)?
2. Who was Huldah (vv. 22–28)?
3. What is a covenant (v. 31)?

Discuss the Meaning

1. What did Josiah do to recommit to God's direction?
2. Why do you think Josiah is recorded by history to have been a "good" king?

Lesson in Our Society

When we desire to live for God, we must humbly seek God's direction. The Word of God provides direction from God, but we cannot live for God unless we have a relationship with Him. Develop a relationship with God by spending time with God through prayer and reading the Bible.

When Josiah heard the Book of the Law, he realized that the nation had drifted from God's principles. He expressed sorrow by tearing his clothes and seeking God's direction through a prophetess, Huldah. Today, you can speak to God directly through Jesus Christ, His Son. God cannot excuse sin; but we can turn to Jesus, who died that our sins might be forgiven and we might live according to God's principles and directions.

Make It Happen

A covenant relationship requires knowing the other person. Judah and Israel turned their backs

on God because they didn't know Him. They stopped hearing His Word and following His directives. Unless you know God, you can't really be true to the covenant He requires today. Make a commitment to read your Bible daily and to build your relationship with God as you study His Word and meet Him in prayer.

Follow the Spirit

What God wants me to do:

_____

_____

Remember Your Thoughts

Special insights I have learned:

_____

_____

More Light on the Text

2 Chronicles 34:15, 18–19, 25–27, 29, 31–33

15 And Hilkiah answered and said to Shaphan the scribe, I have found the book of the law in the house of the LORD. And Hilkiah delivered the book to Shaphan. 18 Then Shaphan the scribe told the king, saying, Hilkiah the priest hath given me a book. And Shaphan read it before the king.

Josiah was the 16th king of Judah after David, and was one of the few good kings of the period. He came to the throne at 8 years of age, following the death of his father, Amon, who, like Josiah's grandfather Manasseh, was an extremely wicked ruler. They not only failed to follow God but led the entire nation astray. Like his great-grandfather, Hezekiah, Josiah was a king whose obedience to God brought reform to the nation. By the time Josiah reached 20 years of age, he had undertaken a campaign to urge the nation to get rid of its idolatrous worship practices and return wholeheartedly to God.

Following the destruction of the high places that had been used extensively in worshiping idols, Josiah moved to repair the temple in Jerusalem, which had fallen into disrepair. During that renovation Hilkiah, the high priest, found the "book" (Heb. *sepher*, **SAY-fer**) of the "Law" or Torah (Heb. *towrah*, **toh-RAH**), The book that was found is believed to have been the book of Deuteronomy, part of the Law of Moses, the sacred writings given by God when Israel was in the wilderness.

While the term *sepher* is most often translated "book," another term, *megillah* (**meg-il-LAH**), actually means "scroll." Despite the distinction, what Hilkiah found were more akin to scrolls than to books in the sense of our modern bound materials. A scroll was a written document that was sealed, only to be read by specific individuals.

The text says that Hilkiah "answered," a term that seems awkward in this context. A better translation of the word for "answered" (Heb. *'anah*, **ah-NAH**) is "shouted." In reality the find was so amazing that Hilkiah let out a cry of excitement and got the attention of Shaphan, the scribe.

Hilkiah's role as high priest was to oversee the work of restoring the temple. Shaphan's responsibility was that of a "scribe" (Heb. *saphar*, **sah-FAR**), one who is learned in the written word. In the remodeling project, it was possibly Shaphan's responsibility to serve as a bookkeeper, recording the various transactions and events of the project. When the book was discovered, Hilkiah went immediately to Shaphan and gave him the book. Shaphan, like Hilkiah, realized that this was no ordinary writing and that it must be taken to the king.

Shaphan read the text "before the king." The word. In Hebrew the word "read" is rendered *qara'* (*kah-RAH*). Together we have a picture of Shaphan declaring the Word of God right in the king's face! What Shaphan read was really a proclamation of God's Law, a declaration of words so important that they could not be taken lightly. This was obviously a binding document, and it revealed that while Josiah had done all he thought to do in honoring God, he and the nation had fallen far short of the mark and far from God.

19 And it came to pass, when the king had heard the words of the law, that he rent his clothes.

In response, Josiah "rent" (Heb. *qara'*, **kah-RAH**) or tore his clothes into pieces. In biblical times, the tearing of one's clothes was traditionally viewed as a sign of grief or repentance. The word for "heard" (Heb. *shama'*, **shah-MAH**) means "to listen carefully and pay attention for the purpose of giving obedience and heed." When confronted by the Law, Josiah was keenly aware of his need to repent because of the treachery and deceit that had taken over the kingdom. Josiah was so distraught that he desperately wanted to know what to do. The situation seemed hopeless; however, he was willing to seek God's mercy

on behalf of himself and the people. In response, Josiah wanted greater insight into how to abate the wrath of the Lord. According to verse 21, Josiah sent Hilkiah, Shaphan, and several others to seek advice regarding what consequences Judah faced for failing to heed the covenant of the Law, which God made with Moses. In response, the men went to the prophetess Huldah. This woman faithfully reported what God would do because of Judah's failure to keep the Law. She also gave a special prophecy regarding Josiah.

25 Because they have forsaken me, and have burned incense unto other gods, that they might provoke me to anger with all the works of their hands; therefore my wrath shall be poured out upon this place, and shall not be quenched.

Verse 25 records Huldah's response as she interprets God's words. The word for "forsaken" (Heb. *'azab*, **ah-ZAHB**) means "to leave, loose, depart from, abandon, or neglect." The people of God had broken the covenant made between God and Moses. They had failed to keep the covenant God made with David. They had gone so far as to offer sacrifices to other gods. God responded to this breach with His "wrath" (Heb. *chemah*, **khay-MAH**), meaning "God's rage, hot displeasure, and indignation." God's anger was so intense that He declared it would not be "quenched" (Heb. *kabah*, **kah-BAH**), meaning "extinguished."

26 And as for the king of Judah, who sent you to enquire of the LORD, so shall ye say unto him, Thus saith the LORD God of Israel concerning the words which thou hast heard; 27 Because thine heart was tender, and thou didst humble thyself before God, when thou heardest his words against this place, and against the inhabitants thereof, and humbledst thyself before me, and didst rend thy clothes, and weep before me; I have even heard thee also, saith the LORD.

While the previous verses describe God's righteous anger, these verses show God's desire to be compassionate and forgiving. Josiah's immediate response to the finding of the Book of the Law grabbed God's attention. Josiah was willing to beg for God's forgiveness. He was not haughty and arrogant. Neither did he lose hope. In the face of sin, Josiah recognized that only God could provide forgiveness; therefore, he had turned to God, going to the prophetess to see what he could do to gain God's compassionate grace.

This portion of Huldah's prophecy turns from the nation to the individual. In verse 27, God says that Josiah's "heart" (Heb. *lebab*, **lay-BAHB**) was "tender" (Heb. *rakak*, **rah-KAHK**). The term for "heart" can also be translated "will" or "mind" while "tender" means "softened or afraid." When Josiah heard the reading of the Law, he yielded his will to God's will. He realized that while he had made every effort to rectify their sin and to turn the people to the Lord, he had not come near to seeking forgiveness for the hundreds of years the nation had been unfaithful to God. It was Josiah's will that the nation turn, but he yielded to God's will by asking what he could possibly do on behalf of the people to turn God's anger aside.

Verse 27 says that Josiah "humbled" (Heb. *kana'*, **kah-NAH**) himself. The phrase means that he bent his knee; he bowed himself before Almighty God in humiliation for the sin that was explained to him. Before finding the book, Josiah and the others did not know the degree of their sin. Nevertheless, when he was confronted with the nation's sin, Josiah was not haughty, declaring himself to be the ruler of the land. Instead, he had torn his clothes and "cried" (Heb. *bakah*, **bah-KAH**) or "wailed" before God. Josiah's cry had been a lamentation, a plea for God's help as the king surrendered before the Jehovah Elohim. As a result, God "heard" (Heb. *shama'*, **shah-MAH**) Josiah's plea.

29 Then the king sent and gathered together all the elders of Judah and Jerusalem. 31 And the king stood in his place, and made a covenant before the LORD, to walk after the LORD, and to keep his commandments, and his testimonies, and his statutes, with all his heart, and with all his soul, to perform the words of the covenant which are written in this book.

We are reminded by this verse of how both David and Solomon had come before the people. In this case, Josiah lead the people into a renewal of the covenant God made with David. Josiah responded to the word of the Lord by summoning the elders to witness the making of his covenant (Heb. *beriyth*, **ber-EETH**) with the Lord.

"And the king stood in his place, and made a covenant before the LORD, to walk after the LORD, and to keep his commandments, and his testimonies, and his statutes, with all his heart, and with all his soul, to perform the words of the covenant which are written in this book" (2 Chronicles 34:31)

The people and their king made a pledge to do three things. First, they would "walk after the Lord." The word for "walk" (Heb. *yalak*, **yah-LAHK**) refers to the lives they intended to lead. They would follow God and change their lives to indicate that they were no longer following false gods and the ungodly worship practices of their idolatrous neighbors. Second, they would "keep" (Heb. *shamar*, **shah-MAR**) God's commandments, testimonies, and statutes. To "keep" means "to build a hedge around something in order to protect it." Their intention was to guard the Law, making sure that they fulfilled what God wanted them to do. They would be careful to obey God's "commandments" (Heb. *mitsvah*, **mits-VAH**), or code. God's "testimonies" (Heb. *'eduwth*, **ay-DOOTH**) are the witness of what God demands. God had spoken and His words were recorded in the Book of the Law as a testimony of what God wanted. "Statutes" (Heb. *choq*, **khohk**) means "ordinance or boundaries." Finally they vowed to "perform" (Heb. *'asah*, **ah-SAH**), which means to accomplish, to fulfill, or show faithfulness. God's word indicated that certain behaviors, actions, and practices were contrary to God's will. By entering into covenant, the people joined Josiah in vowing not to partake in unethical behaviors anymore and to seek God's forgiveness.

The nation was not entering into an agreement to do lip service. No one was agreeing to simply follow the crowd by acquiescing to what the king wanted. The people were to follow God with all their "heart" (Heb. *lebab*, **lay-BAHB**) and "soul" (Heb. *nephesh*, **NEH-fesh**). These terms combined mean that each person was committing to following God's commandments. Josiah was totally committed to maintaining the covenant contained within the Torah with every part of his being, and he was leading the people to do the same.

32 And he caused all that were present in Jerusalem and Benjamin to stand to it. And the inhabitants of Jerusalem did according to the covenant of God, the God of their fathers. 33 And Josiah took away all the abominations out of all the countries that pertained to the children of Israel, and made all that were present in Israel to serve, even to serve the LORD their God. And all his days they departed not from following the LORD, the God of their fathers.

Josiah first made both a personal covenant with God. He then had gathered all the children of Judah and required them to pledge themselves to the Lord.

This was the assurance that the national dedication to Jehovah would be restored. By doing this, Josiah was returning the nation to their roots in God, to the covenant of their fathers. Verse 32 says that Josiah gathered all of the people in Jerusalem and the territory of Benjamin. Josiah called the people to "stand to it" (Heb. *'amad*, **ah-MAHD**). In other words, he called on them to take a stand. He wanted them to declare that day that they were on God's side.

Josiah was aware of the abominations the people committed, and subsequently he cleaned house. First, he took away everything that was considered an "abomination" (Heb. *tow'ebah*, **toh-ay-BAH**), which when used in an ethical sense means anything that was disgusting or wicked. Not only did Josiah destroy the idols and the high places of false worship in Jerusalem, his campaign was to rid the entire nation of idolatrous symbols and restore faithful worship of Jehovah, the Almighty God.

Under Josiah, Judah did not "depart" (Heb. *suwr*, **soor**) or turn away from God to follow any other tradition or worship. They remained loyal to God and "followed" (Heb. *'achar*, **ahkh-AR**) God. The Hebrew word *'achar* is a preposition meaning "to stay behind." Literally they walked behind God; He led them—just as He had led their fathers. Once again, because of Josiah's obedient and humble spirit, God was honored throughout Israel as the "LORD God" (Heb. *Yehovah. 'Elohiym*, **yeh-ho-VAH el-oh-HEEM**).

Daily Bible Readings

M: Revive Me
Psalm 119:25–32

T: Josiah Seeks God's Way
2 Chronicles 34:1–7

W: A Big Discovery
2 Chronicles 34:8–18

T: Josiah Repents
2 Chronicles 34:19–21

F: God Hears Josiah
2 Chronicles 34:22–28

S: The Covenant Renewed
2 Chronicles 34:29–33

S: Teach Me
Psalm 119:33–40

TEACHING TIPS

April 6
Bible Study Guide 6

1. Words You Should Know

A. Purposed in his heart (Daniel 1:8) *suwm leb* (Heb.)—To make up one's mind, determination.

B. King's meat (vv. 8, 13, 15) *melek pathbag* (Heb.)—These were food items selected by the king for the captive youth of Judah. The intent was to strengthen the young men so they could serve as leaders of Babylon.

C. Pulse (vv. 12, 16) *zeroa* (Heb.)—Something that is sown; such as vegetables, seeds, beans, or peas.

2. Teacher Preparation

Unifying Principle—Holding to Your Convictions! Often people find themselves in situations where they may feel pressure to conform. How can believers keep true to who they are and what they believe?

A. Read the Bible Study Guide. As you read, create a timeline that shows how events in today's lesson follow the captivity of the southern kingdom of Judah.

B. Create a list of "Five Little Things" people do without realizing they are compromising their Christian walk (for instance, not alerting a cashier who gave you too much change).

C. Identify a time when you have taken a stand or missed the opportunity to do so. What were the results? Be ready to share one experience.

D. Make a "starter list" of modern Daniels who have taken a stand when it was unpopular. Include people like Martin Luther King Jr. and people in your church, community, or neighborhood.

3. Starting the Lesson

A. Open class with prayer and then display your timeline. Review incidents in Judah's history that led to events in today's lesson.

B. Share the "Five Little Things" list and ask the class to add to it. Discuss why it is easy to fall into these patterns. Ask if these "little sins" really mean much.

4. Getting into the Lesson

A. Teach today's lesson using the At-A-Glance outline and Search the Scriptures questions.

B. Divide the class into groups. Give each group a question from the Discuss the Meaning section, and ask them to prepare and share a response.

5. Relating the Lesson to Life

A. Have someone read the In Focus story. Relate Darlene's situation to the "Five Little Things" list. Ask the class whether Darlene's response was realistic and why.

B. Briefly share your testimony of taking a stand or failing to stand up. Ask a few other people to share a similar testimony or respond to the In Focus question at the end of the story.

C. Share your "starter list" of modern Daniels. Ask class members to add to the list. Then ask what qualities these people had that helped them take a stand.

6. Arousing Action

A. Read the Make It Happen section.

B. Have the class brainstorm ways to help yourself and others take a stand. Ask the class what role the Holy Spirit has when we take a stand. Ask the class to hold hands for prayer and to pray for the strength of the ones whose hands they hold.

Worship Guide

For the Superintendent or Teacher
Theme: Daniel Keeps Covenant in a Foreign Land
Theme Song: "Stand Up, Stand Up for Jesus"
Devotional Reading: Psalm 141:1–4
Prayer

DANIEL KEEPS COVENANT IN A FOREIGN LAND

Bible Background • DANIEL 1
Printed Text • DANIEL 1:8–20 Devotional Reading • PSALM 141:1–4

AIM for Change

By the end of the lesson, we will:

KNOW that our commitments to God are worth every sacrifice;

ASPIRE to keep those commitments; and

COMMIT to live for Christ at any cost.

Keep in Mind

"But Daniel purposed in his heart that he would not defile himself with the portion of the king's meat, nor with the wine which he drank: therefore he requested of the prince of the eunuchs that he might not defile himself" (Daniel 1:8).

Focal Verses

KJV **Daniel 1:8** But Daniel purposed in his heart that he would not defile himself with the portion of the king's meat, nor with the wine which he drank: therefore he requested of the prince of the eunuchs that he might not defile himself.

9 Now God had brought Daniel into favour and tender love with the prince of the eunuchs.

10 And the prince of the eunuchs said unto Daniel, I fear my lord the king, who hath appointed your meat and your drink: for why should he see your faces worse liking than the children which are of your sort? then shall ye make me endanger my head to the king.

11 Then said Daniel to Melzar, whom the prince of the eunuchs had set over Daniel, Hananiah, Mishael, and Azariah,

12 Prove thy servants, I beseech thee, ten days; and let them give us pulse to eat, and water to drink.

13 Then let our countenances be looked upon before thee, and the countenance of the children that eat of the portion of the king's meat: and as thou seest, deal with thy servants.

14 So he consented to them in this matter, and proved them ten days.

15 And at the end of ten days their countenances appeared fairer and fatter in flesh than all the children which did eat the portion of the king's meat.

16 Thus Melzar took away the portion of their meat, and the wine that they should drink; and gave them pulse.

NLT **Daniel 1:8** But Daniel was determined not to defile himself by eating the food and wine given to them by the king. He asked the chief of staff for permission not to eat these unacceptable foods.

9 Now God had given the chief of staff both respect and affection for Daniel.

10 But he responded, "I am afraid of my lord the king, who has ordered that you eat this food and wine. If you become pale and thin compared to the other youths your age, I am afraid the king will have me beheaded."

11 Daniel spoke with the attendant who had been appointed by the chief of staff to look after Daniel, Hananiah, Mishael, and Azariah.

12 "Please test us for ten days on a diet of vegetables and water," Daniel said.

13 "At the end of the ten days, see how we look compared to the other young men who are eating the king's food. Then make your decision in light of what you see."

14 The attendant agreed to Daniel's suggestion and tested them for ten days.

15 At the end of the ten days, Daniel and his three friends looked healthier and better nourished than the young men who had been eating the food assigned by the king.

16 So after that, the attendant fed them only vegetables instead of the food and wine provided for the others.

17 As for these four children, God gave them knowledge and skill in all learning and wisdom: and Daniel had understanding in all visions and dreams.

18 Now at the end of the days that the king had said he should bring them in, then the prince of the eunuchs brought them in before Nebuchadnezzar.

19 And the king communed with them; and among them all was found none like Daniel, Hananiah, Mishael, and Azariah: therefore stood they before the king.

20 And in all matters of wisdom and understanding, that the king enquired of them, he found them ten times better than all the magicians and astrologers that were in all his realm.

17 God gave these four young men an unusual aptitude for understanding every aspect of literature and wisdom. And God gave Daniel the special ability to interpret the meanings of visions and dreams.

18 When the training period ordered by the king was completed, the chief of staff brought all the young men to King Nebuchadnezzar.

19 The king talked with them, and no one impressed him as much as Daniel, Hananiah, Mishael, and Azariah. So they entered the royal service.

20 Whenever the king consulted them in any matter requiring wisdom and balanced judgment, he found them ten times more capable than any of the magicians and enchanters in his entire kingdom.

In Focus

Darlene took a job at a local discount clothing store that paid hourly wages. She thought she could make up for the low pay by using her employee discount to buy clothes for herself and her children. After accepting the job, Darlene found this store did not offer employee discounts. The supervisor who trained Darlene showed her an illegal way to ring up merchandise at a lower price. "This is how you can get a discount," the supervisor said.

Darlene was taken aback by the suggestion and told the supervisor that "God will make a way." Darlene kept the job and worked well. The supervisor never again mentioned "the discount," and Darlene was thankful that God was blessing her. Despite the low wage, she was faithful in paying her tithes and was able to pay her bills.

The following spring, when Darlene returned from a one-week vacation, the boss called her into his office. "I have been carefully watching the registers, and I know that several employees have been skimming. I've tracked what they did and I let them go last week. You, on the other hand, are one of the few who have never tried to do anything underhanded. You are always pleasant, good with the customers, and helpful to other employees. I've reviewed your application, and I see that you have a background that is underused in this job. I need someone who can help me run this store, and I need more people like you to do that. Would you be interested in a managerial position? It would mean a huge increase in pay and I

would feel comfortable knowing that a person of integrity is in management."

Darlene accepted the position, left the office, and thanked God for His faithfulness.

It is easy to compromise in the "little things" in order to gain what we see as necessary. God, however, calls us to be consistently faithful—as He is. Where in your life have you struggled to keep the covenant and been blessed by the sacrifice?

The People, Places, and Times

Daniel. Unlike other prophets, Daniel was primarily an interpreter of dreams and a recipient of visions. Daniel was carried captive into Babylon as a teenager (Daniel 1:1–4), and the rest of his life was spent in exile from Jerusalem. Daniel lived a long and useful life in the courts and councils of some great monarchs such as Nebuchadnezzar, Cyrus, and Darius. Despite his close association with these heathen kings, Daniel remained faithful to God, and God made Daniel the statesman and man of business that he was.

Babylon. In ancient times this civilization was called Shinar. The original city, Babylon, was built by Nimrod, son of Ham and a great-grandson of Noah (see Genesis 9:18–10:10). At the time of Nebuchadnezzar's rule, Babylon had developed into one of the most beautiful and prestigious cities of all time. With over a million inhabitants, the city was lush with parks and gardens.

Nebuchadnezzar. This king of Babylon became the leader of his aged father's armies in 609 B.C. In

605 B.C. he annihilated Egypt's army at the Battle of Carchemish. This victory affirmed Babylonia as the new world power. Nebuchadnezzar then led a successful military campaign against Judah. Some 115 years after the destruction of the northern kingdom of Israel, God used the Babylonian Empire to execute His wrath on the southern kingdom of Judah.

Source:
Lockyer, Herbert. *All the Men in the Bible.* Grand Rapids, Mich.: Zondervan Publishing House, 1958.

Background

God's plan was to use the tribes of Israel to bring salvation to all people of the world; therefore, God extended His covenant grace to the Hebrew nation so that it would be a "light of the Gentiles" (Isaiah 42:6). However, the people and their leaders chose to disobey God and practice idolatry; they failed to bring God's truth to all nations.

After King Solomon's death, Israel was split into two separate kingdoms: the northern kingdom of Israel and the southern kingdom of Judah. All of Israel's kings were ungodly and disregarded God's laws. Because of their disobedience, God used Assyria, a heathen nation, to destroy the northern kingdom in 721 B.C.

While several of Judah's kings respected God's laws, these kings were unable to permanently alter the people's slide into idolatry and immorality. God sent several prophets to warn the people to repent of their ungodly ways and return to Him. But Judah, like Israel, stubbornly refused to listen and was taken captive by Babylon in 586 B.C.

Judah's defeat and captivity took place during Daniel's teenage years. He and other select princes of Judah were taken to Babylon to serve in Nebuchadnezzar's royal court. Daniel lived the rest of his life as an exile in Babylon.

At-A-Glance

1. Daniel's Commitment (Daniel 1:8–10)
2. Daniel's Plan (vv. 11–16)
3. Daniel's Victory (vv. 17–20)

In Depth

1. Daniel's Commitment (Daniel 1:8–10)

Nebuchadnezzar planned to annihilate the nation of Judah. Part of his plan was to take the young Hebrew princes of Judah and convert them to Babylonian beliefs and a heathen lifestyle. He even had Ashpenaz change their Jewish names into names honoring Babylonian gods (see Daniel 1:6–7). Daniel's name, which means "God is my judge" was changed to Belteshazzar, which means "May Bel protect his life." Of Daniel's three companions, Hananiah, whose name means "Yahweh is gracious" became known as Shadrach, meaning "command of Aku" (the Babylonian moon god). Mishael's Hebrew name means "one who is as God," but the Babylonians changed it to Meshach, which means "who is Aku." Finally Azariah, whose name meant "Jehovah has helped," was given the name Abednego, which means "Servant of Nebo."

The boys knew the food from the king's table was strictly forbidden for them to eat. In heathen nations, food and wine were often sacrificed to pagan gods; thus, Jews who knowingly ate the tainted food were considered participants in idolatrous worship. Nebuchadnezzar intended to force the Hebrew boys into compromising their religious convictions by offering them only the foods that he personally chose for their diets.

Verse 8 of the text tells us that Daniel "purposed in his heart" not to defile himself with the king's food—regardless of the consequences. "Purpose" is a strong word that means "to be devoted to a principle or committed to a course of action." Daniel made up his mind he would not compromise his convictions even if it cost him his life.

When Daniel took a stand for God, God worked for Daniel. God gave Daniel favor with Ashpenaz (Daniel 1:3). So, when Daniel approached Ashpenaz with his petition to abstain from the king's food and wine, the overseer was sympathetic but understood the danger of going against the king's wishes. Daniel then asked Melzar, the steward, for permission to eat other foods. At first, Melzar did not agree with this special arrangement. He was afraid the boys would not look as healthy as the other youths who were eating the king's food. Besides, Melzar thought that Daniel's plan could cost him his job and his head (v. 10).

2. Daniel's Plan (vv. 11–16)

Daniel suggested an experiment in which he and his friends would be allowed a diet of vegetables and water for 10 days. After the 10-day trial period, the steward could compare them to those who ate the food from the king's table. Then Melzar could decide whether to let them continue their diet. Melzar agreed, and at the end of the 10-day period, Daniel and his three friends looked healthier than all the other youths (v. 15). From that point, Melzar excused the Hebrew boys from eating the king's diet.

Daniel and his three friends had acted only on their faith. They had no idea how the test would turn out, but they depended on God. Resisting the temptation to compromise their beliefs, they took a stand for God and God stood up for them.

3. Daniel's Victory (vv. 17–20)

When Nebuchadnezzar inspected the young captives, he found that Daniel, Hananiah, Mishael, and Azariah were doing better and were smarter than all of the other young men he had identified for his court. Not only did they excel in stature and health, but their minds and abilities were excellent as well. Daniel 1:20 says that these three young men had ten times the knowledge and skill in all learning and wisdom than was exhibited by anyone else. Nebuchadnezzar had assembled what he considered to be the greatest "think tank" and corporate leaders to date. But these young men, who had kept their integrity and refused to compromise their stand for God, far exceeded anyone the king had.

Search the Scriptures

1. What did Daniel and his three friends make up their minds not to do (Daniel 1:8)?

2. How did God intervene in Daniel's behalf (v. 9)?

3. How long was the test period Daniel suggested for his diet (v. 12)?

4. What was the result of Nebuchadnezzar's examination of the Hebrew boys (vv. 17–20)?

Discuss the Meaning

1. Compare the challenges Daniel and his three friends faced to those of modern-day Christians. In what ways are the situations similar?

2. What do you think helped Daniel make the right choice when faced with a dilemma? Is that resource available to us today?

Lesson in Our Society

Modern-day Christians often find themselves in situations where they feel they have to compromise their beliefs in order to win people to Christ or gain some personal benefit. If the four Hebrew boys were alive today they might be told, "It's OK to compromise. Go along with the program. It will win you favor with the king. You may even be able to talk to the king about God."

What are some of the pitfalls of this kind of reasoning? How is Christianity compromised today? What problems can arise from such compromises?

Make It Happen

It is easy to make the right choice when you are in church. However, when you are faced with a compromising dilemma, how do you respond? For instance, do you laugh at dirty jokes at work? Do you watch inappropriate movies or television programs because they are currently popular? Do you keep the extra change the cashier mistakenly gave you at the grocery checkout? This week, examine your life for areas of compromise. Then "purpose in your heart" to take a stand for God and His Word.

Follow the Spirit

What God wants me to do:

_____

_____

Remember Your Thoughts

Special insights I have learned:

_____

_____

More Light on the Text

Daniel 1:8–20

8 But Daniel purposed in his heart that he would not defile himself with the portion of the king's meat, nor with the wine which he drank: therefore he requested of the prince of the eunuchs that he might not defile himself.

Following the defeat of Judah, Daniel and his friends Hananiah, Mishael, and Azariah were among the young men taken into exile in Babylon. Going into captivity meant that the people of Judah would be subjected to the traditions and practices of Babylon, a pagan nation. Daniel 1 records that these young men were given new Babylonian names. Each of their Hebrew names contained a name for the true God ("el" or "iah," an abbreviation for El Elyon and Yahweh). Each Babylonian name contained the name of a pagan deity.

The deportation of these young men fulfilled the warning Isaiah had given King Hezekiah in 2 Kings 20:17–18. It was forbidden by the Law of Moses for God's people to eat certain foods or participate in pagan rituals and practices. To do so was to be declared ceremonially unclean for worship or defiled.

As a captive, Daniel was subject to Babylonian law. Daniel loved God and "purposed in his heart" (Heb. *suwm leb*, **soom labe**) to remain loyal to the worship of Jehovah. He refused to let anything "defile" (Heb. *ga'al*, **gaw-AL**) his heart. One way to remain ceremonially pure was to refuse to eat the "king's meat" (Heb. *melek pathbag*, **MEH-lek path-BAG**). This refers to portions of food or delicacies reserved for a king. The translators of the King James Version were probably correct in assuming that meat was the most conspicuous delicacy on the king's table. The New American Standard, a modern English translation, renders this word "choice food."

Daniel also refused drink. The word used for "which he drank" in verse 8 and "that they should drink" in verse 16 is *mishteh* (mish-TEH), a Hebrew term meaning "feast" or "banquet." Its use in this context could be understood to communicate that daily meals in the king's household were feasts, especially when compared to the type and quantity of food and drink most people were able to obtain on a regular basis.

The text is unclear why partaking of the king's food would have defiled Daniel. It could have been that the food provided for Daniel had been used in pagan festivals and offerings. Genesis 9:3–4 and Leviticus 7:26–27 prohibited the consumption of meat from certain kinds of "unclean" animals (Leviticus 11:3–8, 26–39). Likewise, drunkenness has always been regarded as both a moral failure (Deuteronomy 21:20; Ephesians 5:18) and an ill-advised lapse of self-control (Proverbs 20:1; 23:20–21).

In his refusal, Daniel exercised wisdom and obedience, and created a distinction between himself and the Babylonians who surrounded him. In his situation, the strong temptation would have been to conform to the local customs in an attempt to demonstrate loyalty to the regime and gain acceptance by powerful men. Daniel, however, made it clear that his first allegiance was to the God of Israel.

Daniel made his request to the prince of the eunuchs. The word for "eunuch" (Heb. *sariys*, **sah-REECE**) refers literally to "an emasculated man." However, it was also used figuratively to refer to "officials" or "chambermaids." On this basis, some English translations render the phrase "commander of the court officials."

9 Now God had brought Daniel into favour and tender love with the prince of the eunuchs.

The word for "favour" (Heb. *checed*, **KHEH-sed**) means "goodness" or "kindness." It is often translated "loving-kindness" in the Old Testament to describe God's gracious acts to preserve and redeem His people. The word for "tender love" (Heb. *racham*, **RAKH-am**) means literally "loving feeling" or "tender mercy." In a few other places in the Old Testament, these words are used together to form an expression that describes God's feelings toward His children (see Psalm 103:4; Hosea 2:19; Jeremiah 16:5).

God gave Daniel such favor with the "prince of the eunuchs." Although we typically think about this story as concerning Daniel's courage to stand up for his convictions, this passage actually points out God's faithfulness. Daniel and his friends were experiencing the consequences of Judah's disobedience. Were it not for the failure of their fathers, they would probably have been in Jerusalem instead of being forcibly relocated to Babylon as slaves in pagan culture. But God doesn't forget His people, even when He is chastening them severely. He promised to always respond to those who sincerely seek Him (see Deuteronomy 4:29–31; Leviticus 26:40–45). By causing the eunuch to be sympathetic toward Daniel, God was acting in faithfulness to His promise and honoring the prayers of righteous men from ages past.

10 And the prince of the eunuchs said unto Daniel, I fear my lord the king, who hath appointed your meat and your drink: for why should he see your faces worse liking than the children which are of your sort? then shall ye make me endanger my head to the king.

The word for "appointed" (Heb. *manah*, **mah-NAH**) is the same word used in verse 5 to tell us that the king personally designated food from his table for the Jewish youths. The chief eunuch believed that changing the diet of those under his care would be directly disobedient to the king's orders. This was no trivial matter, because the king had absolute power! During the chief eunuch's service, he had no doubt seen what happened to people who dared to contradict the king.

The verb translated "worse liking" (Heb. *za'aph*, **zaw-AF**) literally means "to fret, be sad, or out of humor." The only other place this term occurs in the Old Testament is in Genesis 40:6 where it refers to a dejected facial expression. The concern of the chief eunuch was that Daniel's health would suffer in comparison with the health of the other young men who would remain on the king's diet. Other English translations use words like "thin," "haggard," or "malnourished" to convey the concept of poor health.

The phrase "endanger my head to the king" could be translated more literally "make my head guilty." The chief eunuch could have been an extremely conscientious man who really didn't want to act on his own initiative without authorization from his superior, or he might simply have been intimidated by the thought of capital punishment. The latter seems most likely given the conspicuous use of the word "head." In this text, the eunuch believed that giving in to Daniel would be putting his "head" (in English we would normally say "neck") on the line.

11 Then said Daniel to Melzar, whom the prince of the eunuchs had set over Daniel, Hananiah, Mishael, and Azariah, 12 Prove thy servants, I beseech thee, ten days; and let them give us pulse to eat, and water to drink.

The chief eunuch did not deny Daniel's request outright, but indicated that he was not comfortable with the proposition. Daniel then made his request to the steward assigned to him. Melzar was a

Babylonian title, perhaps meaning "guardian." Modern English translations interpret the word as a title, not a name, and describe this man as "steward," "warden," or "overseer." Regardless of whether or not Melzar was actually his name, he was obviously charged with caring for Daniel and his friends.

Daniel asked Melzar to "prove" (Heb. *nacah*, **nah-SAW**) or perform a test to see how well Daniel and his comrades would survive on a diet that was more fitting for them. The phrase "I beseech thee" tells us that Daniel had intensified his request. Some English versions use the word "please" to convey the mood of Daniel's request. He was appealing to Melzar's high opinion of him, but doing so in a respectful and courteous manner.

Daniel asked for "pulse" (Heb. *zeroa*, **zay-RO-ah**), which means "that which is sown" and refers to vegetables. Daniel wanted a diet of only vegetables (v. 12.) This implies that the king's diet included an abundance of meat, a luxury item. While Daniel's concern seems to be religious and not a dietary issue for health purposes, it is still notable to realize that few people—probably only the king and members of the nobility—would have owned enough land to produce meat for consumption on a regular basis. The average person may have eaten meat as little as once or twice per year, and primarily on special religious observances.

13 Then let our countenances be looked upon before thee, and the countenance of the children that eat of the portion of the king's meat: and as thou seest, deal with thy servants.

It seems likely that Daniel asked for the 10-day test as a way to acknowledge the concerns of the eunuchs. By our thinking, 10 days on an alternate diet would neither be long enough for their appearance to suffer nor long enough to allow significant improvement. But Daniel's faith was in God, and in 10 days Daniel knew that God would make the difference and give the favor. If the Lord wanted him to stand for righteousness by abstaining from the king's food, God would direct the heart of the men who had the power to make it possible for him. Daniel could only have faith to believe that God would reveal Himself in the midst of the test, proving to all that He was God Almighty.

14 So he consented to them in this matter, and proved them ten days. 15 And at the end of ten days their countenances appeared fairer and fatter in flesh than all the children which did eat the portion of the king's meat.

At the end of the text, the "countenances" (Heb. *mar'eh*, **mar-EH**) or "appearances" of Daniel and his friends were better than those of the children who ate from the king's table. The term "appeared" is a Hebrew word, *ra'ah* (**raw-AW**), which means to look intently or inspect. The test of 10 days ended with a close inspection of the progress made by Daniel, Hananiah, Mishael, and Azariah.

Their countenances were "fairer" (Heb. *towb*, **tobe**), a common Old Testament word normally translated "good." Some English translations render it "better." The word "fatter" (Heb. *bariy'*, **baw-REE**) seems to imply that they had not wasted away, but had fared well, looking more stout and healthy than their counterparts who had eaten the king's food. In the ancient Near East, girth was a sign of wealth. The common people worked too hard and had too little food available to gain weight. In the ancient world, like underdeveloped regions today, food was scarce and fitness was threatened by malnourishment. If Daniel and the others gained weight, God did it!

16 Thus Melzar took away the portion of their meat, and the wine that they should drink; and gave them pulse.

Up to this point, the text has only indicated that vegetables and water were added to Daniel's supply of food. No doubt the king's meat was delivered daily even if it wasn't eaten. Now Melzar took away the "meat" and "wine." The word for "took away" (Heb. *nasa'*, **naw-SAW**) literally means "to lift or carry." Melzar took action to completely fulfill Daniel's wish.

17 As for these four children, God gave them knowledge and skill in all learning and wisdom: and Daniel had understanding in all visions and dreams.

Daniel and the four princes received "knowledge" (Heb. *madda'*, **mad-DAW**) and "wisdom" (Heb. *chokmah*, **khok-MAW**) in abundance. Wisdom is a common word in the Old Testament with a variety of possible connotations, including skill or aptitude, experience, good sense, shrewdness, intellectual capacity,

and godly insight. "Skill" (Heb. *sakal*, **saw-KAL**) is a verb that means "to be prudent." Other English translations render this word "intelligence." "Learning" (Heb. *cepher*, **SAY-fer**) literally means "writing" or "book."

God gave Daniel and his friends exactly what the king was looking for when he established their training program. The Hebrew words used for "knowledge," "skill," "learning," "wisdom," and "understanding" are the exact words used in Daniel 1:3–4 when Nebuchadnezzar outlined his goals for the young captives. Daniel was blessed with the ability to understand visions and dreams—an indication that God was truly with him and would speak through him (see Numbers 12:6) as he did in several instances recorded in this book (see 2:19; 7:1; 8:1).

The question then is, did God do this for Nebuchadnezzar? No, God blessed Daniel and the others so that His will could be enacted. Even in the midst of trial and the depths of situations that seem to be against us, God will show favor to His people and elevate them to give glory to His name.

18 Now at the end of the days that the king had said he should bring them in, then the prince of the eunuchs brought them in before Nebuchadnezzar.

The eunuchs honored Daniel's wishes with regard to diet. The moment of truth, however, came when Daniel and his friends were to stand before the king. After three years of first-class education and accommodations (see 1:4), would the Hebrew youth measure up to the king's expectations? To be certain, the careers—perhaps even the lives—of the men who cared for and trained Daniel and his friends hung in the balance.

19 And the king communed with them; and among them all was found none like Daniel, Hananiah, Mishael, and Azariah: therefore stood they before the king.

The word for "communed" (Heb. *dabar*, **daw-BAR**) literally means "to talk." The king likely interrogated the young men, either individually or in groups, to discern the depth of their understanding. Daniel, Hananiah, Mishael, and Azariah stood head and shoulders above the rest of the captives.

While these four young men distinguished themselves before Nebuchadnezzar, they also distinguished themselves before God through their courage and faithfulness to God's commands. We know that there were many other Jewish youth enrolled in the same program of education and leadership development. But only these four—certainly a minority—are recorded to have maintained steadfast loyalty to their God.

The phrase "stood before the king" is a literal rendering of the Hebrew. The words are the same ones used in verse 5, which indicates these young men would be working for the king. Some English versions translate the phrase "entered the king's service." The conversation with the king was a combination final exam and job interview!

We see here a principle of privilege coupled with responsibility. God entrusted Daniel and his friends with great gifts, but those gifts came with an obligation. The four young men had power, prestige, and possibly wealth. But God called them to stand with courage and conviction repeatedly throughout the time of their service. The king, as the rest of the book shows, was a demanding and unjust man at times. God gives good gifts, but not necessarily to make our lives easier or more comfortable. Frequently He calls His most gifted servants to exercise great courage and count any present happiness as loss for the sake of advancing His eternal kingdom.

20 And in all matters of wisdom and understanding, that the king enquired of them, he found them ten times better than all the magicians and astrologers that were in all his realm.

Daniel and his three friends were not only found to be wiser than all their peers—they outdid even the king's diviners. The words for "magicians" (Heb. *chartom*, **khar-TOME**) and "astrologers" (Heb. *ashshaph*, **ash-SHAWF**) refer to those who sought secret knowledge through communication with the spirit world. The diviners believed these spirits to be gods and the spirits of deceased people. It was common in the ancient world for rulers to consult experts in the occult. The Scriptures do not allow the practice of divination by the people of God (see Deuteronomy 18:10–14). Rather, we are to listen to those through whom God has chosen to speak (see Deuteronomy 18:15). God calls His people to live in faith, trusting that whatever He ordains is right and that He will tell us what we need to know at the right time.

In Daniel 2:24 and 5:11 we learn that Daniel was actually appointed chief of the magicians and wise men, because Nebuchadnezzar realized that Daniel was filled with the Spirit of God and was actually correct in his interpretations and predictions unlike the king's magicians. Of course, Daniel disavowed the techniques and beliefs of the pagan magicians entirely. In Daniel 2:27–30 he explains that only God can reveal mysteries and men can only have access to divine knowledge when God chooses to reveal Himself.

Daniel, Hananiah, Mishael, and Azariah were "rising stars" in Babylon after their interview with the king. At the time of their exile, no one would have predicted their ascent to the upper echelons of Babylonian government in the next three years. After all, they were basically prisoners of war. But God called them to act courageously, and He honored their faithfulness by using them to leave a powerful and lasting testimony of the one true and living God. By sticking to their convictions, they experienced the power of God in incredible ways.

Daily Bible Readings

M: A Prayer for God's Support
Psalm 141:1–4

T: God's House Besieged
Daniel 1:1–2

W: The King's Plan
Daniel 1:3–7

T: Daniel's Resolution
Daniel 1:8–10

F: The 10-Day Test
Daniel 1:11–14

S: Four Fine Young Men
Daniel 1:15–17

S: Tested and True
Daniel 1:18–21

TEACHING TIPS

April 13
Bible Study Guide 7

1. Words You Should Know

A. Decree (Daniel 3:10) *te'em* (Heb.)—A judgment, command, declaration, or announcement of authority that must be obeyed.

B. Serve (vv. 12, 17, 18) *pelach* (Heb.)—To worship, revere, and minister to someone.

2. Teacher Preparation

Unifying Principle—Holding on to Your Faith It might have been easier for the three Hebrew boys to bow, rather than to believe God to deliver them. It took more faith, however, to trust a God they could not see to deliver them from a king they could see. We must learn to trust God in the face of difficult times.

A. Because this passage is so familiar, it is easy to miss the current application of this text to our lives. Ask God's direction.

B. The Bible Study Guide will help you establish the background of the text.

C. If possible, secure a recording or video of "Long as I Got King Jesus" by Vickie Winans. The seven minute music video relates this lesson to the plight of African Americans through several generations.

D. Prepare two sheets of chart paper, each with two columns labeled "Gains" and "Losses." Create a matching handout for use in the group activity.

E. Have index cards ready to use in this lesson.

3. Starting the Lesson

A. As your class enters the room, play the video or audio recording of "Long as I Got King Jesus."

B. Pass out index cards. Ask the class to write on one side of an index card a phrase that reminds them of a time when they faced persecution for their faith. Then have them write on the back a statement about how their faith helps them in times of trouble. Allow brief sharing.

4. Getting into the Lesson

A. Discuss the Focal Verses using the At-A-Glance outline. Encourage discussion using the Search the Scriptures and Discuss the Meaning questions.

B. After class discussion, have the class record on one of the Gains and Losses sheets what the Hebrew boys, the king, and the accusers gained or lost because of their stance.

5. Relating the Lesson to Life

A. Assign each of three groups one of the following sections: Group 1: Make It Happen; Group 2: Lesson in Our Society; and Group 3: In Focus. Have each group read the assigned section and complete a "gains and losses" statement on the handout. Allow time for each group to present.

B. Have the class members refer to the index card they used earlier and consider what the gains and losses were in their situations. Record their responses on the second Gains and Losses chart.

6. Arousing Action

A. Have the class read Revelation 12:11. Relate this to the Hebrew boys and explain that God allows us to share our testimonies so that our faith and others' can be strengthened.

B. Ask class members to either respond to the Follow the Spirit or Remember Your Thoughts section.

C. Close class by praying for the strength of class members who are facing adversity.

Worship Guide

For the Superintendent or Teacher
Theme: Three Refuse to Break Covenant
Theme Song: "Long as I Got King Jesus"
Devotional Reading: Psalm 121
Prayer

THREE REFUSE TO BREAK COVENANT

Bible Background • DANIEL 3
Printed Text • DANIEL 3:10–13, 16–18, 21, 24 Devotional Reading • PSALM 121

AIM for Change

By the end of the lesson we will:

LEARN to trust God when things are difficult;

BECOME CONVINCED that faith in God is more important than faith in man; and

DECIDE to live and reflect on the value of a faith-filled life.

Keep in Mind

"If it be so, our God whom we serve is able to deliver us from the burning fiery furnace, and he will deliver us out of thine hand, O king. But if not, be it known unto thee, O king, that we will not serve thy gods, nor worship the golden image which thou hast set up" (Daniel 3:17–18).

Focal Verses

KJV

Daniel 3:10 Thou, O king, hast made a decree, that every man that shall hear the sound of the cornet, flute, harp, sackbut, psaltery, and dulcimer, and all kinds of musick, shall fall down and worship the golden image:

11 And whoso falleth not down and worshippeth, that he should be cast into the midst of a burning fiery furnace.

12 There are certain Jews whom thou hast set over the affairs of the province of Babylon, Shadrach, Meshach, and Abednego; these men, O king, have not regarded thee: they serve not thy gods, nor worship the golden image which thou hast set up.

13 Then Nebuchadnezzar in his rage and fury commanded to bring Shadrach, Meshach, and Abed-nego. Then they brought these men before the king.

3:16 Shadrach, Meshach, and Abednego, answered and said to the king, O Nebuchadnezzar, we are not careful to answer thee in this matter.

17 If it be so, our God whom we serve is able to deliver us from the burning fiery furnace, and he will deliver us out of thine hand, O king.

18 But if not, be it known unto thee, O king, that we will not serve thy gods, nor worship the golden image which thou hast set up.

3:21 Then these men were bound in their coats, their hosen, and their hats, and their other garments, and were cast into the midst of the burning fiery furnace.

3:24 Then Nebuchadnezzar the king was astonied, and rose up in haste, and spake, and said unto his counsellors, Did not we cast three men bound into the midst of the fire? They answered and said unto the king, True, O king.

NLT

Daniel 3:10 You issued a decree requiring all the people to bow down and worship the gold statue when they hear the sound of the horn, flute, zither, lyre, harp, pipes, and other musical instruments.

11 That decree also states that those who refuse to obey must be thrown into a blazing furnace.

12 But there are some Jews—Shadrach, Meshach, and Abednego—whom you have put in charge of the province of Babylon. They pay no attention to you, Your Majesty. They refuse to serve your gods and do not worship the gold statue you have set up."

13 Then Nebuchadnezzar flew into a rage and ordered that Shadrach, Meshach, and Abednego be brought before him. When they were brought in,

3:16 Shadrach, Meshach, and Abednego replied, "O Nebuchadnezzar, we do not need to defend ourselves before you.

17 If we are thrown into the blazing furnace, the God whom we serve is able to save us. He will rescue us from your power, Your Majesty.

18 But even if he doesn't, we want to make it clear to you, Your Majesty, that we will never serve your gods or worship the gold statue you have set up."

3:21 So they tied them up and threw them into the furnace, fully dressed in their pants, turbans, robes, and other garments.

3:24 But suddenly, Nebuchadnezzar jumped up in amazement and exclaimed to his advisers, "Didn't we tie up three men and throw them into the furnace?" "Yes, Your Majesty, we certainly did," they replied.

In Focus

Jonathan and Evan are teachers in the local high school and active in the same church. When their principal retired and an interim principal was named, they were happy that the spot would be filled immediately and that the school could move forward with its plans for a new building with only limited interruptions. It turned out, however, that the interim principal, Dr. Clark, had a reputation as an outspoken atheist who felt that any statements of faith were an affront to her constitutional freedom.

Dr. Clark's first act was to demand that Evan get a new coffee cup if he planned to leave his in the break room. His cup read "God Can," and Dr. Clark felt that such a public statement was inappropriate. Evan kept his cup. When she objected to Jonathan's desk calendar that displayed a picture of his church, Jonathan explained that his calendar was on his desk in the staff office and not on display in the classroom. They soon realized that they would have to take a public stance against her but prayed that her interim term would end soon and they could move on. Unfortunately, Dr. Clark remained.

Finally she sent out an e-mail in opposition to the staff prayer that was held every third Friday at 6:30 a.m. The prayer had been going on for over 10 years and had started when the school was facing a crisis following the death of a student. About 15–20 teachers attended the meeting periodically. It occurred two hours before school started and half an hour before the official start time for staff.

At the next prayer group meeting only Jonathan and Evan attended. They proceeded to pray aloud as always and included the various needs of the school and the staff. In the middle of their prayer, Dr. Clark stormed in. The men continued to pray as she stood resolutely expecting them to stop. Instead, they prayed for her and asked God to grant her wisdom and success as she led the school's initiative. They prayed for her family and for her health. When they finished, Dr. Clark was gone and an e-mail was sent rescinding the ban on staff prayer.

Consider the ways, large or small, that you take a stand for your faith in Christ. How is your faith benefiting the community in which you live and work? How is it encouraging others?

The People, Places, and Times

Aramaic. While most of the Old Testament is written in Hebrew, much of the book of Daniel uses words in Aramaic, which was the commercial and diplomatic language of Babylon. Many documents were written in this original Babylonian language, which was once called Chaldee, to reflect the location of the empire.

Background

Nebuchadnezzar, the king of Babylon, had a golden image made to reflect the power of Babylon and king. The statue, which measured about one hundred feet tall and nine feet wide, was placed in Dura, a plain about six miles southeast of Babylon.

Pagan rulers often called themselves gods. For example, both Pharaoh and Caesar were considered gods by their countrymen. With this view, the worship of the image was not particularly unusual to people who practiced the various pagan rites. However, this was not an acceptable practice for the followers of Jehovah.

The execution of those who disobeyed the king was commonplace. Additionally, the furnace was used during biblical times as one form of execution.

At-A-Glance

1. The Accusation (Daniel 3:10–13)
2. The Stand (vv. 16–18)
3. The Result (vv. 21, 24)

In Depth

1. The Accusation (Daniel 3:10–13)

The statements recorded in verses 10–13 of the text were spoken by the Chaldean magicians to the king. It was known throughout the kingdom that the Hebrew captives, especially Daniel and his three companions, were committed to the worship of Jehovah and would not bow to any other god.

In these verses, the instructions for worship are restated. When the music sounded, the people were to fall prostrate on the ground and worship the image of the king. Prostration is a stance of total submission. One's face should be on the ground as the person is helplessly surrendered. Furthermore, the people were not simply to be quiet during this "ceremony." They were to worship the image. Whether there was a formula to be repeated is unclear, but the fact that the image of Nebuchadnezzar was to be revered indicates that the king thought himself to be a god. He believed that he had absolute power and authority, and he was exercising that authority in this instance.

The accusers came before the king to "tell on" the Hebrews. It was expected that the Hebrews would not bow, and now the magicians who had been basically dethroned by the success of Daniel and the others were using this as an excuse to have their Hebrew enemies destroyed.

Notice that it was not enough to say that the Hebrews would not bow or even to name them in the accusation. Their positions were also listed: "whom thou hast set over the affairs of the province of Babylon" (v. 12). By stating their positions and the fact that Shadrach, Meshach, and Abednego were ignoring the king's edict, the accusers were positive that the king would be enraged, kill the offenders, and then give their positions to these more worthy and loyal citizens who had brought the accusation.

Verse 13 details that result of the accusation. The king was livid and had the three men brought before him immediately.

2. The Stand (vv. 16–18)

The accusers were correct. Shadrach, Meshach, and Abednego would not bow to the golden image. They were Jehovah's servants and they would not engage in idolatry. The three had stood with Daniel earlier in refusing to eat food from the king's table. Now, knowing that their lives were in danger, they refused to have their faith shaken. They fully understood that their lives had no meaning if they bowed to the idol. They determined instead to endure persecution and even death rather than be unfaithful to God.

While the accusers saw this as a time to celebrate the wrath of the king on the Hebrews, the king probably saw it as a time to make an example of these subjects who refused his command. Shadrach, Meshach, and Abednego saw it as a time to witness for God. First, they explained that they were not afraid to speak before the king. They were not coming as cowering and whimpering slaves; they were standing before him as men of faith in Jehovah. They wanted King Nebuchadnezzar to know that they had consid-

ered the consequences they faced but had decided to stand for Jehovah.

Next, they explained that regardless of what the king thought He could do to them, God was more powerful and, if He desired, would deliver them even from the king's hand and the fiery furnace. Nebuchadnezzar was presenting them with the most feared death he had available and they were saying that they were not afraid, because their God was more powerful than anything the king could present.

By taking a stand, they showed that there was one before whom they would bow. They were willing to bow to the will of Jehovah, the God of their people. If the Lord wanted them to die, they would gladly die accepting His will for their lives. Regardless of what happened to them, they would not compromise their belief. They let it be known before the king, the entire assembled court, and the accusers: "We will not serve thy gods, nor worship the golden image which thou hast set up."

3. The Result (vv. 21, 24)

While we know this often-quoted passage, we should concentrate on the two things that occur in the printed text for today. First, the men were thrown bound and fully clothed into the furnace. If they would not bow, then Nebuchadnezzar would see that they were unable to worship anything or anyone else. He had them bound! They would have no way to get out, fight their way out, or even hold on to anything on the way to the furnace! They would bow or never make another move.

Second, the king was astonished. Verse 19 indicates the fire was so hot that it consumed the men who threw them in; but the thing Nebuchadnezzar had expected to occur had not. His anger just moments before could not be abated. Then he was out of his chair and looking into the fire, apparently not concerned that it might consume him! He began to question himself. Hadn't he called for the execution of three people? Hadn't he had them bound with all their clothes and thrown into the very hottest part of the furnace?

King Nebuchadnezzar, who had declared himself to be a god—all-knowing and eternal, was now questioning his own sight. Something had occurred that he could not explain, and his bewilderment would not allow him to keep quiet. Shadrach, Meshach, and Abednego had declared the truth about God before the king and now God wanted the king to know that they had spoken the truth.

Search the Scriptures

1. Who is speaking in Daniel 3:10–12?

2. What did the king demand be done when his subjects heard the music played (v. 10)?

3. What was the response of Shadrach, Meshach, and Abednego to the decree (vv. 12, 18)?

4. What was Nebuchadnezzar's response to the accusation brought against Shadrach, Meshach, and Abednego (vv. 13, 21)?

Discuss the Meaning

1. Discuss the reasons people who profess to be Christians find it difficult to take a stand for Christ in the midst of their trials.

2. Shadrach, Meshach, Abednego, and Daniel entered captivity as teens. Throughout their lives they continued to stand for God during the most trying times. What does their faith say to parents and youth workers today?

3. How does the speech Shadrach, Meshach, and Abednego made before the king show their understanding of what the king was asking them to do? How does it show their understanding of what God expected from them?

Lesson in Our Society

We live in a society that is often spiritual but not at all biblical. While the United States Constitution affirms religious tolerance, Christianity seems to have been ousted. At Christmas and Easter, Christ is often banned, and the Internet has constant warnings about the status of "under God" in the Pledge of Allegiance. On the other hand, there are those who use the Bible and Christianity as shields for personal agendas that often fail to encompass biblical principles. Buzz words such as "family" or "morality" are often used to name programs that totally disregard the sensibilities of one group while embracing the cultural standards of another. Claims that we want our children to know a world of peace are countered by media messages that flood them with violence and anxiety.

Prayerfully consider the societal issues currently challenging faith in your community. What conse-

quences and outcomes are evident? What suggestions can you make to address the issue in order to make a stand for God in your home, community, or church?

Make It Happen

What issues do you think Christians in your community should address by taking a biblical stand? Are these issues clouded by personal and political agendas? If so, how can you help others get to the core of the issues without being sidetracked? How can you enlist the help of others in both prayer and human interaction to stand against that which is not bringing glory to God and encouragement to people in need?

Follow the Spirit

What God wants me to do:

_____

_____

Remember Your Thoughts

Special insights I have learned:

_____

_____

More Light on the Text

Daniel 3:10–13, 16–18, 21, 24

10 Thou, O king, hast made a decree, that every man that shall hear the sound of the cornet, flute, harp, sackbut, psaltery, and dulcimer, and all kinds of musick, shall fall down and worship the golden image. 11 And whoso falleth not down and worshippeth, that he should be cast into the midst of a burning fiery furnace.

The lesson text for today begins with a speech made by the deposed chief magicians who had once been key figures in the king's court. Verse 8 calls these men Chaldeans. Chaldea, located in the lower Euphrates and Tigris area, was known throughout the world for being a place where people practiced magical powers. Chaldeans were respected as interpreters of dreams who were able to perform the highest feats of magic in royal courts. But God had given to Daniel the ability to interpret dreams. When his gift was put to the test by Nebuchadnezzar, Daniel was placed in charge of the king's advisors, who were called wise men or magicians. Daniel's elevation over the whole province of Babylon was assured, and he asked that his companions be appointed as his assistants. They were (see Daniel 2:49). It is no wonder, then, that the Chaldeans were the accusers ready to denounce the Hebrews to King Nebuchadnezzar.

The backdrop for today's lesson is an edict proclaimed by King Nebuchadnezzar. After conquering most of the known world, Nebuchadnezzar desired to unite Babylon and solidify his power base. To prove that he was the supreme and feared ruler, he built a pure gold statue of himself "whose height was threescore cubits, and the breadth thereof six cubits" (Daniel 3:1). Essentially Nebuchadnezzar was calling for all subjects throughout the empire of Babylon to worship an idol—the image of the king.

To carry out this decree, the king instructed his subjects to play a myriad of musical instruments. The sackbut (Heb. *cabbeka*, **sab-bek-AW**) and the psaltery (Heb. *picanteriyn*, **pis-an-tay-REEN**) were stringed instruments similar in style to a modern lyre. Both resembled small versions of today's harp. The word "dulcimer" in Hebrew is *cuwmpowneyah* (**soom-po-neh-YAW**) and refers to a wind instrument that could best be described as akin to a bagpipe. The other instruments—the coronet, flute, and harp—are more similar to our modern instruments of similar names, and are often mentioned in ancient music. Our previous studies this quarter indicated that these instruments were played in Jerusalem, and they are prominently mentioned in the book of Psalms. Taken collectively, the instruments probably played a sort of royal theme song; therefore, when the instruments sounded, all of the people under the reign of Nebuchadnezzar were to bow to the image and worship it. (For more on musical instruments see lesson 1—March 2.)

The punishment for failing to bow and worship was death. This punishment did not follow accusation and trial. It was to be immediate, occurring "at the same hour" as the offense (v. 6). Such an edict was an open invitation to destroy one's enemies. The mere accusation of failure to worship would unquestioningly lead to death. The execution was by burning, an act that was not a slow, agonizing "burning at the stake." This was a total consumption that began as soon as the accused neared the oven. The device called the "burning fiery furnace" is taken literally from *yeqad nuwr 'attuwn* (Heb. **yek-AD noor at-TOON**). It appears to

have been an industrial device that was probably used for baking bricks or melting metals. The intensity of the flames can well be imagined. The brutality of this threat was probably enough to make most people just fall down anyway! However, while this means of death was merciless, the cause of the Lord was critical.

Likely, the astrologers didn't believe that Nebuchadnezzar was a god either, but that was beside the point. In truth, their motives were purely selfish. The king's magicians wanted to be rid of the Hebrews who had come to Babylon and essentially stolen the respect the king had for them and been given prominent positions within the Babylonian government (v. 12). Daniel's outstanding skills as an interpreter of dreams had not placed him in a position to be loved by these enemies, and his relationship with Shadrach, Meshach, and Abednego made them into targets as well. No doubt Daniel also didn't bow; but at this point, the accusers would make examples of these men who were known to be avid and faithful lovers of Jehovah. True to form, the accusing astrologers wanted to make sure that King Nebuchadnezzar's decree was carried out to the letter so that their plot to get rid of the Hebrews would be successful.

12 There are certain Jews whom thou hast set over the affairs of the province of Babylon, Shadrach, Meshach, and Abednego; these men, O king, have not regarded thee: they serve not thy gods, nor worship the golden image which thou hast set up.

The decree recorded in verses 1–7 stated that everyone regardless of race, nationality, or language was to fall down and "worship" (Heb. *cegid*, **seg-EED**) Nebuchadnezzar's golden "image" (Heb. *tselem*, **TSEH-lem**). The king had expected—even commanded—that everyone, including Shadrach, Meshach, Abednego, and all of the Hebrew captives, would revere the idolatrous image.

The instructions were that everyone would lie prostrate upon the ground to pay homage to this golden statue of Nebuchadnezzar. Verse 12 says that Shadrach, Meshach, and Abednego had "not regarded" the king. This phrase essentially means that the three were disregarding the king's command. Their crime was not just refusing to bow; it was refusing to acknowledge the divinity of the king. The three were instead maintaining their covenant commitment to the one, true God and refusing to put anyone or anything in place of their worship of Him.

The three determined in their hearts that they would not bow to the idol. Their watchful accusers were more than happy to carry the delightful news to King Nebuchadnezzar. When it was learned, as it was expected, that Shadrach, Meshach, and Abednego were refusing to bow, the accusers pointed out that the Hebrew boys were in direct violation of Nebuchadnezzar's order.

13 Then Nebuchadnezzar in his rage and fury commanded to bring Shadrach, Meshach, and Abednego. Then they brought these men before the king.

Shadrach, Meshach, and Abednego's rebellion enraged the king. Nebuchadnezzar acted swiftly to carry out his punishment for their insurrection. Immediately, they had to face the consequences of their actions. They had stood for God and would now face dire consequences from God's enemies.

The text describes Nebuchadnezzar as being infuriated by the refusal. In truth, it was arrogance that made Nebuchadnezzar declare himself a god and build a statue to be worshiped. It was also arrogance that led him to throw the Hebrews into the fiery furnace as an affront to their God. Nebuchadnezzar would not be outdone. He would be worshiped and they would be the example to prove him worthy of worship. His indignation and immediacy in carrying out the sentence was not as much against the Hebrews as it was against their God.

3:16 Shadrach, Meshach, and Abednego answered and said to the king, O Nebuchadnezzar, we are not careful to answer thee in this matter. 17 If it be so, our God who we serve is able to deliver us from the burning fiery furnace, and he will deliver us out of thine hand, O king. 18 But if not, be it known unto thee, O king, that we will not serve thy gods, nor worship the golden image which thou hast set up.

"If it be so, our God whom we serve is able to deliver us from the burning fiery furnace, and he will deliver us out of thine hand, O king. But if not, be it known unto thee, O king, that we will not serve thy gods, nor worship the golden image which thou hast set up" (Daniel 3:17–18).

It would have been pointless for Shadrach, Meshach, and Abednego to take their punishment without speaking up for the Lord. The word "careful" in Hebrew is *chashach* (**khash-AKH**). It means "in the sense of readiness or to have need of." The phrase "to answer" is translated from Hebrew as *tuwb* (**toob**), and means "to restore, give back, or to return." Finally, the Hebrew term for "matter" is *pithgam* (**pith-GAWM**), and it means "command, affair, or decree." They were dedicated to God, and neither the king nor his decree would intimidate them. In other words, with regard to anything pertaining to the king's decree, they had no intention of being obedient; instead, they were going to obey their God.

By refusing to bow, the three declared their faith in God. They had long ago taken up a position for God, and they were not going to yield any ground to the idolaters. They were covenant keepers, and their answer showed their covenant commitment, faithfulness, fortitude, and tenacity to be all that God had called them to be, even in exile. Regardless of their fate, they were going to be faithful to their God. They would not engage in infidelity by worshiping any being other than Jehovah. Even in life-threatening circumstances, they were determined to obey their God and not engage in spiritual adultery.

They fully believed that if God so desired, He could deliver them. It is interesting that they were not begging to be exempt from the punishment. The word for "able" (Heb. *yekel*, **yek-ALE**) implies "to prevail or to overcome." In this light, the Hebrew boys believed that their God could triumph in their dire situation. On the other hand, they were prepared to accept God's will; even if God chose not to deliver them, they vowed that they would never bow to Nebuchadnezzar's image.

3:21 Then these men were bound in their coats, their hosen, and their hats, and their other garments, and were cast into the midst of the burning fiery furnace.

The king was true to his decree; the punishment came quickly. In his anger, Nebuchadnezzar had Shadrach, Meshach, and Abednego tied up and thrown into the furnace fully clothed.

The fire, according to verse 19, had been heated seven times hotter than normal as a result of Nebuchadnezzar's rage. Subsequent verses indicate that the fire was so hot that the men who took the three Hebrews to the fire were killed by flames of the furnace as they were putting Shadrach, Meshach, and Abednego inside.

3:24 Then Nebuchadnezzar the king was astonied, and rose up in haste, and spake, and said unto his counsellors, Did not we cast three men bound into the midst of the fire? They answered and said unto the king, True, O king.

Apparently the king was so angry that he wanted to see these men die. It is not clear how he and his counselors saw into the furnace, but they did. His thirst for revenge, however, was not to be satisfied. Instead he was "astonied" (Heb. *tevahh*, **tev-AH**) or "startled, alarmed, even amazed." The king could not believe what his own eyes showed him. According to verse 25, there were now four people in the furnace, not the three that had originally gone in.

What Nebuchadnezzar did not realize and what the three Hebrew boys understood was that when persons remain faithful in times of testing and pressure, they open themselves to experience God's strength and emerge with a deeper faith. Daniel and his friends showed more faith in God than in man. God graciously intervened in the plight of His people—God did not leave them alone.

Daily Bible Readings

M: God's Protection Forevermore
Psalm 121:1–4

T: King Nebuchadnezzar's Golden Statue
Daniel 3:1–7

W: The Refusal to Worship the Statue
Daniel 3:8–15

T: Brought before the King
Daniel 3:16–23

F: Not a Hint of Fire
Daniel 3:24–27

S: A New Decree
Daniel 3:28–30

S: God Will Keep You
Psalm 121:5–8

TEACHING TIPS
April 20
Bible Study Guide 8

1. Words You Should Know
A. Kingdom (Daniel 6:4, 7, 26) *malkuw* (Heb.)—Royal realm or reign, the area ruled by a king or emperor.

B. Statute (v. 7) *qeyam* (Heb.)—A decree, pronouncement, or judgment.

2. Teacher Preparation
Unifying Principle—Faith Without Compromise! What does it matter if you compromise your convictions? Sometimes we will be confronted with real-life issues that can compromise our relationship with God. When the order went out to not pray for 30 days, Daniel refused to compromise his beliefs or hide his actions.

A. Prepare for the lesson by studying The People, Places, and Times, Background, More Light on the Text, and In Depth sections.

B. Prepare a display of recent headlines or newspaper and magazine articles that depict situations that seem unjust.

C. Compile a list of volunteer opportunities through your church or community groups. Prepare to share this during the Arousing Action activity.

3. Starting the Lesson
A. After opening with prayer, have the class examine the display of headlines and articles.

B. Poll the class, asking which articles captured their attention and why. Explain that Daniel faced an unjust situation and responded to it regardless of the threat to him.

4. Getting into the Lesson
A. Because of the familiarity of many people with this biblical account, be certain to focus your class discussion on the AIM for Change.

B. Incorporate the Words You Should Know and the insights gathered from your Background study so that the class will be encouraged to search out fresh insights from this account.

5. Relating the Lesson to Life
A. Have the class read the In Focus story and respond to both Denise's action and the final question.

B. Have the group respond to the Lesson in Our Society section.

C. Remind the class that Daniel did not compromise, negotiate, or bargain with his faith. Then have the class respond to the articles they examined at the start of class by answering two questions: (1) What would make this situation right? (2) What would it cost you to help make this situation right?

6. Arousing Action
A. Read the Make It Happen challenge. Allow those who have been involved in volunteering to discuss the benefit that has been garnered for them and others through their volunteer experiences. Encourage other class members to share their ideas or ask questions about how to get started with volunteering.

B. Share the volunteer information you gathered during the week.

C. Close class with prayer.

Worship Guide

For the Superintendent or Teacher
Theme: Daniel's Life-and-Death Test
Theme Song: "Be Still, God Will Fight Your Battles"
Devotional Reading: Psalm 121
Prayer

DANIEL'S LIFE-AND-DEATH TEST

Bible Background • DANIEL 6
Printed Text • DANIEL 6:4–7, 10, 16, 19, 21, 25–26 Devotional Reading • PSALM 119:57–64

AIM for Change

By the end of the lesson, we will:

EXPLORE how Daniel's faith enabled him to resist the temptation to compromise his core values;

BECOME CONVINCED that standing firm in one's faith honors God; and

AFFIRM our faith in and obedience to God.

Keep in Mind

"Now when Daniel knew that the writing was signed, he went into his house; and his windows being open in his chamber toward Jerusalem, he kneeled upon his knees three times a day, and prayed, and gave thanks before his God, as he did aforetime" (Daniel 6:10).

Focal Verses

KJV
Daniel 6:4 Then the presidents and princes sought to find occasion against Daniel concerning the kingdom; but they could find none occasion nor fault; forasmuch as he was faithful, neither was there any error or fault found in him.

5 Then said these men, We shall not find any occasion against this Daniel, except we find it against him concerning the law of his God.

6 Then these presidents and princes assembled together to the king, and said thus unto him, King Darius, live for ever.

7 All the presidents of the kingdom, the governors, and the princes, the counsellors, and the captains, have consulted together to establish a royal statute, and to make a firm decree, that whosoever shall ask a petition of any God or man for thirty days, save of thee, O king, he shall be cast into the den of lions.

6:10 Now when Daniel knew that the writing was signed, he went into his house; and his windows being open in his chamber toward Jerusalem, he kneeled upon his knees three times a day, and prayed, and gave thanks before his God, as he did aforetime.

6:16 Then the king commanded, and they brought Daniel, and cast him into the den of lions. Now the king spake and said unto Daniel, Thy God whom thou servest continually, he will deliver thee.

6:19 Then the king arose very early in the morning, and went in haste unto the den of lions.

6:21 Then said Daniel unto the king, O king, live for ever.

NLT
Daniel 6:4 Then the other administrators and high officers began searching for some fault in the way Daniel was handling government affairs, but they couldn't find anything to criticize or condemn. He was faithful, always responsible, and completely trustworthy.

5 So they concluded, "Our only chance of finding grounds for accusing Daniel will be in connection with the rules of his religion."

6 So the administrators and high officers went to the king and said, "Long live King Darius!

7 We are all in agreement—we administrators, officials, high officers, advisers, and governors—that the king should make a law that will be strictly enforced. Give orders that for the next thirty days any person who prays to anyone, divine or human—except to you, Your Majesty—will be thrown into the den of lions."

6:10 But when Daniel learned that the law had been signed, he went home and knelt down as usual in his upstairs room, with its windows open toward Jerusalem. He prayed three times a day, just as he had always done, giving thanks to his God.

6:16 So at last the king gave orders for Daniel to be arrested and thrown into the den of lions. The king said to him, "May your God, whom you serve so faithfully, rescue you."

6:19 Very early the next morning, the king got up and hurried out to the lions' den.

6:21 Daniel answered, "Long live the king!

6:25 Then king Darius wrote unto all people, nations, and languages, that dwell in all the earth; Peace be multiplied unto you.

26 I make a decree, That in every dominion of my kingdom men tremble and fear before the God of Daniel: for he is the living God, and stedfast for ever, and his kingdom that which shall not be destroyed, and his dominion shall be even unto the end.

6:25 Then King Darius sent this message to the people of every race and nation and language throughout the world: "Peace and prosperity to you!

26 "I decree that everyone throughout my kingdom should tremble with fear before the God of Daniel. For he is the living God, and he will endure forever. His kingdom will never be destroyed, and his rule will never end.

In Focus

One evening as Denise was going home, she noticed her boss, Mr. Duncan, reading a memo on the union bulletin board. He seemed upset. As she got closer she saw that the notice was for a candle-light prayer service in opposition to the company's planned increases to medical benefits for retirees and a proposed layoff. The event would be held on Monday morning outside the corporate headquarters. The rally organizers were calling for media coverage and they would likely get it.

Mr. Duncan angrily said, "I can't believe that the company is allowing that type of demonstration. I definitely do not agree with the concept. People need to consider how the company will feel about this. Costs are going up. I'm sure everyone has to be aware of it. These people are retired; they already have benefits and Medicare. I'm sure they can make it just fine."

"Can they, Mr. Duncan?" Denise asked. "Last week I went to visit Louise—remember her? She worked here for 35 years and recently retired. Her husband has been ill and his medications are quite costly, even with the co-payments. She can't take the cut. And what about the people who will be laid off? Many won't receive any benefits because they are either part-timers or have not been on the job long enough. You know the old saying, 'There but for the grace of God go I'? I don't know about you, but I think this is a situation that calls for all of us to stand together and show a united front to the powers that be. I realize that even though my position is not in jeopardy right now, I can't compromise what I believe in and simply go along to get along. If prayer is being held on the street in front of TV cameras, so be it. I'll be found praying, Mr. Duncan. You're welcome to join me."

It is easy to forget that our call to faithfulness in Christ is about more than our personal comfort and advancement. We, like Daniel, are called to speak out as a matter of justice.

The decision to follow Christ can be costly. What sacrifice are you willing to make to reflect Christ in your community?

The People, Places, and Times

Darius, the Mede. Darius in Daniel 6 is the ruler who took Babylon from Belshazzar. Darius was the ruler of the Medo-Persian Empire.

Decrees. The decrees of a Persian king could not be overruled by a lower official. A king could not withdraw an order due to the royal code. If a king reconsidered a previous decision, it reflected negatively upon his leadership.

Background

Under King Nebuchadnezzar's reign, Daniel was appointed a governor in Babylon. Daniel was an advisor to King Nebuchadnezzar during the building of the new Babylonian Empire when Babylon was one of the most magnificent cities of the ancient world. Since Daniel lived to be an elderly statesman, he served several rulers faithfully and received honor from each. Daniel was governor in the Medo-Persian reign after the fall of Babylon.

At-A-Glance

1. The Enemies Plot (Daniel 6:4–7)
2. Daniel Believes (vv. 10, 16)
3. God Delivers (vv. 19, 21, 25–26)

In Depth

1. The Enemies Plot (Daniel 6:4–7)

Daniel had been a high official of the Babylon Empire for many years and was now a lead statesman in the Persian government. As a result of his faithful prophecies, Darius had placed Daniel in charge of key areas within the Babylonian government. However, the leaders of the provinces, who had been overlooked for key positions while Daniel and other Hebrew captives were given prime responsibilities, did not like Daniel. In order to have Daniel removed, they created a law that they knew would conflict with the law of Daniel's God. They acted out of jealousy, knowing that Daniel would continue his commitment to prayer and worship rather than obeying the king's decree. Daniel would not compromise his faith.

The proclamation said that no one would be allowed to pray to anyone other than the king for 30 days. In effect, the proclamation made Darius a god for 30 days. Once King Darius signed the document, it was law and everyone had to obey it. No one was excluded. A royal decree could not be changed by anyone, including the king. If anyone did not obey the proclamation, they would be thrown into the lions' den.

2. Daniel Believes (vv. 10, 16)

When Daniel prayed in spite of the law, his accusers informed the king that Daniel did not follow the king's command. Notice that they referred to Daniel as one of the "children of the captivity of Judah" (Daniel 6:13). They intensified the breach by telling Darius that Daniel was so defiant that he prayed three times a day.

Daniel's enemies knew when Daniel would be praying; they knew that he would not alter his worship pattern. Regardless of the law, Daniel remained devoted to God. He continued to pray to God three times a day with his windows open and his face turned toward Jerusalem. As expected, Daniel made his choice, and his choice was Jehovah.

Darius did not want to throw Daniel into the lions' den. His heart was heavy as he considered how he could save Daniel. While Daniel's enemies were happy, the king was saddened. Pressed by the leaders who had tricked him into signing this document, Darius could find no way out. He ordered Daniel to be brought before him. Even as he was executing punishment, the king was concerned for Daniel's life. Just as he sent Daniel to what seemed to be a likely death, Darius uttered a prayer that Daniel's God would deliver him from certain death.

Apparently Daniel entered the den without argument or complaint. Daniel did not fear the lions because he knew that he was safe in God's hands. He had made his point; he had stood for God. His routine of prayer had not been curtailed and he had not been intimidated. God had been glorified through Daniel's consistency in prayer and God would be glorified in this final trial as well. When we have completed God's will for our lives, we are still safe in His arms eternally.

Finally Daniel was placed into the lions' den, which was then sealed for the night to ensure that no one could come in and Daniel could not get out. The royal seal and the seal of the king's lords were placed on the lid.

3. God Delivers (vv. 19, 21, 25–26)

The king fasted that night, but Daniel trusted in God. The king was miserable all night because he really did not know Daniel's God. He knew that Daniel trusted God wholeheartedly, but Darius had depended on himself to save Daniel; therefore, he did not have peace. During that night he realized that only Daniel's God could save him.

The next morning Daniel was safe because God had protected him. The lions did not harm him. Because of their malicious plotting, the jealous accusers and their families were thrown into the lions' den, according to Persian custom. The execution was transferred to the accusers because God had saved Daniel, an elderly statesman whose faith was never compromised.

When the world does not follow God, we should continue to stand for God. Regardless of where we are, God knows our situation. Our faith will sustain us until God answers. Like Daniel, keep your faith in God and He will deliver you.

Search the Scriptures

1. What royal proclamation was drafted by Daniel's enemies (Daniel 6:4)?

2. Why couldn't King Darius reverse the law when he discovered it would harm Daniel (v. 10)?

3. What things did Daniel do in violation of the decree (v. 10)?

4. What was the punishment for not following the royal proclamation (vv. 7, 16)?

5. What was the king's reaction when he realized that Daniel had not followed the decree (v. 16)?

6. What was Darius's reaction in response to Daniel's salvation (vv. 25–26)?

Discuss the Meaning

1. Is it possible to remain committed to God in an environment that rejects God?

2. How can the body of believers help strengthen one another to remain steadfastly committed to God during times of conflict?

3. How important is it that Christians take a stand for justice for others?

Lesson in Our Society

Daniel was a high-profile leader in Babylon, but he was willing to take a stand in a life-or-death situation, regardless of what it would cost him. Daniel chose to engage in an act of civil disobedience because he felt it was more important to be consistent in his faith than to accept an unjust law.

Today we are surrounded with life-and-death situations that call Christians to take a stand for godly justice. Some high-profile issues that get attention are abortion and the plight of undocumented foreigners. However, matters of homelessness, hunger, inadequate education, rising medical cost, racial profiling, and the struggle for a living wage are also issues worthy of our attention. At what point should Christians take a stand? Is it ever important to take a stand regardless of what it might cost you personally? What obstacles restrict you from speaking out for justice?

Make It Happen

Every day there are any number of national and local organizations that need our help. While many of us are challenged with making a living, making ends meet, or even making dinner for the family, it is also critical that we make a difference in the lives of others. Conduct a search of your church, local charities, and nearby organizations that can use your help and commit to spending personal time volunteering. Whether it is answering telephones at a free health facility, serving meals to the homeless, sending cards and letters to U.S. troops, or being a mentor to a child, each of us is called, like Daniel, to let our faith be seen.

Follow the Spirit

What God wants me to do:

_____

_____

Remember Your Thoughts

Special insights I have learned:

_____

_____

More Light on the Text

Daniel 6:4–7, 10, 16, 19, 21, 25–26

4 Then the presidents and princes sought to find occasion against Daniel concerning the kingdom; but they could find none occasion nor fault; forasmuch as he was faithful, neither was there any error or fault found in him. 5 Then said these men, We shall not find any occasion against this Daniel, except we find it against him concerning the law of his God.

After reigning for 43 years, Nebuchadnezzar, king of Babylon, died. Daniel was over 80 years old and Darius was the new king. Daniel was one of the top three administrators in the regime. Daniel was still considered an alien because of his Hebrew birth. He had come to Babylon as a teen and been faithful in his work. Nevertheless, there were those in government who still sought to discredit and kill him because he did his job so well. Daniel had always proved to be diligent and responsible, and that made him enemies. The Scriptures declare that Daniel was "faithful" or 'aman (Heb. **am-AN**). Daniel was trustworthy. Neither "error" (Heb. shaluw, **shaw-LOO**) nor "fault" (Heb. shechath, **shekh-ATH**) were found in him.

Daniel was not popular among the "princes" (Heb. 'achashdarpan, **akh-ash-dar-PAN**) of the Persian provinces and the foreign "presidents" (Heb. carek, **saw-RAKE**) or overseers because each of the kings he served preferred him above the other leaders. As the jealous administrators maliciously conspired to get rid of him, they decided to make a strategic attack against his religion. Verse 4 indicates that plots had been laid and discussed before, but it was obvious that only his dedication to God could be used against him.

6 Then these presidents and princes assembled together to the king, and said thus unto him, King Darius, live for ever. 7 All the presidents of the kingdom, the governors, and the princes, the counsellors, and the captains, have consulted together to establish a royal statute, and to make a firm decree, that whosoever shall ask a petition of any God or man for

thirty days, save of thee, O king, he shall be cast into the den of lions.

Before they met with the king, the Persian princes and foreign kings hatched their sinister plot to trap Daniel. The phrase "have consulted together" in Hebrew is *ye'at* (**yeh-AT**), which means "to advise" or "take counsel." They held a meeting, strategized, and then met with the king. They agreed unanimously that the king should sign into law and strictly enforce a decree concerning worshiping other gods.

They presented a united front before the king, declaring that all the relevant leaders of the court were party to this decision. This is the first falsehood, because Daniel was not included in the discussion although they made it sound as if the group were totally inclusive. In addition to the leaders already mentioned, they claimed to have included the prefects or "governors" (Heb. *cegan*, **seg-AN**), the viziers or "counselors" (Heb. *haddabar*, **had-daw-BAWR**), and the "captains" (Heb. *pechah*, **peh-KHAW**) of the various regions in the empire.

The purpose of this caucus was supposedly to "establish" (Heb. *quwm*, **koom**) a royal decree or "statute" (Heb. *qeyam*, **keh-YAWM**). Here is the second fault. Royal decrees are developed by royalty; only the king could create such a decree. They took the initiative to draft a document for Darius's signature and presented it in language and under circumstances they knew he would accept. They did not have the power to oppose Daniel so they decided to manipulate the king, using his power for their own wicked purposes.

This law, of course, involved praying to no one but the king for 30 days, at risk of being thrown into the lions' den. Again, this was a direct attack on Daniel's spiritual covenant with the living God. The third fault in their plan is that the law would declare it impossible for anyone to ask for anything from anyone for the 30-day period. The law was not restricted to gods only. It clearly stated the people were included as well. Since their own jobs were to hear the petitions of the people they ruled, they could not be asked anything either! No doubt this wording was designed to circumvent questions that would have revealed their plot against Daniel. The "politically correct" wording needed to be so general that the real intent would remain hidden.

Their plan went beyond just developing a document. Daniel's accusers wanted the king to put in place a law that must be obeyed to the letter or the perpetrator would suffer the gravest consequences for disobedience. The penalty for disobedience was to be thrown into the lions' den. Furthermore, Persian law was immutable; it could not be changed.

Here, then, is the fourth fault. This punishment was much too severe for a 30-day injunction against prayer. Had they been serious about worship, the decree would have addressed a public and prolonged stance. Their intention was to buy just enough time to be rid of Daniel. They probably weren't sure if he would stop praying at all, but they knew that he would not curtail his worship for an entire 30-day period.

6:10 Now when Daniel knew that the writing was signed, he went into his house; and his windows being open in his chamber toward Jerusalem, he kneeled upon his knees three times a day, and prayed, and gave thanks before his God, as he did aforetime.

Daniel was not ignorant of the king's decree. We cannot tell whether Daniel spoke out against the law or not. He probably didn't. He was accustomed to these attacks against his faith. Whether there was a decree or not would not change his devotion to God. For Daniel this was spiritual warfare, but it was not a decision he was hard-pressed to make. Daniel knew full well the consequences of his actions, but he remained devoted and faithful to Almighty God. He would obey God rather than man because he was a covenant keeper. Regardless of the consequences, Daniel would continue his consistent practice of prayer.

Daniel's method for praying was to kneel in his private room with his windows open as he faced toward Jerusalem. He did this three times each day. Even though his actions were in his home, they were publicly known and publicly witnessed. Daniel's consistency showed no fear. He could have closed his windows and prayed. No one would have known if he was praying or not.

Daniel, however, understood that to do any of these things would have been to break his covenant with God. Daniel was not ashamed of the God he served or the faithfulness with which he served.

6:16 Then the king commanded, and they brought Daniel, and cast him into the den of lions. Now the king spake and said unto Daniel, Thy God whom thou servest continually, he will deliver thee.

"Now when Daniel knew that the writing was signed, he went into his house; and his windows being open in his chamber toward Jerusalem, he kneeled upon his knees three times a day, and prayed, and gave thanks before his God, as he did aforetime" (Daniel 6:10).

Darius's decision to execute Daniel was not at all easy. Verses 11–15, which are not in today's selected text, explain that the men who developed the decree immediately came to see if Daniel was praying—and he was. Without delay they went to the king. Oddly, they did not immediately say that Daniel was at fault. They asked if the king recalled signing the decree and if he remembered what the punishment was for disobedience. Of course he remembered, and he remembered that his sovereign word could not be changed.

Only then did they disclose the intent they had from the beginning. Everything they harbored in their hearts came tumbling out. "That Daniel . . ." There was the accusatory note. Not only was it "that Daniel" but he was of the "children of captivity of Judah." Herein was the disdain for Daniel and his people. His crime was disregarding the king and the decree. Furthermore, Daniel's crime was compounded because he not only prayed, he prayed three times per day!

This of course was not totally true. The opening verses of the chapter say that Daniel had always been faithful to the king and to the work he did on the king's behalf. The decree was unjust and they knew it. Daniel's reaction then can be considered "civil disobedience" rather than disregard.

If their intent was to corner the king and make him dislike Daniel, they failed. The king, according to verses 14 and 15, was totally distraught. Only at this point did he realize what he had been cajoled into doing. He had not considered the impact upon Daniel of this law. He now set about trying to find an avenue of escape for his trusted servant. The king spent the balance of the day trying to find a loophole in his own law.

Finally, the accusers returned and forced the king's hand. He "commanded" (Heb. *'amar*, **am-AR**), or declared his pronouncement, so that Daniel would be brought before him for sentencing. Darius had no alternative. The immutable character of the law meant that Daniel had to pay the penalty; he would be thrown into the den of lions. The only thing that even Darius could hope was that Daniel's God, who Daniel "servest" (Heb. *pelach*, **pel-AKH**) or "worshiped continually," would deliver him. Instead of the king denouncing Daniel's faithfulness to God, the king decided that he also had no choice but to trust Daniel's God.

6:19 Then the king arose very early in the morning, and went in haste unto the den of lions.

According to verse 18, the king was so distraught that he did not sleep that night. Instead he fasted, meditated, worried, wondered, hoped, and prayed that Daniel would be alive. The king was anxious to see if Daniel's God had delivered him, and therefore he went "in haste" (Heb. *behal*, **be-HAL**) to the lions' den the next morning to assess the situation.

Because a stone had been placed in front of the entrance to the den, Darius could not see Daniel. He called out to Daniel asking if Daniel's God, indeed, had been able to rescue him from the lions. His question was not simply, "Daniel, are you alive?" Darius asked if God had been able to deliver (see v. 20). The king realized that what he was asking was beyond human capacity. His inquiry was into the health of Daniel, but his question was to the ability and power of God.

6:21 Then said Daniel unto the king, O king, live for ever.

Daniel answered him in the affirmative, saying in essence, "Long live the king!" With these words, Daniel let the king know that he was alive and well. His God had shown up right on time to deliver him. God does everything very well; so well in fact that not a scratch was found on Daniel's body. The decree, which was designed to stop Daniel from asking God for favor, had actually resulted in having the king ask God for mercy. Darius believed God and now he knew for certain that the God of Daniel, the God of the Hebrews, was greater than any power he had ever known.

6:25 Then king Darius wrote unto all people, nations, and languages, that dwell in all the earth; Peace be multiplied unto you. 26 I make a decree, That in every dominion of my kingdom men tremble and fear before the God of Daniel: for he is the living God, and stedfast for ever, and his kingdom that which shall not be destroyed, and his dominion shall be even to the end.

King Darius made another decree. This message was to the people of every race, nation, and language throughout the world. Darius's decree was meant for everyone. Just as King Darius learned the power of Daniel's God, he wanted others to do so as well.

The king declared that all of the people of the Empire should tremble and fear before Almighty God. This is a statement regarding God's awesome power. God is not to be disregarded or underestimated. After seeing how God delivered Daniel from the jaws of death, King Darius decreed that men and women everywhere should honor and obey Daniel's God. Daniel had been faithful, and God had delivered him from the lions' den. King Darius was now convinced that Daniel's God was the living and omnipotent God. Daniel's devotion to God was a testimony to this ruler and to rulers throughout the world.

Sources:
Life Application Study Bible, NLT. Wheaton, Ill.: Tyndale House Publishers, Inc., 1996.
Strong, J. *The Exhaustive Concordance of the Bible* (electronic ed.). Ontario, Canada: Woodside Bible Fellowship, 1996.

Daily Bible Readings

M: Prayer and Commitment
Psalm 119:57–64

T: An Honest Leader
Daniel 6:1–4

W: A Dishonest Plot
Daniel 6:5–9

T: The King's Distress
Daniel 6:10–14

F: The Charge Stands
Daniel 6:15–18

S: Daniel Trusted in God
Daniel 6:19–23

S: The Living God
Daniel 6:24–28

TEACHING TIPS

April 27
Bible Study Guide 9

1. Words You Should Know

A. Books (Daniel 9:2) *cepher* (Heb.)—Scroll, letters of instruction, or written decrees; here referring to the writing of the prophet Jeremiah.

B. Supplications (vv. 3, 17–18) *tachanuwn* (Heb.)—Earnest prayer or entreaty for help.

C. Servant (v. 17) *'ebed* (Heb.)—A slave or bond servant. Daniel describes himself as a servant of the Most High God.

2. Teacher Preparation

Unifying Principle—Intercession in Crisis It sounds natural, but when a crisis arises, it is often harder to pray.

A. Compare Daniel's prayer to the acronym **ACTS**, whose letters stand for items that compose a prayer: **A** (Ask), **C** (Confession), **T** (Thanksgiving), and **S** (Supplication or Request). Prepare a handout of the **ACTS** acronym.

B. Read the Bible Study Guide and More Light on the Text sections to become familiar with the lesson and its background. Read the Focal Verses in several translations (see the *Precepts For Living*® CD-ROM).

C. Prepare to present the Words You Should Know.

D. Display the AIM for Change on a chalkboard or flip chart.

3. Starting the Lesson

A. Ask each class member to give a one-word testimony about a time God answered a prayer. Then ask how that increased their faith.

B. Ask for prayer requests. Have a volunteer compile them into a prayer list.

C. Open with prayer, including the requests.

D. Review today's AIM for Change. Ask the students to identify times of crisis that required intercessory prayer. Explain that Daniel prayed to save his people.

4. Getting into the Lesson

A. Present a brief background of today's lesson, including The People, Places, and Times, Words You Should Know, and Background sections.

B. Use the At-A-Glance outline and the Search the Scriptures questions to drive discussion.

C. Close this portion of the class with the Discuss the Meaning questions.

5. Relating the Lesson to Life

A. Read the Lesson in Our Society and Make It Happen sections. Encourage members to work together to develop a long-term plan of intercession for their communities and nation.

B. Many feel they cannot pray effectively and are intimidated by public prayer. Share the ACTS pattern, then ask the students what they would say in each part.

6. Arousing Action

A. Remind the students to use the Daily Bible Readings at home. Suggest that they review the Daily Bible Readings for Daniel 9 to examine the power and importance of prayer.

B. Close with an intercessory prayer circle. Take prayer requests and intercede for your pastor and church leadership as well as for personal and unspoken needs of class members.

Worship Guide

For the Superintendent or Teacher
Theme: Daniel's Prayer for the People
Theme Song: "Somebody Prayed for Me"
Devotional Reading: Psalm 130
Prayer

DANIEL'S PRAYER FOR THE PEOPLE

Bible Background • DANIEL 9
Printed Text • DANIEL 9:1–7, 17–19 Devotional Reading • PSALM 130

AIM for Change

By the end of the lesson, we will:

EXPLORE principles of prayer as reflected in Daniel's prayer;

REFLECT on times when prayers have been answered; and

IDENTIFY times when prayer should supersede all else.

Keep in Mind

"Now therefore, O our God, hear the prayer of thy servant, and his supplications, and cause thy face to shine upon thy sanctuary that is desolate, for the Lord's sake" (Daniel 9:17).

Focal Verses

KJV

Daniel 9:1 In the first year of Darius the son of Ahasuerus, of the seed of the Medes, which was made king over the realm of the Chaldeans;

2 In the first year of his reign I Daniel understood by books the number of the years, whereof the word of the LORD came to Jeremiah the prophet, that he would accomplish seventy years in the desolations of Jerusalem.

3 And I set my face unto the Lord God, to seek by prayer and supplications, with fasting, and sackcloth, and ashes:

4 And I prayed unto the LORD my God, and made my confession, and said, O Lord, the great and dreadful God, keeping the covenant and mercy to them that love him, and to them that keep his commandments;

5 We have sinned, and have committed iniquity, and have done wickedly, and have rebelled, even by departing from thy precepts and from thy judgments:

6 Neither have we hearkened unto thy servants the prophets, which spake in thy name to our kings, our princes, and our fathers, and to all the people of the land.

7 O Lord, righteousness belongeth unto thee, but unto us confusion of faces, as at this day; to the men of Judah, and to the inhabitants of Jerusalem, and unto all Israel, that are near, and that are far off, through all the countries whither thou hast driven them, because of their trespass that they have trespassed against thee.

9:17 Now therefore, O our God, hear the prayer of thy servant, and his supplications, and cause thy face to shine upon thy sanctuary that is desolate, for the Lord's sake.

18 O my God, incline thine ear, and hear; open thine eyes, and behold our desolations, and the city which is called by thy name: for we do not present

NLT

Daniel 9:1 It was the first year of the reign of Darius the Mede, the son of Ahasuerus, who became king of the Babylonians.

2 During the first year of his reign, I, Daniel, learned from reading the word of the LORD, as revealed to Jeremiah the prophet, that Jerusalem must lie desolate for seventy years.

3 So I turned to the LORD God and ~~pleaded with him in prayer and fasting~~. I also wore rough burlap and sprinkled myself with ashes.

4 I prayed to the LORD my God and confessed: "O Lord, you are a great and awesome God! You always fulfill your covenant and keep your promises of unfailing love to those who love you and obey your commands.

5 But we have sinned and done wrong. We have rebelled against you and scorned your commands and regulations.

6 We have refused to listen to your servants the prophets, who spoke on your authority to our kings and princes and ancestors and to all the people of the land.

7 Lord, you are in the right; but as you see, our faces are covered with shame. This is true of all of us, including the people of Judah and Jerusalem and all Israel, scattered near and far, wherever you have driven us because of our disloyalty to you.

9:17 "O our God, hear your servant's prayer! Listen as I plead. For your own sake, Lord, smile again on your desolate sanctuary.

18 "O my God, lean down and listen to me. Open your eyes and see our despair. See how your city—the city that bears your name—lies in ruins. We make this our supplications before thee for our righteousnesses, but for thy great mercies.

19 O Lord, hear; O Lord, forgive; O Lord, hearken and do; defer not, for thine own sake, O my God: for thy city and thy people are called by thy name.

plea, not because we deserve help, but because of your mercy.

19 "O Lord, hear. O Lord, forgive. O Lord, listen and act! For your own sake, do not delay, O my God, for your people and your city bear your name."

In Focus

Stacy and James had watched their best friends, Clarence and Maggie, face what seemed like one crisis after another. Before Clarence and Maggie came to the Lord three years earlier, their lives had not been shining examples for their children; but since then, they had turned their lives around. However, their son C. J. had gotten involved with a bad crowd, was arrested for his involvement in a crime, and was given a year's probation. At that time, Clarence's mother was gravely ill, and Maggie lost her job—a job they needed to make ends meet.

Stacy and James saw these situations taking a toll on their friends. They realized that just telling Clarence and Maggie to pray was not enough. They believed they should do something. They invited them over for dinner, and Stacy slipped a little money into Maggie's hand. Although Maggie tried to protest, she was appreciative. James gathered information about resources for Clarence's mom. His own father had faced health challenges, and he had contacts with some local agencies. Still the couple felt they could do more.

One Monday morning, James said, "I've asked the Lord about this, and He told me to 'push back the plate.' I'm going to start a fast and ask God's help for Clarence and Maggie."

"I'm with you," Stacy answered.

The two fasted and prayed for their friends for three days. After the fast, they continued to intercede, asking God to help direct and strengthen Clarence and Maggie. Within a month, they had received three calls. The first one was from Maggie, overjoyed that C. J. had talked to the pastor about being baptized. She later learned that his conviction had been overturned. The second call came from Clarence, who reported how well his mother was doing and how blessed she was by the caregiver the agency had sent. The last call was to invite Stacy and James to dinner to celebrate Maggie's new job.

Stacy and James never told their friends they had fasted. They just thanked God for answered prayer.

Sometimes we, like Daniel, need to intercede in prayer for others. Who is on your prayer list?

The People, Places, and Times

Jeremiah. Jeremiah was a prophet during the thirteenth year of Josiah's reign. He proclaimed God's judgment against Judah and Jerusalem and continued to speak to the exiles when they were in Babylon. Jeremiah is called "the weeping prophet" because he was saddened by the spiritual condition of Israel.

Sackcloth and Ashes. In biblical times, the tradition for prayer and supplication before God was to don sackcloth and ashes. Sackcloth was worn for mourning; ashes were a symbol of shame. To wear sackcloth and ashes was to admit a need for God's intervention on a dire matter (see Daniel 9:3).

Background

The time frame for today's lesson is the same as that of last week's study in Daniel 6. Because time was identified by events rather than dates, Daniel mentions the reign of several kings. It was in 605 B.C. that God used King Nebuchadnezzar to take Daniel, the three Hebrew assistants, and thousands of other Hebrews into captivity. God also allowed the complete destruction of Jerusalem and the Temple. Darius, the king mentioned in today's lesson, came to leadership after Babylon fell to Persia.

When God sent prophets to warn the nation to change, His message was ignored. When Daniel was taken captive in 605 B.C. (the final deportation was in 586 B.C.), Jeremiah, who became a prophet in 627 B.C., was still prophesying. It is the writings of Jeremiah that Daniel mentions in today's text. In this lesson, Daniel mourns the plight of his people and nation, and he goes to God as a prophet and intercessor on their behalf.

At-A-Glance

1. Daniel Prepares to Pray (Daniel 9:1–3)
2. Daniel Confesses on Behalf of the People (vv. 4–7)
3. Daniel Makes His Request Known (vv. 17–19)

In Depth

1. Daniel Prepares to Pray (Daniel 9:1–3)

Judah sinned against God, and that sin would be punished. Prior to captivity, God in His mercy sent prophets with warnings that Israel and Judah should repent of their wicked ways and return to God. One such prophet was Jeremiah, who prophesied to the southern kingdom, Judah. He foretold the exile of Judah and prophesied that the nation would be captive in Babylon for 70 years. The people continued to be disobedient and, as God warned, Judah was defeated.

God punished the nation for their sin by sending Judah to a strange land. This also was meant to encourage them to turn to God. The punishment was severe but God was merciful. Judah's exile in Babylon was not to be permanent. God would end the exile, reunite the nation, and restore the temple. Still, they were a nation in crisis. They needed to learn to pray and to recommit their dependence on God.

Daniel prayed to God. God's plan had been put in motion. God had allowed Judah to be exiled in Babylon and Babylon to be overthrown by Persia. The time prophesied by Jeremiah for the return from captivity was drawing near, and Daniel realized that he needed to pray and fast to know the Lord's will for His people. He put himself into sackcloth and ashes because he wanted to be humbled before God as he asked God's mercy upon the people of Judah and the city of Jerusalem.

2. Daniel Confesses on Behalf of the People (vv. 4–7)

Daniel's first act was to acknowledge God's sovereignty. We cannot come to God properly unless we realize that He is righteous and right! In verse 4, Daniel confessed who God is. He called God *Jehovah* (Lord) and therefore recognized God as the eternal and self-existent One. He acknowledged that God did not need them; they needed God. He called God "my God" or "my *Elohiym*," the righteous Judge of all, the divine Ruler of all people. He called God *Adonai* saying, "O Lord." Using this national name of Lord, Daniel confessed that he knew God. In doing so, he admitted that he was unworthy to come before Him.

Daniel recognized God as "the great and dreadful God, keeping the covenant and mercy to them that love him, and to them that keep his commandments" (v. 4). Again without even yet identifying Israel's specific sins, Daniel humbly confessed that God is mighty and to be feared because of His power. God is faithful and keeps His covenant with those who keep covenant with Him. God is merciful and lovingly bestows His mercy on those who love Him by following His commandments. Already Daniel saw and confessed that he and the nation were unworthy to even approach God.

Then Daniel confessed the sins of the people before this righteous God. In verse 5 he says, "We have sinned." Daniel was not flippant and knew that just lumping together everything under the banner of "sin" was not actually and sincerely confessing the wrong they had done to God. Therefore Daniel identified the sin. The nation had (1) committed iniquity, (2) done wickedly, (3) rebelled, (4) departed from God's precepts, (5) disregarded the Lord's judgments, and (6) ignored the servants, God's prophets. This was among the worst of the errors, because these men had brought warnings that could have offset the punishment they were due for the other things they had done. The sin was more than just individual sin, because the prophets had gone in God's name to the leaders of the nation as well as to the populace with warnings from God. To speak in God's name means this was done with God's full power and authority behind it. When a police officer issues a ticket, it is not on behalf of that individual officer but in the full authority of the government. Such was the case when the Hebrew nation ignored the warnings of God's prophets.

Daniel honestly acknowledged that God's punishment was just because the Hebrew people were at fault and brought their own punishment on themselves. They had broken their covenant commitment to a holy God, thereby drinking from His cup of wrath the full 70 years of captivity to the Babylonians and Persians. It did not matter where they were; the people could not escape what had been done to offend God, and Daniel included all of the people in his prayer. He expressed the shame they carried in direct contrast to the righteousness that belonged to God.

Like disobedient children who deserved the punishment in the first place, Judah and Israel had remained defiant and brought the full wrath of God upon themselves.

3. Daniel Makes His Request Known (vv. 17–19)

Daniel repented for himself and on behalf of the people, and asked God's forgiveness. He knew the power of prayer and was confident that God would respond to his cry as he asked God about His will for the future of the nation. Prayer reflects our dependence on God and our need for God's direction. Daniel went to God in sincerity, humility, and respect for God's will and righteousness.

Daniel knew that the time of punishment and banishment was ending, but he also knew that the only way the people could return to Jerusalem was by God's mercy. Daniel prayed for God to "incline thine ear, and hear; open thine eyes, and behold our desolations" (Daniel 9:18). Judah needed God.

Daniel's plea was not just for the people or even for the sake of the nation. Daniel pleaded with God so that God could be glorified by all nations as the mighty God who delivered His people and restored His temple. God's name was most important. God would receive the glory, and God's people would lead the praise of His name as they returned to the temple and showed the nations the power of the great and terrible God they served. Daniel sought God's forgiveness and restoration. Daniel did not give into the crisis; he turned to God. So should we.

Search the Scriptures

1. Which prophet wrote the "books" Daniel mentioned (Daniel 9:2)?

2. How did Daniel physically humble himself before God (v. 3)?

3. In addition to confessing the wrong Judah had committed, what else did Daniel confess (vv. 4, 7)?

4. What did Daniel want God to do in forgiving His people (vv. 17–19)?

Discuss the Meaning

1. What benefit was there to Daniel's fasting and wearing the clothes of shame and mourning?

2. How would you describe Daniel's plea for forgiveness?

3. What can we learn about the spiritual disciplines of prayer and fasting from this lesson?

Lesson in Our Society

In today's lesson, Daniel interceded for the nation and asked God's forgiveness. As you prayerfully consider the sins of our nation, how have we been disobedient as a nation before God? What biblical warnings have we ignored? How do our communities reflect our neglect of God's mandate to glorify Him before everyone?

Like Daniel, we must recognize sin and then move to ask God's forgiveness and direction. What can we, as faithful Bible students, do to intervene on behalf of our country and our communities?

Make It Happen

Create a group that makes a commitment to God to intercede for others. Remember that the fellowship of believers provides strength and encouragement.

Follow the Spirit

What God wants me to do:

_____

_____

Remember Your Thoughts

Special insights I have learned:

_____

_____

More Light on the Text

Daniel 9:1–7, 17–19

1 In the first year of Darius the son of Ahasuerus, of the seed of the Medes, which was made king over the realm of the Chaldeans; 2 In the first year of his reign I Daniel understood by books the number of the years, whereof the word of the LORD came to Jeremiah the prophet, that he would accomplish seventy years in the desolations of Jerusalem.

In ancient cultures, time was reckoned by events rather than dates. Daniel established the time of the events in this chapter by identifying the king he served. It was during the first year of King Darius's reign over the kingdom of the Chaldeans (522 B.C.) that Daniel began a study of the writings of the prophet Jeremiah, which revealed stirring information about the plight of the Hebrew people. King Darius was the son of Ahasuerus and a Mede, meaning that he was descended from the lineage of people from Madai in central Asia. This group of people claimed a heritage dating from Japheth, Noah's third son. As the ruler of the Chaldeans, Darius's kingdom included the area that bordered Persia near the lower Tigris and Euphrates Rivers in Mesopotamia.

Daniel's phrase "by books" refers to the writing of Jeremiah, who had prophesized that the Israelites would be in captivity for 70 years and then they would return to their homeland. In fact, Jeremiah declared, "And this whole land shall be a desolation, and an astonishment; and these nations shall serve the king of Babylon seventy years" (Jeremiah 25:11; see also 29:10). The word "accomplish" in Hebrew is *male'* (**maw-LAY**) and means "to fulfill or complete." In this light, from the prophecy of Jeremiah, Daniel understood that the time of captivity as appointed by God was nearing an end. He had no doubt that the length of their Babylonian captivity and the period of time that Jerusalem would be in "desolations" (Heb. *chorbah*, **khor-BAW**) or ruin because of the sin of God's people were in the hands of the almighty God.

3 And I set my face unto the Lord God, to seek by prayer and supplications, with fasting, and sackcloth, and ashes.

It was as a prophet that Daniel interceded in prayer for the Hebrew people. By "setting his face unto the Lord," Daniel was determined to go to the only source of help. Despite his work in the powerful government of King Darius and his history of service to the thrones of the Babylonian and Persian Empires, Daniel knew that only God could deliver his people.

Daniel was totally dependent upon "the Lord God." The term "Lord" or *'Adonay* (**ad-o-NOY**) was a term of reverence spoken in place of the name *Yahweh*. Because the Hebrews would not write or pronounce the entire name of Yahweh, they used this term instead. "God" or *'Elohiym* (**el-oh-HEEM**) is written as "Elohim" in English and is a reference to the Lord as the Supreme Ruler. Daniel esteemed, respected, and honored God and had an intimate relationship with Him. Because Daniel knew God as a deliverer in his life, he felt he could ask Him to deliver God's chosen people.

Daniel had been faithful in serving God, and God had delivered him during life-threatening circumstances; yet Daniel did not approach God with haughtiness or even familiarity. He sought God through prayer and supplication as he donned humility by placing himself in sackcloth and ashes as he prayed. "Sackcloth" (Heb. *saq*, **sak**) was a mesh fabric worn in times of mourning. The wearer would then cover himself in "ashes" (Heb. *epher*, **AY-fer**) as a sign of his own unworthiness. This self-humiliation

was a confession that people recognized their need for God's intervention in their situation. Daniel, whose heart was broken because of the sin and captivity of his people, humbly sought God's intervention and mercy.

Daniel knew that it was only through prayer and supplication that God could be asked to intervene. The word used here for "prayer" is *tephillah* (Heb. **tef-il-LAH**). It means "to ask for intercession." "Supplications" (Heb. *tachanuwn*, **tahkh-ahn-OON**) mean "to seek favor." Collectively, then, this phrase means that Daniel earnestly sought God's intervention and mercy. He begged God to deliver the people and to turn aside His anger.

4 And I prayed unto the LORD my God, and made my confession, and said, O Lord, the great and dreadful God, keeping the covenant and mercy to them that love him, and to them that keep his commandments;

On the outside Daniel was covered in sackcloth and ashes, symbols of his sorrowful spirit. On the inside he was truly repentant and sought God's mercy as one of those who had transgressed God's Law. Daniel called upon Jehovah Elohim. The word used for "Lord" in this case is the Hebrew *Yehovah*. This is the national name for God and declares Jehovah to be the self-existent and eternal God. This word recognizes that God is the Creator of all things and that by Him all things exist. Jehovah is self-existent. He does not depend on others and is all-powerful.

Daniel's prayer was not a simple statement of, "Sorry, Lord. I did it." Daniel poured out his heart before God. He first acknowledged the right of God to exact punishment for the sins committed against Him. Then he confessed for himself and his people. This righteous man acknowledged his own need for God's forgiveness for his transgressions of God's laws. The Hebrew term for "confession," *yadah* (**yah-DAH**), means "to cast down or give up that which is yours." Daniel acknowledged that the sin of his people was his sin. He did not attempt to say that the deeds prophesied by Jeremiah were committed by a previous generation. He did not put himself above other Hebrews by reminding God of how he personally had been faithful all the days of his captivity. He had refused the king's food, denied the unjust laws forbidding prayer, and faced the lions' den; but Daniel knew that those things showed God's power, not his own determination. God had delivered, and Daniel was humbled by God's mercy.

Again Daniel addressed God as "Adonay" and said, "the great and dreadful." In Hebrew "great" is *gadowl* (**gah-DOHL**), which means "large in magnitude and extent." With this word Daniel admitted that the God of Judah is larger than Judah. God's power and majesty extend far beyond the boundaries of the holy city, Jerusalem. There in Persia, in the capital city of a foreign land, the power of God was felt. Furthermore, Daniel called God "dreadful" (Heb. *yare'*, **yah-RAY**). God is to be feared and reverenced by all people. His might is so great that He must be given the honor due His name.

In addition, Daniel confessed God as a covenant keeper and a giver of mercy. Through their entire period of sin and judgment, God had never failed His people. Despite their so often forgetting God, He had never forgotten them. God had interceded on behalf of those who kept His commandments.

Daniel's own life had shown that God was faithful. As Daniel tried to serve God faithfully in a strange land, he found that God was present. And Daniel was not alone in this. The Hebrew young men who had been thrown into the furnace were witnesses as well. But Daniel's confession of God's merciful grace goes beyond even those few. God's faithfulness had been demonstrated to their fathers—from Adam to Noah, from Abraham to Jacob, through the judges and the prophets, God had been faithful.

5 We have sinned, and have committed iniquity, and have done wickedly, and have rebelled, even by departing from thy precepts and from thy judgments: 6 Neither have we hearkened unto thy servants the prophets, which spake in thy name to our kings, our princes, and our fathers, and to all the people of the land.

"Now therefore, O our God, hear the prayer of thy servant, and his supplications, and cause thy face to shine upon thy sanctuary that is desolate, for the Lord's sake" (Daniel 9:17).

Daniel surrendered completely as he spoke to Jehovah. He knew that God was a covenant keeper, despite the fact that the Children of Israel were covenant breakers. The Hebrew people had openly rebelled against God and incurred His wrath. It was their own fault that God had punished them by allowing them to go into bondage to the Babylonians. It was because of their sin that the punishment had continued upon their children for multiple generations. In all of this, God was not only blameless but had been merciful toward them. The Hebrew people could blame no one but themselves and could turn to no one but the Lord.

In addition, they had committed "iniquity" (Heb. *'avah*, **aw-VAW**). They had perverted God's Law and done wrong before Him. They had twisted His edicts and failed to follow His will in His way. To further show how they did not follow God's directives, Daniel said that the people "have done wickedly." This phrase in Hebrew is *rasha'* (**raw-SHAH**) and means "to be guilty and condemned" because of wicked ethical and religious acts. There was no doubt in Daniel's mind that God was just in condemning the idolatry and unfaithfulness of His people.

The Hebrew word *shama'* (**shaw-MAH**) means "hearkened" to say that the people had not heard and been obedient to God's Word. To *shama'* means to listen with the intention of obeying, to pay strict attention to what is said and then to yield to the will of the one who gives direction. Daniel knew that as the people and nation walked in sin, they broke their covenant relationship with a Holy God. They had refused to listen and obey. They had willfully refused to yield to God's servants, the prophets who had spoken on God's behalf. These spokesmen had warned them again and again that departing from God's precepts and judgments would kindle the hot anger of Almighty God and He would punish them. There was no excuse for their disobedience, because the prophets spoke to their kings, princes, forefathers, and all the people of the land.

But the people and their leaders failed to listen; they would not hear. They would not heed. Consequently, they had to suffer the consequences of their disobedience—captivity again! Their history had revealed God's deliverance from Egypt, but their actions had caused them to again be placed under the thumb of oppressors as their places of worship and their homes were destroyed and their children were led away to other lands.

7 O Lord, righteousness belongeth unto thee, but unto us confusion of faces, as at this day; to the men of Judah, and to the inhabitants of Jerusalem, and unto all Israel, that are near, and that are far off, through all the countries whither thou hast driven them, because of their trespass that they have trespassed against thee.

Daniel again acknowledged God as his Lord. He recognized the righteous attributes of the God he served. Daniel admitted to God that God was right in His punishment of Israel. He had dealt righteously with His people. They, on the other hand, were the possessors of "confusion" (Heb. *bosheth*, **BO-sheth**) or "shame." Because of Israel's disobedience, their faces were covered with shame, while God's glory is righteous. Daniel also confessed that the people of Judah, Jerusalem, and all Israel, scattered far and near, were to bear the shame of being in captivity. Daniel knew they were scattered because of their own disobedience—their own breaking of God's covenant. God would not tolerate their disloyalty. Neither did God merit their unfaithfulness to Him; He had been too good to the Israelites.

9:17 Now therefore, O our God, hear the prayer of thy servant, and his supplications, and cause thy face to shine upon thy sanctuary that is desolate, for the Lord's sake.

Here Daniel cried out to the Lord because of his deep concern for the nation and the city of Jerusalem where God had placed His sanctuary. Daniel reminded Elohim that Israel was His special possession. The nation was God's chosen people, elected by Him to be representatives of His power and glory to the rest of the world. God had ordained them to be examples to other nations of the power of the Holy God.

Daniel also pleaded with God to hear his prayer, the prayer of God's servant. The phrase "of thy servant" means bondsman or slave in Hebrew. Daniel acknowledged again that he was a servant who served as a prophet or spokesman of the Most High God. It was in his service to God that he appealed to God to hear his petition and supplications.

Daniel then asked that the Lord, for the Lord's own sake, to smile again on His temple. The temple at Jerusalem had been foreshadowed by the tabernacle in the wilderness; it had been promised to David, then built by Solomon. It was destroyed in the destruction of Jerusalem and then sat desolate, a mockery to the power of God. The word used for "sanctuary" is the Hebrew word *miqdash* (**mik-DAWSH**) and refers to the sacred or holy place of worship. In essence, Daniel asked God to restore His holy temple in Jerusalem, God's "sacred place," so that all people would know His name and His power.

18 O my God, incline thine ear, and hear; open thine eyes, and behold our desolations, and the city which is called by thy name: for we do not present our supplications before thee for our righteousnesses, but for thy great mercies.

Daniel asked God to do three things: to "incline" (Heb. *natah*, **naw-TAW**) his ear, to "open" (Heb. *paqach*, **paw-KAKH**) His eyes, and to "behold" (Heb. *ra'ah*, **raw-AW**) the desolation. Daniel asked Almighty God to extend or stretch forth His ear to hear Daniel's petitions for the people and the nation. He begged God to look intently on the pressing situation of His chosen people. He wanted God to open His eyes and see their wretchedness, to see Jerusalem in ruin.

Since Daniel was the intercessor for the Israelites, he told God that he and the people were not asking because they deserved God's help. In fact, Daniel and the nation knew they deserved God's wrath and punishment. But Daniel asked God for help because He is merciful. Daniel acknowledged that God is a God of great compassion. Even though God judges sin, He still shows mercy to those who love Him and are faithful to Him.

19 O Lord, hear; O Lord, forgive; O Lord, hearken and do; defer not, for thine own sake, O my God: for thy city and thy people are called by thy name.

Finally Daniel, in making intercession for the Israelites and the nation, begged God to forgive the people and the nation. The Hebrew word for "forgive" is *calach* (**saw-LAKH**). Daniel asked God to pardon the people individually and the nation collectively for their sin. Daniel came in prayer to his God with a broken and contrite heart, a repentant spirit. He did not come before God trying to make excuses or to place blame. Daniel knew that the omniscient and omnipresent God knew the full extent of their transgressions and disobedience; therefore, Daniel wanted God to hear his pleas and to act on their behalf.

Daniel wanted God to make things right, to put things back together again. He wanted God to put Jerusalem and the temple back in order. The urgency of Daniel's prayer is that he asked God not to defer (Heb. *'achar*, **aw-KHAR**) or delay this work. Daniel

wanted God to answer his prayer quickly. He realized that the 70 years prophesied by Jeremiah was almost up, and he knew that the sins of the people were still counted against them.

It was not, however, for selfish reasons that Daniel wanted God's swift reconciliation. He wanted God to set things right "for thine own sake, O my God." In other words, since the Children of Israel were God's own special possessions, Daniel reminded God that His mercy was needed for His own glory, for the restoration of Jerusalem and the temple, for the return of the city and the people called by God's name. Once more Daniel reminded God that the Israelites were elected by God; they were His chosen people.

Daniel's prayers and supplications are marvelous examples of how we are to take our petitions to God. We must not go blaming God or others. We must come before God acknowledging our own sins and asking Him for forgiveness, because the failure is not in God, but in us!

Sources:
Life Application Study Bible, NLT. Wheaton, Ill.: Tyndale House Publishers, Inc., 1996.
Pfeiffer, Charles F., Howard F. Vos, John Rea, eds. *Wycliffe Bible Dictionary*. Peabody, Mass.: Hendrickson Publishers, Inc., 1998.
Strong, J. *The Exhaustive Concordance of the Bible* (electronic ed.). Ontario, Canada: Woodside Bible Fellowship, 1996.

Daily Bible Readings

M: The Assurance of Redemption
Psalm 130
T: Preparing to Pray
Daniel 9:1–3
W: A Righteous God
Daniel 9:4–10
T: God's Response to Sin
Daniel 9:11–14
F: Hear, O God
Daniel 9:15–19
S: A Word Gone Out
Daniel 9:20–23
S: God's Strong Covenant
Daniel 9:24–27

TEACHING TIPS

May 4
Bible Study Guide 10

1. Words You Should Know

A. Time (Haggai 1:2) *'eth* (Heb.)—Now or due time.

B. Cieled (v. 4) *caphan* (Heb.)—Covered.

C. Waste (v. 4) *chareb* (Heb.)—Desolate.

D. Messenger (v. 13) *mal'ak* (Heb.)—A bearer of news.

2. Teacher Preparation

Unifying Principle—First Things First There are some things that God will ask us to do simply because it honors Him. What determines your priorities? We must never choose our own ambitions over God's plans for us.

A. Read The People, Places, and Times, In Depth, More Light on the Text, and Background sections. Next, read the book of Haggai, the Bible Background, and Daily Bible Readings.

B. Study the Focal Verses from several translations (see the *Precepts For Living*® CD-ROM). Make notes of pertinent differences to help you explain the verses to the class.

C. Review the AIM for Change to focus your teaching.

D. Prepare a chart listing the characteristics of prophecy and the history of Haggai, the prophet.

E. Create a timeline to review the events that led to captivity and that occurred in captivity in the first two units of study (March and April).

F. Gather a flip chart and two different colored markers.

3. Starting the Lesson

A. Open class with prayer, asking God to help the students understand how to apply to their lives the word that was sent to the exiles.

B. Review the events of the timeline and explain that this unit examines the return of the captives to Jerusalem.

C. Present a short lecture on Haggai and the nature of prophecy.

4. Getting into the Lesson

A. Follow the At-A-Glance outline, and use the Search the Scriptures and Discuss the Meaning questions to discuss the Focal Verses.

B. Refer the students to the Words You Should Know as they arise.

5. Relating the Lesson to Life

A. Ask a volunteer to read the In Focus section. Discuss Darren's attitude and relate it to the lesson.

B. Ask the class to brainstorm ways we demonstrate that our priorities are contrary to God's value system. Record these comments in a single column with one marker.

C. Assign one or more items from the list above to small groups of class members. Ask each group to identify strategies for changing and rectifying these errors in priorities. Allow groups to share and record their responses in the second color.

D. Have the class read Lesson in Our Society and discuss the questions.

6. Arousing Action

A. Encourage the class to complete the Make It Happen assignment. Discuss the benefits of a prayer journal. Have those who have kept journals share their experiences.

B. Ask for prayer requests from class members. Close in prayer, lifting up students' concerns.

Worship Guide

For the Superintendent or Teacher
Theme: The Temple Rebuilt
Theme Song: "Trust and Obey"
Devotional Reading: Psalm 84:1–4
Prayer

THE TEMPLE REBUILT

Bible Background • HAGGAI 1; EZRA 5
Printed Text • HAGGAI 1:1–4, 7–10, 12–15 Devotional Reading • PSALM 84:1–4

AIM for Change

By the end of the lesson, we will:

EXPLORE why God withheld His blessings from His people;

SENSE times when our own ambitions are contrary to God's plans for us; and

DECIDE that we will do exactly as God has commanded.

Keep in Mind

"Go up to the mountain, and bring wood, and build the house; and I will take pleasure in it, and I will be glorified, saith the LORD" (Haggai 1:8).

Focal Verses

KJV Haggai 1:1 In the second year of Darius the king, in the sixth month, in the first day of the month, came the word of the LORD by Haggai the prophet unto Zerubbabel the son of Shealtiel, governor of Judah, and to Joshua the son of Josedech, the high priest, saying,

2 Thus speaketh the LORD of hosts, saying, This people say, The time is not come, the time that the LORD's house should be built.

3 Then came the word of the LORD by Haggai the prophet, saying,

4 Is it time for you, O ye, to dwell in your ceiled houses, and this house lie waste?

1:7 Thus saith the LORD of hosts; Consider your ways.

8 Go up to the mountain, and bring wood, and build the house; and I will take pleasure in it, and I will be glorified, saith the LORD.

9 Ye looked for much, and, lo, it came to little; and when ye brought it home, I did blow upon it. Why? saith the LORD of hosts. Because of mine house that is waste, and ye run every man unto his own house.

10 Therefore the heaven over you is stayed from dew, and the earth is stayed from her fruit.

1:12 Then Zerubbabel the son of Shealtiel, and Joshua the son of Josedech, the high priest, with all the remnant of the people, obeyed the voice of the LORD their God, and the words of Haggai the prophet, as the LORD their God had sent him, and the people did fear before the LORD.

13 Then spake Haggai the LORD's messenger in the LORD's message unto the people, saying, I am with you, saith the LORD.

NLT Haggai 1:1 On August 29 of the second year of King Darius's reign, the LORD gave a message through the prophet Haggai to Zerubbabel son of Shealtiel, governor of Judah, and to Jeshua son of Jehozadak, the high priest.

2 "This is what the LORD of Heaven's Armies says: The people are saying, 'The time has not yet come to rebuild the house of the LORD.'"

3 Then the LORD sent this message through the prophet Haggai:

4 "Why are you living in luxurious houses while my house lies in ruins?

1:7 "This is what the LORD of Heaven's Armies says: Look at what's happening to you!

8 Now go up into the hills, bring down timber, and rebuild my house. Then I will take pleasure in it and be honored, says the LORD.

9 You hoped for rich harvests, but they were poor. And when you brought your harvest home, I blew it away. Why? Because my house lies in ruins, says the LORD of Heaven's Armies, while all of you are busy building your own fine houses.

10 It's because of you that the heavens withhold the dew and the earth produces no crops.

1:12 Then Zerubbabel son of Shealtiel, and Jeshua son of Jehozadak, the high priest, and the whole remnant of God's people began to obey the message from the LORD their God. When they heard the words of the prophet Haggai, whom the LORD their God had sent, the people feared the LORD.

13 Then Haggai, the LORD's messenger, gave the people this message from the LORD: "I am with you, says the LORD!"

14 And the LORD stirred up the spirit of Zerubbabel the son of Shealtiel, governor of Judah, and the spirit of Joshua the son of Josedech, the high priest, the spirit of all the remnant of the people; and they came and did work in the house of the LORD of hosts, their God,

15 In the four and twentieth day of the sixth month, in the second year of Darius the king.

14 So the LORD sparked the enthusiasm of Zerubbabel son of Shealtiel, governor of Judah, and the enthusiasm of Jeshua son of Jehozadak, the high priest, and the enthusiasm of the whole remnant of God's people. They began to work on the house of their God, the LORD of Heaven's Armies,

15 on September 21 of the second year of King Darius's reign.

In Focus

Darren was alienated from his family at age 22. He and his parents argued because of his drinking and refusal to work. He had moved in with various friends or acquaintances until his family no longer knew how to contact him and his friends no longer wanted him around.

Now, at age 40, he had turned his life around, married, and fathered three children who had never seen their grandparents. However, Darren's parents never stopped loving him and never stopped trying to find him.

One day in a mall with his family, Darren saw a childhood friend. After some catching up, the man said, "You must know that your parents are concerned about you. They have never given up hope of reuniting with you. They are older now. Your dad has been ill, and it has been a difficult time for them financially and physically. They have held on to the house in case you ever return, but it is clearly too much for them."

Darren was ashamed and said, "I have been away so long, and there are many hurt feelings between my parents and me."

To this the man responded, "You can still come back home."

But Darren went on. "I thought I would come back to my parents when I had accomplished something and made a life for myself. However, when that happened, I told myself that I would come back when I had made enough money. Then the Lord blessed me with money, and I said I would come back when the Lord blessed me with children. But I never came back."

Then the man asked him, "Do you think it is right for you to live in a mansion while your parents struggle to live? Do you suppose it is good for you to have your children while your parents lose the opportunity to be with their own child? Do you suppose it is good for you to have wealth while your parents have spent every dime they had looking for you?"

Darren admitted his shame, and as soon as he left the mall, he went to his parents' house, still very nervous about what would happen next.

In today's lesson we see a nation of people who, in spite of God's love for them, created a priority system that was out of touch with the will of God who brought them from exile. Consider how poor priorities impact all of the relationships in our lives as well as our relationship with God.

The People, Places, and Times

Haggai. Haggai was an Old Testament prophet and author of the book of Haggai. The name Haggai is derived from the Hebrew word *hag*, meaning "feast" or "festival." This term usually refers to the three pilgrimage feasts of the Jewish religious calendar (Feast of Unleavened Bread, Feast of Weeks, and Feast of Tabernacles). The prophet may have been born during the celebration of one of these feasts. As God's spokesman, Haggai encouraged the captives who returned to Jerusalem to complete the reconstruction of the temple.

Remnant. The part of a community or nation that remains after a dreadful judgment or devastating calamity, especially those who have escaped and remain to form the nucleus of a new community. The survival of a righteous remnant rests solely on God's providential care for His chosen people and His faithfulness to keep His covenant promises.

Zerubbabel. Zerubbabel became the Persian governor of Judah under Darius, and was placed in charge of the returning Jews and given the title "Governor of Judah." After much delay, Zerubbabel succeeded in leading the rebuilding of the temple in Jerusalem in the sixth century B.C. (see Ezra 3:8–10 and Haggai 1:14). This reconstruction lasted longer than the temples of Solomon and Herod the Great combined.

Background

The Lord had provided wondrously for the Children of Israel, but they sinned against Him. In His mercy, He promised to deliver them from the hands of their captors. He also gave careful instruction through the prophets regarding how and when to rebuild the temple in Jerusalem. Once the captives were allowed to return to Jerusalem, they set up an altar and laid the temple foundation. The work of rebuilding the temple started shortly after the first exiles returned from Babylon in 538 B.C., but the building activity was soon abandoned because of discouragement and oppression as they faced multiple fronts of opposition. They became so frustrated that even when the opposition was lifted, they were slow in rebuilding the temple. They settled comfortably into their own homes and were content to neglect the temple work. It is this breech of promise that is addressed in today's lesson. Beginning in 520 B.C., Haggai and his fellow prophet Zechariah urged the people to resume the task. The temple was completed four years later in about 516 B.C. (see Ezra 5:1; 6:15).

At-A-Glance

1. The Message of the Prophet
(Haggai 1:1–4)
2. A Prophetic Challenge (vv. 7–10)
3. Obedience and Transformation
(vv. 12–15)

In Depth

1. The Message of the Prophet (Haggai 1:1–4)

The book of Haggai had a message for the Hebrew people who returned from the exile imposed by Babylon in 586 B.C. Even though the Hebrew people had more than 70 years in captivity to learn about the priority of divine things, they returned to their old pattern of misplaced priorities and a few years after returning from exile again misunderstood their purpose. Haggai's prophecies declared God's displeasure with Judah's ingratitude.

God made it clear through King Cyrus that the reason for the return was to rebuild the house of the Lord and to resume worship in it. But after the people received their freedom, they put other priorities

before those of God and made excuses for not doing God's task. The first excuse was that there was no time. They basically said, "What is the rush? It can wait." They had been freed from physical bondage, but they were still bound by the tyranny of time. It is amazing how we suddenly acquire the gift of patience when it comes to doing the things that God has commanded us!

The returning remnant could not say they did not know how to go about the work, because God had given them specific instructions on how to do it. They could not say that they had no money, because God had provided the monies. They could not say that they had no experts, for God had provided skilled workers. In spite of all the providential preparation, they said that it was not time yet to rebuild.

Their own comfort had become their god. In short, they had become their own god. What they wanted took precedence over what God wanted. Look at the way God poses the question to them in verse 4: "Is it time for you . . . ?" This implies that it was not an issue of time but of their view of God's place in their lives. Such an attitude calls for self-examination.

2. A Prophetic Challenge (vv. 7–10)

This call to self-examination implies that if the Hebrew people weighed things carefully, they would notice their way was not working; they struggled to maintain the bare minimum. God, having been put on the back shelf, was withholding His blessings. These people were like so many of us; we want the gifts but not the Giver. We need to be reminded that God is our source. We must keep in mind that God is the reason we have what we possess. How soon we forget!

God revealed that there was an imbalance in their lives because of their procrastination and disobedience. In verses 7 and 8, He tells how they can get back on track. First, He tells them, "Consider your ways." Second, He tells them to prioritize. There was a way of escape from their hopelessness. God says to go and "build the house" (v. 8). Notice that God does not change the command; He merely gives them a second chance. Obedience to God realigns us with His will and puts us in the place where we are able to receive from the Lord.

They were in trouble, which they had brought upon themselves. They chose their own houses instead of God's house. The desolation of God's house led to the desolation of their houses. Everything that happened to them directly related to something they did or refused to do in relation to God. He had provided everything they needed, yet there was not a house for Him. The law of recompense was in progress: they reaped what they sowed.

3. Obedience and Transformation (vv. 12–15)

God is pleased when we hear His rebuke and repent. The people repented after Haggai revealed what God was saying to them. They did what God said to do; they considered their ways. Haggai then assured them of God's presence (v. 13). Once the people obeyed, God reassured them by saying, "I am with you." This reassurance caused the people to complete the work they started. Their spirits were stirred, and they were ready to work.

Search the Scriptures

1. When did the events in today's lesson take place (Haggai 1:1)?
2. What contrast did God draw between His house and the houses of the returning remnant (v. 4)?
3. What were the people to do, and how was God going to respond (vv. 7–10)?
4. When was the temple completed (v. 15)?

Discuss the Meaning

1. Why does God say He "blew" on what they had (v. 9)? How does this relate to what we gain through ill-placed priorities?
2. What does the procrastination of these returnees say about how people regard God's grace and favor?
3. Why do you think God was so patient? How is He patient with us?

Lesson in Our Society

If we are honest with ourselves, we will discover that many (not all) of the calamities we face are a direct result of our disobedience to God's Word. God has told us the way to succeed, but we have chosen to go our own way. He says, "Left," and we say, "Right." He says, "Up," and we say, "Down." He says, "No," and we say, "Yes."

Consider a time when God revealed His desire that you build a life that honored Him, but you failed to obey. How did your disobedience manifest itself in other areas of your life? How have you learned to heed God's voice? What advice can you give others to do the same?

Make It Happen

Make a list of some circumstances in your life that are not going favorably. Search the Scriptures beginning with today's lesson, asking God to reveal where you should honor Him in your life. Ask the Holy Spirit to give you the courage and determination to make God's priorities your priorities and to lift your anxiety as you focus more on being in His will. Keep a prayer journal during this time to record the changes and encouragement God gives you spiritually and physically as you see Him change you in the midst of the situation.

Follow the Spirit

What God wants me to do:

_____

_____

Remember Your Thoughts

Special insights I have learned:

_____

_____

More Light on the Text

Haggai 1:1–4, 7–10, 12–15

1 In the second year of Darius the king, in the sixth month, in the first day of the month, came the word of the LORD by Haggai the prophet unto Zerubbabel the son of Shealtiel, governor of Judah, and to Joshua the son of Josedech, the high priest, saying,

This text describes events that took place during the second year of the reign of King Darius, ruler of the Medo-Persian Empire. As was customary, Haggai dated his prophecy by identifying the ruling power of his day. Darius was relatively new to the throne at the time the Lord directed Haggai to speak to the people regarding the repair of the temple. This center of worship had been desecrated by Nebuchadnezzar when Judah was taken captive in about 586 B.C. At that time the temple was sacked and the sacred artifacts of worship were taken to Babylon. Babylon fell to Persia in about 539 B.C. It was in this succession of wars and kings that formed the Persian Empire, which Darius led starting in 522 B.C.

Jerusalem was central to the religious and national identity of the Hebrew people. Even in their Diaspora (or scattering abroad) whenever they prayed, they faced the direction of Jerusalem because the temple and, therefore, God's presence, was there (see 1 Kings 8:48 and Jonah 2:7). When King Cyrus began allowing the people to return, their primary concern was with repairing the temple of God.

In about 537 B.C., King Cyrus issued a decree allowing a remnant of the Hebrew captives and their offspring to return to Jerusalem. This group immediately made an altar to offer sacrifices, and soon thereafter laid the foundation for a restructured temple. Their return and work to rebuild the temple, however, precipitated anger and opposition by the Samaritans. These descendants of the northern kingdom of Israel had already repopulated Jerusalem after their return from captivity. When the captives from the southern kingdom of Judah returned and resumed work on the temple, the Samaritans claimed they wanted to help with the rebuilding effort. However, because the Samaritans were not considered "true Israel," their request was rejected (see Ezra 4).

Opposition continued to frustrate efforts until finally a letter was sent by the Samaritans to King Artaxerxes asking a halt to the work. When Artaxerxes complied by issuing a decree, the work on the temple stopped (see Ezra 4). Fourteen years later, King Darius came to power and found the original decree written by King Cyrus. This reinstated the authority for the restoration of the temple, and the work should have resumed immediately (see Ezra 4:24). Instead, the captives had become comfortable with the situation and were spiritually lethargic. They were preoccupied with building their own homes and found excuses for neglecting the house of the Lord by claiming the timing wasn't right.

God called His "prophet" (Heb. *nabiy'*, **naw-BEE**) to urge the people to complete the temple. The phrase "thus speaketh the LORD of hosts" makes it clear that the words the prophet spoke were not merely his but God's. A similar phrase, "saith the LORD," is repeated throughout the book of Haggai (1:7, 13; 2:4, 6–9, 11, 14, 23) and points to Haggai as an instrument through whom God speaks.

Haggai addresses God's concerns to Zerubbabel, the governor of Jerusalem, and Josedech, the high priest. As "governor" (Heb. *pechah*, **peh-KHAW**), Zerubbabel was the captain over the returning remnant of Judah. He is referred to as being the son of Shealtiel who was a descendant of the House of David. Thus, a descendant of David was still "on the throne" or in leadership of Judah. Clearly Zerubbabel was not a king, but his lineage was important to the heritage of the people.

In this same verse, Joshua, the son of Josedech, was the high priest. This also follows a line of succession. Joshua was the great-grandson of the high priest Hilkiah. It was Hilkiah who found the Book of the Law in the temple during the renovations ordered by King Josiah (refer to lesson 5—March 30). Hilkiah's son, Seraiah, also served as high priest. Hilkiah's son likely served after captivity but before deportation. Josedech was the son of Seraiah and the father of the high priest Joshua. Josedech was probably a captive and never served in the temple. In this text, Josedech is honored as the father of Joshua who served as high priest immediately following the exile.

Zerubbabel and Joshua were the highest ranking officials in the repopulated Jerusalem and represented both governmental and religious leadership. It was fitting that the word of rebuke given by God to Haggai be directed to the people who could make a difference.

2 Thus speaketh the LORD of hosts, saying, This people say, The time is not come, the time that the LORD's house should be built.

Haggai's first words on God's behalf attacked their excuses for not completing the building project. God begins by addressing the people as "this people" rather than "my people." The word for "people" (Heb. *'am*, **am**) refers to a national identity of related kinsmen. God's condemnation was delivered to the leadership but encompassed each member of the family of Abraham. Since they had neglected His service, the returning captives were met with the accusatory and reproachful tone of "this people," showing their estrangement from God.

The excuse the people most often used to explain their neglect of God's work was that the "time" had not come. In other words, the proper time for building the temple had not arrived. The leaders claimed that the interruption in the work caused by their enemies proved that it was not yet the "proper time" to rebuild the temple. Their real motive, however, was self-centered. They did not want the trouble, expense, and danger from enemies. Politically, they were without excuse since King Darius was sympathetic to their cause. Haggai began with what the people "say" (Heb. 'amar, **aw-MAR**). By indicating what the people said, Haggai presented not just the words but also the thoughts behind them. Not only were the people giving an excuse, but they believed it! Their excuse had become their way of life, and they had become comfortable with it.

3 Then came the word of the LORD by Haggai the prophet, saying, 4 Is it time for you, O ye, to dwell in your cieled houses, and this house lie waste?

The "LORD" (Heb. Yehovah, **yeh-ho-VAW**) is God's covenant title. It implies God's consistent and unchanging faithfulness in keeping His promises to His people. His faithfulness was in direct response to the unfaithfulness of the people He had delivered. In response to their complaint regarding time, God asked how it seemed to be a good time for them to build their own houses and to dwell there at ease.

God's words are "O ye," or literally, "you, you." The repetition of the pronoun shows the shameful contrast between their concern for themselves and their unconcern for God (see 1 Samuel 25:24 and Zechariah 7:5 for similar uses of repetition). The word "cieled" is from the Hebrew caphan (**saw-FAN**) and means "paneled" or "covered." It refers to the walls and ceilings of the people's homes, which were not only comfortably furnished but luxurious. This was in sad contrast to God's house, which was not merely unadorned; its walls were not raised above the foundations.

1:7 Thus saith the LORD of hosts; Consider your ways. 8 Go up to the mountain, and bring wood, and build the house; and I will take pleasure in it, and I will be glorified, saith the LORD.

"Consider your ways" translates two Hebrew words. The first, siym (**seem**), means "to set, put, or establish." The second, lebab (**lay-BAWB**), means "heart" and therefore implies "conscience or mind." The phrase is literally, "Set your heart" or "Give care-

ful consideration." The implication is to consider both what they had done and what they had allowed.

The "mountain" is probably a reference to the mountains around Israel where trees were plentiful. Though not to the exclusion of other materials such as stones, wood was the primary material necessity in building the temple.

God declared, "I will take pleasure" and "I will be glorified" in the newly built temple. "Pleasure," which derives from the Hebrew ratsah (**raw-TSAW**), denotes "delight in" or "to be pleased with." Ratsah frequently describes God's pleasure with His servants. "Glorified" is from kabed (**kaw-BADE**), meaning "to be honored or renowned." God is saying that He would be favorable to supplicants in the temple and receive the honor due to Him, which had been withheld by neglecting the temple that represented His presence.

9 Ye looked for much, and, lo, it came to little; and when ye brought it home, I did blow upon it. Why? saith the LORD of hosts. Because of mine house that is waste, and ye run every man unto his own house. 10 Therefore the heaven over you is stayed from dew, and the earth is stayed from her fruit.

The Hebrew infinitive here expresses continued looking and expectation. The people hoped to increase their own possessions while neglecting the temple. As they sought to prosper in their homes and through the agriculture of the land where they settled, they kept finding themselves in the position of thinking they had enough but finding it was too little. Even if their idea was only to make ends meet, God reminds them in this verse that whatever they got for their toil was never enough.

Furthermore, God brings to their minds the fact that "when ye brought it home, I did blow upon it." In case they thought they were working hard but just not making enough or that someone was cheating them in their business dealings, God lets them know that He alone was responsible for their lack. It was God who scattered even the little crop the people harvested and stored in their barns. God caused their crops to perish with His breath, probably a reference to the wind and heat. The result was scattered and blighted wheat. Why did God deal so harshly with His people? Because His house was in ruin while the people rushed to pursue their own selfish interests. This is a classic sign of being not blessed; they would not

"Go up to the mountain, and bring wood, and build the house; and I will take pleasure in it, and I will be glorified, saith the LORD" (Haggai 1:8).

prosper as long as they neglected God and the temple that had been erected in His name.

Verse 10 says that the sky (heaven) is "stayed" or literally "stays itself." Here sky is personified, implying that even inanimate nature, as represented by heaven and earth, obeys God's will and withholds its goods from disobedient people. God identifies Himself as the invisible first cause and declares it to be His doing. God "calls for" famine, drought, and poverty as instruments of His wrath. The Hebrew word for "drought," *choreb* (**KHO-reb**), sounds like *chareb* (**khaw-RABE**), which means "waste," and describes God's house (vv. 4, 9), implying the correspondence between the sin and its punishment. The people had let God's house "be waste," and He, in turn, sent a drought on all that was theirs: the crops, the cattle, and the people. The phrase "labour of the hands" refers to the fruit of

lands, gardens, and vineyards obtained by the labor of workers' hands.

1:12 Then Zerubbabel the son of Shealtiel, and Joshua the son of Josedech, the high priest, with all the remnant of the people, obeyed the voice of the LORD their God, and the words of Haggai the prophet, as the LORD their God had sent him, and the people did fear before the LORD.

Zerubbabel the political leader and Joshua the high priest gathered all of those who returned from the exile. Their response was not only to listen to Haggai as he voiced God's complaint, but to obey God's call to complete their divinely appointed task. "Obeyed" is translated from the Hebrew word *shama'* (**shaw-MAH**), which literally means "to hear" and implies "to give undivided attention." The people heard the message and responded with heartfelt obedience, even though the work on the temple had not yet begun. They responded to the "LORD" (Heb. *Yehovah*, **yeh-ho-VAW**) their "God" (Heb. *elohiym*, **el-o-HEEM**). These terms define God as the self-existent and supreme Ruler. In essence, they were accepting not only the words but the authority of God in their lives. They were submitting to God's will, repenting of their neglect, and purposing in their hearts to be obedient.

The Hebrew word *dabar* (**daw-BAW**) means "the words," and in this case refers to the word of the Lord as presented by Haggai. The "word of the Lord" is the essential content of God's revelation through His prophets or messengers. As a result, the people "did fear" (Heb. *yare'*, **yaw-RAY**). This doesn't mean they operated out of terror. Instead, they began to reverence God with the honor and respect due His name.

13 Then spake Haggai the LORD's messenger in the LORD's message unto the people, saying, I am with you, saith the LORD.

The Lord's "messenger" (Heb. *mal'ak*, **mal-AWK**) depicts an ambassador who carries a message, performs some specific commission, or serves as a representative of the one who sent him. In this case, Haggai was the commissioned spokesperson to deliver God's message, which was four simple but profound words: "I am with you." It is a promise of God's ever-present empowerment to all those He commissions to service. As the people entered into the service of the Lord by being obedient to God's command to rebuild the temple and to establish it as the center of worship and national life, God would be with them.

The people's attitude had changed, and even before they set to work, God's tone changed from reproving to tenderness. He immediately forgot their past unfaithfulness and assured them that their obedience led to blessing.

14 And the LORD stirred up the spirit of Zerubbabel the son of Shealtiel, governor of Judah, and the spirit of Joshua the son of Josedech, the high priest, and the spirit of all the remnant of the people; and they came and did work in the house of the LORD of hosts, their God.

The rebuilt temple at Jerusalem is often referred to as Zerubbabel's temple. This could be because of the deep personal interest he took in the project or the fact that he oversaw the work as the governor of Judah. In any event, the Scriptures say that the "Lord stirred up the spirit" in Zerubbabel and Joshua. This means that God blessed them with enthusiasm and perseverance to complete the good work, even though they had been slothful in not rallying the people to the work.

As a result, the people eagerly "came and did work," collecting the wood, stones, and other materials necessary for building. The recorded time of this turnaround was the 24th day of the sixth month during the second year of Darius's reign. Within 23 days from the start of Haggai's prophecy, the people and their leaders had harkened to the prophet and turned their hearts and efforts to properly serve and honor God.

Daily Bible Readings

M: In God's House
Psalm 84:1–4

T: Time to Rebuild the Temple
Haggai 1:1–11

W: The Work Begins
Haggai 1:12–15

T: Rebuilding the Foundation
Ezra 3:8–13

F: Help Rejected
Ezra 4:1–4

S: The Rebuilding Questioned
Ezra 5:1–5

S: The Decree of King Cyrus
Ezra 5:6–17

TEACHING TIPS

May 11
Bible Study Guide 11

1. Words You Should Know

A. Sepulchres (Nehemiah 2:5) *qeber* (Heb.)— Places of burial.

B. Reproach (v. 17) *cherpah* (Heb.)—A cause or occasion of blame, discredit, or disgrace.

2. Teacher Preparation

Unifying Principle—Following a Visionary Leader! Many of us have the challenge of following men and women who have been given great assignments. How do we discern a worthy vision and recognize a visionary leader? We can honor God by helping them to complete what God calls us to assist in completing. Nehemiah was so serious about rebuilding the wall that he would not allow anyone to distract him from the goal.

A. Read the Background, More Light on the Text, and In Depth sections to determine how these facts can be presented to develop the AIM for Change.

B. Be sure you can explain the events and ruling kings who took Persia's throne between today's lesson and the one last week.

C. Use the *Precepts For Living*® CD-ROM to study a map of the areas mentioned in today's lesson, including the walls of the temple area and the city.

3. Starting the Lesson

A. After prayer, share the map with the class, explaining each location and the history that connects that place and its leaders to Israel's history.

B. Turn the class's attention to today's text by having several class members read the parts of the Scripture that convey the conversations between Nehemiah, the king, and the people.

4. Getting into the Lesson

A. Discuss the events of the lesson using the Search the Scriptures and Discuss the Meaning questions to drive discussion.

B. Ask a class member to read the In Focus story. Lead the class in a discussion of whether Robert and William are typical of today's community leaders. Ask if the class members think the outcome of the story is realistic and why.

5. Relating the Lesson to Life

A. Divide the class into small groups. After each group reads Lesson in Our Society and Make It Happen, instruct them to develop a list of areas where the class could consider undertaking a task that will encourage and strengthen others in the church or community.

B. Ask for a volunteer to type the lists and e-mail them to class members or post them for next week. If your class can arrange for the activity in Arousing Action, have the copies available for that gathering.

6. Arousing Action

A. Ask class members to try to meet for dessert or coffee during the week to identify one or more projects they can complete as a group over the next few weeks or months.

B. Share their vision with the pastor and celebrate God's faithfulness in helping you complete the task when it is done.

REBUILDING THE WALL

Bible Background • NEHEMIAH 1:1–2:20
Printed Text • NEHEMIAH 2:1–8, 11, 17–18 Devotional Reading • PSALM 137:1–7; 138:1–5

AIM for Change

By the end of the lesson, we will:

DISCOVER how God's people assisted Nehemiah, God's leader, in rebuilding the walls;

RECOGNIZE that working in God's kingdom is good; and

DECIDE to volunteer for a project that helps build God's kingdom here on Earth.

Keep in Mind

"Then I told them of the hand of my God which was good upon me; as also the king's words that he had spoken unto me. And they said, Let us rise up and build. So they strengthened their hands for this good work" (Nehemiah 2:18).

Focal Verses

KJV Nehemiah 2:1 And it came to pass in the month Nisan, in the twentieth year of Artaxerxes the king, that wine was before him: and I took up the wine, and gave it unto the king. Now I had not been beforetime sad in his presence.

2 Wherefore the king said unto me, Why is thy countenance sad, seeing thou art not sick? This is nothing else but sorrow of heart. Then I was very sore afraid,

3 And said unto the king, Let the king live for ever: why should not my countenance be sad, when the city, the place of my fathers' sepulchres, lieth waste, and the gates thereof are consumed with fire?

4 Then the king said unto me, For what dost thou make request? So I prayed to the God of heaven.

5 And I said unto the king, If it please the king, and if thy servant have found favour in thy sight, that thou wouldest send me unto Judah, unto the city of my fathers' sepulchres, that I may build it.

6 And the king said unto me, (the queen also sitting by him,) For how long shall thy journey be? and when wilt thou return? So it pleased the king to send me; and I set him a time.

7 Moreover I said unto the king, If it please the king, let letters be given me to the governors beyond the river, that they may convey me over till I come into Judah;

8 And a letter unto Asaph the keeper of the king's forest, that he may give me timber to make beams for the gates of the palace which appertained to the house, and for the wall of the city, and for the house that I shall

NLT Nehemiah 2:1 Early the following spring, in the month of Nisan, during the twentieth year of King Artaxerxes' reign, I was serving the king his wine. I had never before appeared sad in his presence.

2 So the king asked me, "Why are you looking so sad? You don't look sick to me. You must be deeply troubled." Then I was terrified,

3 but I replied, "Long live the king! How can I not be sad? For the city where my ancestors are buried is in ruins, and the gates have been destroyed by fire."

4 The king asked, "Well, how can I help you?" With a prayer to the God of heaven,

5 I replied, "If it please the king, and if you are pleased with me, your servant, send me to Judah to rebuild the city where my ancestors are buried."

6 The king, with the queen sitting beside him, asked, "How long will you be gone? When will you return?" After I told him how long I would be gone, the king agreed to my request.

7 I also said to the king, "If it please the king, let me have letters addressed to the governors of the province west of the Euphrates River, instructing them to let me travel safely through their territories on my way to Judah.

8 And please give me a letter addressed to Asaph, the manager of the king's forest, instructing him to give me timber. I will need it to make beams for the gates of the Temple fortress, for the city walls, and for a house for myself." And the king granted these enter into. And the king granted me, according to the good hand of my God upon me.

2:11 So I came to Jerusalem, and was there three days.

2:17 Then said I unto them, Ye see the distress that we are in, how Jerusalem lieth waste, and the gates thereof are burned with fire: come, and let us build up the wall of Jerusalem, that we be no more a reproach.

18 Then I told them of the hand of my God which was good upon me; as also the king's words that he had spoken unto me. And they said, Let us rise up and build. So they strengthened their hands for this good work.

requests, because the gracious hand of God was on me.

2:11 So I arrived in Jerusalem. Three days later,

2:17 But now I said to them, "You know very well what trouble we are in. Jerusalem lies in ruins, and its gates have been destroyed by fire. Let us rebuild the wall of Jerusalem and end this disgrace!"

18 Then I told them about how the gracious hand of God had been on me, and about my conversation with the king.

In Focus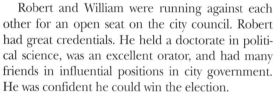

Robert and William were running against each other for an open seat on the city council. Robert had great credentials. He held a doctorate in political science, was an excellent orator, and had many friends in influential positions in city government. He was confident he could win the election.

William also had good credentials, although at first glance they did not appear as impressive as Robert's. William had a master's degree in city planning and a heart to serve his community. A lifelong resident of the city, William had a tremendous vision to move the neighborhood forward. Because he was one of the community members who remained in the area, most of William's friends were the lower- to middle-class constituents of his ward. Despite what promised to be a glowing campaign by his competitor, William, a devout Christian, believed that God had called him to run for city council. He had prayed daily and sought godly council before entering the race.

William knew his win would be an upset the more powerful politicians did not expect, but he believed that God was providing a means for him to be victorious. While his opponent spent funds on commercials, William spoke at local churches, community meetings, neighborhood councils, and private homes. He shared his vision and his faith. He wanted people to know who he was and that he was on a mission because God had called him to help his neighbors and to honor the memory of his own parents who had always lived in the area.

On election night, William was victorious, and in his acceptance speech he thanked God and the people who had come together for a vision to rebuild the neighborhood that had once been the pride of their families.

Like Nehemiah, William had a heart to rebuild the community, not for the political and social status such an endeavor would bring, but to glorify God through the restoration of a better life for the people. Consider how your work or passion to help your community is an outgrowth of God's impact on your life. While everyone is not a politician, every Christian can engage in meaningful restoration in some area of their life. What have you considered doing?

The People, Places, and Times

Nehemiah. The name means "God has consoled." Nehemiah, a soldier and statesman, was born in exile, but he grew up in the faith and he loved Jerusalem. As the king's cupbearer, he held a high place of honor (Nehemiah 1:11), and he had confidential access to the king.

King Artaxerxes. The reign of Artaxerxes followed that of Darius. Artaxerxes funded Nehemiah's return to Jerusalem and the rebuilding of the walls. He came to the throne in about 465 B.C. The events recorded in today's lesson occurred during the twentieth year of his reign, about 445 B.C.

Background

Nehemiah was a contemporary of Ezra. His book completes the history of the remnant's return from exile and Jerusalem's restoration. Nehemiah records the events of the third and final return to Jerusalem and the rebuilding of the city's walls.

Twelve years after Ezra's return to Judah, Nehemiah was informed of the continuing ruined conditions of Jerusalem's walls and gates. As the cup-bearer to King Artaxerxes, Nehemiah's job was to taste the king's food and beverages to insure that they were not poisoned. This position afforded him a great deal of influence with the king. Yet Nehemiah did not rely on his friends in high places when he needed help. His first impulse was to seek God. When Nehemiah received bad news about the Jews who had returned to Jerusalem, he was so deeply affected that he immediately began praying and fasting for his people.

When King Artaxerxes noticed Nehemiah's concern, God prepared Nehemiah to ask for the king's assistance. The king supported Nehemiah's vision for rebuilding Jerusalem and gave him access to the supplies and materials he needed. Once Nehemiah arrived in Jerusalem, he completed the task of rebuilding the walls in only 52 days.

In his role as a political leader, Nehemiah led the nation in both religious reform and spiritual awakening in the midst of a city that was dangerous to those who were attempting to rebuild for God. Nehemiah was a sterling example of what it means to be a good leader in God's kingdom. He labored for the purity of public worship, the integrity of family life, and the sanctity of the Sabbath. He was a coura-geous, God-fearing man, who labored selflessly and served with an unswerving loyalty to God.

Nehemiah's memoirs form the bulk of his book. They reveal a picture of a man of spirit who was pas-sionately concerned for his people's needs. He was quick to respond to the appeals of brotherhood, and he was zealous about the purity of Jewish worship (1:4–9). Above all, Nehemiah was a leader who was always conscious of God and his need for God.

At-A-Glance

1. Prayer Before Action (Nehemiah 2:1–8)
2. Action After Prayer (vv. 11, 17–18)

In Depth

1. Prayer Before Action (Nehemiah 2:1–8)

Following captivity, the Jews who had been held in Babylon and Assyria began to return to Jerusalem.

They restored the temple and attempted to restore the city itself. When news reached Nehemiah that Jerusalem was still in shambles with burned walls and gates, he knew he had to do something—but what and how? Nehemiah did not just sit down and formulate a plan of action. First, he prayed to God for direction. In fact, he prayed and fasted for several days while going about his normal duties in the palace of Artaxerxes in Shushan. He had no idea when or how the Lord would answer his prayer, but he faithfully continued to pray and seek God's direction.

As the king's cupbearer, Nehemiah served King Artaxerxes his wine each day. When Nehemiah's dis-tress showed on his face, the king took notice (Nehemiah 2:1). This was a dangerous action for a palace servant since the king's servants were expected to display a constantly cheerful appearance before him. Even wearing mourning clothes in the palace was forbidden. The king could execute any-one who displeased him. But Nehemiah had prayed and knew that he had to take the chance.

The *New International Version* of the Bible gives us a clear idea of the conversation between Nehemiah and King Artaxerxes. Instead of being angry, the king was concerned about Nehemiah and asked, "Why does your face look so sad when you are not ill?" The king's question gave Nehemiah the opportunity to present his request. After Nehemiah explained the problem, the king asked what he wanted. Once again, Nehemiah prayed knowing that only God could cause the king to grant his requests.

After uttering his brief prayer, Nehemiah got straight to the point. He asked the king to allow him to travel to Jerusalem. Naturally, the king had a few questions (v. 6). Nehemiah had no idea of the amount of work before him or how long he would be gone, but he gave the king a time frame. The Bible does not record Nehemiah's exact answer, but according to Nehemiah 5:14 and 13:6, he stayed in Jerusalem for 12 years. The king granted Nehe-miah's first request—time and assistance to go to Jerusalem—so Nehemiah pressed on. He asked the king for letters to give to the governors of the land he would travel through to guarantee safe passage, and he asked for a letter to Asaph, the king's forest keeper, authorizing him to give Nehemiah timber for Jerusalem's walls.

The "good hand of . . . God" was on Nehemiah (2:8). This meant several things. First, Nehemiah was being used for God's purposes. Second, he was being led by God, and God was granting him favor and assistance. Finally, God was empowering Nehemiah to succeed.

Nehemiah made it a habit to pray before acting. He spent an extended period of time praying and fasting before he approached the king; he prayed briefly before answering the king; and on several other occasions, he called out to God spontaneously in times of need (see Nehemiah 5:19; 6:9, 14; 13:14, 22). The key to Nehemiah's success as a leader of his people was his dependence on God.

2. Action After Prayer (vv. 11, 17–18)

When Nehemiah arrived in Jerusalem, he had the full support of the king, but he did not immediately rush into action or expose his plan. Instead, Nehemiah secretly inspected the wall to assess the damage and estimate the work needed to rebuild and repair the breaches (vv. 12–13).

After determining what was needed, Nehemiah was ready to lead the people to action. He began by telling them, "Ye see the distress that we are in, how Jerusalem lieth waste, and the gates thereof are burned with fire: come, and let us build up the wall of Jerusalem, that we be no more a reproach" (v. 17). With these words, Nehemiah appealed to the people's pride in Jerusalem as God's holy city. Then he appealed to their love for God and their desire not to bring shame or "reproach" on the Lord. Finally, he acknowledged God and His divine guidance in the plan to rebuild the wall before recounting the conversation he had had with King Artaxerxes.

Leadership ability is often confirmed by the followers' attitudes and actions. When Nehemiah completed his brief speech, the people exclaimed, "Let us rise up and build" (v. 18). Nehemiah challenged and inspired the people, "so they strengthened their hands for this good work" (v. 18).

The work Nehemiah undertook was substantial, but his approach gives us several suggestions for leadership. First, Nehemiah enlisted the help of others. He knew that even though God had given him a vision and an outstanding cause, he needed help. God led Nehemiah to seek help from the king and the leaders and workers who were in Jerusalem.

Nehemiah's motives were unselfish, and as a result, he was convinced that the work he had to do was worthwhile and would benefit the people of God. Finally, Nehemiah himself undertook the task. His position in the palace was prestigious, and it would have been easy to let others do the hard work of rebuilding. However, Nehemiah volunteered to engage in the hard work of building, of leading, and of inspiring others for the restoration of God's glory in the land of his forefathers.

Search the Scriptures

1. What did Nehemiah do when the king asked him to state his request (Nehemiah 2:4)?

2. What two questions did the king ask Nehemiah (v. 6)?

3. Why was the letter to Asaph, the forest keeper, necessary (v. 8)?

4. What did the people in Jerusalem do to show they were ready to follow Nehemiah in rebuilding the wall (v. 18)?

Discuss the Meaning

1. Sometimes difficult situations arise without warning and require an immediate response. How are believers supposed to consult God during these times? What example did Nehemiah set?

2. What did Nehemiah mean by the statements, "If it please the king . . ." and "If thy servant has found favour in thy sight . . ." (2:5)? What lessons can we learn from Nehemiah to help our relationships with employers, church leaders, and colleagues?

3. In what ways did Nehemiah's leadership show wisdom? How did he exhibit faith?

Lesson in Our Society

Ours is a society where people often find it easy to stand aside and allow someone else to get things done. Yet, when disasters strike, we are painfully aware that we must be involved in order to make a difference. While catastrophic events call our attention to the need to be involved for the good of ourselves and others, we are actually confronted daily with opportunities to take a stand for God in making conditions or situations better.

Consider the areas in your community where your leadership and support could make a difference. How can you become involved?

Make It Happen

Building God's kingdom is about helping others succeed through service. It is our responsibility as Christians to ask God what we can do to assist the leadership in our communities, workplaces, and churches. For example, helping with the homeless ministry at church, volunteering to assist your boss or a coworker with a special project, or organizing a spring cleanup crew to help beautify your community are just a few ideas. Develop a list of suggestions that you and fellow Christians can undertake to help build God's kingdom here on earth and to encourage others.

Follow the Spirit

What God wants me to do:

_____

_____

Remember Your Thoughts

Special insights I have learned:

_____

_____

More Light on the Text

Nehemiah 2:1–8, 11, 17–18

1 And it came to pass in the month Nisan, in the twentieth year of Artaxerxes the king, that wine was before him: and I took up the wine, and gave it unto the king. Now I had not been beforetime sad in his presence.

In our last lesson, Judah was taken into captivity by King Nebuchadnezzar of Babylon in 586 B.C. Nebuchadnezzar died in 539 B.C., leaving behind a weakened empire. Meanwhile, Persia, under the leadership of Cyrus, unified the Medes and Persians. In 539 B.C. they overthrew Babylon and emerged as the major world power. Persia's kings—Cyrus, Xerxes, and Artaxerxes—figured prominently in the history of the Jewish nation's return to Jerusalem.

Even before this time, however, the leaders of Babylon and Assyria had started to allow some captives and their descendants to return to Jerusalem. The first major group to return, however, was led by Zerubbabel in 538 B.C. The returnees rebuilt the temple in 516 B.C., although it lacked the splendor of Solomon's (see Haggai 2:1–4).

In 458 B.C., a second group returned to Jerusalem led by Ezra, the priest, scribe, and reformer who wrote the book of Ezra. The events of the first two re-entries are recorded in Ezra 1, 2, and 7. Today's lesson references the third group of captives as they returned to their homeland in 445 B.C. and began rebuilding the walls of Jerusalem under the leadership of Nehemiah.

The book of Nehemiah, written between 445 and 432 B.C., is the last of the Old Testament historical books. It records the history of this third group, their work in rebuilding the city's walls, and details about how Nehemiah came to leadership. Nehemiah served in the Persian government as the personal assistant and cupbearer for King Artaxerxes. This position was a prime responsibility, that of a butler. Not only was he responsible for preparing the wine the king was to drink but testing it as well. In other words, Nehemiah was required to put his life on the line. If the wine was poisoned, Nehemiah would die first. If the king was poisoned, Nehemiah would be put to death for allowing such a thing to happen. Such a close and personal position required tremendous trust.

Today's Scripture text begins with a specific time and place. Of the Hebrew calendar's 12 months, Nisan is the first. According to this verse, these events happened during the twelfth year of King Artaxerxes' reign (453 B.C.). The first chapter of the book of Nehemiah records that God had already placed on Nehemiah's heart what he had to do—gather the means for going to Jerusalem to undertake the building project. Consequently, Nehemiah was sad in the king's presence. This was dangerous because the king could execute anyone who displeased him. The king noticed Nehemiah's countenance.

2 Wherefore the king said unto me, Why is thy countenance sad, seeing thou art not sick? this is nothing else but sorrow of heart. Then I was very sore afraid, 3 And said unto the king, Let the king live for ever: why should not my countenance be sad, when the city, the place of my fathers' sepulchres, lieth waste, and the gates thereof are consumed with fire?

The observant king asked Nehemiah why he looked so sad since he was not ill. The word "sore" in Hebrew is *rabah* (**raw-BAW**), which means "greatly" or "exceedingly." In short, the king saw that whatever was bothering Nehemiah had him filled with sorrow. Nehemiah's countenance had never been down before. Immediately, Nehemiah became afraid. The word for "afraid" (Heb. *yare'*, **yaw-RAY**) indicates two things. First, the king could have Nehemiah killed if Nehemiah's presence displeased him. Second, the term *yare'* also means "to reverence" or "be astounded." Certainly Nehemiah did not expect the king to give him an audience, but God was making a way.

Because Nehemiah had the king's ear, he could appeal for what was needed to rebuild the walls of Jerusalem. The phrase "the place of my fathers' sepulchres" translates the following words: The first, "the place," or *bayith* (**BAH-yith**), means "family of descendants" and refers to a person's lineage. The word "sepulchres" in Hebrew is *qeber* (**KEH-ber**) and means "burying places, graves, tombs." Nehemiah shared his heart by telling him that the palace was not his place. Nehemiah's home, the home of his ancestors, was in Jerusalem. Nehemiah explained that his heart was saddened because Jerusalem, where his forefathers were buried, was still lying in ruin with walls that had been burned to the ground. Nehemiah was grieved. He knew that something had to be done and someone had to do it. He believed he was the person God was calling to the task.

4 Then the king said unto me, For what dost thou make request? So I prayed to the God of heaven.

The king asked Nehemiah what he wanted him to do about the situation. Before Nehemiah gave an answer, while he was yet talking to the king, he went into prayer. The phrase "to the God" in Hebrew is *'elohiym* (**el-oh-HEEM**) and means "the true God." Thus, before Nehemiah answered the king, he went to the true God for help. Nehemiah wanted to return to Jerusalem to reunite the Jews and remove the shame of her broken-down walls. In order to do all this, he needed the all-powerful God to assist him.

5 And I said unto the king, If it please the king, and if thy servant have found favour in thy sight, that thou wouldest send me unto Judah, unto the city of my fathers' sepulchres, that I may build it.

The phrase "if it please" in Hebrew is *towb* (**tobe**) and means "be joyful, be beneficial, be pleasant, be happy, be right." The phrase "have found favour" in Hebrew is *yatab* (**yaw-TAB**) and means "to do well, do right." In this light, Nehemiah wanted the king to know that he hoped his service to the king was favorable and that he had acted responsibly in his duties. If he had, then he would be honored if the king would recognize his faithfulness by sending him to Jerusalem, the city of Nehemiah's forefathers' graves, so he might rebuild the walls.

6 And the king said unto me, (the queen also sitting by him,) For how long shall thy journey be? and when wilt thou return? So it pleased the king to send me; and I set him a time.

Nehemiah was in the presence of both king and queen. This statement addresses how faithful Nehemiah was that he should be present when the royal family dined. The fact that Nehemiah records the queen's presence probably means that the queen was influential and was also concerned about Nehemiah's plight.

The king wanted to know how long Nehemiah would be gone and when he would return. Even though the Bible does not record his answer, we know that Nehemiah stayed in Jerusalem 12 years (see 5:14; 13:6). We also know that it took time for Nehemiah to prepare for the journey. Historians place the date of his arrival in Jerusalem at 445 B.C.

7 Moreover I said unto the king, If it please the king, let letters be given me to the governors beyond the river, that they may convey me over till I come into Judah; 8 And a letter unto Asaph the keeper of the king's forest, that he may give me timber to make beams for the gates of the palace which appertained to the house, and for the wall of the city, and for the house that I shall enter into. And the king granted me, according to the good hand of my God upon me.

Nehemiah was a man of order and purpose. God gave him the vision to rebuild, but Nehemiah knew he needed others' help to get the job done. Nehemiah was respectful but faithful as he moved ahead elaborating on his plan. It is obvious that he had prayed about this moment and considered what it would take to complete the task successfully (see chapter 1). Therefore after getting permission from the king to go to Jerusalem, Nehemiah asked the king for additional help. The phrase "if it please the king" again prefaces Nehemiah's request. It is the equivalent of "please" but also acknowledges that he realized that the king's offer was already more than generous. Nehemiah was asking the king in faith. He had prayed and believed that God, who had granted him an impromptu audience with the king, would also soften the king's heart to provide everything he needed.

The first letters Nehemiah requested would be given to the governors beyond the river. This is a reference to the cities he would encounter between Shushan, the capital of Persia, and Jerusalem, the capital of Judah. The phrase "that they may convey me over" in the Hebrew is 'abar (aw-BAR) and means "to pass or cross over." Nehemiah wanted additional help getting to his destination.

Nehemiah also wanted a letter to give to Asaph, the keeper of the king's forest, in order to gather the timber or supplies he needed for his construction projects. He was concerned about the walls, but that task was massive. It included rebuilding the "beams for the gates of the palace." The NIV translation calls this the "'citadel' by the temple." There was also a need for repairs to be made to all the city walls, along with a need of a place for Nehemiah to stay. He knew the king had the means to help him, and because of his faith in God, he was not afraid to ask for additional favors. God's hand upon the king moved the king to come to Nehemiah's aid.

11 So I came to Jerusalem, and was there three days.

The action of Nehemiah's journey is summarized in verses 9 and 10. In verse 11, Nehemiah had already made his way to Jerusalem. Upon his arrival, Nehemiah spent three days carefully observing and assessing the damages to the walls. The verses not included in our text provide the plan Nehemiah used to inspect the situation. He was indeed a wise man. He did not want to act in haste, nor did he want people to know what he was doing before it was time to reveal his plan. Even though he took a few people with him, he did not reveal what God had given him. Nehemiah 1 records both the physical condition of the city and the political and social opposition the returning Hebrews faced, revealing that Nehemiah knew there were few people to be trusted and that the discouraged returnees needed to be encouraged

by sound and positive advice. Therefore, he quietly gathered firsthand information regarding the size and magnitude of the job he was undertaking.

2:17 Then said I unto them, Ye see the distress that we are in, how Jerusalem lieth waste, and the gates thereof are burned with fire: come, and let us build up the wall of Jerusalem, that we be no more a reproach.

Armed with the necessary information and a plan inspired by God, Nehemiah presented a realistic strategy to Jerusalem's leaders and returnees who were going to help with the rebuilding project. God had placed a desire and a plan in Nehemiah's heart, but Nehemiah had to find a practical strategy for sharing and proceeding with that plan.

After realistically assessing the building project, Nehemiah went to the leaders, the people, and the workers and presented his plan. He began by outlining the situation. They could "see" (Heb. ra'ah, raw-AW) that the city was in "distress" (Heb. ra', rah). Nehemiah was describing what was obvious. Inspection of the situation showed how bad things were. In fact, the word ra' indicates a moral evil. Jerusalem was the place where Judah had declared God as their source. The city that had been the pride of their nation, the place of the covenant with God, the site where the Ark of the Lord had been housed, was in ruins. They were no longer being held captive by foreign nations, but they were still in disgrace because their homeland was deplorable.

Second, Nehemiah gave a challenge to those who are present: "Let us build up the wall of Jerusalem." There was quite a bit of work to be done, and Nehemiah had not previously shared what God had given him. To "build up" (Heb. banah, baw-NAW) actually means "to rebuild and reestablish the walls of the city." In ancient days, a city unprotected by walls was vulnerable. Jerusalem was not only the holy city of Judah, it was also Judah's capital. It represented the national identity and had been blessed with God's presence in the temple during the days of Solomon. Walls were erected not only to protect the city; they were a symbol of power and beauty. Building the walls was more than just lending a hand to the work that had already been undertaken. Building the walls was essentially reestablishing Jerusalem as the center of Hebrew life.

"Then I told them of the hand of my God which was good upon me; as also the king's words that he had spoken unto me. And they said, Let us rise up and build. So they strengthened their hands for this good work" (Nehemiah 2:18).

The phrase "that we be no more a reproach" in Hebrew is *cherpah* (**kher-PAW**), meaning "an object of shame, disgrace, scorn." Nehemiah invited them to partner with him and help build the walls of Jerusalem so they would no longer be a source of shame, disgrace, or scorn to the one, true God. Nehemiah was realistic. He knew that the sins of God's chosen people had incited God's wrath and caused the desolation of the temple and its walls in the first place. Their fathers had been taken captive by Babylon to live in a strange land. Only a small fragment had returned to the nation's capital. While exile had been a shameful condition for them to bear, it had also brought shame on their God. They were the people who were to have held up the Lord God, Jehovah, so that others would know His might. Their fall and the destruction of the city and the temple showed that they had failed God as well as themselves. It was now time to restore the city, the walls, and the honor that had been lost.

18 Then I told them of the hand of my God which was good upon me; as also the king's words that he had spoken unto me. And they said, Let us rise up and build. So they strengthened their hands for this good work.

The phrase "the hand" in Hebrew is *yad* (**yawd**) and means "strength, power, support." Now that he

had presented the situation and enlisted their help, he shared with the leaders how God's strength, power, and support had been with him from the beginning, when God gave Nehemiah a vision and a burden to help in Jerusalem. Nehemiah told the leaders of his encounter with King Artaxerxes and the king's willingness support this work. Specifically, Nehemiah wanted the leaders to know that he was not just acting on his own. He had God's guidance and the king's support. With these words, the leaders were ready to follow through and get the job done.

The phrase "so they strengthened" in Hebrew is *chazaq* (**khaw-ZAK**). It means that the people were made strong or bold by Nehemiah's words. They stood together, firmly determined to see the work through. The leaders were encouraged to proceed as a team, as they proceeded with the project. They were ready to encourage and inspire others to carry out God's plan.

Sources:
Life Application Study Bible, NLT. Wheaton, Ill.: Tyndale House Publishers, Inc., 1996.
Strong, J. *The Exhaustive Concordance of the Bible* (electronic ed.). Ontario, Canada: Woodside Bible Fellowship, 1996.

Daily Bible Readings

M: A Lament for Jerusalem
Psalm 137:1–7
T: Weeping and Fasting
Nehemiah 1:1–4
W: Nehemiah's Confession
Nehemiah 1:5–11
T: Permission to Return
Nehemiah 2:1–10
F: A Secret Inspection
Nehemiah 2:11–16
S: Determination to Rebuild
Nehemiah 2:17–20
S: Giving Thanks to God
Psalm 138:1–5

TEACHING TIPS

May 18
Bible Study Guide 12

1. Words You Should Know

A. Wroth (Nehemiah 4:1) *charah* (Heb.)—To be incensed, grow indignant, or act zealously; to display the heat of anger.

B. Breaches (v. 7) *parats* (Heb.)—To break through or to tear down.

2. Teacher Preparation

Unifying Principle—Finishing the Task! It seems that finishing is a difficult task. Many people start things they never seem to find time to complete. However, when we embark on a God-given assignment, we must exercise perseverance and determination to complete the task.

A. Read the various sections of the Bible Study Guide and More Light on the Text.

B. Prepare to again display last week's map of Jerusalem's walls.

C. Prepare a display of key words using Words You Should Know, selected Hebrew terms from More Light on the Text and In Depth along with the *Precepts For Living*® CD-ROM.

D. Prepare "encouragement cards." On one side of each index card, write or place a printed label of a Scripture verse that gives encouragement in hard times. Leave the other side blank for student use.

3. Starting the Lesson

A. After opening with prayer, review lesson 11 and display the map.

B. Be prepared to present a mini-lecture on the context using The People, Places, and Times and Background if the class is unfamiliar with this information.

4. Getting into the Lesson

A. Discuss the Focal Verses using the At-A-Glance outline. Encourage the students to ask questions.

B. Incorporate the Search the Scriptures and Discuss the Meaning questions, using the key word visual to help the class grasp the full measure of opposition Nehemiah faced.

5. Relating the Lesson to Life

A. Have the class respond to the In Focus story using the AIM for Change and responses to the final question.

B. Have small groups respond to the final question for Lesson in Our Society.

C. Pass out the encouragement cards blank-side up. Ask each person to write a word or phrase on the blank side that reminds them of a difficult time in their life when they felt that they could not go on. Have any student who wishes share a one- or two-word description of that time.

D. Have class members read the Scripture on the card. If possible, you might want all the students who received the same Scripture to gather and discuss how the verse was useful. If you choose to not have the class move, they can share in small groups regarding the Scripture each received.

6. Arousing Action

A. In groups or as an entire class, discuss the major concepts in Make It Happen: (1) developing leadership; (2) examining our attitude in times of opposition; and (3) the importance of having a relationship with Christ as a foundation for facing adversity.

B. Remind the class to complete the Follow the Spirit and Remember Your Thoughts sections during the week.

C. End with prayer, thanking God for His Word and for completing the work He began in each student through this lesson.

Worship Guide

For the Superintendent or Teacher
Theme: Up Against the Wall
Theme Song: "No Ways Tired"
Devotional Reading: Psalm 70
Prayer

339

UP AGAINST THE WALL

Bible Background • NEHEMIAH 4–6
Printed Text • Nehemiah 4:1–3, 7–9, 13–15; 6:15 Devotional Reading • PSALM 70

AIM for Change

By the end of the lesson, we will:

REALIZE the importance of persevering in order to complete a task;

REFLECT on the appropriate sense of accomplishment we feel when we complete a task; and

COMPLETE God-given assignments despite seemingly insurmountable circumstances.

Keep in Mind

"So built we the wall; and all the wall was joined together unto the half thereof: for the people had a mind to work" (Nehemiah 4:6).

Focal Verses

KJV

Nehemiah 4:1 But it came to pass, that when Sanballat heard that we builded the wall, he was wroth, and took great indignation, and mocked the Jews.

2 And he spake before his brethren and the army of Samaria, and said, What do these feeble Jews? will they fortify themselves? will they sacrifice? will they make an end in a day? will they revive the stones out of the heaps of the rubbish which are burned?

3 Now Tobiah the Ammonite was by him, and he said, Even that which they build, if a fox go up, he shall even break down their stone wall.

4:7 But it came to pass, that when Sanballat, and Tobiah, and the Arabians, and the Ammonites, and the Ashdodites, heard that the walls of Jerusalem were made up, and that the breaches began to be stopped, then they were very wroth,

8 And conspired all of them together to come and to fight against Jerusalem, and to hinder it.

9 Nevertheless we made our prayer unto our God, and set a watch against them day and night, because of them.

4:13 Therefore set I in the lower places behind the wall, and on the higher places, I even set the people after their families with their swords, their spears, and their bows.

14 And I looked, and rose up, and said unto the nobles, and to the rulers, and to the rest of the people, Be not ye afraid of them: remember the LORD, which is great and terrible, and fight for your brethren, your sons, and your daughters, your wives, and your houses.

15 And it came to pass, when our enemies heard that it was known unto us, and God had brought their

NLT

Nehemiah 4:1 Sanballat was very angry when he learned that we were rebuilding the wall. He flew into a rage and mocked the Jews,

2 saying in front of his friends and the Samarian army officers, "What does this bunch of poor, feeble Jews think they're doing? Do they think they can build the wall in a single day by just offering a few sacrifices? Do they actually think they can make something of stones from a rubbish heap—and charred ones at that?"

3 Tobiah the Ammonite, who was standing beside him, remarked, "That stone wall would collapse if even a fox walked along the top of it!"

4:7 But when Sanballat and Tobiah and the Arabs, Ammonites, and Ashdodites heard that the work was going ahead and that the gaps in the wall of Jerusalem were being repaired, they were furious.

8 They all made plans to come and fight against Jerusalem and throw us into confusion.

9 But we prayed to our God and guarded the city day and night to protect ourselves.

4:13 So I placed armed guards behind the lowest parts of the wall in the exposed areas. I stationed the people to stand guard by families, armed with swords, spears, and bows.

14 Then as I looked over the situation, I called together the nobles and the rest of the people and said to them, "Don't be afraid of the enemy! Remember the Lord, who is great and glorious, and fight for your brothers, your sons, your daughters, your wives, and your homes!"

counsel to nought, that we returned all of us to the wall, every one unto his work.

6:15 So the wall was finished in the twenty and fifth day of the month Elul, in fifty and two days.

15 When our enemies heard that we knew of their plans and that God had frustrated them, we all returned to our work on the wall.

6:15 So on October 2 the wall was finished—just fifty-two days after we had begun.

In Focus

Jeneen had overdrawn her checking account again and was tired of living like this. When she gave her life to Christ two years ago, she thought her financial problems would end. In response to the teaching at her church, she began to tithe faithfully and sow financial seeds. She had prayed, fasted, anointed her bills with oil, and confessed God's Word over them, but nothing seemed to turn her financial situation around.

Fed up, Jeneen realized that faith alone was not going to change her situation; she needed to act on her faith. A friend put her in touch with a financial planner named Tim, who immediately put her on a tight budget that included a debt payment plan and a savings strategy. He also suggested that Jeneen get a part-time job.

Jeneen followed his advice, but here she was five months into a new budget plan and was still bouncing checks. "Why can't I get this right!" she yelled. She felt like giving up but decided to call Tim. "I can't do this," she complained. "It's too hard."

Tim encouraged Jeneen by pointing out the progress she'd already made. In five short months, she had received no calls from creditors. She had saved almost 500 dollars, and more than half of her debt had been paid off. In addition, she had only bounced one check instead of the usual three or four per month. Tim advised her to transfer what she needed to cover the bad check from her savings account, but to make plans to put it back as soon as possible. After speaking with Tim, Jeneen realized that she had, in fact, made progress. Her perseverance was paying off.

In today's lesson, Nehemiah accomplished a huge task as he rebuilt the walls of Jerusalem despite adverse circumstances. Jeneen's obstacle was financial discipline. What are some other areas where we find ourselves feeling hopeless and overwhelmed?

The People, Places, and Times

Walls of Jerusalem. These were originally built by David and Solomon. They enclosed Zion and Mount Moriah. After Nebuchadnezzar destroyed Jerusalem in 586 B.C., Jerusalem was in ruins for nearly a century and a half. Most of the damage to the walls had been by fire, causing the stones to crack and crumble. Nehemiah's walls were smaller than the original walls but were rebuilt eight feet thick.

Sanballat. At the time of Nehemiah, Sanballat, a Moabite, was governor over Samaria, the region just north of Judea where Jerusalem was located. Some Bible scholars believe that he had political plans to also become governor of Judea. He saw Nehemiah's project as a hindrance to his political aspirations; therefore, he opposed the rebuilding of Jerusalem's wall and made trouble consistently. Whatever his reason, he led others with him in a campaign of contempt for the work of repairing the city's walls.

Source:
Smith, William. *Smith's Bible Dictionary.* Peabody, Mass.: Hendrickson Publishers, Inc., 2000.

Background

Just seeing the massive ruin of Jerusalem's walls was enough to squash anyone's desire to rebuild them. Several miles of rubbish—cracked and crumbled walls, ash, and irreparable gates—lay dormant for nearly a century and a half. It took Nehemiah three days to inspect the damage. Only God knew how long it would take to rebuild it.

Previous attempts to rebuild the wall had been made but were quickly aborted. It was a tremendous challenge, and in addition, their enemies opposed the work. Jerusalem's enemies knew that if the city was walled and secured, it would be formidable. Using everything in their power, these enemies worked to keep Jerusalem unsecured so they could swallow it up at any time.

Only a person with deep faith could accomplish such a task. Nehemiah's prayer and fasting, leadership qualities, organizational skills, quick responses to trouble, and confidence in God qualified him as a great leader and man of God.

At-A-Glance

1. The Work Begins (Nehemiah 4:1–3)
2. The Work Is Opposed (vv. 7–9)
3. The Workers Are Discouraged (vv. 13–15)
4. The Work Is Completed (6:15)

In Depth

1. The Work Begins (Nehemiah 4:1–3)

Our lesson passage opens with the phrase "But it came to pass. . . ." Those words are generally translated to mean "it happened." A literal translation, however, is more interesting because the phrase means "it was sent to happen." This suggests purpose and is the underlying theme behind the work of Nehemiah and the returning Jews.

When Sanballat, Nehemiah's chief enemy, heard about the rebuilding project, he did not hesitate to show his anger. He made the project the subject of his ridicule and considered it a foolish undertaking. He did not see Nehemiah's efforts to rebuild the wall as any different from previous attempts. He thought this would come to naught too. He made fun of Nehemiah's plans by mocking the Jews, calling them weak and stupid. "What will they do for materials?" he scoffed. "They'll only last a day. How can they work one day and keep the Feast of Dedication with sacrifice the next?" Tobiah, the Ammonite, was not to be outdone. He added his insults as well. What he and Sanballat failed to realize was that talk was cheap.

2. The Work Is Opposed (vv. 7–9)

When Sanballat and Tobiah realized it would take more than tongue-lashing to stop Nehemiah from fulfilling his purpose, they aligned themselves with the Arabians, the Ammonites, and the Ashdodites. The scoffers had decided that the only way to stop the building would be to kill the builders, and they couldn't wait to surprise Nehemiah with an attack.

Enemies will fight each other all day long but will join together to fight against someone else. Such was the case with Sanballat, Tobiah, and the aforementioned groups. They had their own differences but put them aside to stop the work of the Lord. The text reads that they "conspired all of them together." They unanimously agreed that Nehemiah's work had to be stopped.

Imagine how angry the enemies must have been at Nehemiah and his men for working so quickly. In such a short time, Jerusalem's walls were up halfway, forming a line of defense. Nehemiah and his men would not be caught off guard.

3. The Workers Are Discouraged (vv. 13–15)

Nehemiah was an intelligent man who placed the guards carefully. In the lower places, where they could easily be seen, he put guards behind the wall so they would agitate the enemies and encourage them to climb up. In higher places, where the wall was raised to its full height, he set guards to throw rocks or darts upon the enemies' heads. Further, he set guards according to families, knowing that relatives would assist each other more than if they were simply neighbors. Even rulers and nobles were persuaded to work and fight with him.

In spite of this intelligent plan of action, Nehemiah noticed that the people were weary from working and fighting, and that fear had set in. He encouraged them by bringing their attention to two things: (1) who they fought under and (2) who they fought for. If it were only Nehemiah's plan to rebuild the wall, and if they were only dependent on his intelligence to fight, then they had reason to be discouraged and afraid. But Nehemiah reminded them that God was a better leader than he was. He told them, "Remember the LORD, which is great and terrible." In other words, he told them if they thought their enemies were great and terrible, they should consider how great and terrible God is, especially to those who oppose Him. It is hard to fear man when you reverentially fear the Lord.

Finally, Nehemiah told them not to give up because everything and everyone they loved was at stake. He encouraged them, saying they had not come as far as they had just to give up. He admonished them to fight for their children, spouses, neighbors, and all that they had worked for.

Then the enemies had heard another piece of news—Nehemiah had learned of their surprise attack. It was pointless for them to attack knowing the Jews would be on guard. Even the enemies recognized that God was on Nehemiah's side, and they retreated. Meanwhile, Nehemiah and his men returned to their work.

4. The Work Is Completed (6:15)

In just 52 days, the 40 or so groups of workers under Nehemiah's leadership had completed the wall around Jerusalem! One and one-half miles of an eight-foot-thick wall had been constructed in less than two months. Biblical scholars differ on whether the completion of the wall refers to the construction and hanging of the gates (compare 6:1 and 7:1) or to the entire construction of the wall. The Jewish historian Josephus states that the rebuilding project took two years and four months, but he included such additional tasks as strengthening, embellishing, and beautifying various sections. In either case, the project was completed 52 days after it was started.

Search the Scriptures

1. How did Nehemiah's enemies respond when they learned that he was rebuilding the wall (Nehemiah 4:2–3)?

2. What did the enemies do when they heard the wall was partially rebuilt (v. 8)?

3. What was Nehemiah's response to the increased opposition (v. 9)?

4. Why and how did Nehemiah encourage the people (v. 14)?

5. How long did it take to rebuild the wall (6:15)?

Discuss the Meaning

1. Why is it hard to finish what you start? Why is it often difficult to complete God-given tasks?

2. How can conflict weaken or strengthen our faith?

3. What characteristics can we adopt from Nehemiah that will enable us to persevere?

Lesson in Our Society

In today's lesson, Nehemiah prayed and executed a plan to contend with opposition. He blended faith with action. Though we confess that faith without works is dead (James 2:17), many of us try to accomplish great tasks by faith or works alone. To exercise one without the other is futile, and we forfeit God's assistance.

Consider areas where we act either by prayer alone or by "doing our thing" without consulting

God. What outcomes can we expect if we combine faith and works under God's direction?

Make It Happen

Two key ideas surface in today's text. The first is the issue of Nehemiah's ability as a leader. Some of us have the innate ability to lead, while the others must learn how to lead. Consider reading a book on effective Christian leadership.

The second issue is how to appropriately respond to success or deal with adversity. Today's lesson presented three groups of people: (1) Sanballat and Tobiah who were resentful of others' progress; (2) the returning remnant who became so fearful they had to be reminded that God was bigger than their problem; and (3) Nehemiah who prayed and handled his business. What causes us to be in one category or the other? What can we do to focus our efforts on being more like Nehemiah?

Regardless of where we find ourselves on these two issues, we must remember that life is tough and there are times when we or our loved ones are discouraged and searching for clear leadership. Those are the times when Christians must affirm their commitment to follow Christ by developing spiritual disciplines such as prayer and Bible reading. Only a relationship with Christ can provide the power to persevere in the midst of opposition. Where do you find yourself today?

Follow the Spirit

What God wants me to do:

_____

_____

Remember Your Thoughts

Special insights I have learned:

_____

_____

More Light on the Text

Nehemiah 4:1–3, 7–9, 13–15; 6:15

1 But it came to pass, that when Sanballat heard that we builded the wall, he was wroth, and took great indignation, and mocked the Jews.

The Jews hated the Samaritans. They considered them racially impure, a mixed race that arose when Jews in the northern kingdom of Israel intermarried with their pagan neighbors and their Assyrian captors. Because of the clash between the two cultures, there was bound to be trouble. After all, they had a history of conflict.

When Zerubbabel attempted to rebuild the temple, he told the Samaritans that they could have no part in the rebuilding of the temple or in the worship of God (see Ezra 4). The Samaritans set about opposing the work and were successful in getting the Persian government to halt the rebuilding for a time. In Nehemiah 2:19, Sanballat, Tobiah, and Geshem came to mock the workers and disrupt the work of repairing the walls. The three were told by Nehemiah that they had no part in the work, the worship, or the heritage of Jerusalem. Nehemiah 4, therefore, records the continuation of this conflict.

Sanballat was a Moabite governor of Samaria. His anger turned to fury as he attempted to disrupt the building project. In Hebrew the phrase "was wroth" is *charah* (**khaw-RAW**) and means "to be hot or furious; to burn with anger." The word "indignation" in Hebrew is *ka'ac* (**kaw-AS**), and means that a person is provoked to wrath. "Mocked" in Hebrew is *la'ag* (**law-AG**) and means "to ridicule someone." In his anger Sanballat turned first to ridicule and scorn to discourage the Hebrew remnant from building the wall, then his derision grew into fury and outrage as he became more and more bitter concerning this work.

2 And he spake before his brethren and the army of Samaria, and said, What do these feeble Jews? will they fortify themselves? will they sacrifice? will they make an end in a day? will they revive the stones out of the heaps of the rubbish which are burned?

Sanballat made no effort to hide his anger. He was a governmental agent for the area who wielded his power to disrupt the work of restoration. He spoke boldly in the faces of the "army" (Heb. *chayil*, **KHAH-yil**) of Samaria and stirred his "brethren" (Heb. *'ach*, **awkh**) to join in his mockery of the returning Jews. In essence, Sanballat vented his frustrations to those who would help him carry out his sinister plans—his relatives, tribesmen, and the army of Samaria, men who thrived on fighting and killing their enemies.

Sanballat raised five questions in his attempt to discourage the workers. In the first question he called them "feeble" (Heb. *'amelal*, **am-ay-LAWL**) or weak Jews and asked what they thought they were doing.

He made light of their work and their purpose. He ridiculed them as unskilled and unlearned workers. This was an effort to debase and undermine the Jews. Apparently, Sanballat thought that by calling the workers weak, he could dampen their enthusiasm and cause them to abort the project.

His second question focused on the work itself. The query, "Will they fortify themselves?" can be restated as, "Will they really build a wall that protects them?" Sanballat was saying that the work would not amount to anything substantial. It was a waste of time to assume that this remnant of the former Judah could create something that would protect the area.

Sanballat's third and fourth questions attacked the urgency of the work. He might have asked, "What's your rush? Are you planning on making a sacrifice in this place today?" Nehemiah and the others were working furiously to complete the task. Sanballat wanted them to believe that their progress was no progress at all. In reality there was a rush based on the fact that the wall had been desolate too long. The grief Nehemiah felt at the unfinished work in Jerusalem had given him the boldness to approach the king (Nehemiah 2; see also lesson 11—May 11). He would not be deterred by the remarks Sanballat made. There was urgency in restoring the wall because it was a symbol that God was restoring His people.

The final question was aimed at reminding the former captives how desolate the area had become in their absence and to make a mockery of what they had done up to that point. Sanballat presented the situation as he saw it: They could repair all they wanted, but the walls had been burned and were good for nothing. The material the men were using was junk, "rubbish" (Heb. *'aphar*, **aw-FAWR**) born from the ashes of decay and war. Together the questions were aimed at saying, "You're wasting your time and your energy. This will never again be the place where you can sacrifice and worship. Your materials are substandard and your abilities are lacking. You're stuck with your past and have no possibilities for a meaningful future!"

3 Now Tobiah the Ammonite was by him, and he said, Even that which they build, if a fox go up, he shall even break down their stone wall.

Sanballat did not come alone. He brought with him Tobiah, a Jewish-Ammonite governor who joined forces with Sanballat to oppose the building project. Tobiah viciously quipped that a fox would be able to break down the wall. If the intent was to fortify the city from the onslaught of neighboring countries, Nehemiah and the others had already failed. A "fox" (Heb. *shuw'al*, **shoo-AWL**) is a relatively small but stealthy animal. What Sanballat and Tobiah did not know was that God was empowering the Jews to do what He had called them to do, and with God behind the project, the wall had added protection.

4:7 But it came to pass, that when Sanballat, and Tobiah, and the Arabians, and the Ammonites, and the Ashdodites, heard that the walls of Jerusalem were made up, and that the breaches began to be stopped, then they were very wroth, 8 And conspired all of them together to come and to fight against Jerusalem, and to hinder it.

According to Nehemiah 4:6, one-half of the wall was soon repaired. This was done because the people "had a mind to work." It was not long after the original taunting that the walls of Jerusalem were "made up." This phrase comes from two Hebrew words. The first is *'aruwkah* (**ar-oo-KAW**) and means "healing or restoration." The second is *'alah* (**aw-LAW**) and means "to ascend, to climb upward." In contradiction to the words of Sanballat, the walls of the city of Jerusalem grew from the rubble and ash, from the decay that had been left when the city was sacked, the people were taken, and Jewish worship was disrupted. Now God was enabling His people to restore that which had been stolen.

Tobiah, too, had been proven wrong. Not only was the wall too strong for a fox, but it was too sturdy for people to breach as well. The word "breaches" in Hebrew is *parats* (**paw-RATS**), which means "to break through or to tear down." All of the broken-down places of the damaged wall were being sealed by the new and repaired structure. The people were successful in their endeavor because they were blessed by God to have a mind to work, and the work was blessed by God to succeed.

The project of rebuilding the walls progressed so well that it incurred the wrath of those who opposed it. When the adversaries saw that their intimidation did not deter the progress, they were incensed. As the work continued and the wall was fortified, the naysayers led by Sanballat grew in number. In verse 8, the term "conspired" (Heb. *qashar*, **kaw-SHAR**) means "to come together in a league and for a purpose." Now, in addition to the tribesmen and the army of Samaria, the leaders of the neighboring countries were part of the opposition: the Arabians, the Ammonites, and the Ashdodites. The team consisted of pagan leaders who were enemies of God and His chosen people. This collective group was determined to spoil the building plans of God.

9 Nevertheless we made our prayer unto our God, and set a watch against them day and night, because of them.

Nehemiah was a praying man, a man of character and persistence. He carefully considered what to do and the way God was directing. He depended on God to finish what He had begun. But Nehemiah was not alone in this prayer; the group was collective in their growing faith and prayer life. When people have a praying leader who teaches them how to pray and how to wait on God, they begin to see the value of prayer; and as prayers are answered, they begin to depend on God for themselves.

Verse 9 says that "nevertheless we made our prayer unto God." This phrase in Hebrew consists of one word, *palal* (**paw-LAL**), which means "to intervene through prayer." This was intercessory prayer. They prayed for one another. They prayed for the project. They prayed for wisdom. And they did this despite the opposition. The word "nevertheless" should be considered carefully. Prayer was their intent. They were not driven to pray because of events; they were already praying and kept praying despite the events.

We cannot tell whether Nehemiah had the idea to "set a watch" (Hebrew *'amad mishmar*, **aw-MAD mish-MAWR**), and then prayed about it or if in the midst of prayer, God told him to post guards at every juncture of the work. What we do know is that God can direct us regarding whether or not the idea is a good one, and He can give us an idea when we are at our wits' end. Nehemiah combined prayer with thought, preparation, and effort. As a result, the building team trusted God to handle the matter, and they were vigilant in watching out for the enemy day and night. Hard work had just gotten harder, but they were still not deterred from the task.

"So built we the wall; and all the wall was joined together unto the half thereof: for the people had a mind to work" (Nehemiah 4:6).

4:13 Therefore set I in the lower places behind the wall, and on the higher places, I even set the people after their families with their swords, their spears, and their bows.

The situation soon became so dangerous that the people in Judah had to finally admit they were worn out from the work. The amount of rubble and stone was so great that they were having difficulty with removing the debris (see vv. 10–12). There was only a remnant available to do the work,

and the same people were rebuilding the walls as well as removing the trash!

Added to this was the task of watching out for the enemy. The Jews who lived in outlying areas reported repeatedly that the enemies were gathering with a plan to attack the workers at every place along the wall. The final decision, therefore, was to set a watch by people armed with swords, spears, and bows. Nehemiah took his watch behind the wall as a fortification to those who, along with their families, were watchmen and workers on the higher places along the wall.

14 And I looked, and rose up, and said unto the nobles, and to the rulers, and to the rest of the people, Be not ye afraid of them: remember the LORD, which is great and terrible, and fight for your brethren, your sons, and your daughters, your wives, and your houses.

Nehemiah "looked" (Heb. *ra'ah*, **raw-AW**) at the people with the eyes of a leader. He saw their pain and he perceived their anxiety. In his mind's eye he inspected not only what they had done, the sacrifices they were already making, but he also recognized what they would have to face. If he did not listen to the Lord and remain prayerful, some of these people would lose their lives, and many of them would be afraid of the enemies of the Lord.

So Nehemiah "rose up" (Heb. *quwm*, **koom**). He not only stood on his feet before the crowd, he took a stand on the side of the Lord. Nehemiah stood with clarity about what had to be done. He was not deterred. Instead he was determined not to allow the others to be afraid. He did not rise to beg them to help; he rose to validate God's presence with them. Nehemiah stood to confirm that they were on God's side and doing the work God had ordained no matter how the enemy presented himself. Nehemiah rose with the intent of having others rise with him.

Many factors worked against Nehemiah and the building crew. They had to accomplish a huge building program, deal with enemies who were trying to hinder them, and cope with battle fatigue. Nehemiah had to encourage the people. He spoke to the "nobles" (Heb. *chor*, **khore**), who were the administrators of the project, and to the "rulers" (Heb. *cagan*, **saw-GAWN**), the leaders assigned to various smaller groups. Nehemiah understood, however, that success would require input from outside the leadership. It was necessary that "the rest" (Heb. *yether*, **YEH-ther**) of the "people" (Heb. *'am*, **am**) be involved in the decision as well. In order to be successful, the entire remnant of Judah, including all members of the tribe and nation, had to be of one accord. They had demonstrated that they had a mind to work (see verse 6). Now they were called upon to risk their lives for the work of the Lord.

The first thing Nehemiah had to do was to calm their fears. When rumors, and even truths, about anything that is going to devastate a person's world abound, the level of anxiety increases. Those who were not afraid at first were now losing hope. Those who were already weak or who were concerned with the safety of their wives and children were placed in an awkward situation. They wanted to help, but they wanted to see their families safe. Second thoughts crept in regarding what would happen next.

The second thing was to remember that their God had outstanding attributes. The word "remember" in Hebrew is *zakar* (**zaw-KAR**), which means "to recall" or "bring to mind again something that has gone before." Nehemiah asked the people to call to mind who God was and what He had done for them and their families in the past. They were working for the Lord (Heb. *'Adonay*, **ad-o-NOY**), and it was the Lord who would protect them.

The Hebrew word for "great" (*gadowl*, **gaw-DOLE**) means "large in number and intensity." The enemy seemed to have been growing in allies, but only the Lord was truly great. The numbers among the enemy forces had been increasing. They had started with the taunts of Sanballat, and now other nations were standing against them. They needed to understand that God was mightier and "terrible" (Heb. *yare'*, **yaw-RAY**). They would have no need to fear the enemy, but the enemy had a need to fear God. The term *yare'* also means "to reverence." God would show Himself strong and powerful so that all would reverence His name. The Jews would give all glory to God for His deliverance of them in the present age. They knew the stories of God's deliverance of their parents and ancestors, but now they would know God's deliverance of them.

In addition, the enemy would know that the God who delivered His people from the hand of Egypt under Moses was still delivering His people. The enemy would have to acknowledge that *'Adonay* had delivered into the hand of His people the land which they claimed during the conquests of Joshua. God had no intention of allowing what He had given to the nation to be taken by the enemy. In short, the God they served was to be reverenced, honored, and respected. He would be feared and revered. Who could be a match for the all-powerful God? The enemy would fear Him and know that He was in full control and that the people who were called by His name were doing the work He had ordained—and that work would be successful.

Finally Nehemiah assured them that with this knowledge they could proceed to "fight for your brethren, your sons, and your daughters, your wives, and your houses." They would fight as a nation, as one unified people under God. They would fight for the heritage that would be delivered to their sons. They would fight for their daughters, who would give birth to their legacy, and for their wives, who had borne their children. Lastly, they would fight for their houses (Heb. *bayith*, **BAH-yith**). This term does not mean just for the places where they were to live. They were to fight for their lineage, the house of their fathers, which had continued through them despite war and captivity. Now that they had returned, they were to fight for the houses that would be established in their names as a legacy for the future of the nation.

15 And it came to pass, when our enemies heard that it was known unto us, and God had brought their counsel to nought, that we returned all of us to the wall, every one unto his work.

The enemy was no match for Almighty God! They were thwarted before they even began. In fact, they heard that Nehemiah and his crew knew of their sinister plot. Their careful planning and conniving scheme had been found out and counteracted. The people were both on and inside the wall ready for their attack; but more importantly, the Lord was present and had already shown Himself able to mock their plans. Sanballat and his confederates realized that it was God who had undermined and destroyed their strategy. The phrase "to nought" in Hebrew is *parar* (**paw-RAR**), which means "to break, frustrate, violate, make ineffectual, shatter." In verse 3, Tobiah had predicted that the wall would be so flimsy that a fox could destroy it. Now Tobiah and Sanballat, as well as the leaders of the surrounding nations, realized that their fortified and well-hidden plans had been shattered by the God who was able to break every stronghold and device they could envision.

6:15 So the wall was finished in the twenty and fifth day of the month Elul, in fifty and two days.

The lesson text now moves to the end of the story and provides for us the conclusion of the matter: the wall was finished. The word "so" in English means "as a result of something." "Was finished" in Hebrew is *shalam* (**shaw-LAM**) and means "a covenant of peace" or "to be completed in soundness." Despite the turmoil, the covenant of peace with God for restoration of His city was complete and was demonstrated through the building of the wall. The enemy had said that it couldn't be done, that the effort was useless and would not amount to anything. Now it was obvious that Nehemiah and the nation of Judah served a great God who always finishes what He starts.

Not only was it done, but it was done in 52 days! Sanballat had asked about the urgency, and God had answered by allowing the work to be completed in only 52 days. Those days had been filled with the ridicule of onlookers who were enemies of the people and of God. The 52 days had been filled with the backbreaking work of hauling debris and digging among the ashes for useable rocks and boulders. There had been 52 days of standing watch and then working, of taking shifts and going without sleep. At times, the 52 days had been filled with concern, doubt, and fear, when the enemy had assumed that their backs were against the wall. Now it was known that God had their backs so that on the 53rd day they could shout with victory and proclaim, "It is finished."

Sources:

Life Application Study Bible, NLT. Wheaton, Ill.: Tyndale House Publishers, Inc., 1996.

Pfeiffer, Charles F., Howard F. Vos, and John Rea, eds. *Wycliffe Bible Dictionary*. Peabody, Mass.: Hendrickson Publishers, Inc., 1998.

Strong, J. *The Exhaustive Concordance of the Bible* (electronic ed.). Ontario, Canada: Woodside Bible Fellowship, 1996.

Daily Bible Readings

M: A Cry for Help
Psalm 70

T: Mocking Enemies
Nehemiah 4:1–6

W: A Plot to Confuse the Builders
Nehemiah 4:7–11

T: The Plot Is Foiled
Nehemiah 4:12–15

F: Always at the Ready
Nehemiah 4:16–23

S: Attempts to Stop the Building
Nehemiah 6:1–14

S: The Wall Is Finished
Nehemiah 6:15–19

TEACHING TIPS

May 25
Bible Study Guide 13

1. Words You Should Know

A. Amen (Nehemiah 8:6) *'amen* (Heb.)—A term of agreement meaning "it is so."

B. Gave the sense (v. 8) *suwm sekel* (Heb.)—To establish an understanding or insight.

2. Teacher Preparation

Unifying Principle—Restored and Renewed Relationships falter daily. Every day we should strive to make our relationships better with God and with others, knowing that if we do not maintain our relationships, they can falter.

A. Prepare for this lesson by studying the Focal Verses in at least two different translations. Also, become familiar with resources that help you glean from the original text and culture of the Bible. Prepare to share the names of these resources with interested class members.

B. Read The People, Places, and Times, Background, In Depth, and More Light on the Text sections carefully.

3. Starting the Lesson

A. Set the atmosphere for class by playing praise music from a CD as the class gathers.

B. After prayer give each person a copy of today's Focal Verses in a different language and ask them to read it in unison. After the initial confusion, explain that the people in today's text could not understand the language of the Law, so Ezra provided a translation and interpretation for them.

C. End this section by having the students stand as you play the taped Focal Verses.

4. Getting into the Lesson

A. Discuss the Focal Verses, using the At-A-Glance outline. Incorporate The People, Places, and Times in your discussion at appropriate times.

B. Have the students work in groups to examine the Scriptures that explain the Feast of Tabernacles. Ask each group to outline the highlights of the festival.

C. Have groups report and post their findings. Lead a brief discussion comparing both texts and determining how closely Ezra and the people followed the instructions.

5. Relating the Lesson to Life

A. Sound the ram's horn and explain its significance in calling people to careful listening and application of God's Word.

B. Have the class read the In Focus story and respond to David's dilemma.

C. Have the class brainstorm about what calls us to God's Word today, such as our need for comfort, our commitment to learning God's Word, and the need to explain and apply a specific biblical truth. We are also called to Bible reading as part of our worship experience or a Bible study group or class.

D. Have the class consider how our commitment to God should provide an internal call to study God's Word.

6. Arousing Action

A. Read the Make It Happen section and respond to the questions posed.

B. Briefly display the resources for better Bible understanding. Ask the students who have used these resources to offer comments. Allow time after class for the students to examine copies or ask questions in detail.

C. Encourage the class to read the Daily Bible Readings leading up to next week's lesson and, if possible, to use a resource as part of their study.

D. Close the class with prayer.

Worship Guide

For the Superintendent or Teacher
Theme: A Call to Renew the Covenant
Theme Song: "I Have Decided to Follow Jesus"
Devotional Reading: Psalms 19:7–14; 27:11–14
Prayer

A CALL TO RENEW THE COVENANT

Bible Background • NEHEMIAH 8

Printed Text • NEHEMIAH 8:1–3, 5–6, 13–14, 17–18 Devotional Reading • PSALMS 19:7–14; 27:11–14

AIM for Change

By the end of the lesson, we will:

EXPLORE the significance of a restored relationship with God;

RENEW our commitment to be obedient and serve God; and

PRAY for strength to keep our commitments to God and man.

Keep in Mind

"And he read therein before the street that was before the water gate from the morning until midday, before the men and the women, and those that could understand; and the ears of all the people were attentive unto the book of the law" (Nehemiah 8:3).

Focal Verses

KJV
Nehemiah 8:1 And all the people gathered themselves together as one man into the street that was before the water gate; and they spake unto Ezra the scribe to bring the book of the law of Moses, which the LORD had commanded to Israel.

2 And Ezra the priest brought the law before the congregation both of men and women, and all that could hear with understanding, upon the first day of the seventh month.

3 And he read therein before the street that was before the water gate from the morning until midday, before the men and the women, and those that could understand; and the ears of all the people were attentive unto the book of the law.

8:5 And Ezra opened the book in the sight of all the people; (for he was above all the people;) and when he opened it, all the people stood up:

6 And Ezra blessed the LORD, the great God. And all the people answered, Amen, Amen, with lifting up their hands: and they bowed their heads, and worshipped the LORD with their faces to the ground.

8:13 And on the second day were gathered together the chief of the fathers of all the people, the priests, and the Levites, unto Ezra the scribe, even to understand the words of the law.

14 And they found written in the law which the LORD had commanded by Moses, that the children of Israel should dwell in booths in the feast of the seventh month.

8:17 And all the congregation of them that were come again out of the captivity made booths, and sat under the booths: for since the days of Jeshua the

NLT
Nehemiah 8:1 all the people assembled with a unified purpose at the square just inside the Water Gate. They asked Ezra the scribe to bring out the Book of the Law of Moses, which the LORD had given for Israel to obey.

2 So on October 8 Ezra the priest brought the Book of the Law before the assembly, which included the men and women and all the children old enough to understand.

3 He faced the square just inside the Water Gate from early morning until noon and read aloud to everyone who could understand. All the people listened closely to the Book of the Law.

8:5 Ezra stood on the platform in full view of all the people. When they saw him open the book, they all rose to their feet.

6 Then Ezra praised the LORD, the great God, and all the people chanted, "Amen! Amen!" as they lifted their hands. Then they bowed down and worshiped the LORD with their faces to the ground.

8:13 On October 9 the family leaders of all the people, together with the priests and Levites, met with Ezra the scribe to go over the Law in greater detail.

14 As they studied the Law, they discovered that the LORD had commanded through Moses that the Israelites should live in shelters during the festival to be held that month.

8:17 So everyone who had returned from captivity lived in these shelters during the festival, and they were son of Nun unto that day had not the children of Israel done so. And there was very great gladness.

18 Also day by day, from the first day unto the last day, he read in the book of the law of God. And they kept the feast seven days; and on the eighth day was a solemn assembly, according unto the manner.

all filled with great joy! The Israelites had not celebrated like this since the days of Joshua son of Nun.

18 Ezra read from the Book of the Law of God on each of the seven days of the festival. Then on the eighth day they held a solemn assembly, as was required by law.

In Focus

Three years ago, when David placed his faith in God, his life was in pretty bad shape. He had made a number of poor decisions and had broken relationships with his family and friends. Having reached a low point in his life, he realized that his only hope was in God. His zeal after confessing his faith was extraordinary. He served in the kitchen and worked on the parking lot. He attended Bible class regularly and was always the first person in Sunday School and worship services.

After two years, David was well on the way to a restored life. He had met a young woman in the church and asked her to marry him. However, he wanted to be sure he was financially able to make the commitment. His job offered him the opportunity to move into management, but the promotion also required a move to another city. After prayer, the two decided that David should take the job and their wedding would take place after he was settled in the new city.

David worked hard on his new job, but the city was very different. He had a difficult time finding a church, and with such a heavy workload, he soon stopped looking for a permanent place to worship. He also found himself very tired and eventually stopped being as faithful about keeping the early morning prayer and Bible-reading routine he had kept previously. Because his schedule was so hectic, he also stopped calling his fiancee as often. In his mind, he was still committed and wanted to marry her, but he knew she would understand how hectic things were.

When he called her one evening, she asked him to come home for the weekend. She wanted to talk to him. When he arrived, she spoke candidly. She challenged his commitment to God and told him how she had seen a difference in him. He confessed that he had been lax in Bible study and prayer. She replied that she could not see marrying someone

who could put aside God and other people when times became difficult. They talked for hours.

Finally David asked her to pray with him. He recommitted his life to the Lord and to her. They went to see the pastor, who counseled them on the coming marriage and gave David a number of pointers for getting back on track. He even gave David a list of churches in his new city and the names of several pastors and young men who would be willing to open their fellowship to him.

The Bible, the living Word of God, is available to help us live our lives as committed Christians who honor God and our commitments to others. Today's lesson is about getting acquainted with God's Word. What is your commitment to God's Word? How can you strengthen your covenant relationship with God and others through the Bible?

The People, Places, and Times

Ezra. Ezra was held captive in Babylon. He was a learned man who loved to read and teach. He dedicated himself to teaching the Jews the Word of God, which he studied faithfully. When granted permission by King Artaxerxes to return to Jerusalem, Ezra entered into a program of teaching and preaching (see Ezra 7). He led a revival among the returning Jews and others who were in the land (see Ezra 9–10). Ezra also trained the Levites and priests in reading and understanding the Scriptures, which were written in Hebrew, a language they no longer read or understood. It was these leaders who assisted him in presenting the Word to the people (see Nehemiah 8).

Levites. The Levites were chosen by God to serve in the temple. They were descendants from the tribe of Levi, and their job was to do the work in the temple that included preparing the materials and artifacts for worship. In the days of Moses, the Levites carried the tabernacle in the wilderness and were responsible for setting it up at each camp (see Numbers 1:47–53). Under David, the nation regained the Ark of the Covenant, and Jerusalem was the center of national worship. The Levites, who no longer had to carry the tabernacle, continued the upkeep of the tabernacle and items of worship. David also engaged them as musicians and singers to lead the people in worship (see 1 Chronicles 15:14–28).

Background

Israel was in exile for more than 150 years and Judah for 70 years. When Judah was conquered, the Babylonians took the scrolls from the temple and the temple artifacts. The captives were forced also to abandon their native language in favor of the language of their captors. Aramaic was the language of business for Babylon and later Persia. As was the case in most cultures, only the most elite in society were literate. With the scrolls of God's Word taken and a new language spoken, the people only knew God's Word through the stories of their families and other captives. They had neither seen the words given to Moses nor heard them. Their faith in God was largely based on the accounts that were kept by those who remembered the Word.

In 538 B.C., 70 years after Israel had been exiled, the first group of Israelites returned to Judah under the leadership of Zerubbabel. A number of years later, in 458 B.C., under the leadership of Ezra, a second group returned. Under Ezra's faithful teaching, most of the people turned from their sins and agreed to reestablish their relationship with God and follow His will for their lives. In 444 B.C., 14 years after Ezra, Nehemiah returned and succeeded in rebuilding the walls. The book of Nehemiah overlaps the book of Ezra as indicated in today's lesson where this covenant renewal occurs.

At-A-Glance

1. Gathering (Nehemiah 8:1–3)
2. Blessing (vv. 5–6)
3. Worshiping (vv. 13–14, 17–18)

In Depth

1. Gathering (Nehemiah 8:1–3)

After the returned exiles were settled in their towns, all the people gathered in the square before the water gate in Jerusalem and asked Ezra to bring the Book of the Law (vv. 1–2). As they gathered, Ezra read from morning to midday to all who could understand, and they listened attentively (v. 3). This is a sign that these exiles took the Word of God seriously. The term "Law of God" generally refers to the Decalogue or the Ten Commandments; but the word used here to describe the Law is "Torah," a reference to the word God gave to Moses. Attending to the Law of God, then, is not just paying attention to the do's and don'ts but giving oneself completely to all that God has revealed.

The returning exiles were focused on the Lord and dedicated to the renewal of their covenant with Him. They were determined not to be deterred. They could have attended to their own houses, for the houses of their ancestors had been destroyed by their enemies. They could have attended to their own safety. They could have chosen to stay at home and worship the Lord. But paying attention to all of these things would not have satisfied their need for security and belonging. Attending to the Law of the Lord provided them with the opportunity to enter into the sphere of the covenant that God made with their ancestors. They realized that without the Law they would not grasp the breach that caused them to be exiled in the first place. Attending to the Word leads to a readiness for divine transformation. They had been in exile, and now that they were in their homeland, they needed to cleanse themselves from the reproach of Babylon. They depended on Ezra to read the Word of God, knowing that it would cleanse their hearts from the negative experiences of oppression.

In our modern context, many people rely on pastors alone to decipher the Word of God and then to provide everything their congregants need to follow the Lord. The opposite is seen in this text. The people wanted Ezra to read God's Word to them, not to give his opinion of it. While ministers should take the lead in expounding God's Word, they must not be the only ones for whom God's Word is a priority.

The people gathered to hear Ezra because the Law was important, and they wanted to hear every word. The depth of their attention is seen in the amount of time they spent listening. There is no intimation that the people thought Ezra was taking too long reading the Scriptures. They listened attentively "from early morning until midday" (v. 3).

2. Blessing (vv. 5–6)

By entering into the process of covenant renewal through prayer and worship, Ezra and the people demonstrated their appreciation for God's Law. We cannot discern how long it had been since they had heard the Word read before them. In that culture few people were literate, so hearing the Word would have been the normal way to receive instruction from God. Many of the younger men and women were born in captivity and had probably never heard the Scriptures. From the context it is clear that many could not understand the Word because of a language barrier. The Scriptures were written in Hebrew, and those who had been born in captivity learned to speak Aramaic.

Their appreciation was shown not only in the fact that they listened attentively, but also that they stood when Ezra began to read. Standing indicated that they were ready to move on what was heard. This sign of reverence suggests that the people took a posture of readiness for action. They lifted their hands, indicating their surrender or submission to God's will as they sought to renew covenant with Him. This appreciation acknowledged the fact that God had brought them back to the land of their fathers and mothers.

Ezra "blessed the LORD, the great God," and the people responded by saying, "Amen, amen." By their verbal appreciation they showed that they distinguished the Lord from other gods. They had been held in a pagan land, where the Babylonians and Persians worshiped idols. They had spent their years compelled to obey people who did not know Jehovah, the one, true God. Now they could declare the Lord as the only great God. Their appreciation is seen in their verbal response to Ezra's blessing; their words flowed with praise and thanksgiving. How could they not respond with outbursts of praise, knowing that "the LORD, the great God" had chosen to speak a word into their situation of despair and had transformed them?

3. Worshiping (vv. 13–14, 17–18)

While the renewal of the covenant was a solemn act, the people's worship celebrated God's deliverance and their joy at His mercy and at hearing His Word. The events in the previous verses occurred on the first day of their gathering before Ezra. At the end of the day, the people had been convicted because of their transgression and were ready to mourn, but Ezra and the Levites told them that "the joy of the LORD" would be their strength. They were to rejoice in knowing what God wanted and who God was rather than being downcast for their earlier ignorance (vv. 9–12.)

The next day the leaders of the families, the Levites, and the priests returned to learn more about God's will and the covenant He desired them to keep. In this reading, they discovered the Feast of Tabernacles, a celebration ordained when Israel was delivered from Egypt. This time of staying in booths was a remembrance of the time when the children of Abraham had no homes and no homeland, when God provided for them on their sojourn across the wilderness.

Immediately they gathered themselves to reinstate the Feast of Tabernacles. They realized that God had provided for them as they wandered in a strange land away from their ancestral home. The alert was sounded by messengers on foot and by the sounding of the alarm or ram's horn. Special instructions were given regarding the materials that were to be gathered for the building of the booths or temporary dwellings (see v. 15).

The obedience was so great that booths were built in the streets and on housetops. The people gathered before the temple and at the gates. Their worship was not with tears but with overwhelming gladness at what God had done. They worshiped God and celebrated His covenant. In accordance with the Law, they spent each day learning more of God's Word and purposing in their hearts to be obedient to the Law.

On the eighth day, they held a solemn assembly, as instructed by Moses. On that day, they officially entered the covenant and offered prayers and sacrifices to God in accordance with His Word. They worshiped God, the Covenant Giver, and determined to be covenant keepers as they carried His Word in their hearts.

Search the Scriptures

1. Who read the Law to the returning exiles (Nehemiah 8:1)?

2. Who was present at the reading of the Book of the Law (v. 2)?

3. How long did Ezra read the Word to the exiles (v. 3)?

4. What did the people do when Ezra read the Word (v. 5)?

5. What festival was reinstated as a result of their reading the Book of the Law (vv. 13–14)?

6. What event was held on the final day of the festival (v. 18)?

Discuss the Meaning

1. Why was it necessary for the book to be translated and interpreted? Is this relevant to how we read the Bible today?

2. What signs of eagerness to know God's Word were demonstrated throughout this text?

3. Describe the various types of honor the returnees gave to the Book of the Law.

Lesson in Our Society

Today's text reveals a number of ways to celebrate and honor God's Word. In many worship services today, we see these same actions take place: crying, standing, raising hands, rejoicing, and solemn acts of worship. The context for all of this, however, is hearing God's Word. What Ezra and the Levites presented was not a commentary on God's Word, but the Word itself in clear language. They realized that the original language in which the Book of the Law was written was not the contemporary language of the people.

The same is true today. The Bible was originally written in Hebrew (Old Testament) and Greek (New Testament). Without a clear translation, we would be confused regarding what God's Word says. Fortunately, we don't each have to be Hebrew or Greek scholars to appreciate God's Word. God has provided scholarship by men and women who have developed materials to help every believer understand the words as closely as possible to the original language. The *Precepts For Living*® CD-ROM, for example, provides multiple translations, and the More Light on the Text section provides words and definitions of original language. There are also reference books that provide translations, and dictionaries and encyclopedic resources that help us understand not only the words but the social and political contexts of the times in which the Bible was written.

Make It Happen

How well do you understand God's Word? What is hindering you from making a commitment to get closer to the original text and ideas so that you can better appreciate your covenant with Him? Investigate bookstores, libraries, and on-line resources that will enlighten and strengthen you to follow God's Word in your life.

Follow the Spirit

What God wants me to do:

_____

_____

Remember Your Thoughts

Special insights I have learned:

_____

_____

More Light on the Text

Nehemiah 8:1–3, 5–6, 13–14, 17–18

1 And all the people gathered themselves together as one man into the street that was before the water gate; and they spake unto Ezra the scribe to bring the book of the law of Moses, which the LORD had commanded to Israel.

If we place the book of Nehemiah in context, then prior to the events of this text, several major events have taken place in the history of the Jews who returned from captivity and resettled in Jerusalem. The temple had been restored (Haggai 1:14; lesson 10—May 4; also see Ezra 6:10). The walls of Jerusalem had been rebuilt and restored (Nehemiah 6:15; lesson 12—May 18). Everything was set in place for the people to embark on spiritual revival as they renewed their covenant with the Lord, a covenant established by the patriarchs. The covenant renewal begins with the reading of the Law under the leadership and priesthood of Ezra.

Ezra was the leader, and the people were eager to initiate the revival of their covenant with God. They assembled themselves "as one man into the street that was before the water gate." The word for "street" (Heb. *rechob*, **rekh-OBE**) does not mean a narrow road with houses arranged on both sides as it would be today. The Hebrew term refers to a spacious, open area where a multitude of people gather for important meetings or events. The word itself means a broad or open space, a plaza, much like a town square of the Igbo tradition in Nigeria.

Ezra records that the people assembled together "as one man." The people who had labored together in restoring Jerusalem as the national center apparently gathered voluntarily in unity and cooperation because they were hungry for the Word of God. Every adult member of the nation able to understand the seriousness of the covenant commitment they were making was included and involved.

"And he read therein before the street that was before the water gate from the morning until midday, before the men and the women, and those that could understand; and the ears of all the people were attentive unto the book of the law" (Nehemiah 8:3).

The assembly gathered before the "water gate" in the recently rebuilt wall of Jerusalem. The Bible speaks of many gates around Jerusalem and the temple. Each had a specific purpose and could be used to identify specific areas within the city or temple. As the people gathered, they called on Ezra, the scribe, to bring the Book of the Law. It was time for Ezra to teach God's Word to God's people.

A "scribe" (Heb. *caphar*, **saw-FAR**) was a transcriber of the Law. Ezra is referred to as a "ready scribe" in Ezra 7:6 because of his extensive knowledge of the Mosaic Law. Ezra, who had been held captive in Babylon, was granted permission by King Artaxerxes to return to Jerusalem to help with the restoration. "Ezra had prepared his heart to seek the law of the LORD, and to do it, and to teach in Israel statutes and judgments" (7:10). Ezra did not just copy the Scriptures; he was the custodian of the Law of Moses, which included the Pentateuch, the first five books of our modern Bible. Ezra also interpreted the Law and was prepared to teach the Law to this generation of returnees who no longer knew the language or traditions of their people.

2 And Ezra the priest brought the law before the congregation both of men and women, and all that could hear with understanding, upon the first day of the seventh month. 3 And he read therein before the street that was before the water gate from the morning until midday, before the men and the women, and those that could understand; and the ears of all the people were attentive unto the book of the law.

Verse 1 of our text refers to Ezra, a descendant of Aaron, as a scribe (see Ezra 7:6). Verse 2 refers to him as a priest. According to Jewish law, it was the duty of the priest to teach the people the Word of God (see Deuteronomy 17:9–12). It was in his dual role of priest–scribe that Ezra brought the Book of the Law before the congregation.

The gathering took place on the first day of the seventh month. In their return to the sacred land, the people wanted to do everything God proclaimed. After all, for the years of their captivity they had been denied the right to freely worship Jehovah and were forbidden from returning to Jerusalem, which was the sacred place of worship. The Law required that every seven years the people gather for the reading of the Law (see Deuteronomy 31:9–13). The seven-year

period was in honor of the freedom the nation acquired from Egypt and was to be acknowledged with the release of all slaves and debts. The people had returned from Babylon; they were free and wanted to honor the Law by paying special attention and honor to God's Word.

Verse 3 gives a summary of the events of the day as the book was opened before the people. Ezra "read" (Heb. *qara'*, **kaw-RAW**) in a manner that was much like preaching. He proclaimed aloud the words of the Law from morning until midday, probably over six hours of teaching. This was not an easy task. The crowd included "the men and the women, and those that could understand." While in Babylonian captivity Ezra had studied the Hebrew Scriptures carefully; but the Jewish captives had acquired a new language, Aramaic. The people had to be able to not just hear, but to understand the Scriptures as they were translated for this new generation of Jews. During the reading of the Law, Ezra was flanked by Levites who assisted in the process of translation (see vv. 4, 7). The people paid close attention because they wanted to embrace the Word of God, which was new to them. This was a time of solemnity, respect, and reverence to the Word of God.

8:5 And Ezra opened the book in the sight of all the people; (for he was above all the people;) and when he opened it, all the people stood up: 6 And Ezra blessed the LORD, the great God. And all the people answered, Amen, Amen, with lifting up their hands: and they bowed their heads, and worshipped the LORD with their faces to the ground.

This was not an impromptu gathering. Ezra stepped onto a wooden pulpit or podium, which had been made for such a purpose. Ezra opened the "book" (Heb. *cepher*, **SAY-fer**), which was likely a scroll, and when it was unfurled, "all the people" stood in reverence to God's Word.

Ezra then offered a blessing for the Word and for the task they were about to undertake. Ezra "blessed" (Heb. *barak*, **baw-RAK**) the Lord. This means that he kneeled before the congregation. He did not take this time, for which he had prepared for years, to proclaim what he had learned and needed to share. He began with such reverence for God that he was driven to his knees. Ezra blessed God because he recognized Him as the "LORD" (Heb. *Yehovah*, **yeh-ho-VAW**), the "great" (Heb. *gadowl*, **gaw-DOLE**) "God" (Heb. *'elohiym*, **el-o-HEEM**). Ezra knew that God was self-existent and eternal. He honored God as "great," which can be translated as God's having a powerful and mighty presence. Ezra called God "Elohim," the supreme ruler of all humanity and the judge of all people. Ezra's gesture of falling to his knees was a sign of humility as he recognized his and the people's unworthiness as they were honored to read God's Word before the rebuilt temple which bore His name.

Simply put, Ezra opened the meeting with a prayer of thanksgiving and praise to the Lord. The people lifted their voices in consent and testimony as they agreed with Ezra's actions and words. The "people" are identified by the word *'am*, which in Hebrew means all of the kinsmen, the nation. The collective shout was "Amen, Amen," a direct rendering of the Hebrew *'amen*, meaning "so be it." They "worshipped" (Heb. *shachah*, **shaw-KHAW**), which means to bow or lay prostrate facedown on the ground. This was public worship with full participation by the people as they paid homage to God.

This praise and reading continued for the entire day until Ezra and the designated Levite leaders "gave the sense, and caused them [the people] to understand the reading" (v. 8). The people then returned home, having been comforted by the Levites.

8:13 And on the second day were gathered together the chief of the fathers of all the people, the priests, and the Levites, unto Ezra the scribe, even to understand the words of the law. 14 And they found written in the law which the LORD had commanded by Moses, that the children of Israel should dwell in booths in the feast of the seventh month.

The magnitude of the day and the tedium of the task required more than one day's reading. The reading continued on the second day. It is not clear, however, that all of the people returned. Listed in our text are the "chief" (Heb. *ro'sh*, **roshe**) of the fathers (Heb. *'ab*, **awb**), or the heads of each household. By them, all of the people were accounted for and included in this second day of instruction and worship. Also gathered were the "priests" (Heb. *kohen*,

ko-HANE), who were the officiating officers of the temple, and the Levites, who had been designated by God to oversee the service in the temple.

All of these came before Ezra, the scribe, "to understand the words of the Law." The term "understand" is from the Hebrew word *sakal* (**saw-KAL**), and means "to gather wisdom and instruction from the Law." The leaders were there to fully comprehend the words of the Pentateuch, specifically Deuteronomy or the Mosaic Law, so they could implement its rituals and commands in the life of the nation. They wanted to know how God wanted the Jews to behave and to conduct their affairs. They had been rejected and taken into captivity in a strange land. Having returned to their homeland, they never wanted to be faced with such a challenge again. Most importantly, they wanted to honor God with their obedience.

Now, having listened to the Word of God, they discovered something. They had built the temple and restored the walls, but they had not been obedient to God's direction. The Feast of Tabernacles was to be celebrated on the fifteenth day of the seventh month, which was the month they were currently observing (see Leviticus 23:34; Deuteronomy 16:13). The Feast of Tabernacles, which lasted seven days, was an observance of the deliverance of Israel from Egypt and marked the time of the harvest. During this time, the Children of Israel were to leave their houses and dwell in "booths" (Heb. *cukkah*, **sook-KAW**) or temporary shelters. By doing this, they recognized God's provision for them, the same provision He had given to Moses and the Children of Israel when they were in the wilderness and which he had provided for these families when they were taken from captivity and returned to their homeland.

The Feast of Tabernacles was to be celebrated by all of the people. In order to gather, there was a need to publish the news (see v. 15). This was to be done in two ways. First, a *shofar* or ram's horn was to be blown throughout the nation to proclaim the observance. Second, messengers were sent from household to household to ensure that everyone was made aware of the coming event and that they gathered materials for the celebration of God's provision.

8:17 And all the congregation of them that were come again out of the captivity made booths, and sat

under the booths: for since the days of Jeshua the son of Nun unto that day had not the children of Israel done so. And there was very great gladness. 18 Also day by day, from the first day unto the last day, he read in the book of the law of God. And they kept the feast seven days; and on the eighth day was a solemn assembly, according unto the manner.

The people eagerly complied with the directive to dwell in booths. There were so many people who had come out of captivity and were eager to be involved in proper worship of the Lord that those who owned homes created booths on their housetops or in the courtyards of their houses. Others placed their booths in the courtyards of the temple or in the streets before one of the gates of the city (see v. 16). The outpouring was greater than the Feast of Tabernacles had been at any time since the days of Joshua when the nation had entered the Promised Land.

They not only complied with the Law, they were excited about the Law and the opportunity to celebrate God's deliverance. Gladness permeated the entire event, which is described in verse 17 as "very" (Heb. *me'od*, **meh-ODE**) "great" (Heb. *gadowl*, **gaw-DOLE**) "gladness" (Heb. *simchah*, **sim-KHAW**). There was intense joy and gaiety. Although this was a serious and solemn matter, it was a joyous occasion. The people had been delivered from captivity and were now free to share in worship, to rebuild the celebrations of the Law and God's mercy as they recommitted themselves to their covenant relationship with Him. They rejoiced at what had been done in their lives and, no doubt, at the realization of how connected they were through the religious rituals to the ancestors of old who had been brought out of Egypt (see Leviticus 23:42–43).

The celebration of the Feast of Tabernacles continued for the required seven days. Each day Ezra read from the Book of the Law, proclaiming the goodness of God. Each day they learned more about God's Law. The more they learned, the more they rejoiced over hearing the Word of God. The more they learned, the greater was their assurance that God was able to strengthen them because He had done so time after time.

On the last day of the feast they kept a "solemn assembly" (Heb. '*atsarah*, **ats-aw-RAW**) (see also Leviticus 23:36). This Hebrew term means "to gather," as on a holy day; however, the reference is followed by a call to do no servile work (labor) and to offer a sacrifice. Obviously the solemn assembly was a Sabbath day of worship and praise. The tone for this day seems to have been different from the first seven days; yet the entire experience was part of the renewal of their covenant with God.

In today's lesson, the captives have returned home and renewed their covenant with God as a result of finding the Law and obeying it. Unlike the returning Hebrew children, our covenant with God is based on the sacrifice of Jesus Christ. By grace we are kept in covenant relationship with the Father; however, there are things that we can do to enhance our walk with God. From today's lesson, we learn that reading the Word of God with careful understanding so that we have the sense of it is the first step in the process. We see also in this lesson that obedience to God's way will bring results that glorify Him. Let us examine our covenant relationship with God, apply His Word to our lives, and purpose in our hearts to renew our commitment to give Him glory.

Daily Bible Readings

M: Take Courage
Psalm 27:11–14
T: The Festival of Booths
Leviticus 23:33–43
W: Do Not Appear Empty-Handed
Deuteronomy 16:13–17
T: Hear the Word
Nehemiah 8:1–6
F: Teach the Word
Nehemiah 8:7–12
S: Study the Word
Nehemiah 8:13–18
S: Delight in God's Law
Psalm 19:7–14

JUNE 2008
QUARTER-AT-A-GLANCE
Images of Christ

All three units in this quarter display the images of Christ as found in the letter to the Hebrews, all four Synoptic Gospels, and the letter of James.

UNIT 1 .
IMAGES OF CHRIST IN HEBREWS

The writer of Hebrews reveals Jesus Christ as superior to anything or anyone else. The recipients of this letter were putting angels, Moses, and the high priests above Jesus, so Hebrews shows us, with a healthy helping of Old Testament Scriptures, that Jesus is supreme.

Lesson 1: June 1, 2008
Jesus as God's Son
Hebrews 1:1–4, 8–12

Jesus is far superior to angels because He is the Son of God. This means that His substance is exactly the same as God the Father. He existed from the beginning and participated in Creation. The angels are magnificent beings, but they too must bow down to worship the Lord Jesus Christ.

Lesson 2: June 8, 2008
Christ as Intercessor
Hebrews 7:20–28

The Old Testament foretold that Jesus would come as a priest of a different order than the Levitical priests. The priesthood of Jesus would last forever. Not only did Jesus give Himself for our sins as the only perfect sacrifice, but He also continues interceding for us. He is continually representing us before the Father.

Lesson 3: June 15, 2008
Christ as Redeemer
Hebrews 9:11–18; 10:12–14, 17–18

Jesus boldly entered into the heavenly sanctuary for us because, unlike the imperfect Old Testament sacrifices, He had made the perfect sacrifice. He shed His own blood. Because of His sacrifice for our sins, we can have our consciences cleansed from guilt. God now sees us as holy. He no longer remembers our sins.

Lesson 4: June 22, 2008
Christ as Leader
Hebrews 12:1–13

In the previous chapter the writer of Hebrews gave examples of faith. Now the writer tells us to follow their example; even more we should follow the example of our Lord. This is a race in which we encounter suffering, which our Father allows in our lives in order to teach us. God allows these trials because He loves us and wants us to share in His holiness.

Lesson 5: June 29, 2008
The Eternal Christ
Hebrews 13:1–16

The writer of Hebrews concludes with a number of exhortations. We are urged to live lives of generosity and kindness to others, as well as lives free from sexual sin and greed. Such lives are possible because God has promised to help us and never leave us.

UNIT 2 .
IMAGES OF CHRIST IN THE GOSPELS

One passage from each Gospel is included in the lessons for the month of July, with each revealing another aspect of Jesus. Jesus is presented as Teacher in Luke, Healer in Mark, Servant in John, and Messiah in Matthew.

Lesson 6: July 6, 2008
Christ as Teacher
Luke 4:31–37; 20:1–8

People were amazed that when Jesus taught, He taught with authority; He did not need to quote rabbinical teachers as the religious teachers of His day did. People were amazed that Jesus had the power and authority to cast out demons. The religious leaders were questioning Jesus' authority, but Jesus recognized their question for what it was and threw it back to them.

Lesson 7: July 13, 2008
Christ as Healer
Mark 1:29–45

Jesus' home base was in Capernaum, where he healed Peter's mother-in-law and many with diseases and demon possession. From there Jesus traveled throughout Galilee preaching and driving out demons. As a result, Jesus became so popular as a healer that He had to stay away from populated areas. But still people sought Him out and found Him.

Lesson 8: July 20, 2008
Christ as Servant
John 13:1–8, 12–20

Jesus demonstrated by example how the disciples were to serve one another. At the Last Supper no servants were present to wash their feet, so Jesus performed the job of the lowliest servant by washing the dirty feet of His disciples. Jesus said that just as He served them, they were to serve one another. Jesus promised that we would be blessed if we would serve one another in the same fashion.

Lesson 9: July 27, 2008
Christ as Messiah
Matthew 16:13–23

Jesus challenged the disciples to think through His identity. First He asked them who the general population thought He was. Then He confronted them with who they said He was. Peter identified Jesus as the Christ, the Son of the living God. Then Jesus said, "Upon this rock I will build my church."

UNIT 3.
IMAGES OF CHRIST IN US

These lessons help us to be Christlike by obeying God's Word, by accepting all people as made in the image of God, by being careful in the words we say, by submitting ourselves to God, and by being prayerful people.

Lesson 10: August 3, 2008
Doers of the Word
James 1:17–27

God the Father gives us the new birth in which we are born into His family through His Word. Since we have been born again, we should look into God's Word and do what it says to do. God desires us to control our tempers, live lives of purity, and care for the poor and vulnerable of this world.

Lesson 11: August 10, 2008
Impartial Disciples
James 2:1–13

James tells believers not to discriminate against people because of their lower socio-economic status. The early Christians often experienced exploitation and persecution for their faith at the hands of the very rich people that they were favoring. "Love your neighbor as yourself" is the summation of how we are to treat one another and demands that we show love to the poor.

Lesson 12: August 17, 2008
Wise Speakers
James 3:1–10, 13–18

James points out that some use their tongues to praise God and curse their brothers and sisters. This should not be. There are two kinds of wisdom—earthly and heavenly. Earthly wisdom involves envy and selfish ambition. Heavenly wisdom is demonstrated by the fruit of the Spirit.

Lesson 13: August 24, 2008
People of Godly Behavior
James 4:1–12

A worldly spirit is proud, but God desires to give us a humble spirit. When we humble ourselves and come to God, He purifies our hearts. We are not to slander and judge one another. Only God is the Judge.

Lesson 14: August 31, 2008
Prayerful Community
James 5:13–18

In his closing exhortations, James urges us to pray when we're in desperate circumstances, when we're happy, when we're sick, and when we have sinned. In other words, pray in any situation.

THEMATIC ESSAY

JESUS CHRIST—THE LAMB WITHOUT BLEMISH

by Evangeline Carey

When God made His world, He said that it was "very good" (Genesis 1:31). The word "very" in Hebrew is *me'od* (**meh-OHD**), and it means "exceedingly, abundance, to a great degree, with muchness." The word "good" in Hebrew is *towv* (**tohv**) and means "excellent (of its kind), rich, valuable in estimation." Therefore, when God made His world and put Adam and Eve in the Garden of Eden, all He created was excellent, rich, and valuable in estimation. Even Adam and Eve were perfectly made in body, mind, and spirit. In fact, God made Adam and Eve in His own image and after His likeness (v. 26). They were created to be a reflection of His character: love, patience, forgiveness, kindness, and faithfulness. However, He gave them the ability to choose whether to have an intimate, personal relationship with Him.

Unfortunately, when Adam and Eve chose to sin, they opened the floodgates of evil and allowed it to come into God's perfect world. Because they disobeyed God and questioned His goodness, sin then snaked across the history of all humanity. In fact, after the spiritual fall of Adam and Eve, humanity is now born in sin and iniquity. King David said in Psalm 51:5, "Behold, I was shapen in iniquity, and in sin did my mother conceive me." Consequently, God set in motion the only way our relationship with Him could be restored—a way that we would not have to be eternally separated from a holy God.

In the Old Testament, the Israelites, God's chosen people, had to engage in animal sacrifices to atone for sin (pay the penalty for breaking God's commands or laws). The animals had to be without blemish or defect, and the animals' blood covered the sins of God's people. Even the priest had to sacrifice an animal to atone for his own sins (Leviticus 9:7; Hebrews 7:27). This old covenant was later replaced by a new one. God set in place His own plan of salvation wherein humanity could believe in God's Son, Jesus Christ, and what He did on the Cross at Calvary, and be saved (John 3:16). Animals had to be sacrificed again and again for the Israelites' sins. However, Jesus only had to shed His blood one time, for all believers.

Biblical history tells us that from Abraham and Sarah's seed, God chose for Himself an instrument that He could use to model *how to* and how *not to* walk with God. He elected a people called "the children of Israel," Jacob's—Israel's—12 sons and their descendants (Genesis 12:1–25:19). Even though the Israelites broke their covenant commitment to God time and time again, after 42 generations God used their lineage—the Abrahamic line—for the "Messiah Seed" (Jesus Christ) to come through. Jesus is 100 percent God and 100 percent man, the perfect Lamb without spot or blemish (sin). His sole purpose for coming to Earth was to save believers from their sins—to restore our intimate relationship with a holy God by dying on the Cross.

Jesus' birth, death, and resurrection also set in place a new covenant, the covenant of grace. Under this new covenant, God promised Israel and all believers, even Gentiles, that He would put His law in our inward parts and write it in our hearts; and He would be our God and we would be His people (Jeremiah 31:33). This covenant is fulfilled through Jesus Christ. "With his own blood—not the blood of goats and calves—he entered the Most Holy Place once for all time and secured our redemption forever" (Hebrews 9:12, NLT).

Jesus is indeed the Saviour for all those who believe on Him. As we cover the lessons in this quarter, we will find that not only is He our Lord and Saviour, but He is many other things to those who believe on His name. Jesus is:

- our eternal Christ—"Jesus Christ the same yesterday, and to day, and for ever" (Hebrews 13:8).
- our example of a Servant—"For I have given you an example, that ye should do as I have done to you" (John 13:15).
- our Healer—"And he healed many that were sick of divers diseases, and cast out many devils; and suffered not the devils to speak, because they knew him" (Mark 1:34).
- our High Priest—"For such an high priest became us, who is holy, harmless, undefiled, separate from sinners, and made higher than the heavens; Who needeth not daily, as those high priests, to offer up sacrifice, first for his own sins, and then for the people's: for this he did once, when he offered up himself" (Hebrews 7:26–27).
- our Intercessor—"Wherefore he is able also to save them to the uttermost that come unto God by him, seeing he ever liveth to make intercession for them" (Hebrews 7:25).
- our Leader—"Looking unto Jesus the author and finisher of our faith; who for the joy that was set before him endured the cross, despising the shame, and is set down at the right hand of the throne of God" (Hebrews 12:2).
- our Messiah—"And Simon Peter answered and said, Thou art the Christ, the Son of the living God" (Matthew 16:16).
- our Redeemer—"Neither by the blood of goats and calves, but by his own blood he entered in once into the holy place, having obtained eternal redemption for us" (Hebrews 9:12).
- our Teacher—"And they were astonished at his doctrine: for his word was with power" (Luke 4:32).

In the Old Testament, the Israelites looked forward to Jesus' first coming as Saviour. In the four Gospels, He came, suffered, bled, died, and rose again. In Acts 2, Jesus ascended to heaven and sent His Holy Spirit so that His church could have the power she needs to carry out the "Great Commission"—to go and make disciples of others so that they too can experience God's great salvation. Finally in the book of Revelation, Jesus is coming back again. He is coming not as Saviour, but as Judge.

Clearly, Jesus was and is the perfect sacrifice for the sins of all humanity, and He has won the victory over sin, Satan, and death. Therefore, because of who Jesus is and who we are to Him, we can "lay aside every weight, and the sin which doth so easily beset us, and . . . run with patience the race that is set before us, Looking unto Jesus the author and finisher of our faith" (Hebrews 12:1–2).

Because Jesus is the Lamb without blemish, who paid our sin penalty in full, you and I can have hope, we can have peace, and, as we await His Second Coming, we can live like Jesus. We can be people who display godly behavior, who are doers of the Word, who are sold-out disciples, who are rich in faith, who are wise speakers, and who are always prayerful.

Sources:

Strong, J. *The Exhaustive Concordance of the Bible* (electronic ed.). Ontario, Canada: Woodside Bible Fellowship, 1996.

The Life Application Study Bible, New Living Translation. Wheaton, Ill.: Tyndale House Publishers, 1996.

Evangeline Carey is a staff writer for UMI and has been an adult Sunday School teacher for more than 25 years.

MOTIVATING CHRISTLIKE BEHAVIOR

by Kathy Steward

Image is everything—so a once popular advertising slogan used to tell us. We were encouraged through this advertisement to emulate the people we saw on television, to imitate them and mold our lives similar to theirs. We do need to be modeling our lives after someone who is worthy of imitating. We can't, however, look to the television or pop culture for that person. The only One whose image we should model our lives after is Christ Jesus.

When we explore the images of Christ this quarter, as illustrated in the Gospels and in the books of Hebrews and James, we will see Jesus as Teacher, Healer, Leader, Intercessor, and the only way to salvation. But we will also see Jesus as servant. We will see a humble Jesus serving His disciples—showing by example how to live out the Word. We take from these lessons the knowledge of who Jesus is and what it means to live out the Word.

We may already know a lot about Jesus' life and His instructions to us. Do we act on what we know? Do we integrate our biblical knowledge into our day-to-day lives? Do we recall the familiar biblical commands—love one another, be kind to one another, seek first the kingdom of God—and live them out each day? Do we encourage our students to do the same? As Christian educators, how can we motivate students into transforming what they learn into what they do?

Motivation is "something that energizes, directs, and sustains behavior; it gets students moving, points them in a particular direction, and keeps them going." Students are not all motivated by the same things. Some students are motivated by extrinsic factors, such as earning high grades, being rewarded with special privileges, or receiving the praise of others. Even in some Sunday School and Bible study classes, students memorize a Scripture or answer questions because they are rewarded with a tangible gift or teacher approval.

External motivators have their place and can be effective if used cautiously, especially when working with younger students. The problem with external motivators, however, is that once they are taken away, oftentimes the desired behavior leaves as well. Christians' motivation to live out the Word should be intrinsic—it should come from within, from the heart. It should be rooted in faith and love (John 14:15). It should come from the fact that we are born again—new creations in Christ (2 Corinthians 5:17) with a heart and mind to serve Him. He should be our focus each day.

We must realize that the students we encounter have varying levels of spiritual maturity and faith and various reasons for being in class. Although the motivation to be Christlike should be intrinsic and heartfelt, it may not initially be in some cases. Educational psychologists have suggested, however, that students can come to adopt the values and priorities of those around them as their own—internalized motivation—and that several educational strategies can affect a student's level of motivation. So, Christian educators can do certain things in a learning environment to foster intrinsic motivation in their students and encourage them to live as the Bible instructs.

Encourage students to relate lessons to their personal lives. People tend to value things more and act more quickly and genuinely when they are personally vested in something or can relate it to their own lives. As you discuss a biblical topic, encourage the students to stop and examine how the topic directly affects them. For example, James 2:1–13 instructs Christians to be impartial in our treatment of others. Allow students to think about times when they may have been mistreated or have experienced someone receiving preferential treatment over them. How did they feel? How would they have liked to have been treated instead? Would they want to make someone else feel that way? Now ask them, What can they do to ensure that they treat people impartially? You may suggest that students keep an application journal that helps them relate lessons to their own lives.

Challenge students to set goals. Goals drive what people do, state an intention, and direct activities. Goals must be personally meaningful to a student. Students are more likely to meet a goal when they help to set it, and when they believe the goal is reasonable, achievable, and can be broken down into manageable tasks.

When it comes to integrating our biblical knowledge into our day-to-day lives, James has stated the long-term goal for us: "Be ye doers of the word" (James 1:22). In order to live lives that reflect images of Christ in us, we must do what the Bible instructs us to do. This is not an unreasonable goal, nor is it an unachievable goal. In fact, quite the opposite is true. We can become doers of the Word by yielding to God's will and authority, by resisting Satan, and by humbling ourselves (James 4:7, 10). We can allow the power of God to transform us (Romans 8:5).

While James has provided the long-term goal, your students can self-direct how they can achieve the goal. They can decide how to break the goal into smaller tasks: to love their neighbor as themselves (James 2:8); to be thoughtful and discipline their speech (James 3:5–12); to recognize that fighting, greed, and other sins come from a lack of submission to God, and thus, they need to submit to Him (James 4:1–12); to meditate on God's Word through daily Bible study; and to pray (James 5:16).

Model a Christlike way of living. Social learning theorists believe that people can learn from one another by observing each other and through techniques such as imitation and modeling. A popular example of modeling is a child watching a parent read a book. If over time children observe parents, say, turning off a television and enjoying silent reading, they will imitate what they see and learn reading as an appropriate behavior.

Actually, this concept is not new—it's biblical. When it comes to modeling a Christlike way of living, we should point students toward Jesus—the perfect example. But, we, too, are to live our Christian lives, as instructed in 1 Peter 5:3, as examples to others. We have to let students see Christ in our actions and conduct, and hear Him in our speech, so we can urge them to imitate us, as Paul did (2 Thessalonians 3:9). It's quite easy to study the Bible and tell others what they are supposed to do, but quite another matter—and more effective—to teach by example.

Encourage your students to find their strength in Christ. Lack of motivation is sometimes caused by low self-efficacy. Self-efficacy is people's belief that they have the ability to successfully do something. When people have low self-efficacy, they don't believe that they can accomplish a task and will do things such as give up, not make any genuine attempts to perform the task, or refuse to do the task. When it comes to living out the Word, people dismiss their lack of effort or motivation to try by saying, "I'm not perfect; I'll never be perfect." Counter this with two important points: First, God knows that we are not perfect, and second, help is available. God's Word and the Holy Spirit can lead and guide us.

Bible study is ineffective if the knowledge gained is not put into action. To truly believe what the Bible teaches is to live out what it says. Like the apostle Paul, like James, Christian educators must be diligent in motivating others to action.

Source:

Ormrod, Jeanne Ellis. *Educational Psychology: Developing Learners.* Upper Saddle, N.J.: Pearson Education, 2006.

Kathy Steward *is the editor of UMI's Juniorway® and holds a master of science degree in psychology.*

POINT OF VIEW ESSAY

A DIVERSE CHRIST

by Darcy Ingraham

Every life, though born a single soul, has many faces. A newborn baby is someone's daughter or son and someone's grandchild. He or she may be a brother or sister, a niece or nephew, or even an aunt or uncle. Throughout life we will all play different and ever changing roles, much like characters in a play: friend, student, teacher, coworker, employee, employer, spouse, parent, and more.

Christ also had many roles to fulfill during His life on Earth. The different stages of Christ's life and ministry didn't happen by chance. His entire life was according to God's perfect plan. Beginning at conception, every event in Christ's life happened in divine order so that God's purposes would be fulfilled. Indeed, the conception of Jesus within the womb of a young virgin was nothing short of miraculous.

It certainly sparked curiosity in the people. God had the world's attention, and He intended to keep it.

The supernatural appearances surrounding the conception of Jesus and His birth, including the appearance of the angel to the shepherds, provided evidence that this was of God. "And the angel said unto them, Fear not: for, behold, I bring you good tidings of great joy, which shall be to all people. For unto you is born this day in the city of David a Saviour, which is Christ the Lord" (Luke 2:10–11). Yet the humble birth of Jesus provided a human element that allowed ordinary people to connect with the divine. "And she brought forth her firstborn son, and wrapped him in swaddling clothes, and laid him in a manger; because there was no room for them in the inn" (Luke 2:7).

Little is written about Jesus' childhood, but much is written about His adult life. The poignant account of Jesus' baptism clearly introduces us to three distinct persons who are all God: God the Father, Jesus the Son of God, and God the Holy Spirit, together making up the Trinity. "And Jesus, when he was baptized, went up straightway out of the water: and, lo, the heavens were opened unto

him, and he saw the Spirit of God descending like a dove, and lighting upon him: And lo a voice from heaven, saying, This is my beloved Son, in whom I am well pleased" (Matthew 3:16–17). In order to know one, we must know them all.

The conception of Christ would not have happened without the Holy Spirit. "And the angel answered and said unto her, The Holy Ghost shall come upon thee, and the power of the Highest shall overshadow thee: therefore also that holy thing which shall be born of thee shall be called the Son of God" (Luke 1:35).

The gift of salvation and the promise of eternal life could not be offered to us were it not for the martyrdom of Christ as sanctioned by God the Father. "Jesus saith unto him, I am the way, the truth, and the life: no man cometh unto the Father, but by me" (John 14:6). Three images of Christ. Each one with a specific purpose. The Gospels portray Christ as a teacher, a healer, and a servant, earthly roles that He would successfully fulfill even if He took some unorthodox methods. According to Martin Luther King Jr., "The question is not whether we will be extremists, but what kind of extremists we will be."

Perhaps this is why controversy seemed to follow Jesus wherever He went. The Son of God was on a mission, and He did whatever was necessary to succeed. Jesus was a great teacher who knew how to touch the hearts of the people. He certainly wasn't afraid to stir things up. He got in there among the people. He fraternized with the lowlifes of His day despite the whispers, and He didn't care if His run-in with the money changers in the temple raised a few eyebrows.

Yet He interacted compassionately with those who would hear Him. Healing the sick and broken bodies of people was an important part of Jesus' ministry. It was a demonstration of His great love and the strength of faith, as well as divine power.

Healing bodies was also a testament of Jesus' ability to heal lost and broken souls. Let's look at just one place in Scripture where the connection is explicit: "And when they could not come nigh unto him for the press, they uncovered the roof where he was: and when they had broken it up, they let down the bed wherein the sick of the palsy lay. When Jesus saw their faith, he said unto the sick of the palsy, Son, thy sins be forgiven thee. But there were certain of the scribes sitting there, and reasoning in their hearts, Why doth this man thus speak blasphemies? who can forgive sins but God only?" (Mark 2:4–7).

What was Jesus' response to the doubts of the scribes? "Whether is it easier to say to the sick of the palsy, Thy sins be forgiven thee; or to say, Arise, and take up thy bed, and walk? But that ye may know that the Son of man hath power on earth to forgive sins, (he saith to the sick of the palsy,) I say unto thee, Arise, and take up thy bed, and go thy way into thine house. And immediately he arose, took up the bed, and went forth before them all; insomuch that they were all amazed, and glorified God, saying, We never saw it on this fashion" (Mark 2:9–12).

Jesus' role as a servant is profound. It places Him on a very human level to which everyone can relate. Perhaps you've heard the phrase, "Everyone serves someone." Jesus knew this to be true as well. He demonstrates the essence of servanthood to His disciples in one of the most beautiful and moving stories in the New Testament. In John 13, after washing His disciples' feet, Jesus said, "Ye call me Master and Lord: and ye say well; for so I am. If I then, your Lord and Master, have washed your feet; ye also ought to wash one another's feet. For I have given you an example, that ye should do as I have done to you. Verily, verily, I say unto you, The servant is not greater than his lord; neither he that is sent greater than he that sent him. If ye know these things, happy are ye if ye do them" (John 13:13–17).

Christ lived what He taught, and He expects us also to live those same truths and not just talk about them. The images of Christ as a doer of the Word, a person of perfect behavior and prayerfulness, are found throughout the New Testament. Just as Jesus reached people through example, that is also how we lead others to Christ. How can we invite others to church and expect them to come if we don't attend ourselves? How can we endorse the blessings of godly living if we don't lead godly lives? And how can we encourage others to pray and demonstrate to them that prayer really does work, if we have nothing to show for it ourselves? Obviously, we can't.

James 1:22–25 says, "But be ye doers of the word, and not hearers only, deceiving your own selves. For if any be a hearer of the word, and not a doer, he is like unto a man beholding his natural face in a glass: For he beholdeth himself, and goeth his way, and straightway forgetteth what manner of man he was. But whoso looketh into the perfect law of liberty, and continueth therein, he being not a forgetful hearer, but a doer of the work, this man shall be blessed in his deed."

Indeed, it matters not where we came from, but how we get to where we're going. Living a godly life, in the image of Christ's character, should be our legacy.

We should recognize the biblical images of Christ, honor them, and most important, emulate them. Then ask yourself, "Can others see the image of Christ in me?" If your answer is yes, then you can surely rejoice in where you're going.

Darcy Ingraham *is a freelance writer who lives in upstate New York. She resides with her husband of 23 years and four sons. She is a fill-in pianist and teaches Junior Church.*

REVEREND ALEXIS FELDER: DOING GOD'S WORK IN AFRICA

Reverend Alexis Felder had never been out of the U.S. before, but in 2005, she and her husband, Reverend Dr. Trunell Felder, took 40 members of their church to Ghana, West Africa, on a missions trip to an area where their church supports full-time national missionaries. Reverend Alexis says, "I felt like I was home, like this was what I was created to do."

Reverend Alexis continues to be active in a number of missions in this country—to the homeless, those in the criminal justice system, people in hospice centers, and residents of low-income housing. And she heads up programs to communities in poverty just 25 miles east of their comfortable church, New Faith Baptist Church, in the Chicago suburb of Matteson, Illinois.

Since this church has many medical personnel, they decided to do medical projects in Ghana. During six days of clinics they treated 1,200 to 1,800 people, offered needed surgeries, and provided whatever medications were needed, including heart medications. Their focus was on treating malaria, TB, typhoid, and ringworm, and providing immunizations.

The missions work of Reverend Alexis and the missionaries from her church is based on relationships with the people of Ghana. The missionaries listen to local Ghanaians as to what the needs are, and their full-time staff members in Ghana are all nationals. They support all the schools in two villages, preschool through high school. And they are building 20 wells, two to a village, this year alone.

The missionaries keep in mind the spiritual needs of the people. As they meet the physical needs of people, many Muslims are coming to faith in Jesus Christ. So the missionaries have also built churches in five villages, and they support the churches' pastors and provide for their theological training. The church devotes 10 percent of its annual budget to missions, local and global.

Reverend Alexis says that Africans want to see their African American sisters and brothers. They say, "Welcome home!"

"Then shall he answer them, saying, Verily I say unto you, Inasmuch as ye did it not to one of the least of these, ye did it not to me" (Matthew 25:45).

TEACHING TIPS

June 1
Bible Study Guide 1

1. Words You Should Know

A. Divers (diverse) (Hebrews 1:1) *polutropos* (Gk.)—In many ways, various.

B. Brightness (v. 3) *apaugasma* (Gk.)—A shining forth of light from a luminous body, not to be confused with a reflection of light.

C. Sceptre (v. 8) *rhabdos* (Gk.)—A royal staff used as a symbol of power and authority. The use of the sceptre originated from the idea that the ruler was a shepherd of his people.

D. Vesture (v. 12) *peribolaion* (Gk.)—Something that covers or cloaks. Also used to refer to a piece of clothing or garment that is thrown around as a covering, such as a mantle or veil.

2. Teacher Preparation

Unifying Principle—Finding Deeper Meaning in Life People search for authoritative and credible voices to answer life's questions. Who can speak to us about the deeper meanings of life? God spoke to us through His beloved Son, Jesus Christ.

A. This week begins the unit called "Images of Christ in Hebrews." Begin your personal study by reviewing the background materials on the *Precepts For Living*® CD-ROM.

B. Next, read Hebrews 1–5. After completing the Scripture reading, get an overview of Unit 1 by reading the Thematic Essay.

C. Finally, read Bible Study Guide 1 and complete the corresponding lesson from the *Precepts For Living*® *Personal Study Guide* to round out your lesson preparation.

3. Starting the Lesson

A. Begin the lesson with prayer according to the AIM for Change.

B. Before getting into this week's lesson, take some time to review the highlights from the last lesson.

C. Ask for volunteers to share their experiences from last week's Make It Happen suggestion.

4. Getting into the Lesson

A. Have the students silently read the Thematic Essay. Then explain the unit theme using the descriptions from the Quarter-At-A-Glance.

B. To focus attention on today's lesson, ask a volunteer to read the In Focus story aloud.

C. Ask the students why they think it is important for Jesus to be superior to anyone or anything in all creation; and how knowing Christ provides deeper meaning to their lives.

5. Relating the Lesson to Life

A. Explain the information from Background and The People, Places, and Times. Ask volunteers to read the Focal Verses according to the At-A-Glance outline. Briefly give an overview of the important points found in the In Depth section.

B. Solicit individual students to answer the Search the Scriptures questions.

6. Arousing Action

A. To help the students relate the lesson to modern-day situations, discuss the Lesson in Our Society and Discuss the Meaning questions.

B. Review the Make It Happen suggestion and challenge the students to put it into practice.

C. Assign next week's reading and encourage the students to use the passages in the Daily Bible Readings as a part of their daily devotions.

Worship Guide

For the Superintendent or Teacher
Theme: Jesus as God's Son
Theme Song: "Jesus, Name Above All Names"
Devotional Reading: Proverbs 8:22–31
Prayer

JESUS AS GOD'S SON

Bible Background • HEBREWS 1
Printed Text • HEBREWS 1:1–4, 8–12 Devotional Reading • PROVERBS 8:22–31

AIM for Change

By the end of the lesson, we will:

EXPLORE the truth of Christ's deity;

REJOICE in the truth that Jesus Christ is the Son of God and worthy of our worship;

DISCOVER life's deeper meaning by drawing closer to Christ through prayer, worship, and reading God's Word.

Keep in Mind

"Who being the brightness of his glory, and the express image of his person, and upholding all things by the word of his power, when he had by himself purged our sins, sat down on the right hand of the Majesty on high" (Hebrews 1:3).

Focal Verses

KJV **Hebrews 1:1** God, who at sundry times and in divers manners spake in time past unto the fathers by the prophets,

2 Hath in these last days spoken unto us by his Son, whom he hath appointed heir of all things, by whom also he made the worlds;

3 Who being the brightness of his glory, and the express image of his person, and upholding all things by the word of his power, when he had by himself purged our sins, sat down on the right hand of the Majesty on high;

4 Being made so much better than the angels, as he hath by inheritance obtained a more excellent name than they.

1:8 But unto the Son he saith, Thy throne, O God, is for ever and ever: a sceptre of righteousness is the sceptre of thy kingdom.

9 Thou hast loved righteousness, and hated iniquity; therefore God, even thy God, hath anointed thee with the oil of gladness above thy fellows.

10 And, Thou, Lord, in the beginning hast laid the foundation of the earth; and the heavens are the works of thine hands:

11 They shall perish; but thou remainest; and they all shall wax old as doth a garment;

12 And as a vesture shalt thou fold them up, and they shall be changed: but thou art the same, and thy years shall not fail.

NLT **Hebrews 1:1** Long ago God spoke many times and in many ways to our ancestors through the prophets.

2 And now in these final days, he has spoken to us through his Son. God promised everything to the Son as an inheritance, and through the Son he created the universe.

3 The Son radiates God's own glory and expresses the very character of God, and he sustains everything by the mighty power of his command. When he had cleansed us from our sins, he sat down in the place of honor at the right hand of the majestic God in heaven.

4 This shows that the Son is far greater than the angels, just as the name God gave him is greater than their names.

1:8 But to the Son he says, "Your throne, O God, endures forever and ever. You rule with a scepter of justice.

9 You love justice and hate evil. Therefore, O God, your God has anointed you, pouring out the oil of joy on you more than on anyone else."

10 He also says to the Son, "In the beginning, Lord, you laid the foundation of the earth and made the heavens with your hands.

11 They will perish, but you remain forever. They will wear out like old clothing.

12 You will fold them up like a cloak and discard them like old clothing. But you are always the same: you will live forever."

In Focus

Many people desire to have a life full of power, fortune, and fame, but they are unsure how to make the connection between living a better life and making sure that life has meaning and purpose. The things most of us worry about, including our careers, paying the bills, rearing children, and relationship issues, are all important, but they pale in comparison to knowing life's deeper meaning.

People often seek out persons of authority who can help them in understanding life's meaning, but the Bible tells us that a meaningful, fulfilling, and abundant life must be centered in Jesus Christ. Not only does a relationship with Christ give our lives meaning, but developing a powerful image of Christ will bring hope to many who have little or no power in their lives. Every day we allow ourselves to be caught up in the daily concerns of life, never realizing that we have greater spiritual needs than physical ones. However, believing that Jesus Christ is God's Son and superior to all makes us more likely to trust in the powers and promises found in God's Word.

In today's lesson, the writer of Hebrews made it very clear that Jesus Christ is God's Son and the ultimate authority. He is greater than any of the Old Testament prophets and the angels. Only through Christ can one find peace and the real meaning of life.

The People, Places, and Times

Angels. Spiritual creatures who witnessed the creation of the physical universe even though they did not participate in it (Job 38:7). Except for those who followed Satan in his heavenly rebellion, angels possess unquestioned integrity and goodwill and are perfectly obedient to God.

Angels serve many functions, but Hebrews 1:14 defines their primary functions as messengers and ministers of God to humanity. They bring God's specific commands (1 Kings 19:5–6; Matthew 1:20–21). They assist people in times of distress (1 Kings 19:5–7) and sometimes even carry out military missions (Daniel 10:13, 21; 12:1). The book of Daniel records the first references to angels by proper names (Daniel 8:16; 10:13, 21). Psalm 91 brought out the possibility of angels who act as personal guardians (v. 11). Jesus indicated the existence of personal guardian angels (Matthew 18:10). The New Testament closely associates angels with the giving of the law (Acts 7:53;

Hebrews 2:2) and final judgment (Matthew 16:27; Mark 8:38).

Background

Jesus prophesied that believers would suffer great persecution for His sake (Matthew 10:17–20), and after His death that prophecy was coming true. Jewish believers were not only being hounded by Roman authorities, but their own people had turned against them.

Judaism was a legal religion in the Roman Empire, and in Christianity's beginning, Roman authorities considered it a Jewish sect and paid little attention to it. In Antioch all that began to change. A large number of Gentile believers heard the Gospel and converted. People in the city began referring to believers as Christians for the first time (Acts 11:20–26).

Jews began ostracizing Christian believers. Jewish Christians were forbidden to participate in temple worship, and many were driven from their homes and families. They were brought before Jewish councils, imprisoned and beaten, and some were even killed. At the same time, because of the Christians' refusal to offer worship to Caesar, the Romans began their persecution of the infant religion. Things were bad, and many Jewish believers began to reconsider the wisdom of their conversions.

The original readers of the Letter to the Hebrews faced a dilemma. As Jews, they had been taught and had practiced Judaism all their lives. When the apostles and other Christian believers presented the Good News of salvation to them, many had turned to Christ as Lord and Saviour. However, some were beginning to wonder how an unknown son of a carpenter from the obscure village of Nazareth could be greater than their forefathers and prophets like Moses. These harried believers needed to be reminded of the essential truth of their new faith. The writer of Hebrews demonstrated that Jesus Christ was superior in His nature, His name, and His position over creation, including the greatest heroes of faith and the angels.

At-A-Glance

1. Christ's Superior Nature (Hebrews 1:1–4)
2. Christ's Superior Name (vv. 8–9)
3. Christ's Superior Position (vv. 10–12)

In Depth

1. Christ's Superior Nature (Hebrews 1:1–4)

The first two verses establish the theme for the entire book: the superiority of Christ. The writer begins this message to the Hebrews by stating that God has revealed Himself to humanity through two different eras, past and present.

The phrase "in time past" (v. 1) refers to the Old Testament period that began when Moses received the Law and continued until the cessation of prophecy in the days of Malachi. In those times, God used prophets as His means of communicating His truths to His people. God spoke to the prophets at different times and in various ways. In other words, God gradually revealed His mind and His will to them. He added one revelation after another as their understanding of Him increased. In addition to the messages from the prophets, God used various means to reveal Himself to His people, such as angels, dreams, and visions.

"But in these last days he has spoken to us by his Son" (v. 2, NIV). The phrase "last days" refers to the Church Age, which extends from the initial advent of Christ to His Second Coming. Jesus is the final and complete revelation of God. Christ's superior revelation is based on several facts:

A. He was appointed heir of all things. Two meanings are implied by the word "heir": lordship and possession. Christ's death and resurrection reclaimed the dominion over the earth that Adam surrendered to Satan in Eden. When Christ returns, He will exercise authority over heaven and earth. This has been God's plan from the very beginning: "That in the dispensation of the fulness of times he might gather together in one all things in Christ, both which are in heaven, and which are on earth; even in him" (Ephesians 1:10).

B. Christ made the worlds. In this passage, "worlds" refers to God's total creation, which encompasses the entire universe. Christ was not an instrument or an inferior in the creation process. God spoke the universe into existence, and Christ is God's own eternal Word, Wisdom, and Power.

C. Christ is the brightness of God's glory and the express image of God's person (v. 3). These expressions are strong affirmations of Christ's deity. Christ is the light of God's glory: In the Old Testament, *glory* expressed the grandeur of divine manifestation and confirmed God's presence. Christ does not reflect God's glory; He is the actual outshining of it. The apostle John phrased it this way: "And the Word was made flesh, and dwelt among us, (and we beheld his glory, the glory as of the only begotten of the Father,) full of grace and truth" (John 1:14).

D. Christ "sat down" on the right hand of the majesty (v. 3). The fact that He is seated indicates a contrast between the priesthood of Christ and the Aaronic priesthood. Once a year, on the Day of Atonement, the high priest entered the Holy of Holies and stood in holy reverence ministering to the Lord for the sins of the people. After he had completed his sacrificial offering, he departed. Christ, on the other hand, after His one offering entered into heaven itself. He entered the presence of God, not to minister in humility but to share the throne and participate in the divine glory and majesty.

At least one cult teaches that Jesus is an archangel, but Scripture clearly denounces such teaching. Because of His divinity, the pre-incarnate Christ was always infinitely more excellent than the angels. When He voluntarily took a human body and a human nature, He became a human being without ever ceasing to be God. When the man Jesus of Nazareth proved faithful even unto death, the Father exalted Him to the highest place of honor (His right hand) and gave Him a name that is above all names, including those of the angels.

2. Christ's Superior Name (vv. 8–9)

What is the name that is so superior? The name is Son of God. Just as Jesus is the superior revelation because of His superior nature, He is superior to angels because of His superior name. Although angels are collectively called "sons of God" (Job 1:6), only Christ bears the title "Son of God." When the angel Gabriel originally announced the coming of Christ, he told Mary: "He will be great and will be called the Son of the Most High" (Luke 1:32, NIV). Later in the same revelation, the angel explained, "The Holy Spirit will come upon you, and the power of the Most High will overshadow you. So the holy one to be born will be called the Son of God" (v. 35, NIV).

From all eternity, Christ had been God's Son. In the Incarnation, the Son humbled Himself, became a man, and offered Himself on the Cross. For this reason "God also hath highly exalted him, and given him a name which is above every name" (Philippians 2:9).

In Hebrews 1:8, God refers to Jesus as God; in verse 9, still talking to Jesus, God refers to Himself as "your God" (NIV). This distinction is consistent with the Trinitarian teaching of God the Father, God the Son, and God the Holy Spirit. God's command that the angels worship Christ is further proof of His deity. In His wilderness test, Jesus quoted Deuteronomy 6:13 to Satan: "Thou shalt worship the Lord thy God, and him only shalt thou serve" (Luke 4:8). Scripture never affords worship to angels; only God is to be worshiped. However, speaking of Jesus, Scripture declares, "Worthy is the Lamb that was slain to receive power, and riches, and wisdom, and strength, and honour, and glory, and blessing" (Revelation 5:12).

Christ's love of righteousness is best shown by His joy in doing God's will (Hebrews 10:7), but He hates wickedness as much as He loves righteousness. Because of this, God has set Him above all created beings and anointed Him with the oil of gladness. This anointing refers to the glory and authority that God restored to Christ after His resurrection (see John 17:5).

3. Christ's Superior Position (vv. 10–12)

Jesus occupies the eternal throne of heaven. He is the superior revelation of God and holds a superior position over creation. From the beginning He formed both the heavens and the earth. In Colossians, Paul describes Jesus as "the image of the invisible God" and the Creator of all things (1:15–17). In his epistle, John emphatically declares, "All things were made by him; and without him was not any thing made that was made" (1:3).

To support his argument for the eternal existence and the power of Christ, the writer of Hebrews echoes the Old Testament imagery of Psalm 102: "Of old hast thou laid the foundation of the earth: and the heavens are the work of thy hands. They shall perish, but thou shalt endure: yea, all of them shall wax old like a garment; as a vesture shalt thou change them, and they shall be changed: But thou art the same, and thy years shall have no end" (vv. 25–27). Jesus not only created the world, He will change it. At the end of time as we know it, Christ will fold up this worn-out world like we fold our clothes. However,

even after the world passes away, He remains the unchangeable, eternal, sovereign Lord.

The writer has clearly detailed Jesus' superiority to all created beings. Because of His superiority, the Hebrew Christians who received this letter were to understand that Christianity is superior to all other religions. All other religions are defective. "Salvation is found in no one else, for there is no other name under heaven given to men by which we must be saved" (Acts 4:12, NIV).

Search the Scriptures

1. In Old Testament times, who did God use to speak to the people (Hebrews 1:1)?

2. After completing His sacrifice on Calvary for the forgiveness of our sin, where did Jesus go (v. 3)?

3. What are two reasons that Jesus is superior to angels (v. 4)?

4. In view of the person and work of Jesus, how should believers react to His message?

Discuss the Meaning

1. Because Christianity claims that Jesus is the only way to God, Christians are often accused of being narrow-minded and haughty. How would you answer this accusation?

2. What is the significance of Christ's superiority for your life? How does it apply to any personal situation you may be facing today?

Lesson in Our Society

Throughout history, people have looked to leaders, governmental systems, or science to overcome society's difficulties. Every human element that we have trusted has failed, yet people continue to look to human ingenuity to relieve the problems of the human condition.

Christians believe that Christ is the answer to what ails our world. If this is true, why haven't more people put their faith in Him? What can individual believers do to convince people to trust Christ?

Make It Happen

God's call to salvation is not just a call out of sin; it is a call into service. God has gifted believers with abilities to build up His church. Our responsibility is to perfect or develop our gifts to their highest level.

Take some time this week to explore some ways that you can perfect your gift.

Follow the Spirit

What God wants me to do:

_____

_____

Remember Your Thoughts

Special insights I have learned:

_____

_____

More Light on the Text

Hebrews 1:1–4, 8–12

These passages of Scripture underscore the uniqueness and superiority of Jesus and the finality of God's revelation in Him.

1 God, who at sundry times and in divers manners spake in time past unto the fathers by the prophets, 2 Hath in these days spoken unto us by his Son, whom he hath appointed heir of all things, by whom also he made the worlds;

The first four verses of the book of Hebrews are only a single sentence in the Greek text. Unlike modern translations that have three or four sentences, the King James Version (KJV) retains the sense of the original Greek text in one rich and complete sentence.

In this epistle, the writer begins with God. God is the initiator of revelation; therefore, the focus is upon Him and not upon man. The first and second verses compare the methods of communication God used in the past and uses in the present. The phrase "at sundry times and in divers manners spake" refers to the fact that God chose the times and the methods to communicate. The Old Testament records the angelic visitations, dreams, visions, etc., that God used to communicate with His people. God also used the prophets to reveal what He was saying. The reference to "prophets" here is not limited to the traditional prophets but includes men of God like Moses, David, and Solomon, to mention a few.

The phrase "in these last days" refers to both the present and end times. We see a clear sense that God has reached the climax of His self-revelation. He has saved the best for last. There is a definite intention to show that this last revelation of God is superior to what He has done in the past. The fact that God has already "spoken unto us by his Son" suggests that Jesus was the ultimate revelation and the climax of history.

Even though most English translations say "his son" or "the Son," the Greek has no definite article. It simply says "a Son." The writer assumes that the readers know whom he is talking about. The use of the indefinite article "a" makes this statement stronger. Instead of identifying whom God spoke through, it emphasizes the nature of the one whom God spoke through. Unlike the prophets, the Son is more than a messenger. His divine nature makes Him the right and only capable bearer of God's complete revelation. The book of Hebrews explains this truth and the identity and superiority of the revelation of God though Jesus Christ.

The phrase "appointed heir of all things, by whom also he made the worlds" indicates that Christ embodies a dual motif of sonship and priesthood. When speaking of Jesus as God's heir, Psalm 2:7–8 says, "Thou art my Son; this day have I begotten thee. Ask of me, and I shall give thee the heathen for thine inheritance, and the uttermost parts of the earth for thy possession." Everything God has belongs to Jesus. The Bible also reveals that Jesus is co-creator with God (Colossians 1:16–17).

The word translated as "worlds" or "universe" (Hebrews 1:2, NIV) is *aion* (**eye-OHN**) in Greek. It literally means ages or times. The preferred interpretation is "ages," which suggests that Jesus not only created the world but also controls the events of history.

3 Who being the brightness of his glory, and the express image of his person, and upholding all things by the word of his power, when he had by himself purged our sins, sat down on the right hand of the Majesty on high;

In verse 3, we get a complete Christology. The first part of the verse talks about the Son's relationship with God, the second part deals with the work of Christ, and the third part refers to His exaltation: the pre-existence, incarnation, and exaltation of Christ. The phrase "brightness of his glory" could mean that Jesus is either the reflection or the radiance of the glory of God. The Bible tells us that God is inapproachable, but that Jesus makes it possible to know Him truly and intimately. What a blessing! The "express image of his person" literally means "the imprint or seal of God's nature," and the word translated as "person" literally means "the reality or actuality of His being." Thus, Jesus fully represents God (cf. Colossians 2:9). The exaltation of Christ is an allusion to Psalm 110; "the Majesty" is a term for God.

4 Being made so much better than the angels, as he hath by inheritance obtained a more excellent name than they.

The phrase "better than" or "superior to" is used 13 times in the Christology presented in the book of Hebrews. Verse 4 introduces the major subjects of the discussion that is to follow, Christ and the angels. To counter the worship of angels, the writer shows the real position of the angels in relation to Christ.

1:8 But unto the Son he saith, Thy throne, O God, is for ever and ever: a sceptre of righteousness is the sceptre of thy kingdom. 9 Thou hast loved righteousness, and hated iniquity; therefore God, even thy God, hath anointed thee with the oil of gladness above thy fellows.

These verses are a direct quotation of Psalm 45:6–7. Psalm 45 is a marriage psalm calling a princess of Tyre (vv. 12–14) to heed the king's call and "forget also thine own people, and thy father's house" (v. 10) in order to enter the king's palace, where there is great joy. This king loves righteousness and hates sin. This psalm has many Messianic applications. Hebrews 1:8–9 refers to the Son as God and says that His throne is exalted forever. Christ is superior to the angels—"anointed with the oil of gladness above thy fellows." The Son of God is above all prophets, priests, and kings that have served God on earth.

10 And, Thou, Lord, in the beginning hast laid the foundation of the earth; and the heavens are the works of thine hands: 11 They shall perish; but thou remainest; and they all shall wax old as doth a garment; 12 And as a vesture shalt thou fold them up,

and they shall be changed: but thou art the same, and thy years shall not fail.

These verses declare the pre-existence and immutability of the Lord Jesus Christ. Just as a king remains a king when he takes off his royal robes, folds them, and puts them away, Christ will remain the sovereign Lord when He lays aside the heavens and earth. He created this world by His power, and He will change it by His divine authority. Verse 12 says of Jesus: "You will roll them [the heavens and the earth] up like a robe; like a garment they will be changed. But you remain the same, and your years will never end" (NIV). Jesus Christ is the beginning and the ending (Revelation 1:8); He is the first and the last (v. 11); and He is the same yesterday, today, and forever (Hebrews 13:8). Christ is both immutable and immortal; His years shall not fail.

Daily Bible Readings

M : From the Beginning
Proverbs 8:22–31

T: Appointed Heir
Hebrews 1:1–5

W: In the Beginning
John 1:1–5

T: The Firstborn
Hebrews 1:6–9

F: The Work of God's Hands
Hebrews 1:10–12

S: Full of Grace and Truth
John 1:14–18

S: Heir of All Things
Hebrews 1:13–14

TEACHING TIPS

June 8
Bible Study Guide 2

1. Words You Should Know

A. Order of Melchisedec (Hebrews 7:21) *taxis Melchisedek* (Gk.)—The "manner" or "likeness in official dignity" of Melchisedec, the king of Salem whose priesthood superceded Aaron's.

B. Make Intercession (v. 25) *entugchano* (Gk.)—To meet in order to converse or make a request for others; pleading in prayer or petition on behalf of another.

2. Teacher Preparation

Unifying Principle—Who Can Speak for Us? Sometimes we need someone to speak up for us, to take our side. Who speaks on your behalf? God chose Jesus to be the perfect and permanent intercessor for humanity.

A. Pray that God will enlighten you with His Word.

B. Start early in the week to conceptualize the AIM for Change, while studying the Focal Verses, Background, and In Depth sections.

C. Read The People, Places, and Times and More Light on the Text sections.

D. Study from your *Precepts For Living*® CD-ROM and complete lesson 2 in the *Precepts For Living*® *Personal Study Guide.*

3. Starting the Lesson

A. Before the students arrive, write the lesson title, At-A-Glance outline, and the word "intercession" on the chalkboard or flip chart.

B. When the students arrive, open the class with prayer, including the AIM for Change objectives as a guide.

C. Ask the students to define "intercession." Explain that today's lesson introduces Christ as our High Priest and Intercessor who represents us before the Father.

D. Have a volunteer read the In Focus story.

4. Getting into the Lesson

A. Help the students gain an understanding of the context for today's lesson. Encourage the students to ask questions.

B. Ask the students to imagine receiving this letter telling of a new priesthood: "Priests will no longer be appointed by inheritance, nor will they need to offer sacrifices for their sins and for the people. The old system—with earthly priests, temples, and sacrifices—is no longer effective." Ask the students to discuss why this information might have been hard for them to receive.

5. Relating the Lesson to Life

A. Just as the recipients of this letter may have had trouble accepting the new and better priesthood, some believers today struggle with doing things Christ's way. Some are still trying to obtain perfection, righteousness, and holiness through earthly means. Identify and discuss some ways in which believers do this.

B. Discuss the benefits of having Christ as our High Priest and Intercessor. How does the new priesthood make life easier and better for us?

6. Arousing Action

A. Direct the students' attention to the Lesson in Our Society and Make It Happen sections. Formulate a list of the class members' prayer concerns.

B. Have class members exchange e-mail addresses or cell phone numbers. At some point during the week either e-mail or text message members of the class, offering encouraging words concerning their prayer concerns.

C. Close the class with prayer, thanking God for giving His Son Jesus Christ, in whom we have a perfect, permanent intercessor.

Worship Guide

For the Superintendent or Teacher
Theme: Christ as Intercessor
Theme Song: "What a Friend"
Devotional Reading: Jeremiah 31:31–34
Prayer

CHRIST AS INTERCESSOR

Bible Background • HEBREWS 7
Printed Text • HEBREWS 7:20–28 Devotional Reading • JEREMIAH 31:31–34

AIM for Change

By the end of the lesson, we will:

RECOGNIZE that Jesus intercedes with the Father on our behalf;

DISCUSS what it means to be a modern-day intercessor; and

DISCOVER how to approach God through prayer and intercession.

Keep in Mind

"Wherefore he is able also to save them to the uttermost that come unto God by him, seeing he ever liveth to make intercession for them" (Hebrews 7:25).

Focal Verses

KJV **Hebrews 7:20** And inasmuch as not without an oath he was made priest:

21 (For those priests were made without an oath; but this with an oath by him that said unto him, The Lord sware and will not repent, Thou art a priest for ever after the order of Melchisedec:)

22 By so much was Jesus made a surety of a better testament.

23 And they truly were many priests, because they were not suffered to continue by reason of death:

24 But this man, because he continueth ever, hath an unchangeable priesthood.

25 Wherefore he is able also to save them to the uttermost that come unto God by him, seeing he ever liveth to make intercession for them.

26 For such an high priest became us, who is holy, harmless, undefiled, separate from sinners, and made higher than the heavens;

27 Who needeth not daily, as those high priests, to offer up sacrifice, first for his own sins, and then for the people's: for this he did once, when he offered up himself.

28 For the law maketh men high priests which have infirmity; but the word of the oath, which was since the law, maketh the Son, who is consecrated for evermore.

NLT **Hebrews 7:20** This new system was established with a solemn oath. Aaron's descendants became priests without such an oath,

21 but there was an oath regarding Jesus. For God said to him, "The LORD has taken an oath and will not break his vow: 'You are a priest forever.'"

22 Because of this oath, Jesus is the one who guarantees this better covenant with God.

23 There were many priests under the old system, for death prevented them from remaining in office.

24 But because Jesus lives forever, his priesthood lasts forever.

25 Therefore he is able, once and forever, to save those who come to God through him. He lives forever to intercede with God on their behalf.

26 He is the kind of high priest we need because he is holy and blameless, unstained by sin. He has been set apart from sinners and has been given the highest place of honor in heaven.

27 Unlike those other high priests, he does not need to offer sacrifices every day. They did this for their own sins first and then for the sins of the people. But Jesus did this once for all when he offered himself as the sacrifice for the people's sins.

28 The law appointed high priests who were limited by human weakness. But after the law was given, God appointed his Son with an oath, and his Son has been made the perfect High Priest forever.

In Focus

My ability to write well is a gift from God, but I inherited my love for writing from my father. My father and I are full-time writers and novelists. We have found strength and maturity through writing, as it develops our faith, patience, discipline, and tenac-

ity. We work daily in silence and solitude, through financial feast or famine, doing what we feel we are called to do—sharing our messages with readers around the world through the printed word.

We write in completely different genres—I write Christian fiction and he writes urban literature. Our styles are different—his books contain social and

political messages, while my writing is conversational and deals with emotional and moral issues. But our reason for writing is similar: Writing has enabled both of us to speak on behalf of those who have suffered societal injustices. We both act as advocates, using our penchant for writing to speak to others about issues facing our families, our friends, and the community at-large. We choose to use our "voice" to speak on behalf of those who would otherwise not have a voice to speak or express themselves and their opinions.

Who speaks on your behalf? Many people encounter problems that they cannot face alone and that require someone to speak on their behalf. The writer of Hebrews calls Jesus our High Priest, the One who goes into the Holy of Holies for us. He is our Advocate—our Intercessor—the One who defends our rights before God the Father.

The People, Places, and Times

Levitical Priesthood. Synonymous with Aaronic priesthood and derived from the Law of Moses, this system restricted priestly duties to the tribe of Levi. Levitical priests were appointed by inheritance and were ever-changing. They offered up animal sacrifices to the Lord daily for their own sins and for the people. This system was imperfect, impermanent, and ineffective.

Melchisedec. He held the offices of both king of Salem and a priest. He is characterized as a type of Christ in his priestly ministry. Greater than Levitical priests, Melchisedec blessed Abraham and received tithes from him. The Scriptures do not mention his ancestry, priestly pedigree, or birth and death, thereby typifying the eternal existence and unending priesthood of Christ. In the Old Testament his name is spelled Melchizedek, and it means "King of Righteousness." Salem, the name of his city, signified "peace." Thus, as king of peace, he typified Christ, the Prince of Peace, the One whose saving work reconciles God and man.

Sources:
King James Version Study Bible. Grand Rapids, Mich.: Zondervan, 2002.
Smith, William. *Smith's Bible Dictionary*. Peabody, Mass.: Hendrickson Publishers, 2000.

Background

In the first six chapters of Hebrews, the writer warms up the recipients of the letter before making his point. Knowing that many of his readers were wavering in their faith, he began the epistle with a subject they could easily digest—that Jesus Christ is supreme over all. He then emphasized God's faithfulness to His Word and His promise of rest for believers. At the end of chapter 4, the writer introduces an unfamiliar concept referring to Christ as our great High Priest. To prevent losing his readers, he immediately moves into describing the credentials for the priesthood as they know it (chapter 5). Gently, he discusses the qualifications of a priest and contrasts them to qualify Jesus.

Although the writer mentions Melchisedec in chapter 5 and wants to discuss his priesthood in greater detail, he doesn't elaborate at this point. Instead, he writes that the readers are spiritually immature and "dull of hearing" (see Hebrews 5:11–14). But he doesn't leave them hanging; he warns them of the danger of failing to grow in faith and tempers his rebuke with encouragement by saying, "But, beloved, we are persuaded better things of you . . ." (Hebrews 6:9).

Finally, in chapter 7 the writer introduces this king who was also a priest, Melchisedec. As if anticipating their questions, he recounts how this king–priest met Abraham and blessed him and received tithes from him. He also explains that the name Melchisedec means "king of righteousness" and "king of peace" and tells readers that his genealogy and dates of birth and death are not known. This description exalted Melchisedec above Abraham and portrayed the king-priest as a type of Christ, representing Jesus' eternal existence and unending priesthood.

Hebrews 7:11–14 reveals a transition of great significance: Anyone who turned to Christ and His priesthood must reject the Levitical priesthood and its law. The Levitical system as they knew it disqualified Jesus from becoming a priest since He was from the tribe of Judah. However, Jesus' priesthood was of a higher order, not an earthly and imperfect one like the Levitical priesthood.

At-A-Glance

1. Christ: The Priest Established by Oath (Hebrews 7:20–22)
2. Christ: The Priest Appointed as Intercessor (vv. 23–25)
3. Christ: The Priest Qualified Through Perfection (vv. 26–28)

In Depth

1. Christ: The Priest Established by Oath (Hebrews 7:20–22)

This new priesthood was marked by many changes. One such change was God's endorsement of the priest. God swore Jesus in with a solemn oath, "Thou art a priest for ever after the order of Melchisedec" (v. 21). Never had God done that in the Levitical priesthood. Jesus' priesthood, pledged in Psalm 110, was superior because it was divinely affirmed with an oath.

Another change of the priesthood was that of its dispensation, or the way in which it was administered. The duties of the Levitical priesthood had to be carried out daily. Priests of the law were sinful and had to offer daily sacrifices for their own sins and for those of the people. And the important Day of Atonement (Leviticus 23:27), in which the high priest entered the Holy of Holies, came yearly. It was a "shadow of heavenly things" according to Hebrews 8:5. But the Gospel dispensation was surer. With Christ as surety (7:22), man's reconciliation with God was guaranteed through an everlasting covenant. Christ, the Mediator, united the divine and human nature in His own Person. What animals' blood couldn't do, Jesus' blood did—once and fully.

2. Christ: The Priest Appointed as Intercessor (vv. 23–25)

According to verse 25, this Mediator of the new covenant "ever liveth to make intercession for them." This signified another change in the priesthood—Christ's priesthood was permanent and unchangeable. Whereas priests of the law died, leaving a vacancy in the priesthood until they were replaced, with Jesus Christ as High Priest there would never be a vacancy in the priesthood. At all times, in all things, He would be available to negotiate our spiritual concerns in heaven, by interceding with the Father on our behalf.

In 1 Timothy 2:1–5, Paul urges followers of Christ to pray for all people and make their requests known to God. In his writing about Timothy's church member Epaphras, Paul says this servant of Christ "prays earnestly for you, asking God to make you strong and perfect . . . following the whole will of God" (Colossians 4:12, NLT). Based on these passages, it is obvious that the primary function of an intercessor is to petition God's throne of grace through prayer.

3. Christ: The Priest Qualified Through Perfection (vv. 26–28)

Another difference between these priesthoods was the moral qualifications of the priests. Verse 26 records that Jesus was "holy, harmless, undefiled, separate from sinners, and made higher than the heavens." Priests of the law were mortal and sinful; therefore, they had their share of physical infirmities and defects.

No lawful priest could have qualified to make atonement for sin and intercession for sinners except Christ, who was excellent Himself.

Search the Scriptures

1. How was Christ made Priest (Hebrews 7:20–21)?

2. Christ was made priest after the order of what king-priest (v. 21)?

3. Why were there many priests (v. 23)?

4. What unique characteristics did Christ have as Priest (vv. 26–27)?

5. What didn't Christ have to do (v. 27)?

Discuss the Meaning

1. Compare and contrast the Levitical priesthood and Jesus' priesthood.

2. Compare and contrast Jesus and Melchisedec.

3. Which priesthood do we rely upon today? Explain your answer.

Lesson in Our Society

In today's society communication is king. Staying "connected" is the important thing. Everyone has a cell phone or a PDA (personal digital assistant). We send e-mails, we send text messages, we send IMs (instant messages). A lot of people (at least between the ages of 18 and 34) have a Web site or a video on Facebook or YouTube. The goal is to stay as "connected" to one another as possible. With all of this *communication* going on, becoming a modern-day intercessor should be very easy. We all have the capacity to intercede for one another readily. Ask yourself, "What kind of moral support am I providing (or receiving) that affects my family, friends, coworkers in a positive manner?"

Make It Happen

Are you struggling with a particular area in your life—financial burdens, a toxic relationship, sexual impurity, filthy communication, etc.? This week, commit it to prayer and intercession. Establish a prayer chain or a prayer group and commit to intercessory prayer for one another. Know that Christ, your High Priest, goes to the Father on your behalf. Give your problem to Him and ask for His help in turning away from it.

Follow the Spirit

What God wants me to do:

_____
_____

Remember Your Thoughts

Special insights I have learned:

_____
_____

More Light on the Text

Hebrews 7:20–28

During the early period of the Old Testament era, a priestly system was instituted with Aaron and his sons as priests from the tribe of Levi who would offer up sacrifices for the sins of the people. But the priests had to offer up sacrifices every day for their own sins as well. The sacrifices were never perfect or complete. Moreover, the high priest always had to be replaced when he died.

The Old Testament prophets saw the need for a priest of a different order than the Levitical priests. Acting as God's mouthpiece, they foretold that Jesus would come as a holy Priest, and therefore have no need to make sacrifices for His own sins.

Writing long after the life, death, resurrection, and ascension of Jesus Christ, the writer of Hebrews affirms that Jesus is the Priest about whom the prophet Isaiah spoke: "He had done no violence, neither was any deceit in his mouth . . . and he bare the sin of many, and made intercession for the transgressors" (Isaiah 53:9, 12).

The writer of Hebrews notes that with the coming of Jesus, the Levitical priesthood was set aside because it was weak and unprofitable (Hebrews 7:18). "A better hope" was introduced, "by the which we draw nigh unto God" (v. 19). Jesus did not sacrifice an animal; He sacrificed Himself for our sins. Therefore, no other sacrifice is needed—ever. We have now and will have forever Jesus, who intercedes with the Father for us. Therefore, it is written: "He is able also to save them to the uttermost that come unto God by him, seeing he ever liveth to make intercession for them" (v. 25). It is against this background information that our Scripture text begins with a note of exclamation.

20 And inasmuch as not without an oath he was made priest:

This is the writer's way of saying the priesthood of Jesus is of a higher order than Levitical succession. Jesus' priesthood was established by God with an oath, meaning God has sworn and will not change His mind. Just as God kept His covenant with Abraham, He will keep His promise regarding Jesus' priesthood. Jesus' priesthood is permanent, in contrast to the Levitical priesthood.

21 (For those priests were made without an oath; but this with an oath by him that said unto him, The Lord sware and will not repent, Thou art a priest for ever after the order of Melchisedec:)

The Levitical priesthood established under Aaron (Exodus 28:1) was conditional. It was instituted without an oath and therefore lacked permanence. Christ's priesthood was confirmed by an oath, and He is therefore "a priest for ever." The fact that Jesus' priesthood is confirmed by divine oath leaves no room for qualification because of any human weakness, sin, or failure.

The writer of Hebrews aims to show that Christ's priesthood is superior to the Levitical priesthood. To strengthen the argument, the writer references Psalm 110:4, which is understood to be God's comment to Christ: "Thou art a priest for ever after the order of Melchisedek." Hebrews is the only New Testament book that makes a direct reference to Melchisedec. This name appears twice in the Old Testament, spelled Melchizedek. In Genesis 14:18–20 he is referred to as "the king of Salem" and "the priest of the most high God." While there are several extra-biblical references to Melchisedec, and it appears that some early Christian writers were aware of a Melchisedec tradition, he remains a mysterious figure. The lack of clarity regarding Melchisedec's role in biblical history, however, does not diminish the truth of the superiority and permanence of Christ's priesthood.

22 By so much was Jesus made a surety of a better testament.

Here the writer of Hebrews surprisingly moves his line of reasoning from that of the priesthood to that of a testament or covenant. The Greek word *diatheke* (**dee-ah-THAY-kay**, translated "testament" or "covenant," which carries the idea that a promise has been made) is used in conjunction with the Greek word *egguos* (**ENG-goo-oss**, translated "surety," meaning the guarantee that a promise will be fulfilled). These two words are meant to make perfectly clear the incontestability of God's oath whereby Jesus was made "a priest for ever." God made the promise, and Jesus is the guarantee that the promise will be fulfilled.

It is understood that a will or testament is final and absolute and therefore cannot be successfully challenged except by the testator. God has laid the terms of Christ's priesthood down once and for all time. Jesus' life and God's oath make unnecessary a succession of priests after Christ.

Again, this is the writer's way of saying *Christ's priesthood is forever!* Christ Jesus is our Intercessor. He now intercedes with the Father for us. Indeed, He "ever liveth to make intercession for" us (Hebrews 7:25).

23 And they truly were many priests, because they were not suffered to continue by reason of death:

The writer of Hebrews continues to contrast Jesus with the Levitical priests. Historians tell us that from the time of Aaron to the destruction of the temple in A.D. 70, there were between 80 and 85 high priests. Because they were all subject to death, there was need for numerous replacements. Jesus, on the other hand, overcame death and therefore qualified to be the eternal guarantee or "surety" of God's promise. Given such superiority over the Levitical priesthood, Jesus can indeed speak for us. He can go before God and plead our case.

24 But this man, because he continueth ever, hath an unchangeable priesthood.

Unlike the Levitical priests, Jesus' priesthood "continueth ever." He has "an unchangeable priesthood." The Greek word *aparabatos* (**ahp-ar-AH-bah-toss**, translated "unchangeable," meaning something that cannot be transgressed or transferred to another) conveys the idea that Jesus' priesthood lives with Him through eternity. Since Jesus "continueth ever," His priesthood is "unchangeable." Jesus' priesthood cannot be transferred to another. It extends into eternity. Thus, He is able to intercede for us and for all people in every generation yet unborn. Moreover, His eternal priesthood cannot be matched by the mortal priests of the past. It is little wonder that such a priest as Jesus Christ "is able also to save them to the uttermost that come unto God by him" (v. 25).

25 Wherefore he is able also to save them to the uttermost that come unto God by him, seeing he ever liveth to make intercession for them.

The basic and most significant content of this verse is contained in the Greek verb *sozo* (**SOHDzoh**, translated "to save," also meaning to deliver, make whole, or to preserve safe from danger, loss, and destruction). More specifically, in the context of Hebrews, it is salvation in its broadest and fullest meaning. It implies complete deliverance, no matter what our need, including deliverance from the punishment resulting from sin. In Jesus, we have a Saviour who is able to bring complete salvation to all who "come unto God by him."

Jesus lives to make intercession for us! Because He lives forever, His priestly concern for us never ends. Whatever our need, at any time or in any place, Jesus Christ stands ready to petition God the Father in our behalf. He is able and always available to speak for us, and to go before God and plead our case. Hallelujah! What a Saviour.

26 For such an high priest became us, who is holy, harmless, undefiled, separate from sinners, and made higher than the heavens;

All priests who served in the temple where God's presence dwelled were obliged to be holy, harmless, undefiled, and separate from sinners. In essence, they were to be free of any Levitical impu-

"Wherefore he is able also to save them to the uttermost that come unto God by him, seeing he ever liveth to make intercession for them" (Hebrews 7:25).

rity—any of the actions or circumstances that would render them unclean according to the Mosaic Law. Any defilement rendered the priest incapable of interceding for the people. When the priest and the Levite refused to help the half-dead man on the road from Jerusalem to Jericho (Luke 10:29–32), their refusal may have been based on the fear that while helping him he might die. Their contact with a dead man would disqualify them from performing their priestly duties.

The writer of Hebrews wants his readers to know that Jesus fulfills *all* of these requirements. He is holy, harmless, and undefiled, and although He is a friend of sinners, He has been "made higher than the heavens." While Jesus is apart from sinners, He nonetheless intercedes for sinners in ways that show His capacity to identify with the least of these. In fact, Hebrews 4:14–15 reminds us, "Seeing then that we have a great high priest, that is passed into the heavens, Jesus the Son of God, let us hold fast our profession. For we havenot an high priest which cannot be touched with the feeling of our infirmities; but was in all points tempted like as we are, yet without sin." Christ's undefiled character attests to His capacity to go before God on our behalf. Unlike the Levitical priests, Jesus has no need to offer a sacrifice for Himself. By virtue of His undefiled character, He was qualified to offer Himself as the atoning sacrifice for our sins. He was the "lamb without blemish and without spot" (1 Peter 1:19).

27 Who needeth not daily, as those high priests, to offer up sacrifice, first for his own sins, and then for the people's: for this he did once, when he offered up himself.

This verse presents meticulous students of the Scriptures with a problem. A careful reading of the relevant text will show that while sacrifices were offered daily, the high priest was not required to offer them personally. Those sacrifices requiring the high priest's attention were offered yearly, not daily (cf. Hebrews 9:7, 25; 10:1). However, the writer wishes to make the point that Jesus has no need to offer sacrifices daily or yearly for His own sins, because He was sinless (4:15). His perfect sacrifice was sufficient for all time, "for this he did once, when he offered up himself."

The writer's use of the phrase translated "for this he did once" is a critically important affirmation. It speaks not only of the eternal completeness and efficacy of Christ's sacrifice of Himself, it also nullifies every other sacrificial system. Christ's sacrifice of Himself was final, complete, and eternally adequate for our salvation.

28 For the law maketh men high priests which have infirmity; but the word of the oath, which was since the law, maketh the Son, who is consecrated for evermore.

Here another comparison is made between the Levitical priests and Jesus. Under Levitical law, which was imperfect, priests were appointed by ordinary men from among ordinary men. Therefore priests, even the high priest, are limited, just as all men are limited. They have *astheneia* (Gk. **ahs-THEN-ay-ah**, translated "infirmity" or "weakness"). They are subject to death.

Standing in clear contrast to the law is "the word of the oath," which came much later than the law. One could ask: If the law was perfect, making provi-

sion for the appointment of perfect priests, what need would there have been for "the word of the oath"? The mere fact that "the word of the oath" came after the law points to the inadequacies of the Aaronic priesthood.

This verse is really a summary of the preceding verses. It reiterates the thought that Jesus, the Son, is superior to all the priests appointed under the law. The continuous replacement of imperfect priests is contrasted with the permanent placement of Jesus "who is consecrated [or perfected] for evermore." Praise God that we have a perfect High Priest who can speak for us! Who would want to turn away from such a One who is able and available to plead our case before God? May it please God that we will all avail ourselves of His gracious and merciful redeeming grace.

Daily Bible Readings

M: Preparing for a New Covenant
Jeremiah 31:31–34
T: The Old Order of Priests
Hebrews 5:1–4
W: King Melchizedek
Genesis 14:17–20
T: Introduction of a New Order
Hebrews 7:4–17
F: The Permanent Priesthood
Hebrews 7:18–24
S: Interceding for All Who Approach God
Hebrews 7:25–26
S: Perfect Forever
Hebrews 7:27–28

TEACHING TIPS

June 15
Bible Study Guide 3

1. Words You Should Know

A. Redemption (Hebrews 9:12, 15) *lutrosis* (Gk.)—Deliverance from some evil by payment of a price.

B. Sanctifieth/Sanctified (v. 13; 10:14) *hagiazo* (Gk.)—Separation of the believer from evil things and ways.

C. Purge (9:14) *katharizo* (Gk.)—To cleanse.

D. Testament (v. 15) *diatheke* (Gk.)—A covenant or an agreement.

E. Transgressions (v. 15) *parabasis* (Gk.)—The breaking of the law.

F. Sacrifice (10:12) *thusia* (Gk.)—The act of offering.

2. Teacher Preparation

Unifying Principle—Guilt Removed People feel a need to be absolved of their wrongdoing. Who can take away our guilt? In Hebrews, we read that Jesus shed His blood for the redemption of humanity.

A. Begin with prayer and then read the Devotional Reading Scriptures and Focal Verses.

B. Read the AIM for Change objectives and the Unifying Principle.

C. Look up the definition of "blood" in the dictionary or consult a medical reference book to gain insight on the significance of human blood in relation to sustaining life.

3. Starting the Lesson

A. Open with prayer.

B. Briefly explain today's AIM for Change objectives and Unifying Principle.

C. Ask a student to volunteer to read the In Focus story. Ask the class to reflect on situations or circumstances for which they are currently carrying guilt.

D. Ask the students to explain their understanding of how human blood sustains life within the body.

4. Getting into the Lesson

A. Recap the Background and The People, Places, and Times sections to provide the students with a clearer picture of the setting of today's lesson.

B. Review the terms in the Words You Should Know section.

C. Break the class into three groups and assign each group an In Depth section and corresponding Discuss the Meaning questions to review and discuss.

5. Relating the Lesson to Life

A. Reassemble the class and ask each group to report its conclusions.

B. Ask two or three students to share how we can identify specific people with whom to share the power of Christ's forgiveness through His blood.

6. Arousing Action

A. Have the students reread the AIM for Change aloud in unison.

B. Remind the class that the shedding of Jesus' blood has washed away our sins and we no longer have to feel guilty because of our past transgressions. We have to share the Good News of His redeeming power with those who are not saved.

C. Close the class with prayer.

Worship Guide

For the Superintendent or Teacher
Theme: Christ as Redeemer
Theme Song: "Amazing Grace"
Devotional Reading: John 4:21–26
Prayer

CHRIST AS REDEEMER

Bible Background • HEBREWS 9:11–10:18
Printed Text • HEBREWS 9:11–18; 10:12–14, 17–18 Devotional Reading • JOHN 4:21–26

AIM for Change

By the end of the lesson, we will:

UNDERSTAND why the blood of Jesus washes away our sins;

FEEL SECURE in the forgiveness of our sins through the blood of Jesus; and

TESTIFY to a friend or neighbor as to how God has forgiven our sins through the blood of Jesus.

Keep in Mind

"Neither by the blood of goats and calves, but by his own blood he entered in once into the holy place, having obtained eternal redemption for us" (Hebrews 9:12).

Focal Verses

KJV

Hebrews 9:11 But Christ being come an high priest of good things to come, by a greater and more perfect tabernacle, not made with hands, that is to say, not of this building;

12 Neither by the blood of goats and calves, but by his own blood he entered in once into the holy place, having obtained eternal redemption for us.

13 For if the blood of bulls and of goats, and the ashes of an heifer sprinkling the unclean, sanctifieth to the purifying of the flesh:

14 How much more shall the blood of Christ, who through the eternal Spirit offered himself without spot to God, purge your conscience from dead works to serve the living God?

15 And for this cause he is the mediator of the new testament, that by means of death, for the redemption of the transgressions that were under the first testament, they which are called might receive the promise of eternal inheritance.

16 For where a testament is, there must also of necessity be the death of the testator.

17 For a testament is of force after men are dead: otherwise it is of no strength at all while the testator liveth.

18 Whereupon neither the first testament was dedicated without blood.

NLT

Hebrews 9:11 So Christ has now become the High Priest over all the good things that have come. He has entered that greater, more perfect Tabernacle in heaven, which was not made by human hands and is not part of this created world.

12 With his own blood—not the blood of goats and calves—he entered the Most Holy Place once for all time and secured our redemption forever.

13 Under the old system, the blood of goats and bulls and the ashes of a young cow could cleanse people's bodies from ceremonial impurity.

14 Just think how much more the blood of Christ will purify our consciences from sinful deeds so that we can worship the living God. For by the power of the eternal Spirit, Christ offered himself to God as a perfect sacrifice for our sins.

15 That is why he is the one who mediates a new covenant between God and people, so that all who are called can receive the eternal inheritance God has promised them. For Christ died to set them free from the penalty of the sins they had committed under that first covenant.

16 Now when someone leaves a will, it is necessary to prove that the person who made it is dead.

17 The will goes into effect only after the person's death. While the person who made it is still alive, the will cannot be put into effect.

18 That is why even the first covenant was put into effect with the blood of an animal.

10:12 But this man, after he had offered one sacrifice for sins for ever, sat down on the right hand of God;

13 From henceforth expecting till his enemies be made his footstool.

14 For by one offering he hath perfected for ever them that are sanctified.

10:17 And their sins and iniquities will I remember no more.

18 Now where remission of these is, there is no more offering for sin.

10:12 But our High Priest offered himself to God as a single sacrifice for sins, good for all time. Then he sat down in the place of honor at God's right hand.

13 There he waits until his enemies are humbled and made a footstool under his feet.

14 For by that one offering he forever made perfect those who are being made holy.

10:17 Then he says, "I will never again remember their sins and lawless deeds."

18 And when sins have been forgiven, there is no need to offer any more sacrifices.

In Focus

Nine years earlier, Jazmine had celebrated her 21st birthday at a party with all her friends. During the party, someone offered her drugs. Although she initially refused the offer, eventually she gave in to the peer pressure and took some cocaine.

At the end of the party, Jazmine and two friends got into her car, and Jazmine got behind the wheel to drive home. On the way, she lost control of the car and crashed into a van, killing the van's occupants and her two friends. Later she discovered that the family riding in the van was the youth minister of her church and his wife, who was pregnant with twins.

Jazmine served nine years in prison. At the age of 30, Jazmine returned home from prison. For nine years she had been overcome with the guilt of her crime and the death of her friends. Although many people had visited her in prison and told her of the forgiving power of Jesus Christ, she turned away from God, thinking she did not deserve forgiveness since she was a murderer. Her thinking did not change once she returned home. She even refused to attend church anymore, afraid of what people would say. All she heard in her mind was "Killer! Child Murderer!" over and over.

Her parents explained to Jazmine that the enemy was tormenting her, but Jesus wanted her to be free of the guilt of her sins: "Jazmine, the sacrifice of Christ and the blood offering He made on our behalf makes possible the forgiveness of my sins and yours and frees us from the torment of guilt. Just ask God to forgive you, believe in your heart that Christ's sacrifice covers your sins, and receive God's gift of salvation and forgiveness."

In today's lesson, we learn about the sacrifice Jesus made by shedding His blood for the forgiveness of our sins. In Christ, we are made righteous and are no longer condemned by our past transgressions.

The People, Places, and Times

Author. Many people have been suggested as the author of Hebrews, including Paul, Luke, Barnabas, and others. However, the name of the author is not given in the text. We do know that the author was writing to the Hebrew Christians who were wavering between the Christian faith and a return to Judaism.

Time. Hebrews was probably written before the destruction of the temple in Jerusalem in A.D. 70. The religious sacrifices and ceremonies are referred to in the book, but no mention is made of the temple's destruction.

Background

The writer of Hebrews presents the sufficiency and superiority of Christ. Many Hebrew Christians were wavering between the practice of the traditional religion of Judaism and their new faith in Christ as the Messiah. They did not want to abandon the old to accept the new. Some were considering returning to Judaism because of the disconnection in relation to Christianity.

Hebrews describes how Christ fulfilled all the promises and prophecies of the Old Testament. Moreover, Jesus Christ is superior to everything in the Jewish tradition because He is God (1:1–3). He is greater than the angels (1:4–2:18), greater than Moses (3:1–4:13), and greater than the Old Testament priesthood (4:14–7:28).

The writer shows the connection between the old covenant under Moses and the new covenant in Christ.

Source:

The Life Application Study Bible, New Revised Standard Version. Wheaton, Ill.: Tyndale House Publishers, 1989.

At-A-Glance

1. Christ, the Perfect Sacrifice (Hebrews 9:11–14)
2. Christ, the Great Mediator of a New Testament (vv. 15–18)
3. Christ, the Redeemer (10:12–14, 17–18)

In Depth

1. Christ, the Perfect Sacrifice (Hebrews 9:11–14)

Under the old covenant of Moses, only the high priests, who were from the tribe of Levi, entered the tabernacle's inner sanctuary. The high priests entered once a year into the inner room to offer atonement for their sins first and then for the nation's. The blood of animals was sprinkled on the Ark of the Covenant. This sacrifice ceremonially covered the sins of the people externally, but it could not cleanse them from the defilement of sin that lay within the conscience. There needed to be a more perfect sacrifice.

Christ came as the One appointed by God with superiority above all previous high priests (5:5–10). He is High Priest of a tabernacle not made with hands, conceived of the Holy Ghost and born of the virgin Mary. Jesus' priesthood surpassed Aaron's (7:11) and Melchisedec's (7:15–17), and it contains the perfection missing in the older sacrificial system (7:18). He entered into heaven by the sacrifice of His own blood, which was not tainted by sin. "There was no sin found in Him." His sacrifice was sufficient for eternity, not just a year's pardon (7:27; 9:12).

Furthermore, Christ's sacrifice transforms our lives and hearts and purifies the conscience. Christ offered Himself to God without spot, without any sin-

ful blemish either in His nature or life, just as required of animal sacrifices. However, the sacrifices of animals could not do what the blood of Christ accomplished. By His blood alone, we are forgiven and our consciences cleared of all guilt. It purges the guilt, which separates God and sinners, through the sanctifying power of the Holy Spirit (9:14). We are no longer enslaved by the power of sin and death. Christians are free to serve God, having been eternally redeemed by the blood of the Lamb.

2. Christ, the Great Mediator of a New Testament (vv. 15–18)

In these verses, the Gospel is considered as a testament, the new and last will and testament of our Lord and Saviour Jesus Christ. A will and testament is a voluntary act and deed of an individual person, executed and witnessed to, bestowing legacies on the persons described and identified by the testator; a will can only take effect upon the person's death. A will is legally binding and can rarely be amended by anyone except the testator.

All people have sinned and are guilty before God. God is so gracious and merciful that He permitted the blood of bulls and goats to be a temporary sacrifice. But Jesus became the Mediator of a new, permanent testament by shedding His blood to make atonement for our sins.

For the New Testament to become valid, Christ had to die (9:16). His act of sacrifice on the Cross redeemed all those who believe and are called to receive the promise of an eternal inheritance, salvation (5:9). Christians have an inheritance that will never perish but continues into eternity (7:23–25). This promise gives us confidence in our positions as children of God. Because of Christ, we do not have to doubt we are forgiven. Christ became the perfect sacrifice sufficient to atone for sin once and for all.

3. Christ, the Redeemer (10:12–14, 17–18)

Christ's sacrifice on the cross redeemed us from the curse of the law. Because His work is complete, "he sat down on the right hand of God." In contrast, the Old Testament priests had to continually stand and make sacrifices. Their work was never finished. The description of Christ sitting down symbolizes that His sacrifice completed the work that God appointed Him to do. There is no need for another

The work you sent me to do is FINISHED.

sacrifice. "It is finished!" We need not try to gain eternal life through good works. Only through faith in Jesus Christ as Lord and Saviour can we inherit eternal life.

Christ is not only our Redeemer, but He is also our Defender. Jesus is the Messiah who will ultimately defeat the wicked (Psalm 110:1; Revelation 6–9). We, bearing the righteousness of God through Christ, do not have to fear the future. Our Redeemer has secured our future for eternity through His sacrifice. Thus, we can live victoriously.

Source:
"Matthew Henry's Commentary." *Precepts For Living*® CD-ROM. Chicago: Urban Ministries, Inc., 2005.

Search the Scriptures

1. Where did Christ enter to shed His own blood (Hebrews 9:12)? *The Most Holiest Place*

2. What does the blood of Jesus Christ do for us that the blood of bulls and goats could not (vv. 13–14)? *Purifies our Conscience*

3. How was the new testament made valid (9:15–18)? *Christ's death*

4. How often will Christ remember our sins (10:17)? *He will remember them Never.*

5. Do we have to continue to offer sacrifices for our sins (v. 18)? *Christ died ONCE 4 all.*

Discuss the Meaning

1. Look up the meaning of the word "redeemer" in the dictionary. How does the definition clarify your understanding of Christ as our Redeemer?

2. Do you ever condemn yourself for past sins? What did you learn from the Scriptures?

3. As a Christian, what impact does Jesus' sacrifice have on your life today and for eternity?

Lesson in Our Society

Sin often causes guilt and self-condemnation. Many people, like Jazmine in the In Focus story, are suffering because of past sins. She was even afraid to attend church because she thought she would be ostracized and rejected. She did not understand that the sacrifice Christ made was sufficient to cleanse her from all sin and guilt. Thankfully, someone reached out to Jazmine to testify of the forgiving power of God available to us through the blood of Jesus.

All Christians need to reach out to others and testify how God has forgiven us through the blood of Jesus. His love is so powerful that it can reach anyone.

Make It Happen

This week pray and ask God to direct you to someone who needs to know about the forgiveness available through Jesus Christ. Show the person from the Scriptures why Jesus had to shed His blood. Share your testimony of being reconciled to God through Jesus Christ's sacrifice. Your testimony may change the life of a lost soul.

Follow the Spirit

What God wants me to do:

_____

_____

Remember Your Thoughts

Special insights I have learned:

_____

_____

More Light on the Text

Hebrews 9:11–18; 10:12–14, 17–18

Having explained the inability of the ceremonial proceedings of the Levitical system to clear the worshiper's conscience (Hebrews 9:1–10), the writer of Hebrews showed that Christ's sacrifice of Himself is far superior to that of animal sacrifices. Although the "carnal ordinances" of the old covenant served a provisional purpose until the inauguration of the new covenant (Hebrews 9:10), they could not facilitate intimacy with God. Worship under the Levitical system focused upon ceremonial purity and did little to reconcile people's hearts to God and enhance moral purity. Sacrifices made by humans were ultimately unacceptable to God because we are all tainted by sin.

This description of worship under the old covenant of the Levitical priesthood highlights by contrast the "good things" (Hebrews 9:11) that accompany worship under the new covenant and Christ's priesthood. Christ's sacrifice of Himself for our sin accomplished what the sacrifices of the old covenant could not accomplish. Because of Christ's sacrifice for our sins, we can have our consciences cleansed from guilt. Indeed, Jesus was the only One

"Neither by the blood of goats and calves, but by his own blood he entered in once into the holy place, having obtained eternal redemption for us" (Hebrews 9:12).

who could pay the penalty for our sins. Therefore, He—and He alone—qualifies as our Redeemer!

11 But Christ being come an high priest of good things to come, by a greater and more perfect tabernacle, not made with hands, that is to say, not of this building;

Since this text was written long after the life, death, and resurrection of Jesus, the Greek phrase *genomenon agathon* (**gen-o-MEN-ohn ah-gah-THOHN**, here translated "good things to come") is the present tense active voice and should probably be translated "the good things that are already here." Although the author does not identify what these good things are, it is reasonable to conclude that this is a reference to the current *and future* blessings Christ affords those who by faith accept His saving grace.

By referring to "a greater and more perfect tabernacle, not made with hands, that is to say, not of this building," the writer seeks to convey the heavenly and eternal nature of Christ's redeeming work and compares it to the earthly nature of ceremonial proceed-

ings that took place in the temple built by human hands. The tabernacle of Moses was built with earthly and corruptible materials. The more perfect tabernacle that Christ's saving work creates within the hearts of the redeemed (Revelation 21:3; see also 1 Corinthians 3:16) is heavenly, "incorruptible, and undefiled, and . . . fadeth not away" (1 Peter 1:4). This was accomplished not by the continuous flow of goats' and calves' blood, but by the once-and-for-all-time shedding of the blood of Christ, which was far superior to earthly sacrifices.

12 Neither by the blood of goats and calves, but by his own blood he entered in once into the holy place, having obtained eternal redemption for us.

Every time the high priest went into the Holy of Holies he took the blood of goats and calves with him (Hebrews 9:7) to sprinkle on the ark. The goats' blood symbolized the cleansing of the people and the calves' blood symbolized the cleansing of the priests. In radical contrast to this annual ritual performed by the high priest, Christ "obtained eternal redemption for us" by entering "once into the holy place." When the high priest entered the Holy of Holies, it was believed that he had entered into the presence of God. The Holy of Holies, however, was built by human hands, as was the ark upon which the blood of animals was sprinkled by imperfect priests.

In contrast to the priest, Christ did not enter the same Holy of Holies; rather, He who knew no sin entered the true sanctuary above—the heavenly sanctuary—and offered up His own blood in the very presence of God in heaven (Hebrews 8:1; see also Hebrews 9:24).

13 For if the blood of bulls and of goats, and the ashes of an heifer sprinkling the unclean, sanctifieth to the purifying of the flesh: 14 How much more shall the blood of Christ, who through the eternal Spirit offered himself without spot to God, purge your conscience from dead works to serve the living God?

Verses 13–14 form one rhetorical question. The implied answer highlights the superiority of Christ's sacrifice over the sacrifices of animals. The inadequacy of animal sacrifices under the old covenant to "purge the conscience from dead works to serve the living God" has been established. The blood of Christ (i.e., Christ's death) is far more efficacious than "the blood of bulls and of goats, and the ashes of an heifer."

Here the writer reaffirms the point that while animal sacrifices may have given worshipers the feeling of external cleansing, only the blood of Christ can purge our consciences and liberate us from the guilt of sin. God's holy character demanded a perfect sacrifice in order to achieve reconciliation for us. The Spirit worked in and with Christ, making sure our redemption is secure and we through faith in Christ are set free "to serve the living God." Christ is our Redeemer!

15 And for this cause he is the mediator of the new testament, that by means of death, for the redemption of the transgressions that were under the first testament, they which are called might receive the promise of eternal inheritance.

The writer goes on to amplify what Christ's death achieved. Central to the writer's explanation is the use of the Greek word *kleronomia* (**klay-ron-om-EE-**

ah), translated "inheritance." Generally speaking, an inheritance is received through the will or "testament" of someone who died. Christ died and bequeathed redemption to us and to all those who believe in Him.

Because Christ's death achieved what the old covenant could not achieve, He is the mediator of "the new testament" (i.e., the new covenant), which supersedes the old covenant.

16 For where a testament is, there must also of necessity be the death of the testator. 17 For a testament is of force after men are dead: otherwise it is of no strength at all while the testator liveth.

Verse 16 affirms the fact that a testament or a will is activated only after the death of the person who made the will. Verse 17 repeats the point that without the death of the testator, the will has no force. In essence, this is the writer's way of illustrating the necessity of Christ's death. The inheritance referenced in verse 15 could not have been given and received by us apart from the death of Christ. Christ had to die in order for the new covenant to have been put in force. Just as a will becomes valid after the testator's death, so our eternal inheritance could only be received after the death of Christ.

18 Whereupon neither the first testament was dedicated without blood.

Having argued that death must occur in order for a will to be put in force, the writer now argues the same point from the perspective of the Law. Under the Law, for sin to be forgiven blood had to be shed. Here the writer reasons that just as a death was required under the old covenant, so also was a death required under the new covenant. This point is reiterated in Hebrews 9:22: "And almost all things are by the law purged with blood; and without shedding of blood is no remission."

10:12 But this man, after he had offered one sacrifice for sins for ever, sat down on the right hand of God;

The writer again contrasts the work of Jesus with that of the priests. While this has been the writer's theme all along, it is stated here with emphasis that Jesus offered one sacrifice and "sat down." The work of the Levitical priests was never finished.

Therefore, figuratively speaking, the priests could never sit down. They were always standing and working, always required to offer up sacrifices. Because Christ's work is done, He is free to take on the posture of rest and sit "down on the right hand of God." This is the writer's way to say that the atoning work of Christ is both finished and complete. The Greek words he uses are *eis to dienekes* (**ayss tah dee-ay-neh-KESS**), translated "for ever" or "for all time." The meaning here is twofold: Christ's sacrificial work is *finished for all time* and He can sit "down on the right hand of God for ever." It should also be noted that to be seated at the right hand of God is to be in a position of exalted and highest honor. Jesus Christ is our *exalted* Redeemer!

It is little wonder, and somewhat ironic, that when Jesus claimed this rightful position for Himself, the high priest tore his robe in anger and accused Jesus of blasphemy (Mark 14:60–64).

13 From henceforth expecting till his enemies be made his footstool.

With the redemptive work of Christ completed, this verse seems to anticipate the day when all the forces of evil will be overthrown. In the words of the psalmist, He is sitting in heaven "till his enemies be made his footstool" (see Psalm 110:1). Let us receive Christ's saving grace and so live our lives that we will not be numbered among His enemies.

14 For by one offering he hath perfected for ever them that are sanctified.

The Greek word *teleioo* (**tel-ay-O-oh**), here translated "perfected," is best understood in terms of our standing with God. In other words, for the writer of Hebrews, to be perfected is to be fully cleansed from sin and thus made fit to be in fellowship with God. This is often referred to as justification. Christ's one offering justifies us and puts us on a track of being *hagiazo* (**hahg-ee-AHD-zoh**) or "sanctified" (i.e., those being made holy). Justification is *what we are* through faith in the saving work of Jesus Christ. Sanctification is *what we are becoming* as we learn to walk in His will and live by the Spirit.

10:17 And their sins and iniquities will I remember no more.

This verse alludes to a statement by Jeremiah (see Jeremiah 31:33–34), which seems to anticipate the salvific work of Christ described in Hebrews: "After those days, saith the Lord, I will put my law in their inward parts . . . and will be their God, and they shall be my people . . . . I will forgive their iniquity, and I will remember their sin no more." The writer of Hebrews makes the point that the new covenant spoken of by the prophet and established by Christ provides for the forgiveness of sins.

18 Now where remission of these is, there is no more offering for sin.

This verse summarizes the writer's argument and conveys the conviction that Christ has effectively dealt with sin; nothing more need be done to remove our guilt and give us a clear conscience before God. There is no need for any further sacrifices. We can feel secure in the forgiveness of our sins through the blood of Jesus.

Daily Bible Readings

M: "I Am He"
John 4:21–26
T: Mediator of a New Covenant
Hebrews 9:11–15
W: On Our Behalf
Hebrews 9:16–24
T: Once for All Time
Hebrews 9:25–28
F: A One-Time Sacrifice
Hebrews 10:1–10
S: For Our Sanctification
Hebrews 10:11–14
S: Forgiveness Forever
Hebrews 10:15–18

TEACHING TIPS

June 22
Bible Study Guide 4

1. Words You Should Know

A. Witnesses (Hebrews 12:1) *martus* (Gk.)—One who can verify a particular truth based on what he has seen, heard, or knows.

B. Chastening (vv. 5, 7) *paideia* (Gk.)—Education or training; by implication, it also means disciplinary correction.

2. Teacher Preparation

Unifying Principle—Trustworthy Leadership People want to follow leaders who will give them direction. What makes a leader credible? By His action and godly discipline, Jesus demonstrates that He is a leader who can be trusted.

A. Familiarize yourself with Hebrews 11 and 12.

B. Review the Words You Should Know and the AIM for Change.

C. Make a list of some of the struggles African Americans have had to endure so that they could enjoy the standard of living they have today. Scripture presents suffering as a discipline that purifies and strengthens one's faith and builds character.

3. Starting the Lesson

A. Open the class with prayer, asking God to help the class understand how suffering can lead to disciplined and holy living.

B. Ask the students to share some of the ways they have suffered and dealt with adversity. Ask them if the experience was beneficial or harmful in the end. What lessons have they learned from suffering?

C. Have the students silently read the In Focus story. Follow up by posing the following questions: What do you think of when you think of leadership? Have you ever thought of yourself as a leader?

4. Getting into the Lesson

A. State the AIM for Change objectives and tie them into the Unifying Principle by stating that Jesus is a leader who can be trusted.

B. Briefly summarize the Background and The People, Places, and Times sections. Ask the class to comment on how they would respond to suffering if they lived in a similar setting.

C. Discuss why God allows His children to suffer for righteousness' sake.

5. Relating the Lesson to Life

A. Have volunteers respond to the Discuss the Meaning questions. Then explain that 2 Corinthians 13:5 teaches that we are to examine ourselves to see whether we are "in the faith."

B. In light of today's lesson, have students reflect and ask themselves: "Am I following Jesus' leadership?"

C. Ask the students: What can we learn from suffering for Christ's sake? Have we denied ourselves, taken up our cross, and followed Jesus? Are we following Jesus' example of godly discipline? Or are we inauthentic in our Christian witness?

6. Arousing Action

A. Ask the students to encourage someone who is going through some difficulty by sharing some of their trials and tribulations that have made them stronger in the faith.

B. Instruct the students to prepare for next week's lesson by reading the Daily Bible Readings for next week.

Worship Guide

For the Superintendent or Teacher
Theme: Christ as Leader
Theme Song: "I Am on the Battlefield for My Lord"
Devotional Reading: Proverbs 3:5–12
Prayer

CHRIST AS LEADER

Bible Background • HEBREWS 12:1–13
Printed Text • HEBREWS 12:1–13 Devotional Reading • PROVERBS 3:5–12

AIM for Change

By the end of the lesson, we will:

DISCUSS what makes a credible leader;

REFLECT on what makes Jesus a credible leader; and

COMMIT to following Jesus' example of godly discipline.

[handwritten notes: Strong Godly, Stable/committed, Knowledge/understanding, Integrity, Common ground.]

Keep in Mind

"Wherefore seeing we also are compassed about with so great a cloud of witnesses, let us lay aside every weight, and the sin which doth so easily beset us, and let us run with patience the race that is set before us" (Hebrews 12:1).

Focal Verses

KJV

Hebrews 12:1 Wherefore seeing we also are compassed about with so great a cloud of witnesses, let us lay aside every weight, and the sin which doth so easily beset us, and let us run with patience the race that is set before us,

2 Looking unto Jesus the author and finisher of our faith; who for the joy that was set before him endured the cross, despising the shame, and is set down at the right hand of the throne of God.

3 For consider him that endured such contradiction of sinners against himself, lest ye be wearied and faint in your minds.

4 Ye have not yet resisted unto blood, striving against sin.

5 And ye have forgotten the exhortation which speaketh unto you as unto children, My son, despise not thou the chastening of the Lord, nor faint when thou art rebuked of him:

6 For whom the Lord loveth he chasteneth, and scourgeth every son whom he receiveth.

7 If ye endure chastening, God dealeth with you as with sons; for what son is he whom the father chasteneth not?

8 But if ye be without chastisement, whereof all are partakers, then are ye bastards, and not sons.

9 Furthermore we have had fathers of our flesh which corrected us, and we gave them reverence: shall we not much rather be in subjection unto the Father of spirits, and live?

10 For they verily for a few days chastened us after their own pleasure; but he for our profit, that we might be partakers of his holiness.

NLT

Hebrews 12:1 Therefore, since we are surrounded by such a huge crowd of witnesses to the life of faith, let us strip off every weight that slows us down, especially the sin that so easily trips us up. And let us run with endurance the race God has set before us.

2 We do this by keeping our eyes on Jesus, the champion who initiates and perfects our faith. Because of the joy awaiting him, he endured the cross, disregarding its shame. Now he is seated in the place of honor beside God's throne.

3 Think of all the hostility he endured from sinful people; then you won't become weary and give up.

4 After all, you have not yet given your lives in your struggle against sin.

5 And have you forgotten the encouraging words God spoke to you as his children? He said, "My child, don't make light of the LORD's discipline, and don't give up when he corrects you.

6 For the LORD disciplines those he loves, and he punishes each one he accepts as his child."

7 As you endure this divine discipline, remember that God is treating you as his own children. Who ever heard of a child who is never disciplined by its father?

8 If God doesn't discipline you as he does all of his children, it means that you are illegitimate and are not really his children at all.

9 Since we respected our earthly fathers who disciplined us, shouldn't we submit even more to the discipline of the Father of our spirits, and live forever?

10 For our earthly fathers disciplined us for a few years, doing the best they knew how. But God's discipline is always good for us, so that we might share in his holiness.

11 Now no chastening for the present seemeth to be joyous, but grievous: nevertheless afterward it yieldeth the peaceable fruit of righteousness unto them which are exercised thereby.

12 Wherefore lift up the hands which hang down, and the feeble knees;

13 And make straight paths for your feet, lest that which is lame be turned out of the way; but let it rather be healed.

11 No discipline is enjoyable while it is happening—it's painful! But afterward there will be a peaceful harvest of right living for those who are trained in this way.

12 So take a new grip with your tired hands and strengthen your weak knees.

13 Mark out a straight path for your feet so that those who are weak and lame will not fall but become strong.

In Focus

Myra, a 35-year-old single mom, had worked for a Fortune 500 company for five years. She was well-liked, hardworking, and a team player; yet she had been laid off. So many questions ran through her mind as she struggled to understand why the Lord had allowed her to lose her job. After all, she had a young child to support and bills to pay. She was distressed and disappointed and couldn't understand why she was undergoing this fiery trial.

Her world had turned upside down at the news of her layoff. There were times when she felt like giving up. She couldn't see how she was going to pay her bills once her unemployment checks stopped coming. *What should I do?* she wondered. *How am I going to make it with no job and no money coming in?*

Everyone had a well-intentioned piece of advice to give her. Her mother told her to find a good husband. Her girlfriend told her to get a roommate. A former coworker suggested she beg for her old job back. Finally, Myra stopped feeling sorry for herself and did something about her situation. She remembered God's promise, "All things work together for good to them that love God, to them who are the called according to his purpose" (Romans 8:28).

She began to trust God for what direction she should take, and her faith began to increase. She decided to go back to school and get her MBA. Times were tough for her and her daughter, but they survived. She finally earned her MBA and soon thereafter found a better-paying job that had more prestige and responsibility.

Now she looks back on the day she got laid off and calls it a blessing in disguise. Without that trial, she never would have had the courage to go back to school. As she began to think more about it, she understood that the Lord allowed the suffering so that she would have the discipline to get her MBA degree. She discovered that her response to this trial brought out the best in her.

What do you think of when you think of leadership? In today's lesson, we see that Jesus set the perfect example as the leader who was tempted but did not give in. He endured the pain and shame of the Cross to achieve the joy and victory of eternal life with God.

The People, Places, and Times

Rome. As the capital city of Italy, it was the center of commerce, culture, and religion. A myriad of religions dotted the social landscape at the time this letter to the Hebrews was circulated. Rome was known to tolerate a plethora of religions. Judaism and Christianity were allowed to coexist here with other religions in a cornucopia of religious expression.

Believers in Rome. It was not easy or politically correct to be a Christian during this time. Christians in Rome had to deal with the threat of persecution by the Roman authorities, although none of them had become martyrs like Jesus, Stephen, and others. Because they were still alive, the writer encouraged them to continue to run their race and not give up. He reminded them that Jesus never gave up and neither should they.

Background

The letter to the Hebrews was written in response to the threat that believers might renounce Christianity and revert to Judaism. The writer wanted to inform his vacillating readers that Jesus Christ, the object of God's final revelation, is superior to the greatest of Judaism's heroes.

The writer also wanted to highlight and remind his audience of the efficacy of Jesus' power of salvation. He reminded them that whereas the Jewish legal sacrificial system was powerless to remit sins,

Jesus, the eternal High Priest, "is able also to save them to the uttermost that come unto God by him, seeing he ever liveth to make intercession for them" (Hebrews 7:25). Furthermore, the writer explains the need for patient endurance amid the persecution and sufferings to which the heirs of eternal salvation are inevitably exposed.

He suggests that all Christians emulate Jesus' suffering and patience if they anticipate an eternal reward.

At-A-Glance

1. Believers Must Run the Race (Hebrews 12:1–2)
2. Believers Must Develop Endurance (vv. 3–6)
3. Believers Must Learn to Enjoy the Discipline of the Lord (vv. 7–11)
4. Believers Must Increase Their Discipleship and Become an Example (vv. 12–13)

In Depth

1. Believers Must Run the Race (Hebrews 12:1–2)

The writer encourages the Christian readers to continue to run their race of discipleship no matter what tries to hinder them. He tells them to "lay aside every weight."

Being a Christian was not an easy thing back then, and it still isn't today. It is a lifelong commitment that involves peaks and valleys, good times and bad times, and sunshine and rain. Christian discipleship is not a sprint; it is a marathon. That is why the author tells his audience to run with "perseverance" (v. 1, NIV). Perseverance is an inner quality that allows one to continue in some course of action in spite of difficulty or opposition. To persevere is to be steadfast in a particular purpose.

Disciples of Jesus Christ must always look to Jesus as the ultimate model of perseverance. In His ministry He suffered insults and attempts on His life. He persisted even though His hometown and relatives rejected Him. He overcame the obstinacy of His followers and betrayal by one of His own. He never faltered during the unjust criminal trial that accused Him of sedition and heresy—or the beating by the Roman police force. Finally, He did not waver on the Cross at Calvary. He did all of that not only so future generations of believers would have access to a spiritual power potent enough to change the world, but

also to set an example of the perfect leader who was tempted but did not give in.

As we continue to live as ambassadors of Christ, let us persevere on our jobs, in our homes, and in our communities. God demands our best in this life. No matter what hardships we go through, our history is peppered with credible leaders who have overcome greater hardships than we have ever had to imagine. We can learn from them. If they made it, surely we can make it. With God on our side and "a great cloud of witnesses" cheering us on, we can get through any adverse situation we face.

2. Believers Must Develop Endurance (vv. 3–6)

The writer of Hebrews encouraged the Christians in Rome to consider Jesus' life when they began to complain about the adversity they had to face. He supported his argument by testifying that they had not faced persecution to the degree that they had shed their own blood. He also let them know that trials suffered for righteousness' sake could be viewed as the "chastening of the Lord" (v. 5). The Lord's chastening is not arbitrary or without direction—it always has a purpose. The writer suggests that trials could be disciplinary correction and a part of God's overall plan to edify His children. Corrective discipline is always a good thing and a symbol of love. When an earthly father exercises discipline on his child, it is beneficial to the child so the same wrong actions will not be repeated. Our heavenly Father operates in the same way. Because God loves us, He disciplines us so we will not commit the same sins or something worse.

3. Believers Must Learn to Enjoy the Discipline of the Lord (vv. 7–11)

The writer of Hebrews presents yet another reason that believers should cheerfully bear affliction when it comes. Christians are encouraged to endure the discipline of the Lord because it is the mark of sonship as well as the way to become more holy and righteous.

The Bible is clear that those who suffer for righteousness' sake glorify God: "Beloved, think it not strange concerning the fiery trial which is to try you, as though some strange thing happened unto you: But rejoice, inasmuch as ye are partakers of Christ's sufferings; that, when his glory shall be revealed, ye may be glad also with exceeding joy" (1 Peter 4:12–13). Second Timothy 2:12 says, "If we suffer, we shall also reign with him: if we deny him, he also will deny us." The writers insist that we must look on all the hardships of life as the discipline of God—sent to work, not for our harm, but for our ultimate and highest good.

Consider the failure to discipline a child who is disobedient. It is not a mark of trustworthiness or love, but of apathy and unconcern. Likewise, God's willingness to discipline us is a mark of our sonship. It is never pleasant to be corrected and disciplined by God, but His discipline is a sign of His deep love for us. When God corrects you, see it as proof of His love and His ability to lead you in the right direction, and ask Him what He is working to teach you.

4. Believers Must Increase Their Discipleship and Become an Example (vv. 12–13)

Since we know that hardship, trials, and suffering are a part of the Christian journey, we should face them with courage. To accept Christ into our lives is to allow the prospect of facing hardship. Jesus told His disciples, "If any man will come after me, let him deny himself, and take up his cross, and follow me" (Matthew 16:24).

We are to be an example for future generations. We are to be guides and role models for our children, who are standing on our shoulders. If we shrink in the midst of painful trials, what kind of example will we set for them? We must not live with only our own survival in mind. Others will follow our example, and we definitely have a responsibility to them if we are living for Christ. We also have a responsibility to support weaker Christians who may get discouraged by the Lord's discipline. We are to bear the burdens of the weak, for this is what Christ did. Suffering brings us into higher levels of compassion. As a people, where would we be without enduring struggles?

Frederick Douglass once said, "Without struggle there can be no progress." The great Civil Rights martyr, Rev. Dr. Martin Luther King Jr., said, "If a man has not found a cause worth dying for, then he is not fit to live." Any cause worth giving your life for will involve suffering for righteousness' sake. But we have an eternal promise from Jesus. He told His disciples to be of good cheer because He had overcome the world (John 16:33).

Therefore, no matter what comes against us in the world, whether rumors of war, the fear of terrorist attacks, the elimination of affirmative action, job layoffs, or trouble in our marriages, we know that God is our refuge and a very present help in the time of trouble (cf. Psalm 46:1; 91:1–9). We cannot shrink in the midst of painful trials. If we believe that our God will deliver us, then we cannot live in fear or anger when we face fiery trials.

Does your behavior in the midst of a trial make it easier for others to believe in and follow Christ, and to mature in Him? Or would those who follow you end up on the wrong path, lost and confused?

Search the Scriptures

1. What should inspire Christians to hold on to their faith (Hebrews 12:1)?

2. Why is our Christianity never to be stationary (v. 1)?

3. Who are we to model ourselves after (v. 2)?

4. How are we to handle the Lord's chastening (vv. 5–6)?

5. What is the purpose of trials and tribulations (v. 7)?

6. What is the end result of God's chastening (vv. 10–11)?

Discuss the Meaning

1. What makes Jesus a credible leader? How would you have turned out if the Lord had not chastised you? Think about your children or children you know. Imagine how they would turn out without someone to discipline them.

2. Why is it so hard for Christians to adjust to suffering? Have you been told that once you give your life to Jesus, everything will be all right? Have we been anesthetized into believing that children of God are exempt from suffering?

3. Many of us have needed to be disciplined into spiritual shape. As you look back over your life, in what ways has God disciplined you? How did you feel while going through it? How did you benefit from it?

Lesson in Our Society

Before a professional sports team takes the field, it goes through training camp. Training camp is a fiery trial that most players hate. However, veterans and rookies alike must endure training camp in order to learn new plays, to get into shape, and, most important, to learn how to become a disciplined and victorious team.

If we Christians are going to be victorious, we have to go through our own version of training camp. God, our coach (leader), wants to turn us into a well-coached, well-trained, and well-disciplined body of believers. In order to do that, God allows some adversity into our lives. Christians are like tea bags. In order for our rich and robust flavor to come out, we have to be placed in some hot water.

Make It Happen

Many great biblical and historical characters had to endure much suffering for the causes they supported, whether it was for the spread of Christianity or in the fight for civil rights. Remember that life is a marathon, not a sprint. If we are going to be successful, individually and collectively, we have to keep our eyes on the prize. Individually, that prize is the likeness of Jesus Christ; collectively, the prize is to make the kingdom of God a reality in our midst.

Commit to following Jesus' example of godly discipline. Continue working toward the goals that you have, never giving up, and keeping your eyes on the prize. Anything worth having is worth all of the suffering, trials, and tribulations that come along on the journey. Therefore, embrace the struggle because it will bring discipline to your life; and once you achieve your goals, you can give God the glory for the marvelous things He has done.

Follow the Spirit

What God wants me to do:

_____

_____

Remember Your Thoughts

Special insights I have learned:

_____

_____

More Light on the Text

Hebrews 12:1–13

1 Wherefore seeing we also are compassed about with so great a cloud of witnesses, let us lay aside every weight, and the sin which doth so easily beset us, and let us run with patience the race that is set before us,

In this verse, the "great cloud of witnesses" is referring to those persons mentioned in chapter 11. Here, the writer is saying that those who have gone before are an example to living the life of faith. God has confirmed their faithfulness, and they can be seen as examples of those who endured. Therefore, in light of our inspiring audience, we must rid ourselves of "every weight" and "run with patience."

The Greek word for "patience" is *hupomone* (**hoo-po-mo-NAY**), which is derived from two Greek words: *hupo* (**hoo-PAW**), meaning "under," and *meno* (**MEN-oh**), meaning "to remain." In other words, the Greek root suggests that by remaining under some trial, we may be molded to fit God's purposes.

2 Looking unto Jesus the author and finisher of our faith; who for the joy that was set before him endured the cross, despising the shame, and is set down at the right hand of the throne of God. 3 For consider him that endured such contradiction of sinners against himself, lest ye be wearied and faint in your minds.

To run the race, one must stay focused on Jesus, as implied here by the use of the Greek word *aphorao* (**ahf-or-AH-oh**), translated as "looking." To *aphorao* means "to turn the eyes away from other things and fix them on something else"—namely Jesus. We do so because Jesus is the "author" (Gk. *archegos*, **ar-khay-GOSS**), meaning chief leader, and the "finisher" (Gk. *teleiotes*, **tel-ay-o-TAYSS**), which means "perfecter, of faith." In other words, Jesus' life is the perfect example of faith.

The word *endured* comes from *hupomeno* (Gk. **hoop-om-EN-oh**), meaning "to remain or tarry." Jesus chose to remain on the Cross and bear the shame of crucifixion in order to save humanity. Jesus focused on the future and finished the work of our redemption, bringing many to glory (Hebrews 2:10).

4 Ye have not yet resisted unto blood, striving against sin.

Here the readers are reminded that although they may have suffered great persecution (Hebrews 10:32–34), none have shed blood and died as Jesus did. None had yet become martyrs because of having confessed Jesus as their Messiah or Saviour.

5 And ye have forgotten the exhortation that speaketh unto you as unto children, My son, despise not thou the chastening of the Lord, nor faint when thou art rebuked of him: 6 For whom the Lord loveth he chasteneth, and scourgeth every son he receiveth.

In verses 5 and 6 the author quotes Proverbs 3:11–12. The Lord disciplines those He loves. In these verses, the reader is reminded of the parent-child relationship. Undisciplined children are unloved children. In this instance, the use of the Greek word *paideia* (**pie-DAY-ah**) means to nurture or give instruction. The writer is saying that one should not make light of God's instruction, but welcome it as a means of spiritual growth.

7 If ye endure chastening, God dealeth with you as with sons; for what son is he whom the father chasteneth not? 8 But if ye be without chastisement, whereof all are partakers, then are ye bastards, and not sons.

Christians should view trials as a form of divine discipline. Just as a parent would discipline a child, so too God deals with the sinner. No wise father would allow his children to continue exhibiting bad behavior and not correct it. Therefore, receiving discipline can be viewed as a sign of God's Fatherly love.

9 Furthermore we have had fathers of our flesh which corrected us, and we gave them reverence: shall we not much rather be in subjection unto the Father of spirits, and live?

God here is called "the Father of spirits" (an expression that occurs only here in the New Testament)—in contrast to the human "fathers of our flesh." The writer makes a comparison between an earthly father and the Heavenly Father. The argument being, if earthly parents discipline us and we respect them for it over the long run, then we should respect our Heavenly Father even more.

10 For they verily for a few days chastened us after their own pleasure; but he for our profit, that we might be partakers of his holiness.

Verse 10 points out the difference between human discipline and heaven's discipline. The Greek word for "profit" is *sumphero* (**soom-FEHR-oh**), which means "to help, to be profitable, or to be expedient." Our earthly parents discipline us "for a few days," whereas God's discipline gives us an eternal benefit. Human discipline is often inconsistent and usually provides a temporary benefit. However, the long-range goal in God's discipline is that we might be "partakers" (Gk. *metalambano*, **met-ahl-ahm-BAHN-oh**) of His holiness. Nothing pleases God more than children who grow to emulate Him.

11 Now no chastening for the present seemeth to be joyous, but grievous: nevertheless afterward it yieldeth the peaceable fruit of righteousness unto them which are exercised thereby.

Present discipline seems painful because it is! The purpose of our pain is to produce Christlike behavior. Sometimes we have to endure painful discipline. The Greek word for "exercised" is *gumnazo* (**goom-NAHD-zoh**), and as used here it implies exercise of the mind in order to endure persecution. God desires for His children to have fruitful lives, and oftentimes that requires pain and sacrifice.

12 Wherefore lift up the hands which hang down, and the feeble knees; 13 And make straight paths for your feet, lest that which is lame be turned out of the way; but let it rather be healed.

Running God's race is not easy. Hands, knees, and feet are key body parts for any runner (cf. Isaiah 35:3). While our eyes need to be fixed on Jesus, we need straight paths for our feet. In Greek the word "straight" is *orthas* (**or-THOSS**), which means "upright." Therefore, if we strive to keep our path in life straight and run faithfully, at the end of life's track meet we will be rewarded by the greatest Runner— the One whose discipline included crucifixion wounds in His hands and feet!

Daily Bible Readings

M: Seek God's Leadership and Discipline
Proverbs 3:5–12
T: Endure the Race
Hebrews 12:1–3
W: Endure Trials and Discipline
Hebrews 12:4–7
T: Necessity of Discipline
Hebrews 12:8–11
F: Be Strong and Be Healed
Hebrews 12:12–13
S: Be Humble Like Christ
Philippians 2:1–4
S: Follow Christ's Example
Philippians 2:5–11

TEACHING TIPS

June 29
Bible Study Guide 5

1. Words You Should Know
A. **Without Covetousness** (Hebrews 13:5) *aphilarguros* (Gk.)—To be free from the love of money.

B. **Helper** (v. 6) *boethos* (Gk.)—A term that signifies God's assistance of His saints.

2. Teacher Preparation
Unifying Principle—Finding Stability and Permanence Today Times change, but Jesus never changes. In a world of rapid change, people seek stability. Where can we find such grounding? God gave Jesus eternal life so that humans would have a firm foundation for living in relationship to God and others.

A. To prepare for today's lesson, pray that you will clearly communicate the Word of God and that in your attitudes and actions you will be a leader who imitates Christ.

B. Do a personal assessment as you study the AIM for Change, the Focal Verses, Background, and In Depth sections for this lesson. Ask yourself, "How can I guide learners by modeling for them a positive Christian example?"

C. Read The People, Places, and Times and More Light on the Text sections.

D. Study the related information found in the *Precepts For Living*® CD-ROM and *Precepts For Living*® *Personal Study Guide.*

3. Starting the Lesson
A. Begin the lesson with a time of prayer and meditation using the Devotional Readings as a guide.

B. Before starting today's lesson, ask for volunteers to share their experiences from last week's Make It Happen suggestion.

C. Next, reinforce the AIM for Change objectives and Unifying Principle for today's lesson by reminding the class that today's Scripture text offers several admonitions of how to love and care for one another.

D. Ask a volunteer to read the In Focus story aloud. Ask the class members how they react when they are approached by a stranger in need.

4. Getting into the Lesson
A. Divide the class into three groups and assign each group a section of the Focal Verses and In Depth based on the At-A-Glance outline. Have the groups discuss the sections and appoint a speaker to present the highlights to the class.

B. Allow 15 minutes for the discussion, and then bring the class back together for the presentations.

5. Relating the Lesson to Life
A. Give the students time to answer the Search the Scriptures and Discuss the Meaning questions to help them relate the text to their personal lives.

B. Reserve some time for thoughts on the Lesson in Our Society to help the students apply the lesson to some of today's social concerns.

6. Arousing Action
A. Help the students organize and put into practice this week's Make It Happen suggestion, or challenge them to think of their own ideas and put them into action.

B. Encourage the students to read the Daily Bible Readings for next week. This will reinforce the lesson and foster good Bible study habits.

C. Close the class with prayer.

Worship Guide

For the Superintendent or Teacher
Theme: The Eternal Christ
Theme Song: "Jesus, Use Me"
Devotional Reading: Psalm 118:5–9
Prayer

FEEL MY PAIN

THE ETERNAL CHRIST

Bible Background • HEBREWS 13:1–16
Printed Text • HEBREWS 13:1–16 Devotional Reading • PSALM 118:5–9

AIM for Change

By the end of the lesson, we will:

RECOGNIZE that we can live godly lives based upon our relationship to our unchanging Lord;

OFFER a sacrifice of praise to our Lord, who is the same yesterday, today, and forever; and

DECIDE to express our faith by reaching out in service to the people in our communities.

Keep in Mind

"Jesus Christ the same yesterday, and to day, and for ever" (Hebrews 13:8).

Focal Verses

KJV

Hebrews 13:1 Let brotherly love continue.

2 Be not forgetful to entertain strangers: for thereby some have entertained angels unawares.

3 Remember them that are in bonds, as bound with them; and them which suffer adversity, as being yourselves also in the body.

4 Marriage is honorable in all, and the bed undefiled: but whoremongers and adulterers God will judge.

5 Let your conversation be without covetousness; and be content with such things as ye have: for he hath said, I will never leave thee, nor forsake thee.

6 So that we may boldly say, The Lord is my helper, and I will not fear what man shall do unto me.

7 Remember them which have the rule over you, who have spoken unto you the word of God: whose faith follow, considering the end of their conversation.

8 Jesus Christ the same yesterday, and to day, and for ever.

9 Be not carried about with divers and strange doctrines. For it is a good thing that the heart be established with grace; not with meats, which have not profited them that have been occupied therein.

10 We have an altar, whereof they have no right to eat which serve the tabernacle.

11 For the bodies of those beasts, whose blood is brought into the sanctuary by the high priest for sin, are burned without the camp.

12 Wherefore Jesus also, that he might sanctify the people with his own blood, suffered without the gate.

NLT

Hebrews 13:1 Keep on loving each other as brothers and sisters.

2 Don't forget to show hospitality to strangers, for some who have done this have entertained angels without realizing it!

3 Remember those in prison, as if you were there yourself. Remember also those being mistreated, as if you felt their pain in your own bodies.

4 Give honor to marriage, and remain faithful to one another in marriage. God will surely judge people who are immoral and those who commit adultery.

5 Don't love money; be satisfied with what you have. For God has said, "I will never fail you. I will never abandon you."

6 So we can say with confidence, "The LORD is my helper, so I will have no fear. What can mere people do to me?"

7 Remember your leaders who taught you the word of God. Think of all the good that has come from their lives, and follow the example of their faith.

8 Jesus Christ is the same yesterday, today, and forever.

9 So do not be attracted by strange, new ideas. Your strength comes from God's grace, not from rules about food, which don't help those who follow them.

10 We have an altar from which the priests in the Tabernacle have no right to eat.

11 Under the old system, the high priest brought the blood of animals into the Holy Place as a sacrifice for sin, and the bodies of the animals were burned outside the camp.

12 So also Jesus suffered and died outside the city gates to make his people holy by means of his own blood.

13 Let us go forth therefore unto him without the camp, bearing his reproach.

14 For here have we no continuing city, but we seek one to come.

15 By him therefore let us offer the sacrifice of praise to God continually, that is, the fruit of our lips giving thanks to his name.

16 But to do good and to communicate forget not: for with such sacrifices God is well pleased.

13 So let us go out to him, outside the camp, and bear the disgrace he bore.

14 For this world is not our permanent home; we are looking forward to a home yet to come.

15 Therefore, let us offer through Jesus a continual sacrifice of praise to God, proclaiming our <u>allegiance to his name.</u>

16 And don't forget to do good and to share with those in need. These are the sacrifices that please God.

In Focus

On Kathy's annual trip down South, she loved stopping at one of her favorite soul food restaurants along the way. As she neared the restaurant, all she could think about was how good those buttered biscuits with honey were going to taste.

When she arrived at the restaurant, she got her food and made her way to a nearby table. A man approached her asking for spare change. He said he needed the money to take his little girl to a doctor. Kathy had some extra change she could have given him, but his appearance caused her to doubt his honesty. Without even thinking, she told the man she didn't give money to strangers, especially not to men. She added somewhat sarcastically that she expected men to give her money.

Kathy watched the man leave the restaurant with the little girl trailing behind him. Then that still, small voice she had come to recognize as the Holy Spirit spoke to her heart.

Just as outward appearances influence the way we respond to strangers, our actions affect the way non-Christians view Christianity. Today's lesson focuses our attention on the nature of Jesus' servanthood and how serving one another is important.

The People, Places, and Times

Prisons. Christians in the early church were sometimes imprisoned for their faith. When this occurred, other Christians ran to their aid. They tried to redeem their imprisoned brethren by any means necessary. If they could not redeem them, they stood by them until they were either executed or released.

Licinius. A Roman emperor who passed legislation declaring that anyone showing kindness to prisoners would receive the same punishment as those they helped. In spite of this, Christians continued to comfort their imprisoned brethren.

Background

Hebrew Christians in the early church often suffered persecution, ridicule, and open hatred by other Jews. Giving up long-held religious traditions to follow Christ cost these believers dearly. The unknown writer of Hebrews teaches how emulating Christ's superior lifestyle through fellowship (Hebrews 10:19–31), perseverance (10:32–12:13), sanctification (12:14–29), and a life of service to others (13:1–21) would demonstrate the reality of the living Christ to their unsaved loved ones.

At-A-Glance

1. Loving, the Mark of Christianity
(Hebrews 13:1–6)
2. Submitting to Godly Leadership
(vv. 7–8)
3. Offering Acceptable Sacrifices
(vv. 9–16)

In Depth

1. Loving, the Mark of Christianity (Hebrews 13:1–6)

Hebrew Christians suffered great persecution and rejection because of their faith in Christ. Because the persecution came from family and former friends, it was vital for believers to form healthy relationships among themselves. That's why the writer of the epistle admonishes these second-generation Christians to remember to keep on loving one another (13:1).

Evidence of a healthy Christian life is the way Christians get along with each other. One of the ways we demonstrate our love for others is through Christian hospitality. Hebrew Christians were encouraged to offer hospitality to strangers. This hospitality involved both housing and caring for the needs of their guests. The writer alludes to Abraham opening his tent to three travelers, two of whom turned out to be angels, and the third one God Himself (Genesis 18:1–8).

Christian love never forgets. The writer instructs his readers to remember those who have been imprisoned for their faith. These prisoners were dependent on people outside for warm clothes and healthy food. Because the church is one body, whenever one suffers, all suffer, and all pitch in to help.

The first place love should be demonstrated is in marriage. God Himself formed the institution of marriage to be a permanent, monogamous, heterosexual union (Genesis 2:24). The marriage covenant is honorable in God's sight (Hebrews 13:4), and those who violate this covenant "God will judge"—execute divine vengeance on.

Believers show love for their communities through godly behavior ("conversation," v. 5). The key to dealing with others is integrity. Integrity results from being content with what God has blessed us with and depending on God, who will never leave us or forsake us (v. 6), to meet our needs. Covetousness is the enemy of integrity, just as greed is the enemy of contentment. The believer's contentment comes from knowing that God is our source and helper.

2. Submitting to Godly Leadership (vv. 7–8)

Living responsibly also includes submitting to godly leadership. Godly leaders have a responsibility to protect the purity of the Gospel and transfer the Gospel message to future generations. Leaders who preach the truth of God's Word and live holy lives serve as examples of faith and holiness.

The phrase "have the rule over you" (v. 7) also appears in verses 17 and 24. The phrase refers to all those who had preached and taught the Word of God to them. The word "remember" may suggest that these particular leaders have died (perhaps martyred) and should not be forgotten. Christian leaders who have fought the good fight and finished their course should be remembered for their wisdom and their godly lives.

The Hebrew believers could imitate their leaders' faith and remember their victories. The words and deeds of godly leaders all point to Christ as the ultimate example of faithfulness. Church leaders live and die, come and go, but Christ remains the same yesterday, today, and forever (v. 8).

3. Offering Acceptable Sacrifices (vv. 9–16)

Christians find stability in Christ. This stability should stop us from being blown around by "every wind of teaching and by the cunning and craftiness of men" (Ephesians 4:14, NIV). The writer of Hebrews warned his audience against being carried away by strange doctrines (Hebrews 13:9). Some of these strange doctrines included adding Jewish religious practices such as animal sacrifice to Christian worship.

He explained that Christians do not need to perform animal sacrifices. Jesus has become our living sacrifice once and for all. Following the old sacrificial system could influence behavior, but it could not change hearts. To continue under the old system would deny the effectiveness of Christ's sacrifice.

Under the Levitical system, priests were allowed to eat the meat of ordinary sacrifices, but on the Day of Atonement they were not. The bodies of animals sacrificed on this holy day were taken outside of the Israelites' camp and burned (Leviticus 4:21; 16:27). It was the blood that provided the ceremonial cleansing under the old covenant. The blood was taken into the sanctuary to be sprinkled on the lid of the Ark of the Covenant. Just as sacrificial animals were burned outside the camp, Jesus suffered and died outside the city's gate (John 19:17–20). His blood accomplished what animal sacrifices could never accomplish—sanctification for God's people.

The writer parallels the burning of sacrificial animals outside the camp with Jesus' body being hung outside of Jerusalem's walls. He encourages his readers to forsake Jewish sacrificial rites and be clearly identified with Jesus. In those days, to be "outside the camp" meant to be unclean. Those who followed Christ had to be ready to endure the reproach of their people. They would be considered unclean by their Jewish brethren.

True Christianity often carries with it a stigma that believers must be prepared to bear. Bearing the shame of identification with Jesus becomes easier when we recognize that our home is not in a city made by human hands, but a kingdom established eternally in the heavens (Hebrews 13:14).

Under the new covenant all believers are priests (1 Peter 2:5). A part of our responsibilities as priests is to offer sacrifices to God. However, these sacrifices are not the offering of animals; they are submitted hearts manifested through sacrifices of praise that exalt God's holy name.

Search the Scriptures

1. Christians are encouraged to offer hospitality to strangers. How were some believers who followed this advice blessed (Hebrews 13:2)?

2. What will happen to those who violate their marriage vows (v. 4)?

3. What assurance do we have as believers to help us to be content in this life (v. 5)?

4. Jesus was crucified on a hill called Calvary. Where was this hill in relation to the city (v. 12)?

5. What is the sacrifice that all Christians should offer to God (v. 15)?

Discuss the Meaning

1. The Hebrew Christians were instructed to remember those who were in bonds. How can we comfort those who are in prison?

2. Scripture admonishes us to not be carried away with various strange doctrines (v. 9). What strange doctrines are infiltrating the modern-day church? How can believers protect themselves from being "carried away" by them?

Lesson in Our Society

Times change, but the love and faithfulness of Jesus never changes. Jesus Christ, our High Priest, "is the same yesterday, and to day, and for ever" (v. 8). His grace and mercy, as well as His standards for holy living, endure unchanged through every generation. While the culture around us may appear to be getting increasingly wicked, Jesus is available to help us "walk worthy of the vocation wherewith [we] are called" (Ephesians 4:1).

Make It Happen

Christians should let our light shine by showing brotherly love, being hospitable, and having sympathy for those in trouble. This week look for ways you can be of service to someone in your neighborhood. It would be even better if the person or people you help were strangers. Use your service as an opportunity to share the Gospel with them. Be prepared to share your experiences with the class next week.

Follow the Spirit

What He wants me to do:

_____

_____

Remember Your Thoughts

Special insights I learned:

_____

_____

More Light on the Text
Hebrews 13:1–16

The writer of Hebrews reminds us that we can walk worthy of our calling because Christ our eternal Intercessor and Redeemer has promised to help us and never leave us. To this end our study of Hebrews concludes with a number of exhortations urging us to live chaste lives and to extend generosity, kindness, and love toward others.

1 Let brotherly love continue.

There is no greater virtue than *philadelphia* (Gk. **fil-ah-del-FEE-ah**), translated here as "brotherly love." Brotherly love is the love Christians have for one another, which grows out of a common spiritual life. It stands to reason that those who share in the saving work of Christ should also have Christ's kind of love for one another.

2 Be not forgetful to entertain strangers: for thereby some have entertained angels unawares.

In addition to demonstrating brotherly love toward one another, Christians are also urged to *philonexia* (Gk. **fil-on-ex-EE-ah**), translated here "to entertain strangers." A more accurate translation would read "to be hospitable toward strangers." This translation is also in keeping with the cultural and social values of that day. According to *The Handbook of Social Values*, in the world of the Bible, hospitality was shown by receiving strangers, not by entertaining family and friends. Hospitality was the way outsiders were received and changed from strangers to guests.

The phrase "entertained angels unawares" does not promote hospitality as a way to gain friendship with an angel. Instead, it refers to the possibility that one may unwittingly entertain angelic guests. The phrase is also the writer's way to say that good things tend to follow acts of hospitality.

Source:
Pilch, John J., and Bruce J. Malina, eds. *Handbook of Biblical Social Values.* Peabody, Mass.: Hendrickson Publishers, 1998).

3 Remember them that are in bonds, as bound with them; and them which suffer adversity, as being yourselves also in the body.

Here we are reminded that compassionate concern for prisoners is a vital part of the Christian's witness. Such a witness was critically important in the world of the Bible because prisoners were not treated well. In fact, they were often mistreated. Consequently, they were dependent upon persons outside the penal system for basic necessities such as food and clean clothing. Christians were, therefore, encouraged to reach out and relate to prisoners "as bound with them . . . as being yourselves also in the body." In other words, believers were to relate to prisoners as if they themselves were fellow prisoners. The same compassionate concern was to be extended to all who are mistreated and who "suffer adversity."

4 Marriage is honourable in all, and the bed undefiled: but whoremongers and adulterers God will judge.

In biblical days, many ascetics held marriage in dishonor (1 Timothy 4:3–5). Under the old Levitical covenant, every act of sexual intercourse, even within marriage, was defiling (Leviticus 15:16–18). Moreover, the prevailing secular culture of the day viewed chastity as an unreasonable demand.

In opposition to these views, the writer makes a quick reference to the Christian stance toward marriage, the marriage bed, and all forms of sexual sin. Marriage is to be held in honor. There is nothing defiling about the marriage bed—the term "marriage bed" is a euphemism for sexual intercourse within marriage. Thus, the writer teaches that sexuality within marriage is honorable. However, all sexual

sins—any sexual activity with someone to whom you are not married—are a violation of God's plan. Those who engage in such activity will come under the "judgment" (Gk. *krino*, **KREE-noh**, translated with emphasis) of God!

5 Let your conversation be without covetousness; and be content with such things as ye have: for he hath said, I will never leave thee, nor forsake thee.

Love of money is an ever-present temptation. It is the root of all evils; and those who have yielded to this temptation "have erred from the faith, and pierced themselves through with many sorrows" (1 Timothy 6:10). Thus, the relevance of the author's exhortation: "Let your conversation be without covetousness; and be content with such things as ye have." The covetous always want and chase after more and tend to fear losing what they have, but those who have accepted the eternal Christ as their Lord feel secure in knowing that God will never leave them nor forsake them. The Lord is their Shepherd, and they shall not want. Even though they may have little, the eternal Christ enables them to live as though they possessed everything (2 Corinthians 6:10).

With faith in the eternal Christ, it is possible for all believers to live in the knowledge that God is our helper.

6 So that we may boldly say, The Lord is my helper, and I will not fear what man shall do unto me.

When God is on our side, we can trust Him and not worry about other people or our circumstances. Admittedly, it will take courage to do so, but we can give up the covetous concern for money and live free from worry like the birds of the air, knowing that our Heavenly Father will provide. It is little wonder that people of such faith can "boldly say (Gk. *tharrhountas hemas legein*, **thar-ROON-toss hay-MAHSS LEG-ayn**), The Lord is my helper, and I will not fear what man shall do unto me."

7 Remember them which have the rule over you, who have spoken unto you the word of God: whose faith follow, considering the end of their conversation.

While many Scriptures talk about how leaders should behave, fewer talk about how believers should relate to their leaders. Here Christians are admonished to "remember" (Gk. *mnemoneuo*, **mnay-mon-YOO-oh**), but the intended meaning is to bring to the surface of your memory and with respect and honor keep in mind constantly those who have authority over you.

What are believers to remember about their leaders? They are to remember that their leaders have shared the Word of God with them. They are to remember their leaders' faith and imitate such faith in their own lives. Finally, if the leaders they remember are dead, they should remember and learn valuable lessons from the outcome of their lives.

8 Jesus Christ the same yesterday, and to day, and for ever.

This verse should probably be understood in comparison with earthly leaders, who come and go. But Jesus Christ is eternal. He is with us forever, and His call for us to live godly lives never changes. Therefore, we can confidently base our conduct upon His unchanging character and Word.

"Jesus Christ the same yesterday, and to day, and for ever" (Hebrews 13:8).

(1 Corinthians 8:8); only His grace can strengthen and establish our hearts in ways that please God.

9 Be not carried about with divers and strange doctrines. For it is a good thing that the heart be established with grace; not with meats, which have not profited them that have been occupied therein.

We are not told what "divers and strange doctrines" are in question. The writer may be responding to a resurgence of the teachings of the Judaizers (those who would return Christian believers to keeping the Mosaic Law, including circumcision and dietary laws). It is sufficient to know that both the author and his original readers knew. It appears from the writer's use of the word "meats" (Gk. *broma*, **BROH-mah**) that the erroneous teachings had something to do with foods, but we cannot be certain. We can know, however, that the teachings were in radical opposition to those accepted by the writer.

In any event, readers of the text are urged to remember that spiritual growth occurs not by the foods we eat, but by the grace afforded us through faith in the eternal Christ. "For the kingdom of God is not meat and drink; but righteousness, and peace, and joy in the Holy Ghost" (Romans 14:17). Food that enters the stomach will not commend us to God

10 We have an altar, whereof they have no right to eat which serve the tabernacle. 11 For the bodies of those beasts, whose blood is brought into the sanctuary by the high priest for sin, are burned without the camp. 12 Wherefore Jesus also, that he might sanctify the people with his own blood, suffered without the gate.

Verses 10–13 form another brief and distinct exhortation. The central message of this exhortation is in the opening confessional phrase: "We have an altar." What are we to understand about this altar, and who are the people who "have no right to eat"? Neither of these questions is easily answered, and there is little agreement when possible answers are offered.

Given the distinctions made throughout Hebrews between the old and new covenants, our "altar" should probably be understood metaphorically as a reference to the sacrifice of the eternal Christ.

In answer to the second question, the writer goes on to make the point that since the meat of sacrificial animals under the old covenant was not eaten by the high priest but rather burned outside ("without") the camp, so also did Christ suffer outside the gate "that he might sanctify the people with his own blood" (v. 12).

13 Let us go forth therefore unto him without the camp, bearing his reproach.

Since Jesus suffered outside the gate, the author's readers are now encouraged "to go to Jesus outside the camp," meaning outside of Judaism, outside the earthly city, and outside of the confines of the old covenant. For to remain with the ways of the old covenant is tantamount to living apart from Christ. Finally, those who identify themselves with Christ outside the camp should anticipate "reproach," but the scorn and reproach cannot compare with the joy that comes from being in fellowship with the eternal Christ.

14 For here have we no continuing city, but we seek one to come.

Again, Christians are encouraged to go to Jesus outside the camp, but this time for an additional reason: They have no stake in a city and way of life regulated by the old covenant. Christians are seeking an eternal city where Christ abides.

15 By him therefore let us offer the sacrifice of praise to God continually, that is, the fruit of our lips giving thanks to his name.

The writer's readers are here reminded that acceptable sacrifices are offered to God through Jesus Christ and not through the priests of the old covenant. Moreover, their sacrificial offerings are to be words of praise voiced with hearts overflowing with gratitude for what God has done through Christ and a commitment to confess His name.

16 But to do good and to communicate forget not: for with such sacrifices God is well pleased.

The writer brings his timely exhortations to a close with the mention of two more sacrifices of praise that Christians can offer to God: doing good and sharing in Christian fellowship with other believers. The Greek word *koinonia* (**koy-nohn-EE-ah**), translated here as "to communicate," is best translated "fellowship."

In the final analysis, our response to what Christ has done involves our offering praise, acts of kindness, and love through various expressions of love and concern toward all persons for whom Christ died outside the gate. Our response to what Christ has done also involves our testifying to others about how God has forgiven our sins through the blood of Jesus. What He has done for us, He stands eternally ready to do for others.

Daily Bible Readings

M: Take Refuge in God
Psalm 118:5–9
T: Christ as Supreme and Eternal
Colossians 1:15–20
W: Show Hospitality and Courage
Hebrews 13:1–6
T: True Leaders to Imitate
Hebrews 13:7–9
F: Confess Christ's Name
Hebrews 13:10–16
S: A Leader Who Professes Christ
Philippians 3:12–16
S: A Leader Looking to Christ Eternal
Philippians 3:17–21

TEACHING TIPS

July 6
Bible Study Guide 6

1. Words You Should Know
A. Doctrine (Luke 4:32) *didache* (Gk.)—Teachings or principles that form the basis of a religious belief system.

B. Word (v. 32) *logos* (Gk.)—Sayings or statements.

C. Authority (20:2, 8) *exousia* (Gk.)—The source from which ability and authority to rule is drawn.

2. Teacher Preparation
Unifying Principle—Teaching That Transforms Many teachers bombard us with competing information. How do we discern which teachers give information of lasting value? Jesus taught as no other teacher, with the power to transform lives.

A. Today's lesson is unique for you, the teacher, because it focuses on the attributes of Jesus' teaching ministry. Ask God to give you wisdom, knowledge, and understanding as you prepare to teach others.

B. Read the Daily Bible Readings, Devotional Reading, Focal Verses, and AIM for Change for today's lesson.

C. Using the questions found in the In Focus section, develop a questionnaire that allows students to evaluate your effectiveness as a teacher. Give the following instructions to students: "On a scale of 1 to 5, 1 being the lowest and 5 being the highest, evaluate the effectiveness of the weekly teaching you receive." The purpose of this exercise is to help you gain a better understanding of your abilities.

3. Starting the Lesson
A. Open with prayer.

B. Read the In Focus story aloud and pass out paper copies of the evaluation. Allow the students several moments to reflect and complete the evaluation.

C. Ask the students to give feedback on how they might improve the class. Allow the students a few minutes to share their ideas.

4. Getting into the Lesson
A. Briefly summarize for the class the Background and The People, Places, and Times sections.

B. Review the Words You Should Know and allow the students a few moments to silently read the Focal Verses.

C. Discuss the In Depth section with your class, emphasizing Jesus' authority and power as an effective teacher among the common people as opposed to the religious leaders.

D. Review the Search the Scriptures questions and allow the students to search out the answers.

5. Relating the Lesson to Life
A. Review the Discuss the Meaning section with the class.

B. Provide the class with examples of how God acted through people to give authoritative witness to their teaching and ministry.

C. Ask for suggestions on how class participants might demonstrate their spiritual authority as they "teach" the Good News of the Gospel to others.

6. Arousing Action
A. Reinforce the Lesson in Our Society and Make It Happen suggestions by encouraging the class to become better students of God's Word.

B. Provide the class with a suggested list of in-depth study materials such as the *Precepts For Living*® CD-ROM or the *Precepts For Living*® *Personal Study Guide*, study Bibles, and concordances to prepare them to be an authoritative witness for Christ.

C. Instruct the class to read the Daily Bible Readings in preparation for next week's teaching.

Worship Guide

For the Superintendent or Teacher
Theme: Christ as Teacher
Theme Song: "Tis So Sweet to Trust in Jesus"
Devotional Reading: Isaiah 11:1–3
Prayer

CHRIST AS TEACHER

Bible Background • LUKE 4:31–37; 20:1–8
Printed Text • LUKE 4:31–37; 20:1–8 Devotional Reading • ISAIAH 11:1–3

AIM for Change

By the end of the lesson, we will:

RECOGNIZE the complete dependability of the teaching of Jesus;

UNDERSTAND the complexity and power of Jesus' teachings; and

EQUIP ourselves to become effective, authoritative teachers of God's Word.

Keep in Mind

"And they were astonished at his doctrine: for his word was with power" (Luke 4:32).

Focal Verses

KJV **Luke 4:31** And came down to Capernaum, a city of Galilee, and taught them on the Sabbath days.

32 And they were astonished at his doctrine: for his word was with power.

33 And in the synagogue there was a man, which had a spirit of an unclean devil, and cried out with a loud voice,

34 Saying, Let us alone; what have we to do with thee, thou Jesus of Nazareth? art thou come to destroy us? I know thee who thou art; the Holy One of God.

35 And Jesus rebuked him, saying, Hold thy peace, and come out of him. And when the devil had thrown him in the midst, he came out of him, and hurt him not.

36 And they were all amazed, and spake among themselves, saying, What a word is this! for with authority and power he commandeth the unclean spirits, and they come out.

37 And the fame of him went out into every place of the country round about.

20:1 And it came to pass, that on one of those days, as he taught the people in the temple, and preached the gospel, the chief priests and the scribes came upon him with the elders,

2 And spake unto him, saying, Tell us, by what authority doest thou these things? or who is he that gave thee this authority?

3 And he answered and said unto them, I will also ask you one thing; and answer me:

4 The baptism of John, was it from heaven, or of men?

5 And they reasoned with themselves, saying, If we shall say, From heaven; he will say, Why then believed ye him not?

NLT **Luke 4:31** Then Jesus went to Capernaum, a town in Galilee, and taught there in the synagogue every Sabbath day.

32 There, too, the people were amazed at his teaching, for he spoke with authority.

33 Once when he was in the synagogue, a man possessed by a demon—an evil spirit—began shouting at Jesus,

34 "Go away! Why are you interfering with us, Jesus of Nazareth? Have you come to destroy us? I know who you are—the Holy One sent from God!"

35 Jesus cut him short. "Be quiet! Come out of the man," he ordered. At that, the demon threw the man to the floor as the crowd watched; then it came out of him without hurting him further.

36 Amazed, the people exclaimed, "What authority and power this man's words possess! Even evil spirits obey him, and they flee at his command!"

37 The news about Jesus spread through every village in the entire region.

20:1 One day as Jesus was teaching the people and preaching the Good News in the Temple, the leading priests, the teachers of religious law, and the elders came up to him.

2 They demanded, "By what authority are you doing all these things? Who gave you the right?"

3 "Let me ask you a question first," he replied.

4 "Did John's authority to baptize come from heaven, or was it merely human?"

5 They talked it over among themselves. "If we say it was from heaven, he will ask why we didn't believe John.

6 But and if we say, Of men; all the people will stone us: for they be persuaded that John was a prophet.

7 And they answered, that they could not tell whence it was.

8 And Jesus said unto them, Neither tell I you by what authority I do these things.

6 But if we say it was merely human, the people will stone us because they are convinced John was a prophet."

7 So they finally replied that they didn't know.

8 And Jesus responded, "Then I won't tell you by what authority I do these things."

In Focus

Noted Christian educator Dr. Alvin Lewis states that "Christian education takes on a relevant meaning when it orders the way we live, reflects how we respond to God, and shapes how we behave toward each other. Therefore, effective teaching is based on where people live, work, and play. It touches every facet of the adult's spiritual, social, and psychological being."

Teaching, therefore, is more than giving out information. It has the power to transform lives. It provides learners with a method of sorting through the vast amounts of information they receive in order to determine that which is of lasting value. An integral part of our Christian education is the effectiveness of the teacher's abilities to reach learners and transform lives. According to Jesus' Great Commission we are all called to teach (Matthew 28:18–20). Fortunately, however, God already knows our strengths and weaknesses, even though we are sometimes blind to them ourselves. Those who stand week after week to train and teach God's Word are indeed individuals with a special calling on their lives. Spend a few moments contemplating the following questions and evaluate your teacher to gain a better understanding of his or her ability to function as an effective teacher.

(1) Do you feel the teacher is prepared and knowledgeable to teach each lesson? (2) Does the teacher assist learners to be honest in expressing their ideas and/or feelings? (3) Does the teacher assist learners in making plans for changing their behavior based on what they discover? (4) Does the teacher talk to students freely about his or her own faith walk (both successes and failures)? (5) Does the teacher pay attention to the individual growth needs of the learners? (6) Does the teacher allow learners plenty of room to explore and discover God's truth for themselves? (7) Does the teacher give time to learners out-side of class, as needed? (8) Does the teacher stick to the specific learning objectives given?

Jesus was the ultimate teacher. He was able to teach with power and authority because He is God and God is all-knowing. Today's exercise is not meant to criticize your teacher's abilities, but to provide feedback and help you have a better understanding of their attributes as an effective teacher.

Source:
Lewis, Alvin. *Strategies for Educating African American Adults.* Chicago: Urban Ministries, Inc., 2006.

The People, Places, and Times

Capernaum. It was the nearest village to the River Jordan on the northwest shores of the Sea of Galilee. Capernaum was a wealthy city due to fishing and trade. It was a densely populated, culturally diverse city occupied by both Greeks and Romans. It housed the Roman troops' headquarters. It also suffered from great sin and decadence. Jesus moved there from Nazareth. It was Jesus' home base during His ministry in Galilee. He possibly moved to Capernaum to get away from the intense opposition in Nazareth, to have an impact on the greatest number of people, and to have access to more resources for His ministry. Capernaum was home to several disciples (Matthew 4:13–19) and the place where Matthew accepted his call to be a disciple (Matthew 9:9). Jesus condemned the city for the people's unbelief (Matthew 11:23; Luke 10:15).

Synagogue. This is the Jewish place of worship where people gathered for prayer and reading of the Torah. It also served as a gathering point and a meeting place where the people could congregate whenever it was necessary to take counsel over important community affairs.

Temple. This is the religious center of the Jewish nation and the place where the people expected the Messiah to arrive. Herod the Great rebuilt and remodeled the temple 15 years before Jesus was born (20 B.C.). It was not completed until A.D. 64. Herod made it the most beautiful building in Jerusalem, to appease the Jews. It was composed of three parts: the courts for all the people, the holy place where only the priests could enter, and the most holy place where the Ark of the Covenant was stored and the high priest entered once a year to offer sacrifices to atone for the sins of the people. With Christ's death, the barrier between God and man was split in two. Now all people have access to God directly through Christ (Hebrews 9:1–14; 10:19–22).

Priests. They worked as ministers in the temple, managing its upkeep, teaching the people God's Word, and directing the worship services.

Scribes. They were experts in the study of the Law of Moses. They recorded and preserved the oral law in written form and faithfully handed down the Hebrew Scriptures. Sometimes the scribes were considered legalistic because they felt the oral law was more important than the written law (Matthew 7:5ff).

Sources:

The Life Application Study Bible, New Revised Standard Version. Wheaton, Ill.: Tyndale House Publishers, 1989.

Unger, Merrill. *The New Unger's Bible Handbook.* Chicago: Moody Press, 1984.

Background

The Gospel according to Luke was written to present an emphasis on the perfect humanity of Christ, whom it presents as the Son of Man and Saviour. Luke the physician wrote it primarily for Greeks around A.D. 60. He gives special attention and details on the birth, childhood, and human development of Jesus.

During Jesus' baptism in the Jordan, the Trinity was present (3:21–22). Jesus was full of the Holy Spirit and afterward was led into the wilderness for 40 days to be tempted by the Devil. Jesus resisted the temptation by the power of the Word of God (4:1–13). Jesus then returned to Galilee "in the power of the Spirit," where he preached and taught in the synagogues.

He returned home to Nazareth and went to the synagogue to teach. He read from Isaiah 61:1–2 and proclaimed, "This day is this scripture fulfilled in your ears" (4:21). Jesus was making it known to all listening that He was the One who would bring this prophecy to pass. Those in His hometown did not accept Him. His words caused such outrage within the people that they drove Him out of town. Thereafter, Jesus traveled to Capernaum to continue ministering.

At-A-Glance

1. Teaching with Authority (Luke 4:31–32)
2. Exercising Authority (vv. 33–37)
3. Questioning Authority (20:1–2)
4. Source of Authority (vv. 3–8)

In Depth

1. Teaching with Authority (Luke 4:31–32)

Jesus went to Capernaum, a city in Galilee, after leaving Nazareth. He visited the synagogues to teach on the Sabbath. The synagogue was the Jewish place of worship that included prayer and reading of the Torah. Jesus took advantage of their policy of allowing visitors to teach. Itinerant rabbis were always welcome to speak to those who gathered each Sabbath in the synagogues.

Jesus' authoritative teaching surprised the people. He did not need to quote rabbinical teachers as the religious teachers of His day did. He was "the Word made flesh" (John 1:14). Jesus' authority came from being the visible image of God. "I am in the Father and the Father is in me" (John 14:10). He has the same power as God because He is God! In addition, "He was full of the Holy Ghost" (Luke 4:1).

We too have been given the power of the Holy Spirit who "shall teach you all things" (John 14:26). As we read and study the Scriptures, the Spirit illumines our minds. This illumination helps us to understand how to use the Word in whatever situation we find ourselves. "For the Word of God is quick, and powerful, and sharper than any twoedged sword, piercing even to the dividing asunder of soul and spirit, and of the joints and marrow, and is a discerner of the thoughts and intents of the heart"

(Hebrews 4:12). The Word not only teaches but also reveals and transforms the hearts and minds of the hearers.

2. Exercising Authority (vv. 33–37)

In the midst of the people gathered in the synagogue, there was a man who had a demon (v. 33). Demons are evil spirits ruled by Satan and sent to harass people and tempt them to sin. They are fallen angels who have joined Satan in rebellion against God (Isaiah 14:12–15; Revelation 12:7–9).

Jesus' authoritative teaching stirred the demon in the man (v. 34). He wanted Jesus to leave them (demons) alone so the man could continue to be possessed. Satan does not want to leave willingly. He recognized that the power of God's Word would destroy them. The demon called Jesus by name, since speaking someone's name was an exercise of power over that person or power. Jesus spoke a word, which had the power to cause the demon to be quiet and leave the man (v. 35). The man fell to the floor as the demon left him, but he was not physically harmed.

The people were amazed at the power of Jesus' words to cast out demons. His deeds began to spread quickly in the densely populated town of Capernaum (vv. 36–37). As God's people, it is vital to meditate on His Word day and night (Psalm 1:2). Satan cannot stand against the Word.

Every day Christians in other countries endure persecution for their faith. Many are kidnapped, imprisoned, starved, beaten, and ostracized from society. But still their faith is strong because they recognize the dependability of Jesus and His words. We may never experience this type of suffering, but trials and temptations will come. "In all these things we are more than conquerors through him that loved us" (Romans 8:37). Satan is already defeated because Jesus arose from the grave with all power. "All power is given unto me in heaven and in earth" (Matthew 28:18).

3. Questioning Authority (20:1–2)

The scene switches to a later time in Jesus' ministry. He had just triumphantly entered Jerusalem with the crowds rejoicing and praising God, saying, "Blessed be the King that cometh in the name of the Lord: peace in heaven, and glory in the highest" (19:38). Before the celebration was over, Jesus lamented over the spiritual condition of the city

(19:41–44). He saw the need for repentance and forgiveness of sin. It's no surprise He proceeded to cleanse the temple of corruption (19:45–46). How could "He without sin" enter a place of worship corrupted by sin and not purge it? He purified it in order for it to become a place of His own ministry of teaching (19:47).

Daily, Jesus was teaching and preaching the Gospel in the temple, which caused strong opposition from the religious leaders. They wanted to kill Him (19:47–48). The religious leaders felt their positions of authority were being threatened. In the temple, the priests exercised authority by managing the daily upkeep, teaching the Word, and directing worship. The priests of the family of Levi were appointed to these positions by God as a tribe to minister at the altar. It differed from the synagogue, where visiting rabbis were granted the privilege of speaking and teaching to the people gathered.

Jesus' interrogators wanted to know "by what authority doest thou these things? Or who is he that gave thee this authority?" (20:2). The leaders wanted to set a trap for Jesus with their questions. The priests knew their authority came from God to minister to the people. But their question was: Who gave Jesus the authority to teach and preach in the temple? After His baptism, Jesus was filled with the Holy Spirit and God the Father identified Jesus as His Son, which granted Him authority.

4. Source of Authority (vv. 3–8)

Jesus' did not allow Himself to be caught in a trap. He responded to the question with a question. Jesus asked, "The baptism of John, was it from heaven, or of men?" (v. 4). His question about John's ministry gave the religious leaders an opportunity to explain their assessment of another person who recently had come preaching the word of God's coming reign. The leaders hated and criticized John the Baptist, and Jesus received the same treatment.

After much discussion among themselves, they admitted not knowing the answer. In truth they were saying, "We will not say." Jesus simply responded, "Neither tell I you by what authority I do these things" (v. 8). Jesus' authority came from God, but His question answered their opposition and silenced their challenge.

Search the Scriptures

1. Who taught in the synagogue of Capernaum on the Sabbath (Luke 4:30–31)?

2. Who cried out with a loud voice as Jesus was teaching (v. 33)?

3. What was Jesus' response (v. 35)?

4. How did the religious leaders question Jesus (20:2)?

5. How did Jesus avoid being trapped by their questions (vv. 4, 8)?

Discuss the Meaning

All throughout today's Scripture text, we see Jesus as an authoritative teacher. Both narratives demonstrate that Jesus was more accepted by the common people than the religious leadership. The call of Christ to all is to labor in God's vineyard (Matthew 20:1–16) and expand the kingdom of Christ in the lives of others. The fact remains, however, there are many who have never viewed themselves as teachers of the Gospel, nor have they been taught to share their faith with others. As Christians we are all called to spread the Good News of Christ and teach others to do the same (Matthew 28:18–20). How can you become an effective teacher of God's Word? How can your teaching have the authority of Jesus? What are some examples of God acting through people to give authoritative witness to their teaching and ministry?

Lesson in Our Society

There are many people who claim to be God's prophets. However, some of them are teaching false doctrines that are misleading and twisted. On a daily basis, we hear about these false prophets telling their followers to do foolish things like live in a bunker and prepare for Armageddon; kill others in the name of God; commit mass suicide; and so on. The only defense we have is the true Word of God. God wants us to study His Word and share the Gospel with the world. When the truth is shared, the power of God overcomes evil and transforms lives. People are set free to live a new life with Christ. It is vital that we teach others what God has revealed to us.

Make It Happen

Make an effort to attend Bible study on a regular basis to learn more about God's Word. You can also visit a Christian bookstore and purchase a concor-dance and Bible dictionary as study aids. Or use the *Precepts For Living*® CD-ROM for more in-depth studying. Think about a family member, co-worker, or neighbor who needs to hear an encouraging word. Ask God for an opportunity to spend time sharing Scripture with them. God has given you the authority to teach others about His saving grace.

Follow the Spirit

What God wants me to do:

_____

_____

Remember Your Thoughts

Special insights I have learned:

_____

_____

More Light on the Text

Luke 4:31–37; 20:1–8

Every verse in this first section of today's Bible text shows a positive example of the goals for this lesson. The second section shows the negative results when those positive lessons are rejected.

31 And came down to Capernaum, a city of Galilee and taught them on the Sabbath days.

Luke began describing this incident by saying Jesus "came down." Came from where? Jesus came from Nazareth, His hometown, where He had grown up. This was literally true. Nazareth was located 1,300 feet above sea level on the hilly spine that ran down the center of Palestine. Capernaum, on the Sea of Galilee's coast, was nearly 700 feet below sea level. Nazareth was a largely Jewish backcountry village, whereas Capernaum was a thriving Gentile town. So when a Jew went to Capernaum, it was a comedown both literally and figuratively.

Luke expected that many of his first readers would not know Palestine geography well, so he explained its location as, "a city of Galilee." The way that Luke told this story provides a good example for Christians today who want to share their faith with others. They need to follow his example by making sure that the words they use make sense to the person they're talking to. As was true with first-century non-Christians, many people today would have little idea about where Capernaum was. Christians should remember that words that are commonly used at church—washed in the blood, hiding behind the Cross, sanctified, and so on—may be meaningless or confusing to people outside of it.

When Luke wrote that Jesus "was teaching," he was referring to something Jesus did repeatedly because the verse ends by saying, "on the Sabbath days." Notice Luke wrote "days," not day. Jesus understood that hearing something once is seldom enough. Similarly, just knowing the facts of the Gospel isn't enough. Once a person grasps the nature of God's call to faith in Jesus, that person still has to decide to accept his or her need for God, for repentance, for spiritual rebirth, and the need to grow spiritually. Peter understood this well, which explains why he wrote those early Christians, "So I will always remind you of these things, even though you know them well and are firmly established in the truth you now have. . . . I will make every effort to see that . . . you will always be able to remember these things" (2 Peter 1:12, 15, NIV).

32 And they were astonished at his doctrine: for his word was with power.

The King James Version uses the perfect word here when it says those hearing Jesus teach "were astonished at his doctrine." Luke used the Greek word *ekplesso* (**ek-PLAYSS-so**), indicating that people were astounded over and over by what Jesus said. As people listened, they may have shaken their heads in amazement. Unlike most teachers at that time, Jesus didn't constantly quote other scholarly rabbis. Rather, He spoke simply, which is probably why Mark 12:37 says, "The common people heard him gladly." The word "doctrine" (Gk. *didache*, **did-ahkh-AY**) simply means teaching, not a complicated system of beliefs.

Luke wrote that people marveled about what Jesus said, but also about how He said it: "His word was with power." Power often referred not just to speaking forcefully, but to authority and giving commands, which Jesus went on to do. In verses 33–35, Luke recorded events which showed that Jesus' words had power to overcome the domination of evil in a person's life.

33 And in the synagogue there was a man, which had a spirit of an unclean devil, and cried out with a loud voice,

Notice that the man was in the synagogue where Jesus was teaching. He came to a place where he might get help. This is a good illustration of what Jesus referred to when He said that faith no greater than "a grain of mustard seed" could bring about miraculous results (Luke 17:6). This man had the bare minimum of faith needed to show up at the synagogue, but that was enough for his life to be transformed.

Luke does not say how the demonic spirit revealed itself in the man's life. Many times the Bible records that satanic spirits attacked people through physical ailments (Luke 4:40–41; 11:14; 13:11). Likewise, in addition to physical ailments, Satan uses emotional problems in people's lives to lead them to doubt, to be afraid, to get angry, or to escape from physical or emotional pain in ways that hurt themselves or others or dishonor God. Like this man long ago, every Sunday people come into church overwhelmed by some power of evil controlling their lives. Maybe the problem is alcohol or drugs; maybe it's hate, violence, depression, or countless other ways sin gains control over people's lives.

This man wasn't struggling against only one demon. Although one demon was in charge, the man's question is, "What have we to do with thee?" (v. 34). After Jesus freed the man from the evil powers in him, the onlookers in the synagogue also recognized that He had driven out more than one demonic spirit. Being freed from the satanic spirits controlling the man's life wasn't easy or painless. Luke says that he cried out to Jesus. The same Greek word that Luke used (*anakrazo*, **ahn-ahk-RAHD-zoh**) was also used of the cries of a woman giving birth. The *New Living Translation* says the demon "began shouting"; the New International Version adds to that, "at the top of his voice."

34 Saying, Let us alone; what have we to do with thee, thou Jesus of Nazareth? art thou come to destroy us? I know thee who thou art; the Holy One of God.

Luke described the demons' outburst in verse 34 with a two-letter word that can mean either an order to get away, as the King James Version renders it, or an irritated grunt such as "Ha!" like the *New International Version* suggests. Either way, the demons controlling the man's life did not want Jesus around.

The demons assumed rightly that Jesus had the power to destroy them and feared that He might do so. Jesus' purpose, though, wasn't to destroy evil but to defeat it. Sin is an unavoidable, ever-present reality of life (Romans 3:23). Every person must choose whether to allow it to dominate his or her life, but only God has the power to defeat that sin and evil permanently. That happens only when a person trusts Him enough to allow Him to do it.

35 And Jesus rebuked him, saying, Hold thy peace, and come out of him. And when the devil had thrown him in the midst, he came out of him, and hurt him not. 36 And they were all amazed, and spake among themselves, saying, What a word is this! for with authority and power he commandeth the unclean spirits, and they come out.

Jesus' reply to the demon speaking through the man was short: "Hold thy peace." The word Luke used (Gk. *phimoo*, **fee-MO-oh**) generally referred to muzzling an animal. The *New International Version* translates Jesus as saying, "Be quiet!" In other words, the phrase "Shut up" would not be incorrect. When the demon spoke, Jesus refused to listen.

After dismissing the demons, He commanded them to get out of the man's life. Gaining release from the demonic hold on his life wasn't easy for the man. He ended up being thrown to the ground, but he got up unhurt in the end.

The other people in the synagogue were amazed, because driving the demons from the man's life proved that Jesus wasn't all talk. What Jesus said contained the power to transform the man's life. Those teaching the Bible should be strengthened by the knowledge that God's Word can still do that today—and does.

The once-demon-possessed man was now freed from demonic control. In verse 35, the phrase "in the midst" (Gk. *mesos*, **MESS-oss**) can apply either to the man being thrown down or to the demons being expelled. The *New Living Translation* manages to make it apply to both by rendering it, "The demon threw the man to the floor as the crowd watched." Either way, Luke wants to make it plain that this

wasn't a story he made up but an event that many people saw take place.

Verse 36 seems to express pure astonishment by those present in the synagogue at what Jesus' words had accomplished. But Luke states more than that. The rest of verse 36 is a question. People saw the man miraculously freed from demonic oppression, but they couldn't understand how mere words could have such transforming power. The explanation was that they weren't just words, but the words filled with God's power, just as the Bible is the Word of God for people today.

37 And the fame of him went out into every place of the country round about.

In this verse, Luke says that what Jesus said and did in Capernaum that day was repeated all over Galilee. When Luke says that Jesus' "fame . . . went out," he used the Greek word *echos* (**ay-KHOSS**), from which the modern English word "echo" comes. It meant to ring, resound, or reverberate. People discussed Jesus' words and actions over and over. Luke mentions that this happened again and again, eventually spreading beyond Galilee (see Luke 5:15; 7:17).

The unwillingness of the Jewish leaders to learn from what Jesus said and did is seen. This confrontation between Jesus and the Jewish priests and lay leaders was only one of many. Mark's Gospel, the earliest of the four, tells how from the very beginning of Jesus' ministry, Jewish lay leaders began plotting to kill Him (Mark 3:6). John's Gospel reports that as soon as Jesus came in contact with the leaders in Jerusalem and the temple, they likewise conspired to kill Him (John 7:1, NIV).

20:1 And it came to pass, that on one of those days, as he taught the people in the temple, and preached the gospel, the chief priests and the scribes came upon him with the elders,

One day during the week before Jesus' crucifixion, He was teaching people who had come to the temple. Since that was the week before Passover, the most sacred time among Jews, people likely filled the temple. The enthusiastic reception He had received when He entered Jerusalem (Luke 19:37) had probably ballooned the size of the crowd that came to hear Jesus teach, as did the widespread belief by many that He was a true prophet. While He was teaching, a group that included priests, temple officials, and lay leaders came up to Jesus.

2 And spake unto him, saying, Tell us, by what authority doest thou these things? or who is he that gave thee this authority?

This time they didn't ask politely or address Jesus with any term of respect as they had at previous encounters (Matthew 12:38; Mark 12:14; Luke 18:18; John 3:2). The demand for an answer took the form of a blunt command: Tell us what gives You the right to teach what You're teaching and do what You're doing! Who gives You the authority?

The purpose for Jesus' miracles had been to answer this question more powerfully than anything He could say (Luke 5:24). Just as poll taxes and literacy tests in the past weren't meant to determine a citizen's qualifications to vote, Jesus knew that neither was the intent behind their question to gain needed understanding. Rather, with their minds made up to reject Him, they were seeking some way to discredit Him before His followers or something that would give them an excuse to destroy Him.

3 And he answered and said unto them, I will also ask you one thing; and answer me: 4 The baptism of John, was it from heaven, or of men?

Jesus agreed to answer their question if they agreed to answer one of His. His question put them in the same bind they had planned for Him. God's approval of Jesus had been seen and heard at His baptism (Luke 3:21–22). Jesus asserted that His right to forgive sin was confirmed by His miraculous healings (5:24).

5 And they reasoned with themselves saying, If we shall say, From heaven; he will say, Why then believed ye him not? 6 But and if we say, Of men; all the people will stone us: for they be persuaded that John was a prophet. 7 And they answered, that they could not tell whence it was. 8 And Jesus said unto them, Neither tell I you by what authority I do these things.

As they weighed how to answer Jesus' question, they realized that if they said John's baptism originated with God, their earlier rejection of John would immediately discredit them (7:30). If they gave that answer, they foresaw Jesus asking how the official leaders of God's people could reject John if they had known he was God's spokesman. If, on the other hand, they dismissed John's baptism as merely something he had dreamed up, they risked the general population's outrage and being stoned to death. Most people were fully convinced that John had been martyred as God's prophet.

Finding a response to Jesus' question that would both save face and save their bodies, they bounced from one possibility to another. The word "reasoned" (Gk. *sullogizomai*, **sool-log-ID-zom-eye**) that Luke chose to describe their struggle meant to debate. Finally, they accepted that either response would work against them, so they told Jesus they didn't know. Jesus replied that if they weren't going to answer His question, He wouldn't answer theirs.

Their squabbling over how to reply to Jesus' question makes clear that their intention wasn't to discover new truth, but rather to confirm the opinions they already held. Bible students need to understand that the value from their study comes not from merely knowing what the Bible says, but in opening themselves to its truth and its application to their lives. That means that Bible study needs to go beyond learning the truth to living it, something these men were unwilling to do. But that can—and does—happen whenever we accept the Bible as our trustworthy source of truth about how we and our world can know life at its fullest through God's revelation and faith in Jesus.

Daily Bible Readings

M: Spirit-Anointed Teacher
Isaiah 11:1–3

T: Filled with God's Spirit
Luke 4:14–15

W: With Authority
Luke 4:31–37

T: Blessed Are You
Luke 6:17–23

F: Woes and Blessings
Luke 6:24–31

S: Love Your Enemies
Luke 6:32–36

S: Authority Questioned
Luke 20:1–8

TEACHING TIPS

July 13
Bible Study Guide 7

1. Words You Should Know

A. Synagogue (Mark 1:29) *sunagoge* (Gk.)—A gathering together. The word is used more than 50 times in the New Testament to refer to the place of worship where Jews assembled together to offer prayers and listen to the reading and teaching of the Scriptures.

B. Minister (v. 31) *diakoneo* (Gk.)—To serve, provide care for, or supply the things that are necessary to sustain life.

2. Teacher Preparation

Unifying Principle—Finding Healing and Wholeness Many people are looking to be made whole. Jesus was able to heal anyone who came to Him for help. His miracles of healing demonstrated His deity and His compassion.

A. Complete lesson 7 in the *Precepts For Living® Personal Study Guide,* paying particular attention to Jesus' treatment of those who suffered physically, mentally, and spiritually.

B. Consider asking a person who has been healed to share his or her experience with the class.

C. *Optional:* Many of the sicknesses and diseases that African Americans suffer, like high blood pressure, diabetes, and high cholesterol, are preventable or controllable with exercise and proper nutrition. Consider inviting a nutritionist to speak with the class.

3. Starting the Lesson

A. Before the students arrive for class, write the phrase "THE UNTOUCHABLES" on the chalkboard in capital letters.

B. Ask one student to lead the class in prayer.

C. Give a brief synopsis of Background and The People, Places, and Times, and discuss the AIM for Change and Unifying Principle objectives.

C. Draw the students' attention to the chalkboard. Brainstorm and create a list of people or groups that our society considers misfits or outcasts. Ask: Do you find it difficult to minister to these people? If so, why?

D. Ask the class to silently read the In Focus story and share stories of a time when physical and spiritual healing took place in their lives or the life of someone they know.

4. Getting into the Lesson

A. Have the students read the Focal Verses and In Depth section according to the At-A-Glance outline.

B. After reading the In Depth section, ask the class to discuss the characteristics of spiritual wholeness. Compare the healing ministry of Jesus while on Earth with His healing ministry today.

C. Complete the Search the Scriptures questions.

5. Relating the Lesson to Life

A. Instruct the students to take out a pencil and paper and jot down their responses to the Discuss the Meaning questions.

B. Read the Lesson in Our Society exercise.

6. Arousing Action

A. Direct the students' attention to the Make It Happen section.

B. Pass out a list of your church's outreach organizations. Encourage class members to AIM—get ACTIVE IN MINISTRY.

C. Close the class in prayer.

D. Remind the students to read the Daily Bible Readings leading up to next week's lesson.

415

CHRIST AS HEALER

Bible Background • MARK 1:29–45
Printed Text • MARK 1:29–45 Devotional Reading • ISAIAH 61:1–4

AIM for Change

By the end of the lesson, we will:

COMPARE the healing ministry of Jesus while on Earth with His healing ministry today;

FEEL COMPASSION toward these who are suffering physically, mentally, spiritually, or otherwise; and

REACH out to those in our community who are suffering.

Keep in Mind

"And he healed many that were sick of divers diseases, and cast out many devils; and suffered not the devils to speak, because they knew him" (Mark 1:34).

Focal Verses

KJV
Mark 1:29 And forthwith, when they were come out of the synagogue, they entered into the house of Simon and Andrew, with James and John.

30 But Simon's wife's mother lay sick of a fever, and anon they tell him of her.

31 And he came and took her by the hand, and lifted her up; and immediately the fever left her, and she ministered unto them.

32 And at even, when the sun did set, they brought unto him all that were diseased, and them that were possessed with devils.

33 And all the city was gathered together at the door.

34 And he healed many that were sick of divers diseases, and cast out many devils; and suffered not the devils to speak, because they knew him.

35 And in the morning, rising up a great while before day, he went out, and departed into a solitary place, and there prayed.

36 And Simon and they that were with him followed after him.

37 And when they found him, they said unto him, All men seek for thee.

38 And he said unto them, Let us go into the next towns, that I may preach there also: for therefore came I forth.

39 And he preached in their synagogues throughout all Galilee, and cast out devils.

40 And there came a leper to him, beseeching him, and kneeling down to him, and saying unto him, If thou wilt, thou canst make me clean.

NLT
Mark 1:29 After Jesus left the synagogue with James and John, they went to Simon and Andrew's home.

30 Now Simon's mother-in-law was sick in bed with a high fever. They told Jesus about her right away.

31 So he went to her bedside, took her by the hand, and helped her sit up. Then the fever left her, and she prepared a meal for them.

32 That evening after sunset, many sick and demon-possessed people were brought to Jesus.

33 The whole town gathered at the door to watch.

34 So Jesus healed many people who were sick with various diseases, and he cast out many demons. But because the demons knew who he was, he did not allow them to speak.

35 Before daybreak the next morning, Jesus got up and went out to an isolated place to pray.

36 Later Simon and the others went out to find him.

37 When they found him, they said, "Everyone is looking for you."

38 But Jesus replied, "We must go on to other towns as well, and I will preach to them, too. That is why I came."

39 So he traveled throughout the region of Galilee, preaching in the synagogues and casting out demons.

40 A man with leprosy came and knelt in front of Jesus, begging to be healed. "If you are willing, you can heal me and make me clean," he said.

41 And Jesus, moved with compassion, put forth his hand, and touched him, and saith unto him, I will; be thou clean.

42 And as soon as he had spoken, immediately the leprosy departed from him, and he was cleansed.

43 And he straitly charged him, and forthwith sent him away;

44 And saith unto him, See thou say nothing to any man: but go thy way, shew thyself to the priest, and offer for thy cleansing those things which Moses commanded, for a testimony unto them.

45 But he went out, and began to publish it much, and to blaze abroad the matter, insomuch that Jesus could no more openly enter into the city, but was without in desert places: and they came to him from every quarter.

41 Moved with compassion, Jesus reached out and touched him. "I am willing," he said. "Be healed!"

42 Instantly the leprosy disappeared, and the man was healed.

43 Then Jesus sent him on his way with a stern warning:

44 "Don't tell anyone about this. Instead, go to the priest and let him examine you. Take along the offering required in the law of Moses for those who have been healed of leprosy. This will be a public testimony that you have been cleansed."

45 But the man went and spread the word, proclaiming to everyone what had happened. As a result, large crowds soon surrounded Jesus, and he couldn't publicly enter a town anywhere. He had to stay out in the secluded places, but people from everywhere kept coming to him.

In Focus

Mr. Ryan, an elderly, eccentric loner, had become the subject of small-town gossip. Companionless and shunned by his neighbors, he lived quietly on a corner lot. One evening after leaving Bible study, a young boy named Billy and a few of his friends witnessed Mr. Ryan's house being burglarized. The thugs raced out of the house as the old man lay unconscious on the front steps. Billy begged his friends to help Mr. Ryan, but they laughed at him and left, saying the old man got what he deserved for being so mean. Nevertheless, Billy stayed to help the old man and called 911. The ambulance rushed the old man to the hospital. A few weeks later Mr. Ryan was released from the hospital, fully recovered from his injuries. Billy discovered that his actions helped save the old man's life, and he began visiting him on the weekends.

Billy found out that Mr. Ryan was a disabled war veteran. Mr. Ryan shared many stories of his experiences in the war, and Billy shared the Word of God with Mr. Ryan. The two developed a close friendship. Before he died, Mr. Ryan attended church regularly and received Jesus Christ as Saviour. He thanked Billy for not only helping him to heal physically, but also helping him to heal spiritually. Today, Billy is a youth pastor in his old neighborhood. He continues to share God's Word and Mr. Ryan's story with others. He hopes sharing his story will convince others that God heals physical as well as spiritual wounds.

In today's lesson, we examine Christ as a healer. Jesus heals us because He wants us to be whole. No matter who that individual is, faith in the power of Jesus Christ will lead to wholeness—spiritual, physical, or otherwise.

The People, Places, and Times

Leper. This is a person afflicted with a chronic and extremely infectious disease. The disease is characterized by noticeable changes in the skin and damage to peripheral nerves and mucous membranes. Individuals afflicted with the disease experience loss of sensation to touch, loss of skin pigment, and paralysis of the face, legs, or hands. In Jesus' day, lepers were considered outcasts and shunned by the community.

Background

The gospel of Mark depicts Jesus Christ as the Saviour, Son of God, and a servant of man. According to some scholars, the gospel of Mark was written by John Mark, son of a certain woman named Mary from Jerusalem (Acts 12:12). He accompanied the apostle Paul and Barnabas on the first missionary tour (Acts 13:5). The gospel of Mark is the shortest of all the four Gospels (Matthew, Mark, Luke, and John). In the book of Mark, we "see" Jesus in action. Words used by the writer, such as "straightway" and "immediately," portray Jesus' behavior as dynamic and energetic. We see Jesus doing more acting than speaking. There is less emphasis on Old Testament prophecies and more emphasis placed on Jesus as the miracle-working servant. Many of the parables written in the gospels of Matthew, Luke, and John are omitted in Mark. The target audience for Mark is the Gentile (Roman and not Jewish) community. The author presents Jesus as the prevailing, magnificent, and awesome Son of God whose words reign supreme in both the spiritual and natural realms. Not only is Jesus depicted as the Redeemer who died as a ransom for many, but He is also seen as displaying incredible compassion for humankind.

The book of Mark gives Christians a clear picture of God's love for suffering and hurting people. Mark presents numerous illustrations of God's divine healing through Jesus. Jesus' behavior is an example of how we should respond to one another and those around us. These incidents not only reveal the power God has over sickness and demonic influences, but they also reveal His heart. It pleases the heart of God to see people living healthy and productive lives. Equally pleasing to His heart is our response toward those seeking God. The Lord's compassion is extended to anyone who seeks after Him.

At-A-Glance

1. God Heals Compassionately (Mark 1:29–34)
2. God Heals Impartially (vv. 35–45)

In Depth

1. God Heals Compassionately (Mark 1:29–34)

In today's text, we see compassion in action. Jesus left the synagogue to visit the home of His disciples Simon (Peter) and Andrew. The disciples informed Jesus that Simon's mother-in-law suffered from a disabling fever. Jesus immediately went to her bedside, touched her, and lifted her from her sickbed (v. 31). The Bible does not tell us how long Simon's mother-in-law had been sick or what caused her illness. All we know is that Jesus healed her, and once restored to health, she ministered to Jesus and His disciples. From this passage of Scripture we can learn powerful principles concerning healing, God's compassion toward the suffering, and the appropriate response to His kindness.

The first principle we learn is not to condemn or judge the sick. In these verses, we notice how Jesus responded to Simon's mother-in-law with love and compassion. He did not condemn or find fault with her or any of His disciples. He simply healed her! When we encounter the sick, we should always pray for the Lord's intervention, healing, and deliverance. Nevertheless, in all our fasting, praying, and declaring the Word, we should never forget that God is sovereign. Our response toward the suffering should be Christlike; we should not condemn or judge the sick. Instead, we should imitate Jesus' reaction to the suffering and respond with love.

Another principle illustrated in these passages of Scripture is the Lord's response to petitions. Jesus responded to His disciples' request right away (v. 31). He went to the bedside of Simon's mother-in-law and immediately healed her. Sometimes our prayers are not answered with an instantaneous response from God. While some are healed miraculously, the Lord may cure others by way of medicine and surgery, and recovery may take days, months, or even years. Healing might mean that an individual is made well on this side of eternity (while a person is still alive) or on the other side of eternity (when a person dies and goes home to be with the Lord). No matter how the Lord chooses to heal, our situations do not negate the fact that God is a healer and deliverer. "If we live, we live to the Lord; and if we die, we die to the Lord" (Romans 14:8, NIV).

Yet another principle we must recognize is the proper response when God shows compassion toward us. After being touched and healed by Jesus, Simon's mother-in-law began to minister unto the Lord (v. 31). What an awesome revelation! We must not view the mother-in-law's response to Jesus as a role that only women fulfilled in those days. If we relegate this task to the role of women or minimize the significance of serving, we miss the meaning behind the Lord's command to love the Lord our God with all our heart, soul, mind, and strength (Mark 12:30). Serving the Lord is an honor and not something we should take lightly. It is one of the primary ways we show our gratitude and love for the Lord. Serving God comes from a thankful heart and is an outward expression of our love for God. Anytime God delivers us out of sickness, our first response should be to serve Him.

We also should desire to serve our families. Simon's mother-in-law served Simon, a member of her family. A servant's heart is a humble heart, neither boastful nor prideful, naïve, or weak. When we serve God first, we are able to provide care to our family members. The Lord commands that we serve Him and others. Serving others does not mean we neglect our own needs. The mother-in-law could not serve while suffering with a fever. Jesus had to heal her first. When He made her well, she had the capacity to extend hospitality to her family.

We should also serve those in the body of Christ. Peter's mother-in-law served the other disciples. We are to serve in our local church, extend hospitality in our homes, and fellowship with one another. We cannot serve each other unless we are in fellowship with one another.

Jewish leaders declared that it was against the Mosaic Law to heal on the Sabbath day (Matthew 12:10; Luke 13:14). Out of fear of the Jewish leaders and in obedience to the law, people sought Jesus after the sun went down. The Lord did not discourage anyone from coming to Him. The people brought their loved ones, friends, and neighbors to Jesus because they knew He could transform their lives.

When Jesus cast out demons, He commanded them to remain silent. He did not allow demons to boast of their knowledge of Him (v. 34). The evil spirits knew He was the Son of God. By exercising His authority over demonic influences, Jesus demonstrated His control over the situation. Jesus silenced the demonic voices because they would have distorted the truth about God. No satanic influence is more powerful than God. This truth should give us the strength to trust God's Word in every situation.

2. God Heals Impartially (vv. 35–45)

In those days, anyone suffering from leprosy was considered an outcast in society. They were cut off from living productive lives within the community. Jesus took the time to listen attentively, touch, and speak kindly to anyone in need. Jesus healed the leper, and His willingness to heal was not hindered by the leper's social status.

As Christians, we have a responsibility to respond in a Christlike manner toward those suffering around us. Jesus was no respecter of persons. He healed all kinds of people who sought His help. Like Christ, our compassion should extend beyond our immediate and biological family. Although Jesus is not on earth in the flesh today, His presence dwells in every believer by way of the Holy Spirit. We are His eyes, hands, and feet—His representatives on the earth. Through us, people will see the loving, compassionate heart of God. The need for compassion is paramount in our society today.

During Jesus' earthly ministry, His healing power convinced the people who He was and taught the disciples the true identity of God. Today, Jesus is still convincing people around the world that He is God. When we hear stories from around the world of how God miraculously healed people with life-threatening and crippling diseases, we are in awe of His power. These stories remind us of His divine mercy and goodness. Each time we experience restoration from sickness to wellness, we realize how intimately God is involved in every aspect of our lives. It also reminds us of the importance of sharing our testimonies. Our testimony about the Lord should be equally as powerful. People should have a curiosity about the Lord based on what we say and the changes they see in our lives. Our testimony is not just about how we live but also what we say!

Search the Scriptures

1. Describe the various ways people came to Christ for healing. What does this tell you about the Lord's capacity to heal (Mark 1:32–34, 40–42)?

2. Jesus told the leper not to tell anyone about his healing. The leper was so excited that he shared his testimony with everyone. What does this tell us about testifying about the Lord (vv. 40–45)?

Discuss the Meaning

Evaluate your ideology on healing. Ask yourself the following questions:

1. What is my response to those who are sick?

2. Do I judge their level of faith?

3. Do I measure their trust in God by their current situation?

4. Do I hurl accusations and blame their actions for causing their own predicaments?

5. Do I gently point them to the loving mercies of God?

Lesson in Our Society

If you ever doubt the need for compassion today, just read the newspaper or turn on the television. Better yet, just listen to voices in the pews, at work, or in our communities. We would soon discover the world is full of hurting individuals who are discouraged, desperate, and disgusted with life. Many struggle aimlessly without hope, not knowing Jesus is a healer and refuge. The church is a hospital, and there should always be room in the pews for the displaced, brokenhearted, and sick. Echoing cries of the suffering should fill the sanctuary. Imagine the impact in the kingdom of God if believers regularly shared their testimony with others! How many people have heard your testimony?

Make It Happen

Decide to get involved in one of your church's outreach ministries. If your church does not have an outreach program, extend an act of kindness to someone in your congregation or community (for example, buy groceries for an elderly neighbor). Often people avoid those who are labeled "misfits," including those who are maimed, crippled, or poor. Can you think of someone you can reach out to? Make an effort to minister to that person during the upcoming week. How did you feel? Share your experience with the class next week.

In addition to getting involved and taking practical action, you can also take spiritual action. Pray for God's healing for those suffering from physical, emotional, spiritual, or mental illness. When we pray for God's healing to take place in a person's life, we demonstrate faith in God and acknowledge Him as the source of healing. List the names of people you know who need God's healing and pray for them.

Follow the Spirit

What God wants me to do:

_____

_____

Remember Your Thoughts

Special insights I have learned:

_____

_____

More Light on the Text

Mark 1:29–45

Our text for today's lesson picks up in Mark's gospel where Luke's gospel left off in last week's lesson. Taken together, we have the first account of a whole day in Jesus' ministry.

As Jesus began the pursuit of His goal on Earth, Mark says that "Jesus came into Galilee, preaching.... The time is fulfilled, and the kingdom of God is at hand: repent ye, and believe the gospel" (Mark 1:14–15). The Good News from God, which is the meaning of "Gospel," was that God's dominion would soon be revealed.

Jesus came to make known that entry into God's realm was possible by turning from self and sin and trusting God's Son, Jesus. Mark recorded examples of how Jesus showed that participation in God's dominion did not merely involve accepting a set of beliefs, but trusting Jesus enough to live by those beliefs.

29 And forthwith, when they were come out of the synagogue, they entered into the house of Simon and Andrew, with James and John.

Mark begins this section with one of his favorite Greek words, *euthus* (**yoo-THOOS**), a word he used 4 times in today's text and over 40 times in his Gospel. The word means "immediately, at once, or soon." The King James Version renders it as "forthwith" in verses 29 and 43, as "anon" in verse 30, and as "immediately" in verse 42. Mark used the word as a way of emphasizing that Jesus had only a limited time to deliver the revelation that God the Father had commissioned Him to deliver. Jesus was keenly aware of His purpose and went directly from one task to the next.

Although Nazareth, 20 miles west, was Jesus' hometown, He chose Capernaum at the north end of the Sea of Galilee as His home base. This mainly Gentile town is the only place where any of the Gospels refer to Jesus as being at "home" (Mark 2:1, NIV). From the beginning, Jesus reached out to people who were not religious insiders. The first four disciples He chose were working men, fishermen. Peter and Andrew may not have owned a boat like James and John. Perhaps they eked out their living fishing from the bank. None of the four were from Jerusalem, the religious center for Jews. They weren't even from Judea; instead, they were from Galilee, in far-north Palestine, and cut off from a direct connection with Jerusalem by Samaria, where a perverted form of the Israelite religion was practiced.

30 But Simon's wife's mother lay sick of a fever, and anon they tell him of her. 31 And he came and took her by the hand, and lifted her up; and immediately the fever left her, and she ministered unto them.

Women were considered inferior to men in every way—physically, intellectually, emotionally, and spiritually. Of the first two healings described by Mark, one was a man (Mark 1:23–26), but the second was a woman, Peter's mother-in-law, who was probably a widow, which made her even lower on the social scale.

When Peter came home with Jesus, James, and John as guests, he was told that his mother-in-law was in bed with a fever. The *New Living Translation* says "with a high fever." The Greek word that Mark used, *puresso* (**poo-REHS-soh**), came from their word for fire. We might say today that she was burning up. When Mark wrote that she "lay" sick, the imperfect tense of the Greek word that he used, *katakeimai* (**kaht-AHK-ay-my**), meant that she was sick again. She was seriously ill. In that time, before the discovery of aspirin or antibiotics, a fever was not a small matter.

When Jesus was told of her condition, He went to her bedside and healed her. Two lessons can be learned here. The first is how Jesus healed the woman. He did it privately, not publicly, not in a synagogue or the temple. God wants to work in people's lives wherever they are, not just at church. He healed her fever not to impress the crowds, but out of concern for her individually.

Second, when they told Jesus about her condition, He went to her bedside, took her hand, and healed her. Jesus often touched people when He healed them (Matthew 8:3; Luke 13:13). Why? It was not because these actions were necessary to complete their healing. Sometimes He did not touch the person at all (Luke 17:12–14). Sometimes the person to be healed was not even present, but even then Jesus was able to heal the person (Luke 7:3, 10; John 4:46–52).

The phrase "took her hand" is mild for what Mark wrote. The word he used (Gk. *krateo*, **kraht-**EH-oh**) meant "to grab hold of something or to get a grip on it." His firm grip assured the woman that she was cared for as well as cured.

Mark also wrote that Jesus lifted her up. The *New Living Translation* says He "helped her sit up." He helped her get up and then supported her. The application for Christians is that often people need support to believe they can change and make a new beginning. Jesus modeled the behavior that those who trust and follow Him should imitate: Do what you can to help. Jesus could heal, so He did.

Mark says that when Jesus touched the woman and took hold of her, the fever left. When a person trusts God and lets Him touch his or her life, God's purpose is not merely to save that person from a besetting sin or a life-threatening illness. The woman's actions after Jesus got rid of her fever show this well.

Curing the woman's fever resulted in service to Jesus and His disciples. Our text, the King James Version, says that she "ministered unto them"; the *New International Version* says that she "began to wait on them," and the *New Living Translation* states that she "prepared a meal." Each version conveys Mark's meaning. The church gets the word "deacon" from the word Mark used (Gk. *diakoneo*, **dee-ahk-on-EH-oh**), which means "to serve in a lowly position."

The word described something the woman did over and over. God's purpose in healing, whether physical, emotional, or spiritual, is to free a person to live fully and become involved with serving God and meeting the needs of others.

32 And at even, when the sun did set, they brought unto him all that were diseased, and them that were possessed with devils. 33 And all the city was gathered together at the door.

A Jewish Sabbath began on Friday night at sundown and ended at sundown on Saturday. To carry anything, even a sick person, to a healer on the Sabbath was considered work. Consequently, only after sunset on Saturday would a faithful Jew feel free to do that. That is likely why Mark notes that it was "at even, when the sun did set" that the people started bringing others to Jesus for healing.

34 And he healed many that were sick of divers diseases, and cast out many devils; and suffered not the devils to speak, because they knew him.

When this verse says "he healed many . . . and cast out many devils," it sounds like Jesus healed some people but not others.

Jesus' willingness to become involved with all kinds of problems should remind Christians that when a person chooses to follow Jesus, that person takes on the responsibility to do as Jesus did. His healing and other miracles were given as proof that His teaching and preaching were from God. His goal was to free people from the power and the penalty of sin in order to make possible a new relationship with God (John 1:12; 3:16–17; Ephesians 2:1–7).

Jesus' main focus at this point was not to proclaim His own status with God (John 4:34; 6:38), so He repeatedly commanded demons and even close disciples not to reveal His divine nature (Mark 5:43; 8:30).

The demons knew who Jesus was, but this was not the same as knowing Him (James 2:19). Knowing meant more than being able to describe who He was with words. Knowing Him is possible only when people, like the demon-possessed man and Peter's mother-in-law, are willing to trust Jesus enough to obediently put themselves into His hands.

35 And in the morning, rising up a great while before day, he went out, and departed into a solitary place, and there prayed. 36 And Simon and they that were with him followed after him. 37 And when they had found him, they said unto him, All men seek for thee.

Jesus' commitment to prayer shows that the strength to care for the problems of so many people did not come without a price. Prayer was never a minor add-on in Jesus' life, or something He did to enhance His reputation as a religious leader. Instead, all four Gospel writers recorded incidents that revealed that prayer was a priority for Jesus (Matthew 26:39, 44; Luke 6:19; 9:18). He rose early, before others, or when everyone else was gone, to make time for prayer (Mark 6:46; Luke 5:16; 6:12). Three times He prayed before His arrest and crucifixion. The first and last words He spoke while dying on the Cross were prayers.

The priority Jesus gave prayer illustrates the place it should have in the lives of His followers. Just as it gave Jesus strength to zero in on His goal rather than chasing public attention, or frittering away His life on piddling issues, it can do the same for us. Although Mark frequently used the word "immediately" (Gk. *euthus*, **yoo-THOOS**) in his Gospel, in these verses he seemed to slow down to in order to emphasize that Jesus' commitment to prayer was crucial. Overcoming Satan's power and the problems of life comes not from phenomenal human ability, such as Michael Jordan's athletic prowess or Booker T. Washington's intellect. Prayer is the key for keeping faith in our Father strong and following God's will.

We Christians should never allow ourselves to believe we have arrived spiritually (Philippians 3:12; 1 Corinthians 10:12). Neither should we fool ourselves into thinking that we are following Jesus if all we want is to get what He can do for us. That is what some half-hearted followers did after He miraculously fed five thousand people with a few pieces of bread and a couple of fish. Many of those who came seeking Him in this case may have been like that.

38 And he said unto them, Let us go into the next towns, that I may preach there also: for therefore came I forth. 39 And he preached in their synagogues throughout all Galilee, and cast out devils.

Probably the disciples who came to escort Jesus back to Capernaum, where people were hunting for Him, were surprised when He said they were moving on. They may have wondered why Jesus would choose to leave a bustling town on a major trade route and go to little villages. Although the King James Version calls them "towns," Mark used a word (Gk. *komopolis*, **koh-MOP-ol-is**) that combined the words "town" and "village." The term referred to villages that had a market day so that farmers in the area could sell their produce to local people. Villages like that were scattered all over the province of Galilee.

Jesus' desire to share God's message in backwater, backwoods places showed that He was not just concerned that the wealthy, the influential, or the religious heard His message from God. Leaving Capernaum and going to those villages made plain that He wanted everyone to hear it. The phrase in the text that says "therefore came I forth," if written today might read "that's what I'm here for." Jesus' statement to His disciples back then should remind believers today that every person needs to hear God's Word, whether they live downtown, in the suburbs, or out in the country, whether they live in their own homes, in crowded apartments, in abandoned buildings, or out on the street. In all those little places, Jesus taught and healed just as He had in Capernaum. Everywhere He went, He found people with the same spiritual, emotional, and physical needs.

40 And there came a leper to him, beseeching him, and kneeling down to him, and saying unto him, If thou wilt, thou canst make me clean. 41 And Jesus, moved with compassion, put forth his hand, and touched him, and saith unto him, I will; be thou clean. 42 And as soon as he had spoken, immediately the leprosy departed from him, and he was cleansed.

In a nameless village, a man with leprosy approached Jesus. Leprosy was highly contagious and incurable, at least for humans. Contracting the disease made the victim a living corpse suffering a slow death sentence. It cut a person off from other people (Leviticus 13:46). A leper was forbidden from entering the temple, participating in worship, or bringing sacrifices there.

This man was obviously desperate. What he did violated the quarantine of the Mosaic Law, which commanded that lepers keep away from other people (Leviticus 13:46). Instead, he came to Jesus (almost certainly not in a synagogue), knelt before Him, and begged Him to consider healing him. Even though the rabbis said healing leprosy was as hard as raising the dead, the leper's request expressed faith that Jesus could heal him. He realized, though, that Jesus might not be willing to do so. The conditional phrase "If thou wilt" (Gk. *thelo*, **THEL-oh**) meant if Jesus was willing, but could also mean "If you wish to" or "If you want to," which is how *The Message* renders it. Rabbis often thought leprosy was deserved punishment for the sin of slander, which was breaking the ninth commandment.

The man's condition aroused pity and caring in Jesus. In response to the leper's request, Jesus did what would have been unthinkable to most people at that time. He touched the leper and said, "I will; be thou clean." By healing the man, Jesus restored him both physically and spiritually.

Jesus' compassion for hurting people prompted many of His miracles, such as raising Lazarus from the dead (John 11). Just as the suffering of individuals stirred Jesus' compassion, the sinful, self-destructive attitude of society did also (Matthew 9:36; Mark 6:34).

43 And he straitly charged him, and forthwith sent him away; 44 And saith unto him, See thou say nothing to any man: but go thy way, shew thyself to the priest, and offer for thy cleansing those things which Moses commanded, for a testimony unto them.

After Jesus healed the man's leprosy, He immediately gave him orders about how to behave. Jesus told him to show himself to a priest and do all that was required by the Mosaic Law (Leviticus 14:1–32). Jesus did not ignore the regulations of the law in the least, nor did He encourage others to do so. The principle here still applies today—if a person genuinely trusts Jesus, that person will obey Him (John 14:15).

Being healed of leprosy made a new life possible for the man. When a person asks for and accepts the forgiveness from sin provided by Jesus' crucifixion, that person is born again spiritually. That opens for the person a new life socially in the church, intellectually in Bible study, and spiritually in prayer (2 Corinthians 5:17).

When Jesus sent the healed man away to confirm his restored health by a priest, verse 43 says Jesus "straitly charged him" (Gk. *embrimaomai*, **em-brim-AH-om-eye**). The *New International Version* says that "Jesus sent him away . . . with a strong warning." Mark used a word that implies anger, displeasure, or irritation. Maybe He sensed that the man wasn't going to obey Him. The following verse suggests that was His concern because Jesus instructed the man not to talk to anybody, but to go directly to find a priest and follow the instructions for cleansing. Also, the final phrase in the verse indicates that Jesus wanted the man to act quickly. The word "forthwith" in modern English means "at once." The literal meaning of "sent" (Gk. **ekballo, ek-BAHL-loh**) is "to throw out." Jesus sent the man off to fulfill the law's demands as soon as He healed him.

"So Jesus healed many people who were sick with various diseases, and he cast out many demons. But because the demons knew who he was, he did not allow them to speak" (Mark 1:34, NLT).

Apparently, the man did not do as Jesus instructed him. Instead, he went all over the place, fervently telling people how Jesus had healed him of leprosy. As a result, Jesus could no longer go into any town to teach and preach. Soon He had to go outside town into open fields. In fact, when Jesus tried to get away with His disciples to rest, thousands of people chased after Him. The result was the only miracle recorded in all four Gospels, the feeding of 5,000 people with only five loaves of bread and two dried fish. The remarkable and wonderful lesson is that Jesus did not get angry at the interruption. Instead, when He saw the huge mob that had followed and found Him, "he had compassion on them. . . . So he began teaching them many things" (Mark 6:34 NLT).

Sources:

Nineham, D. E. *The Gospel of Saint Mark: The Pelican New Testament Commentaries.* New York: Penguin Books, 1969.

Plummer, Alfred. *Thornapple Commentaries, The Gospel According to St. Mark.* Grand Rapids, Mich.: Baker Book House (originally published in 1914 as part of the *Cambridge Greek New Testament for Schools and Colleges*).

Schweizer, Eduard. *The Good News According to Mark.* Translated by Donald H. Madvig. Atlanta, Ga.: John Knox Press, 1970.

Jesus' instructions to the healed leper give useful guidelines for any person today to express his or her faith in obedience. Jesus was saying, "Do not dawdle: Go and do this right now!"

Jesus ends His instructions by saying to do this "for a testimony unto them." Similarly, when God touches a person's life today and makes a new life possible, that person needs to share that good news with others. What God has done in one person's life can be a testimony to what He can do in others if they decide to trust Him.

45 But he went out, and began to publish it much, and to blaze abroad the matter, insomuch that Jesus could no more openly enter into the city, but was without in desert places: and they came to him from every quarter.

Daily Bible Readings

M: Anointed by God
Isaiah 61:1–4

T: He Cured Many
Mark 1:29–34

W: To Neighboring Towns
Mark 1:35–39

T: The Word Spread
Mark 1:40–45

F: The Needs for Healing Grow
Mark 2:1–2

S: Healed by Faith
Mark 2:3–5

S: Astonished Beyond Measure
Mark 7:31–37

TEACHING TIPS

July 20
Bible Study Guide 8

1. Words You Should Know

A. Wash (John 13:5) *nipto* (Gk.)—To bathe, especially the washing of living objects or persons. Usually expresses the washing of a part of the body.

B. Clean (v. 10) *katharos* (Gk.)—Free from pollution or dirt; pure or clear.

2. Teacher Preparation

Unifying Principle—To Be a Servant The whole purpose of the life of Jesus was to serve. How are we to know who and when to serve? Jesus Christ demonstrated what it means to be a humble servant.

A. To prepare, you may want to take time to examine the word "servanthood." You can look it up in a regular dictionary. Then refer to a Bible dictionary for further clarity.

B. As you read through the passage and the commentary, examine your attitudes and actions about serving others. Spend some time in prayer about the subject, and ask God to examine your heart on this matter. Look at this passage as if you were one of Jesus' disciples in the Upper Room and He were talking directly to you.

C. Complete the Make It Happen exercise to use as an example during the class time.

D. Materials needed: Bible, newsprint or chalkboard.

3. Starting the Lesson

A. If possible, have a foot-washing demonstration with a few students in the class, or wash each of your students' feet. Lead a discussion about how those who were washing and those who received the washing felt and what it meant to them.

B. Have the students read the Focal Verses silently and put the Search the Scriptures statements in order.

C. Read the AIM for Change and ask one of the students to pray with this in mind.

4. Getting into the Lesson

A. Ask the students to read The People, Places, and Times and the Background sections of the lesson.

B. Put the At-A-Glance outline on the board and read it over.

5. Relating the Lesson to Life

A. Have the students answer the questions in the Discuss the Meaning section, and help them relate the answers to their own lives. Challenge them to answer the questions in light of the Focal Verses and the AIM for Change.

B. Discuss their thoughts about the Lesson in Our Society section. Ask: What do you believe is our society's attitude about servanthood?

6. Arousing Action

A. Use the Make It Happen exercise as a closing class project. Make this a fun time. You may want to use the one you completed when you prepared for class.

B. Encourage the students to use the Daily Bible Readings. Ask a couple of students to share how reading their devotions has helped them.

C. Allow each student to share one thing they plan to do differently to be a better servant.

CHRIST AS SERVANT

Bible Background • JOHN 13:1–20
Printed Text • JOHN 13:1–8, 12–20 Devotional Reading • ISAIAH 53:4–6

AIM for Change

By the end of the lesson, we will:

EXPLORE the significance of Jesus washing His disciples' feet;

BE AWARE of the need to serve others humbly; and

DECIDE to serve someone during the coming week.

Keep in Mind

"For I have given you an example, that ye should do as I have done to you" (John 13:15).

Focal Verses

KJV

John 13:1 Now before the feast of the passover, when Jesus knew that his hour was come that he should depart out of this world unto the Father, having loved his own which were in the world, he loved them unto the end.

2 And supper being ended, the devil having now put into the heart of Judas Iscariot, Simon's son, to betray him;

3 Jesus knowing that the Father had given all things into his hands, and that he was come from God, and went to God;

4 He riseth from supper, and laid aside his garments; and took a towel, and girded himself.

5 After that he poureth water into a bason, and began to wash the disciples' feet, and to wipe them with the towel wherewith he was girded.

6 Then cometh he to Simon Peter: and Peter saith unto him, Lord, dost thou wash my feet?

7 Jesus answered and said unto him, What I do thou knowest not now; but thou shalt know hereafter.

8 Peter saith unto him, Thou shalt never wash my feet. Jesus answered him, If I wash thee not, thou hast no part with me.

13:12 So after he had washed their feet, and had taken his garments, and was set down again, he said unto them, Know ye what I have done to you?

13 Ye call me Master and Lord: and ye say well; for so I am.

14 If I then, your Lord and Master, have washed your feet; ye also ought to wash one another's feet.

15 For I have given you an example, that ye should do as I have done to you.

NLT

John 13:1 Before the Passover celebration, Jesus knew that his hour had come to leave this world and return to his Father. He had loved his disciples during his ministry on earth, and now he loved them to the very end.

2 It was time for supper, and the devil had already prompted Judas, son of Simon Iscariot, to betray Jesus.

3 Jesus knew that the Father had given him authority over everything and that he had come from God and would return to God.

4 So he got up from the table, took off his robe, wrapped a towel around his waist,

5 and poured water into a basin. Then he began to wash the disciples' feet, drying them with the towel he had around him.

6 When Jesus came to Simon Peter, Peter said to him, "Lord, are you going to wash my feet?"

7 Jesus replied, "You don't understand now what I am doing, but someday you will."

8 "No," Peter protested, "you will never ever wash my feet!"

13:12 After washing their feet, he put on his robe again and sat down and asked, "Do you understand what I was doing?

13 You call me 'Teacher' and 'Lord,' and you are right, because that's what I am.

14 And since I, your Lord and Teacher, have washed your feet, you ought to wash each other's feet.

15 I have given you an example to follow. Do as I have done to you.

Is any thing more important than Learning God's Word? Doing it!!

16 Verily, verily, I say unto you, The servant is not greater than his lord; neither he that is sent greater than he that sent him.

17 If ye know these things, happy are ye if ye do them.

18 I speak not of you all: I know whom I have chosen: but that the scripture may be fulfilled, He that eateth bread with me hath lifted up his heel against me.

19 Now I tell you before it come, that, when it is come to pass, ye may believe that I am he.

20 Verily, verily, I say unto you, He that receiveth whomsoever I send receiveth me; and he that receiveth me receiveth him that sent me.

16 I tell you the truth, slaves are not greater than their master. Nor is the messenger more important than the one who sends the message.

17 Now that you know these things, God will bless you for doing them.

18 "I am not saying these things to all of you; I know the ones I have chosen. But this fulfills the Scripture that says, 'The one who eats my food has turned against me.'

19 I tell you this beforehand, so that when it happens you will believe that I AM the Messiah.

20 I tell you the truth, anyone who welcomes my messenger is welcoming me, and anyone who welcomes me is welcoming the Father who sent me."

In Focus

When most African Americans think about servanthood in America, it is usually not in a positive way. One picture that comes to mind may be one of a mistreated slave being forced to do unpleasant tasks for a harsh slave master. Another picture may be of butlers with big smiles on their faces, showing all their teeth, while balancing a silver tray, serving tables full of White people. Another may be a woman on her hands and knees scrubbing a huge kitchen floor while her employer sits at the table drinking a leisurely cup of coffee.

Our picture of servanthood from slavery until now is not a pretty picture. Because we have suffered injustice and racial discrimination, the terms "slave" and "servant" often present a negative image. However, to be a servant of God is a very different occupation. It is to follow Jesus' example. Our love for the Lord empowers us to serve as His servants without apology or offense.

In this lesson, we learn that Jesus defines our discipleship by our servanthood, and that the Word of God enables us to change our outlook, mind-set, and attitude about servanthood by following Jesus Christ's example.

The People, Places, and Times

John's Gospel. John is the only Gospel that outlines certain events in the Upper Room, such as the foot washing and the identifying of Judas as the betrayer by the dipping of the bread. Matthew, Luke, and Mark all mention Jesus instituting the Last Supper. John does not. John's Gospel differs from the other writers' and puts a unique emphasis on particular events. John underscores Jesus' teaching concerning these events and their meaning, rather than just reporting the facts of the occasion.

Passover. The Passover began when the Israelites were released from Egypt. The final plague on the Egyptians was the death of their first-born sons. On the night this was to take place, God instructed His people to place blood from a blemish-free lamb on the doorposts of their houses. When the death angel saw the blood, he would *pass over* that home. The blood indicated that this home belonged to God and provided protection. Each year the nation of Israel was to celebrate this historical event with a feast. An unblemished lamb once again was to be slain and used for the meal.

Jesus was crucified during the Passover celebration. This symbolized that He had become the Passover Lamb and His blood would protect believers from the angel of death.

Background

John 12 recounts the conclusion of Jesus' public ministry. After this point He says nothing more to the multitudes. There are only a few words addressed to those who examined Him. In the remaining chapters of the gospel of John, Jesus turns His attention exclusively to His disciples and describes for them His coming death, burial, and resurrection.

Jesus knew all about His disciples' fear and confusion as His time to depart was drawing near. Therefore, He used this valuable time to speak about resources available to the disciples after His departure. As He sat at the table in the Upper Room, He knew that in less than 24 hours He would be on the Cross. This was Jesus' final opportunity to reinforce the constructive lessons that would carry the disciples through a very challenging future. John wrote specific details about this intimate time.

At-A-Glance

1. Jesus Exemplified Humility (John 13:1–5)
2. Jesus Explained Cleansing (vv. 6–8)
3. Jesus Encouraged Servanthood (vv. 12–17)
4. Jesus Examined the Heart (vv. 18–20)

In Depth

1. Jesus Exemplified Humility (John 13:1–5)

Before the foot washing, John set the stage. The Passover meal sat before Jesus and His disciples. This would be His last Passover with His disciples before His crucifixion. Jesus, with a heavy heart, probably looked around the table at these 12 men with whom He had worked intimately for the last three years. He loved each one and desired to express His love on this final night together. He also realized that whatever He said to His disciples in these final hours was of utmost importance.

John used the phrase "his hour had come" to describe this particular time. It was time for Jesus to complete His mission. At the time of Jesus' birth, He began His journey to the Cross. He had come to this earth to die for the sins of mankind. Several times the religious leaders tried to put Him to death because they did not agree with His bold statements, yet they were unable to harm Him because "His time had not come." But tonight the long-awaited suffering loomed large in the mind of the Saviour. It was time.

Jesus and the disciples had walked from Bethany to the Upper Room to celebrate the Passover feast. Ordinarily, a servant of the lowest position on the staff washed the feet of the guests who entered the house before the meal. However, this meal with Jesus and His disciples was to be entirely private. No host

or servant was present to wash feet; yet in place were the water in a jug, the basin, and the linen apron intended to serve also as a towel.

In those times, the roads were dusty and dirty and the people wore sandals. The tables were low, like a coffee table. Dinner guests sat on pillows and reclined at the table. (They were not seated on a bench as some pictures of the Upper Room scene suggest.) Therefore, clean feet were essential to the enjoyment of the meal.

The disciples proceeded to recline upon the couches in the fashion common at the time for dining. No one said or attempted to do anything about the dirty feet. Peter and John had gotten everything in order for the meal, so they probably thought, *We've done enough.* Maybe the disciples expected Jesus to tell someone to do it. That would probably have indicated to them this person was the lowliest of the disciples. No one volunteered.

The phrase "he rises from the supper" indicates that Jesus had waited a while. Finally, Jesus took off His robe, placed Himself in the position of a lowly servant, poured water into a basin, knelt down and removed the men's sandals, and one by one began to wash the dirty feet of each disciple.

Although Jesus through His ministry had taught these 12 men about servanthood and demonstrated it time after time, the disciples still were not following His example.

John interjected into his account of this moving Upper Room experience an interesting fact. The devil had already taken over the heart of Judas to betray Jesus. Jesus served not only the faithful disciples that He knew were going to stay true to Him and be His servants after His death, but Jesus also served His enemy. Judas' feet were washed along with all the rest.

2. Jesus Explained Cleansing (vv. 6–8)

When Jesus came to Simon Peter to wash his feet, Peter objected. Peter might have thought, *This is the King of kings and the Lord of lords on His knees, washing dirty feet.* This proved to be too much for Peter to take. The use of his old name, Simon, in this passage indicates that he was operating out of the old man and not the new one.

"Lord, are you going to wash my feet?" (13:6, NLT). Peter, being the bold, outspoken one, probably was voicing what many of the disciples felt—that

Jesus shouldn't be doing this. Peter still did not understand that to be a godly leader, one must be a servant. Jesus replied, "Peter, you may not understand now, but everything I've done, including this, will make sense to you in the long run." He might have been referring to the time when the Holy Spirit would come and help the disciples understand Jesus' teaching and ministry once He was gone.

This response was still not adequate for impetuous Peter. He continued to protest strongly. Jesus responded to Peter again, "But if I don't [wash your feet], you can't be my partner." In other words, "Peter, if I don't wash your feet, you are not accepting all of who I am, only the parts you pick and choose. To be my disciple you have to accept all of Me and all of who I am, even if I have aspects to my life or personality that you feel are not right or not befitting to a king."

Symbolically, John also used the word "wash" to mean the washing away of one's sins. This is necessary before one can become a Christian. Apart from this type of cleansing, one cannot have any part of Jesus Christ.

After this explanation, Peter went to the other extreme, "Well, Lord, then give me a total bath." Once again, Jesus patiently replied, "He who has bathed needs only to wash his feet." Just as in the natural life, a man who has bathed needs only to wash the dust off his sandaled feet when he returns home, so in the spiritual life a person who has been cleansed from his or her sins through faith in Christ need only confess those sins to be entirely clean again (1 John 1:9).

Jesus took this opportunity as He talked about cleanliness to point out that not everyone in the room was clean. He was referring to Judas. Jesus wanted Judas to know that He was fully aware of Judas' intentions and that this act would mark him as unclean. Jesus was trying to jar Judas into reality and give him an opportunity to repent. But there was no confession or repentance on the part of Judas.

3. Jesus Encouraged Servanthood (vv. 12–17)

Once Jesus finished washing His disciples' feet, He replaced His robe and sat back down at the table. "Do you understand what I was doing?" He asked (13:12, NLT). With this question, Jesus intimated He desired for them to learn more than the idea that when you come for dinner, someone needs to wash feet, so you

might as well do it. He was not merely rebuking their pride. Jesus' act was an example of true love—love that is ready to render the lowest kind of service to others. He was not so much concerned about them being humble as He wanted them to catch on and follow His example.

Jesus talked to His disciples about the titles they used for Him: Teacher (referring to the words He uttered) and Lord (referring to divine power manifested in Him). Jesus explained that He was certainly their honored Teacher and God in the flesh, yet He had taken the place of a servant and washed their feet. Therefore the disciples, who were not as great, surely should wash one another's feet.

The phrase "verily, verily" indicates that the next statement is important. Jesus reminds His followers of their status as "slaves" and "men sent." They were not to stand on their dignity or think too highly of themselves. If their Master and Lord performed a lowly action, the slaves and the sent ones should not consider menial tasks beneath their dignity. Jesus teaches servanthood and humility to His disciples on four other occasions. Obviously, He felt these lessons were important.

Jesus knew that what kept His disciples from being servants was an attitude of superiority, so He gave them Himself for comparison. If any one of the disciples should ever think he was too great to stoop to perform menial tasks in serving his fellow disciples, he would be thinking that he was greater than Jesus.

In verse 17, Jesus spoke to those who not only knew the significance of what Jesus had done for them, but who also live in light of it and in obedience to His call. It is important that we not only hear God's Word, but do it.

4. Jesus Examined the Heart (vv. 18–20)

In verse 18, Jesus told the disciples that His betrayer was one of them. Even though Jesus knew which one of His disciples would betray Him, He still showed affection and loyalty to all of them, even to the one who would betray Him. In the culture of Jesus' day, to eat bread with someone was a gesture of friendship and trust. Jesus revealed that someone at this meal—one of His own disciples—would not only fellowship and eat with Him . . . but would also "lift up his heel against him." Jesus quoted from Psalm 41:9, which describes an act of treachery by one's close friend: "Yea, mine own familiar friend, in whom I trusted, which did eat of my bread, hath lifted up his heel against me." It was a dramatic description of Judas's response to Jesus—like a heel lifted up to kick someone in the face who had offered only their love and friendship. The expression "lifted up his heel against me" in John 13:18 indicates an act of violence.

Jesus said the Scripture would be fulfilled literally: "I have told you these things before they happen, that when it happens—because they will happen—you will know that I am the one of whom that psalm was speaking" (v. 19, paraphrased).

It was not obvious that Judas was the betrayer. After all, he was the one who was trusted to keep the money. Judas was one of the Twelve who had seen devils cast out, people healed, and the dead raised. However, Judas refused to believe because he had never "received" the Lord. Though he was called a disciple, his heart had never yielded to Jesus' Lordship nor surrendered to His will. Although Judas appeared to follow Jesus, he was a betrayer and an unbeliever. In spite of this, Jesus still demonstrated His love for Judas by eating with him and washing his feet.

Search the Scriptures

Place the following events in order of their occurrence.

1. _15_ Jesus said, "You see my example; now follow it."
2. _11_ Jesus said that not everyone in the room was clean.
3. _12_ Jesus asked the disciples if they understood what He had done.
4. _8_ Peter objected to having his feet washed.
5. _18_ Jesus explained that He would be betrayed.
6. _5_ Jesus washed the disciples' feet.

Discuss the Meaning

1. How do you think love was demonstrated to Jesus' disciples through the foot washing?
2. Why did Jesus wash Judas' feet, knowing he would betray Him?
3. What were Peter's objections, and why did they prove that he did not understand Jesus totally?
4. What was Jesus attempting to convey to His disciples and why?

Lesson in Our Society

A major city in Wisconsin faced a serious flood last spring. Many homes that had never experienced a problem with water in their basement suffered major problems. A retired city worker gave his opinion of the situation. "When I worked for the city, we kept a crew that went down into the sewers and cleaned them out. We got down there with the rats and the smelly water. That is no longer the case today. No one wants that kind of job. Therefore, many of the sewage-ways are blocked. I believe this contributed to the problem."

It is true, not only among city workers but also in the home, the church, and many other areas of our society, that no one wants the unpleasant job. No one wants the lowly position. How different this is from what Jesus taught and demonstrated in His ministry.

Make It Happen

Fill in the acrostic below with words that characterize biblical servanthood.

S _UFFER — STRUGGLE_
E _NCOURAGE_
R _ESPONSIBILITY_
V _ISION_
A _CTION_
N _OMAD_
T _RIBULATION_

Check the ones that are true of you and put an X by the ones you need to pray about.

Follow the Spirit

What He wants me to do:

_____

_____

Remember Your Thoughts

Special insights I have learned:

_____

_____

More Light on the Text

John 13:1–8, 12–20

The events recorded in this chapter through chapter 17 relate to the last day before the Passover. Jesus is with his disciples, and he is about to teach them in practical terms some of the most important doctrines. Here Jesus gives them some final instructions before His departure from this world.

The picture is like that of a father, or the head of a family, about to take a long trip from home. Because He is going to be away for a long time, Jesus gathers His disciples to give them instruction on how to live with one another until He returns. Jesus encourages and instructs them regarding how to live as children of God in a world full of evil. He talks to them about serving one another and living in love and harmony.

Love is the trademark of all believers. It is through love for one another that the world will know that we are His disciples. Through love, the world will recognize that He is truly from the Father. And it is through love that we show that we love Him. We keep His commandment when we love one another, for love to Him is the greatest commandment.

1 Now before the feast of the passover, when Jesus knew that his hour was come that he should depart out of this world unto the Father, having loved his own which were in the world, he loved them unto the end. 2 And supper being ended, the devil having now put into the heart of Judas Iscariot, Simon's son, to betray him;

The opening verses (1–3) of this chapter give a summary statement of the spiritual importance of the events that are about to follow. Note Jesus' deep awareness of the dawning of the hour (time) for the fulfillment of His mission—that is, His death, His consistent love for His people, and the work of the Devil, which results in His betrayal. This summary includes Jesus' awareness of the divine origin and destiny of His work.

John starts his narrative by telling us the time period of the events—the eve of the Feast of the Passover. Jesus is aware "that his time has come." John uses this phrase six other times in his Gospel (compare John 2:4; 7:30; 8:20; 12:23, 27; 17:1). The first five instances are in the negative, while this verse and 17:1 are in the positive sense—for example, "What have I to do with thee? Mine hour is not yet come" (2:4) and "No man laid hands on him, because his hour was not yet come" (7:30).

The significance of the statement is notable. It tells of the divine nature of Christ. Although He walked on Earth as a human, He maintained His divine nature. He was totally aware of all things, including the purpose of His coming to earth, and precisely the time for His departure. This separates Him from ordinary humans.

John introduces here the subject of love, which will play an important role in the narrative. Love, as noted above, is the hallmark of all things that Jesus did. The phrase "having loved His own which were in the world, He loved them unto the end" shows Christ's readiness to give up Himself on behalf of His people. The phrase "the devil having now put into the heart of Judas Iscariot, Simon's son, to betray him" (v. 2) qualifies the arrival of the time for His departure. It is one of the signs of the time.

3 Jesus knowing that the Father had given all things into his hands, and that he was come from God, and went to God; 4 He riseth from supper, and laid aside his garments; and took a towel, and girded himself.

Verse 3 also supports the fact of Christ's divinity. Jesus "knowing" (Gk.. *eido*, **AY-doh**) means "to be aware, having the knowledge, or being conscious" that the Father has given all things into His hands. John says that Jesus is conscious of the authority He has from the Father, His divinity, and the coming glory just before His next teaching on humility and servitude symbolized by the washing of the apostles' feet.

It seems that His knowledge, both of the coming moment of His departure and His divine authority and glory, prompted Him for this teaching. The reason for this teaching must have been the disciples' argument about who would be "the greatest" among them (see Luke 22:24).

Before this time, Jesus had rebuked this type of spirit by setting a little child in their midst, saying that they had to become as little children in humility and not seek to lord it over one another (see Matthew 18:1–10). He also had rebuked this spirit on earlier occasions (see Matthew 20:20–28; Mark 10:35–45). Months had passed, and it seemed that the disciples had not yet learned their lesson on this subject. With the time for His departure drawing near, Jesus sought to get rid of this worldly passion. He resorted to using a visual aid to teach the same truth. There was no better time for such teaching than when He was conscious of His glorified position.

5 After that he poured water into a basin, and began to wash the disciples' feet, and to wipe them with the towel wherewith he was girded.

It seems that the washing of the disciples' feet was done before the supper and not at the end of it. It seems that Jesus and the disciples are set and ready for dinner. While everyone is attentive, Jesus gets up, takes off His outer robe, ties a towel around Himself, and starts to wash their feet. Apart from the real teaching of this event of humility and servitude (v. 12 ff), Jesus is following the Jewish custom. It is customary for a host to wash the feet of his guests as a symbol of affection and reverence. Supplicants, in making important requests, also practiced it. One writer indicated that conquered people practiced foot washing as a token of subjection and obedience. However, to Greeks and Romans, the washing of feet was the duty of the lowest slave.

6 Then cometh he to Simon Peter: and Peter saith unto him, Lord, dost thou wash my feet? 7 Jesus answered and said unto him, What I do thou knowest not now; but thou shalt know hereafter. 8 Peter said unto him, Thou shall never wash my feet. Jesus answered him, If I wash thee not, thou hast no part with me.

Peter understands the lowliness of this act so well that when it is his turn, he refuses to have the Lord wash him. The question here, "Lord, dost thou wash my feet?" is rhetorical. Peter, ignorant of the spiritual and moral implications of this act, refuses to be washed by Jesus. Jesus makes it clear to Peter that there is a motive behind what He is doing and promises to explain it shortly to him. Still, Peter stubbornly refuses to yield to the washing and emphatically says to Jesus *ou me nipses mou tous podas* (Gk. **oo may NIP-sayss moo toos PO-dahss**), which means "By no means, or never, will you wash my feet." "I consider it far beneath your dignity," Peter seems to say.

Notice the word "Lord" (Gk. *kurios*, **KOO-ree-oss**) that Peter uses in verse 6. This is translated "owner" or "master," and means one with full authority. It is used also as a title of honor or respect. It is the opposite of servanthood. Peter, using this word, signifies

how highly he regards the Lord and how lowly he sees himself. Peter emphasizes that he is not worthy for the Lord to wash him.

The word "wash" (Gk. *nipto*, **NIP-toh**), which means "to cleanse," is used about seven times to describe the act of washing part of the body (see Matthew 6:17; 15:2; John 9:7–15). Peter's understanding of this act is only physical. But he later learns that something more than mere washing of feet is involved here. There is also a spiritual dimension. Jesus' reply to him, "If I wash thee not, thou hast no part with me," brings out this dimension. What does Jesus mean here? The word "part" (Gk. *meros*, **MEHR-oss**) can also mean "share, portion, piece, or allotment." Some suggestions include that Peter's refusal would mean that he would not share or participate in the work of Christ. The washing of feet, therefore, is more than an example. It is a means by which the disciples could participate in His humiliation and suffering.

13:12 So after he had washed their feet, and had taken his garments, and was set down again, he said unto them, Know ye what I have done to you? 13 Ye call me Master and Lord: and ye say well; for so I am. 14 If I then, your Lord and Master, have washed your feet; ye also ought to wash one another's feet.

After washing their feet, Jesus sits down and then proceeds to teach the application of this service and the implications of His action. He begins by asking them whether they understand what He has done. Of course, the answer is no. He knows how limited their understanding is. His intention is to get their attention and to make them think.

To answer His own question, Jesus appeals to His relationship with them and reminds them of that Lord and servant relationship. They call Him their Master and Lord. The word translated here as "Master" is the Greek word *didaskalos* (**did-AHS-kahl-oss**), meaning "one who teaches." The word "Lord" is the equivalent of the Greek word *kurios* (**KOO-ree-oss**), which is sometimes translated "Master." Jesus uses His double title of Teacher and Lord to strike an important note, which He would explain later. The disciples by inference know what it means to be a teacher or lord. It does not include the washing of feet.

That is the puzzling thing about the whole event. To the ordinary Jew, Greek, or Roman, it

"For I have given you an example, that ye should do as I have done to you" (John 13:15).

15 For I have given you an example, that ye should do as I have done to you. 16 Verily, verily, I say unto you, The servant is not greater than his lord; neither he that is sent greater than he that sent him. 17 If ye know these things, happy are ye if ye do them.

Jesus emphasizes this principle in verses 15 and 16. He tells them that He has set an example for them to follow and calls on them to imitate Him.

Using the phrase "verily, verily" (Gk. *amen, amen,* **ahm-AYN, ahm-AYN**) or "truly, truly, I say unto you," Jesus emphasizes the importance of this example. He argues that a servant is never greater than his master, referring to Himself and the disciples. It is well understood that a servant had no rights at all in his master's house. Therefore, if He, the Master, could condescend to do the menial job of washing their feet, how much more should they who are the servants do likewise to one another. This principle is repeated in two other Gospels (see Matthew 10:24–25; Luke 6:40).

Jesus closes this teaching by emphasizing the practical aspect of the teaching—of servitude and the benefit of doing so (Revelation 2:7, 11, 17; 3:5). To Jesus, knowing without doing has no value (Matthew 7:24–25; Luke 11:28). James, the brother of Jesus, echoes this in his own epistle (James 1:25).

does not make any sense for a teacher to stoop down and wash his servants' feet. With this understanding, Jesus now goes on to make His point, which is the climax of the narrative—how to serve one another as disciples and, yes, as Christians. The message is clear. He says, "If I, being your Master and Lord, would condescend to do this, you should be willing to do the lowest service for one another." This act is revolutionary in the human realm, since humility was despised in the ancient world as a sign of weakness. Jesus calls on them "to wash one another's feet." This is specific in the context of Jesus' act, but the principle is clear. They are to serve one another.

Some Christians take the washing literally and observe the act of foot washing during Communion. However, the principle is to be considered more important than the act.

18 I speak not of you all: I know whom I have chosen: but that the scripture may be fulfilled, He that eateth bread with me hath lifted up his heel against me.

The word translated "speak" here is *lego* (Gk. **LEG-oh**), which means "to teach, exhort, or command." Jesus qualifies His statements by saying that His words are directed to all but one. Jesus declares, "I know whom I have chosen."

The Greek word translated "know" is *eido* (Gk. **AY-doh**), which means "to see or perceive with the senses; to observe, notice, or discern." It also can mean "to discover, inspect, or examine the state or condition of someone or something." Jesus knew from the beginning who would fail to believe and ultimately betray Him (see John 6:64). He had plainly stated, "Have not I chosen you twelve, and one of you is a devil?" (6:70). There was one among the disciples who, in reality, was the very opposite of a disciple.

Judas was "chosen" (Gk. *eklegomai*, **ek-LEG-om-eye**) as a disciple, but he did not choose to follow Christ. After receiving the call and privilege of following the Master, his heart, instead, chose another allegiance. Scripture points out that after Mary of Bethany poured costly oil on the feet of Jesus and wiped them with her hair, Judas asked angrily, "Why was not this ointment sold for three hundred pence, and given to the poor?" (John 12:5). His response could imply that Judas cared more about the poor than he cared for Jesus. But the writer goes on to explain that Judas said this "not that he cared for the poor; but because he was a thief, and had the bag, and bare what was put therein" (12:6).

The Scripture Jesus mentions when He says "but that the scripture may be fulfilled" is a reference to Psalm 41:9: "Mine own familiar friend, in whom I trusted, which did eat of my bread, hath lifted up his heel against me." To share a meal with someone was a sign of fellowship. Here Judas, the disciple that Jesus had instructed and even trusted to carry the money bag, fellowships with the Lord before going out to betray Him.

The Greek word translated "hath lifted up" is *epairo* (**ep-EYE-roh**), which means "to raise, to lift up, or to take up." It is also used as a metaphor for being lifted up with pride or exalting one's self. Similarly, to lift up the "heel" (Gk. *pterna*, **PTEHR-nah**) is a metaphorical expression that means to attack a person in an underhanded manner under the pretense of friendship, so as to gain an advantage when the person is unprepared.

19 Now I tell you before it come, that, when it is come to pass, ye may believe that I am he.

By this statement Jesus tells the disciples that when one of them betrays Him, they should not become discouraged, because the event was known and foretold by Christ Himself. He makes this announcement, partly for the sake of Judas—possibly to give him one more opportunity to repent or to prevent him from excusing his act of betrayal—and partly for the sake of the others, to encourage them to continue in faith after He is betrayed. It is as if Jesus

admonishes them, "Don't let his treachery shake your confidence in Me." Or, as the *New Living Translation* puts it, "I tell you this beforehand, so that when it happens you will believe that I am the Messiah."

The phrase "that I am he" means that Jesus is that Messiah who had been promised and prophesied about in the Scriptures. He is the Son of God who knows and declares things before they come to pass, and our Saviour and Redeemer who loves us and died for us. Jesus used this same phrase in John 8:24: "I said therefore unto you, that ye shall die in your sins: for if ye believe not that I am he, ye shall die in your sins."

20 Verily, verily, I say unto you, He that receiveth whomsoever I send receiveth me; and he that receiveth me receiveth him that sent me.

The word "verily" is used to mark the importance of the truth about to be uttered. Thus, "verily, verily" is am emphatic statement that could also be translated "truly, truly." John records Jesus using the double form 25 times. Matthew quotes the single "verily" 30 times, Mark 14 times, and Luke 7 times. Whoever, then, does not receive the ministers of the Gospel, rejects Christ who sent them and rejects God who sent His Son to be the Saviour of the world.

Daily Bible Readings

M: The Suffering Servant
Isaiah 53:4–6
T: To the End
John 13:1–2a
W: Unless I Wash You
John 13:2b–11
T: An Example
John 13:12–17
F: Whoever Receives Me
John 13:18–20
S: What Do You Want?
Matthew 20:20–23
S: Not to Be Served
Matthew 20:24–28

TEACHING TIPS

July 27
Bible Study Guide 9

1. Words You Should Know

A. Prevail against (Matthew 16:18) *katischuo* (Gk.)—To be superior in strength; to overcome.

B. Rebuke (v. 22) *epitimao* (Gk.)—To admonish sharply; a chiding or reproof.

C. Savourest (v. 23) *phroneo* (Gk.)—To think, regard, or be like-minded.

2. Teacher Preparation

Unifying Principle—Getting to Know a Person We come to know people not by what others say about them but by a personal relationship with them. How well do we ever really know somebody? Establishing a right relationship with God is dependent upon our understanding of who Jesus really is. Peter's confession of Jesus was a milestone in his understanding of Jesus as the Messiah.

A. To prepare for today's lesson, pray that God will enlighten you with His Word.

B. Study the Bible Background and Focal Verses. Familiarize yourself with the information in the More Light on the Text section.

C. Watch the movie *The Passion of the Christ* and record your thoughts and insights as preparation to lead the class discussion.

3. Starting the Lesson

A. Open the class with prayer.

B. Read the AIM for Change out loud.

C. Read Focal Verses and the Keep in Mind verse together with the class. Ask for volunteers to read the In Depth section and explain the verses.

4. Getting into the Lesson

A. Have the students read the In Focus story. Ask the students to share similar experiences with the class.

B. Invite the students to discuss how often they share the Word of God with friends, coworkers, neighbors, strangers, and family members.

5. Relating the Lesson to Life

A. Ask the students if they have seen the movie *The Passion of the Christ*, and invite them to share insights with the group.

B. Ask a volunteer to read the Lesson in Our Society section aloud.

C. Spend as much time as possible sharing thoughts and discussing the questions raised in the Lesson in Our Society section.

6. Arousing Action

A. Challenge the students to use the Make It Happen assignment.

B. Refer to the Search the Scriptures and Discuss the Meaning questions. Continue the discussion.

C. If there are any students who have not given their lives to the Lord, remind them that you are available to pray with them after class. Inquire if there are any prayer requests and then end the session with prayer, keeping the AIM for Change in mind.

Worship Guide

For the Superintendent or Teacher
Theme: Christ as Messiah
Theme Song: "We Praise You for Your Glory"
Devotional Reading: Isaiah 43:1–7
Prayer

CHRIST AS MESSIAH

Bible Background • MATTHEW 16:13–23
Printed Text • MATTHEW 16:13–23 Devotional Reading • ISAIAH 43:1–7

AIM for Change

By the end of the lesson, we will:

DEFINE the meaning of "the Christ, the Son of the living God";

WORSHIP Christ as Saviour and God; and

RECEIVE Jesus as Saviour if we have not already done so, or decide to share the Gospel with someone during the coming week.

Keep in Mind

"He saith unto them, But whom say ye that I am?" (Matthew 16:15).

Focal Verses

KJV **Matthew 16:13** When Jesus came into the coasts of Caesarea Philippi, he asked his disciples, saying, Whom do men say that I the Son of man am?

14 And they said, Some say that thou art John the Baptist: some, Elias; and others, Jeremias, or one of the prophets.

15 He saith unto them, But whom say ye that I am?

16 And Simon Peter answered and said, Thou art the Christ, the Son of the living God.

17 And Jesus answered and said unto him, Blessed art thou, Simon Barjona: for flesh and blood hath not revealed it unto thee, but my father which is in heaven.

18 And I say also unto thee, That thou art Peter, and upon this rock I will build my church; and the gates of hell shall not prevail against it.

19 And I will give unto thee the keys of the kingdom of heaven: and whatsoever thou shalt bind on earth shall be bound in heaven: and whatsoever thou shalt loose on earth shall be loosed in heaven.

20 Then charged he his disciples that they should tell no man that he was Jesus the Christ.

21 From that time forth began Jesus to shew unto his disciples, how that he must go unto Jerusalem, and suffer many things of the elders and chief priests and scribes, and be killed, and be raised again the third day.

22 Then Peter took him, and began to rebuke him, saying, Be it far from thee, Lord: this shall not be unto thee.

23 But he turned, and said unto Peter, get thee behind me, Satan: thou art an offence unto me: for thou savourest not the things that be of God, but that be of men.

NLT **Matthew 16:13** When Jesus came to the region of Caesarea Philippi, he asked his disciples, "Who do people say that the Son of Man is?"

14 "Well," they replied, "some say John the Baptist, some say Elijah, and others say Jeremiah or one of the other prophets."

15 Then he asked them, "But who do you say I am?"

16 Simon Peter answered, "You are the Messiah, the Son of the living God."

17 Jesus replied, "You are blessed, Simon son of John, because my Father in heaven has revealed this to you. You did not learn this from any human being.

18 Now I say to you that you are Peter (which means 'rock'), and upon this rock I will build my church, and all the powers of hell will not conquer it.

19 And I will give you the keys of the Kingdom of Heaven. Whatever you forbid on earth will be forbidden in heaven, and whatever you permit on earth will be permitted in heaven."

20 Then he sternly warned the disciples not to tell anyone that he was the Messiah.

21 From then on Jesus began to tell his disciples plainly that it was necessary for him to go to Jerusalem, and that he would suffer many terrible things at the hands of the elders, the leading priests, and the teachers of religious law. He would be killed, but on the third day he would be raised from the dead.

22 But Peter took him aside and began to reprimand him for saying such things. "Heaven forbid, Lord," he said. "This will never happen to you!"

23 Jesus turned to Peter and said, "Get away from me, Satan! You are a dangerous trap to me. You are seeing things merely from a human point of view, not from God's."

In Focus

Anna and four of her girlfriends decided to go to the diner to get a bite to eat. While eating, they began discussing aspects of a film that challenged the identity of Christ and the truth of the Bible. Although the movie challenged the identity of Jesus and contradicted the truth of the Bible, Anna knew that it also opened an opportunity to share her faith with her friends.

Anna listened intently as her friends spurred accusations against her faith and tried to rattle her cage. After praying silently for the Holy Spirit's guidance, she calmly shared her testimony about Jesus. Speaking the truth in love, she began to introduce them to the *real* Jesus Christ. She explained that Jesus was the Son of the Living God who loved them so much that He died so they could be saved.

Her girlfriends were dumbfounded and ashamed. They did not expect Anna to respond so graciously. Her serene demeanor reflected a quietness and peace that only God could provide. The conversation soon shifted from talking about the movie to church, and how Anna became a Christian. A few months later two of her girlfriends gave their lives to Christ.

People are always watching what we say and what we do. Our response can be the catalyst that draws them to God. We do not have the power to save; only God can save, but we do have the responsibility to plant the seed (the Word of God) or water the seed that has already been planted and watch God do the rest!

The People, Places, and Times

Jerusalem. This is called the "City of Peace," which has known very little peace throughout its history. Jerusalem is a mountainous city that sits on the edge of one of the highest tablelands in Palestine. The city is situated 48 miles from the Mediterranean Sea and 18 miles west of the Jordan River. Under Kings David and Solomon, Jerusalem became the capital of the kingdoms of Israel and Judah. At the time of Jesus, the city had fallen under the authority of King Herod and the Roman Empire.

Background

The Jewish community waited patiently for a leader that would overthrow the oppressive Roman Empire. They believed that this leader, the "Anointed One," would establish a new kingdom and improve the condition of their lives. This new king would rule the world with justice. Unfortunately, many Jewish citizens disregarded the part of the prophetic message that proclaimed that this king would be rejected, killed, and named the "suffering servant." So it stands to reason that many rejected Jesus. Those who rejected Him viewed Him as the son of a carpenter and blatantly refused to accept Him as Christ the Messiah! Matthew, a Jewish tax collector and one of Jesus' faithful disciples, penned this Gospel for his fellow Jews to prove Jesus is the Messiah and to reveal God's kingdom.

At-A-Glance

1. Jesus, Son of the Living God
(Matthew 16:13–19)
2. Jesus, Plan of the Living God (vv. 20–23)

In Depth

1. Jesus, Son of the Living God (Matthew 16:13–19)

Jesus asked His disciples, "Who do men say that I am?" Jesus, being God, already knew the community's perspective, so why did He ask the question? He asked the question in order to hear His disciples' interpretation of public opinion. Is this same question relevant for believers today? Yes, it is as equally significant today as it was back then. How we interpret and respond to the world's portrayal of Jesus will disclose our own perceptions of Him. Do we agree or disagree with the anti-Christ depictions? If we concur with the counterfeit images we see on television or in movies, articles, newspapers, and magazines, then we need to question our understanding of Jesus. These deceptive representations can shake and challenge the faith of a new believer. For the mature in Christ, it should reinforce the necessity to stay grounded in our convictions and strengthen our desire to share the Gospel with others. If our faith is tossed to and fro by every new icon that surfaces in the media about Jesus, we need to reevaluate our attitude about the Christian faith and ask the question, "Do I really believe Jesus is who He says He is, the Messiah?"

To avoid being persuaded by media hype, Christians need to be immersed in the Word of God and rooted in the fundamental truth of the Gospel. Jesus was never moved by contradictory and antagonistic attitudes. He remained focused on teaching and preaching the Gospel and fulfilling His destiny. Similarly, when the Word is practiced in everyday living, the truth of God's Word is clearly visible in the life of a believer. We should not be panic-stricken by what society says about our Lord. It should only create in us perseverance, an attitude that we will never succumb to the world's folly.

If the Lord were to ask you, "Who do you say that I am?" what would be your response? It is amazing how varied these responses would be, even within the body of Christ. When Jesus asked Peter this question, Peter answered by the inspiration of the Holy Spirit and said that Jesus is the Son of the living God. The term "Son of the living God" reflects Jesus' eternal and personal Sonship. Before the foundation of the world and prior to taking on human flesh, Jesus enjoyed an intimate relationship with the Father in heaven. Jesus is called the Son of God because His incarnation and birth into the human race were created by the Holy Spirit. When we accept Jesus into our hearts as Lord and Saviour, we are adopted into the family of believers. However, Jesus alone is the only begotten Son of God. In these passages of Scripture the Lord is revered as the "Living God." The word "living" is used to stress the significance in knowing that the God we serve is alive, active, and sitting on the throne!

Interpreters of the Bible say different things about what Jesus meant when he said "upon this rock" He would build His church. They have said that the "rock" is Jesus; His work on the Cross; Peter, the first great leader of the church; and Peter's confession of faith. The most straightforward interpretation is that "rock" refers to Peter.

There is much debate as to what Jesus meant by "keys of the kingdom." Some scholars interpret the "keys of the kingdom" as Jesus' open invitation to all people (Jews and Gentiles) and a call to salvation, readily available to anyone who believes Jesus is the Messiah and accepts Him as Lord and Saviour. Jesus is the only doorway to heaven. Through our faith in Jesus, we have access to the Father in heaven.

2. Jesus, Plan of the Living God (vv. 20–23)

Peter did not understand what Jesus was saying when He told them He would die at the hands of men and be raised up on the third day. Sometimes the harsh truth about God's Word pierces our hearts. We take offense when He tells us something contrary to what we want. Peter was not necessarily "rock solid" in his character, for right after announcing Jesus was the Christ, he proceeded to rebuke the Master for saying He would be crucified. Jesus had to reprimand Peter for standing in disagreement with God's plan for human redemption.

Peter provides an example of how easily we can slip outside the will of God when we don't understand the ways of God. It is possible Peter was trying to protect Jesus, but again, Peter may have been looking out for his own best interests. He was afraid Jesus would abandon him. After all, he did give up his livelihood to follow Jesus. What would happen to Peter if Jesus died? Peter's fear consumed him to the point that he neglected to hear Jesus say He would rise again. Peter had no idea of the impact of his statement. He had no clue that his actions were unintentionally and unconsciously attempting to thwart the redemptive plan of God! What a revelation!

Many of us have read these verses of Scripture and have either bad-mouthed Peter or shook our heads in annoyance over Peter's zealous reaction. However, if we were honest with ourselves, we could easily recall incidents where we overreacted to God's Word, and fear catapulted us into error or paralyzed us into immobilization. Fortunately for us, no one has the ability to override God's Word or frustrate His plan. Jesus told His disciples His plan to go to the Cross in order to prepare them for the future. Today, God still gives us His plan by way of the Bible. We are God's ambassadors! He has equipped us with the Word of God in order to change the future of the unsaved and to make a difference in our world.

Search the Scriptures

1. Who did Peter say that Jesus is (Matthew 16:16)?

2. How did Jesus respond to Peter's answer (vv. 17–19)?

3. What did Jesus charge His disciples to do (v. 20)?

4. Why did Jesus rebuke Peter (vv. 22–23)?

Discuss the Meaning

1. In your own words, describe the meaning of the term "Son of the living God."

2. How would you describe the relationship between God the Father and Jesus Christ the Son?

3. Why do you think the writer emphasized the word "living" in referring to the living God?

4. Think about your own life. Is God "living" in your heart today?

Lesson in Our Society

The movie *The Passion of the Christ* portrayed a vision of the graphic, horrific, and bloody death of Jesus. The movie must have left undeniable imprints on the minds of unbelievers, forcing them to consider the question: "Is Jesus the Messiah?"

It also left memorable impressions on the hearts of every believer, reinforcing their conviction that Jesus is Lord! With all the negative press that is purposed to discredit our God, we must know, without a shadow of doubt, that Jesus is the Messiah, our Lord and Redeemer. How strong is your conviction? What is your response to unbelievers when they ask you why you serve Jesus Christ?

Make It Happen

Without Christ, life is unfulfilling; there is no forgiveness of sin, no peace, and no hope. God called us to salvation because He loves us. No greater love has ever been witnessed than that of our Lord Jesus Christ.

Have you made Him your Lord? If not, you can do so by praying this prayer: "Father God, in the name of Jesus, I know that I have sinned and I need Your forgiveness. I pray and ask Jesus to be Lord over my life. I believe in my heart that Jesus has been raised from the dead. I receive Him as Lord and Saviour over my life. Thank You for making me Your child."

Share the Good News of Jesus with others. In Christ, we have hope for the hopeless, joy for the fearful, love for the lonely, rest for the weary, and peace for the fretful. Continue studying God's Word, and ask the Lord to open up a door of opportunity for you to share the Gospel with someone. Share your experience with the class the next week.

Follow the Spirit

What God wants me to do:

_____

_____

Remember Your Thoughts

Special insights I have learned:

_____

_____

More Light on the Text

Matthew 16:13–23

For more than two years, Jesus had recruited and taught 12 men as the core group of His disciples. This getaway with them was the first time that He openly admitted He was the Messiah, whose arrival Israelites had anticipated for over a thousand years. When Jesus asked who the people understood Him to be, Peter's answer was correct. However, his reaction when Jesus described what that required of Him was way off base. Only a short period of time remained for Jesus to change that before the climax of God's purposes for His coming.

13 When Jesus came into the coasts of Caesarea Philippi, he asked his disciples, saying, Whom do men say that I the Son of man am?

Jesus had tried to get away so that He and the disciples could regain their strength after a time of intense ministry. A mob of thousands followed Him and frustrated that plan. Jesus' compassion would not allow Him to send them away confused and hungry without teaching and feeding them (Mark 6:31–32, 44).

This time Jesus went to the northernmost edge of Israelite territory. He and his disciples stopped near Caesarea Philippi, a city set on a rocky mountain ledge. From the south slope of Mount Hermon, it overlooked a lush green plain 1,700 feet below. The reference to "the coasts" of the area is misleading. No large body of water was near. The Sea of Galilee was 25 miles south, and the Jordan River was only a trickle since its headwaters took shape in that area.

Jesus and His disciples were worn out from preaching, teaching, and healing. Getting away to rest and relax in a place of picturesque scenery may have seemed like a holiday at first. Jesus brought them back to His mission with the question, "Who are people saying that I, the Son of Man, am?"

Some 27 times the Gospels quote Jesus referring to Himself as the Son of Man. That term enabled Jesus to balance His humanity with theirs. Over 60 times in the book of Ezekiel the term is used in almost the same way—almost, but not quite. Ezekiel spoke of himself as a "son of man," whereas Jesus called Himself "*the* Son of Man." The prophet Daniel foretold the coming of One whom God would send with authority to create an eternal kingdom. Many Jews imagined that the Messiah would be like Daniel's son of man. That seemed to be the idea when Jesus used the term.

14 And they said, Some say that thou art John the Baptist: some, Elias; others, Jeremias, or one of the prophets.

When Matthew says "he asked his disciples," the tense of the word "asked" (Gk. *eratao*, **er-oh-TAH-oh**) meant "to ask repeatedly." He kept asking, "What else?" He got several responses. Jesus was different things to different people, just as He is today. The first answer was John the Baptist, even though John had been beheaded (Matthew 14:6–11). People guessed that because of the miracles Jesus did, He must be John the Baptist come back to life (Matthew 14:2). Even Herod's son, Antipas, who had John executed, believed that (Mark 6:14–16).

A second response was that Jesus was Elijah. That meant that these people viewed Jesus as the forerunner of the Messiah. This belief had a biblical basis because Malachi, the last book of prophecy, said, "I will send you Elijah before the coming of the great and dreadful day of the LORD" (Malachi 4:5). Jesus Himself quoted that verse to testify that John was the Elijah (Matthew 11:14; also 17:11–12).

Some people also thought Jesus was the prophet Jeremiah. In some collections of Jewish Scripture, Jeremiah was placed first in the books of prophecy. Other unnamed prophets were mentioned. Some non-biblical books, such as the book of Enoch, which was popular then, predicted that prophets of old would come back to announce the arrival of the Messiah.

John the Baptist, Elijah, and Jeremiah were accepted as prophets and authorized messengers from God. However, most Jewish leaders thought that God no longer sent prophets.

15 He saith unto them, But whom say ye that I am?

Jesus' goal was not just to be accepted as someone out of the ordinary, or an unusual prophet, or even one with extraordinary gifts. What He was seeking to determine was whether people, especially the disciples, understood who He was. This concern is evident in the way Matthew wrote Jesus' question. Unlike English, in biblical Koine Greek a person and the action of that person are usually one word. If a writer used separate words to identify the person and the action taken, it was a way of emphasizing the importance of the person's action. The order of the words also indicated what the writer wanted to spotlight in a statement.

A third difference between English and biblical Greek was the use of pronouns. In English, the same word can refer to one person or to a group of people, as the word "you" does in English. Greek had one word for speaking to a single person (Gk. *sou*, **soo**) and another word if addressing a group (Gk. *humeis*, **hoo-MAYSS**). All three of those differences are repeatedly important for Jesus' question and Peter's answer.

The first word in Jesus' question was the plural "you." His question was addressed to all the disciples. The crowds had heard and seen Jesus here and there. Now He asked those closest to Him who, unlike the crowds, had watched and listened to Him up-close and personal for more than two years, "Who do you guys think I am?"

16 And Simon Peter answered and said, Thou art the Christ, the Son of the living God.

Peter was impetuous. He often took the lead. When Jesus called for Peter and Andrew to follow Him, Mark 1:18 says, "At once they . . . followed him." At Jesus' transfiguration, Peter was the one who suggested building shelters and staying on the mountaintop with Jesus, Elijah, and Moses. When Jesus' arrest and execution neared, Jesus revealed to the disciples that He foresaw all of them abandoning Him. Peter immediately said, "Even if all fall away, I will not. . . . Even if I have to die with you, I will never disown you" (Mark 14:29, 31a). Then Mark finished by adding, "And all the others said the same." Peter often expressed what others felt but did not say. Here Peter became spokesman for the Twelve.

After saying Jesus was the Messiah, he added "the Son of the Living God." The second psalm recorded that Hebrew priests quoted similar words at the coronation for any new king. This was the first time in the Bible that any specific person was called the Son of God. Abraham was not, nor was Moses or David; neither were any of the prophets.

This was exactly the point in John 3:16 when Jesus was called God's "only begotten Son." Jesus was—and is—the only person ever born the Son of God. Everyone else since Adam has had to choose to become God's sons and be born again through repentance and faith.

Peter used the word "you" for a single person to show he meant a specific individual: You Yourself, or maybe You alone, are the Christ. "Christ" (Gk. *christos*, **khris-TOSS**) is the Greek form of the Hebrew word for "Messiah" (Heb. *mashiyach*, **mah-SHEE-ahkh**). Both words mean "the anointed one." When a new Jewish king or high priest was installed, oil was poured onto his head and rubbed into his hair and over his face. Sometimes it was perfumed. The oil made the man's hair and face shiny and indicated gladness and celebration. Ordinary Jewish people would often rub oil over their hair and face on holidays.

No clear picture of the Messiah was held among Jewish people. Only twice is the term used prophetically of a person God would send to Israel. In some prophecies, the Messianic hope was strong. Isaiah 9:1–7 gives an exalted sketch of promises the Messiah would fulfill. Other prophetic books emphasize a messianic period more than the Messiah as a person.

17 And Jesus answered and said unto him, Blessed art thou, Simon Barjona: for flesh and blood hath not revealed it unto thee, but my Father which is in heaven.

When Matthew wrote that Jesus addressed Peter as Simon Barjona, something is revealed that likely few Bible students realize. The term "Barjona," meaning "son of Jonah," is Aramaic, which was similar to Hebrew and the language used by most people throughout Palestine.

Although the Old Testament was written almost completely in Hebrew, and the New Testament in Koine Greek, Jesus probably seldom used either language. That means that all of Jesus' teaching in the Gospels was translated from Aramaic into Greek. The Christian New Testament was written in Greek because of its wide use across the Roman Empire, just as English is spoken across the world today.

A few Aramaic phrases remain. Probably the best known is Jesus' cry to God during His crucifixion, found in Matthew 27:46. The *New International Version* translates the Aramaic words *Eloi, Eloi, lama,*

sabachthani as "My God, my God, why have you forsaken me?" These Aramaic fragments remind Bible students how close to the original events and how tied to their actual locations these accounts are.

The King James Version renders what Jesus said exactly as Matthew wrote, "Blessed art thou," not "You are blessed" as the *New Living Translation* gives it. His emphasis was on the result of Peter's faith. However, the word "blessed" comes across as confusing and empty of meaning to many people today. "Blessed" (Gk. *makarios*, **mahk-AR-ee-oss**) had two basic uses. One use described a person's feeling about life—happy or fortunate. The other described a positive condition in the person's life—privileged or favored, especially by God. In this instance, Jesus declares to Peter that he should regard himself as privileged by God.

Peter was privileged because his statement of faith in Christ was graciously bestowed by a loving God, not discovered by dogged human effort. As Ephesians 2:8 (NIV) says, "For it is by grace you have been saved, through faith—and this not from yourselves, it is the gift of God."

Jesus wanted Peter and His disciples to realize fully that knowing God did not come from the rationalism of the Sadducees or the ritualism of the Pharisees or the acclaim of the masses. Instead, it is by faith, trusting that the Messiah that God had sent could reveal fully who He is and could save anyone who comes to God through faith in Him.

18 And I say also unto thee, That thou art Peter, and upon this rock I will build my church; and the gates of hell shall not prevail against it.

Jesus reminded Peter what He had said he could be when they first met (John 1:42): a "rock" (Gk. *petra*, **PET-rah**), firm and unchanging. Peter's faith was not flawless, but whose is? Yet Peter was first to recognize Jesus as the Messiah and first among the Twelve to see Jesus after His resurrection. The firmness of Peter's faith gleamed brightest when, less than two months after Jesus' crucifixion in Jerusalem, he stood to speak before thousands of zealous Jews who had come there for the Feast of Pentecost. Peter bravely declared the crucified Jesus to be "a man approved of God" (Acts 2:22). He then confronted those present as guilty of His murder. What Jesus said to Peter applied to him personally, but it also applied to the other disciples for whom Peter was spokesman, except Judas, who inwardly rejected Jesus.

Because Peter's name means "rock" and Jesus then says He will build His church on "this rock," some Christians have thought Jesus intended for Peter to be the foundation of His church. In a sense that was true because Peter plays a unique role in the beginning of the church. In Acts 1–15, we read that Peter is the prominent leader who lays the foundation for the church. This does not, however, lead to the conclusion that Peter is the pope, a "first among equals" who is Christ's primary representative on earth.

A second reason that denies Peter was the head of the church or the person on which Jesus would build the church was Peter's lack of ultimate authority in the early church. Acts 11:2 shows that he was not given overarching rule. Acts 6 shows plainly that he had no supernatural ability to dictate solutions for the church's problems, and in Acts 15, at the council in Jerusalem, the final decision is handed down by James, not Peter.

The word rendered as "hell" was the Greek word *hades* (**HAH-dace**), which was not the place of punishment after God's judgment, "gehenna" (Gk. *geenna*, **GHEH-en-nah**). Both words are translated "hell" in the King James Version, but *hades* referred to the abode of all who died and awaited resurrection.

The phrase "the gates of hell shall not prevail against it" sounds as if the forces of evil are laying siege against the church but will not succeed. But Jesus was saying death would not be able to hold those who trusted Him as Messiah. It could not prevail against (Gk. *katischuo*, **kaht-is-KHOO-oh**) faith in Him. Death would not be victorious in keeping its gates locked shut.

19 And I will give unto thee the keys of the kingdom of heaven: and whatsoever thou shalt bind on earth shall be bound in heaven: and whatsoever thou shalt loose on earth shall be loosed in heaven.

This verse is the biblical basis some Christians have for believing that Jesus made Peter the head of the church. In verse 15, Jesus had asked the whole body of disciples, using the plural Greek word for "you" (*humeis*, **hoo-MAYSS**), who they thought He was. After Peter answered that He was the Christ, in this verse Jesus used the Greek word "you" for a single person (*sou*, **soo**). That sounds like Jesus was giving a

single individual authority over what Christians should and should not believe and do. However, two chapters later (18:18), Matthew showed that was not the case when Jesus repeated the same statement to all the disciples. That showed that what Jesus said to Peter as their spokesman applied to all the disciples.

At that time, Jewish rabbis decided what was "bound," meaning permissible under the Mosaic Law, and what was "loosed," meaning not allowed by it. Jesus told Peter and the other disciples that they could decide what was permissible for the Christian church and what was not. But Matthew said more than that. When Matthew wrote "whatsoever thou shalt bind on earth shall be bound in heaven," the phrase "shalt be" refers to a condition that is already in effect, not something that is going to begin in the future. The form of the word used here, the Greek perfect tense, refers to past action that has continuing effect in the present. Jesus was saying that whatever His church does in obedience to Him reflects what has already been established as God's will in heaven.

20 Then charged he his disciples that they should tell no man that he was Jesus the Christ.

Even though Peter used the correct words, his actions soon revealed that he did not understand what they meant. Peter's scolding of Jesus revealed that he held the common misconception of an exalted Messiah. If Peter proclaimed Jesus' sacrificial mission in those terms, he would have made a difficult task more difficult.

What being the Messiah and the "only begotten" Son of God meant would not become fully understood until Jesus was crucified and resurrected. Therefore, Jesus gave Peter and the other disciples the same stern instructions He had given the demon-possessed man at Capernaum and the leper whom He healed while traveling through Galilee (Luke 4:33–36; Mark 1:40–45).

21 From that time forth began Jesus to shew unto his disciples, how that he must go unto Jerusalem, and suffer many things of the elders and chief priests and scribes, and be killed, and be raised again the third day.

With this declaration, Jesus entered the final stage before the fulfillment of His mission on earth.

Although He continued to heal and teach people who came to Him, His public ministry was mostly over. Matthew says that in His final six months Jesus "began . . . to show" (Gk. *deiknuo*, **dayk-NOO-oh**) the Twelve His sacrificial role and what it would make possible. He did not expect to accomplish this overnight. This should be a reminder to those trying to teach God's Word. Jesus understood that a process accomplishes this goal, not a one-time event.

When He told the disciples that He must go to Jerusalem, the word "must" (Gk. *dei*, **day**) meant "to feel a moral or spiritual obligation," not "a physical necessity or personal desire" (Gk. *chre*, **khray**). Jesus' statement that He must go to Jerusalem to suffer, be killed and be raised from the grip of death shows that this was not an unforeseen accident or flaw in God's plan. No, this happened because a just but loving God chose to let it happen. God's plan was to bring those cut off from Him back into a loving relationship with Him and His purposes by trusting in Jesus.

22 Then Peter took him, and began to rebuke him, saying, Be it far from thee, Lord: this shall not be unto thee.

When Peter heard Jesus say that He would be killed in Jerusalem, he did not hear anything else. Although he had just called Jesus the Messiah, he pulled Him away from the others and in confusion started scolding Jesus. Peter could not bear to hear what Jesus was saying. Rather than "this shall not be," Matthew quotes Peter as saying this shall "never" (Gk. *ou me*, **oo may**) be. In other words, "Absolutely not!"

23 But he turned, and said unto Peter, Get thee behind me, Satan: thou art an offence unto me for thou savourest not the things that be of God, but those that be of men.

The phrase "Jesus turned" likely means He turned His back to Peter. Then He said to Peter almost exactly what He said to Satan in the wilderness, "Get behind me." Luke 14:27 reports Jesus saying, "And whosoever doth not bear his cross, and come after me, cannot be my disciple." Peter's exclamation rejected God's will and purposes for

His Son, the Messiah. Jesus gave Peter the choice to get behind Him and go away, or to get behind Him and follow where He led.

Daily Bible Readings

M: The Promise of a Saviour
Isaiah 43:1–7

T: Who Am I?
Matthew 16:13–16

W: Tell No One
Matthew 16:17–20

T: Get Behind Me
Matthew 16:21–23

F: Transfigured
Matthew 17:1–4

S: Acclaimed
Matthew 17:5–8

S: Elijah Has Already Come
Matthew 17:9–13

TEACHING TIPS

August 3
Bible Study Guide 10

1. Words You Should Know

A. Firstfruits (James 1:18) *aparche* (Gk.)—A beginning of sacrifice. James referred to the early Christian believers as the beginning of God's harvest that would eventually yield an abundance of born-again believers in the ages to come.

B. Superfluity (v. 21) *perisseia* (Gk.)—Abundance.

2. Teacher Preparation

Unifying Principle—Committed Living Being born again should bring about a change in behavior. However, what is the appropriate relationship between knowing what to do and acting on that knowledge? James tells us that as God's people we must not only hear the Word of God but also respond to it with transforming action.

A. Pray and ask God for insight and clarity as you study the lesson and prepare to teach.

B. Read and study the Bible Background passage and the Focal Verses in two or three different Bible versions.

C. Read the AIM for Change and the In Depth section to familiarize yourself with the lesson content.

D. Study the More Light on the Text section to expand your knowledge of the lesson.

E. To test your understanding, complete the exercises for lesson 10 in the *Precepts For Living® Personal Study Guide.*

3. Starting the Lesson

A. Begin the lesson with a prayer and include the AIM for Change objectives.

B. Read the Keep in Mind verse to the class and then ask the class to repeat it three times in unison.

C. To introduce the topics to the class, have someone read the At-A-Glance outline.

4. Getting into the Lesson

A. Have a volunteer read the In Focus story. Ask how many in the class are familiar with the tale. Ask the students to share insights into applications of how this story relates to life experiences today.

B. Ask volunteers to read the Focal Verses.

C. Read the Search the Scriptures questions and solicit answers from the class. Refer to the In Depth commentary section when necessary to generate answers and discussion.

5. Relating the Lesson to Life

A. Ask the students to respond to the Discuss the Meaning questions.

B. Have a volunteer read the Lesson in Our Society section and follow the instructions. Be prepared to record responses either on paper or a chalkboard.

C. To recall God's Word of instruction, remind the students to use the Remember Your Thoughts and Follow the Spirit sections to write down any special insights they may have gained during the class discussion.

6. Arousing Action

A. Read the Make It Happen suggestion. Remind the class that we are to be "doers" of God's Word. Encourage them to put forth an effort to complete the activity.

B. Encourage the students to prepare in advance for next week's class and to read the Daily Bible Readings for each day of the coming week.

C. Close the class with prayer.

Worship Guide

For the Superintendent or Teacher
Theme: Doers of the Word
Theme Song: "I Have Decided to Follow Jesus"
Devotional Reading: Psalm 92:1–8
Prayer

DOERS OF THE WORD

Bible Background • JAMES 1
Printed Text • JAMES 1:17–27 Devotional Reading • PSALM 92:1–8

AIM for Change

By the end of the lesson, we will:

STUDY God's plan for faithful and active discipleship;

IDENTIFY ways to integrate Bible study into our daily lives; and

ALLOW God's Word to transform the way we live.

Keep in Mind

"But be ye doers of the word, and not hearers only, deceiving your own selves" (James 1:22).

Focal Verses

KJV
James 1:17 Every good gift and every perfect gift is from above, and cometh down from the Father of lights, with whom is no variableness, neither shadow of turning.

18 Of his own will begat he us with the word of truth, that we should be a kind of firstfruits of his creatures.

19 Wherefore, my beloved brethren, let every man be swift to hear, slow to speak, slow to wrath:

20 For the wrath of man worketh not the righteousness of God.

21 Wherefore lay apart all filthiness and superfluity of naughtiness, and receive with meekness the engrafted word, which is able to save your souls.

22 But be ye doers of the word, and not hearers only, deceiving your own selves.

23 For if any be a hearer of the word, and not a doer, he is like unto a man beholding his natural face in a glass:

24 For he beholdeth himself, and goeth his way, and straightway forgetteth what manner of man he was.

25 But whoso looketh into the perfect law of liberty, and continueth therein, he being not a forgetful hearer, but a doer of the work, this man shall be blessed in his deed.

26 If any man among you seem to be religious, and bridleth not his tongue, but deceiveth his own heart, this man's religion is vain.

27 Pure religion and undefiled before God and the Father is this, To visit the fatherless and widows in their affliction, and to keep himself unspotted from the world.

NLT
James 1:17 Whatever is good and perfect comes down to us from God our Father, who created all the lights in the heavens. He never changes or casts a shifting shadow.

18 He chose to give birth to us by giving us his true word. And we, out of all creation, became his prized possession.

19 Understand this, my dear brothers and sisters: You must all be quick to listen, slow to speak, and slow to get angry.

20 Human anger does not produce the righteousness God desires.

21 So get rid of all the filth and evil in your lives, and humbly accept the word God has planted in your hearts, for it has the power to save your souls.

22 But don't just listen to God's word. You must do what it says. Otherwise, you are only fooling yourselves.

23 For if you listen to the word and don't obey it, it is like glancing at your face in a mirror.

24 You see yourself, walk away, and forget what you look like.

25 But if you look carefully into the perfect law that sets you free, and if you do what it says and don't forget what you heard, then God will bless you for doing it.

26 If you claim to be religious but don't control your tongue, you are fooling yourself, and your religion is worthless.

27 Pure and genuine religion in the sight of God the Father means caring for orphans and widows in their distress and refusing to let the world corrupt you.

In Focus

Perhaps you may recall the story of the Little Red Hen. Although it is a fictitious account, it is amazing how true to life this story becomes when we consider human behavior, particularly people within the church. Remember how difficult it was for the Little Red Hen to get some of the other farm animals to be involved with her noble project: the baking of bread? Mr. Pig was too tired to help plant the seed for the wheat grain. Mrs. Cow had no interest in cutting and sifting the grain after it had grown. And Mr. Cat was simply too sleepy to help take the grain to the mill to make flour.

But then what happened after the Little Red Hen and her chicks completed all the work by themselves and baked their bread? The sweet smell of freshly baked bread brought all the lethargic farm animals to the hen's back door. Now they were all ready to partake of the hen's labor—that delicious bread!

Many devoted pastors and Christian workers have had a similar experience. A challenge from the Word of God is set before the people. They hear it, but little action follows.

Bridging the gap between hearing God's Word and doing something about it in our lives is what this week's lesson is all about. Only when we endure our trials and temptations with faith and patience, seeking God's wisdom and receiving His Word, can the gap be closed.

The People, Places, and Times

Jerusalem. Dating from the third millennium B.C., the city of Jerusalem is one of the world's most renowned cities. This ancient city has been deemed as sacred by three prominent religions: Judaism, Christianity, and Islam. An abundance of traditions reflecting all three faiths is found within the city's limits. In Isaiah 52:1, Jerusalem is described as the holy city. Although the city predates the Israelites, the Hebrew phrase *'iyr haqqodesh* (**eer hah-koh-DESH**) literally means "the city of holiness." It was given this name most likely because the temple was built in Jerusalem.

Source:
Douglas, J. D., ed. *The Illustrated Bible Dictionary Part 2.* Wheaton, Ill.: Tyndale House Publishers, 1980.

Background

This letter was written by James, pastor and leader of the Jerusalem congregation. He was, therefore, writing to a Jewish Christian audience, as he addresses the "twelve tribes scattered among the nations" (James 1:1). It is generally thought that this group of believers were members of the early Jerusalem church. After Stephen's murder, believers spread themselves across the land, reaching as far as Phoenicia, Cyprus, and Syrian Antioch (Acts 8:1; 11:19). James wrote to instruct, rebuke, and encourage a scattered people as they were confronted with much adversity.

The New Interpreter's Bible presents the fact that the canonization (acceptance as part of the Holy Bible) of James's letter came relatively late; that is, toward the end of the fourth century. However, it also asserts, "When read on its own terms, James is a powerful witness to both the diversity in early Christianity and the moral imperative of Christian identity in every age."

Sources:
Barker, Kenneth, ed. *The NIV Study Bible 10th Anniversary Edition.* Grand Rapids, Mich.: Zondervan Publishing House, 1995.
The New Interpreter's Bible, Vol. XII. Nashville: Abingdon Press, 1998.

At-A-Glance

1. Receiving Gifts from God
(James 1:17–18)
2. Dealing with Anger (vv. 19–21)
3. Hearing and Doing (vv. 22–25)
4. Experiencing True Religion (vv. 26–27)

In Depth

1. Receiving Gifts from God (James 1:17–18)

James is offering some much-needed encouragement by letting the church know that the Father in heaven showers His children with good and perfect gifts. He has just finished teaching about enduring trials and temptations as believers. James has admonished them to continue exercising faith in God, practicing perseverance under trial, and ultimately they will receive their crown in glory. James also exhorts those who must deal with poverty to be lifted up, because a position in God is much to be thankful for.

Conversely, he urges the wealthy to embrace trials that could result in a loss of wealth and material stature but will surely gain the eternal gift of life.

As pastor of his congregation, his concern for their spiritual growth is very obvious. He wants them to avoid confusion in their thinking and therefore delivers his words of counsel in a straightforward manner. In verse 16 (NIV), James issues the warning, "Don't be deceived, my dear brothers." James is informing them that they must adhere to what he is teaching them about falling into temptations and blaming God for bringing the temptation. He clearly states that God cannot be tempted by evil and neither does God tempt anyone (v. 13). Rather, people are tempted by allowing their evil desires to consume them (v. 14).

All of this instruction leads up to the blessed culmination that God provides good and perfect gifts. These gifts are not necessarily tangible gifts that one would expect to receive as a part of birthday or holiday celebrations. Rather, God's gifts include some wonderful, intangible blessings that we could not manufacture on our own, even if we tried. For example, earlier in this passage James offers, "If any of you lacks wisdom, he should ask God, who gives generously to all without finding fault, and it will be given to him" (v. 5, NIV). Godly wisdom is a priceless commodity that only comes from the Spirit of God and cannot be imitated.

In verse 17, James uses the phrase when referring to God, "with whom is no variableness, neither shadow of turning." God, then, is the only One that can be counted on not to change. *The New Interpreter's Bible* describes James's definition of God: "God is defined in terms of complete and generous goodness. God is associated with light, rather than darkness; with stability and consistency, rather than change and alteration; with the giving of gifts, rather than with the grasping characteristic of desire." This means that we can depend on God, who is perfect and trustworthy in all of His ways.

Verse 18 continues to express the goodness God has shown to His creation of humanity. James teaches that God has made us to be the "firstfruits of his creatures." Not only did God create humans in His own image and likeness and gave us dominion over the things of earthly nature (Genesis 1:26–28), God has taken His gift-giving even further and bestowed upon humanity the gift of rebirth or regeneration.

Moreover, God declared His creation to be born by the Word of truth that He utilized to will humans into being. God chose human beings to be the firstfruits, or the highest level of earthly creation, that would represent all of God's creation in its entirety. This is how much the God of all creation loves mankind, His highest expression of nature.

Source:
The New Interpreter's Bible, Vol. XII. Nashville: Abingdon Press, 1998.

2. Dealing with Anger (vv. 19–21)

James speaks here in very practical terms as he calls his readers' attention to his next instruction: "You must all be quick to listen, slow to speak, and slow to get angry. Human anger does not produce the righteousness God desires" (vv. 19–20, NLT). This is sound counsel, as James is keenly concerned with godly communication among believers. Words are not idle talk, but powerful instruments of disclosing one's heart intentions. Thus, Christians must take care how we speak to one another. There is great wisdom in the admonition to be "slow to speak." Proverbs 10:19 (NIV) also shares insight on this subject: "He who holds his tongue is wise."

Many of the senseless murders and violent altercations that take place in this society occur among family members and close friends. Murders of passion, as they are called, are often the result of arguments of very little significance. A word spoken in haste and in the heat of a moment often invites negative reactions that can escalate into extremely dangerous situations. God desires that His children live righteous lives. James warns that an uncontrolled, angry temper works in direct contrast with the righteousness of God (v. 20). He goes on to direct his audience to separate themselves of immorality and evil behavior and instead embrace the Word of God that has been instilled within the hearts of believers (v. 21). The message of the Gospel of Jesus Christ, which is implanted in our hearts, will point the way to salvation and righteous living. Anything that goes contrary to the Word of God only reaps distortion and corruption and must therefore be completely eliminated.

3. Hearing and Doing (vv. 22–25)

The bottomline issue of James's message did not escape from his sermon. The Christian must not only hear the Word, but he or she must become a doer of the life-transforming Word of God (v. 22). How often have we listened to a great sermon or heard sound biblical teaching without ever applying the truth to our lives? If we actually apply the Word in practical, everyday situations, it will do what it has the power to do—it will bring about a real change in our lives. No doubt James remembered Jesus' story about building on solid rock (Matthew 7:24–27). It is the wise man, Jesus said, "who hears these words of mine and puts them into practice." James cautions that we are only deceiving ourselves if we do anything less.

In verse 23, he uses the example of a man who looks at his face in a mirror. After he looks at himself, the man walks away and very soon fails to remember his own appearance. This is the same as when people hear God's Word and immediately behave in a manner that is contrary to truth. They do not act on the Word and fail to allow its instruction to touch their hearts and effect a lasting change within them.

Yet James offers a wonderful promise: If we refuse to be forgetful hearers and instead become faithful doers of the Word, God will bless our good deeds. The Christian life does not lend itself to the practice of "do your own thing." Instead, believers in Christ are called to be free (Galatians 5:1, 13) and must therefore submit themselves to the law of liberty, that is, the freedom from sin that is found in Christ Jesus.

4. Experiencing True Religion (vv. 26–27)

James challenges his hearers concerning the nature of true religion. The pretense of religion that does not translate into Christian acts of love and mercy is worthless. A misinformed, hypocritical religious person with a "loose tongue" is probably one of the most dangerous people alive. His own self-deception hurts more people than one can imagine. For James, the tongue becomes the most powerful weapon in the hands of a "pseudo-religious" person, and that tongue must be bridled because such a person will speak false truths in the name of the Lord.

In contrast, James uses the term "pure religion," which defines the Christian character by taking responsible action and demonstrating godliness. The two are inseparable. Observing those who are in need, which James refers to as "visiting the fatherless and widows in their affliction" (v. 27), compels the individual who is putting the Word of God into prac-

tice to do everything within his or her power to meet that need. At the same time, this action produces godliness that fuels the believer in Christ to continue doing good deeds. The Spirit of God empowers Christians to perform deeds that reflect a heartfelt desire to please God. The Spirit also enables every Christian to "keep oneself from being polluted by the world" (v. 27, NIV).

Romans 12:9–21 provides a firm foundation on which sincere Christian believers should model their lives. In this passage, the apostle Paul further describes the practical manner in which Christians should conduct themselves. In essence, he is explaining what pure religion really means when acted out in its truest form.

Search the Scriptures

1. Wherefore, my beloved brethren, let every man be swift to _____, slow to _____, slow to _____ (James 1:19).

2. What practical advice does James offer for dealing with anger (v. 21)?

3. What is the result of hearing God's Word but not doing God's work (v. 22)?

4. What is the definition of "pure religion" that James describes to his readers (v. 27)?

Discuss the Meaning

1. Discuss some honest feelings people may experience when confronted by trials and temptations. Where can one find peace and discover God's wisdom for these kinds of situations?

2. In spite of the rhetoric and personal opinion that is often prominent in some churches, do you believe that overall the church as a whole is doing a significant work for Christ in our communities?

3. What are some practical ways that we can enhance communication and relationships in our churches by the proper use of the tongue?

Lesson in Our Society

At the time of James's writing, the church was going through troubled times. The saints of God needed some encouragement, and James addressed their need. He first reminded them of God's generous and beneficent nature toward His creation. He warned them against letting their anger get out of control because this type of behavior is not pleasing to God. He instructed them in the necessity of not only listening to God's Word, but afterward, putting the Word into action. James's final warning was about using the tongue to bless God and practicing godly living to experience what true religion is all about.

Examine the passage again, James 1:17–27, and give some serious thought to how James's instructions can apply to our current situation. On a chalkboard or a sheet of paper, list the categories of James's instruction: "Receiving Gifts from God," "Dealing with Anger," "Hearing and Doing," and "Experiencing True Religion." Discuss the relevance of this teaching for today's church and record the group's answers.

Make It Happen

This week take some time to reflect on something that you have personally heard from God's Word but you have yet to act on in your life. Be open and honest and allow the Holy Spirit to direct you. Offer a prayer of faith that He will help you to act on what God is showing you to do. Share with a close friend or prayer partner the action you plan to take, and ask for prayers and support as you seek to do God's will.

Follow the Spirit

What God wants me to do:

_____

_____

Remember Your Thoughts

Special insights I have learned:

_____

_____

More Light on the Text

James 1:17–27

17 Every good gift and every perfect gift is from above, and cometh down from the Father of lights, with whom is no variableness, neither shadow of turning.

As the number of believers grew and scattered, James became the leader of the church in Jerusalem. He wrote this letter to the Jewish believers (the Twelve Tribes) who, scattered by persecutions, had fled to Gentile countries abroad. This new sect of Judaism was neither purely Gentile nor purely Jewish

in nature; therefore, followers of Jesus became economic and social outcasts everywhere they traveled and were mistreated by both Jews and Gentiles.

In the opening verses of this letter, James encouraged his readers to patiently endure trials and persecutions. He wanted them to know that they were going to be tempted to turn away from Christ and from the conviction of their faith. He encouraged them to seek wisdom and patience and to realize that God was not the author of this temptation. James explains that good and perfect gifts are from God. The word "good" (Gk. *agathos*, **ahg-ahth-OSS**) means "beneficial" and the term "perfect" (Gk. *teleios*, **TEL-ay-oss**) means "complete." God's gifts are useful; He gives believers everything they need for successful and constructive lives.

On the first day of Creation, God said, "Let there be light" (Genesis 1:3). In James 1:17, James refers to God as the "Father of lights." Light here is a metaphor and refers to a beacon or beam, illuminating our way. As light flows from the Father, we are shown the way not only to the Father but also the connection of our daily lives to the will of God. As we face life under the guiding light of God's love and direction, our paths in helping others and standing upon our confession of faith become brighter.

James explains that there is no "variableness" (Gk. *parallage*, **par-ahl-lahg-AY**) or variance in God; the light of the Father does not flicker. He is steady and His light continues to move us forward. There is no shadow, no indication that the light of God will change or that the course He has set for us in His Son, Christ Jesus, will turn. God, the Father of lights, is consistent.

18 Of his own will begat he us with the word of truth, that we should be a kind of firstfruits of his creatures.

God is the Father of light, and as such He begot us as His children through Jesus Christ, the Light of the World (John 8:12). Jesus declared that His followers would not walk in darkness but have the fullness of life. Followers of Jesus Christ are to be lights in this world (Matthew 5:14). It is in this context that God begot us through the "word" (Gk. *logos*, **LOG-oss**) of "truth" (Gk. *aletheia*, **ahl-AY-thay-ah**) to be followers of His only begotten Son, Jesus Christ. There is no variableness in God; therefore, God is Truth. His Word, spoken from the foundation of the world and brought to life in Jesus Christ, is also true and faithful. What God has ordained will come to pass. James points out that the adoption of believers into the life of Christ was done by God's "will" (Gk. *boulomai*, **BOO-lom-eye**). Christians are not accidents of fate or circumstance. God's intention has always been to restore humanity to proper relationship with Him, and this was accomplished through Jesus' sacrifice on Calvary. James's readers should have been encouraged to know that they had not made a mistake in following Christ and should not consider turning back under the pressure of their trials.

James tells his readers that they are the "firstfruits" of Jesus Christ. The phrase "firstfruits" (Gk. *aparche*, **ahp-ar-KHAY**) is a reference to the Feast of the Harvest (Exodus 23:16). James's readers were Jews (the Twelve Tribes) with a complete understanding of Jewish rituals. God commanded that the first of all crops should be offered to Him in thanksgiving for His provision. When the harvest was brought forth, the Jewish community gave the first of the crop as a sacrifice to the Lord. James is not calling for these believers to offer sacrifices; he is pointing out that Jesus Christ has given His followers to the Father as His "firstfruits." Christians become new creatures (2 Corinthians 5:17) who enter life anew by the sacrifice of Jesus Christ.

19 Wherefore, my beloved brethren, let every man be swift to hear, slow to speak, slow to wrath:

James begins verse 19 with the term "wherefore" (Gk. *hoste*, **HOHS-teh**). This word connects verses 18 and 19. It means that since believers are the firstfruits of Jesus Christ presented to the Father of lights, they must act in a manner that shows their relationship to God. James wrote this letter addressing the actions of these converts out of his authority as the head of the church and the shepherd of this flock. We can infer from his words that James was concerned that the persecution and turmoil these followers faced was causing them to be anxious and afraid. It is natural to assume that they might have been responding to situations with anger and frustration.

James's words in the opening verses of his letter may seem harsh but he tempers this with the opening words of verse 19, indicating that his instructions are from his heart. He refers to the Jewish Christians as his "beloved brethren." The Greek term for "beloved" (*agapetos*, **ahg-ahp-ay-TOSS**) is akin to a term often used in churches today, *agape*, to refer to the genuine and unselfish love that believers are to have for one another. This is the same love Christ showed by going to Calvary as a sacrifice for our lives. By calling the readers "beloved brethren," James reminds them that they are one with him and with each other. They are family in Christ Jesus and must reconcile their behavior to a love that places its concern for others above its own desires and needs.

James gives three guidelines that Christians should follow in order to demonstrate the *agape* love he has just mentioned. His instruction is that they should be "swift to hear," "slow to speak," and "slow to wrath." The phrase "swift to hear" is translated in *The Message* as "lead with your ears." Our first response, then, in fellowship, communion, and unity with others, is to listen. The term "hear" (Gk. *akouo*, **ahk-OO-oh**) means "to listen attentively" and implies more than simply waiting your turn to speak in the conversation. It means to discern what others are saying. James tells the followers to listen swiftly (Gk. *tachus*, **tahkh-OOS**). They are to be prompt, ready, and willing to listen. Basically this implies that Christians are to take listening as a responsibility or duty. We are not to listen with a begrudging spirit, compelled to impatiently pay attention like a child. Listening is a sign of maturity and implies a decision to understand what the other party means. A misunderstanding of words and terms can lead to hurt or even the destruction of relationships. James's advice is the first step in practical living: Listen!

In contrast to the eagerness with which we should attend to the words and meaning of others, we must be cautious in speaking. While we can appreciate the adage regarding "sticks and stones," we must admit that words can hurt. Spoken words cannot be taken back. The irreparable danger of hasty speech or harmful statements will linger long after the conversation ends. James reminds us that our words can be a source of discouragement that broods in the mind of the hearer and impacts decisions and attitudes then and later.

James also tells his readers to be slow to "wrath" (Gk. *orge*, **or-GAY**). There is an implication here of becoming emotional and acting impulsively. Taking time to listen and think curtails our instinct to respond with haste and anger when we are opposed to the words or actions of another person. Proverbs 15:1 reminds us that "a soft answer turneth away wrath." James gives his readers a practical strategy for doing just that.

20 For the wrath of man worketh not the righteousness of God.

James explains that wrath does not produce the "righteousness" (Gk. *dikaiosune,* **dik-ah-yos-OO-nay**) of God. James uses a Greek term (*katergazomai,* **kaht-ehr-GAHD-zom-eye**) for "work," which means to fully accomplish. In other words, rash behavior that arises from an emotional outburst is not acceptable to God because it does not accomplish His will. As the first-fruits of the sacrifice of Jesus Christ, our behavior should reflect the relationship we have with the Father of lights. James's statements about being "swift to hear, slow to speak, slow to wrath" are ultimately about the believer's relationship with God. Christians are advised to listen to others and prayerfully discern what they are saying.

Understanding the intent and meaning of another person is a first step in active listening. Before speaking, followers of Christ should seek God's wisdom in how to respond and then respond slowly, as they seek God for the "right" words in that situation. God, who gives His children light, directs them in saying the words that will be beneficial to the other person and the situation. In the end, followers will not be given to anger and hasty judgment. Such Christian action will actually demonstrate that the believer is in right standing with God.

21 Wherefore lay apart all filthiness and superfluity of naughtiness, and receive with meekness the engrafted word, which is able to save your souls.

If our words are to reflect righteousness in God, our actions must also follow. In verse 21, James admonishes his readers to put off ("lay aside," Gk. *apotithemi,* **ap-ot-EETH-ay-mee**) behaviors that are not helpful to their testimony as followers of Christ. "Filthiness" is a Greek term (*rhuparia,* **hroo-par-EE-ah**) that means "to make foul." It is a reference to defiled and dishonorable behaviors and attitudes. "Superfluity" (Gk. *perisseia,* **per-is-SAY-ah**) means "overabundance" and "naughtiness" (Gk. *kakia,* **kak-EE-ah**) means "malice, wickedness, or depravity." James is referring to actions that harm others, that are willful and malicious intentions, including lawbreaking.

"Walk the talk" has become a popular phrase meaning that our actions should reflect our public profession of our beliefs. James 1:22 goes to the root of this phrase by urging us to "be ye doers of the word and not hearers only." James's use of the word "be" coupled with the word "but" carries a mandate to become doers. It is difficult to "become" something, to carry yourself in a particular manner, when your actions, upbringing, and former beliefs are contrary to what you are to become. This was the case with the first-century Jewish believers that James addresses. Their lives, like ours prior to following Christ, did not automatically please God. Those who become Christians must learn to think and act in new ways as new creatures in Christ. While this letter was written to Jews who had only recently become followers of Jesus Christ, it gives sage advice to all believers.

It is obvious that we are not reconciled to God's standard when we do not listen and curtail our speech with prayerful submission to God's will and guidance. Hasty speech and behavior breed more than just personal injury. James indicates that these actions also bring injury upon others and interfere with our ability to hear God's direction in our lives. In order to change these behaviors, James advises that believers receive with meekness the "engrafted" (Gk. *emphutos,* **EM-foo-toss**) Word of God, which is inborn or implanted in believers by the Spirit of God. In Ezekiel 11:19, God promised to remove the stony heart of His people and replace it with a heart of flesh. In 2 Corinthians 3:2, Paul describes believers as epistles of God, written on the heart. God has placed His Word in the heart so that it will effectively save our souls.

"Meekness" (Gk. *prautes,* **prah-OO-tayss**) stands in sharp opposition to anger and impulsivity. Meekness is mildness and gentleness. It is a quality that gives preference to another rather than responding harshly to behavior that might be offensive. James tells believers to receive the engrafted Word with this attitude. "Receive" (Gk. *dechomai,* **DEKH-om-eye**) means "to accept or grab hold." While James does not deny that trials are upon the believers through political and social persecution, he leaves no doubt that the real healing and salvation of Christ's followers is a matter of the soul that connects us with eternity in Christ Jesus.

22 But be ye doers of the word, and not hearers only, deceiving your own selves.

James says that we are to be "doers" (Gk. *poietes*, **poy-ay-TAYSS**) of the Word. If the Word is written in our hearts and if Jesus Christ is the manifestation of the Word in flesh, then we must be obedient to God's Word. It should be impossible to hear the Word and not act upon it if, in fact, it is within you. It is equally impossible to ignore the direction of God when your very heart is attuned to His guidance.

James warns his readers that if they act in disobedience to what God, through the Holy Spirit, has placed in their hearts, they are "deceiving" (Gk. *apatao*, **ahp-aht-AH-oh**) themselves with faulty reasoning. Paul uses the same word in Colossians 2:4 when speaking of people who are deceived by enticing words. Given that definition, James's admonition includes the responsibility of the listener to discern what the speaker is saying. To hear the words and not clarify the meaning so we can properly follow sound instruction in the Word of God is equal to fooling oneself into going on the wrong path. If we are true followers of God, we will be obedient to His Word and not deny that we are His. If we are not followers of God, it will become evident in our actions and our masquerade, as believers will be uncovered.

James admonishes the people of God to realize that they are not just converts because they have heard the sermons and been part of the fellowship. Instead, they are called to become those who act upon the teaching of Jesus Christ in their daily circumstance. To do otherwise is a form of self-deception. The Word of God has as its main purpose "doctrine, reproof, correction, and instruction in righteousness" (2 Timothy 3:16). The instruction in the Word of God is given for the understanding and application of God's words of inspiration and correction to our lives. We miss the point and fall short of receiving the true joy and blessing of living in ways that are pleasing to God and beneficial to others when we fail to act on what we learn. James, therefore, warns followers to avoid self-deception.

23 For if any be a hearer of the word, and not a doer, he is like unto a man beholding his natural face in a glass: 24 For he beholdeth himself, and goeth his way, and straightway forgetteth what manner of man he was.

James explains the idea of inaction in a simple illustration. Having the Word and refusing to accept the guidance of it is like looking in a mirror and refusing to accept that your hair is undone or you need a shave! Such a person looks in the mirror, sees the situation, and immediately moves on without acting upon the obvious, forgetting the purpose of looking in the mirror in the first place. Mirrors allow us to see ourselves as others see us. They provide a way for us to "get it together" so that we can be properly represented in public. Failure to adjust ourselves based on what the mirror reveals means that we have forgotten to fix ourselves for proper display to the world. The same is true of God's Word: Failure to align with God's will as expressed in His Word means that our effort to display Christian character to the world will be faulty.

25 But whoso looketh into the perfect law of liberty, and continueth therein, he being not a forgetful hearer, but a doer of the work, this man shall be blessed in his deed.

James says that the law of liberty, the Gospel of Christ, is like a mirror that helps us see if we are aligned with God's Word and His direction. Those who examine themselves in light of the Gospel message, who respond to the guidance of God, will be blessed as "doers of the word." The person who aligns with God's mirror of liberty acts in a manner that shows the Word of God is effective in his or her life. This person stands in stark contrast to the one who forgets or fails to listen to the Lord's guidance.

26 If any man among you seem to be religious, and bridleth not his tongue, but deceiveth his own heart, this man's religion is vain.

James likens those who fail to line up with the Word of God with those who "seem" to be religious (Gk. *threskos*, **THRAYS-kos**) and do those things that they think followers of God do. In modern times, perhaps such people give offerings and attend worship services. They might be members of church groups and sing in the choir. They do all of the things that appear to be proper for followers of God; but they do not do those things that indicate they are true followers. James warns that one true mark of followers is that they "bridle" (Gk. *chalinagogeo*, **khal-in-ahg-ohg-EH-oh**) their tongues. To not restrain one's words (i.e., "bridle the tongue") is to disobey James's admonition of being "slow to speak." A person who speaks without restraint may spew words that are spiteful and unhelpful to those who are in need of encouragement and strength. James wanted the believers to know that their irrational words did more harm than good and led people away from, rather than to, the Father of lights.

James says that such people make a show of religion that is in vain (Gk. *mataios*, **MAHT-ah-yoss**). This Greek term means "lacking in truth, power, and results." In short, such seemingly religious activity is useless. Our actions must point people to the light of God. Doing religious things might be beneficial in that some help may come to someone; however, James is very clear that it is the meek and honest obedience to what God has engrafted in our hearts that proves a person is a child of God.

27 Pure religion and undefiled before God and the Father is this, To visit the fatherless and widows in their affliction, and to keep himself unspotted from the world.

Finally James explains what pure religion is. First, "pure" (Gk. *katharos*, **kahth-ar-OSS**) religion is ethically without blame or guilt. The term can be used of a vine that is pruned and has had the dead and useless branches removed. The result is a plant that is totally committed to bringing forth fruit. There is no doubt that the honest practice of worship and spiritual discipline is directed by the Father of lights and aligned with the engrafted Word in the heart of the believer. Pure religion is without blame and will, in fact, be a witness to others. The practitioner of pure religion does not bring an attack upon the name of the Lord or harm to the members of Christ's body. Pure religion is evident in our actions. Specifically, James admonishes his reader to visit the fatherless and widows and to keep themselves "unspotted" (Gk. *aspilos*, **AHS-pee-loss**), free from censure and vice. In other words, the person who practices pure religion does not bring reproach to the body of Christ or themselves.

"Visiting" (Gk. *episkeptomai*, **ep-ee-SKEP-tom-eye**) means more than stopping by to say hello. It means to look upon and give help to another. It means to be of benefit and to give care. The persecution of the church was tearing families apart and leaving in its wake people who were totally without support. During the first century, it was the norm for women and children to be completely destitute if the father, husband, or breadwinner of the family was incapacitated or dead. Without an income, those who were without fathers and husbands were at the mercy of society. They had no means of support, no way out of their homeless and impoverished circumstances. Without the help of the church, there was no hope.

James has already told these believers to follow the Father of lights, to be obedient and mindful of the engrafted Word that the Holy Spirit has placed in their hearts. He has told them to be honest in their service to the body of Christ and to avoid superfluous and meaningless religiosity. Now he uses a harsher term, "keep" (Gk. *tereo*, **tay-REH-oh**), which means "to guard against that which is not helpful to the individual." The term "world" (Gk. *kosmos*, **KOS-moss**) means more than just the universe. It refers to governmental systems as well as the entirety of people who populate the world. More specifically, it refers to the ungodly multitude that does not follow God, whose lives are in contrast to the will of God. James calls his readers to a higher standard of accountability. His final words in this chapter are a call to service and worship that advances the cause of Christ and encourages the body of believers.

Daily Bible Readings

M: The Full Effect of Endurance
James 1:1–4

T: Ask in Faith
James 1:5–8

W: How to Boast
James 1:9–11

T: Endure Temptation
James 1:12–15

F: Everything Is from God
James 1:16–21

S: Blessed in Doing
James 1:22–27

S: How Great Are Your Works
Psalm 92:1–8

TEACHING TIPS

August 10
Bible Study Guide 11

1. Words You Should Know

A. Vile (James 2:2) *rhuparos* (Gk.)—Dirty, cheap, or shabby.

B. Raiment (v. 2) *esthes* (Gk.)—To clothe; dress: apparel, clothing, robe.

2. Teacher Preparation

Unifying Principle—Honoring All People God does not judge people based upon income, and neither should we. James teaches that Christians should make no distinctions in their treatment of others because of their material wealth.

A. Begin by meditating on the Devotional Reading: Matthew 25:31–46.

B. Review the Bible Background information and read the Focal Verses in two different Bible versions.

C. Study More Light on the Text to expand your knowledge of the lesson.

D. Complete the exercises for lesson 11 in the *Precepts For Living® Personal Study Guide.*

3. Starting the Lesson

A. Have a volunteer read the AIM for Change. Begin with prayer.

B. Write the letters L-O-V-E on the chalkboard in vertical order. Ask the students to make words from each of the letters that reflect God's love for His children. For example: L=Live, O=Others, V=Valuable, E=Everyone.

C. After several words have been given for each letter, ask for volunteers to make sentences with the words. For example: *Live for others because everyone is valuable.*

D. Have volunteers read the In Focus story. Ask the students why it is important to show love and respect to everyone, not just to people who look a certain way.

4. Getting into the Lesson

A. To introduce the lesson, read the At-A-Glance outline to the class.

B. Have a volunteer read the Background section.

C. Ask for volunteers to read the first section of the In Depth commentary. Generate a discussion about people showing favoritism in the church. Apply what James is teaching in vv. 1–7 of the Scripture passage.

D. Ask the students to share experiences they have had when they obey God's command to "love your neighbor as yourself." Did they encounter difficulties when doing so?

5. Relating the Lesson to Life

A. Ask a volunteer to read The People, Places, and Times information.

B. Have the students share the most significant point they have learned from the lesson and how they plan to use it during the coming week.

6. Arousing Action

A. The Make It Happen section offers suggestions about ways to practice the principles taught in the lesson. Ask the students for other ways your church can reach out.

B. Remind the students that we are to be impartial disciples for Christ, who always treat poor people with dignity. Emphasize that we are to share out of God's abundance and bless those in need.

C. Close the class with prayer.

Worship Guide

For the Superintendent or Teacher
Theme: Impartial Disciples
Theme Song: "All Creatures of Our God and King"
Devotional Reading: Matthew 25:31–46
Prayer

IMPARTIAL DISCIPLES

Bible Background • JAMES 2
Printed Text • JAMES 2:1–13 Devotional Reading • MATTHEW 25:31–46

AIM for Change

By the end of the lesson, we will:

RECOGNIZE that God cares for all people, especially the poor;

RESPECT all people regardless of their socioeconomic status; and

DEVELOP strategies to show the love of God to all people.

Keep in Mind

"Hearken, my beloved brethren, Hath not God chosen the poor of this world rich in faith, and heirs of the kingdom which he hath promised to them that love him?" (James 2:5).

Focal Verses

KJV **James 2:1** My brethren, have not the faith of our Lord Jesus Christ, the Lord of glory, with respect of persons.

2 For if there come unto your assembly a man with a gold ring, in goodly apparel, and there come in also a poor man in vile raiment;

3 And ye have respect to him that weareth the gay clothing, and say unto him, Sit thou here in a good place; and say to the poor, Stand thou there, or sit here under my footstool:

4 Are ye not then partial in yourselves, and are become judges of evil thoughts?

5 Hearken, my beloved brethren, Hath not God chosen the poor of this world rich in faith, and heirs of the kingdom which he hath promised to them that love him?

6 But ye have despised the poor. Do not rich men oppress you, and draw you before the judgment seats?

7 Do not they blaspheme that worthy name by the which ye are called?

8 If ye fulfil the royal law according to the scripture, Thou shalt love thy neighbour as thyself, ye do well:

9 But if ye have respect to persons, ye commit sin, and are convinced of the law as transgressors.

10 For whosoever shall keep the whole law, and yet offend in one point, he is guilty of all.

11 For he that said, Do not commit adultery, said also, Do not kill. Now if thou commit no adultery, yet if thou kill, thou art become a transgressor of the law.

12 So speak ye, and so do, as they that shall be judged by the law of liberty.

13 For he shall have judgment without mercy, that hath shewed no mercy; and mercy rejoiceth against judgment.

NLT **James 2:1** My dear brothers and sisters, how can you claim to have faith in our glorious Lord Jesus Christ if you favor some people over others?

2 For example, suppose someone comes into your meeting dressed in fancy clothes and expensive jewelry, and another comes in who is poor and dressed in dirty clothes.

3 If you give special attention and a good seat to the rich person, but you say to the poor one, "You can stand over there, or else sit on the floor"—well,

4 doesn't this discrimination show that your judgments are guided by evil motives?

5 Listen to me, dear brothers and sisters. Hasn't God chosen the poor in this world to be rich in faith? Aren't they the ones who will inherit the Kingdom he promised to those who love him?

6 But you dishonor the poor! Isn't it the rich who oppress you and drag you into court?

7 Aren't they the ones who slander Jesus Christ, whose noble name you bear?

8 Yes indeed, it is good when you obey the royal law as found in the Scriptures: "Love your neighbor as yourself."

9 But if you favor some people over others, you are committing a sin. You are guilty of breaking the law.

10 For the person who keeps all of the laws except one is as guilty as a person who has broken all of God's laws.

11 For the same God who said, "You must not commit adultery," also said, "You must not murder." So if you murder someone but do not commit adultery, you have still broken the law.

12 So whatever you say or whatever you do, remember that you will be judged by the law that sets you free.

13 There will be no mercy for those who have not shown mercy to others. But if you have been merciful, God will be merciful when he judges you.

In Focus

It had been a long climb for Charles to make it back to working-class society. Two years earlier, he had been walking from trash can to trash can, trying to find a meal for the day. He recalled a soul-stirring message from an evangelist who had come to the area to bring food and to preach the Word of God. For many nights after that visit, he remembered those soul-lifting words.

On the Fourth of July, he got up the nerve to go forward. He had not changed clothes in a long time and his shoes had worn soles, but he pushed his way through the crowd and stood before the evangelist. "Preacher," he called, waving his arm. At that moment, a strong push thrust him backward and a voice bellowed, "Get out of the way, you bum!" With head hung down, he turned to walk back into the crowd.

"Sir, sir," the voice of the evangelist called out. "Did you want to say something?"

Without hesitation he asked, "Can I be saved in these dirty old clothes?"

Looking into his pain-filled eyes, the evangelist replied, "Yes, you certainly can. Jesus is not concerned with your clothes; He cares about you."

Today's lesson emphasizes that the Christian view of the poor should be informed by the value of all people in God's sight. Believers must know that God does not judge people based upon their income, and neither should we. The way we treat the poor should be motivated by God's command to love our neighbors as ourselves. We are called by God to be impartial disciples.

The People, Places, and Times

James. The writer of the book of James is self-identified as "James." Two persons named James are mentioned in the New Testament: James, the son of Zebedee, who with his brother, John, was among the first Jesus called as his disciples (Mark 1:19; 5:37; 9:2; 10:35); and James, the brother of Jesus (Mark 6:3; 1 Corinthians 15:7; Galatians 1:19), a prominent leader of the Jerusalem church who relied upon Scripture and tradition to settle the dispute concerning Gentile conversion requirements (Acts 15:13–29; Galatians 2:1–14). The evidence is greater in support of the author being the brother of Jesus than the son of Zebedee. The latter was martyred around 44 C.E. by Herod Agrippa I (Acts 12:2) before the book is believed to have been written, and the former in 62 C.E. according to the Jewish historian Josephus and the Christian historian Eusebius. Nevertheless, the Greek style of writing employed by the writer, called the diatribe, suggests that the book was written by a Hellenistic Jew rather than a Palestinian Jew. The one thing we do know is that the writer identifies himself as a teacher (James 3:1).

The book of James is referred to as one of the catholic (meaning universal) letters because it is not addressed to a particular church, but rather appears to be a general letter written to several churches.

Background

The letter from James was written to a people under pressure. Christians were apparently not being martyred, but they were suffering economic persecution and oppression, and the church was breaking under the strain. In a response to the difficulties they faced, James admonished believers to pull together and help one another. Otherwise, they would compromise with the world and become divided because of the constant adversity. Helping one another would have been the ideal choice, but it seems that these believers were more focused on the struggle to get ahead in the world.

There is no other letter in the New Testament that refers to the teachings of Jesus as does this letter. Although James does not directly quote Jesus, he uses phrases and ideas that originated with Jesus. Most of these teachings are found in the Sermon on the Mount, in Matthew 5–7, and the Sermon on the Plain, in Luke 6:17–49.

The apostle James is an excellent example of a New Testament church leader who highlighted the Lord's teaching and applied it to the problems found within the church. This also makes James's teaching a model of practical advice for the contemporary church on how to apply the teachings of Jesus in troublesome times.

Source:
Vincent, Marvin R. *Word Studies in the New Testament*. Peabody, Mass.: Hendrickson Publishers, 1888.

At-A-Glance

1. Warning against Favoritism (James 2:1–7)
2. Encouragement to Love (vv. 8–13)

In Depth

1. Warning against Favoritism (James 2:1–7)

As a concerned leader of the Christian church, James began with a warning to the believers: Beware of favoritism. In his day, it was not unusual for people to show partiality to the rich and blatant disregard for the poor. To address this ungodly practice, James wrote to let the believers in Christ know that such behavior is unacceptable (v. 1).

To prevent any misunderstanding about what he was trying to convey, James demonstrated his point by using the illustration of two men who enter the house of God. One man would immediately be regarded as well-to-do because he was wearing a gold ring and fine clothes. The other man, however, was considered poor because he wore shabby clothes (v. 2). Partiality begins when the believer who greets them pays more attention to the man of higher status, offering him the best seat. At the same time, the poor man is directed to sit apart from the rest of the congregation (v. 3). James pointed out that the tendency to show a preference to those with prestige and position over the poor and less fortunate is incompatible with the teachings and actions of our Lord Jesus.

James continued his teaching by asking the question: "Hath not God chosen the poor of this world [to be] rich in faith, and heirs of the kingdom which he hath promised to them that love him?" (v. 5). Jesus' parables often highlighted a noticeable emphasis in favor of the poor and against the haughty rich (Luke 12:16–21; 16:19–31). This is not to say that Jesus was against rich people, but Jesus definitely had a heart for the poor. Abraham Lincoln suggested that the reason God made so many poor people is because He loves them so. James reminds us that God has "chosen those who are poor in the eyes of the world to be rich in faith and to inherit the kingdom" (v. 5, NIV). God will not deny a place in the kingdom for rich persons, but this verse emphatically states that the poor, who are so often dishonored and oppressed by the rich (vv. 6–7), are not only welcome but celebrated in the kingdom of God. James points out that poor people are honored by God and therefore should not be dishonored by those who profess to be His children.

2. Encouragement to Love (vv. 8–13)

James continues to teach by saying that it is not enough to merely tolerate poor people and refrain from mistreating them. Rather, believers must go farther and actively show love to the less fortunate, even as we love ourselves (v. 8). James referred to this commandment as "the royal law." Here he drew from the strength of the words spoken by Moses in the book of Leviticus, "You shall love your neighbor as yourself" (Leviticus 19:18). Under Levitical law, the concept of holiness affected not only the relationship each individual had with God, but also the relationship of sharing neighborly love and respect with one another.

Similarly, Jesus taught the commandment that is found at the heart of all godly relationships, "Do to others as you would have them do to you" (Luke 6:31, NIV). In our relationships with others, Jesus requires us to put this command into action. Conversely, if we disobey God's law, it will lead to the sin of showing partiality (v. 9).

James refers to those who commit such an action as "transgressors," which means God's law has been broken (v. 9). Since this is a violation of God's commandment, James further explains that we cannot expect God to overlook it when we are found guilty of practicing favoritism. As a result of committing one disobedient act against God, that individual becomes guilty of violating God's law in its entirety (v. 10).

In verse 11, James gives examples of what he means. God has declared that believers must not commit adultery, nor should we commit murder. James explains if you do not commit adultery, but you do commit murder, you are a transgressor of God's law. In simpler terms, God has declared that we must have no other god before Him. He has also commanded that we must not steal. Someone who can claim that they do not steal from others, but places their earthly possessions above God, is guilty of breaking God's law just the same.

James ends this teaching by admonishing his readers to show their obedience and allegiance to God by speaking and acting toward one another with mercy, because the day will come when all believers will receive their just reward.

He ends with a strong statement that receiving mercy will be the result of showing love and impartiality toward everyone—those who have and those who have not. This is God's way, and as believers, we have been given the mandate to follow God's way of having mercy for others in order to receive mercy in return (v. 13).

Source:

Barker, Kenneth, ed. *The NIV Study Bible*. Grand Rapids, Mich.: Zondervan Publishing House, 1995.

Search the Scriptures

1. Hath not God ____the ____ of this world rich in ____, and heirs of the _____ which he hath promised to them that _____ (James 2:5)?

2. If ye fulfill the royal law according to the Scripture, _____, ye do well (v. 8).

3. But if ye have respect to persons [or show partiality], ye commit ____ (v. 9).

4. For he shall have _____ without _____, that hath [showed] _____ mercy (v. 13).

Discuss the Meaning

1. What should be the attitude of the believer toward the rich and the poor in our congregations?

2. Describe what James means by the term "royal law" in verse 8. What does he mean when he wrote that we would do well to fulfill the law?

3. What are some distinct ways believers in the church today despise the poor?

4. According to the apostle James, what trait of God must we show others if we want to be judged by God in the same way?

Lesson in Our Society

In many metropolitan areas, it appears as if highways are built so that commuters don't have to drive through poor communities. This strategy represents an extreme attempt to keep poor people trapped in a marginalized state where society can avoid the issue of improving the quality of life of an underserved population. But God has called His church to be impartial disciples who do not show partiality toward the rich. Instead, we are to fulfill God's royal law and show the love of God to all people, treating everyone as we would like to be treated—with no respect to a person's social status. To the extent that an unfortunate situation involving favoring the rich and ignoring the poor affects African Americans, and therefore African American Christians, we must soberly consider what we can do to help improve the economic conditions of poor neighborhoods.

Make It Happen

1. Plan a fundraiser and use the proceeds to buy trees and plant them around the community.

2. If there is a nearby community that is being underserved, make up flyers to be distributed in that area. Include your church's name, address, telephone number. With a message based on James 2:5, use these flyers to let the residents know that God loves them and that they are welcome to your church.

3. Do a self-evaluation to discover a time you judged someone unfairly. Repent and ask the Lord to help you fulfill James 2:13.

Follow the Spirit

What God wants me to do:

_____

_____

Remember Your Thoughts

Special insights I have learned:

_____

_____

More Light on the Text

James 2:1–13

1 My brethren, have not the faith of our Lord Jesus Christ, the Lord of glory, with respect of persons.

The writer James began this teaching by immediately addressing a serious issue that the New Testament church faced. Surprisingly enough, the church of the twenty-first century still struggles with aspects of that same issue today. James wanted his brothers in Christ to know that God is not pleased when those who profess to be His own show favoritism and partiality toward people less fortunate than themselves. For this cause, he delivers a significant warning in an attempt to guide the believers away from such an ungodly practice.

James makes it very clear to his audience that as believers who claim to have faith in the Lord Jesus Christ, they must follow God's Word. He is taking a direct approach to the danger of showing respect of persons. The apostle Peter also brought out the truth that God Himself is no respecter of persons (Acts 10:34). How, then, can one claim to be a believer in Christ if that person displays behavior that is contrary to what our Lord expects? This is James's message to the church.

2 For if there come unto your assembly a man with a gold ring, in goodly apparel, and there come in also a poor man in vile raiment; 3 And ye have respect to him that weareth the gay clothing, and say unto him, Sit thou here in a good place; and say to the poor, Stand thou there, or sit here under my footstool: 4 Are ye not then partial in yourselves, and are become judges of evil thoughts?

James is an excellent teacher. He uses an example to follow up his point. His desire is to make the message clear enough so that the intention cannot be missed. He poses a scenario that illustrates what he is attempting to convey. Imagine two men coming into the church at the same time. These two people have extremely different appearances. One man is wearing fine clothing and a gold ring, and the other man is poorly dressed in tattered clothing. James suggests that if anyone offers the man who is well dressed a prominent seat while communicating to the poor man that he is unworthy by relegating him to a lesser seat, that person is exercising judgment based on outward appearances. In the society of the day, Craig S. Keener's writing confirms the preferential treatment that existed: "Moralists and satirists mocked the special respect given to the wealthy, which usually amounted to a self-demeaning way to seek funds." Whatever the motive, James stressed this type of behavior as being clearly unacceptable to God.

It stands to reason that the wealthy people owned many articles of clothing, while the poor probably possessed one garment, more than likely torn and dirty. To protect the poor, Jewish law specifically forbade partiality based on economic stature (Leviticus 19:15). However, James was forced to ask the question in verse 4, "Are ye not then partial in yourselves, and are become judges of evil thoughts?" "Partiality" is from the Greek word *prosopolepteo* (**pros-oh-pol-ayp-TEH-oh**), which means to make distinctions among people based on their rank and influence while showing preference for the rich and powerful. The person who is guilty of such action has, in effect, made himself a judge of both the wealthy and the poor. These thoughts are in direct contradiction to God's Word, and James rightfully renders them as coming from an evil motive. How often today do we observe injustice conferred on those who are less fortunate simply due to their low economic status?

5 Hearken, my beloved brethren, Hath not God chosen the poor of this world rich in faith, and heirs of the kingdom which he hath promised to them that love him?

James asks a very serious question that believers of any era cannot deny. Although he is posing a question, he is making his point very clear in verse 5. He reminds those that have a tendency toward showing favoritism that it is God, in His infinite wisdom, who has shown favor by choosing those considered by the world to be poor. It is also God who has given those with such distinction the ability to be rich in faith. Having faith in God demonstrates a love for God; therefore, these circumstances are pleasing in God's sight and He has decreed that the poor will inherit His kingdom.

6 But ye have despised the poor. Do not rich men oppress you, and draw you before the judgment seats? 7 Do not they blaspheme that worthy name by the which ye are called?

Poor people often find themselves in a vulnerable state. Simply because they do not possess money and power to wield, they are in a position to be misused and oppressed by persons who seemingly have the upper hand. This is what James means when he charges his audience with a staggering fact, "But ye have despised the poor." The NIV uses the word "insulted," which suggests that the poor were treated with contempt. When people who obviously have a measure of stature in life are shown preference over poor people, this is a way of showing dishonor to the latter.

Then he wisely turns the situation around and puts the guilty in that place of being looked down upon. He directs them to consider their own situations. He points out that the rich people are treating them in the same way that they are treating those less fortunate than they. *The New International Commentary on the New Testament* states, "Clearly the discrimination against the poor took more active, serious, and even physical forms than being snubbed in church." James wanted to help his readers to see themselves in the position of being mistreated by the upper echelon in society as a means of correcting their ungodly actions toward the poor. With straightforward words, he charged them with not only disagreeing with God's Word, but also ignoring their own state of being.

How double-minded these Christians were! Ironically, they failed to realize that their desire to come together and lift up the name of Jesus was being corrupted by the fact that they allowed the rich in society to exploit them while they turned on each other with the same type of blatant partiality. James could certainly not be silent on this issue.

8 If ye fulfil the royal law according to the scripture, Thou shalt love thy neighbour as thyself, ye do well: 9 But if ye have respect to persons, ye commit sin, and are convinced of the law as transgressors.

The word "love" used here is the Hebrew word *'ahav* (**ah-HAHV**), which expresses esteem ("to place a high value on; show respect"). James is making reference to the command given in Leviticus 19:18 and also Jesus' words in Luke 6:31. *The NIV Study Bible* states that "The law of love (Leviticus 19:18) is called 'royal' because it is the supreme law which is the source of all other laws governing human relationships." Love for one's neighbor begins with one's own self esteem. It has to do with how one cannot extend love to someone else if that individual does not think of one's self as worthy of receiving love.

James follows up by affirming that the person who fulfills the royal law does a good thing. But on the other hand, if one is guilty of having respect to persons (showing favoritism), they are committing a sin against God. This transgression of the royal law is a serious matter that the writer rightfully refutes. He uses the term to emphasize the significance of God's edict against the practice of favoritism because his readers were familiar with the judicial system and would recognize the term's significance. Craig Keener offers, "A 'royal' law, i.e., an imperial edict, was higher than the justice of the aristocracy, and because Judaism universally acknowledged God to be the supreme King, his law could be described in these terms. Christians could naturally apply it espe-

"Listen to me, dear brothers and sisters. Hasn't God chosen the poor in this world to be rich in faith? Aren't they the ones who will inherit the Kingdom he promised to those who love him?" (James 2:5, NLT).

cially to Jesus' teaching; like some other Jewish teachers, Jesus used this passage in Leviticus 19:18 to epitomize the law."

10 For whosoever shall keep the whole law, and yet offend in one point, he is guilty of all. 11 For he that said, Do not commit adultery, said also, Do not kill. Now if thou commit no adultery, yet if thou kill, thou art become a transgressor of the law.

The New Interpreter's Bible brings clarity to James's statements here: "The person who claims to live by the law of love, yet practices the sort of discrimination that the law of love itself forbids has broken the law of love entirely." Since it is the same God who has declared what constitutes sin, one cannot differentiate on the basis of an individual sin. Even though a person commits one type of sin but refrains from committing another form of sin, in essence that person is rejecting the whole of God's authority and is therefore guilty of committing sin. All people are one in Christ (Galatians 3:28). When partiality and distinctions are shown based on race, gender, position, power, or wealth, sin has entered in and God's law has been violated.

12 So speak ye, and so do, as they that shall be judged by the law of liberty. 13 For he shall have judgment without mercy, that hath shewed no mercy; and mercy rejoiceth against judgment.

This passage ends with James's final words of counsel. He tells his readers to talk and act as though they truly believe what they claim to believe. They must live up to the faith that they profess with their mouths and refrain from betraying God's law of love by showing preferential treatment. It is clear from his teaching that part of living by God's standards involves helping those who are in need. If we show no mercy to others, then we cannot expect mercy from God in return.

The Bible Background Commentary New Testament explains that "Jewish teachers defined God's character especially by two attributes, mercy and justice, and suggested that mercy normally won out over justice. They would have agreed with James that the merciless forfeited a right to mercy. . . ." We would do well to learn that God's mercy triumphs over judgment (v. 13, NIV); otherwise, we have missed the meaning of God's law of love and will reap the consequences.

The final warning here concerns the fact that believers will be judged with the same type of judgment they show to others. James warns that judgment without mercy will be shown to anyone who has not been merciful. In other words, we will fulfill the commandment of God by becoming doers of the Word through showing love and mercy to our brothers and sisters. Jesus said, "Blessed are the merciful, for they will be shown mercy" (Matthew 5:7, NIV). If we would only take heed to James's instructions and follow Jesus' words, we will avoid the trap of deceiving ourselves. The Good News is that, if we obey the Word, we will spend all of eternity with the merciful and loving God of the universe.

Sources:

Bruce, F. F., and James B. Adamson, eds. *The New International Commentary on the New Testament.* Grand Rapids, Mich.: William B. Eerdmans Publishing Co., 1976.

Keener, Craig S. *The IVP Bible Background Commentary New Testament.* Downers Grove, Ill.: InterVarsity Press, 1993.

The New Interpreter's Bible, Vol. XII. Nashville: Abingdon Press, 1998.

Vincent, Marvin R. *Word Studies in the New Testament.* Peabody, Mass.: Hendrickson Publishers, 1888.

Daily Bible Readings

M: Sheep or Goats?
Matthew 25:31–46

T: Acts of Favoritism?
James 2:1–4

W: God's Favored
James 2:5–7

T: The Royal Law
James 2:8–11

F: The Law of Liberty
James 2:12–17

S: Faith and Works
James 2:18–20

S: An Active Faith
James 2:21–26

TEACHING TIPS

August 17
Bible Study Guide 12

1. Words You Should Know

A. Offend (James 3:2) *ptaio* (Gk.)—To stumble, trip; to make a mistake, go astray, sin.

B. Conversation (v. 13) *anastrophe* (Gk.)—Way of life, conduct, behavior.

C. Wisdom (v. 13) *sophias* (Gk.)—Good judgment in the face of demands made by human, and specifically by the Christian, life (practical wisdom).

D. Righteousness (v. 18) *dikaiosune* (Gk.)—Uprightness as the compelling motive for the conduct of one's whole life.

2. Teacher Preparation

Unifying Principle—Thoughtful Speech The words we say can cause great damage. God desires us to have control over our tongues. How can people become kinder in their speech? James exhorts people to discipline their tongues by accepting the wisdom and peace that comes from above.

A. Following prayer, read the background Scripture for the lesson. After you have studied the lesson, look up the Words You Should Know in a dictionary to familiarize yourself with their contemporary usages.

B. Read James 3:1–10, 13–18 from different versions of the Bible utilizing your *Precepts For Living®* CD-ROM, since certain passages differ slightly and can obscure understanding.

C. As you carefully review the lesson, keep your focus on the Unifying Principle.

3. Starting the Lesson

A. Read theAIM for Change.

B. Ask the students to identify teachers in their lives who they consider great and to describe the attributes that make them so.

C. Read the In Focus section, or invite a student to read. Invite the class to share their insights from the story.

4. Getting into the Lesson

A. Ask for volunteers to read the Focal Verses.

B. Answer the questions in the Search the Scriptures section.

C. Read the Background information and The People, Places, and Times section. You might want to explain keys terms such as "diatribe" and "Jewish Wisdom Literature."

D. Ask for volunteers to read the In Depth section and answer any of the questions raised.

5. Relating the Lesson to Life

A. Divide the students into three small groups and assign each group one question from the Discuss the Meaning section, then reconvene the larger group and ask them to share their insights.

B. Use the Lesson in Our Society section to further help the students apply contemporary examples to today's lesson.

C. Ask the students to reflect on the Make It Happen section and to think of a time when they said something hurtful or had something hurtful said to them. Ask them what they would do differently today.

6. Arousing Action

A. Ask the students to spend the rest of the week praying for God to tame their tongues.

B. Remind the students to use the Daily Bible Readings, Remember Your Thoughts, and Follow the Spirit sections.

C. Close with prayer.

Worship Guide

For the Superintendent or Teacher
Theme: Wise Speakers
Theme song: "Use Me (If You Can Use Anything)"
Devotional Reading: Proverbs 15:1–4; 16:21–24
Prayer

WISE SPEAKERS

Bible Background • JAMES 3
Printed Text • JAMES 3:1–10, 13–18 Devotional Reading • PROVERBS 15:1–4; 16:21–24

AIM for Change

By the end of the lesson, we will:

RECOGNIZE that God desires us to have control over the things we say;

SUBMIT our tongues to God by examining our speaking habits; and

ASK God to discipline our speech.

Keep in Mind

"Out of the same mouth proceedeth blessing and cursing. My brethren, these things ought not so to be" (James 3:10).

Focal Verses

KJV

James 3:1 My brethren, be not many masters, knowing that we shall receive the greater condemnation.

2 For in many things we offend all. If any man offend not in word, the same is a perfect man, and able also to bridle the whole body.

3 Behold, we put bits in the horses' mouths, that they may obey us; and we turn about their whole body.

4 Behold also the ships, which though they be so great, and are driven of fierce winds, yet are they turned about with a very small helm, whithersoever the governor listeth.

5 Even so the tongue is a little member, and boasteth great things. Behold, how great a matter a little fire kindleth!

6 And the tongue is a fire, a world of iniquity: so is the tongue among our members, that it defileth the whole body, and setteth on fire the course of nature; and it is set on fire of hell.

7 For every kind of beasts, and of birds, and of serpents, and of things in the sea, is tamed, and hath been tamed of mankind:

8 But the tongue can no man tame; it is an unruly evil, full of deadly poison.

9 Therewith bless we God, even the Father; and therewith curse we men, which are made after the similitude of God.

10 Out of the same mouth proceedeth blessing and cursing. My brethren, these things ought not so to be.

3:13 Who is a wise man and endued with knowledge among you? let him shew out of a good conversation his works with meekness of wisdom.

14 But if ye have bitter envying and strife in your hearts, glory not, and lie not against the truth.

NLT

James 3:1 Dear brothers and sisters, not many of you should become teachers in the church, for we who teach will be judged more strictly.

2 Indeed, we all make many mistakes. For if we could control our tongues, we would be perfect and could also control ourselves in every other way.

3 We can make a large horse go wherever we want by means of a small bit in its mouth.

4 And a small rudder makes a huge ship turn wherever the pilot chooses to go, even though the winds are strong.

5 In the same way, the tongue is a small thing that makes grand speeches. But a tiny spark can set a great forest on fire.

6 And the tongue is a flame of fire. It is a whole world of wickedness, corrupting your entire body. It can set your whole life on fire, for it is set on fire by hell itself.

7 People can tame all kinds of animals, birds, reptiles, and fish,

8 but no one can tame the tongue. It is restless and evil, full of deadly poison.

9 Sometimes it praises our Lord and Father, and sometimes it curses those who have been made in the image of God.

10 And so blessing and cursing come pouring out of the same mouth. Surely, my brothers and sisters, this is not right!

3:13 If you are wise and understand God's ways, prove it by living an honorable life, doing good works with the humility that comes from wisdom.

14 But if you are bitterly jealous and there is selfish ambition in your heart, don't cover up the truth with boasting and lying.

15 This wisdom descendeth not from above, but is earthly, sensual, devilish.

16 For where envying and strife is, there is confusion and every evil work.

17 But the wisdom that is from above is first pure, then peaceable, gentle, and easy to be entreated, full of mercy and good fruits, without partiality, and without hypocrisy.

18 And the fruit of righteousness is sown in peace of them that make peace.

15 For jealousy and selfishness are not God's kind of wisdom. Such things are earthly, unspiritual, and demonic.

16 For wherever there is jealousy and selfish ambition, there you will find disorder and evil of every kind.

17 But the wisdom from above is first of all pure. It is also peace loving, gentle at all times, and willing to yield to others. It is full of mercy and good deeds. It shows no favoritism and is always sincere.

18 And those who are peacemakers will plant seeds of peace and reap a harvest of righteousness.

In Focus

Michael had taken off from work early to attend the open house at his son's school. He had many unfinished tasks on his desk, but he knew how important this evening was to his son, so he had put various papers into piles, put on his jacket, and left the office.

Michael worked for the city as an attorney. His rise to this position was a long and difficult one. He was raised by his grandmother. As hard as she tried to bring him up right, he often rebelled and did just the opposite. He was disruptive in school, and by the time he was in high school he was a frequent truant. No one was more surprised than Michael that his life had taken such a positive turn.

When they arrived at Little Mike's classroom, the teacher approached them to greet them. There was something familiar about her, but Michael could not recall what it was.

"Hi. I'm Mrs. Randall, Mike's teacher," she said as she reached out her hand.

"It's good to see you again, Mrs. Randall. I met you on the first day of school," replied Michael's wife.

"Hello, Mrs. Randall. I'm Michael, Little Mike's father."

"You don't remember me, do you?" Mrs. Randall asked Michael.

"You look familiar, but I can't place you," he replied.

"I was your sixth grade teacher, but you knew me as Miss Carter back then."

Michael stood there frozen. He had behaved badly in Miss Carter's class, but not bad enough for her to tell him that he would grow up to become a bum or a criminal, as she had done. As if reading his mind, Mrs. Randall responded, "I should never have said what I did twenty years ago. I was young and inexperienced."

She continued, "I've been following your career. I've always wanted to apologize, and when I realized that you were Mike's dad, I knew that I would finally get the opportunity."

"You know, Mrs. Randall, your words really hurt me, and I could have ended up just like you said. Instead, I had a teacher in high school who really turned things around for me. He told me that God had great plans for me if only I would submit to Him and follow Him. I took his advice and my life has never been the same."

In today's lesson, we see that our words have the power to change lives.

The People, Places, and Times

Teacher. The Greek term for "teacher" is *didaskalos* (**did-AHS-kahl-oss**) from *didasko* (**did-AHS-koh**), "to teach." *Daskalos* is related to the English word "didactic," derived from the Greek *didaktikos*, and means to be apt or skillful at teaching or imparting wisdom or instruction. The King James Version usually translates it "master" in the British sense of "teacher." In the New Testament, more than thirty instances of its usage are in reference to Jesus. He is not referred to as "teacher" in the official sense, but rather as a title of respect and to recognize His status as the leader of the disciples. In the book of James, a teacher was an official of the Christian church. Teachers in the early church were responsible for instruction or exhortation on various aspects of Christian life and thought for those who had already been converted to the faith by the preached word, but needed guidance in distinguishing right belief from false teachings (see Acts 13:1; 1 Corinthians 12:28; Ephesians 4:11; 2 Timothy 1:11).

Background

The book of James is addressed to "the twelve tribes scattered abroad," or in Diaspora (dispersion). The writer is referring here to the new Israel, representing the church that was now located throughout the known world (Acts 9–28). Besides being written in a formal Greek style, it also resembles and incorporates elements of Jewish Wisdom literature (i.e., Psalms, Proverbs), making it the closest thing to New Testament Wisdom literature.

We do not know anything about the social or economic status of James. However, he appears as an advocate for the victims of social injustice. James demonstrates a special concern for the poor (2:14–26), the orphaned, and the widowed (1:27). He also opposes any form of partiality shown to the rich or discrimination towards the poor (2:1–7). He made famous the words "Faith, if it hath not works, is dead, being alone" (2:17), for faith needed to result in works of compassion toward the poor and not just good thoughts.

At-A-Glance

1. Taming the Tongue (James 3:1–10)
2. Two Kinds of Wisdom (vv. 13–18)

In Depth

1. Taming the Tongue (James 3:1–10)

People have different reasons for going into the teaching ministry. Some believe that God has called them to this ministry, others have a gift for teaching, and still others are mature persons in the faith and have the knowledge and experience required for teaching. Yet some teach for the recognition that comes with the position. James instructs his listeners that not many in the faith should take up the vocation of teaching, since those who teach will be judged with greater strictness. Moreover, because we all stumble and make mistakes, if any of us can go without making a mistake in our speech, then we have the discipline to control our entire body.

The King James Version uses the word "offend." Other translations include "mistake" or "stumble." Many of us today associate the word "offend" with hurting someone's feelings or causing someone to feel resentment or anger. However, the original definition meant to break a law or religious command-

ment, or to commit a sin or crime. By reading our modern concept of the term into the Old English understanding, we miss the seriousness of what it means to offend. We don't just hurt someone's feelings, but we sin against them. Since we know that all have sinned and come short of the glory of God (Romans 3:23), we know just how difficult it must be to have self-control when it comes to speaking.

According to James, teachers are held to an even higher standard of judgment regarding what they say. Teachers have an enormous responsibility in the church because they are trusted with guiding believers, especially the spiritually immature in the faith. Therefore, it is important that teachers speak with humility and good judgment, for James says that anyone who cannot keep their tongue in check deceives themselves and their religion is in vain (1:26). Thus, the old adage "Think before you speak" is especially applicable to teachers.

James speaks of a person who is able not to offend with words, having the ability to bridle the whole body (v. 2). A bridle is a harness that goes over the head of a horse but guides the horse's entire body. Anyone who has ever stood next to a horse knows how large an animal a horse is, and that it might be difficult to control. Yet, as large as a horse is, it is the bit, the smallest part of the bridle that fits into the horse's mouth, that is the means for controlling and communicating with the horse. Likewise, it is the small helm or rudder that guides a great ship (v. 4). On the other hand, something as small as the tongue can cause uncontrollable events, just as a small spark can consume an entire forest. James draws further on the imagery of the small flame causing a forest fire by likening the tongue to a fire with the ability to corrupt the whole body (v. 6). James recognizes the power of speech, and if uncontrolled, the havoc it can wreak.

James notes with irony that the same tongue with which we bless God the Father is the one with which we curse those who are made in the image of God (v. 9). James could have been drawing on the Jewish Wisdom tradition found in the book of Sirach, a text familiar to early Christian communities but only recently introduced to many Protestant Christians: "Honor and dishonor come from speaking, and the tongue of mortals may be their downfall" (5:13, NRSV). In both instances, the contradiction between blessing and cursing coming from the same mouth demonstrates the hypocrisy of claiming to love God on the one hand and condemning the one God made on the other. As 1 John 4:20 says, "If a man say, I love God, and hateth his brother, he is a liar." James asserts that such behavior is unacceptable (v. 10).

2. Two Kinds of Wisdom (vv. 13–18)

James returns to a theme introduced earlier in the book, the importance of demonstrable acts. In this instance it is a demonstration of one's *wisdom* rather than one's *faith* by one's actions. James exhorts the listener to show by their good conduct or way of life that they are wise and understanding. The King James Version reads, "Let him shew out of a good conversation his works with meekness of wisdom" (v. 13). This translation is consistent with James's teaching in verse 1:26 that one's religiosity can be known by the content of one's words. It is also consistent with Jewish Wisdom literature, which teaches that good behavior is a reflection of wisdom.

The opposite of someone whose works are performed with meekness of wisdom is someone whose works reflect bitter envy and selfish ambition. James says that neither should they be boastful nor lie about how they really feel. Moreover, James asserts that such wisdom is not from God (vv. 14–15). He describes two wisdoms that are diametrically opposed: one heavenly and one earthly. One must be careful here not to associate physical matter, including human beings, with bad or evil, and the spirit or mind with good or godly. The early church opposed such teachings in the form of Gnosticism, derived from the Greek word *gnosis* (**GNOH-sis**, "knowledge"). Among other Gnostic teachings considered heretical by the church was the belief called docetism, that Jesus was not really human because God would not enter evil matter. They divided the world into the carnal (evil) and spiritual (good). James is not setting God in opposition to humans who are made in God's image, but rather showing us two different kinds of wisdom.

The earthly wisdom produces envy and strife, which leads to confusion and evil work, as opposed to the good works that come from wisdom from above, which is godly wisdom. Wisdom that comes from God is pure, peaceable, gentle, courteous, full of mercy and good fruits, and without a trace of partiality or hypocrisy. Again, the attributes of wisdom are not just lofty ideals to be reflected on, but are evident in one's behavior. It is clear that we belong to God when we display the wisdom of God by our actions.

Following a list of the fruits of wisdom, James concludes with the fruit of righteousness, which is sown in peace. The Greek word for peace is *irene* (**ihr-RAY-nay**). Peace means to be free from war or conflict. Ironically, many of the conflicts waged in the Middle East during the Crusades of the Middle Ages were led with the charge, "God wills it!" In order to reap peace, peace must be sown by peacemakers. One cannot initiate strife and expect peace to be the outcome.

Search the Scriptures

1. Why does James say that anyone who does not offend in word is perfect (James 3:2)?

2. What does James say comes from the same mouth (v. 10)?

3. How does James say we can show that our works reflect meekness born of wisdom (v. 13)?

4. Describe the attributes of the wisdom that comes from above (v. 17).

5. The fruit of _____ is sown in peace of them that make_____ (v. 18).

Discuss the Meaning

1. Abraham Lincoln is quoted as saying, "It is better to remain silent and thought a fool, than to speak and remove all doubt." What is the significance of this quote to James's lesson on controlled speech?

2. James taught that we should "be quick to listen, slow to speak, and slow to become angry" (1:19, NIV). How does each admonition relate to the other and to our lesson?

3. Which of the attributes of wisdom that come from God would you say describe you best, and why? Which attributes do you think you lack, and what would you do to build these up?

Lesson in Our Society

E-mail can be a wonderful tool for communicating. We can send messages to our friends and colleagues in a matter of seconds. This ability can also be to our detriment. Too often we send messages before we have proofread them or given them sufficient thought. How many times have we sat at our computers and fired off an e-mail to someone with whom we disagreed or we thought was critical of us? On how many of those occasions did we wish we could undo what we had done with the quick press of the "send" button? There is a "recall" option with most e-mail accounts. However, it does not prevent the message from being read; it only indicates that the message was sent unintentionally or that the sender has changed his or her mind. Just like the small bit in the horse's mouth or the rudder guiding the ship, something as small as a button on a keyboard can contribute to the cause of great calamity.

Of course first-century Palestinian Jews did not communicate by e-mail. Few could read and even fewer could write. Learning was primarily by rote, with pupils being taught orally by an instructor. Nevertheless, whether orally or written, what we say can have significant consequences. God expects us to keep control over what we say, especially those of us who are in teaching positions in the church, because we exert tremendous influence over our students. If we cannot control something as small as the tongue, how can we be expected to maintain discipline in other aspects of our life? Moreover, if we cannot control our own lives, how can we be expected to keep the church running efficiently?

Make It Happen

Sometimes we say hurtful or inappropriate things that we don't mean, but are said out of our own feelings of hurt, low self-esteem, or for personal gain. Or we might say things that cause misunderstandings or anger because we lacked the skills to say what we really intended. Either way, the end result often breeds discord. We find ourselves trying to make amends. Today's lesson has taught us that we can submit our tongues to God and ask God to tame our tongues. This week, make a serious effort to cooperate with God and do something to help tame your tongue, such as think before you speak.

Follow the Spirit

What God wants me to do:

_____

_____

Remember Your Thoughts

Special insights you have learned:

_____

_____

More Light on the Text

James 3:1–10, 13–18

1 My brethren, be not many masters, knowing that we shall receive the greater condemnation.

In chapter 2, James states that "faith without works is dead" (v. 26). Words are also works, particularly in the case of those who teach. Teaching plays an important role in the life of the church (1 Corinthians 12:28; Acts 13:1; Romans 12:7; Ephesians 4:11). Since authority and privilege are attached to the teaching ministry, there is a danger in seeing too many people attracted to teaching for wrong motives.

The Greek verb *ginomai* (**GHIN-om-eye**), "to become" or "to arise" in the sense of appearing in public, is imperative. James advises that not many should become teachers. The church needs to know what is involved in teaching. Teachers are continually engaged in passing judgment. They are sometimes severely critical. The more they speak, the more likely they are to stumble and make mistakes. Their words may have destructive consequences. They leave an indelible impact for good or evil upon their listeners. Thus, they will receive "the greater condemnation" or severe judgment (Gk. *meizon krima*, **MAYD-zon KREE-mah**) if they fail to walk according to their teaching (Luke 12:48). Teaching is a heavy responsibility and must not be taken lightly (see Acts 20:26–27; Mark 12:38–40).

The verb "receive" (Gk. *lambano*, **lahm-BAHN-oh**) is in the future tense, indicating that the judgment is future (Gk. cf. 5:7–9 when the Lord returns). The warning "be not many masters [or teachers]" (v. 1) was not meant to discourage those who are called to teach. James, by pointing out the dangers and responsibilities linked to teaching, was seeking to enhance the work of teachers.

2 For in many things we offend all. If any man offend not in word, the same is a perfect man, and able also to bridle the whole body.

The Greek word *polus* (**pol-OOS**) is accusative plural and is used as an adverb to intensify the verb to "offend" (Gk. *ptaio*, **PTAH-yo**). In many directions or at many times we sin. The expression points out the universality of sin. Teachers are not perfect. They are capable of sinning in word (or in speech) just like everyone else.

The tongue is the hardest to control of all the members of the human body. It reveals the state of the heart (see the power of words Proverbs 10:8, 11; 18:7–8; see also the danger of eloquence in history Hitler, Lenin, etc.). The "perfect man" is a person who has his tongue completely under control. Controlling the tongue gives the power to monitor the whole body.

Thus, teachers need to examine themselves and learn to lead under the guidance of the Holy Spirit (2 Corinthians 10:5), for out of the abundance of the heart the mouth speaks (see Matthew 12:34).

3 Behold, we put bits in the horses' mouths, that they may obey us; and we turn about their whole body.

James uses three familiar examples to illustrate his point about the controlling of tongues (vv. 3–6). First, he speaks of how horses, strong and powerful animals, can be controlled by putting bits in their mouths. What is true of horses is also true of people. Our tongues need to be under the control of the Holy Spirit.

4 Behold also the ships, which though they be so great, and are driven of fierce winds, yet are they turned about with a very small helm, whithersoever the governor listeth.

James gives a second illustration, taken from the rudder of a ship. The rudder, though small like the tongue, is the most important part of the ship. The person in control of it controls the whole vessel. The pressure from the rudder of a ship changes the course of the largest ships even when they are being driven by strong winds.

5 Even so the tongue is a little member, and boasteth great things. Behold, how great a matter a little fire kindleth!

The "tongue" (Gk. *glossa*, **GLOHS-sah**), just like a bit or a rudder, can achieve big results—and boast about it. The Greek word *megalaucheo* (**meg-ahl-ow-KHEH-oh**) denotes arrogant boasting (talking big).

James's third illustration shows the destructive power of the tongue in individual lives and in human relationships. Fire, although starting as a small and useful flame, can spread great destruction through an entire forest. The Greek word *hule* (**HOO-lay**), referring to wood in the sense of forest, envisions a wildfire.

6 And the tongue is a fire, a world of iniquity: so is the tongue among our members, that it defileth the whole body, and setteth on fire the course of nature; and it is set on fire of hell.

James equates the tongue with fire and describes its devastating effects. It pollutes the whole body. It exercises its evil influence continuously throughout the whole course of human life. It can create a world of wickedness.

The Greek word *trochos* (**trokh-OSS**, "wheel") was a common symbol for the state of constant change and the completed cycle of human life. Human life was compared to a wheel rolling onward from birth to death through many phases and changes. The evil influence of the tongue spreads out to the entire circumference of human life from birth (Gk. *genesis*, **GHEN-es-is,** "origin, source") onward (Matthew 15:18; cf. 2 Timothy 2:17).

The fire inflames human passion and infects human life throughout its entire existence. It is set alight by the Devil and comes from beneath—the fire of hell, in which the unrepentant sinner is ultimately punished (Matthew 5:22; 18:9).

7 For every kind of beasts, and of birds, and of serpents, and of things in the sea, is tamed, and hath been tamed of mankind:

At Creation, humanity was given dominion over the animal world (Genesis 1:28). Thus, we have under our control all types of creatures. They can be subdued and have been by mankind since the beginning.

8 But the tongue can no man tame; it is an unruly evil, full of deadly poison.

No human being can tame the tongue. Human beings have not yet learned to control the tongue because of the Fall. Man can tame the animals, but cannot control his own unruly nature as typified by the tongue.

The tongue was given to man by God to enable him to communicate with and to enjoy fellowship with other humans. The tongue, which was designed to praise the Creator, has become a means to deceive and to dishonor. Humanly speaking, it is an utter impossibility to have total control of the tongue. The tongue is a "restless evil" (Gk. *akataschetos kakos*, **ahk-aht-AHS-khet-oss kahk-OSS**), a "deadly poison" (Gk.

"Out of the same mouth proceedeth blessing and cursing. My brethren, these things ought not so to be" (James 3:10).

ios, **ee-OSS**, "death bearing"); the same word sometimes means "rust" (see 5:3).

9 Therewith bless we God, even the Father; and therewith curse we men, which are made after the similitude of God.

In essence, the tongue is inconsistent. Believers' use of the tongue to say incompatible things is the evidence of how difficult it is to control the tongue. The tongue can also be used for a beneficial and worthy purpose such as giving glory to God (Gk. *eulogeo*, **yoo-log-EH-oh**, "to bless, to speak in praise of"; cf. the word "eulogy"). It is at the same time used to curse our brothers and sisters, which "are made after the similitude of God." The verb "are made" (Gk. *ginomai*, **GHIN-om-eye**, "made") is in the perfect tense, meaning that man still has upon him the marks of his divine origin. In spite of all the sin and evil inherent in human nature, the image of God (Gk. *homoiosis*, **hom-OY-oh-sis**, "likeness") is still reflected to some extent in every human being. Thus, by cursing our fellow men, we are in fact cursing God Himself and wiping out the previous act of blessing.

10 Out of the same mouth proceedeth blessing and cursing. My brethren, these things ought not so to be.

Using the same tongue for blessing God and cursing men is contrary to the revealed will of God. It is against nature and ought not to be (or to happen or to continue; Gk. *ginomai* **GHIN-om-eye**) among born-again children of God.

3:13 Who is a wise man and endued with knowledge among you? let him shew out of a good conversation his works with meekness of wisdom.

Verses 13–18 describe earthly wisdom and contrast it with the wisdom from above. Earthly wisdom is characterized by lies, the bad use of the tongue. It divides people, sowing hatred and jealousy.

Teaching requires "wisdom" (Gk. *sophos*, **sof-OS**, "wise, experienced"), an expert or professional "knowledge" (Gk. *epistemon*, **ep-ee-STAY-mohn**, "understanding") and "meekness" (*prautes*, **prah-OO-tayss**, "unpretentious," see Matthew 11:29; 2 Corinthians 10:1). A person aspiring to teach is challenged to give practical evidence (Gk. *ergon*, **EHR-gon**, "deed, action or achievements") that he possesses wisdom, understanding, and meekness or humility.

Just as the reality of faith is shown by good work, wisdom is demonstrated by "a good conversation" (Gk. *kales anastrophes*, **kahl-AYSS ahn-ahs-trof-AYSS**, from the root *strepho*, **STREF-oh**, "to turn, to convert, to behave") or a good behavior, a good way of life. It must be obvious to others that the teacher's way of life is good (see 1 Peter 2:12). In order to teach wisdom, one must have it. Wisdom is the source of true teaching.

14 But if ye have bitter envying and strife in your hearts, glory not, and lie not against the truth.

An aspiring teacher should look into his or her heart and see whether it is free from "bitter envying" and "strife," two evils that are most certain to hinder the work of teaching (Romans 13:13; 2 Corinthians 12:20; Galatians 5:20).

The Greek word *zelos* (**DZAY-loss**, "zeal, jealousy," from the root *zeo*, **DZEH-oh**, "boil or be fervent") is used both in a bad sense (see Acts 5:17; Romans 13:13) and a good sense (see John 2:17; Romans 10:2; 2 Corinthians 9:2). Here in James, the bad sense is used and emphasized by the epithet "bitter." Bitter envying is opposed to meekness (v.13; 1:21; 1 Peter 3:4).

The Greek word *eritheia* (**ehr-ith-EE-ah**, "strife") means "ambition" or "party-spirit, faction" (see Romans 2:8; Philippians 1:16). When believers are not paying sufficient attention to God's Word, their actions will spring from earthly motives, bitter jealousy, and ambition.

15 This wisdom descendeth not from above, but is earthly, sensual, devilish.

False wisdom is "earthly" (Gk. *epigeios*, **ep-IG-ay-oss**), characterized by bitter envying and strife. It is natural as opposed to spiritual and diabolical. It owes its origin to earthbound motives even if it is discussing heavenly things. It is limited by the unregenerate mind of man and is from the Devil.

16 For where envying and strife is, there is confusion and every evil work.

Jealousy and selfish ambition are opposed to the very nature of God (cf. 1 Corinthians 14:33; 1 John 1:5). They lead to "confusion" (Gk. *akatastasia*, **ahk-aht-ahs-tah-SEE-ah**, or "instability"), spiritual instability, and spiritual darkness.

17 But the wisdom that is from above is first pure, then peaceable, gentle, and easy to be intreated, full of mercy and good fruits, without partiality, and without hypocrisy.

In contrast to earthly wisdom characterized by rivalry and jealousy, wisdom from above is pure in itself. It has the following beneficial characteristics: peace, gentleness, sensibility, full of mercy and good fruits. Thus, it fosters healthy human relationships.

18 And the fruit of righteousness is sown in peace of them that make peace.

The expression "the fruit of righteousness" is a genitive definition meaning the fruit which consists of righteousness. Such righteousness is the natural harvest of the seed that "is sown in peace by them that make peace" or "behave peaceably."

Daily Bible Readings

M: The Tongue of the Wise
Proverbs 15:1–4
T: With Greater Strictness
James 3:1–4
W: Corralling the Tongue
James 3:5–9
T: Purity of One's Words
James 3:10–12
F: Born of Wisdom
James 3:13–16
S: Sown in Peace
James 3:17–18
S: Wise and Pleasant Speech
Proverbs 16:21–24

TEACHING TIPS

August 24
Bible Study Guide 13

1. Words You Should Know

A. Friendship (James 4:4) *philia* (Gk.)—To befriend or have a fondness for someone.

B. Humble yourselves (v. 10) *tapeinoo* (Gk.)—From a Greek word meaning to make oneself of low condition, with the idea of contrition and penitence toward God.

2. Teacher Preparation

Unifying Principle—Living Responsibly Many people act greedily, engage in disputes, or judge others in order to obtain something they want. James says the key to godly living is submission to God.

A. Pray and ask the Holy Spirit to open your understanding.

B. As you read through the entire Bible Study Guide, keep your focus on the Unifying Principle.

C. Read the More Light on the Text commentary.

3. Starting the Lesson

A. Assign a student to lead the class in prayer.

B. Invite a few students to share their experiences from last week's Make It Happen suggestion.

C. Ask volunteers who have a translation of the Bible other than the King James Version to read the Focal Verses for today's lesson.

D. To introduce the lesson, pass out sheets of lined paper and use the questions in the Search the Scriptures section as a closed Bible quiz. Review the answers together.

4. Getting into the Lesson

A. Divide the class into two groups and direct them to silently read the Background information. Allow 5–7 minutes to complete the reading and then talk about some human desires that conflict with our desire to live righteously. For example, the drive to obtain money is not itself a bad thing. However, when humans make the pursuit of money a priority over godly living, a problem arises.

B. Discuss The People, Places, and Times section to help the students understand that our desires are

not necessarily evil but that giving in to our desires can lead to evil.

5. Relating the Lesson to Life

A. Read verses 4–6 in a modern Bible translation. Ask the class to explain what James means in context when he wrote that God opposes the proud but gives grace to the humble. After everyone has offered their responses, ask the following: Since God gave us desires for pleasure, how is it that when we yield to these desires we become friends of the world and enemies of God? Does God want us to live pleasureless lives?

B. Read the Discuss the Meaning questions and allow time for the students to respond.

C. Allow several minutes for the students to consider the questions asked in the Lesson in Our Society section and offer solutions.

6. Arousing Action

A. Using the Make It Happen section, challenge the students to consider their personal responses to both categories (building earthly and heavenly treasures) and the actions necessary to ensure progress toward their goals.

B. Encourage the students to read the Daily Bible Readings for the upcoming week.

C. Close with prayer.

Worship Guide

For the Superintendent or Teacher
Theme: People of Godly Behavior
Theme Song: "It Is Well with My Soul"
Devotional Reading: Proverbs 3:13–18
Prayer

PEOPLE OF GODLY BEHAVIOR

Bible Background • JAMES 4
Printed Text • JAMES 4:1–12 Devotional Reading • PROVERBS 3:13–18

AIM for Change

By the end of the lesson, we will:

REALIZE that fighting, greed, and other worldly sins come from a lack of submission to God;

IDENTIFY greed, disputations, and judgments in our own behavior; and

HUMBLE ourselves before God in order to become more Christlike.

Keep in Mind

"Draw nigh to God, and he will draw nigh to you. Cleanse your hands, ye sinners; and purify your hearts, ye double minded" (James 4:8).

Focal Verses

KJV

James 4:1 From whence come wars and fightings among you? come they not hence, even of your lusts that war in your members?

2 Ye lust, and have not: ye kill, and desire to have, and cannot obtain: ye fight and war, yet ye have not, because ye ask not.

3 Ye ask, and receive not, because ye ask amiss, that ye may consume it upon your lusts.

4 Ye adulterers and adulteresses, know ye not that the friendship of the world is enmity with God? whosoever therefore will be a friend of the world is the enemy of God.

5 Do ye think that the scripture saith in vain, The spirit that dwelleth in us lusteth to envy?

6 But he giveth more grace. Wherefore he saith, God resisteth the proud, but giveth grace unto the humble.

7 Submit yourselves therefore to God. Resist the devil, and he will flee from you.

8 Draw nigh to God, and he will draw nigh to you. Cleanse your hands, ye sinners; and purify your hearts, ye double minded.

9 Be afflicted, and mourn, and weep: let your laughter be turned to mourning, and your joy to heaviness.

10 Humble yourselves in the sight of the Lord, and he shall lift you up.

11 Speak not evil one of another, brethren. He that speaketh evil of his brother, and judgeth his brother, speaketh evil of the law, and judgeth the law: but if thou judge the law, thou art not a doer of the law, but a judge.

12 There is one lawgiver, who is able to save and to destroy: who art thou that judgest another?

NLT

James 4:1 What is causing the quarrels and fights among you? Don't they come from the evil desires at war within you?

2 You want what you don't have, so you scheme and kill to get it. You are jealous of what others have, but you can't get it, so you fight and wage war to take it away from them. Yet you don't have what you want because you don't ask God for it.

3 And even when you ask, you don't get it because your motives are all wrong—you want only what will give you pleasure.

4 You adulterers! Don't you realize that friendship with the world makes you an enemy of God? I say it again: If you want to be a friend of the world, you make yourself an enemy of God.

5 What do you think the Scriptures mean when they say that the spirit God has placed within us is filled with envy?

6 But he gives us even more grace to stand against such evil desires. As the Scriptures say, "God opposes the proud but favors the humble."

7 So humble yourselves before God. Resist the devil, and he will flee from you.

8 Come close to God, and God will come close to you. Wash your hands, you sinners; purify your hearts, for your loyalty is divided between God and the world.

9 Let there be tears for what you have done. Let there be sorrow and deep grief. Let there be sadness instead of laughter, and gloom instead of joy.

10 Humble yourselves before the Lord, and he will lift you up in honor.

11 Don't speak evil against each other, dear brothers and sisters. If you criticize and judge each other, then you are criticizing and judging God's law. But your job is to obey the law, not to judge whether it applies to you.

12 God alone, who gave the law, is the Judge. He alone has the power to save or to destroy. So what right do you have to judge your neighbor?

In Focus

The story is told of two friends, Bill and Henry. Henry told Bill that he had a trained fish. When Bill asked him what he meant, Henry said that he trained his fish to swim at only one end of his fishpond and only within a two-foot radius. Bill thought it was pretty strange, so he went to check it out. Sure enough, there was the trained fish, swimming around and around, stuck in a two-foot circle. Every time it appeared that the fish would swim into the bigger area of the pond, it would abruptly change direction and go back to the center of this circle.

"This is amazing!" said Bill. He asked Henry how he had trained his fish to do that. Henry then produced a tall, two-foot-in-diameter glass jar. He said that he originally placed the fish in the jar and placed the jar in the pond. At first, the fish kept pounding into the wall of the jar. After a while, it stopped. When Henry removed the jar, the fish stayed put.

Many people are like that trained fish. They are trapped by the limitations of self-gratification. Status, power, and money cloud their vision; the desire for pleasures limits their thinking and inhibits their relationship with God. God challenges His people to seek His kingdom and His righteousness above all else. When we seek the earth's pleasures before God's pleasures, we limit God's blessing in our lives and become like trained fish, swimming around in the realm of the temporal, wondering why nothing works out the way we planned.

In today's lesson, we examine a basic question: Is your primary motivation in life to please God or to gratify your desire for the world's pleasures? This is a question all believers must ask themselves on a daily basis. James explains how sinful desires can shape our world and explores the dangers and consequences of living for temporal pleasures.

The People, Places, and Times

Desire. The word suggests dangerous passions growing out of one's erroneous evaluation of the world and its pleasures. Scripture reveals that the desires that drive human beings are deeply rooted in our sinful human nature. Speaking of our pre-conversion days, Paul says, "All of us also lived among them at one time, gratifying the cravings of our sinful nature [or flesh] and following its desires and thoughts" (Ephesians 2:3, NIV). Driven by these passions, peo-

ple easily fall into sin. So the Bible encourages believers, "Therefore do not let sin reign in your mortal body so that you obey its evil desires" (Romans 6:12, NIV).

Desires in and of themselves are not evil. The capacity to feel pleasure and delight is given to us by God and is a reflection of His own boundless emotional capacity. However, our desire is often tainted because we are flawed by sin. Our desires are shaped by our sinful human nature and often compel us to choose those things that are evil and bad for us. The beauty of our salvation is that our Saviour came to set us free from overwhelming desires that compel us to sin. Our world is no longer shaped by our desires, but by the Holy Spirit. We can reject the old and choose the things that God values, and enjoy the blessings of all the pleasures in God's creation.

Background

In the fourth chapter of this book, James returns to the discussion of the negative results of earthly wisdom (see James 3:15). He has previously identified the basic cause of envy, disorder, selfish ambition, and "every evil practice" (v. 16, NIV) as the love of self rather than a love for God. Those who love the world are self-centered and primarily concerned with their own needs and desires.

From the beginning of time, humanity has fallen into the trap of self-absorption. Satan would not have been able to lure Eve into sin if he had not played on her desire to be like God (Genesis 3:5–6). Eve's desire to be like God was not evil, but the method of satisfying that desire without God is what brought about her downfall. In the same way, our desires are not evil in and of themselves, but when personal satisfaction becomes our priority, we lose sight of God and evil is imminent.

At-A-Glance

1. Submission to the World
(James 4:1–6)
2. Submission to God (vv. 7–10)
3. Submission to God as Supreme
Judge (vv. 11–12)

In Depth

1. Submission to the World (James 4:1–6)

Without preamble, James launches into an explanation of the dangers of pursuing self-gratification. Using his familiar method of rhetorical questioning, James introduces a new thought: "What is causing the quarrels and fights among you?" (James 4:1, NLT). The question is exploratory, designed to make his readers search for the cause of their troubles. The second question is diagnostic: "Don't they come from the evil desires at war within you?" (v. 1, NLT). As the readers search for the cause of the problems among them, James directs the search within themselves. The phrasing of the question implies that the problems are continuous. The human desire for pleasure wages a constant war within God's people. The word "war" highlights the violent nature of the conflict going on inside.

The fallen nature of humanity demands satisfaction. It wants what it wants, and it wants it now. When we submit ourselves to our lustful desires, there are natural consequences: "You quarrel and fight" (v. 2, NIV). Conflicts and disputes among believers are always destructive. Cliques are formed as people line up other people to join them in an alliance against their rivals.

The basic things that people lust after are power, prestige, money, material possessions, and sensual pleasures. When people put these things first in their lives, the natural result is unhealthy competition. Rather than lifting each other up, people try to pull each other down.

The final and possibly worst consequence of yielding to pleasure is that it shuts the door of heaven to our prayers. Selfish pleasure-seekers are doubly frustrated. They are frustrated in what they do not have, and they are frustrated with God because He will not provide what they desire. James sums up their frustration this way: "You do not have, because you do not ask God. When you ask, you do not receive, because you ask with wrong motives, that you may spend what you get on your pleasures" (James 4:2–3, NIV). Some had not even bothered with prayer, so they did not get what they desired. Others had indeed petitioned God for the desires of their hearts but still came up empty because all they wanted was to wallow in their own pleasures. It is an unfortunate truth that selfish people seldom pray correctly. While committed Christians pray, "Your will be done," the selfish pray, "My desires be satisfied." These selfish people are not necessarily praying for sinful things, but they are praying from selfish motivations.

After exposing the futility of self-gratification, James uses Old Testament language to sharply rebuke his readers: "You adulterers" (James 4:4, NLT). He calls them adulterers because they have made the pursuit of pleasure a higher priority than the pursuit of holiness. "Adultery" is a common figurative Old Testament term used to describe Israel's unfaithfulness to God. This is because God once considered Israel, and now considers the church, to be His bride. The prophet Isaiah declared, "For your Maker is your husband—the LORD Almighty is his name" (54:5, NIV). The Lord says, "But like a woman unfaithful to her husband, so you have been unfaithful to me, O house of Israel" (Jeremiah 3:20, NIV). For God's people to turn away from Him and pursue another is spiritual adultery.

We must realize that both God and the world are trying to win our hearts. When we long for pleasure, we form "friendship with the world." Because the world hates God and competes with Him for the hearts of people, anyone who chooses to be a friend of the world becomes an enemy of God (James 4:4, NLT).

2. Submission to God (vv. 7–10)

After explaining how the compulsion for pleasure leads to friendship with the world and hostility to ward God, James offers solutions to the problem in a series of ten essential commands. These commands are practical exhortations to put God back into first place in our lives. The first essential command is to "submit" (James 4:7). God does not force anyone to obey His will. Rather, He desires that we voluntarily submit. Our readiness to submit to His desires is a sure sign of humility.

Submission to God is the key to Christian living, and as such, it affects all of our relationships. We are to submit to governmental authorities (1 Peter 2:13), wives are exhorted to submit to their husbands (3:1), younger people are instructed to submit to the elderly (5:5), servants are expected to submit to their masters (Titus 2:9), and believers are commanded to submit to one another (Ephesians 5:21).

In submitting to God, believers automatically "resist the devil" (James 4:7, NIV). This term is a military metaphor meaning "to take a stand against." The word "devil" means "slanderer." The Devil's evil purpose is to use our own desire to lure us into evil and then slander us before God. However, if you take a stand against the Devil based on your faith in God to supply all that you need, then the Devil will have to "flee from you" (v. 7, NIV).

The next command is to "draw nigh to God" (James 4:8). This means to enter into God's presence and connect with Him as a worshiper. The command to draw near to God also carries a promise: "He will draw nigh to you" (James 4:8). Communion with God is a two-way street; we have fellowship with God, and He has fellowship with us. Our Heavenly Father promises to come near to all who turn away from their sin and call to Him in true repentance. The nearness of His presence brings comfort, peace, grace, and love.

Entering into God's presence requires some preliminary preparation, so James tells us to "cleanse your hands . . . and purify your hearts" (v. 8). King David wrote, "Who may ascend the hill of the LORD? Who may stand in his holy place? He who has clean hands and a pure heart" (Psalm 24:3–4, NIV). James addresses his readers as "sinners" and "double minded" (James 4:8) because they were seeking the pleasures of the world while claiming devotion to God. Their loyalties were divided, and the deeds of their hands were dirty. Those who seek to worship and serve God must pursue a righteous life. Clean hands are hands free from external acts of sin. A pure heart refers to our inner motives, with a primary goal of inward holiness. Clean hands are the outward expression of a pure heart because godly behavior flows from a pure heart. Jesus promised that those with pure hearts would see God (Matthew 5:8).

The next trio of commands seem a little strange at first: "Be afflicted, and mourn, and weep" (James 4:9). To be afflicted, or miserable, implies having a feeling of shame because of sin. The realization of personal sinfulness should produce a feeling of wretchedness similar to what Paul experienced when he examined his own sinfulness:

"What a wretched man I am!" (Romans 7:24, NIV). Falling into sin should make a believer miserable and drive him to his knees in repentance.

"Mourn and weep" are the outward expressions of inner misery. These words are almost synonymous. In fact, in the two accounts of the Beatitudes, Matthew says, "Blessed are those who mourn" (5:4, NIV), while Luke says, "Blessed are you who weep now" (6:21, NIV). Mourning expresses grieving, and agonized weeping is an expression of our mourning.

The command to "let your laughter be turned to mourning, and your joy to heaviness" (James 4:9) is a continuation of James's call to repentance. He is not asking that we turn away from the joy of the Lord. Instead, he is challenging us to give up the shallow laughter and temporary joy that result from sin.

The final command is "humble yourselves in the sight of the Lord" (James 4:10). This command completes the circle and takes us back to verse 6, where God "giveth grace unto the humble." When we enter into God's presence, we must acknowledge our unworthiness. This command also carries a promise: "He shall lift you up" (v. 10). Voluntary humility involves emptying oneself of both self and sin. We are then filled with the Holy Spirit and lifted up by the power of God within us.

The application of this passage is that believers should quit playing with the Devil and become serious about forsaking sin. We should submit ourselves wholeheartedly to God and resist the Devil and his evil schemes in every area of our lives.

3. Submission to God as Supreme Judge (vv. 11–12)

James issues a very serious command in verse 11. Apparently the believers were using their tongues against one another as weapons, speaking ill of each other with slanderous words. With this knowledge, James had already addressed their use of violent words that brought judgment on their fellow brothers and sisters. He had already established the fact that the same tongue was being used to bless God and to curse men (3:1–12). Proverbs 18:21 declares that "Death and life are in the power of the tongue: and they that love it shall eat the fruit thereof." Psalm 34:13 warns, "Keep thy tongue from evil, and thy lips from speaking guile." James's statements support the truth of God's Word as he attempted to redirect the wrong behavior of the people that would lead to their demise.

People were engaging in acts of evil speech without considering the ramifications of their behavior as being in violation of God's law. In God's law, God declared His love for His people and His command for people to love one another as they would love themselves (2:8). Here James teaches that this behavior showed disrespect for God's law since speaking evil of the law was the same as judging, or challenging, God's edicts. He goes on to say there is only one lawgiver, and that One is God alone. God has the sole ability to both save and to destroy. God reserves this right for Himself. Therefore, James asks the question, "Who are you to judge your neighbor?" (v. 12, NIV).

In Matthew 7:1–5, Jesus teaches against the unrighteous act of one man judging another. His warning is that we are asking to be judged in the same manner in which we issue judgment against someone. We would do well to follow Jesus' teaching and avoid the dire consequences that will come from failing to adhere to God's position as the Supreme Judge. This is James's objective, and he delivers a message to prevent his audience from committing acts of judgment that will only bring upon themselves their own condemnation. God is the trustworthy and ultimate judge that will bring about proper punishment and rewards. In His infinite knowledge and wisdom, each individual will receive what he or she deserves.

Search the Scriptures

1. What is the true source of fighting and quarreling among God's people (James 4:1)?

2. Why is it that the prayers of pleasure-seeking people often go unanswered (v. 3)?

3. What is the necessary first step in resisting the temptations of Satan (v. 7)?

4. How does God respond when His people humble themselves before Him (v. 10)?

5. Why should believers refrain from judging one another (v. 12)?

Discuss the Meaning

1. Why is the formula "if God wills" so vital to our future plans, hopes, and dreams?

2. Discuss the meaning of James's statement in verse 11: "If thou judge the law, thou art not a doer of the law, but a judge."

Lesson in Our Society

The media exert tremendous appeal to the basic desires of people. Billboards advertising liquor and cigarettes can be seen from the windows of inner-city schools. Television commercials become more audacious every year. Society teaches us that material things and pleasure are the ultimate ends of life.

The church should be concerned about the pull of the media on our children and society. As the conscience of the nation, how can we get our leaders to take a look at where we are headed? Is speaking out against commercialism and the continuous bombardment of temporal pleasures an attempt to make others follow our beliefs? Or is taking social action against moral depravity an integral part of God's command for us to live responsible and fruitful lives?

Make It Happen

Retirement planning is an excellent means of acquiring wealth for our later years so that we can live responsibly. Many companies offer pension plans and 401(k) savings to help their employees plan for their "golden years." Scripture does not prohibit planning ahead; it admonishes us to acknowledge God in our plans.

This week, prayerfully consider putting aside a certain amount of your earnings toward your retirement years if you are not already doing so. Then prayerfully consider the actions you are taking that build and contribute to your eternal retirement. What are you doing now to lay up treasure in heaven?

Follow the Spirit

What God wants me to do:

_____

_____

Remember Your Thoughts

Special insights you have learned:

_____

_____

More Light on the Text

James 4:1–12

1 From whence come wars and fightings among you? come they not hence, even of your lusts that war in your members?

James is addressing the community as a whole, not individuals. This is a more detailed explanation of the principle mentioned in 3:16 that confusion and disorder result from envy and strife. He asks the believers to identify the origin of "wars" (Gk. *polemos*, **POL-eh-moss**) and "fightings" (Gk. *mache*, **MAH-khay**) among them. These words can be used to describe conflict between both individuals and between nations. The phrase "wars and fightings" can mean heated verbal arguments and serious armed struggle. Paul told Titus, to "avoid . . . strivings [*machai*] about the law; for they are unprofitable and vain" (Titus 3:9). Certainly some things are worth fighting for, or at least defending. However, the struggle must be done in a God-honoring way.

These attitudes come from their "lust" (Gk. *hedone*, **hay-dah-NAY**), which can be translated as "passion." This word is not necessarily negative, because it can also be translated as "pleasure." But in the New Testament it is always used negatively (Luke 8:14; Titus 3:3; 2 Peter 2:13). James continues the military image to suggest that lusts or passions are waging wars within individuals. There is a battle, for example, between the desires of the body and the desires of the spirit. Peter alludes to this type of conflict in 1 Peter 2:11: "Abstain from fleshly lusts, which war against the soul." Paul also mentions this type of internal conflict in Romans 7:23 (NIV): "But I see another law at work in the members of my body, waging war against the law of my mind and making me a prisoner of the law of sin at work within my members."

2 Ye lust, and have not: ye kill, and desire to have, and cannot obtain: ye fight and war, yet ye have not, because ye ask not. 3 Ye ask, and receive not, because ye ask amiss, that ye may consume it upon your lusts.

The first part of this verse explains the implications of frustrated desire. James says the source of these conflicts is lust or desire for something. When such desires are unfulfilled, people commit murder. Again, when a person desires something and cannot get it, fighting and war could result. This pattern of unfulfilled and unchecked desires is present in the New Testament. It was envy that led certain Jewish leaders to arrest Jesus, and Pilate knew this: "For he [Pilate] knew that the chief priests had delivered him [Jesus] for [because of] envy" (Mark 15:10). In the case of Jesus, it led to His death.

James was warning the believers that if they continued in this manner, their unfulfilled desires could lead to killings. His statement (v. 1) already tells us that there have been war and fighting among them. Even today, envy and unfulfilled desires are behind all personal conflicts and national war.

James gives two reasons why the believers do not have what they want. The first reason is simple: They do not have because they do not ask (Gk. *aiteo*, **eye-TEH-oh**). The second reason is connected to the first; when they ask, they do not receive because they ask wrongly. The last part of verse 3 explains what it means to ask wrongly: they ask in order to satisfy their lusts. These believers are still operating within the realm that created their problems in the first place, namely, their lusts. James is appealing to the same principle that Jesus used in prayer, "Ask, and it shall be given you" (Matthew 7:7). In 1 John 5:14, we read, "And this is the confidence that we have in him, that, if we ask any thing according to his will, he heareth us."

4 Ye adulterers and adulteresses, know ye not that the friendship of the world is enmity with God? whosoever therefore will be a friend of the world is the enemy of God.

The phrase "ye adulterers and adulteresses" is one word in Greek: *moichalides* (**moy-khah-LIH-dess**), and it means just adulteresses, not adulterers. The translation "ye adulterers and adulteresses" captures the sense of the word. The phrase "adulterous people" is preferable. Why does James use this feminine term to describe the believers? In the following verses, James quotes heavily from the Old Testament. His use of the term "adulteresses" picks up the imagery of the relationship between God and Israel in the Old Testament. The relationship between God and Israel is sometimes referred to as a marriage (Isaiah 54:1–6; Jeremiah 2:2). Israel's disobedience is considered spiritual adultery. The prophet Hosea used this language profusely (Hosea 2:5, 7, 16, 20). Jesus also used this terminology to describe the Israelites when He called them "an evil and adulterous generation" (Matthew 12:39).

James is justified to call the believers adulteresses because they were developing intimacy with the world. The Scripture is very clear from Genesis to Revelation that we cannot serve God and the world at the same time. James's strong language and position are based on his conviction that the believers' confession must match their lifestyle. They cannot be double-minded.

5 Do ye think that the scripture saith in vain, The spirit that dwelleth in us lusteth to envy?

The "spirit" (Gk. *pneuma*, **PNOO-mah**) that dwells in us could be a reference to the Holy Spirit who dwells in born-again believers (1 Corinthians 3:16). It could also be a reference to the breath of God that is in all human beings right from creation, which is the human spirit. Thus, James could be appealing to the believers that God owns them either by virtue of creation or by virtue of their new life in Christ.

6 But he giveth more grace. Wherefore he saith, God resisteth the proud, but giveth grace unto the humble.

The first part of verse 6 is a quotation of Proverbs 3:34, and the second part is similar to 1 Peter 5:5–9. In fact, a comparison of James 4:6–9 and 1 Peter 5:5–9 shows that the two passages are similar. It seems that the suggestion here is not new to the believers. God is gracious to His children, and He gives them grace to live for Him. However, God resists the proud who live in sin by earthly wisdom. This is a common theme in the Old Testament (Psalm 18:27; 34:18; Isaiah 61:1; Zephaniah 3:11–12).

7 Submit yourselves therefore to God. Resist the devil, and he will flee from you. 8 Draw nigh to God, and he will draw nigh to you. Cleanse your hands, ye sinners; and purify your hearts, ye double minded. 9 Be afflicted, and mourn, and weep: let your laughter be turned to mourning, and your joy to heaviness.

Verses 7–10 are a series of commands. These commands call believers to discard the habits of the old life and to practice these new ones. James recognizes the danger of the Devil and calls for the believers to resist him. Verse 7 connects very well with verse 8, which calls for the believers to draw close to God. Resisting the Devil is crucial because his primary purpose is to do everything he can to ruin believers' lives.

These verses describe the procedure of drawing near to God. The first step is repentance. This is signified by the cleansing of hands, an external action, and by the purification of hearts, an internal action. The issues that the believers are to repent of have already been spelled out. This is demonstrated by the fact that James calls the people double-minded. This passage connects with 1:8, but it also carries the image of these believers who want to be a friend of God and a friend of the world too (4:4). This theme of drawing near to God in worship with clean hands and hearts is an Old Testament concept. The Psalmist said clean hands and a pure heart were necessary for those who would minister before the Lord (Psalm 24:3–4).

James calls the believers to be remorseful and mourn over their sins. This is similar to the prophetic language of calling the Israelites back to God. The Lord called the Children of Israel back to Himself through the prophet Joel because the Day of the Lord was near. He says, "Turn ye even to me with all your heart, and with fasting, and with weeping, and with mourning: And rend your heart, and not your garments, and turn unto the LORD your God: for he is gracious and merciful, slow to anger, and of great kindness" (Joel 2:12–13). Deep sorrow and repentance over our sins is the appropriate response for sinning. Believers can sometimes fall into carelessness about sin by taking it lightly because of Christ's forgiveness. Jesus said, "Blessed are they that mourn: for they shall be comforted" (Matthew 5:4). True joy comes from genuine repentance before God and a knowledge of having peace with God through Jesus Christ.

10 Humble yourselves in the sight of the Lord, and he shall lift you up.

This is the last in a series of commands that James gives. Humility before God is to recognize our true state as human beings. We are poor, wretched, and needy. This state of humility is best exemplified in the parable Jesus told of the two people who came to pray in the temple (Luke 18:10–14). One was a Pharisee and the other was a tax collector. The tax collector recognized his spiritual poverty before God and asked for mercy. Jesus said, "Every one that exalteth himself shall be abased [humbled]; and he that humbleth himself shall be exalted" (v. 14). Deep humility in the Christian life is synonymous with total dependence on God.

11 Speak not evil one of another, brethren. He that speaketh evil of his brother, and judgeth his brother, speaketh evil of the law, and judgeth the law: but if thou judge the law, thou art not a doer of the law, but a judge. 12 There is one lawgiver, who is able to save and to destroy: who art thou that judgest another?

Here James continues his authoritative correction to his audience who has been living in error against the law of God. He has done well in his communication to clearly convey his message. It is apparent that James wanted to leave no room for misunderstanding. These were matters of a very serious nature. He had already shared stern words about their in-fighting, lusting, and becoming friends of the world. He has just told them to resist the Devil and to avoid the temptation to act proud and haughty. Instead of committing these acts of disobedience, James advised them to humbly submit themselves to God. Now James commands them not to speak evil words about their brothers and sisters, and he offers them the reason for not doing so. He is asserting that speaking evil and judging others go together. When humans assume the position of judgment against other humans, they have stepped outside of their duty of obeying the law. In verse 11 he says, "If thou judge the law, thou art not a doer of the law but a judge." This is a state of disobedience to God, and evil words will naturally come forth. Exercising this type of behavior against others is the same as showing disrespect of God's law by speaking evil of it and judging the law of God.

The people knew they were in violation of the law since it was common knowledge among the Jews that God was the true judge. In fact, the courts of the day acknowledged God's supreme authority. The rulers within the court system were required to render judgment according to God's law. They were compelled to thoroughly investigate matters brought before the court, and at least two witnesses were to be produced. If it was found that someone falsely accused another, the accuser was then punished according to the judgment the one being accused would have been given if they had been convicted of the crime.

James reminds his readers that God is the only Lawgiver, and therefore God is the only one who has the right and is able to preserve life or destroy it. Consequently, James tells them they do not have the right to judge another. Furthermore, the writer of Hebrews firmly states, "For we know him that hath said, Vengeance belongeth unto me, I will recompense, saith the Lord. And again, The Lord shall judge his people" (Hebrews 10:30).

Source:
Keener, Craig S. *The IVP Bible Background Commentary New Testament.* Downers Grove, Ill.: InterVarsity Press, 1993.

Daily Bible Readings

M: Understanding and Peace
Proverbs 3:13-18

T: Ask Rightly
James 4:1-3

W: Yearn for God's Spirit
James 4:4-7

T: Humble Yourselves
James 4:8-10

F: Do Not Judge
James 4:11-14

S: Seek God's Wishes
James 4:15-17

S: Living in the Light of God
Ephesians 5:8-11

TEACHING TIPS

August 31
Bible Study Guide 14

1. Words You Should Know

A. Elders (James 5:14) *presbuteros* (Gk.) noun—Older person; the older of two individuals; a church official.

B. Sins (v. 15) *hamartias* (Gk.)—The action itself (sinning), as well as its result (sin); every departure from the way of righteousness.

2. Teacher Preparation

Unifying Principle—Powerful and Effective Living How can we achieve a positive attitude that leads to powerful and effective living? James teaches that our lifestyle is to be shaped by an attitude of prayer.

A. If possible find a copy of the poem "Prayer Is the Soul's Sincere Desire" by eighteenth-century Scottish poet James Montgomery and include it in your personal devotion. If you can locate it, be prepared to share it with the class.

B. Pray and ask God to guide you through the lesson. Read the Focal Verses, reflecting on the significance of the Keep in Mind verse and the Unifying Principle. Also read 1 Kings 17:1; 18:42–45.

C. Review the information in The People, Places, and Times and Bible Background sections.

D. Prepare your answers to the Search the Scriptures questions and consider your responses to the Discuss the Meaning questions.

3. Starting the Lesson

A. Lead the class in prayer.

B. Ask the class to close their eyes as you read the In Focus poem, "My Prayer for You!" aloud. Then invite them to share their personal stories of times when others prayed for them and God answered those prayers.

C. Ask the class to silently review The People, Places, and Times. Ask volunteers to define the term "elder" in general and its meaning in the church. Specifically focus on the role of the elders in the church.

4. Getting into the Lesson

A. Ask someone to read the Focal Verses.

B. If you have a copy of the poem "Prayer Is the Soul's Sincere Desire," read it to the class and allow the students to express their reaction to it. Discuss how the words connect with the Scripture passage.

C. As volunteers read the In Depth section, encourage the students to listen intently. Answer any questions after the reading.

D. Read the Search the Scriptures questions and ask for volunteers to provide the answers.

5. Relating the Lesson to Life

A. Help the students apply the lesson to their lives by leading them in the Discuss the Meaning questions.

B. Use the Lesson in Our Society section to further help the students relate the Scripture lesson to happenings in today's society.

C. Call the students' attention to the Make It Happen section. Lead them in a discussion regarding why some people are uncomfortable praying.

6. Arousing Action

A. Ask the students to practice praying, either by keeping a prayer journal, praying through the Daily Bible Readings, or using the ACTS prayer model found in the Make It Happen section.

B. Remind the students to use the Remember Your Thoughts and Follow the Spirit sections.

C. Close with prayer.

Worship Guide

For the Superintendent or Teacher
Theme: Prayerful Community
Theme Song: "Praise God from Whom All Blessings Flow"
Devotional Reading: 1 Thessalonians 5:16–22
Prayer

PRAYERFUL COMMUNITY

Bible Background • JAMES 5
Printed Text • JAMES 5:13–18 Devotional Reading • 1 THESSALONIANS 5:16–22

AIM for Change

By the end of the lesson, we will:

EXAMINE situations in which God answers prayers;

BECOME CONVINCED that faith in God results in answered prayers; and

DECIDE to develop a habit of praying in each and every situation.

Keep in Mind

"Is any among you afflicted? let him pray. Is any merry? let him sing psalms" (James 5:13).

Focal Verses

KJV **James 5:13** Is any among you afflicted? let him pray. Is any merry? let him sing psalms.

14 Is any sick among you? let him call for the elders of the church; and let them pray over him, anointing him with oil in the name of the Lord:

15 And the prayer of faith shall save the sick, and the Lord shall raise him up; and if he have committed sins, they shall be forgiven him.

16 Confess your faults one to another, and pray one for another, that ye may be healed. The effectual fervent prayer of a righteous man availeth much.

17 Elias was a man subject to like passions as we are, and he prayed earnestly that it might not rain: and it rained not on the earth by the space of three years and six months.

18 And he prayed again, and the heaven gave rain, and the earth brought forth her fruit.

NLT **James 5:13** Are any of you suffering hardships? You should pray. Are any of you happy? You should sing praises.

14 Are any of you sick? You should call for the elders of the church to come and pray over you, anointing you with oil in the name of the Lord.

15 Such a prayer offered in faith will heal the sick, and the Lord will make you well. And if you have committed any sins, you will be forgiven.

16 Confess your sins to each other and pray for each other so that you may be healed. The earnest prayer of a righteous person has great power and produces wonderful results.

17 Elijah was as human as we are, and yet when he prayed earnestly that no rain would fall, none fell for three and a half years!

18 Then, when he prayed again, the sky sent down rain and the earth began to yield its crops.

In Focus

My Prayer for You!

May God give you a measure of faith
Where you stagger not at His promises,
Where there is no room for worry or doubt,
So that when troubles are pressing on every hand,
You will know what complete faith in Him is all about!

May God give you a measure of faith that will keep you,
Yes, keep you constantly in His will,
So that when you go through the valleys so low,
You will render prayer and praises still!

May God grant you a faith that can be used to deliver you
When your heart is dark with pain,
So that you can rest in the fact that He is your Saviour
And trust in Him again and again!
—*Evangeline Carey*
Copyright© 1996 by Evangeline Carey. Used by permission. All rights reserved.

The People, Places, and Times

Elders. The New Testament use of the word "elder" has its origins in the Jewish tradition. Elders in the Old Testament wielded authority in the community. The Hebrew word *zaqen* (**zah-KAYN**), meaning "old," is derived from the root meaning "chin" or "beard," referring to a mature or elderly man in the community. Old age was associated with wisdom, so it is no surprise that positions regarded with such esteem were held by older men. Officials during the Exodus-wilderness period were selected from among the elders (Exodus 18; Deuteronomy 1:15; Numbers 11:16). Elders also functioned in the life of the family, clan, and tribe. Their responsibilities included settling disputes, leading wars, and imparting wisdom.

In New Testament times, elders continued to maintain a position of authority in Jewish communities. Each community had a council of elders, or presbytery. The Sanhedrin council mentioned in the New Testament was composed of elders and priests. The infant church maintained the tradition of having a council of elders, appointing them and ordaining them to serve in the churches founded by Paul and Barnabas in Asia Minor (Acts 14:23; Titus 1:5). Just as they did in the synagogues, elders in the church rendered decisions, at least in the church in Jerusalem (Acts 15:2, 4, 6, 22, 23). Their responsibilities may have included pastoral duties also (Acts 20:28; 1 Peter 5:1–4; James 5:14). By the second century, exhortation and preaching were among the duties of elders.

Prayer. Jesus is the model for when and how to pray in the New Testament. Mark recorded that Jesus often prayed at decisive moments in His ministry, including prior to inaugurating His public ministry (1:35–38); after feeding the multitude (6:46; but not 8:10); before His arrest in Gethsemane (14:36, 39); and from the Cross (15:34). Mark also recorded occasions when Jesus participated in the life of the Jewish community where He would have engaged in prayer, such as at the synagogue (1:21; 6:2) and at home celebrations like the Passover (14:17–26). Mark also mentions Jesus' table blessings (6:41; 14:22–23). Where Mark might have assumed prayer, Luke includes that Jesus was praying (6:12; 9:28).

Sources:

Davies, G. Henton. "Elder in the OT." *Interpreter's Dictionary of the Bible,* Vol. 2. Nashville: Abingdon Press, 1962.

Shepherd Jr., M. H. "Elder in the NT." *Interpreter's Dictionary of the Bible,* Vol. 2. Nashville: Abingdon Press, 1962.

Background

The closing verses of the letter of James concern life in the community of faith. The main emphasis in the verses for this lesson is on practical advice related to prayer. The power of prayer must be exercised as a necessary element within the community of believers in Christ Jesus. The "prayer of faith" James mentions in verse 15 alludes to the fact that whether a believer receives his or her healing through physical medicine or divine healing, the healing ultimately comes from God. Through prayer, we are demonstrating that we rely on the Lord to honor the prayers we pray in faith and believe that He will respond to earnest prayers and raise up the one who is sick.

Scripture further informs us that "if he [the one who is sick] has sinned, he will be forgiven" (v. 15, NIV). This truth is also presented to us in three of the Gospel accounts. When Jesus healed the paralytic man, He first told the man that his sins were forgiven. Moments later, when He discerned the thoughts of His nearby critical observers, Jesus addressed them and explained the reason for His actions, "that ye may know that the Son of man hath power on earth to forgive sins" (Matthew 9:6). Jesus then told the paralyzed man to get up, pick up his bed, and go home. The man immediately demonstrated that He had been healed, obeyed Jesus' command, and went home healed and forgiven (Matthew 9:2–7).

At-A-Glance

1. The Prayer of Faith (James 5:13–15)
2. Pray for One Another (vv. 15–16)
3. Power of Prayer (vv. 16–18)

In Depth

1. The Prayer of Faith (James 5:13–15)

James's exhortation to the Christian community in chapter 5 addresses how the church should respond in difficult situations. He implores believers to pray no matter what they are going through. No fewer than three times does he use the word "pray." Are you afflicted? James says to pray. Are you sick? Again, James says to pray. In whatever circumstances we find ourselves, we ought to be in prayer.

James reminds us to pray when we are suffering, sick, or have fallen. However, he also reminds us that we are not alone. Believers are called to mutuality in love by our oneness in Christ. "Bear ye one another's burdens, and so fulfil the law of Christ," we are urged in Galatians 6:2. How often do we hear of people suffering alone or in silence? Perhaps this is you. But James says that we should call for the elders of the church and have them pray over us. Depending on your faith tradition, this might be an elder, pastor, or priest. Whoever it is, you should have the confidence in knowing that there are leaders in your church who will pray for you.

James adds that the elders should anoint the sick with oil in the name of Jesus. Olive oil was a commonly used emollient in the ancient world that was rubbed on the sick or injured to promote healing (Mark 6:13; Luke 10:34). Today, we would likely visit the doctor, who would prescribe medicine or therapy, but the use of modern remedies does not alleviate the need for prayer and faith to facilitate our healing. Many studies support the view that prayer promotes healing.

While James exhorts us to pray when we are sick or afflicted, he also encourages us to be cheerful in whatever our circumstances (v. 13). He instructs us to sing psalms or songs of praise. Paul also says that we are to sing "psalms and hymns and spiritual songs, singing and making melody in your heart to the Lord; giving thanks always for all things unto God and the Father in the name of our Lord Jesus Christ" (Ephesians 5:19–20).

2. Pray for One Another (vv. 15–16)

The theme of mutuality continues in James's exhortation to confess our sins to one another and to pray for one another so that we may be healed. James links the healing of sickness with the forgiveness of sins. At the time James lived, many believed that sickness resulted from sin, so that physical healing would also bring spiritual restoration. In Mark 2, friends of a paralytic man bring him to Jesus to be healed. His friends went to great lengths to bring him to Jesus. Jesus declared that because of their faith, their friend's sins were forgiven and he was healed. However, Jesus also claimed in John 9 that the condition of the man who had been blind since birth was neither the result of his or his parents' sins, but so that God's works might be revealed in him. In either case, God assures us forgiveness of sins if we confess

our sins (1 John 1:9). Confessing to one another and praying for one another also brings restoration to the community that is threatened by the sins of its members.

3. Power of Prayer (vv. 16–18)

One of the criteria James lists for answered prayer is righteousness. He recalls the prayer of the prophet Elijah as an example of the power of prayer. Gone were their ancestors, who recalled the Lord's deeds and could pass this information down. For them, the Lord was the God of the past. They had tasted of the new gods worshiped by the Canaanites, and the new doctrine and theology was more appealing to them. Yet, when they were being oppressed by the Canaanites and cried out, it was the Israelite God who raised up judges for them that delivered them.

Search the Scriptures

1. According to the Letter of James, when should we pray (James 5:13, 16)?
2. What did James say that the sick should do (v. 14)?
3. Why should you confess your sins to one another and pray for one another (v. 16)?
4. The prayer of the righteous is _____ and _____ (v. 16).

Discuss the Meaning

1. Why do you think that it is important to pray when we are at our most vulnerable, whether it be physical or spiritual adversity?
2. James describes life in the Christian community as being reciprocal. Church leaders are supposed to pray for members, and members are supposed to pray for one another. Why is it important that we share one another's joys and concerns, and bear one another's burdens in the church?
3. Discuss how the example of Elijah in verses 17 and 18 demonstrates the power of prayer.

Lesson in Our Society

In this lesson, James highlighted the importance of prayer in the time of sickness. Speaking directly to the church, he took an authoritative approach to point out why believers need to lift up one another when healing is necessary. Beginning in 5:14, he began conveying to his readers the process of achieving a positive end result: "the prayer of faith shall save the sick, and the Lord shall raise him up." He went one step further and proclaimed that confessing faults and praying for one another brings about healing and forgiveness. The Word of God will become real to those who have faith in it only when we actually do what it says.

As you are reminded of James's counsel, give some serious thought to whether you think we are adhering to his instruction on prayer in society today. Are the leaders of the church today following James's sound counsel on how to pray? What can we do to get us back to following God's Word so that we can reap the rich benefits of practicing it?

Make It Happen

Many people are afraid to pray. They believe that they are not articulate enough or do not know the words to say. However, Romans 8:26 states that we have the assistance from the Holy Spirit to help us when we pray. Even when we do not know what we ought to pray, the Holy Spirit makes intercession on our behalf with sighs too deep for words. We can also practice praying the ACTS model: A—for acknowledge God, C—for confess our sins, T—for thanksgiving, and S—for supplication (asking for God's help for others and ourselves).

Follow the Spirit

What God wants me to do:

_____

_____

Remember Your Thoughts

Special insights you have learned:

_____

_____

More Light on the Text

James 5:13–18

13 Is any among you afflicted? let him pray. Is any merry? let him sing psalms.

James advises believers on how to respond to different life circumstances. The believers experienced times of joy and times of sorrow (vv.13–18; 1:2–3). James urged them to turn constantly to prayer in whatever circumstances life brought their way, even in going through "hard times" (Gk. *kakopatheo*, **kahk-op-ahth-EH-oh**) as well as in "health" (Gk. *euthumeo*, **yoo-thoo-MEH-oh**). Prayer may not remove the afflic-

tion but it most certainly can transform it. Divine help and blessings are conveyed to the Christian in response either to his or her own prayers or the intercessions of other Christians on the individual's behalf. In all circumstances, it is a Christian's duty and privilege to pray.

The Greek word *psallo* (**PSAL-loh**) primarily means to play a stringed instrument and then to sing to the accompaniment of the harp. Here it is referring to every sounding of God's praises, alone or in the company of others, vocally with or without musical instrument (Romans15:9; 1 Corinthians 14:15; Ephesians 5:19). Through singing, we have the ability to express our thanks to God.

14 Is any sick among you? let him call for the elders of the church; and let them pray over him, anointing him with oil in the name of the Lord:

In the case of being severely "sick" (Gk. *astheneo*, **ahs-then-EH-oh**), when the body may be tormented with pain and the mind considerably disturbed, it is not easy to turn one's thoughts in a concentrated manner to prayer. In any case, the exhortation is to call the elders of the church to pray over the sick and anoint the afflicted person with oil in the name of the Lord (as they did in Mark 6:13). The word "oil" (Gk. *elaion*, **EL-ah-yon**) literally means olive oil (from the root *elaia*, **el-AH-yah**, or "olive"). Oil is the symbol of the Holy Spirit, the divine presence (1 John 2:20, 27). In biblical days, it was used for medicinal purposes (Luke 10:34).

The emphasis on "in the name of the Lord" reminds the reader that the Lord is the healer, not the elders. It is neither the oil nor the elders that brings the healing. The Lord Himself is the healer. The anointing of oil is done in His name.

15 And the prayer of faith shall save the sick, and the Lord shall raise him up; and if he have committed sins, they shall be forgiven him.

The expression "shall raise him up" means to restore to physical health. Physical healing is a form of redemption. Here James is offering God's prescription for healing and the forgiveness of sins, which will deliver the believer from eternal perdition. The Greek word used for "the sick" (*ton kamnonta*, **ton KAHM-non-tah**) is the present participle of a verb whose primary meaning is to grow weary in the sense of growing weary by reason of sickness.

The verb *egeiro* (**eg-AY-roh**) is used in the transitive sense with the Lord as the subject. It means to wake up or awaken from sleep (see Matthew 1:24 from sleep; John 11:11–12 from death; 11:29 from sitting). In this verse, the word means to wake up from illness.

The conditional clause "if he have committed sins" does not mean that the sickness is necessarily due to sin. It may or may not be due to a sin. The Bible does not teach that all sickness is due to a sin committed by the person suffering, although the possibility is there (Mark 2:5–11; 1 Corinthians 11:30).

16 Confess your faults one to another, and pray one for another, that ye may be healed. The effectual fervent prayer of a righteous man availeth much.

Confess to one another "your faults" (Gk. *paraptoma*, **par-AHP-toh-mah**) and pray one to another so that your "deviation from the right path" may be brought to the throne of grace and be forgiven (see Matthew 5:23, 24). There is great power in intercessory prayer. The Greek word *deesis* (**DEH-ay-sis**), translated "prayer," has a more restricted meaning. It denotes a petition, a supplication (Matthew 18:19; Acts 12:5–17). Sin is the enemy of personal and community life; it must be confessed before the throne of grace (Proverbs 28:13–14; 1 John 1:8–10; see Psalm 32:1).

A righteous man is a person who fears God and obeys His word. His prayers differ from the prayers of others by virtue of their earnestness and their fervency. God listens to him because he fears God and obeys God's Word. His sins have been confessed and are forgiven. On the other hand, God cannot listen to anyone who is unforgiving and lives in sin.

17 Elias was a man subject to like passions as we are, and he prayed earnestly that it might not rain: and it rained not on the earth by the space of three years and six months.

Here the reader's attention is drawn to one outstanding example of the efficacy of a righteous man's prayer, Elias [Elijah] (see 1 Kings 17–18). The phrase "[Elijah] was a man subject to like pas-

sions as we are" (Gk. *homoiopathes*, **hom-oy-op-ath-AYSS**) means that he was suffering the same things that all human beings suffer. He was not a super human; he was a human being just as we are.

Elias "prayed earnestly" is literally, he "prayed in prayer." James, by using a Hebrew infinitive absolute construction (Genesis 2:17 "to die with death"; Luke 22:14–15 "to desire, I have desired"), points out the earnestness that characterized Elias's prayer. James wants his readers to know that they too can pray this type of prayer. It is possible for all the true followers of the Lord to effectively pray in this way.

18 And he prayed again, and the heaven gave rain, and the earth brought forth her fruit.

Elijah's prayer for rain to return and water the dry land is an illustration of the sick returning to life after the prayer of faith. A time of being sick is like a period of dryness. But the prayers of people made righteous through the blood of Jesus are efficient to bring new life. Elijah had faith in the power of prayer. He prayed with boldness and waited on God in every circumstance. We are called to pray with boldness and to wait on God in every situation that arises (Hebrews 4:16).

Daily Bible Readings

M: Pray without Ceasing
1 Thessalonians 5:16–22
T: The Plight of the Rich
James 5:1–6
W: Patience and Endurance
James 5:7–12
T: Pray for One Another
James 5:13–15
F: The Prayer of the Righteous
James 5:16–18
S: Stay with the Truth
James 5:19–20
S: Prayer for Community Power
Ephesians 3:14–21